Boris Pasternak

a reference guide

Boris Pasternak

a reference guide

MUNIR SENDICH

G.K. Hall & Co.
An Imprint of Macmillan Publishing Company
New York

Maxwell Macmillan Canada
Toronto

Maxwell Macmillan International
New York   Oxford   Singapore   Sidney

G.K. Hall & Co.
An Imprint of Macmillan Publishing Company
866 Third Avenue
New York, NY 10022

Library of Congress Catalog Card Number: 93-27469

Printed in the United States of America

Printing Number
10 9 8 7 6 5 4 3 2 1

Library of Congress Cataloging-in-Publication Data

Sendich, Munir.
  Boris Pasternak: a reference guide / Munir Sendich.
      p. cm. — (A Reference guide to literature)
  Includes bibliographical references and indexes.
  ISBN 0-8161-8992-7
  1. Pasternak, Boris, 1890–1960—Bibliography. I. Title. II. Series.
  Z8662.35.S46 1993
  [PG3476.P27]
  016.89171'42—dc20   93-27469
                                                        CIP

The paper used in this publication meets the minimum requirements of American National Standard for Information Sciences—Permanence of Paper for Printed Library Materials. ANSI Z39.48-1984. ⊗™

891.73
P291ZS

To my wife, Donna Lara Sendich.

Contents

The Author

Munir Sendich is a professor of Russian literature at Michigan State University and editor of the *Russian Language Journal* (since 1974). He is the author/editor of nine books, editor of fifty-six volumes of the *Russian Language Journal,* and author of twenty-four essays on Russian literature and seven bibliographic complilations.

Preface

Boris Pasternak: A Reference Guide consists of six parts: a list of abbreviations; an introduction; "Boris Pasternak's Writings In Russian, 1913–1990"; "Criticism of Boris Pasternak, 1914–1990"; an author index; and a subject index. The list of abbreviations of journals, periodicals, and series editions is the key to both bibliographies. The introductory essay, divided into seven sections (covering poetry, short prose, translations, Pasternak's links with other artists, Pasternak's views of art and literary schools and trends, Pasternak's poetics, and *Doctor Zhivago*), attempts to capture major shifts and changes in the perception of Pasternak as recorded in Pasternak criticism from 1914 to 1990. The bibliography of Pasternak's writings in Russian records 556 entries of various genres published from 1913 through 1990. It includes poetry (single poems, tales in verse, collections, and bilingual collections—in Russian, Italian, German, or English), prose (including excerpts, fragments, chapters, and entire pieces), translations (individual pieces or collections), criticism (critiques, essays, reviews, notes, translations, commentaries, and notes), speeches and lectures, introductions, afterwords, sketches, inscriptions, replies to questionnaires, literary portraits, and correspondence. The annotated bibliography, the primary section of the book, lists entries of Pasternak criticism published during 1914–1990. This bibliography includes 1,049 entries selected from a vast criticism in Russian, English, and the major European and Slavic languages.

When compiling the sources for the annotations, I preferred to focus on recent scholarship in English and Russian, though substantial criticism in other languages has been included. The amount of entries varies from year to year, with the post-*Doctor Zhivago* criticism presented more voluminously and comprehensively than that before 1957; indeed, the early criticism is utterly selective and confined to the most prominent writings, usually by well-established critics, writers, and poets. I have attempted to exclude a great deal of criticism that aims at politicizing its approach to Pasternak or focuses primarily on political interpretations of Pasternak's works or his biography. Such omissions occurred with Vladislav Khodasevich's and Georgy Adamovich's rebuttal over Pasternak in the mid-1920s and with numerous *Doctor Zhivago* reviews wrangling time and again over the novel's political impact.

I attempted in writing the annotations (regardless of the obvious pitfalls) neither to judge or evaluate the Pasternak criticism, and endeavored to present as factually and with as much detail as is reasonably possible the theme and content of each annotated piece. In this manner, criticism speaks for itself—while providing an impartial interpretation of Pasternak's literary legacy and recording shifts and changes in criticism's treatment of Pasternak.

The subject index provides access to a broad range of entries such as titles of works (including, in some instances, entries for first lines of poems), subjects, and proper names (of authors, writers, etc.). Some of the entries for individual works (*Doctor Zhivago* and *My Sister, Life*) and for subjects (poetics, for example) have been broken down into subentries. Cross-references have been made for entries warranting additional information (authors' pseudonyms, related works, etc.).

I have consulted numerous bibliographic sources, some of them included in notes in criticism, others published in chapter bibliographies of Pasternak biographies (Christopher Barnes's Pasternak biography, for example), still others listed in separate bibliographic compilations on Pasternak. Sources of the last type included: (1) *A Bibliography of Works of B. Pasternak and Literature About Him Printed in Russian*, by N.A. Troitsky (New York: All Slavic Publishing House, 1969) and (2) *Pasternak's Doctor Zhivago. An International Bibliography of Criticism (1957–1985)*, by Munir Sendich and Erica Greber (East Lansing, MI: RLJ, 1990).

I have also consulted the following sources: *Arts and Humanities Citation Index*, 1976–1989 (Philadelphia: Institute for Scientific Information); *Book Review Index*, 1965–1988 (Detroit: Gale Research Co.); *British Humanities Index*, 1962–1988 (London: The Library Association); *Canadian Book Review Annual*, 1975–1988 (Toronto: Peter Martin Associates); *Canadian Periodical Index*, 1938–1988 (Ottawa: Canadian Library Association); *Canadian Theses*, 1947–1985 (Ottawa: National Library of Canada); *Chicago Tribune Index*, 1972–1985 (New York: New York Times Co.); *Christian Science Monitor Index*, 1955–1988 (Ann Arbor, MI: University Microfilms International); *Contemporary Literary Criticism*, 1973–1988 (Detroit: Gale Research Co.); *Essays in General Literature Index*, 1900–1988 (New York: H.W. Wilson Co.); *Humanities Index*, 1949–1988 (New York: H.W. Wilson Co.); *Index to Jewish Periodicals*, 1963–1985 (Cleveland Heights: Index to Jewish Periodicals); *Modern Language Association International Bibliography*, 1921–1990 (Baltimore: Modern Language Association); *New York Times Book Review Index*, 1896–1988 (New York: New York Times Co.); *Russian Literature in a Hispanic World: A Bibliography*, compiled by George O. Schanzer (Toronto: University of Toronto Press, 1972); *East European Languages and Literatures. A Subject and Name Index to Articles in English Language Journals, 1900–1977*, compiled by Terry M. Garth (Oxford: Clio Press, 1978), and its supplements: Nottingham, England: Astra Press, 1982, 1985, 1988; *Washington Post Index*, 1971–1983 (Ann Arbor, MI: University Microfilms); and *The Year's Work in*

Modern Language Studies, 1930–1990 (London: Modern Humanities Research Association).

In writing this book, I have adhered to dictates of *A Manual of Style*, 13th ed. (University of Chicago Press, 1982). English translations of titles of bibliographic sources in languages less widely understood (Polish, Russian, Czech, Serbo-Croatian, and Scandinavian languages) have been rendered in brackets following bibliographic entires. Titles in languages commonly used (French, German, Spanish, and Italian) have not been rendered into English. As to transliteration of Russian, I have used two systems: (1) that of the Library of Congress and (2) a system widely accepted for transliteration of names for English-speaking readers. Bibliographic entires have been transliterated by the former system, while names in annotations and in the introduction have been transliterated by the latter—as in the ending of the name of Voznesensky transliterated as **skii** (according to the former) and **sky** (by the latter). Other names follow a similar suit, such as Briusov, Aseev, Tynianov, or Maiakovskii (according to the Library of Congress system) versus Bryusov, Aseyev, Tynyanov, or Mayakovsky (as these names have become familiar to English-speaking readers).

Neither of the two systems has been used to transliterate bibliographic entries that contain Russian which had already been transliterated by another (i.e., "Linguistic") system. The names of Tomaševskij (1968.17) and Xodasevič (1989.25), for example, have been retained as they appear in the original. Similar adherence to the original has been observed in the use of diacritic marks (accents and umlauted vowels included) in French, German (and other Germanic languages), Hungarian, Polish, Czech, and Serbo-Croatian. Titles of journals and magazines have been abbreviated in both bibliographies—with a list of abbreviations compiled separately. The city of publication has been given in brackets only for those journals and magazines whose titles—for their ambiguity—warrant identification of the city of publication. Another list records publishers' acronyms as they appear on respective publications. Names of all other publishers have been recorded in full.

Acknowledgments

During the past four years, a number of individuals have assisted me in the completion of this book. I am deeply indebted to all of them, especially to the staff of the Michigan State University interlibrary loan service and to Michael L. Wolford, a graduate student in the Department of English at MSU, for his assistance in proofreading the annotations and introduction. My profoundest gratitude goes to Donna Lara Sendich for her scrupulous verification of bibliographic entries, proofreading of the entire book, and her countless suggestions to improve the quality of the entire text.

I would also like to express my gratitude to the administration of the Michigan State University College of Arts and Letters for awarding me a College All-University Research Grant for the 1990–1991 academic year. The grant was extended for another year, and I am grateful to Dr. John W. Eadie, dean of the College of Arts and Letters, for his assistance in obtaining the grant extension.

Abbreviations

AB	Al'manakh bibliofila
AM	Atlantic Monthly
AMP	Alma Mater Philippina
AN	Age noveau
AnN	Angelus novus
AR	Antioch Review
AS	The American Scholar
ASEES	Australian Slavonic and East European Studies
ASJ	Anglo-Soviet Journal
AUMLA	Journal of the Australasian Universities Modern Language Association
BA	Books Abroad
BCB	Boletin Cultural y Bibliografico
BIDS	Bulletin of the International Dostoevsky Society
BJA	British Journal of Aesthetics
BLM	Bonniers Litterära Magasin med All världens Berättare
BNYPL	Bulletin of the New York Public Library
BRG	Blätter der Rilke Gesellschaft
CA	Cuadernos Americanos
CASS	Canadian-American Slavic Studies
CC	Christian Century
CDSP	Current Digest of the Soviet Press [Ann Arbor, MI]
CEA	CEA Critic
ČeR	Československá rusistika
ChP	Chitatel' i pisatel'

ChR	Chast' rechi
CI	Contemporary Issues
CiC	La civiltà Cattolica
CJF	Chicago Jewish Forum
CL	Contemporary Literature
CLOS	Cahiers de linguistique d'orientalisme et de slavistique
CMRS	Cahiers du monde russe et soviétique
CQ	Colorado Quarterly
CR	Chicago Review
CRCL	Canadian Review of Comparative Literature
CrQ	Critical Quarterly
CS	Contrat social
CSP	Canadian Slavonic Papers
CSS	Canadian Slavic Studies
CW	Catholic World
DN	Druzhba narodov
DP	Den' poezii
DR	Dublin Review
EC	Essays in Criticism [Oxford]
EJ	English Journal
EP	Essays in Poetics [Keele, England]
ESE	Études slaves et est-europeennes [Quebec]
EUQ	Emory University Quarterly
FH	Frankfurter Hefte
FMLS	Forum for Modern Language Studies [St. Andrews, Scotland]
FN	Filologicheskie nauki
FT	Finsk Tidskrift
GOTR	Greek Orthodox Theological Review
GR	Germanic Review
GrS	Grand Street
GS	Germano-Slavica [Ontario]
GSh	God shesnadtsatyi
HM	Harper's Magazine
HR	Hudson Review

IAN	Izvestiia Akademii nauk. Seriia literatury i iazyka
IaSPFL	Iazyk i stil' proizvedenii fol'klora i literatury
IJSLP	International Journal of Slavic Linguistics and Poetics [Lisse]
IL	Internatsional'naia literatura
ILA	International Literary Annual
InL	Inostrannaia literatura
ISS	Irish Slavonic Studies
IZh	Iskusstvo i zhizn'
JAAC	Journal of Aesthetics and Art Criticism
JD	Jewish Digest
JF	Jewish Frontier
JKU	Journal of the Karnatak University
JRS	Journal of Russian Studies
KhS	Khudozhestvennoe slovo
KN	Krasnaia nov'
KR	Kenyon Review
KrN	Krasnaia niva
KZ	Krasnaia zvezda
KZh	Kultura i zhizn'
Lef	
LG	Literaturnaia gazeta
LI	Literatura i iskusstvo
LiG	Literaturnaia Gruziia
LiN	Literaturnoe nasledstvo
LiR	Literaturnaia Rossiia
LiS	Literaturnyi sovremennik [Munich]
LJ	Library Journal
LK	Literaturnyi kritik
LM	London Magazine
LN	Lettres nouvelles
LO	Literaturnoe obozrenie
LR	Literary Review
LS	Literaturnyi sovremennik
LU	Literaturnaia ucheba

LUK	Listy pro uměni a kritika
LZ	Literaturnoe zakavkaz'e
MA	Moskovskii al'manakh
MFS	Modern Fiction Stories
MG	Molodaia gvardia
MLR	Modern Language Review [Belfast]
MoP	Moskovskii ponedel'nik
MoW	Modern World
MP	Modern Philology
MQ	Meanjin Quarterly [Victoria, Australia]
MR	Massachusetts Review
MSS	Melbourne Slavonic Studies
MT	Musical Times [London]
MW	Moderne Welt
NA	Nuova Antologia [Rome]
NaD	Nashi dni [St. Petersburg]
ND	Nashi dni [Frankfurt am Main]
NDH	Neue deutsche Hefte [Gütersloh]
NDVSh	Nauchnye doklady vysshei shkoly
NeR	New Republic
NeuR	Neue Rundschau
NG	Novyi grad [Paris]
NHQ	New Hungarian Quarterly
NL	Novyi lef
NLH	New Literary History
NLP	Na literaturnom postu
NM	Novyi mir
NoR	Northwest Review
NoS	Nord e Sud
NP	Na postu
NR	National Review
NRF	La Nouvelle revue française
NRK	Novaia russkaia kniga
NRS	Novoye Russkoye Slovo

NS	Neue Sammlung
NVP	Norfolk Virginian-Pilot
NWR	New World Review
NY	New Yorker
NYHTBR	New York Herald Tribune Book Review
NYRB	New York Review of Books
NYTM	New York Times Magazine
NZh	Novyi Zhurnal
OSP	Oxford Slavonic Papers
PaR	Partisan Review
ParR	Paris Review
PC	Problems of Communism
PCL	Perspectives on Contemporary Literature
PF	Pensée française
PL	Philosophy and Literature
PLL	Papers on Language and Literature
PM	Die politische Meinung
PMLA	Publications of the Modern Language Association
PNR	PN Review
PoR	Poiski i razmyshleniia
PP	Psychological Perspectives
PR	Pechat' i revoliutsiia
PSL	Problemy strukturnoi lingvistiki
PSZhSL	Problemy stilia i zhanra v sovetskoi literatury
PTL	A Journal for Descriptive Poetics and Theory of Literature
QQ	Queen's Quarterly [Kingston, Ontario]
RA	Ruski arhiv [Belgrade]
RBPH	Revue belge de philologie et d'histoire
RC	Ruperto-Carola
RD	Reader's Digest
RDN	Revue de defense nationale
ReD	Recherches et débats
RES	Revue des études slaves
RF	Razon y Fe

RGB	Revue générale belge
RI	Russkoe iskusstvo
RIaSh	Russkii iazyk v shkole
RIL	Religion in Life [Nashville, TN]
RiS	Ricerche slavistiche
RL	Russkaia literatura
RLJ	Russian Language Journal
RLT	Russian Literature Triquarterly
RM	Russkaia mysl' [Paris]
RR	Russian Review
RS	Russkii sovremennik
RuA	Russkii al'manakh
RuL	Russian Literature [Amsterdam]
RUO	Revue de l'Université d'Ottawa
RuR	Russkaia rech
RZIa	Russkoe i zarubezhnoe iazykozhanie
SAB	South Atlantic Bulletin
SAJP	South African Journal of Philosophy
ScS	Scando Slavica
SEEJ	Slavic and East European Journal
SEER	Slavic and East European Review
SEES	Slavic and East European Studies
SFQ	Southern Folklore Quarterly
SH	Slavica Hierosolymitana [Jerusalem]
SiO	Sibirskie ogni
SL	Soviet Literature
SlaL	Slavica Lundensia
SlaR	Slavic Review
SlR	Slavische Rundschau
SlS	Slavistički studii [Skopje]
SM	Schweizer Monatshefte
SO	Slavia Orientales
SoR	Southern Review
SoZ	Sovremennyi Zapad

SQ	Shakespeare Quarterly
SR	Saturday Review
SS	Soviet Survey
SSASH	Studia Slavica Academiae Scientiarum Hungaricae
SSF	Studies in Short Fiction
SSR	Scottish Slavonic Review
SSU	Studies on the Soviet Union
ST	Shreveport Times
SV	Sotsialisticheskii vestnik [Berlin]
SVSQ	St. Vladimir's Seminary Quarterly
SZ	Sovremennye zapiski [Paris]
SZh	Svobodnyi zhurnal
TC	Twentieth Century
TD	Tridtsat' dnei
TeC	Teoria e critica
TLL	Teaching Language through Literature
TM	Temps modernes
TP	Tempo presente
TRSF	Trudy po russkoi i slavianskoi filologii
TSLL	Texas Studies in Literature and Languages
TZS	Trudy po znakovym sistemam
UES	Unisa English Studies [Pretoria, South Africa]
UlR	Ulbandus Review
ULR	Universities and Left Review [London]
UQ	Ukrainian Quarterly
UR	Ukrainian Review
USC	Universidad de San Carlos
UZTGU	Uchenye zapiski Tartuskogo gosudarstvennogo universiteta
VF	Voprosy filosofii
VII	Vestnik instituta po izucheniiu SSSR [Munich]
VL	Voprosy literatury [Moscow]
VLGU	Vestnik Leningradskogo gosudarstvennogo universiteta. Seriia istorii, iazyka i literatury
VM	Vol'naia mysl' [Munich]
VMK	V mire knig

VoR	Volia Rossii
VP	Vozdushnye puti [New York]
VQR	Virginia Quarterly Review
VR	Voprosy romantizma
VRSKhD	Vestnik russkogo studencheskogo khristianskogo dvizheniia
VsP	Vstrechi s proshlym
VT	Volia truda
WHR	Western Humanities Review
WLT	World Literature Today
WoW	Wort und Wahrheit
WS	Die Welt der Slaven
WSA	Wiener slawistischer Almanach
WSJ	Wiener slawistisches Jahrbuch
WW	Welt und Wort
WZ	Wort in der Zeit
YR	Yale Review
ZeF	Zemlia i fabrika
ZeS	Zeitschrift für Slawistik
ZF	Zona Frana [Caracas]
ZI	Zhizn' iskusstva
ZOR	Zapiski otdela rukopisei
ZS	Zbornik za slavistiku [Belgrade]
ZSP	Zeitschrift für slavische Philologie

Publishers' Acronyms

AN SSSR	Akademiia nauk Soiuza sovetskikh sotsialisticheskikh respublik
CPCC	Communist Party Central Committee
DETGIZ	Detskoe izdatel'stvo
GIKhL	Gosudarstvennoe izdatel'stvo khudozhestvennoi literatury
GIZ	Gosudarstvennoe izdatel'stvo
GOZPOLIZDAT	Gosudarstvennoe politicheskoe izdatel'stvo
ILP	Izdatel'stvo liubitelei poezii
SOPO	Soiuz poetov
RLJ	Russian Language Journal
TsOPE	Tsentral'noe Ob"edinenie politicheskikh emigrantov iz SSSR

Introduction

In their early criticism of Pasternak, Ehrenburg (1922.4), Tsvetaeva (1922.7), and Aseyev (1923.1) saw Pasternak's poetry as having a magic quality: "Pasternak's magic lies in his syntax"; "It [*My Sister, Life*] has miraculous power"; and "Pasternak's magic is in his syntax, his rhythm, furious and wild in its swiftness." One of the latest critiques, entitled "Miraculousness" and focusing on Pasternak's "holy craft," rounds out that magic theme, which is but one aspect of criticism that is copious, and, above all, variegated as a whole. Indeed, critics have profusely responded to almost the entire of Pasternak's "encyclopedical legacy"; criticism is therefore difficult to survey unless fragmented into certain categories: poetry; short prose; translations; Pasternak's links with other artists; Pasternak's views of art and literary schools and trends; Pasternak's poetics; and *Doctor Zhivago*. Even these categories fail to exhaust the entire spectrum of Pasternak criticism; they only attempt to capture its essence, while stressing shifts and changes in the perception of Pasternak from 1914 through 1990.

I

Even with publications of Pasternak's first collections, his poetry received mixed reviews. Between Shershenevich's scathing review, labeling the poetry of *A Twin in the Clouds* "chaotic" and a "result of insipidness and inner muddle" (1914.1), and Tsvetaeva's prophecy of Pasternak's notoriety: "The majority of significant poets *were*, there were few who *are*, only Pasternak *will be*" (1922.7), lies a myriad of conflicting, often polar, views. In the 1920s, many a leftist critic saw Pasternak as a "contemporary" poet ("truly contemporary with our time" [1924.1]), while others lambasted him for "harming" the "development of a new proletarian literature," a view to be frequently repeated later ("[He] inflicted a severe damage on the Soviet poetry" [1948.1]). Still others argued that Pasternak's poetry was "affected and incomprehensible"; revealed "unintelligibility of means," "social egoism," and "social neutrality"; has "sources of his world views footed in bourgeois culture"; and was written by a "city poet" isolated from

1

"social human emotions"; and that Pasternak "saw life from afar, behind a window sash."

Although this animosity continued even into the most recent criticism, the general reception of Pasternak's poetry was warm, with critics ranking Pasternak as "perhaps the greatest poet of the first incredible forty years," a "universal poet," an "original poet, an innovator," and a "real poet"—"from top to toe, one of a few poets for whom the entire world could become an object of poetic expression." Others stressed various qualities of his poetry, such as "simplicity of Pasternak's verse, the limpid sonority of their form" and "thematic interweaving of life, history, and art," praising his "gift of poetic language and poetic expressiveness," and claiming that "Pasternak's gift was above all to write of how the world feels to an individual full of life that poetry should live by."

Apart from these general views, criticism has thoroughly analyzed the entire canon of Pasternak's poetry, paying tribute to each of his collections and to almost each poem in them. In fact, the vast majority of Pasternak's celebrated poems received criticism's complete attention—resulting in the most thorough analyses of Pasternak's poetics. Some of the poems' variants, "Marburg" (1979.11 and 1979.21) and "Mirror" (1983.27 and 1989.21) in particular, were painstakingly compared to each other in order to examine shifts in Pasternak's poetry. Here again, the criticism fluctuated. Some vehemently argued that Pasternak's poetry "from early to late" showed a concern for simplicity, that changes occurred from a "lyric intonational spaciousness and word repetitiousness of *A Twin in the Clouds*, lyric word play of *Themes and Variations*, sound metaphors and attentiveness to details of things and objects in *My Sister, Life*, epic form in *A High Malady* and three tales in verse to a romance tradition of Fet and Polonosky in *Second Birth*" (1976.25). Yet others attempted to prove that Pasternak's "poetical biography" is cyclical, not evolutionary (1975.4); Pasternak's conception of art formed in the early period is applicable to all of his works; the poetry of "Yuri Zhivago" and *When the Skies Clear* are "internally kindred" to Pasternak's early poetry (1988.8); Pasternak's early poetry displays more simplicity than his "mature" verse (1983.19); and that "there have been no essential changes in Pasternak's way of expression since 1917" (1962.13).

This disparity aside, criticism concurred that *My Sister, Life* and *Themes and Variations* are Pasternak's "high points" and his "lasting accomplishments": the former deemed a "classic" of the twentieth century, a "stepping stone to Pasternak's development as a poet," and "no literary cliche," and the latter as Pasternak's "most expressive book." *My Sister, Life* was also praised for its "unique structure" (each poem individually complete and yet textually dependent on one another), its "saturated lyricism" and "total disappearance of authorial 'I'"—seen as the collection's "most astonishing quality" (1988.8). Some critics attributed that "unique structure" to Blok's influence (in which "single elements achieve their complete meaning only in the context of the whole," [1987.13]), others broadened the influence to include Heine, Bodlair, Annensky, Ivanov, Blok, and Bely (1988.8). Another study perceived the collection's structure as divided into two halves, its narrative form similar to that of a novel, and stressed the significance of the garden and mirror imagery, the love theme, and the motif of separation, concluding that Pasternak's art follows and frames life (1978.33).

Hardly any critique failed to discuss *My Sister, Life*'s poetics, metrical structure, rhymes, sound instrumentation, alliteration, motifs, space and time criteria, allusions, illusions, imagery, ellipses, language, composition, repetition devices, anaphoras, stanzaic instrumentation, syntactic pauses, themes (such as art, music, music and poetry, nature, and love), publication history, text variants, and many other aspects. Textual parallels were drawn between the collection and many a literary work, including *Doctor Zhivago*, Gogol's *The Terrible Vengeance*, *The Lay of Igor's Campaign*, and Dobrolyubov's *From the Unseen Book* (its memorable lines, "So whispered a girl, my Sister"), and, of course, the works of Lenau, Goethe, and Lermontov, and Scriabin's "Third Symphony," to name but a few parallels.

Pasternak's other poetry, poetry of *Doctor Zhivago*, *Above the Barriers*, *Second Birth*, *A High Malady*, and *When the Skies Clear*, also received criticism's acclaim. After the appearance of *Second Birth* and the three tales in verse, criticism began to stress changes in Pasternak's poetics, a "transformation," a shift "from a conspicuous to an inconspicuous style." Changes were particularly noted in *Second Birth*, its genres, the art-and-life relationship, the double meanings of time and space, structure of stanzas, the function of imagery, lexica, rhythm, and rhymes. An analysis of *Lieutenant Schmidt* recorded another form of changes revealing the tale's monometrical structure; its chain, pair, and ring rhymes; the "thematic spheres," an amalgamation of history, nature, and "personal life"; and the function of "authorial language stratum" (1976.18).

Interpretations of more specific features led to other shifts in criticism that focused on Pasternak's use of syntax, the tendency toward anacoluthon, the use of "syntactic displacements," and the "contamination" of syntactical constructions (such as verbal ellipses and imbalance between main and subordinate clauses). Recent criticism began to investigate some neglected aspects of Pasternak's poetry, particularly with new approaches such as decoding and intertextuality, among others. Studies also centered on the function of various motifs, myths, folklore, and plot in Pasternak's lyrics. Others resuscitated criticism's analyses of Pasternak's use of metonymy, now seeing its function both as a trope and as a compositional device. Still others attempted to advance new linguistic approaches to Pasternak's poetics, notably the "poetry and grammar" analyses. The role of music became a frequent subject of criticism too. Some analyzed the musicality of Pasternak's lyrics, finding echoes of Beethoven and Chopin in them. Others underlined the use of "musical forms" in the lyrics' compositions, focusing on melodic motifs and rhythmic patterns, or they interpreted Pasternak's use of interplay of light and color, i.e., synesthesia, as an influence of Scriabin. Many even insisted on Pasternak's cult of music, claiming that Pasternak "entered poetry through his love for music and painting."

II

Early criticism of Pasternak's short prose, like that of his poetry, was inconsistent in its views. For Tsvetaeva (1933.3), *The Childhood of Luvers* was a "work of genius," whereas Mirsky (1925.1) labeled it a "stumbling and incoherent story." Weidle (1928.5) was even more strident when condemning *The Line of Apelles* and *Letters from Tula* as "unsuccessful, chaotic experiments." Both Mirsky and Weidle, however, admired *Aerial Ways*: Mirsky praised it for not having the "dry" prose of *The Childhood of Luvers*, and Weidle for its "wholly original linguistic tissue, unlike any that has ever existed before in Russian prose." Jakobson continued Mirsky's and Weidle's praise of *Aerial Ways*, seeing it as Pasternak's most dramatic story. His study laid the ground for a new approach to the prose, stressing the role of metonymy as Pasternak's figure of speech and proving the interrelationship between Pasternak the poet and the prose writer (1935.1). Gutner (1936.2) further developed both of Jakobson's concepts, expounding that Pasternak the prose writer stems from Pasternak the poet and the Pasternakian metaphor (in *A Safe Conduct*) "shortens the distance between the nature phenomena fixed by his metaphor and the reader's reception." Gutner was among the first critics to compare Pasternak's early prose to that of young Tolstoy, Proust, and Rilke. Except for Aleksandrov's (1937.1) and Schimanskii's (1945.3) critiques, criticism of Pasternak's prose became dormant for almost thirty years. Aleksandrov drew attention to the meaning of detail, while Schimanskii, in his interpretation of *Letters from Tula*, *The Childhood of Luvers*, *The Line of Apelles*, and *Aerial Ways*, evinced that "in every one of the four stories, therefore, something is lost: a notebook in the story from Italy; a life's purpose in the old actor's existence in *Letters*; a child in *Aerial Ways*; and the innocence of childhood in the last story."

Such an emphasis on the poetics was resumed in the 1960s, with Livingstone's study (1964.8) of modes of expression in Pasternak's six prose works and with Aucouturier's interpretation of the theme of the poet-legend in *The Line of Apelles*, *Letters from Tula*, and *The Tale* (1966.4), and his appraisal essay of *The Line of Apelles* (1968.2). Livingstone examined Pasternak's concept of simplicity, which she saw resulting in a shift in emphasis from the "outrageous self-confidence" of the poet in *The Line of Apelles* to its loss in *Letters from Tula*. Aucouturier saw the legend of the poet as the "initial ferment of all the prose work of Pasternak" that only reached its maturity in *The Tale* ("the poet is not the author of his legend, but the servant of the destiny it traces for him" [1966.4]). Aucouturier's findings, in the second article (1968.2), that the title of *The Line of Apelles* points to a symbolic notion of art in this work and that it is futile to distinguish craft from talent, also heralded a new shift in criticism.

Criticism of the 1970s followed that literary approach. It focused on, among other aspects, stylistic traits and imagery, genesis of "literary aspiration" (1976.23), the presence of Pasternak the poet in his prose, the function of coincidences, the author's self-concealment devices, and on specific topics within individual short pieces. Mossman's study (1971.12) examined the stylistic traits in several short prose works, the use in them of neologisms, phonetic progressions, and rhythmization in particular, while deducing that the relativity of time and space was an important trait of Pasternak's short prose. Another Mossman study (1972.14) traced Pasternak's "coming of age" and the art-life theme throughout Pasternak's prose—from the earliest pieces (*History of an Contraoctave, The Line of Apelles, The Childhood of Luvers, Aerial Ways,* and *The Tale*) to *Doctor Zhivago.* Mossman also extended the concept of "tonal realism" of Pasternak's "biographical" realism inspired by Lermontov. Elena Pasternak's two contributions (1976.23; 1977.18) shifted criticism's attention to Pasternak's "first prose attempts," and established a multitude of new traits akin to his early prose. Thus she drew thematic similarities between Pasternak's earliest drafts (under the pen name Relinquimini) and *My Sister, Life* ("for the first time we can here see a personified life image entering a trusting relationship with the poet"). Other types of "early prose attempts" were postulated in Simpliccio's critique (1979.44) of Pasternak's fragments, which are seen to have a "'European,' romanticized background" and "figures from medieval history."

Criticism also moved in a new direction with Carol Jackson's theory of coincidences devices (1978.22) and her identification of three types of coincidences—happenstance (physical), synchronicity (psychic or spiritual), and prophetic (destiny-related)—all seen to occur on three levels: obvious, subtle, and transcendent. Jackson showed that Pasternak's short prose operates more on obvious and transcendent levels than on subtle ones. Ponomareff's study (1979.37), attempting to unmask the self-concealment of authorial speech, highlighted yet another change in criticism of the 1970s. Similar changes occurred with emphasis on individual short prose pieces, such as Katkov's study (1979.23) that considered *Without Love* (in its "fundamental philosophical structure") an embryo of *Doctor Zhivago,* and studies of *A Safe Conduct.*

Ever since Jakobson's critique of *A Safe Conduct* in 1935, criticism has repeatedly paid attention to it. Some regarded *A Safe Conduct* as one of Pasternak's most prominent accomplishments, as important as the *My Sister, Life* collection and *Doctor Zhivago.* Others placed *A Safe Conduct* even higher, calling it "The Bible" of their childhood, as Voznesensky did (1968.18). Still others summed it up as "a series of fascination and original discourses on art, culture, history, psychology, and many other topics" (1977.3), or as a "history of how Pasternak became a poet, and what the life of a poet actually means" (1981.17). It was only in the 1970s that more profound studies of *A Safe Conduct* began to appear, many of them focusing on a single topic instead of making general comments. Aucouturier's essay (1979.3), for example, initiated a new approach to both of Pasternak's autobiographies. It pointed to three features in *A Safe Conduct*—artistic, the displacement of a traditional autobiographical plot, and philosophical—that make *A Safe Conduct* different from Pasternak's second autobiography, *An Essay in Autobiography.* Aucouturier exhibited that a close bond between Pasternak's poetry and *A Safe Conduct* exists, traced a source for its title (in the poem "To a Friend"), and concluded that *A Safe Conduct* is an "attempt to protect art from the encroachment of the time-enslaver and to secure to art a road into eternity." A different shift emerged, too, in Hughes-Raevsky's interpretation (1989.20) of Mayakovsky's suicide in *A Safe Conduct*, contending that the suicide was portrayed "in motion" (a desire to capture the "dynamism" of a Mayakovsky-futurist) and "directly" (including detailed descriptions of weather, nature, and people, with their expressions and experiences), and that *A Safe Conduct* is "still another biographical 'concurrence-non-concurrence' between the two poets—an opposite solution to the question of death and immortality."

Two new approaches, decoding and intertextuality, were introduced in Faryno's (1987.7) and Greber's (1989.17) critiques. Faryno deciphered the most concealed meanings of lexica in *Letters from Tula,* and defined ten lexical levels, "key motifs," while analyzing the story's lexical strata against the poetics of Pasternak's other works. Greber's contextual and intertextual approach to *The Childhood of Luvers*, *Three Chapters from the Tale*, and *The Tale* focused on literary, historical, religious, musical, philosophical, psychological, and anthropological aspects. She found echoes of *The Lay of Igor's Campaign* in *Three Chapters from the Tale*, Chekhov and Dostoevsky in *The Tale*, and most convincingly, Dostoevsky's *Netochka Nezvanova* in *The Childhood of Luvers*. Similar novelty was displayed in another study of *The Childhood of Luvers*, in Szoke's essay (1988.43), defining the function of naming in the tale. Szoke argued that *The Childhood of Luvers* does not focus, as promulgated in other criticism, on the coming of age and upbringing—but on the tale's heroine, Zhenya. Szoke inferred that the tale's major issues, naming and appellation, are beyond the realm of the personality "question," and that naming is linked to the appearance of "objective, 20th-century lyric poetry reflecting perception in the world."

III

Although Pasternak's translations comprise an impressive volume, "greater than that of his own collected works" (1982.14), criticism of them is much less abundant than criticism of his poetry and prose. It was not until 1935 that the first critique appeared, and of a translation of Georgian poets at that, even though Pasternak's translations of many German poets had been published earlier, with his debut of a Kleist translation appearing in 1918. Another five years passed before critiques began to appear, as a result of the *Hamlet* translation in 1940—the year that publicly launched Pasternak as a translator. Yet twenty more years were needed for publications of scholarly studies of Pasternak's translations, by then numerous and including a broad range of poets and writers from various languages, cultures, and time spans. In the 1970s and 1980s, criticism widened its scope even more with critiques of the poetics, focusing frequently on translations of individual poets or their poems, moving beyond Shakespeare, Goethe, Georgian poets, and Rilke translations—regarded as Pasternak's major accomplishments.

Except for a few scathing comments (one by the Polish poet Miłosz, who characterized the translations as of "doubtful quality"), Pasternak's translations have been well received. He was ranked with the most prominent Russian translators of the nineteenth century, and, in several cases, thought superior to others, including Pushkin, Bryusov, and Marshak. Criticism bestowed many compliments upon his skills, above all the ability to recreate a translated work, applying his own concept: "like an original, a translation should produce an impression of life, not of literature" (1968.12). He was especially hailed for his language, which Poggioli characterized as "mosaic" (1958.58), while another critic (1983.16) equated it with the multilayered language of Pasternak's poetry. Others extolled him for establishing his own school of translation—based more on the recreation of the spirit of the original than a lexical truthfulness to the original (1968.17). His Petőfi translations were described as "beyond doubt wonderful," translations of the German impressionist poets as "exemplary," and the translation of Verlaine's "Effect de nuit" as surpassing that of Bryusov's (in conveying the poem's concluding chain of tropes and in its musicality, "inherent in the original poem" [1983.8]). Likewise, he was commended for renditions of Horace's poetry: retention of the original meter, loyalty to the content and "artistic form," "freshness and naturalness of the language," and sound instrumentation—emulating the original's "rustling of trees, burbling of streams, and sea waves" (1966.5). A great portion of the praise was given to the poetics of Pasternak's translations, "in which visual images lose the self-sufficing, sensual thingness owing to the mobility and inner metaphorical quality of his poetic language" (1940.3), to his style, "gravitation" toward a spoken language (1971.13) and to his approach to "overturn" the poets he translated (1968.18).

Criticism paid its greatest tribute to translations of Shakespeare (plays and poetry), ranking the *Hamlet* translation as Pasternak's most celebrated achievement; though some critics found faults with the translation. Such a mixed reaction was true of Russian criticism in general—both praising and condemning Pasternak for his choice of language. Vilyam-Vilmont (1940.3), for example, was thrilled with the language of Pasternak's *Hamlet*: "popular and everyday ... a healthy, lusty language touched by a sudden frost of the historic tragedy." Similarly, another reviewer applauded Pasternak for accurate renditions of many passages, translated "with great mastery, ingenuity, and technical dexterity," yet accused him of "distortions, unnecessary and unjustified modernization, heavy, utterly incomprehensible lexical constructions," and "marked vulgarization" (1940.1). Such an approach was followed by Reztsov (1940.2) and Morozov (1944.2), the former castigating Pasternak for "errors and blunders" caused by "an insufficiently disciplined selection of words," and the latter hailing him for the "enormous merit in his translation," his tendency to simplify and economize Shakespeare's language, and elimination of literalism.

Critics continued in this vein in the 1960s and 1970s, labeling the *Hamlet* translation "A Soviet Hamlet" (1960.23), but leveling criticism at the abundance of "spoken idiomatic turns," bordering "at times on vulgarity" (1979.12). Another stigma was attached, that the *Hamlet* translation conveyed "descriptions of his [Pasternak's] own fate, his polemics with the authorities, and his interaction with the contemporary life" (1960.23). That view was shared by almost all American studies of the *Hamlet* translation, including those of Markov, France, Rowe, and Clayton. Markov thus inferred that the translation illustrated Pasternak's own personality, reflecting his "lyrical confession disguised as translation," a variant of the "Aesopian language" (1961.18). France, too, reiterated that view, insisting the translation downplayed strong images of decay, corruption, and disease used by Shakespeare (1973.4), and changed sexual allusions ("That's fair thought to lie between maids' legs" became "But what a wonderful thought that is—to lie at a young girl's feet!" [1978.15]). Rowe likewise interpreted "departures" from the original as aimed at portraying Pasternak's own life, and noted as well an increased emphasis on Ophelia's sexual innocence, and a muting of the scene of contamination (1976.24). Clayton's conclusion that Pasternak may have viewed the image of Hamlet as an allegory of events in Russia during Pasternak's lifetime (1978.8) reverberated once more to the strains of this familiar interpretation of Pasternak's *Hamlet*.

Pasternak's translations of Georgian and German poets frequently drew criticism's responses, too. Responses to translations of Georgian poets (Titsian Tabidze, Simon Chikovani, Vazha Pshavela, and Baratashvili) reflected some features of criticism of the Shakespeare translations, for example the notion of Pasternak's assimilation of himself into his translations, as presented in Rayfield's survey of Pasternak's affinity with Georgian poets. Rayfield also noted that the accuracy of the translation of Vazha Pshavela's *The Snake-Eater* was questionable, for "Vazha's beeches and elms become puny planes and maples" (1982.17). A similar discrepancy was discussed in a study of a Baratashvili translation (the poem "Two Colors"), badly digressing from the original so that one could talk of "two different poems" connected by an identical theme (1976.1). Laudatory responses, however, prevailed, as in an early review of Pasternak's first collection of Georgian poets, the first "first-class work of poetic translation in all the existence of Soviet poetry" (1935.3), even though Pasternak did the translations, as the review noted, from a language he did not know, using a crib.

Criticism of Pasternak's German translations basically revolved around *Faust* and Rilke, ignoring translations of, for example, Kleist, impressionist poets (such as Becher, Herwegh, Heym, Hoddis, Werfel, and Zech), Schiller, Sachs, and Goethe's lyrics. It again focused on Pasternak's infusion of his creeds into the translations, creating in the *Faust* translation, as was claimed, "Pasternak's Faustian world" (1979.25). The *Faust* assimilation was particularly felt in the recreation of a "newly poetic, musically—which means spiritually—and emotionally different atmosphere" (1979.25), in Pasternak's changing of *Faust*'s heroine (of "minor importance" in the original) into a person who "acquires a matter, breathes the life, the pain into it" (1968.18), and in his tendency to use poetry instead of the prose ("Hier ist ein

Kompositionsplan verwirklicht, der ... das Lied zum tragenden Element macht" [1972.22]). As to Rilke translations, Pasternak's imprint was even more conspicuous; the translations were pronounced as his "own work," as a result of Pasternak's "simplification of syntax" and the use of everyday "expressions" (1986.12), among other reasons.

IV

Criticism of Pasternak's links to other authors could be divided into two major periods, before and after the appearance of *Doctor Zhivago*. In the first, comparisons were made occasionally, with brief comments, comparing, for example, Pasternak's early poetry to Pushkin, i.e., Pushkinian "lucidity and simplicity" (1922.3) or pronouncing Pasternak a "direct descendent of Pushkin" (1945.3). Such generalized comparisons were made to other poets and writers: Lermontov, Tyutchev, Fet, Bely, Bryusov, Apukhtin, Annensky, Balmont, Mandelstam, Akhamatova, Esenin, Severyanin, Mayakovsky, Khlebnikov, T.S. Eliot, Auden, and Rilke. In the second period, a more elaborate criticism prevailed, with Pasternak tied to numerous poets and writers, unknown and renowned, with a list growing to staggering proportions, so much so that one critic doubted the validity of Pasternak's links to "all these poets who have nothing in common with each other" (1959.74). Another defended the links, however: the "roots of Pasternak's talent have deeply and widely made way into the soil of the world and Russian literature" (1960.1). Taken at random, the list includes Derzhavin, Dudintsev, Benediktov, Zhukovsky, Joyce, Jean-Paul Jacob, Ignazio Silone, Sinclair Lewis, Verlaine, Baudelaire, Maria Gironella, Rimbaud, Ibsen, Mann, Mallarmé, Valery, Moravia, Heidegger, Camus, Brodsky, Swinburne, Grigoryev, Griboyedov, Andreas-Salomé, Poe, Bergson, Cervantes, C.F. Meyer, Ferdinand de Saussure, Hemingway, and many others—some of whom were discussed in more detail than others.

Pasternak's propensity for alliteration, inner rhymes, hyperbole, and toying with poems' titles, for example, was attributed to Nietzsche's influence (1966.6), and Nietzsche's Zarathustra, "unable to be happy among men," was compared to Zhivago (1983.21). This critic also drew similarities in the concept of "inwardness" in Kierkegaard and Pasternak, contending that both of them found refuge in turning inward "to create for themselves a more acceptable world" (1983.20). Popper's theory that knowledge is expanded through one's attempt to prove or disapprove current knowledge was compared to Pasternak's view of art as an endeavor to solve the enigmas put forth in the art of one's predecessors (1979.26). The collection *My Sister, Life* was tied to, among others, Helen of Troy from Goethe's *Faust* and Shakespeare; Pasternak's affinity with both Goethe and Shakespeare was repeatedly emphasized in the criticism. Repeated comparisons were made to Eliot, too, starting with suggestions of Eliot echoes in Pasternak's early poetry (1944.1), continuing with an investigation into Eliot's literary sources and allusions (1965.1), and ending with a discussion of literary bonds between Pasternak's poem "Hamlet" and Eliot's *Prufrock* (1983.12). Ibsenian motifs, the purpose of a poet in his internal struggle, and Pasternak's "Gulfstream" metaphor seen as echoed in Ibsen, were also discussed (1966.14). Pasternak was likened to Plato as well, with Pasternak's poem "Uninhibited Voice" reflecting Plato's "Feast" (1988.19).

Pasternak's affinity with Rilke occupies a large segment of criticism, broad in scope and time span, and replete with general remarks and detailed studies. Thus, criticism noted that in *The Childhood of Luvers*, Pasternak rejected Rilke's philosophy of symbolism (1932.1), both Pasternak and Rilke were concerned with transformation of objects and events into symbols (1959.10), both loved to animate objects distinguished in poets by particular imagery (1962.5), and Pasternak has "much more heart" and Rilke "much more intellect" (1962.5). Comparisons of Pasternak's early prose to Rilke's *Aus den Aufzeichnungen des Malte Laurids Brigge* began in early criticism, first with general remarks (1936.2), then with more substantiative comments on similarities of "tone and style" (1958.58), artistic personalities and their aesthetic theory (1972.2), themes and notions, the language, and the poets' temperament (1979.27), and metaphors and themes (1983.18). "Textual echoes" were found in the *A Twin in the Clouds* collection, sharing the "introspective mood and subdued imagery" of *Das Stundenbuch*, in Pasternak's poem "To the Meyerholds," and in the poetry of the *Second Birth* collection, though "the impact of Rilke on Pasternak was ultimately a spur to individual and original activity" (1972.2). Pasternak's "the Garden of Gethsemane" and Rilke's "Ölbaumgarten" were contrasted and compared in terms of various aspects, with one study finding that Pasternak's poem was not a response to Rilke's, that Pasternak displayed more "dramatic highpoints," and that his poem depended more on a biblical text than Rilke's (1963.15). Other Pasternak-Rilke ties—religious poetry, Pasternak's Rilke translations, and Rilke's impact on Pasternak as described in Pasternak's autobiographies—were also noted (1972.21).

Criticism of Pasternak's ties to Russian poets and writers was also voluminous, including most importantly Blok, Mayakovsky, Pushkin, Tolstoy, Dostoevsky, Gogol, Lermontov, Fet, Tyutchev, and three of his literary peers—Tsvetaeva, Akhmatova, and Mandelstam.

The presence of Blok in Pasternak was, for one critic, "through the whole of his [Pasternak's] production" (1959.57), for another Pasternak stood among "the greatest, Alexander Blok and Osip Mandelstam" (1976.11), while a third thought of Pasternak as "the true successor" to Blok in Russian poetry (1967.4). The presence was also defined differently, as echoes, or as "Blok associations" and "shadows" (1960.33), "allegiance," and influence (most strikingly during Pasternak's formative years [1974.9]). Similarities were found in their adherence to literary schools (Pasternak's poetics, like that of Blok, is closer to the poetics of romanticism than that of his immediate predecessors, argued Poggioli [1958.58]), concepts of realism (defined "cross" for Blok, and "self-sacrifice" for Pasternak [1967.4]), and their works. Echoes were noted in many poems ("February" [1980.19], "Hoar-Frost," "Wind," and "Spring in the Forest" [1987.3], "Winter" [1988.3], "Uninhibited Voice"

[1988.19], "Hamlet" [1959.47]) and parallels were drawn between *Doctor Zhivago* and Blok's *Retribution* (1960.16) and "Russia, the Poverty-Ridden Russia" (1961.12); and between Pasternak's "The Star of Nativity" and Blok's *The Twelve* (1978.3), among other comparisons.

Criticism of the Pasternak-Mayakovsky relationship stressed both their affinity and differences. The extent of the affinity shifted throughout the criticism, beginning with a "close association" (1959.74), then detailing an "obsession" with Mayakovsky (1959.66), the fact that Mayakovsky held a special place in Pasternak's life (1958.4), and the idea of Pasternak seeing "a high model and the justification for revolutionary novelty" in Mayakovsky's poetry (1985.3), and ending with emphasis on their "closeness" (1979.15). Yet contrasts repeatedly surfaced in the criticism, juxtaposing, for example, the poetic credo of the two poets (Mayakovsky was a poet of the street, Pasternak a chamber poet [1929.2]), their poetry (Pasternak was a "parthenon of impersonality" after the agonies and perorations of Mayakovsky [1930.2], Pasternak's "private muse" against Mayakovsky's "chaos and violence" [1963.12]), their imagery ("dramatic and pathetic" with Pasternak, "hyperbolic and iconoclastic" with Mayakovsky [1958.57]), their views of time ("panchronistic" with Pasternak, "ahistorical" with Mayakovsky [1968.16]), and their language ("classless, unstyled" with Pasternak, "conscious handling of language" with Mayakovsky [1968.16]), or critics related the two poets' conceptions of art, finding more differences than similarities (1985.4).

Influence of Pushkin's aesthetics on Pasternak attracted a special notice, first as Pasternak's perception of Pushkin "in an impressionistic way" (1928.4), and also as an inference that through his entire creative life, Pasternak found support in Pushkin's aesthetics. Pushkin was constantly present in his consciousness (1989.3). During that period, criticism recorded various degrees of Pasternak's bonds to Pushkin: influence, echoes, "associative links," "concealed quotations," and variations on Pushkin's works, themes, imagery, motifs, language, the poetics in general, and other forms of "enrichment" (1960.1). Pushkin's influence was also seen in Pasternak's conception of art and the artist, attempts to secularize the Russian literary language (1986.14), the poetics of the poem "Theme with Variations" (reflecting Pushkin's nature imagery, references to Greek and Egyptian mythology, and Judeo-Christian tradition [1979.8]), Pasternak's borrowing of an identification of a poet with a wild duck from *Eugene Onegin* that Pasternak used in his poem "Sturdy Marksman" (1986.17), and in *Themes and Variations*, "the most conspicuous example" of Pushkin's presence in Pasternak (1989.3). Aside from noticing influences, criticism drew parallels between Pasternak's *Dramatic Fragments* and Pushkin's *Little Tragedies* (1989.2), *The Childhood of Luvers* and *The Captain's Daughter* (for the story's "rapidly sketched picture of a snowstorm which is almost as vividly powerful as the description of the blizzard in Pushkin's *The Captain's Daughter*" [1963.1]), and *Spektorsky* and *The Fountain of Bakhchisarai* (presentation of a "dual vision of woman" [1974.8]). And Pasternak's variations on Pushkin were found in *Second Birth* (1990.2), the poem "Hamlet" (with its "firmer allegiance" to Pushkin [1959.47]), in the poem "Out of Superstition" (a variant of "I Remember a Marvelous Moment" [1980.22]), several poems from the 1917 edition of *Above the Barriers*, the poem "A Woman Substitute," Pasternak's two "large novels," in which "poetry and prose are combined"—*Spektorsky* plus *The Tale* and *Doctor Zhivago*—and in "concealed quotations" from Pushkin (1989.3), all of which prompted a critic's comment that "Pasternak became a bridge connecting Soviet poets with a Pushkin tradition" (1989.3).

Criticism of Pasternak's links with Tolstoy focused on their similarities and dissimilarities—as reflected in their views of history, art, religion, and works. A common bond, for example, was perceived in their attitudes toward nature and man (1960.42), in concepts of the conflict between nature and history (1968.3), and in Pasternak's "Tolstoyian non-acceptance of violence . . . [that] found its total incarnation in the novel" (1989.28). Similar affinity surfaced between Pasternak's early prose and that of young Tolstoy, with Tolstoyian impact seen on *Letters from Tula* (1980.1) in particular, and between *Doctor Zhivago* and *War and Peace*, with one critic mentioning their common features (1960.16), and others detailing that "kinship," such as their fundamental views of art as a means of illuminating reality, their own versions of simplicity and directness, and their views of the meaning of existence (1967.15). Foremost among those pointing out the dissimilarities was a critique that stressed that "Pasternak was a poet and a musician which Tolstoy was not" (1959.44). Other criticism differentiated Pasternak's and Tolstoy's opposing attitudes toward religion, claiming Pasternak was inspired by the supernatural and Christ's miracles, whereas Tolstoy denied the supernatural (1980.1), and arguing that Pasternak's worldviews are based on a metaphysical approach, Tolstoy's on a rational (1961.19), among other contrasts. Comparisons of Pasternak to Dostoevsky were also instituted on various levels, regarding their concepts of beauty and femininity (1959.80), and specific links between their works. Criticism detected, more specifically, links between Pasternak's "Bad Dream" and Ivan Karamazov's "accusation against God" (1987.5); between Zhivago and Raskolnikov, the protagonists of *Doctor Zhivago* and *Crime and Punishment* (1960.20); and between Zhivago and Myshkin (the hero of Dostoevsky's *The Idiot*)—similar in their Christ-like positive attributes toward sexual love, suffering, and individualism (1968.7). One critic likened in particular *The Childhood of Luvers* to Dostoevsky's *Netochka Nezvanova*, matching similarities in their plots, roles of narrators, relationships between the parental couples, the motifs of a fallen woman and children's secret readings, and the theme of feminine adolescence, concluding that "Pasternak's reference to Dostoyevsky is disguised and can be decoded only in roundabout ways" (1988.15). Criticism of Pasternak's links with Gogol was identified in several critiques: Pasternak's use of Gogol's epigraph in his poem "Collapse" (1937.1), comparisons between Pasternak's play *Blind Beauty* to *Dead Souls* (1969.9), comparisons of *My Sister, Life* to Gogol's *The Terrible Vengeance* (1988.36), and views of Pasternak's prose as an "intersection between Gogol's and Dostoyevsky's prose" (1971.6).

Ever since Tynyanov's remark on Pasternak-Lermontov "common bonds" (1924.4), criticism repeatedly discussed their affinity, referred to as "literary associations" or influence. Such "associations" were attributed to Pasternak's poems "Hamlet" (1959.47) and "A Woman Substitute," with its title reflecting "the double tradition" of Lermontov and Heine (1971.8), and Lermontov's "biographical realism" (1972.14). The Lermontov influence was confined to *My Sister, Life*, one critic claiming this was the only influence on Pasternak during his work on the collection (1967.12), and another perceiving that influence in the impact of Lermontov's "tragi-romantic hero, the *Demon*" in the collection's epigraph (1988.36). As to Pasternak-Fet ties, specific features of Pasternak's poetics reminded critics of Fet, like meter and semantics in Pasternak's "Mein Liebchen, was willst du noch mehr"—compared with Fet's "Bad Weather-Autumn-You Smoke" (1988.11), and critics discerned echoes between Pasternak and Fet in their "methods of associative leaps" (1976.25), their "contextual bonds" (1971.3), and "common bonds" (1924.4). Mandelstam went so far as to juxtapose Pasternak's "high tide of images and feelings [that] sprang into being again with unprecedented force" against Fet's "the burning salt of undying words" (1923.5). And Pasternak's links with Tyutchev were detected in Pasternak's poems "Night" (1988.3) and "Hamlet" (1959.47), in his poetics (1970.4), and in his theoretic views—specifically, in Pasternak's preference of the term "poesy" over "lyric poetry" (1975.16), among other comparisons.

Of Pasternak's ties to other poets, criticism emphasized his affinity with Tsvetaeva, Akhmatova, and Mandelstam. Pasternak's friendship with Tsvetaeva, poetic and in life, occupied a good portion of criticism, starting with Adamovich's critique of contrasts between the two poets—Pasternak was more a poet than Tsvetaeva, though Pasternak lacked Tsvetaeva's "charm" (1958.2). It continued through the late 1980s, with a critique's conclusion that Tsvetaeva's imitation of Pasternak's style indicates her "absorption" in him at that time, and that "her love for Pasternak may have been displaced . . . but it returned to him deepened and enriched" (1989.35). During that thirty-year period, some critics compared their poetics (1970.4), discussed the depth of their relationship, noting disappointments in their real-life encounters, and contrasted the exuberance of Tsvetaeva's poetic tributes with Pasternak's reticence (1970.5). Others drew parallels between their works, finding echoes (as in Pasternak's poem "All Moods and Voices" [1981.11]) or the influence of each other in them—or critics contrasted their portraiture techniques (1990.66). A critic found Pasternakian images in Tsvetaeva's "From the Sea," equating, for example, the poem's image of "objects washed away by the sea" with a passage from *Doctor Zhivago* describing additional features of Lara (1989.22).

Links with Akhmatova were reflected in their literary bonds, reciprocal poetry dedications to each other (1976.12), and Akhmatova's poem "The Four of Us" (1977.9)—Akhmatova, Mandelstam, Pasternak, and Tsvetaeva—which, of course, was Akhmatova's response to Pasternak's poem "The Three of Us." In addition to recognizing their bonds (1922.4 and 1933.4, for example), critics saw Pasternak's poetics as similar to that of Akhmatova (1970.4 and 1980.13), and they elaborated on the two poets' "long, complex evolution," their interactions with the government, and on shifts in their literary styles (1982.7). Drawing parallels between their works, critics attempted, for example, to define the genre of *Doctor Zhivago* by contrasting it to Akhmatova's *A Poem without a Hero*, a "Gedichtroman" as opposed to *Doctor Zhivago* as "Romangedicht" (1984.3).

Finally, criticism of Pasternak's links with Mandelstam centered on their differences, though also recorded instances of their affinity, similarities between their poetry (1925.1 and 1933.4) and their views of art (1985.4), and dialogic echoes of Mandelstam in Pasternak's poem "All Moods and Voices" (1981.11). Contrasts, however, prevailed, particularly in recent criticism, as in the critique listing "antipodes" between Pasternak and Mandelstam (1985.9).

V

Criticism of Pasternak's association with futurism became controversial from the outset, with one critique labeling Pasternak a "living misunderstanding which occurred among Futurists" (1924.2). The controversy did not question Pasternak's belonging to two futurist groups, "Centrifuge" and "Lyrika," as it did the scope of futurist influence on Pasternak's early works. Many a critic either strongly denied attributing "the Futurist label to any significant body of his verse" (1989.11); insisted Pasternak did not participate in the futurist "activities" (1965.9); or assumed that the influence futurists (including Mayakovsky) were said to have exerted on Pasternak was "nil" (1967.12). At the opposite extreme, critics consented Pasternak was a "'fellow traveller' of the Futurists" (1967.7), or claimed Pasternak inherited his novelty of rhymes from futurism (1959.74). Others became more assertive, contending Pasternak's poetry belonged to futurism (1964.1), or to a right wing of futurism (1929.2); or they claimed Pasternak's style was that of a futurist (1964.9), and his poetry is a combination of "the classical tradition, a symbolist musicality and the colloquial bent of the Futurist" (1964.15); or Pasternak's closeness to futurists could be attested by his involved syntax and estrangement of the futurists with his own directness, confidence, and unique view of life (1943.2). Even a study of Pasternak's poem, "Definition of Poetry," insisted that "in both form and content the poem establishes a metapoetical discussion for and against Futuristic poetics" (1987.10). Two other critiques also attested to futurist features in Pasternak's early poetry, notably "sound-images," "words at freedom" poetics, and "intersyntactical connectedness" discerned by the first critique (1975.13), and parenthetical constructions, a tendency toward anacolutha and ellipses, the idea of "poetry growing out of everything, even out of trivialities," and the varied use of the instrumental pointed out by the second (1968.13). Still another critique reconfirmed that affinity, and, among other things, juxtaposed Pasternak's essay *The Wassermann Test* against an article by Bolashkov, a mediator between Pasternak and Mayakovsky, and identified a number of common concepts in their two essays. It concluded convincingly that "aesthetic declarations of *A Safe Conduct* fully correspond to artistic principles in a futurist painting—a dynamic portrayal of displacement, a registration of several dynamic aspects, with an 'image' of man portrayed in the fixation of 'transition'" (1979.15).

Controversy dominated, too, in criticism of Pasternak's association with other schools and movements: symbolism, imagism, impressionism, realism, and avant-garde poetry. Despite some critics stressing Pasternak's aversion for labeling art with *isms* (1962.1), a number of critics still associated Pasternak with a specific literary school, seeing him as an impressionist (1926.1); or a unique reformer of impressionism, rethinking and recreating it as a literary device (1928.4); or a "major, and perhaps the last writer of the Symbolist novel" (1968.19); or an imagist who puts imagism at the service of a complex and unified vision, using paradoxical or unexpected images that convey an essential truth (1949.1); one critic claimed that "Boris Pasternak is, in decisive impulses of his poetics, a poet of the Avant-garde" (1981.13). Criticism of Pasternak's adherence to the principles of romanticism turned likewise epidemic, seen either as Pasternak's unique blend of romanticism, present in his poetry, though "not one of his poems could have been written before him" (1922.4), or in the interpretation of Pasternak's aesthetic in the romantic tradition, "a view of poetry as a knowledge of the deepest reality of nature as a living whole, and of poetry as primarily myth and symbolism" (1967.17). A critique tied that "Romantic tradition" with Pasternak's views of both romanticism and realism, inferring that a "genuine debate over Romanticism and Realism" occurred in Pasternak's two autobiographies, that Pasternak looked upon romanticism as a "variety" of art and a "false pathos," and that Pasternak "clearly" accepts realism in his essays of the 1940s (1975.8). The concept of realism also incorporates "moral realism," an association with "richness of content," "impressionability, collaboration with real life, seriousness, conscientiousness, and moral responsibility" (1988.28). Consenting to Pasternak's adherence to a "Realism of his own coinage" (1958.59), some critics began to emphasize Pasternak's disassociation from literary schools, and forwarded a date for that detachment. One critic premised that toward the end of the 1920s, Pasternak completely detached himself from symbolism and began to strive for simplicity and naturalness in his poetry (1983.23), while another, suggesting an earlier date, laid down that Pasternak had already in 1915 surmounted the contradictory views on art propounded by symbolists, acmeists, and futurists in the character of Heine (1968.2)—the hero of *The Line of Apelles.*

Views of Pasternak's conception of art and his "artistic method" shifted throughout criticism as well—with the spectrum of controversy widening to diametrical opposites. Quoting Pasternak from an interview, a critic recalled Pasternak's insistence that "he had no philosophy of art except that gained from stark experience" (1960.5). Others attempted to specify that nonexistence of theory more distinctly, proposing Pasternak had no "complete theory of art" but made "claims for certain abstract terms," his "concept of a 'force' or 'power'" (1985.4), and that he never presented a coherent theory as the basis for his writings (1975.16), or they labeled his system of thinking as "very entangled" (1959.74). A critic, disputing these views, categorically insisted "that Pasternak *has* a theory of art," the essence of which lies within three categories: "movement and interaction," "transformation and reunion," and "naming and the lyric truth" (1988.29). Others saw the conception as "traced to two major sources—the author himself and the world in which he lives" (1972.7), or in Pasternak's creative approach of vitalism (1983.26), in his creativity philosophy—categories of quality, conscious, originality, art as an imbibing sponge, "mirror reflection," and concept of time (1988.22), in views of dynamism (1964.10), or in Pasternak's "ability to recreate emotional states by means of utterly trivial correlatives and the unusual choice of images" (1945.3). An attempt to identify the conception in detail was made in another critique, this time through a series of Pasternak's adages on art—art ought to "grasp reality" ("natural, human reality"); a work of art should contain a "rich and profound content"; art should reflect life with its "constant zest"; art should give the "whole show to the world"; and that a creation of an "enlarged image of man," which art is supposed to achieve, is "possible only in the motion" (1964.10). Concerning criticism of Pasternak's "artistic method," two critiques endeavored to define it, one as a three-fold method, combining Tolstoy's epic structure, the symbolist poetics of metaphor and simile, and the polyphonic method of Dostoyevsky (1960.34), and the other as an intuitive and associative method, striving to name that which had not yet been named (1963.3).

VI

From its early start, criticism labored over basic features of Pasternak's poetics, discerning, for example, "downpour" as his favorite image (1924.4); establishing three forms of Pasternak's "technique": self-observation, observation, and "poetic influence" (1927.4); praising Pasternak's unusual skill of combining sounds with sense (1928.5); and noticing that "tonality and harmony of words is the very spring of Pasternak" (1930.2); or admiring unusual rhymes, as in *Spektorsky* (Pasternak "hardly employs any other combinations but 'rhyphmoids'") and commenting that Pasternak's rhymes "often result in daring intellectual adventures" (1931.1). Early criticism also examined Pasternak's "unusual" metaphors and elliptical devices (1933.2); lauded his poetry's compositional structure, rhythm, metaphors, and metrics (a "variety of meters, an efficient combination of various themes and variations in a single small work, and a rich verse instrumentation—all this makes Pasternak's poetic technology musical and expressive" [1934.1]); and declared that metonymy is Pasternak's most essential figure of speech: "Pasternak's lyricism, both in poetry and in prose, is imbued with metonymy" (1935.1).

During the next three decades, criticism continued to elaborate on the poetics features previously discussed. In one instance, it related Pasternak's infatuation with music to Verlaine's influence (his adage, "de la music avant toute chose" [1960.17]), and in other instances, it expounded on rhyme innovations ("in the invention of new rhymes Pasternak has probably no rivals in modern Russian poetry" [1959.57]), rhymes preferred, such as past tense verbal adverb rhymes and "chain rhymes" (1960.37), his propensity for apocopated and near rhymes (1959.59), and Pasternak's ternary meter omissions ("there seems to be no doubt that Pasternak should be regarded as an outstanding renovator of Russian ternary verse" [1968.15]). Criticism also continued to detail the poetics of Pasternak's metaphors and similes, viewing the former as achieved "through successive juxtaposition and superimposition and fragmentation of images," composed of "slang ... next to the most sophisticated reinterpretations of Plato or the most subtle suggestions of tenderness" (1959.57), or so innovative that Pasternak's metaphors stood out among futurists (1959.74), and the latter as void of accessories or ornaments (1961.1). All these aspects prompted a critic to pronounce Pasternak a master of "concrete" detail in his similes and metaphors (1963.19).

Such general views of imagery included criticism of symbols: a symbol of rain corresponding to life, of water as a symbol of Pasternak's heroes' inner experiences, and of snow as a symbol of death (1962.9), among others. Two critiques stood out in their detailed approach to Pasternak's concept of world ("it is world entirely *seen and experienced*"), his "humanization of the world" (1969.14), and to his role as "witness" (opposed to Blok's role as "seer"), ending with the summation that Pasternak's poetics could be defined as "Romanticism with a difference" (1964.4).

Criticism of the 1970s and 1980s either continued the examination of the established features of Pasternak's poetics—sound instrumentation, versification, similes and metaphors, symbolism, and syntax, for example—or shifted to other aspects, such as verse organization, semantics, poetry systematization, structure, thematics, dialogue, mythology, folklore, recurrent motifs, recurrent imagery, and quotations, among other aspects. Again, criticism confirmed that Pasternak did not violate the Russian classical metric system, and conducted his innovations within the five basic traditional meters (1979.13), and that Pasternak's "meter variations" were moderate, with a four-foot iambic prevailing ("a sign of bondage with the Pushkin tradition"), the "movement of verse syntax" corresponded to "the evolution of sound repetitions," approximate rhymes abound (33 percent), with inexact rhymes employed less frequently (12.5 percent), and that an average length of Pasternak's verse is 30.2 lines (1984.1). Another aspect of the poetics was reexamined, Pasternak's apocopated rhymes, referred to as rhymes with final consonant truncations, and seen as "encountered more often in Pasternak's ternary measures than in his binary" (1989.23). Critics also reverted to Pasternak's repetition devices; one critique established four repetition types: Type A (with a stressed vowel), Type B (a stressed vowel with a consonantal echo), Type C (a pure consonantal repetition), and Type D (with an unstressed vowel alone or followed by a consonantal echo) (1978.9). Another critic attempted to prove that Pasternak consciously employed sound repetitions as motifs combined into larger thematic units, and that repetitions are "carriers of lyric action"—not metaphor conduits (1979.9). This analysis paved the way for another critique that defined the role of sound as a thematic motif, and asserted that four sound themes were prevalent in Pasternak's poetry: man/crowd; creativity/absence of creativity; harmony/absence of harmony; and love/absence of love (1989.1). Imagery, simile and metaphor in particular, became once more a repeated subject of criticism, which displayed new approaches, "imagery of spoken language" revealing Pasternak's tendency for "lexical vulgarization" (1986.15), a new interpretation of "metaphorization and demetaphorization" as "regulators" of plot (1979.17), a finding that the vehicle of metaphors and similes reflects "*the* reality" (1985.3), and a theory that two essential lines run through Pasternak's system of similes, "a principal of sensual vision and a compositional principle of purely verbal associations" (1982.12).

New approaches to the poetics were echoed in other criticism, with a critique scrutinizing Pasternak's verse organization, seen to be based on seven devices (development, expansion, repetition, modification, contrast, matching/combination, and presentation [1980.21]). Other critics converged on Pasternak's world conception, insisting Pasternak created an image of the world without using physical elements (1970.4), or they expounded on the function of myth (including the role of folklore) in Pasternak's poetic world (1980.2). Some examined recurring motifs, referential and stylistic, inferring that a communion of the everyday with the eternal is the central theme of Pasternak's poetry (1990.74); others analyzed recurring images, for example "mask" (*maska*), "cast" (*slepok*), "make-up" (*grim*), and "bust" (*biust*) (1987.3). Another critic applied decoding to the study of poetics, suggesting that a candle is a symbol of "human life," a Christmas tree represents an image of "eternity and a myth of childhood," and a window is an "entrance through which the demonic winter world strives to penetrate" (1978.14). Indeed, a window image comprised an entire study that aspired to present it as the most recurrent image, a "sort of recurrent character," as recurrent as Pasternak's art, spring, garden, night, or candle, and to interpret it as an "opening" through which air and fragrances penetrate, a gleam through which visual impressions permeate, and a "part of one's living quarters open to the outside world" (1978.41).

The latest approaches, notably intertextuality (1989.11 and 1985.6), analysis of "distribution contacts" in Pasternak's "poetic diction" (1982.20), and the function of quotations, have likewise unveiled new features in Pasternak's poetics. A study of quotations within Pasternak's poetic world led a critic to formulate five quotation types: quotations used "consciously"; "simply 'rooted' in a literary tradition"; "obviously" influenced by a literary work; based on "correlative description" of text; and quotations involving a repetition of Pasternak's own text (1976.27). Another critique revealed new sides of Pasternak's poetics, while applying Karolina Pavlova's identification of poetry as a "holy craft" to Pasternak's "miraculousness"—"Karolina Pavlova called her craft holy. Marina Tsvetaeva followed that path, too. Boris Pasternak acquired early his craft, which, naturally, flowed into a mastery, and, further, into enchantment. But he achieved that which he himself defined a miraculousness" (1990.47). Finally, a critic saw the shift in the poetics in this way: Pasternak's poetics during the forty years remained the same, and yet experienced an "obvious evolution": in syntax ("expanded steadily"), rhymes ("originality was achieved by a skilled altering of corrected forms"), composition ("structured on a clear, three-part pattern"), and sound instrumentation (1986.18).

VII

None of Pasternak's works received as much attention as *Doctor Zhivago*. In a year's time following the American publication of the novel (5 September 1958), ninety-five critiques appeared in newspapers and magazines in the United States alone, and by the end of 1959, criticism all over the world totaled 658 items', most of them boasting sensational headlines. Some argued whether *Doctor Zhivago* was a factual or political novel, a saga of the Russian family, a pessimistic novel about "snow, blood, and tears," "A Russian Odyssey," a book of a man's life dream, or a novel aspiring to "A Truly Great Work of Art." Although sensationalism began to subside soon, criticism continued to exploit that bombshell fervor, as reflected in a number of titles in the early criticism—"Much Ado about Zhivago," "A Storm About Boris Pasternak," "The Pasternak Affair," or "About Pasternak but Without Sensation." Sensationalism fully exploited, criticism began to underscore the novel's literary values, comparing it to the Bible, Dante's *Divine Comedy*, Goethe's *Faust*, Joyce's *Ulysses*, Steinbeck's *Grapes of Wrath*, Shakespeare's *Hamlet*, and to Russian literary giants—Dostoevsky, Turgenev, Chekhov, Pushkin, and Tolstoy, among others. Other critics accentuated the novel's Russian literature themes—life and death, the tragic nature of the main hero, the relationship of an individual to history, enslavement of the human spirit, and Russian myths and legends—themes that prompted a critic to declare *Doctor Zhivago* as the last "Russian classic." Such a shift in criticism produced a plethora of scholarly studies, forming the axis of future criticism of *Doctor Zhivago*—structure, genre, philosophy, history, religion, evaluation, themes, characters, "ideology," language, symbolism, imagery, and poetry.

The novel's poetry, too, became early criticism's target, unfolding with a review (27 February 1959) that lamented, "One wishes that one might read the poems in the original, so impressive are they in translation" and culminating with scholarly studies and dissertations, which pronounced the last chapter "the conclusive, necessary resolution, the final chord in which a wandering melody has come to rest," "the genesis of a work of art," "integral to the novel, not merely supplementary," and "ein unentbehrlicher Bestandtteil des Werkes." Criticism attempted to determine the arrangement of the poems as well, adjudging they "fall into five groups which follow the procession of the seasons," are arranged "according to an evidently international order which reflects at once the cycle of the seasons," reflect "the three basic themes of the sequence . . . nature, love, and the author's views on the meaning and the purpose of life," and are "like a play within a play." Beyond such generalizations,

---

'According to *Pasternak's Doctor Zhivago. An International Bibliography of Criticism (1957–1985)*, by Munir Sendich and Erica Greber (East Lansing, MI: RLJ, 1990), pp. 2–35.

criticism turned to more specific topics, the relationship, for example, of individual poems to the prose, "Winter Night" and "Hamlet" in particular; it also endeavored to analyze nine of the religious poems through a tripartition of "Entrance," "Hesitation," and "Action"—thus heralding yet another shift in criticism, to be examined below in more detail.

From its very beginning, shifts and changes frequently occurred in *Doctor Zhivago* criticism. Once sensationalism surrendered to scholarly study, critics attempted to separate "sense" from "nonsense," demanding "some sorting out and summing up," which dominated the first five years of criticism, 1957–61. The "sorting out" was triggered by controversies, engulfing almost the entire criticism, the novel's artistic merits, composition, central meaning, bonds with Russian literature, genre, events surrounding the publication, characters, themes, language, style, symbolism, the role of the Revolution, "The Pasternak Affair," the Soviet authorities' victimization of Pasternak, and even Pasternak's reaction to the criticism. Controversies ran so high that some critics both praised and found faults with the novel. A critic saw *Doctor Zhivago* as "an epoch-making novel" in which "everything flows into a common harmony" but detested the novel's "complex" composition (1957.5), another underlined the novel's "Russianness," the abundance of details, the absence of lyrical plot development and plot motivations, the absence of promulgations of systems and concepts, yet disliked the presence of concocted collisions and coincidences (1958.22), and a third declared *Doctor Zhivago* "more than a novel, a piece of revelation," but complained about its debilitating effects of "symmetric duplicity" (1958.34). The discrepancies widened even more with interpretations of the novel's structure, coincidence devices, and criticism's rebuttals. The structure was found to be centered around three women, symbolizing three different worlds, the old, the Revolution, and the new (1959.4); composed of four "sustained moments at which the 'candle burns'" (1959.23); and equated to a play, with the first two acts involving the appearance of the hero, the third the writing and publishing of the novel, the fourth the crowning and humbling of the hero, and the fifth developing into the *denouement*, with the epilogue reflecting "the judgement of posterity" (1958.51). Similar controversy echoed in the use of coincidences, termed a daring enhancement of the novel's verisimilitude (1958.14) and useful in conveying Pasternak notion of the interrelatedness of all things (1959.75)—yet two other critics found the novel marred by obscure language coincidence (1960.20), and "wildly improbable in its use of coincidence" (1958.77).

Rebuttals appeared both in American and foreign criticism, with one Italian critique claiming that the diversity of views stemmed from the critics' political affiliations (1958.21). Such politics did not primarily dominate American rebuttals, as in an Isaac Deutscher and Irving Howe confrontation, but reflected many features typical of the rebuttal criticism of the first five years. Deutscher accused Pasternak of misreading history, writing a novel anachronistic in content and form, with irrelevant and peripheral characters, and marked by a "perplexing contrast between masterful lyrical passages and an inept confusing storyline" (1959.17). Howe's response sought to spurn Deutscher's views, while insisting that the novel is faithful to the "essential history of our time," shows Pasternak's treatment of current political concerns, and portrays recurring, timeless truths—freedom, conformism, and suffering (1959.27). Struve's reaction to the criticism of Deutscher, Richard Stern, Edmund Wilson, and the letter from the editors of *Novy mir* highlighted the rebuttal criticism of the first five years. Struve retorted to Stern that *Doctor Zhivago* "is a poet's novel, a novel of symbolic realism," that coincidences "are deliberate, consciously willed, and skilfully contrived." He lectured Deutscher on the proper use of the term "inside émigré," adding that Deutscher's interpretations are "unadulterated nonsense." Some of Wilson's arguments were dubbed "meaningless and pointless" or "just gibberish" (1962.27). Struve's study, in its endeavor to "sort out" previous criticism, created a sharp turn in the direction of the criticism of the 1960s.

This new direction occurred in criticism's tendency to center on the novel's previously examined literary qualities—the poetics of landscape descriptions, language, comparisons to other literary works, genre, originality, similes, metaphors, allegory, religious symbolism, and other features. Another direction introduced criticism with specific topics, previously mentioned or newly approached, such as the self-realization quest, comparisons of *Doctor Zhivago* to *War and Peace*, the novel's structure, the role of personality, the image of Zhivago, the language, style, artistic merits, plot, the novel's symbol of a wild duck, art and society, water imagery, recurrent imagery, the poems, and adverse criticism. Some of these topics were treated before, yet their re-emergence reflected an important change in the 1960s criticism—in its innovative approaches and scholarly contributions. Parallels between *Doctor Zhivago* and *War and Peace* were drawn from the outset (1957.2), but only the 1960s criticism defined, for example, the novel's common features within a specific area—structure—thus finding both novels divided into fifteen chapters with an epilogue and consisting of three broad sections (1962.17); criticism also revealed more specific bonds between the two authors (1967.15). Criticism of imagery, with emphasis on similes and metaphors, also emerged early, one critique mentioning three types of metaphors (the "instinctive gestures," the "straightforward process," and the "deliberate step" [1959.5]), yet a profound study of imagery came out only in the late 1960s. The critique elaborated on Pasternak's "preoccupation" with figurative language that described inanimate nature, details of daily life, and Lara, declaring that recurrent imagery "is reserved exclusively for Lara," and its use is limited to the good only (1968.9). Criticism of symbolism frequently appeared, too, from the early start, once referred to as "esoteric symbol chopping" (1961.4), but it remained confined to general criticism of the novel. Yet, only in the 1960s, the first critique entirely devoted to a specific aspect of symbolism was published, suggesting that the dead duck in *Doctor Zhivago* echoes the "whole range of hopes, dreams and illusions," and was represented by similar birds in Ibsen's *The Wild Duck* and Chekhov's *The Seagull* (1963.8). Even hostile criticism became more specific, attacking, as in one instance, the novel's composition ("naive, sprawling, disjointed"), characters ("pale and invisible"), and ideology ("untenable ideas on Christianity and the Revolution" [1968.10]), and in another instance finding the "basic faults" in the portrayal of the Revolution and the main hero in his relationship with Lara (1963.6).

Adverse criticism resurfaced in the 1970s as well, though it appeared only occasionally (1979.43), eclipsed as it was by the preponderance of scholarly critiques, some of which continued to lean on the already-established criticism, others paving the way for new interpretations. Following the trends of the previous criticism, critics still profusely treated the novel's structure, religious symbolism, characters, and language; drew parallels between Pasternak's early prose and the novel, including the novel's comparisons to other works; produced criticism with comprehensive views of the novel; and returned to the controversy over the novel's publication, with one critique entitled "After the Storm" (1972.4). New criticism centered on the novel's onomastics (with emphasis on the formation of names, their derivative, diminutive, and patronymic forms [1970.11]), the use of *Doctor Zhivago* in advanced language instruction (1972.10), the novel's dependence on history (Kolchak and the formation of the Far Eastern Republic [1979.22]), analyses of individual poems, and the author's concealment devices (1979.37), and attempted to reveal the novel's literary genesis, and home and mythopoetic imagery.

Criticism of the novel's structure revolved around various topics, including a comparison of the novel's epilogue to epilogues in the major novels of Dostoevsky, Turgenev, and Tolstoy, with the conclusion that sentences ending sections and chapters either emphasize the plot already narrated, hint at the narrative to unfold, or are used as surprise and tension devices (1970.6). A variety of structure devices—duplicity, duality, contrapositions, plurality, and paradox—was examined in another critique (1971.5), followed by still another study that thoroughly grouped sections and chapters and unraveled "interlocking devices" (1974.15). Criticism also drew parallels between *Doctor Zhivago* and Pasternak's early prose, turning back as far as *Dramatic Fragments* (1970.2), *The Story of a Contraoctave*, *The Line of Apelles*, *Letters from Tula*, and *A Safe Conduct*. *A Safe Conduct* was read, in another critique, as the "extension" to *Doctor Zhivago*, with "particular episodes of the novel (the spring in Melyuzeevo, the long journey to the Urals, the return to Varykino) evolving from the most successful experiments in his earlier fiction" (1977.9). As to the novel's genesis, two critiques stood out, noting parallels to Dostoevsky's *The Devils* and *Crime and Punishment*. The portrayal of fanatical and materialist revolutionaries as leading Russia into disintegration and chaos was seen as common to *The Devils* and *Doctor Zhivago* (1978.29), with similarities to *Crime and Punishment* drawn on various planes: between the life stories of Dunya and Lara, the personalities of Svidrigaylov and Komarovsky, and the occurrence of axe murders in both novels (1979.42). Criticism viewed home imagery as serving numerous purposes, "an expression of Zhivago's resentment of Bolshevik Revolution," "the primary symbol of man's nature and of his destiny," the novel's conception of art, and "the problems of death and immortality" (for "man is at home in the universe in death as in life, death being a return to the All—the final homecoming")—all of which was compared to Heidegger's aesthetic theory (1974.4).

Criticism of the 1980s went in two directions as well—it expanded previous criticism and produced criticism with new approaches. As before, there appeared criticism of the novel's genesis, comparisons to other works (Pasternak and others'), and criticism of the novel's concept of history, the function of window imagery in the novel, genre, and the novel's "central" motifs and themes, as well as criticism of criticism and adverse criticism—all of which markedly contributed to the novel's scholarship. The scholarship was likewise enhanced by criticism with new interpretations; for example, modes of characterization, studies of single poems (even of a single line), the function of epiphany, and the novel's railroad motif. The novel's genesis was contrasted in these instances against Pasternak's lesser-known works, a fragment from a 1936 prose piece, a passage from a play, Pasternak's unpublished notes on Dostoevsky's *Diary of a Writer*, and Pasternak's notes on the folklore of the Urals (1983.14). *A Haughty Beggar* and *A District in the Rear* were thought to "come right up to" the novel (1983.24), Pasternak's six "Reliquimini Fragments" were tied to the novel (1984.11), and Bulgakov's *Master and Margarita* was compared to *Doctor Zhivago* on various planes. Of the adverse criticism, Nabokov's views of the novel became most memorable, including his "stylistic observations," "political ideology," and view of "the Jewish question, and the novel's religiosity" (1989.19). The poetics of metaphors and similes ("the figures of analogy") was reexamined in a separate study, claiming that in the novel there exist "entire pages without metaphor or simile," yet "some pages bristle with them," figures of analogy are "confined to . . . the narrator's discourse," occur "in all kinds of forms," "combine elements of nature with aspects of human life," and are "essential techniques for the author to express his view of life" (1985.8). A study that surveyed the entire history of the criticism grouped the early period by themes, evaluation, the protagonist, the novel's suitability for publication in the Soviet Union, and its shortcomings as discussed in criticism. The study paid special attention to criticism of the past decade, the novel's structure, form, the correlation between prose and poetry sections, feminism, intertextuality (quotations, influences, allusions, parallels, borrowings, and adaptations), and the "Joycean approach" (1986.5).

The new approaches to Pasternak revealed many unexplored features of his works. Anderson's study (1987.1) of railroad motifs, imagery, and symbolism found train imagery to be associated with many characters (Zhivago, Lara, Antipov/Strelnikov, Tonya, Kolya, and Prolenko) and discerned in the imagery of the railroad a "system made up of many different intersecting private journeys"—a "train-as-system" view of the symbolic structure. Another critic (1981.4) argued that epiphanies, defined in this instance as "transformations of images to achieve a transcendant effect," were Pasternak's favored method of portraying "striking, brief relevations" in which "conventional logic has no place whatever." Recurrent imagery of death and trains in *Doctor*

Zhivago was cited as evidence of these revelations, and Lara was considered the focal point of Zhivago's epiphanies.

Other analyses of the characters focused on the modes of character descriptions, polyphony, and coincidence devices in relation to Bakhtin's theory of the "ideal" novel (1982.9), and reevaluated Zhivago as an egoist, an antisocial individual, a "trimmer," and a poor family man, among other epithets (1988.32). Both essays discussed the characters of *Doctor Zhivago* in relation to Pasternak. Other critics focused on Zhivago's poetry. Altschuller and Dryzhakova (1985.1) examined the nature and love themes, the role of Hamlet, and Zhivago's affinity with Christ—an embodiment of the "personal, individual outset of the world history." Liapunov and Senderovich (1986.10) analyzed the last line from the poem "Hamlet" ("To live one's life is not to cross a field"), and assessed it in terms of "temporal" and "spatial measurement." They saw it as a "minimal poetic text" governed by Pasternak's poetic laws of "word compression," with the only difference being that his poetry "amplifies expressive means which the proverb avoids."

Pasternak criticism of 1990 experienced a profound resurgence following the 100th anniversary of Pasternak's birth. Alfonsov (1990.2), Asmus (1990.5), Aucouturier (1990.6), Barnes (1990.9), Girzheva (1990.27), Ozerov (1990.48), E.B. Pasternak (1990.50), Pomerants (1990.58), and Zholkovsky (1990.74) all attempted to present a critical summation of Pasternak's works and artistic techniques either in toto or by focusing on one or a combination of aspects—poetry, themes, motifs, poetics, views of art, movement towards simplicity, and other signs of evolution or change in Pasternak's poetics. Other critics, such as Bogomolov (1990.13), Fleishman (1990.20), Gerstein (1990.25), Kats (1990.30), Kazakova (1990.31), Khazan (1990.32), Levi (1990.35), Musatov (1990.45), Ozerov (1990.47), E.B. Pasternak and E.V. Pasternak (1990.52–53), and Smolitsky (1990.68) presented general or specific biographies; attempted to analyze in detail Pasternak's involvement with other writers on a personal plane; and reexamined the role of music, philosophy, literary movements and their journals ("Lyrika" and "Centrifuge"), and Pasternak's acceptance of Tolstoy's teachings (1990.52). Besides attempting to summarize or explain in greater detail Pasternak's works and life, Zh. Pasternak (1990.55), Maslenikova (1990.43), Muravina (1990.44), and Polivanov (1990.57) recounted in memoirs their interactions with Pasternak or their recollections of events in Pasternak's life. Scholarship also looked at the history of the critical reception of *Doctor Zhivago*. One study (1990.72), divided into the sections "Yesterday" and "Today" (1958 and 1988 criticism collections of *Doctor Zhivago*), showed that the adverse reaction of Russian critics to *Doctor Zhivago* in 1958 did not change that much in 1990. Voznesensky (1988.46 and 1990.72) saw such hostile criticism as a failure to read *Doctor Zhivago* "objectively" because of the lies and invectives that have accompanied the Soviet reading of the novel for many years.

Overall, Pasternak criticism, throughout almost eight decades of its history, was positive, and, most significantly, comprehensive. It laboriously examined and unveiled innumerable facets of Pasternak's multifarious literary legacy, while creating a more definitive image of Pasternak the poet, prose writer, translator, essayist, critic, art theoritician, and literary craftsman, among other qualities. Although Pasternak the poet received criticism's ultimate acclaim, criticism placed Pasternak the prose writer and translator almost on the same level with poetry, with numerous critiques repeatedly emphasizing that Pasternak the prose writer and translator stems from Pasternak the poet, and that within Pasternak's oeuvre a continued tenor incontestably existed. Criticism singled out *My Sister, Life*; *A Safe Conduct*; and *Doctor Zhivago* as Pasternak's most prominent accomplishments, and hailed the Rilke and Shakespeare renditions as Pasternak's most celebrated achievements, his "own works."

Critics thoroughly scrutinized his poetics, too; marveled at his "mosaic" language, imagery (simile, metaphor, and metonymy—deemed his most essential poetic figure), rhymes (the innovative richness of which knew no equal), rhythm, verse organization, sound instrumentation, and other aspects; and attempted to prove that the poetics of Pasternak's poetry remained unchanged, though it experienced an "obvious evolution." Others asserted that Pasternak's "poetic biography" was cyclical, that his poetics principles formulated in the early period were carried over into his latest works, and that his early poetry (*My Sister, Life*, for example) was "internally kindred" with his latest (the poetry of *Doctor Zhivago* or the collection *When the Skies Clear*). Such a discrepancy generated yet another controversy, a distinctive feature of Pasternak criticism. Controversy prevailed in criticism of Pasternak's association with literary movements and schools and Pasternak's theory of art, nonexistent for some, and "categorically" conceptualized for others. Criticism also placed emphasis on Pasternak's affinity with and links to other poets and writers, foreign and Russian, exhibiting that Pasternak "widely made way into the soil of the world and Russian literature" (1960.1). Finally, *Doctor Zhivago* remained criticism's watershed, triggering new scholarship in the never-ceasing criticism, as if justifying Tsvetaeva's prophecy of 1922 that "only Pasternak *will be.*"

Boris Pasternak's Writings in Russian
1913–1990

1913

1 "Ia v mysl' glukhuiu o sebe" [Into a vague thought about myself I], "Fevral'. Dostat' chernil i plakat'!" [It's February. To get ink and cry], "Sumerki . . . slovno oruzhenostsy roz" [Dusk . . . as if sword-bearers of roses], "Segodnia my ispolnim grust' ego" [Today we'll fulfill his sorrow], and "Kak bronzovoi zoloi zharoven" [Like bronze ashes of braziers]. In *Lirika. Al'manakh.* Moscow: Lirika, pp. 41–45.

1914

1 "Artillerist stoit u kormila" [Artilleryman stands at the helm]. *KN*, no. 119 (20 November): 7.

2 *Bliznets v tuchakh. Stikhi* [A twin in the clouds. Poems]. Introduction by N. Aseev. Moscow: Lirika, 48 pp.

3 "Tsygane" [Gypsies], "Mel'khior" [Cupronickle], "Ob Ivane Velikom" [About Ivan the Great], "Gramota" [Deed], and *Vassermanova reaktsiia* [Wassermann test]. In *Rukonog. Sbornik stikhov i kritiki*, edited by N. Aseev, S. Bobrov, and I. Zhdanevich. Moscow: Tsentrifuga, pp. 10–12, 31–38.
   Wassermann Test reprinted: 1967.7.

1915

1 "Kak kaznachei poslednii iz planet" [Like the last paymaster of planets]. In *Vzial. Baraban futuristov.* Petrograd: n.p., p. 7.

27

2   "V posade, kuda ni odna noga . . ." [In a suburb whither not a single foot], "Vesna, ty syrost' rudnika v viskakh" [Spring, you are the dampness of a mine in (head) temples], and "Ia klavishei staiu kormil s ruki" [I fed a flock of keyboards from my hand]. In *Vesennee kontragentstvo muz.* Moscow: Studiia D. Burliuka and S. Vermel', pp. 45–47.

3   Trans. "Razbityi kuvshin" [Kleist's *Der zerbrochene Krug*]. *Sovremennik*, no. 5, pp. 25–85.
        Reprinted: 1923.9; 1941.6.

1916

1   "Poliarnaia zvezda (I–II)" [The North Star, I–II], "Toska, beshenaia, beshenaia" [Ennui, mad, mad], and "Chernyi bokal" [Black goblet]. In *Vtoroi sbornik Tsentrifugi. Piatoe turboizdanie.* Moscow: Tsentrifuga, pp. 9–11, 39–44.

1917

1   *Poverkh bar'erov. Vtoraia kniga stikhov* [Above the barriers. The second poetry collection]. Moscow: Tsentrifuga, 94 pp.

1918

1   "Bezliubie" [Without love]. *VT*, no. 60 (26 November): 2.
        Continued: 1918.2.

2   "Bezliubie" [Without love]. *VT*, no. 62 (28 November): 2.
        Continuation of 1918.1.

3   *Il tratto di Apelle. Znamia truda. Vremennik.* Moscow, pp. 17–22.

4   "Po stene sbezhali strelki" [The clock hands raced along the wall] and "Slozha vesla" [With oars at rest]. In *Vesennii salon poetov. Al'manakh.* Moscow: Zerno, pp. 139–40.

1919

1   "Ulichnaia" [Street] and "Raspad" [Decay]. In *Iav'*. Moscow: Iav', pp. 41–43.

1920

1 "Gorod" [The city] and "Zamestitel'nitsa" [The replacement]. In *Liren'. Sbornik*. Moscow: Liren', pp. 15–18.

2 "Margarita" and "Mefistofel'" [Mephistopheles]. In *Bulan'*. Moscow, pp. 24–26.

3 "Potselui" [A kiss] and "Ia sam" [I myself]. In *My. Sbornik stikhov*. Moscow: Chikhi-Pikhi, pp. 32–33.

4 "Pro eti stikhi (Na trotuarakh istolku)" [About these verses (on side-walks I'll pound)]. *KhS*, no. 1, p. 6.

1921

1 "Elene" [To Helene]. *KhS*, no. 2, p. 10.

2 "Kuda chasy nam zatesat'?" [Where are we to rough-hew our time?]. In *Poeziia bol'shevistkikh dnei*. Berlin: Mysl', pp. 118–20.

3 "Matros v Moskve" [A sailor in Moscow]. *KN*, no. 4, pp. 120–22.

4 "Nabroski: 'Osennee,' 'Vesennee,' 'Zimnee'" [Sketches: autumn, spring, winter], "Zimnee utro" [Winter morning], "Nu, i nado zh bylo, tuzhas'" [Well, it was needed, while exerting ourselves], and "Mezhdu prochim, vse vy, chtitsy" [By the way, all of you are women reciters]. In *Kinovar'. Sbornik stikhov*. Ryazan: Ryazanskoe otdelenie, pp. 13–18.

5 "Stantsiia" [Station] and "Rudnik" [The mine]. *KN*, no. 2, pp. 68–71.

1922

1 "Detstvo Liuvers" [The childhood of Luvers]. *NaD* 1: 121–67.

2 "Kreml' v buran 1918 goda" [The Kremlin in the blizzard of 1918]. In *Pomoshch'. Khudozhestvenno-literaturnye i nauchno-populiarnye sborniki*. Vol. 1. Simferopol': Krymsk TsTs Pomgol, p. 6.

3 "Mne v sumerki ty vse—pansionerkoiu" [At dusk you are still to me like a boarder] and "Mozhet stat'sia tak, mozhet—inache" [It can become like that or it can be otherwise]. In *Vserossiiskii Soiuz Poetov. Vtoroi sbornik stikhov*. Moscow: SOPO, pp. 13–16.

4   "Ne trogat'" [Don't touch]. In *Veshch'. Vremennik.* Vols. 1–2. Berlin: Veshch', p. 6.

5   "Neskol'ko polozhenii" [Some propositions]. *Sovremennik*, no. 1, pp. 5–7.

6   "Pamiati Demona" [In memory of *The Demon*], "Ty v vetre, vetkoi probuiushchem" [You are in the wind, testing with a twig], "Dozhd" [The rain], "Do vsego etogo byla zima" [Up till now it was winter], "Iz suever'ia" [Out of superstition], "Podrazhateli" [Imitators], "Obrazets" [A specimen], and "Zamestitel'nitsa" [The replacement]. In *Poeziia revoliutsionnoi Moskvy*, edited by I. Ehrenberg. Berlin: Mysl', pp. 81–91.

7   "Pis'ma iz Tuly" [Letters from Tula]. *Shipovnik* 1: 57–64.

8   "Pushkin." *Abraksas* 1: 31.

9   "Razryv" ("O, angel zalgavshiisia, srazu by, srazu by" [Oh angel, having lied, oh immediately, immediately], "O styd, ty v tiagost, mne! O sovest', v etom rannem" [Oh shame, you burden me! Oh conscience, in this early . . .], "Ot tebia vse mysli otvleku" [I'll shake off all my thoughts of you], "Pomeshai mne, poprobui. Pridi, pokusis' potushit'" [Just try to prevent me. Come, attempt to extinguish], "Zapleti etot liven', kak volny, kholodnykh loktei" [Braid this downpour like waves of cold elbows], "Razocharovalas'? Ty dumala—v mire nam" [You're disillusioned? You thought, in this world for us . . .], "Moi drug, moi nezhnyi, o toch-v-toch, kak noch'iu" [My love, my angel, just as in that night], and "Roial' drozhashchii penu s gub oblizhet" [The trembling piano will lick foam from its lips]). *Sovremennik*, no. 1, pp. 10–12.

10 "Nad Kamoi" [Over Kama], "S tekh dnei stal nad nedrami parka sdvigat'sia" [Since those days I began moving above the bowels of the park], "Poteli stekla dveri na balkon" [The glass of the door to the balcony perspired], and "Tak nachinaiut. Goda v dva" [Thus they begin. When they are two]. *Zhizn'*, no. 1, pp. 104–5.

11 *Sestra moia zhizn'. Leto 1917 g. Stikhi* [My sister, life. Summer, 1917. Poems]. Berlin-Petersburg-Moscow: I.Z. Grzhebin, 136 pp.
    Second edition: 1923.5; Third edition: 1976.3–4.

12 "Sneg idet" [It is snowing]. In *Iuzhnyi al'manakh*. Simferopol: Krymizdat, pp. 18–19.

13 "Tri glavy iz povesti" [Three chapters from the tale]. *MoP*, no. 1 (12 June): 2–3.

14 "Ty v vetre, vetkoi probuiushchem" [You are in the wind, testing with a twig] and "Imelos'" [There was]. *Trilistnik* 1: 31, 76–77.

15 "V lesu" [In the forest] and "Spasskoe." *Peresvet* 2: 46–48.

16 "Vo sne ty bredila, zhena" [My wife, you were delirious in your sleep] and "Strashis' menia, kak. . ." [Fear me like. . .]. *Izvestiia* (15 March): 5.

17 "Vorob'evy gory" [Sparrow hills] and "Sestra moia zhizn'" [My sister, life]. *KN* 2, no. 6: 100–102.

18 Trans. *Tainy* [Goethe's *Die Geheimnisse*]. Introduction by Prof. G.A. Rachinsky. Moscow: Sovremennik, pp. 17–32.

1923

1 "Briusovu" [To Bryusov]. In *1873–1923. Valeriiu Briusovu. Sbornik, posviashchennyi 50-letiiu Ia. Briusova*, edited by P.S. Kogan. Moscow: Kubs, p. 65.

2 "Kreml' v buran kontsa 1918 goda" [The Kremlin in the blizzard of the end of 1918]. *Lef*, no. 1, p. 53.

3 "Matros v Moskve" [A sailor in Moscow]. In *Strugi*. Vol. 1. Berlin: Manfred, pp. 11–13.

4 "1-e maia" [The first of May]. *Lef*, no. 2, p. 15.

5 *Sestra moia zhizn'. Leto 1917 g. Stikhi.* [My sister, life. Summer, 1917. Poems]. 2d ed. Berlin: Z.I. Grzhebin, 115 pp.
    First edition: 1922.11. Reprinted: 1976.3–4.

6 "Tema s variatsiiami (Variatsii 4, 5 i 6)" [A theme with variations (Variations 4, 5, and 6)]. *Krug* 1/2: 7–10.

7 *Temy i variatsii. Chetvertaia kniga stikhov* [Themes and variations. The fourth poetry collection]. Berlin: Helikon, 121 pp.
    Reprinted: 1972.4.

8 "Vesna v Moskve" [Spring in Moscow]. *MA* 1: 15.

9 Trans. "Razbityi kuvshin," "Prints Fridrikh Gomburgskii," "Semeistvo Shroffenshtein," and "Robert Giskar" [Kleist's *Der zarbrochene Krug,*

Prinz von Homburg, Die Familie Shroffenstein, and *Robert Giskar*]. In *Sobranie sochinenii*, by Heinrich Kleist, edited by N.S. Gumilev and V.A. Zorgenfrei. 2 vols. Moscow-Petrograd: Vsemirnaia literatura, pp. 19–148, 149–169.

"Razbityi kuvshin" reprint of 1915.3.

1924

1   "Belye stikhi" [Blank verses]. *Rossiia* 3, no. 12: 85–88.

2   "Otplyt'e" [Sailing away], "Petukhi" [Cocks], "Osen' (Ty raspugal moikh tovarok)" [Autumn. You scared away my buddies], and "Perelet" [Flight]. *RS*, no. 2, pp. 7–10.

3   "Vozdushnye puti" [Aerial ways]. *RS*, no. 2, pp. 85–96.
Reprinted: 1976.8.

4   Trans. "Somnenie," "Nebesnaia zmeia," "Angel smerti. U oblak vid . . . ," by Jakob van Hoddis; "Sumerki," and "Demony gorodov," by Georg Heym. *SoZ*, nos. 1–2, pp. 3–6, 35–36, 44–45, 86, 95–96.

1925

1   [Commentary on the Russian CPCC's resolution on literature.] *Zhurnalist*, no. 10, pp. 10–11.

2   "9 ianvaria" [January 9]. *KN* 2: 32–34.

3   "Iz stikhov B. Pasternaka (Al'manakh 'Kovsh', kn. 2-aia)" [From B. Pasternak's poetry (The almanac "Kovsh," the second book)]. *VoR*, nos. 9–10, p. 206.

4   *Karusel'. Stikhi dlia detei* [Carousel. Poems for children]. Illustrations by D. Mitrokhin. Leningrad: GIZ, 14 pp.

5   "Kruchenykh." In *Zhiv. Kruchenykh. Sbornik statei*. Moscow: Vserossiiskii soiuz poetov, pp. 1–2.

6   "Otryvok iz I-voi glavy romana 'Spektorskii'" [An excerpt from the first chapter of the novel *Spektorsky*]. In *Styk. Pervyi sbornik stikhov Moskovskogo Tsekha Poetov*. Introduction by A.V. Lunacharsky and S.M. Gorodetsky. Moscow: MTP, pp. 102–6.

7   *Rasskazy* [Tales] (Includes: *The Childhood of Luvers, The Line of Apelles, Letters from Tula*, and *Aerial Ways*). Moscow: Krug, 107 pp.

8   "Spektorskii" (chapters 1–3). *Krug* 5: 5–18. Reprinted in *Kovsh* 2: 128–32.
     Continued: 1926.10.

1926

1   [Autobiographical notes.] In *Pisateli. Avtobiografii i portrety sovremennykh russkikh prozaikov*, edited by V.I. Lidin. Moscow: Sovremennye problemy N.A. Stolliar, pp. 225–27.

2   [Comments on the resolution of the XIIIth Congress of the Russian CP.] *Versty*, no. 1, pp. 201–2.

3   "Deviat'sot piatyi god" [The year 1905]. *Proletarii* 1: 149–58.

4   *Izbrannye stikhi* [Selected verses]. Moscow: Uzel, 31 pp.

5   "Leitenant Shmidt" [Lieutenant Schmidt]. Part 1. *NM*, nos. 8–9, pp. 33–42.

6   "Muzhiki i fabrichnye" [Peasants and workers] (A chapter from *The Year 1905*). *Zvezda*, no. 2, pp. 140–42.

7   "Pis'mo k sestre. Otryvok iz poemy 'Leitenant Shmidt'" [A letter to my sister. An excerpt from the tale in verse *Lieutenant Schmidt*]. *MG*, no. 7, pp. 3–5.

8   "Pokhorony Baumana" [Bauman's funeral] and "Studenty" [Students] (A chapter from *The Year 1905*). *KrN*, no. 20, p. 4.

9   "Potemkin" and "Morskoi miatezh" [Mutiny at sea] (A chapter from *The Year 1905*). *NM*, no. 2, pp. 31–36.

10 "Spektorskii" (chapter 4). *Kovsh*, no. 4, pp. 123–35.
     Continuation of 1925.8. Reprinted: 1928.11.

11 Trans. "Podgotovka," "Nas polkovye marshi," "Broneviki," "Berlin," and "Les," by Johannes R. Becher; "Gorozhane," by Franz Werfel; "Tuneiadtsy," "Smert' Zhoresa," and "Voskresen'e Zhoresa," by Walter Hasenclever; "Nebesnaia zmeia," "Somnen'e," "U vid stolovogo bel'ia," and "Angel smerti," by Jakob van Hoddis [Hans Davidsohn]; "Demony

gorodov," "Na sudakh bystrokhodnykh," and "Prizrak voiny," by Georg Heym; "Mertvyi gorod," by Edlef Koeppen; "Mertvyi Libknekht," by Rudolf Leongard'; "Sumerki," by Alfred Lichtenstein; "Golos," by Ludwig Rubiner; and "Sortirovshchitsy," by Paul Zech (Translations of German impressionists). In *Molodaia Germaniia. Antologiia*, edited by G. Petnikov. Kharkov-Kiev: GIZ Ukrainy, pp. 42–43, 72, 73–77; 80–86; 103, 111, 126–29; 143–48; 161–62; 164–67; 219; 245; 279–82; 313–14.
  "Sortirovshchitsy" reprinted: 1930.7.

1927

1 "14 noiabria" [November 14] (A passage from "Lieutenant Schmidt").
   NL 1: 24–25.

2 *Deviat'sot piatyi god. Stikhi* [The year 1905. Poems]. Moscow: GIZ, 97 pp.
     Second edition: 1930.1; Third edition: 1932.1.

3 *Dve knigi. Stikhi* [Two books. Poems]. Moscow: GIZ, 212 pp.
     Second edition: 1930.3

4 "K Oktiabr'skoi godovshchine" [For the October anniversary]. *Zvezda*, no. 11, pp. 5–8.

5 "Landyshi" [Lillies of the valley] and "Prostranstvo" [Space]. *ZeF* 1: 339–42

6 "Leitenant Shmidt" [Lieutenant Schmidt]. *NM*, nos. 2–5, pp. 29–33; 22–27; 30–35; and 39–47.

7 "Leitenant Shmidt" [Lieutenant Schmidt]. *VoR* 2: 34–48.

8 [On the classics.] *NLP*, nos. 5–6, p. 62.

9 [Pasternak about himself.] *NLP*, no. 4, p. 74.

10 "Priblizhenie grozy" [Approach of a storm]. *Zvezda*, no. 9, p. 34.

1928

1 [An untitled article in the section "Sovetskie pisateli o pisateliakh i chitatele."] *ChP*, nos. 4–5 (11 February): 4.
     Reprinted: 1963.2.

2 "Bal'zak." *Zvezda*, no. 4, pp. 46–47.

3 "Kogda smertel'nyi tresk sosny skripuchei" [When the deadly crackling of a creaking pine tree]. *NM*, no. 1, p. 169.

4 "Marburg." *Zvezda*, no. 11, pp. 34–36.

5 "'Peredelka' iz knigi Poverkh bar'eov" [An adaptation from the book *Above the barriers*]; "Mel'nitsy" [Windmills]; "Otryvok iz neizdannoi poemy" [A fragment from an unpublished tale in verse]. *NM*, no. 12, pp. 38–41.

6 "Poka mne rifmy, byli v pervouchinu" [While rhymes were new to me]. In *Turnir poetov*. Moscow: Leningradskii teatr Doma pechati, p. 10.
    Reprinted: 1930.5.

7 "Pripiska k poeme 'Gorod'" [Addition to "The city," tale in verse]. *NM*, no. 12, p. 20.

8 "Proshchanie s romantikoi" [Parting with the romantics] and "Dvadtsat' strof s predisloviem" [Twenty stanzas with a preface]. In *Pisateli-Krymu. Literaturnyi al'manakh*. Moscow: Komissiia po bor'be s posledstviiami zemletriaseniia v Krymu, pp. 36–39.

9 "Siren'" [Lilac]. *ZeF* 2: 378.

10 "Son" [Dream], "Vokzal" [Train station], "Venetsiia" [Venice], and "Zima" [Winter]. *Zvezda*, no. 8, pp. 57–59.

11 "Spektorskii" (chapter 4). *KN*, no. 1, pp. 121–24.
    Continued: 1928.12.

12 "Spektorskii" (chapters 6 and 7). *KN*, no. 7, pp. 154–59.
    Continuation of 1928.11. Continued: 1929.14.

13 "Vysokaia bolezn'" [A high malady], "Gorod" [The city], and "Zimniaia noch'" [Winter night]. *NM*, no. 11, pp. 18–21.

1929

1 "Iz ballady (Vpustite, mne nado videt' grafa)" [From a ballad (Let me in, I must see the count)] and "Iz neokonchennoi poemy (Ia tozhe liubil, i dykhan'e)" [From an unfinished poem (I too loved, and breathing)]. *NM*, no. 1, pp. 107–9.

2   *Izbrannye stikhi* [Selected verses]. Moscow: Pravda, 32 pp.

3   "Ledokhod" [Drifting of ice] and "Posle dozhdia" [After the rain]. In *Moskovskie mastera. Al'manakh*. Vol. 1. Leningrad-Moscow: Zhizn' i znanie, pp. 43–46.

4   [A letter to the editorial staff of *Literaturnaia gazeta*.] *LG*, no. 4 (13 May): 4.

5   [A letter to the editorial staff of *Literaturnaia gazeta* signed by Pasternak and other writers.] *LG*, no. 37 (30 December): 2.

6   "M.Ts." [To Marina Tsvetaeva], "Mgnovennyi sneg, kogda bulyzhnik uzrel" [An instantaneous snow, when cobbelstone beheld], "Anne Akhmatovoi" [To Anna Akhmatova], and "Meierkhol'dam" [To the Meyerholds]. *KN*, no. 5, pp. 158–61.

7   "Nochnoi nabrosok" [A night outline] (A chapter from *The Tale*). *LG*, no. 13 (15 July): 1.

8   "Okhrannaia gramota" [A safe conduct] (chapter 1). *Zvezda*, no. 8, pp. 148–66.
        Continued: 1931.5.

9   "Ottepeliami iz magazinov" [With thaws from stores], "Mel'nitsy" [Windmills], and "Otryvok (Ia spal. V tu noch' moi dukh dezhuril)" [A fragment (I slept. That night my spirit stood watch)]. *NM*, no. 12, pp. 38–41.

10 *Poverkh bar'erov. Stikhi raznykh let* [Above the barriers. Poems from various years]. Moscow-Leningrad: GIZ, 159 pp.
        Revised: 1931.9

11 "Povest'" [The tale] (A chapter from *The Tale*). *KrN*, no. 30, pp. 24–25.

12 "Povest'" [The tale] (A chapter from *The Tale*). *LG*, no. 13 (15 July): 1.

13 "Povest'" [The tale]. *NM*, no. 7, pp. 5–43.

14 "Spektorskii" (chapter 8 to the end of the book). *NM*, no. 12, pp. 119–24.
        Continuation of 1928.12.

15 *Zverinets. Stikhi dlia detei* [Menagerie. Verses for children]. Moscow: GIZ, 16 pp.

16 Trans. "Po odnoi podruge Rekviem." *NM*, nos. 8–9, pp. 63–69.

17 Trans. "Rekviem," by R.M. Rilke. *Zvezda*, no. 8, pp. 167–70.

1930

1 *Deviat'sot piatyi god. Stikhi* [The year 1905. Poems]. 2d ed. Moscow: GIZ, 97 pp.
>   First edition: 1927.2; Third edition: 1932.1.

2 "Drozhat garazhi avtobazy" [The garage depots shake], "Na dache spiat" [They sleep at the country home], and "Dve ballady" [Two ballads]. *KN*, no. 12, pp. 80–81.

3 *Dve knigi. Stikhi* [Two books. Poems]. 2d ed. Moscow: GIZ, 208 pp.
>   First edition: 1927.3.

4 "Pesn' nenavisti" [A song of hate], "Vozzvanie" [An appeal], and "Protiv Rima" [Against Rome]. In *Revoliutsionnaia poeziia Zapada XIX veka*, edited by A. Gatova. Moscow: Ogonek, pp. 72–75.

5 "Poka mne rifmy byli v pervouchinu" [While rhymes were new to me]. In *Turnir poetov*. Moscow: Izd. "Grupy lefovtsev," p. 8.
>   Reprint of 1928.6.

6 "Spektorskii" (An introduction). *NM*, no. 12, pp. 17–19.

7 Trans. "Sortirovshchitsy" [Paul Zech's "Sortiermädchen"]. In *Sovremennaia revoliutsionnaia poeziia Zapada*, edited by A. Efros and Geints-Kogan. Moscow: Ogonek, pp. 44–45.

1931

1 "Godami kogda-nibud' v zale kontsertnoi" [With years, some time at a concert hall], "Ne volnuisia, ne plach', ne trudi" [Don't worry, don't cry, don't bother], "Okno, piupitr" [Window, desk], "Liubit' inykh— tiazhelyi krest" [To love others is a heavy cross], "Vse sneg da sneg" [And still it snows!], "Mertvetskaia mgla" [Deadly haze], "Platki, podbory, zhguchii vzgliad" [Shawls, assortments, a stinging glance], "Liubimaia, molvy slashchavoi" [My sweetheart, of sugary rumor], and "Krasavitsa moia, vsia stat'" [My beauty, you are a match]. *NM*, no. 8, pp. 40–44.

2 "Kavkazskie stikhi ('Vecherelo. Povsiudu retivo,' 'Poka my po Kavkazu lazaem')" [The Caucasus poems ("It grew dark. It is zealous everywhere," "While we are climbing the Caucasus")]. *NM*, no. 12, pp. 54–55.

3 "Leto (Irpen'—eto pamiat')" [Summer (Irpen, this is memory)] and "Drugu" [To a friend]. *NM*, no. 4, p. 63.

4 "Na ulitse voiloka kloch'ia" [A piece of thick felt on the street], "Krugom semeniashcheisia vatoi" [Around with cotton seed bringing in], "Nikogo ne budet doma" [No one will be in the house], "Ty zdes', my v vozdukhe odnom" [You are here, we are nothing but the air], and "Opiat' Shopen ne ishchet vygod" [Again, Chopin does not seek advantages]. *KN*, no. 9, pp. 13–14.

5 "Okhrannaia gramota" [A safe conduct] (chapter 2). *KN*, no. 4, pp. 3–23.
   Continuation of 1929.8. Continued: 1931.6.

6 "Okhrannaia gramota" [A safe conduct] (chapter 3 to the end of the book). *KN*, nos. 5–6, pp. 32–46.
   Continuation of 1931.5.

7 *Okhrannaia gramota* [A safe conduct]. Leningrad: Izdatel'stvo pisatelei v Leningrade, 128 pp.

8 "Pervye vstrechi s Maiakovskim" [First meetings with Mayakovsky] (A chapter from *A Safe Conduct*). *LG*, no. 20 (14 April): 3.

9 *Poverkh bar'erov. Stikhi raznykh let* [Above the barriers. Poems from various years]. 2d ed. Moscow: GIKhL, 168 pp.
   Revision of 1929.10.

10 "Smert' poeta" [The death of a poet]. *NM*, no. 2, p. 117.

11 *Spektorskii. Poema* [Spektorsky. A tale in verse]. Moscow: GIKhL, 62 pp.

12 "Za razvernutuiu samokritiku" [For a large-scale self-criticism] (A letter to the editorial staff of *Literaturnaia gazeta* signed by Pasternak and other writers). *LG* (24 April): 4.

13 Trans. "Alkhimik." In *Dramaticheskie proizvedeniia*, by Ben Johnson. 2 vols. Moscow-Leningrad: Academia, pp. 301–564.

14 Trans. "Kaznennye," by A. Akopian. In *Sovremennaia armianskaia poeziia*. Moscow-Leningrad: GIKhL, pp. 11–12.

1932

1 *Deviat'sot piatyi god. Stikhi* [The year 1905. Poems]. 3d ed. Moscow: GIZ, 97 pp. Reprint. Moscow: Izdatel'stvo pisatelei v Leningrade, 93 pp.

Second edition: 1930.1. Reprinted: 1989.16.

2 [A letter to Stalin upon the death of his wife, Nadezhda Allilueva.] *LG* (17 November): 1.

3 "Uprek ne uspel potusknet'" [The rebuke has not been able to fade], "Stikhi moi, begom, begom" [My verses, run, run], and "Kogda ia ustaiu ot pustozvonstva" [When I tire of idle talk]. *NM*, no. 2, pp. 82–83.

4 "Vesenneiu poroiu l'da ..." [At springtime of ice ...]. *NM*, no. 3, pp. 44–45.

5 "Vesennii den' tridtsatogo aprelia ..." [Autumn day, 30th of April ...] *NM*, no. 5, p. 67.

6 "Volny" [Waves]. *KN*, no. 1, pp. 24–27.

7 *Vtoroe rozhdenie. Stikhi* [Second birth. Poems]. Moscow: Federatsiia, 96 pp. Second edition: 1934.7.

1933

1 *Izbrannye stikhi* [Selected verses]. Moscow: Sovetskaia literatura, 247 pp.

2 *Izbrannye stikhotvoreniia* [Selected poems]. Introduction by A. Tarasenkov. Moscow: GIKhL, 251 pp.

3 *Poemy* [Tales in verse]. Moscow: Sovetskaia literatura, 167 pp.

4 *Stikhotvoreniia v odnom tome* [Poems in one volume]. Leningrad: Izdatel'stvo pisatelei v Leningrade, 430 pp. Second edition: 1935.1; Third edition: 1936.8.

5 *Vozdushnye puti* [Aerial ways] (Includes *The Childhood of Luvers, The Line of Apelles, Aerial Ways*, and *The Tale*). Moscow: GIKhL, 141 pp.

1934

1 *Izbrannye stikhotvoreniia* [Selected poems]. Moscow: GIKhL, 251 pp.

2 [A letter to the editorial staff of *Literaturnaia gazeta* signed by Pasternak and other writers]. *LG* (20 May): 4.

3 *Povest'* [The tale]. Leningrad: Izdatel'stvo pisatelei v Leningrade, 102 pp.

4 "Skorb' i gnev" [Grief and anger]. In *Pisateli—Kirivu. Sbornik*, by L. Leonov, V. Lidin, A. Novikov-Priboi, B. Pasternak, and I. Erenburg. Moscow: GIKhL, p. 17.

5 [Speech of 29 August at the First All-Union Congress of Soviet Writers.] In *Pervyi vsesoiuznyi s"ezd sovetskikh pisatelei. 1934. A stenographic report.* Moscow: GIKhL, pp. 548–49.

6 "Teplo naroda i gosudarstva okruzhaet nas" [The warmth of the people and the government surrounds us]. *Pravda* (31 August).

7 *Vtoroe rozhdenie. Stikhi* [Second birth. Poems]. 2d ed. Moscow: Sovetskii pisatel', 95 pp.
    First edition: 1932.7.

8 Trans. "Ballada spaseniia," by I. Abashidze. In *Molodaia poeziia narodov SSSR*. Moscow: Molodaia gvardiia, pp. 119–22.

9 Trans. "Iz gruzinskikh poetov." "Stalin," by Nikolo Mitsishvili; "Oktiabr'skie stroki" and "S galerki opernogo teatra," by Valer'ian Gaprindashvili; "Pesnia," "Belaia alycha," and "Okrokana" by Kolay Nadiradze (Translations of Georgian poets). *NM*, no. 3, pp. 12–14.

10 Trans. "Iz gruzinskikh poetov." "Stalin," by Paolo Iashvili; "Tiflisskie rassvety" and "Kililai damna," by Georgii Leonidze; and "Sel'skaia noch'," by Titsian Tabidze (Translations of Georgian poets). *KN*, no. 6, pp. 3–5.

11 Trans. "Na smert' Lenina," by P. Iashvili. *TD*, no. 1, p. 13.

12 Trans. "Ushgul'skii komsomol," by S. Chikovani. In *Molodaia poeziia narodov SSSR*. Moscow: Molodaia gvardiia, pp. 123–26.

13 Trans. *Zmeeed. Poema*, by V. Pshavela. Tiflis: Zakgiz, 60 pp.
    Reprinted: 1935.8; 1947.5; 1958.25.

1935

1 *Stikhotvoreniia v odnom tome* [Poems in one volume]. 2d ed. Leningrad: GIKhL, 440 pp.
    First edition: 1933.4; Third edition: 1936.8.

2 Trans. "Ballada spaseniia," by I. Abashidze; "Oktiabr'skie stroki," "Mechta," "More," "Kutias vo vremia vetra," and "S galerki opernogo teatra," by K. Kaladze; "Zima," "Pervyi sneg," "Tiflisskie rassvety," and

"Kalilai damna," by G. Leonidze; "Stalin," by N. Mitsishvili; "Okrokana," "Belaia alycha," and "Pesnia," by K. Nadiradze; "Idu so storony cherkesskoi," "Esli ty brat mne," "Sel'skaia noch'," "Okrokana," and "Ne ja pishu stikhi," by T. Tabidze; "Mingrel'skie vechera" and "Ushgul'skii komsomol," by S. Chikovani; and "Na smert' Lenina," "Stalin," "Utro," "Sobytie sada," "Bez povoda," "Samgor," "Kak khlopan'e parusa," and "Rabota," by P. Iashvili (Translations of Georgian poets). In *Poety Gruzii v perevodakh B. L. Pasternaka i N.S. Tikhonova*. Tbilisi: Zakgiz, pp. 3–6, 9–11, 14–18, 29–30, 43–44, 48, 70–71, 73–76, 81, 85–86, 111–14, 127–28, 130, 132, 136, 142–44, 147–49, 177–79, 182, 184–90.

3   Trans. *Gruzinskie liriki* (Translations of Georgian poets). Moscow: Sovetskii pisatel', 137 pp.
      Reprinted: 1937.4.

4   Trans. "Mingrel'skie vechera," by S. Chikovani. *LZ*, nos. 4–5, pp. 149–51.

5   Trans. "Stalin," by N. Mitsishvili; "Stalin," by P. Iashvili; and "Oktiabr'skie stroki," by V. Gagrindashvili (Translations of Georgian poets). In *Stikhi i pesni narodov Vostoka o Staline*, compiled by A. Chachikov. Moscow: Biblioteka "Ogon'ka," "Zhurgaz," pp. 25–26; 27–28; 30–31.
      Reprinted: 1936.10–11; 1937.5.

6   Trans. "Ushgul'skii komsomol," by S. Chikovani; "Zima," by K. Kaladze; and "Ballada spaseniia," by I. Abashidze (Translations of Georgian poets). In *Molodaia Gruziia. Sbornik*. Moscow: GIKhL, pp. 206–8, 234–35, 241–43.

7   Trans. "Ushgul'skii komsomol," "Zima," and "Ballada spaseniia" (Translations of Georgian poets). In *Sbornik proizvedenii molodykh pisatelei sovetskoi sotsialisticheskoi respubliki Gruzii*. Moscow: Molodaia Gvardiia, pp. 206–8.

8   Trans. "Zmeeed." In *Poemy*, by Vazha Pshvela, edited by V. Gol'tsev and T. Tabidze. Moscow: GIKhL.
      Reprint of 1934.13. Reprinted: 1947.5; 1958.25.

1936

1   "Ia ponial. Vse zhivo" [I grasped. All is alive], "Mne po dushe stroptivyi norov" [I like an obstinate temperament]. *Izvestiia* (1 January): 5.
      Reprinted: 1936.2.

2   "Ia ponial. Vse zhivo" [I grasped. All is alive], "Mne po dushe stroptivyi norov" [I like an obstinate temperament], "Nemye individy" [Mute indi-

viduals], "Vse naklonen'ia i zalogi" [All moods and voices], "Kak-to v sumerki Tiflisa" [Somehow in the twilight of Tbilisi], "Skromnyi dom, no riumka romu" [A humble home, but a shot-glass of rum], and "On vstaet. Veka. Gelaty" [He rises. Centuries. Gelati]. *Znamia*, no. 4, pp. 3–11.
Partial reprint of: 1936.1.

3   "Iz letnikh zapisok" [From summer sketches]. *NM*, no. 10, pp. 87–90.

4   "Novoe sovershennolet'e" [New full age]. *Izvestiia* (15 June): 2.

5   "O skromnosti i smelosti" [On modesty and courage]. *LG*, no. 12 (24 February): 5.

6   [On himself.] *Izvestiia* (1 January): 3.

7   *Stikhotvoreniia*. [Poems]. 2d ed. Moscow: GIKhL, 439 pp.

8   *Stikhotvoreniia v odnom tome* [Poems in one volume]. 3d ed. Leningrad: GIKhL, 440 pp.
Second edition: 1935.1.

9   Trans. "Ne ia pishu stikhi," "Esli ty brat mne," "Idu so storony cherkesskoi," "Okrokany," and "Sel'skaia noch'" (T. Tabidze's poetry). In *Izbrannoe*, by Tsitsian Tabidze, edited by V. Gol'tsev. Moscow: GIKhL, pp. 21, 23, 27–28, 38–39, 42.

10   Trans. "Stalin," by N. Mitsishvili; "Stalin," by P. Iashvili; and "Oktiabr'skie stroki," by V. Gaprindashvili (Translations of Georgian poets). In *Stalin v pesniakh narodov SSSR*. Moscow: Molodaia gvardiia, pp. 16 and 27.
Reprint of 1935.5. Reprinted: 1936.10; 1937.5.

11   Trans. "Stalin," by N. Mitsishvili; "Stalin," by P. Iashvili; and "Oktiabr'skie stroki," by V. Gaprindashvili (Translations of Georgian poets). In *Stikhi i pesni narodov vostoka o Staline*, compiled by E. Zozulia, G. Lakhuti, and A. Chachikov. Moscow: Biblioteka "Ogonka," "Zhurgaz," pp. 25–26; 27–28; 30–31.
Reprint of 1935.5; 1936.9. Reprinted: 1937.5.

1937

1   *1905. Leitenant Shmidt* [1905. Lieutenant Schmidt]. 4th ed. Moscow: GIKhL, 79 pp.]

2   "Iz novogo romana o 1905 g." [From a new novel about 1905]. *LG*, no. 71 (31 December): 3.

3 "On pereidet v legendu" [He will pass into legend]. *LG*, no. 64 (26 November): 3.

4 Trans. *Gruzinskie liriki* (Translations of Georgian poets). Moscow: Sovetskii pisatel', 73 pp.
   Reprint of 1935.3.

5 Trans. "Stalin," by N. Mitsishvili; "Stalin," by P. Iashvili; and "Oktiabr'skie stroki," by V. Gaprindashvili (Translations of Georgian poets). In *Gruzinskie stikhi i pesni o Staline*. Tbilisi: Zaria vostoka.
   Reprint of 1935.5; 1936.11.

1938

1 "Uezd v tylu" [A district in the rear]. *LG*, no. 69 (15 December): 4.
   Reprinted: 1958.14.

2 Trans. "Muzyka" and "Zima," by Shakespeare; "Stansy k Avguste," by Byron; "Nochnoe zrelishche," "Tak brezzhit den'," "Zelen'," and "Iskusstvo poezii," by Verlaine. *KN*, no. 8, pp. 131–35.

1939

1 "Drugu, zamechatel'nomu tovarishchu" [To a friend, a wonderful comrade]. *LG*, no. 11 (26 February): 3.

2 "Nadmennyi nishchii" [The haughty pauper]. *Ogonek*, no. 1, pp. 14–15.

3 "Tetia Olia" [Aunt Olya]. *TD*, nos. 8–9, pp. 31–35.

4 "Zverinets" [Menagerie]. *MG*, no. 4, pp. 97–99.

5 Trans. "Mariia." In *Kobzar*, by Taras Shevchenko. Leningrad: Sovetskii pisatel', pp. 398–416.
   Reprinted: 1947.4; 1956.7; 1964.4.

1940

1 "Ot perevodchika" [From the translator] (An introduction to Pasternak's translation of *Hamlet*). *MG*, nos. 5–6, pp. 15–16.

2 Trans. "Gamlet, prints datskii" [Shakespeare's *Hamlet*]. *MG*, nos. 5–6, pp. 16–131.

Reprinted: 1941.5; Second edition: 1942.3; Third edition: 1947.2; Fourth edition: 1951.2; Fifth edition: 1956.5.

3 Trans. *Izbrannye perevody* [Selected translations]. (Includes: "Prints Fridrikh Gomburskii," by Kleist; "Muzyka," "Zima," "Sonnet 66," "Sonnet 73," by Shakespeare; "Synu," by Raleigh; "Stansy k Avguste," by Byron; "Iz 'Endimona'," "Oda k oseni," "Kuznechik i sverchok," "More," by Keats; "Dvorianin," "Moia liubov'," "Kabaki neredkost'," "Skin', pastikh, ovchinu," "V kontse goda," by Petöfi; "Nochnoe zrelishche," "Tak kak brezzhit den'," "Zelen'," "Iskusstvo poezii," "Tomlenie," "Sred' neobozrimo unyloi ravniny," "Khandra," by Verlaine; "Liuter," by Becher; and "Nemetskaia maslenitsa," "Eilenshpigel' so sleptsami," "Korzina raznoschika," "Fiunzigenskii konokrad i vorovatye krest'iane," by Sachs). Moscow: Sovetskii pisatel', 198 pp.

1941

1 "Leto (Bosoi po ugol'iam idu)" [Summer (Barefoot I walk on coals)] and "Gorod (Kogda s kolodtsa led ne skolot)" [The city (When the ice is not chipped away from the well)]. *MG*, no. 1, pp. 54–55.

2 "Na rannikh poezdakh" [On early trains] and "Bobyl'" [A poor farmer; a loner]. *KN*, nos. 9–10, p. 46.

3 "Smelost'" [Courage]. *LG* (24 September): 2.

4 "Strashnaia skazka" [Terrible tale] and "Zastava" [Gates]. *Ogonek*, no. 39 (14 September): 6.

5 Trans. *Gamlet, prints datskii* [Shakespeare's *Hamlet*]. Moscow: GIKhL, 172 pp.
   Reprint of 1940.2. Second edition: 1942.3

6 Trans. *Razbityi kuvshin. Komediia* [Kleist's *Der zerbrochene Krug*]. Moscow: Iskusstvo, 104 pp.
   Reprint of 1915.3.

1942

1 "Moi novye perevody" [My new translations]. *Ogonek*, no. 47, p. 13.
   Reprinted with a different title: 1968.2.

2   "Smelost'" [Courage] and "Strashnaia skazka" [Terrible tale]. In *V ogne Otechestvennoi voiny*, compiled by G. Petnikov. Nalchik: Nalchikskoe kraevoe izdatel'stvo.

3   Trans. *Gamlet, prints datskii* [Shakespeare's *Hamlet*]. 2d ed. Moscow: DETGIZ, 182 pp.
   First edition: 1941.5. Third edition: 1947.2.

4   Trans. "Kulig" and "Pesnia litovskogo legiona," by Juliusz Słowacki. *KN*, no. 7, pp. 105–7.

5   Trans. "Zima" [Shakespeare's *Winter's Tale*]. In *Ballady i pesni angliiskogo naroda*, edited by M. Morozov. Moscow-Leningrad: DETGIZ, pp. 48–50.

1943

1   "Kreml' v buran kontsa 1918 goda" [The Kremlin in the blizzard of the end of 1918], "Deviat'sot piatyi god" [The year 1905], "Leitenant Shmidt" [Lieutenant Schmidt], "Vysokaia bolezn'" [A high malady], "Volny" [Waves], and "Strashnaia skazka" [Terrible tale]. In *Sbornik stikhov*, compiled by V. Kazin and V. Pertsov. Moscow: GIKhL, pp. 187–212.

2   *Na rannikh poezdakh. Novye stikhotvoreniia* [On early trains. New poems]. Moscow: Sovetskii pisatel', 52 pp.

3   "Poezdka v armiiu" [A trip to the front]. *Trud* (20 November): 4.

4   "Pol' Mari Verlen." *LI*, no. 1 (1 April): 2.

5   "Razvedchiki" [Scouts]. *KZ* (10 December).

6   "Strashnaia skazka" [Terrible tale]. In *Grazhdanskaia i Otechestvennaia voina v poezii*. Kurov: Ogiz, pp. 58–59.

7   "Zarevo" [A glow] and "Vstuplenie k poeme" [Introduction to a tale in verse]. *Pravda* (15 October): 3.

8   "Zima nachinaetsia (priblizhaetsia)" [Winter begins (approaches)]. *LI* (13 November): 2.

9   Trans. *Romeo i Dzhul'etta* [Shakespeare's *Romeo and Juliet*]. Moscow: Vsesoiuznoe upravleniie po okhrane avtorskikh prav, 68 pp.

Second edition: 1944.10; Third edition: 1944.11; Fourth edition: 1951.5; Fifth edition: 1973.4.

10   Trans. "Slavianskii poet," "Poslednee srazhen'e," "Khranitel' zhizni," "Prevrashchen'e," "Zelenyi rynok v Ostrave," and "Grushevskie prudy," by Ondra Lysogorskii. *LI* (21 August): 2.

1944

1   "Afinogenov." *LI* (28 October): 2.

2   "Ozhivshaia freska" [A resuscitated fresco]. *LI* (15 April): 3.

3   "Pobeditel'" [The conqueror]. *Trud* (28 November).

4   "Smert' sapera" [The death of a sapper], "Presledovanie" [Pursuit], and "Letnii den'" [A summer day]. In *V boiakh za Orel*. Moscow: GOSPOLIZDAT, pp. 137–39.

5   "Zametki perevodchika" [A translator's notes]. *Znamia*, nos. 1–2, pp. 165–66.

6   "Zimnie prazdniki" [Winter holidays] (A version of the poem "Zazimki"). *LG* (11 November): 3.

7   Trans. *Antonii i Kleopatra* [Shakespeare's *Anthony and Cleopatra*]. Moscow: GIKhL, 147 pp.

8   Trans. "Indiiskaia serenada," "K . . . ," "Stroki," and "Oda zapadnomu vetru" (Translations of Shelley). *Znamia*, nos. 1–2, pp. 167–68.

9   Trans. "Otello" (The fifth act's third scene of Shakespeare's *Othello*, with notes by Pasternak). *LG* (9 December).

10   Trans. *Romeo i Dzhul'etta* [Shakespeare's *Romeo and Juliet*]. 2d ed. Moscow: GIKhL, 130 pp.
       First edition: 1943.9; Third edition: 1944.11.

11   Trans. *Romeo i Dzhul'etta* [Shakespeare's *Romeo and Juliet*]. 3d ed. Moscow: Detgiz, 123 pp.
       Second edition: 1944.10; Fourth edition: 1951.5.

1945

1   *Izbrannye stikhi i poemy.* [Selected verses and tales in verse] (From the collections *Above the Barriers*; *My Sister, Life*; *Second Birth*, *On Early Trains*, *The Earth's Expanse*, *The Year 1905*, and *Lieutenant Schmidt*). Moscow: GIKhL, 187 pp.

2   "Shopen." *Leningrad*, nos. 15–16, pp. 22–23.

3   *Zemnoi prostor. Stikhi* [Earth's expanse. Poems]. Moscow: Sovetskii pisatel', 47 pp.

4   Trans. "Filosofiia zhizni." In *Vesna. Sbornik*, by S. Vergun. Baku, pp. 28–29.

5   Trans. "Kogda by iz moei serdechnoi rany," "Glukhim, neiasnym, prizrachnym prizyvom," "Dusha—pereletnaia bednaia ptitsa," "V toske ia shel vdol' gornogo kriazha," "U kogo tak noet retivoe," "Iz zhizni vsei," and "Pesnia Zaro." In *Izbrannye stikhi*, by Avetik Isaakian. Moscow: GIKhL, pp. 32, 33, 53, 58–60, 62, 128.
    Reprinted: 1959.11.

6   Trans. "Mechta," by V. Gaprindashvili. In *Antologiia gruzinskoi patrioticheskoi poezii.* Tbilisi: Zaria vostoka, pp. 108–9.

7   Trans. *Otello—venetsianskii mavr* [Shakespeare's *Othello*]. Moscow: GIKhL, 77 pp.
    Second edition: 1945.8; Third edition: 1945.9; Fourth edition: 1951.3.

8   Trans. *Otello—venetsianskii mavr* [Shakespeare's *Othello*]. 2d ed. Moscow: GIKhL, 140 pp.
    First edition: 1945.7; Third edition: 1945.9.

9   Trans. *Otello—venetsianskii mavr* [Shakespeare's *Othello*]. 3d ed. Moscow: GIKhL, 140 pp.
    Second edition: 1945.8; Fourth edition: 1951.3.

10   Trans. "Polden'." In *Stikhotvoreniia i poemy*, by Maksim Ryl'skii. Moscow: GIKhL, p. 92.
    Reprinted: 1958.21.

11   Trans. "Zima." In *Stikhi, pesni, ballady*, by K. Kaladze. Tbilisi: Zaria vostoka, p. 73.
    Reprinted: 1957.20.

1946

1 Trans. "A.O. Kazachkovskomu." In *Izbrannye stikhotvoreniia i poemy*, by Taras Shevchenko. Moscow-Leningrad: DETGIZ, pp. 591–609.

2 Trans. *Gruzinskie poety v perevodakh Borisa Pasternaka* (Translations of Georgian poets). Moscow: Sovetskii pisatel', 123 pp.

3 Trans. "Khranitel' zhizni," "Blagodaren'e," "Nerushimost'," "Poslednee srazhen'e," "Prevrashchenie," "Grushevskie prudy," "Zelennyi rynok v Ostrave," "Venetsianskie mosty," "Radiorupor," and "Komnata v Tashkente." In *Stikhotvoreniia*, by Ondra Lysogorskii. Moscow: Sovetskii pisatel', pp. 38–42, 57–58, 60–61, 63, 75.

4 Trans. "More," "Mechta," "Oktiabr'skie stroki," by V. Gaprindashvili; "Proshchanie so starym Tiflisom," by I. Grishashvili; "Tiflisskie rassvety," "Staryi buben," by G. Leonidze; "Stikhi," by A. Mashashvili; "Pesnia" and "Belaia alycha," by K. Nadiradze; and "Rabota," by S. Chikovani (Translations of Georgian poets). In *Rodina. Poety sovetskoi Gruzii, 1926–1946*. Tbilisi: Zaria vostoka, pp. 49–51, 81–83, 116–19, 132–34, 150–54, 188–89.

5 Trans. "Proshchan'e so starym Tiflisom." In *Stikhi*, by I. Grishashvili, edited by G.N. Obolduev. Moscow: Sovetskii pisatel', pp. 26–28.

6 Trans. *Stikhotvoreniia v perevode Borisa Pasternaka* (Translations of N. Baratashvili). Moscow: Pravda, 47 pp.
   Reprinted: 1948.4; 1957.19.

1947

1 "Ottsy" [Fathers], "Detstvo" [Childhood], "Zarevo" [A glow], and "Vesna (Nas vremia baluet pobedami)" [Spring (Time spoils us with victories)] (Chapters from *The Year 1905*). In *Stikhi i poemy 1917–1947*, compiled and edited by L. Belov, V. Pertsov, and A. Surkov. Moscow: Pravda, pp. 125–32.

2 Trans. *Gamlet, prints datskii* [Shakespeare's *Hamlet*]. 3d ed. Moscow: Detgiz, 190 pp.
   Second edition: 1942.3; Fourth edition: 1951.2.

3 Trans. *Gruzinskie poety. Izbrannye perevody* (Translations of Georgian poets). Tbilisi: Zaria vostoka, 141 pp.

4 Trans. "Mariia." In *Kobzar*, by Taras Shevchenko. Moscow: GIKhL, pp. 591–609.
   Reprint of 1939.5. Reprinted: 1956.7.

5 Trans. "Zmeeed." In *Poemy*, by Vazha Pshvela, edited by V. Gol'tsev and S. Chikovani. Moscow: GIKhL, pp. 115–30.
   Reprint of 1935.8. Reprinted: 1958.25.

1948

1 *Izbrannoe* [Selected works]. Moscow: Sovetskii pisatel', 160 pp.

2 Trans. *Genrikh Chetvertyi. Istoricheskaia khronika v 2 chastiakh* [Shakespeare's *Henry IV*]. Moscow: DETGIZ, 256 pp.
   Second edition: 1949.1.

3 Trans. *Izbrannoe* (Translations of collected works), by Sandor Petöfi. Moscow: GIKhL, 488 pp.

4 Trans. *Stikhotvoreniia* (Translations of N. Baratashvili). Commentary by V. Gol'tsev. Moscow: GIKhL, 80 pp.
   Reprint of 1946.6. Reprinted: 1957.19.

1949

1 Trans. *Korol' Genrikh Chetvertyi* [Shakespeare's *Henry IV*]. 2d ed. Moscow: GIKhL, 164 pp.
   First edition: 1948.2.

2 Trans. *Korol' Lir* [Shakespeare's *King Lear*]. Moscow: GIKhL, 164 pp.
   Second edition: 1949.3.

3 Trans. *Korol' Lir* [Shakespeare's *King Lear*]. 2d ed. Moscow: DETGIZ, 180 pp.
   First edition: 1949.2.

4 Trans. "Na rodine," "Skin', pastukh, ovchinu," "Dobryi staryi traktir-shchik," "Pobyvka u svoikh," "Malaia Kumaniia," "U lesa ptich'ia trel' svoia," "Razvaliny korchmy," "Osen' vnov'," "Step' zimoi," "V kontse goda," "Vnov' zhavoronok nado mnoi," and "Vitiaz' Ianosh." In *Stikhotvoreniia*, by Sándor Petöfi. Moscow-Leningrad: DETGIZ, pp. 27–28; 29–30; 36–38; 43–45; 48–51; 52; 57–60; 73–74; 125–27; 160–62; 165–66; 167–235.

5 Trans. "Sumerki na Mtatsminde," "Tainstvennyi golos," "Noch v Kabakhi," "Razdum'ia na beregu Kury," "Moei zvezde," "Kniazhne E. Chavchavadze," "Odinokaia dusha," "Ia pomniu, ty stoiala," "Moia molitva," "Chto strannogo, chto ia pishu stikhi?," "Muzhskoe otrezvlen'e—ne izmena," "Mogila tsaria Irakliia," "Zlobnyi dukh," "Ty samoe bol'shoe chudo," "Osennii veter u menia v sadu," "Tsvet nebesnyi, sinii tsvet," and "Sud'ba Gruzii," by N. Baratashvili; "Pamiati Gogolia" and "Poet," by A. Tsereteli; "Mechta" and "Oktiabr'skie stroki," by V. Gaprindashvili; "Proshchanie so starym Tiflisom," by I. Grishashvili; "Iz puteshestviia po rodine," "Pervyi sneg," "Tiflisskie rassvety," and "Staryi buben," by G. Leonidze; "Okrokana" and "Belaia alycha," by K. Nadiradze; and "Mingrel'skie vechera," "Poseshchenie rybaka," and "Smert' boitsa Leshkasheli," by S. Chikovani (Translations of Georgian poets). In *Poeziia Gruzii. Antologiia.* Moscow-Leningrad: GIKhL, pp. 213–17, 219–24, 274–75, 364–65, 397–400, 425–26, 445–47, 449.

6 Trans. "U kamina Vazha Pshavely." In *Izbrannoe*, by Simon Chikovani. Moscow: Sovetskii pisatel', pp. 77–79.

7 Trans. *V. Shekspir v perevode Borisa Pasternaka.* Edited by M.M. Morozov. 2 vols. (Vol. 1 includes *Romeo and Juliet*; *Henry IV*; and *Hamlet, the Danish Prince.* Vol. 2 includes *Othello, the Moor of Venice*; *King Lear*; and *Anthony and Cleopatra*). Moscow: Iskusstvo, 608 pp. and 520 pp.
   Second edition: 1950.1.

1950

1 Trans. *V. Shekspir v perevode Borisa Pasternaka.* Edited by M.M. Morozov. 2 vols. (Vol. 1 includes *Romeo and Juliet*; *Henry IV*; and *Hamlet, the Danish Prince.* Vol. 2 includes *Othello, the Moor of Venice*; *King Lear*; and *Anthony and Cleopatra*). 2d ed. Moscow: Iskusstvo, 608 pp. and 520 pp.
   First edition: 1949.7.

2 Trans. *Vitiaz' Ianosh. Povest' v stikhakh* [Sándor Petöfi's *János vitéz*.]. Moscow: DETGIZ, 66 pp.

1951

1 *Kogda razguliaetsia. Stikhi* [When the skies clear. Poems]. Paris: Izdatel'stvo liubitelei poezii B.L. Pasternaka, 51 pp.
   Reprinted: 1959.7.

2　Trans. *Gamlet, prints datskii* [Shakespeare's *Hamlet*]. 4th ed. Moscow: Iskusstvo, 243 pp.
　　Third edition: 1947.2; Fifth edition: 1956.5.

3　Trans. *Otello—venetsianskii mavr* [Shakespeare's *Othello*]. 4th ed. Moscow: Iskusstvo, 228 pp.
　　Third edition: 1945.9.

4　Trans. "Pervyi sneg," "Puteshestvie," "Tiflisskie rassvety," and "Staryi buben." In *Stikhotvoreniia i poemy*, by Georgii Leonidze. Moscow: GIKhL, pp. 78–79, 83–84, 88–90, 104–5.

5　Trans. *Romeo i Dzhul'etta* [Shakespeare's *Romeo and Juliet*]. 4th ed. Moscow: Iskusstvo, 183 pp.
　　Third edition: 1944.11; Fifth edition: 1973.4.

6　Trans. *Tragedii* [Shakespeare's tragedies]. Edited with introduction and notes by M.M. Morozov. Moscow: DETGIZ, 717 pp.

1952

1　Trans. Vol. 1: "Na rodine," "Nadoevshee rabstvo," "Dvorianin," "Pobyvka u svoikh," "Al'fel'd," "Vecher," "Moia liubov'," "Bushuiushchee more . . . ," "Lesnoe zhil'e," "Esli ty tsvetok . . . ," "Smolkla grozovaia arfa buri . . . ," "V derevne," "Staryi dobryi traktirshchik," "Na gore sizhu ia . . . ," "Razvaliny korchmy," "Istochnik i reka," "V lesu," "Kak na letnem nebe," "Liubliu ia . . . ," "Na Kheveshskoi ravnine," "Rozami moei liubvi . . . ," "Dnei osennikh proziaban'e," "V al'bom baryshne Iu. S.," "Vo sne ia videl mir chudes . . . ," "Noch' zvezdnaia, noch' svetlogolubaia," "V al'bom baryshne R.É.," and "Vengerskaia natsiia." Vol. 2: "Kutiakaparo," "Chem liubov' byla mne?," "Skin', pastukh, ovchinu . . . ," "Tsvety," "Stoit mne . . ." "Pyl' stolbom . . . ," "Tetia Shari," "Dorogoiu . . . ," "Puteshestvie po Al'fel'du," "Liubliu li ia tebia?," "U lesa ptich'ia trel' svoia . . . ," "Ia vizhu divnye tsvety vostoka . . . ," "Otvet na pis'mo moei miloi," "Ne obizhaisia," "Prekrasnoe pis'mo," "Zvezdnoe nebo," "Vidal li kto . . . ," "V kontse sentiabria," "Poslednie tsvety," "Strana liubvi," "Nebo i zemlia," "V koliaske i peshkom," "Mogila nishchego," "U Ianosha Arania," "V dushe glubokoi . . . ," "Noch'," "Zimnie vechera," "Step' zimoi," "V rodnykh mestakh," "Malaia Kumaniia," "V gorakh," "Ty pomnish' . . . ," "Osen' vnov' . . . ," "V kontse goda," and "Vnov' zhavoronok nado mnoi. . . ." Vol. 3: "Vitiaz' Ianosh," "Volshebnyi son," and "Shaglo." In *Sobranie sochinenii*, by Sándor Petöfi. Vols. 1–3. Moscow: GIKhL, Vol. 1, pp. 59–60; 94–95; 99; 115–16; 148–49; 152–53; 190; 191; 265–66; 299; 306; 311–12; 313–14; 337; 341–43; 348; 418–19; 420; 438; 440–41; 450; 453–54;

458; 461–63; 470; 472; 481–82. Vol. 2, pp. 9–11; 51–52; 53; 61–62; 75; 81–82; 93–94; 103–7; 117; 128–29; 134–36; 154–55; 162–63; 166–67; 175–76; 192; 197; 200–204; 208–9; 222–23; 227–28; 229–30; 240–42; 262–64; 277–78; 347–48; 351–53; 383–84; 391–92; 411–12; 433–34; 447–48. Vol. 3, pp. 41–86; 91–97; 108–20.
Reprinted: 1958.20.

1953

1 Trans. *Faust* [Goethe's *Faust*]. Introduction and comments by N.N. Vil'mont. Moscow: GIKhL, 619 pp.
Second edition: 1955.2; Third edition: 1957.14; Fourth edition: 1960.4; Fifth edition: 1969.7.

2 Trans. "Pesn' pesnei," "Ty gor'ka, moia zhizn'," "Poet," "Lira," and "Pamiati Gogolia." In *Izbrannye stikhotvoreniia*, by A. Tsereteli. Moscow-Leningrad: DETGIZ, pp. 82–86, 93–94, 105–6.

3 Trans. "Romeo i Dzhul'etta," "Korol' Genrikh IV" (chapters 1 and 2), "Gamlet," "Otello," "Korol' Lir'," "Makbet," and "Antonii i Kleopatra." In *Izbrannye proizvedeniia*, by William Shakespeare, edited by M. Morozov. Moscow: GIKhL, pp. 31–184, 235–431.

4 Trans. "Stansy k Avguste." In *Izbrannye proizvedeniia*, by George Byron. Moscow: GIKhL, p. 50.

1954

1 "Vesenniaia rasputitsa" [Spring floods], "Belaia noch'" [White night], "Mart" [March], "Leto v gorode" [Summer in the city], "Veter" [Wind], "Khmel'" [Hops], "Bab'e leto" [Indian summer], "Razluka" [Parting], "Svidan'e" [Rendezvous], and "Svad'ba" [Wedding] (Poems from *Doctor Zhivago*). *Znamia*, no. 4, pp. 92–95.

2 Trans. "Ballada spaseniia," by I. Abashidze; "Proshchanie so starym Tiflisom," by I. Grishashvili; "Pervyi sneg," "Tiflisskie rassvety," "Puteshestvie," and "Staryi buben," by G. Leonidze; "Ne ia pishu stikhi," by K. Nadiradze; "Tiflisskii rybak," "Poseshchenie rybaka," "Gnezdo lastochki," "U kamina Vazha Pshavely," and "Rabota," by S. Chikovani; and "Stalin," "Sobytie sada," "Kak khlopan'e parusa," "Stol," "Utro," "Obnovlen'e," and "Samgorskim stroiteliam," by P. Iashvili (Translations of Georgian poets). In *Gruzinskaia sovetskaia poeziia*. Tbilisi: Zaria vostoka, pp. 57–58, 133–34, 188–90, 193–95, 271, 328, 329, 342–44, 348–49, 352, 397–400.

1955

1 "Okhrannaia gramota" [A safe conduct]. In *Opal'nye povesti. Sbornik*, edited by V.A. Aleksandrova. New York: Izdatel'stvo im. Chekhova, pp. 67–165.

2 Trans. *Faust* [Goethe's *Faust*]. Introduction and comments by N.N. Vilmont. 2d ed. Leningrad: Khudozhestvennaia literatura, 619 pp.
   First edition: 1953.1; Third edition: 1957.14.

1956

1 "Khleb" [Bread]. *NM*, no. 10, p. 18.

2 "Rassvet" [Dawn] and "Zimniaia noch'" [Winter night] (Two poems from *Doctor Zhivago*). In *DP*, p. 27.

3 "Vo vsem mne khochetsia doiti" [I want to find the essence of all things], "Eva," "Bez nazvaniia" [Without a title], "Vesna v lesu" [Spring in the forest], "Leto" [Summer], "Pervyi sneg" [First snowfall], "Osennii den'" [An autumn day], and "Byt' znamenitym nekrasivo" [It's not nice to be famous]. *Znamia*, no. 9, pp. 74–78.

4 "Zametki k perevodam shekspirovskikh tragedii" [Notes on translations of Shakespeare's tragedies]. In *Literaturnaia Moskva. Sbornik 1*. Moscow: GIKhL, pp. 794–809.

5 Trans. *Gamlet, prints datskii* [Shakespeare's *Hamlet*]. 5th ed. Moscow: DETGIZ, 190 pp.
   Fourth edition: 1951.2.

6 Trans. "Ia rodilsia v sedle," "Moi glaza," "Petukhi poiut na gumnakh," and "V detskom kraiu." In *Lirika*, by A. Grashi. Moscow: GIKhL, pp. 11–16.

7 Trans. "Mariia." In *Sobranie sochinenii*, by Taras Shevchenko. Vol. 2. Moscow: GIKhL, pp. 297–316.
   Reprint of 1947.4. Reprinted: 1964.4.

1957

1 "Aktrisa" [The actress]. *Teatr*, no. 7, p. 108.

2 *Doktor Zhivago. Roman* [Doctor Zhivago. A novel]. Milan: Feltrinelli, 633 pp.
   Reprinted: 1959.3.

3 "Gamlet" [Hamlet], "Mart" [March], "Ob"iasnenie" [Explanation], "Bab'e leto" [Indian summer], "Osen'" [Autumn], "Zimniaia noch'" [A winter night], "Svidanie" [Rendezvous], "Rassvet" [Dawn], and "Zemlia" [Earth] (Poems from *Doctor Zhivago*). *Grani*, no. 36, pp. 3–10.

4 [A letter to S.I. Chikovani.] *VL*, no. 1, p. 198.

5 "Na strastnoi" [Holy week], "Rozhdestvenskaia zvezda" [Star of the nativity], "Chudo" [The miracle], "Durnye dni" [Evil days], "Magdalina I–II," and "Gefsimanskii sad" [The garden of Gethsemane] (Poems from *Doctor Zhivago*). *Grani*, nos. 34–35, pp. 3–13.

6 *Poesie. 1915–1957* (Russian and Italian texts). Translated by A. Ripellino. Turin: G. Einaudi, 552 pp.
   Second edition: 1959.9.

7 "Stoga" [Haystacks], "Lipovaia alleia" [Linden alley], "Tishina" [Silence], "Sneg idet" [Snow is falling]. *LiG*, no. 4, pp. 77–80.

8 "V razgare khlebnaia uborka" [Harvest is in full swing]. *LG* (19 October): 3.

9 "V razgare khlebnaia uborka" [Harvest is in full swing], "Noch'" [Night], and "Muzyka" [Music]. In *DP*, pp. 88–89.

10 "Vesna v lesu" [Spring in the forest], "Leto" [Summer], and "Osennii den'" [Autumn day]. In *Stikhi 1956 goda*. Moscow: GIKhL, pp. 192–94.

11 "Zazimki" [First snows]. In *Antologiia russkoi sovetskoi poezii. 1917–1957*. Vol. 1. Moscow: GIKhL, pp. 314–15.

12 Trans. "Avtoportret," "Peterburg," "Karmensita," "Tanit Tabidze," "Idu so storony cherkesskoi," "Ne ia pishu stikhi," "Likovanie," "Voskhodit solntse, svetaet," "Esli ty—brat mne," "Sel'skaia noch'," "Okrokany," "Stikhi o Mukhranskoi doline," and "Lezhu v Orpiri." In *Izbrannoe*, by T. Tabidze. Moscow: GIKhL, pp. 25, 28, 32–33, 43–44, 47–48, 61–62, 65, 75, 80–83, 89–90, 108–9, 123–24.

13 Trans. "Dusha—pereletnaia bednaia ptitsa," by A. Isaakian; "Kudriavyi mal'chik," by E. Charents; and "Moi glaza," by A. Grashi. In *Antologiia armianskoi sovetskoi literatury*. Erevan: Aipetrat, pp. 42, 140, 340.

14 Trans. *Faust* [Goethe's *Faust*]. Introduction and comments by N.N. Vil'mont. 3d ed. Leningrad: GIKhL, 619 pp.
   Second edition: 1955.2; Fourth edition: 1960.4.

15 Trans. "Monolog muzhchiny," "Vopros," "Obyk-novennaia devushka," "Poslednee pis'mo," "Edinyi golos," "Tsvetok," "Liudi trudiatsia," and "Dragotsennaia pyl' zemli." In *Sochineniia*, by Rabindranat Tagor. Vol. 7. Moscow: GIKhL, pp. 41–44, 130–42, 180–82.

16 Trans. "Oda zapadnomu vetru" and "K. . . ." In *Lirika*, by Percy Shelley. Moscow: GIKhL, pp. 59–62.

17 Trans. "Pervoe znakomstvo." In *Stikhotvoreniia*, by Petro Tychyna. Moscow: GIKhL, pp. 103–10.

18 Trans. "Pesnia pervogo snega," "Puteshestvie," "Tiflisskie rassvety," "Staryi buben," and "N. Baratashvili." In *Stikhotvoreniia*, by Georgii Leonidze. Moscow: GIKhL, pp. 46–48, 65–68, 95–99, 151–53, 174–82.

19 Trans. *Stikhi* (Translations of N. Baratashvili). Moscow: GIKhL, 87 pp. Reprint of 1948.4.

20 Trans. "Zima" and "Dva dereva, oshelomliaiushchikh vzgliad." In *Stikhi, pesni, ballady*, by K. Kaladze. Moscow: GIKhL, pp. 104–6.
    "Zima" reprint of 1945.11.

1958

1 "Doktor Zhivago" (A chapter from the novel). *NZh*, no. 54, pp. 5–58.

2 *Doktor Zhivago. Roman* [Doctor Zhivago. A novel]. Ann Arbor: University of Michigan Press, 567 pp.
   Second edition: 1959.4; Third edition: 1959.5.

3 *Doktor Zhivago. Roman* [Doctor Zhivago. A novel]. Glasgow: Collins, 567 pp.

4 "Gamlet" [Hamlet], "Mart" [March], "Na strastnoi" [Holy week], "Vesenniaia rasputitsa" [Spring floods], "Ob"iasnenie" [Explanation], "Khmel'" [Hops], "Bab'e leto" [Indian summer], "Osen'" [Autumn], "Zimniaia noch" [A winter night], "Razluka" [Parting], "Zemlia" [Earth], "Durnye dni" [Evil days], and "Magdalina I–II" (Poems from *Doktor Zhivago*). *Posev*, no. 49 (7 December): 8–9.

5 "Gamlet" [Hamlet], "Ob"iasnenie" [Explanation], "Osen'" [Autumn], "Skazka" [A tale], "Avgust" [August], and "Zemlia" [Earth] (Poems from *Doktor Zhivago*). *Opyty*, no. 9, pp. 6–15.

6   "Gefsimanskii sad" [Garden of Gethsemane] (A poem from *Doctor Zhivago*). *Posev*, no. 15 (13 April): 5.

7   "Gefsimanskii sad" [Garden of Gethsemane]. *VRSKhD*, no. 48, p. 42.

8   "Iz novogo romana o 1905 g." [From a new novel about the year 1905]. *NRS* (5 October).

9   "Izbrannoe" [Selected poems]. "Kak bronzovoi zoloi zharoven'," "Fevral'," "Vesna," "Marburg," "Posle dozhdia" (In *Above the Barriers*); "Sestra moia zhizn'," "Ty v vetre, vetkoi probuiushchem," "Plachushchii sad," "Pro eti stikhi," "Opredelenie poezii," "Opredelenie dushi," "Bolezni zemli," "Opredelen'e tvorchestva," "Nasha groza," "Toska" (In *My Sister, Life*); "Vesna, ia—s ulitsy, gde topol'—udivlen," "Chirikali ptitsy i byli iskrenni," "Moi stol ne stol' shirok, chob grad'iu vseiu," "Zdes' proshelsia zagadki tainstvennyi nogot'," "Roial' drozhashchii penu s gub oblizhet," "Tak nachinaiut. Goda v dva" (In *Themes and Variations*); "Petukhi," "Otplytie," "Anne Akhmatovoi," "M. Ts," "Drugu" (In *Mixed Poems*); *Lieutenant Shmidt* (Parts 4 and 6); "Ballada," "Ne volnuisia, ne plach', ne trudi ... ," "Poka my po Kavkazu lazaem," "Nikogo ne budet v dome," "Mne khochetsia domoi, v ogromnost'" (In *Second Birth*); "Briusovu" (In *Selected Poems*); "Na rannikh poezdakh," "Opiat' vesna," "Vesna" (In *On Early Trains*); "Veter," "Peremena," "V bol'nitse," "Sneg idet," "Sledy na snegu," "Posle v'iugi," "Posle pereryva" (In *When the Skies Clear*); "Nedotroga, tikhonia v bytu," "Leto," "Osennii den'," "Byt' znamenitym," "Muzyka," "Pronossheisia grozoiu polon vozdukh" (In *The Day of Poetry*). *Grani* 13, no. 40: 11–50.

10 "Kogda razguliaetsia" [When the skies clear], "Pakhota" [Plowing], "Zamorozki" [Frosts], and "Vse sbylos'" [All has come true]. *LiG*, no. 4, pp. 29–31.

11 [Letter to A.A. Bisk about Pasternak's translations of Rilke.] *NRS* (16 March).

12 [A letter to Khrushchev.] *Pravda* (2 November): 1.

13 "Stikhotvoreniia B. Pasternaka k romanu 'Doktor Zhivago'" [B. Pasternak's poems for the novel *Doctor Zhivago*]. In *"Delo Pasternaka."* Munich: TsOPE, pp. 78–112.

14 "Uezd v tylu" [A district in the rear]. In *Mosty. Al'manakh*. Vol. 1. Munich: TsOPE, pp. 11–19.
        Reprint of 1938.1.

15 "Veter—3 otryvka o Bloke" [The wind—three excerpts about Blok], "Peremena" [A change], "V bol'nitse" [In the hospital], "Sneg idet" [It is snowing], "Sledy na snegu" [Footprints in the snow], "Posle v'iugi" [After the blizzard], "Posle pereryva" [After the interval], "Vo vsem mne khochetsia doiti" [I want to find the essence of all things], "Bez nazvani-ia" [Without a title], "Byt' znamenitym nekrasivo" [It is not nice to be famous], and "Pronessheisia grozoiu polon vozdukh" [The air is full of the passing thunderstorm]. *Grani*, no. 40, pp. 11–50.

16 "Zametki k perevodam shekspirovskikh tragedii" [Notes on the transla-tions of Shakespeare's tragedies]. *VRSKhD*, no. 50, pp. 32–48.

17 Trans. "Ballada spaseniia." In *Stikhotvoreniia*, by I. Abashidze. Moscow: GIKhL, pp. 17–22.

18 Trans. "Komsomol v Ushgule," "Megrel'skie vechera," "Tifliiskii rybak," "Prikhod rybaka," "U kamina Vazha Pshavely," "Rabota," and "Gnezdo lastochki." In *Stikhotvoreniia*, by Simon Chikovani. Moscow: GIKhL, pp. 28–32, 46–51, 69–74, 110–13, 116–20.

19 Trans. *Mariia Stiuart* [Schiller's *Maria Stuart*]. Moscow: GIKhL, 231 pp.

20 Trans. "Na rodine," "Nadoevshee rabstvo," "Dvorianin," "Pobyvka u svoikh," "Al'fel'd," "Vecher," "Moia liubov'," "Bushuiushchee more," "Lesnoe zhil'e," "Esli ty tsvetok . . . ," "Smolkla grozovaia arfa buri . . . ," "V derevne," "Staryi dobryi traktirshchik," "Na gore sizhu ia . . . ," "Razvaliny korchmy," "Istochnik i reka," "V lesu," "Kak na letnem nebe," "Liubliu ia . . . ," "Na Kheveshskoi ravnine," "Rozami moei liubvi," "Dnei osennikh proziaban'e," "V al'bom baryshne Iu. S.," "Vo sne ia videl mir chudes . . . ," "Noch' zvezdnaia, noch' svetlogolubaia," "V al'bom baryshne R.É.," "Vengerskaia natsiia," "Kutiakaparo," "Chem liubov' byla mne?," "Skin', pastukh, ovchinu . . . ," "Tsvety," "Stoit mne . . . ," "Tetia Shari," "Dorogoiu . . . ," "Puteshestvie po Al'fel'du," "Liubliu li ia tebia?," "U lesa ptich'ia trel' svoia . . . ," "Ia vizhu divnye tsvety vostoka . . . ," "Otvet na pis'mo moei miloi," "Ne obizhaisia," "Prekrasnoe pis'mo," "Zvezdnoe nebo," "Vidal li kto . . . ," "V kontse sentiabria," "Poslednie tsvety," "Nebo i zemlia," "V koliaske i peshkom," "Mogila nishchego," "U Ianosha Arania," "V dushe glubokoi . . . ," "Zimnie vechera," "Step' zimoi," "V rodnykh mestakh," "Malaia Kumaniia," "V gorakh," "Ty pomnish . . . ," "Osen' vnov' . . . ," "V kontse goda," "Vnov' zhavoronok nado mnoi . . . ," "Vitiaz' Ianosh," "Volshebnyi son," and "Shalgo." In *Izbrannoe*, by Sándor Petöfi. Moscow: GIKhL, pp. 39–40, 50–52, 56–57, 65–66, 68–69, 77, 89–90, 94–98, 102, 104–6, 114–16, 121–30, 132–35, 139–41, 152–54, 158–59, 166, 171–72, 175–79, 181–82, 192–94, 198–99, 203–7, 212–17, 232–34, 238–40, 270, 272–74, 282–83, 286–87, 292–93, 297–99, 305–6, 349–401, 412–24. Reprint of 1952.1.

21 Trans. "Polden'," by M. Ryl'skii. In *Antologiia ukrainskoi poezii v 2 tomakh*. Vol. 2. Moscow: GIKhL, p. 54.
Reprint of 1945.10.

22 Trans. Prologue to the poem "Moisei," by I. Franko. In *Antologiia ukrainskoi poezii v 2 tomakh*. Vol. 1. Moscow: GIKhL, pp. 324–25.

23 Trans. *Stikhi o Gruzii. Gruzinskie poety. Izbrannye perevody* (Translations of Georgian poets). Tbilisi: Zaria vostoka, 256 pp.

24 Trans. "Sumerki na Mtatsminde," "Tainstvennyi golos," "Noch' v Kabakhi," "Razdum'ia na beregu Kury," "Moei zvezde," "Kniazhne E. Chavchavadze," "Ser'ga," "Odinokaia dusha," "Ia pomniu, ty stoiala," "Moia molitva," "Chto strannogo, chto ia pishu stikhi?," "Muzhskoe otrezvlen'e—ne izmena," "Mogila tsaria Irakliia," "Zlobnyi dukh," "Ty samoe bol'shoe chudo," "Osennii veter u menia v sadu," "Tsvet nebesnyi, sinii tsvet," and "Sud'ba Gruzii," by N. Baratashvili; "Pesn' pesnei," "Ty gor'ka, moia zhizn' bestalannaia," "Poet," "Lira," and "Pamiati Gogolia," by A. Tsereteli; "Fioletovyi svet," "Vesna," "Kamennyi olen'," "More," and "Serdtse poeta," by A. Abasheli; "Ballada spaseniia," by I. Abashidze; "Oktiabr'skie stroki," by V. Gaprindashvili; "Proshchanie so starym Tiflisom," by I. Grishashvili; "Pesnia pervogo snega," "Puteshestvie," and "Staryi buben," by G. Leonidze; "Okrokana" and "Belaia alycha," by K. Nadiradze; "Ne ia pishu stikhi," "Idu so storony cherkesskoi," "Voskhodit solntse," and "Stikhi o Mukhranskoi doline," by T. Tabidze; "Rabota," "Prikhod rybaka," "U kamina Vazha Pshavely," "Mingrel'skie vechera," and "Gnezdo lastochki," by S. Chikovani; and "Sobytie sada," "Utro," and "Obnovlen'e," by P. Iashvili (Translations of Georgian poets). In *Antologiia gruzinskoi poezii*. Moscow: GIKhL, pp. 246–70, 344–49, 425–29, 451–53, 489, 518, 582–85, 589–90, 646–47, 681–82, 684–86, 699–701, 703–6, 717, 753–57.

25 Trans. "Zmeeed," by Vazha Pshavela. In *Sochinenia v 2 tomakh*. Vol. 2. Moscow: GIKhL, pp. 267–97.
Reprint of 1947.5.

1959

1 "Avtobiograficheskii ocherk" [Autobiographical sketch]. *NRS* (12–26 January).

2 "Avtobiograficheskii ocherk" [Autobiographical sketch]. *RM* (12–31 December).

3 *Doktor Zhivago. Roman* [Doctor Zhivago. A novel]. Milan: Feltrinelli, 633 pp.
   Reprint of 1957.2.

4 *Doktor Zhivago. Roman* [Doctor Zhivago. A novel]. 2d ed. Ann Arbor: University of Michigan Press, 567 pp.
   First edition: 1958.2; Third edition: 1959.5.

5 *Doktor Zhivago. Roman* [Doctor Zhivago. A novel]. 3d ed. Ann Arbor: University of Michigan Press, 567 pp.
   Second edition: 1959.4.

6 *Doktor Zhivago. Roman* [Doctor Zhivago. A novel]. 2 vols. Paris: Société d'Impression Mondiale, 635 pp.

7 *Kogda razguliaetsia. Stikhi.* [When the skies clear. Poems]. Paris: Izdatel'stvo liubitelei poezii B.L. Pasternaka, 49 pp.
   Reprint of 1951.1.

8 "Nobelevskaia premiia" [The Nobel prize]. *NRS* (21 February).

9 *Poesie. 1915–1957* (Russian and Italian texts). 2d ed. Translated by A. Ripellino. Turin: G. Einaudi, 548 pp.
   First edition: 1957.6.

10 "Za povorotom" [Around the turning], "Vse sbylos'" [All has come true], "Pakhota" [Plowing], "Poezdka" [A trip], "Zimnie prazdniki" [Winter holidays], and "Edinstvinnye dni" [Unique days]. In *Mosty.* Vol. 2. Munich: COPE, pp. 11–20.

11 Trans. "Kogda by iz moei serdechnoi rany," "Glukhim, neiasnym, prizrachnym prizyvom," "Dusha—pereletnaia bednaia ptitsa," "V toske ia shel vdol' gornogo kriazha," "U kogo tak noet retivoe," "Iz zhizni vsei," and "Pesnia Zaro." In *Izbrannye stikhi*, by Avetik Isaakian. Moscow: GIKhL, pp. 32, 33, 53, 58–60, 62, 128.
   Reprint of 1945.5.

1960

1 "Bezliub'e" [Without love]. *NZh*, no. 62, pp. 10–18.

2 *Kogda razguliaetsia. Poems. 1955–1959* (Russian and English texts). Translated by Michael Harari. London: Collins and Harvill Press, 128 pp.

3   *Poeziia. Izbrannoe* [Poetry. Selected works]. Edited by N. Anatol'eva, N. Tarasova, and G. Shishkina. Frankfurt: Posev, 422 pp.

4   Trans. *Faust* [Goethe's *Faust*]. Introduction and comments by N.N. Vil'mont. 4th ed. Leningrad: GIKhL, 619 pp.
       Third edition: 1957.14; Fifth edition: 1969.7.

5   Trans. "Mariia Stiuart" [Schiller's *Maria Stuart*]. In *Izbrannye sochineniia v 2 tomakh.*, by Iu. Slovatskii. Vol. 1. Moscow: GIKhL, pp. 497–578.

6   Trans. "Otello" and "Korol' Lir." In *Polnoe sobranie sochinenii v 8 tomakh*, by William Shakespeare. Vol. 6. Moscow: Iskusstvo, pp. 281–568.

1961

1   Afterword to "Okhrannaia gramota" [A safe conduct]. *RM*, no. 1634 (24 January).

2   [An excerpt from a letter.] *NRS* (19 January).

3   [A letter to K. Becker.] *NRS* (5 February).

4   *Sobranie sochinenii* [Collected works], edited by G.P. Struve and B.A. Fillipov. 4 vols. Vol. 1, 503 pp. *Stikhi i poemy, 1912–1932.* Preface by Jacqueline de Proyart. Introduction, entitled "Boris Pasternak i modernizm" [Boris Pasternak and modernism], by Vladimir Weidle; Vol. 2, 363 pp. *Proza 1915–1958. Povesti, rasskazy, avtobiograficheskie proizvedeniia.* Introduction, entitled "Proza Pasternaka" [Pasternak's prose], by Vladimir Weidle; Vol. 3, 330 pp. *Stikhi, 1936–1959. Stikhi dlia detei. Stikhi, 1912–1957, ne sobrannye v knigi avtora. Stat'i i vystupleniia.* Introduction, entitled "Zavershenie puti" [The end of the road], by Vladimir Weidle; Vol. 4, 567 pp. *Doktor Zhivago.* Ann Arbor: University of Michigan Press.

5   *Stikhotvoreniia i poemy* [Poems and tales in verse]. Moscow: GIKhL, 375 pp.

1963

1   [Letters to Gorky.] *LiN* 70: 295–310.

2   [An untitled article.] *Grani*, no. 53, pp. 78–79.
       Reprint of 1928.1.

1964

1   [Letter to Tamara Iashvili (28 August 1937).] *LiG*, no. 7, pp. 88–89.

2   [Letter to Viacheslav Polonskii (1 June 1927).] *NM*, no. 10, pp. 195–96.

3   [Letters to T. Tabidze (1933–35).] In *Stat'i, ocherki, perepiska*, by T. Tabidze. Tbilisi, pp. 246–51.

4   Trans. "Mariia." In *Stikhotvorenniia i poemy*, by Taras Shevchenko. Moscow-Leningrad: Sovetskii pisatel', pp. 393–418.
    Reprint of 1956.7.

1965

1   "Bessonnitsa" [Insomnia], "Pod otkrytym nebom" [Under the open sky], and "Nezhnost'" [Tenderness]. In *Evtushenko-Pasternak-Akhmatova. Stikhotvoreniia*. Lechworth, Hartfordshire: Bradda Books, pp. 17–23.

2   [Letter to Jozsef Hóra (15 November 15 1935).] In *Glejt*. Prague: Státni nakladatelství Krásne literatury a umění, pp. 182–83.
    Reprinted in 1979.7.

3   [Letters to Jacqueline de Proyart.] *NZh*, no. 80, pp. 75–83.

4   [Letters to Renate Schweitzer.] *Grani*, no. 58, pp. 3–90.

5   [Pasternak's review of Mayakovsky's *Prostoe kak mychanie*, Pasternak's "Zametki perevodchika" (Notes of a translator), and "Shopen."] *LiR* (19 March): 18–19.

6   *Stikhotvoreniia i poemy* [Poems and tales in verse]. Edited by A.A. Ozerov. Introduction by A.D. Siniavskii. Moscow: Sovetskii pisatel', 730 pp.

7   "1917–1942", "Pamiati Mariny Tsvetaevoi" [In memory of Marina Tsvetaeva], "Osvobozhdennyi gorod" [Liberated city], "Speshnye stroki" [Hurried verses], "Poezdka v armiiu" [A trip to the front], "Bessonnitsia" [Insomnia], "Pod otkrytym nebom" [Under the open sky], "Nezhnost'" [Tenderness], and "Gorod. Zimnee nebo" [City. Wintry skies]. *NM*, no. 1, pp. 163–84.

1966

1 [Letters to Georgian writers and Georgian friends (1932–1959).] *VL* 10, no. 1: 166–200.

2 [Letters to Gorky.] *Plamen* 8, no. 6: 52–58.

3 "Neskol'ko slov o novoi gruzinskoi poezii" [A few words about new Georgian poetry]. *VL* 10, no. 1: 170–71.

4 "Pisma druz'iam (1931–1959)" [Letters to friends]. *LiG*, nos. 1–2, pp. 75–91; 83–96.

5 *Stikhi* [Poems]. Edited by Z. Pasternak and E. Pasternak. Introduction by K. Chukovskii. Moscow: GIKhL, 366 pp.

6 [Two poems, "When in my recollections" and "The future will change the view of everything"; and a letter to the Chistopol High School students.] *RuL*, no. 3, pp. 194–95.

7 Trans. *Zvezdnoe nebo. Stikhi zarubezhnykh poetov* (Translations of émigré poets). Moscow: Progress, 155 pp.

1967

1 [Letters to Gustav Herling-Grudzinki.] *Kultura*, no. 240, pp. 111–14.

2 [Letters to Mariia Iudina.] *ZOR*, no. 29, pp. 254–57.

3 "Liudi i polozheniia (Avtobiograficheskii ocherk)" [People and situations (Autobiographical sketch)]. *NM*, no. 43, pp. 204–36.

4 *Sestra moia zhizn'. Leto 1917 goda* [My sister, life. Summer, 1917] (Russian and English texts). Translated by Phillip C. Flayderman. New York: Washington Square Press, 172 pp.
   Reprinted: 1976.5.

5 *Stikhi* [Verses]. Moscow: GIKhL, 63 pp.

6 *Stikhotvoreniia i poemy* [Poems and tales in verse]. Moscow: Sovetskii pisatel', 366 pp.

7 *Vassermanova reaktsiia* [Wassermann test]. In *Die Manifeste und Programmschriften der russischen Futuristen*. Preface by Vladimir Markov

Munich: Wilhelm Fink Verlag, pp. 112–17.
Reprinted from 1914.3.

1968

1   [A speech delivered at the First All-Union Meeting of Translators]. *LiG*, no. 8, pp. 38–41.

2   "Zametki o perevode" [Notes on translation]. In *Masterstvo perevoda, 1966.* Moscow: Sovetskii pisatel', pp. 105–10.
Reprint of 1942.1.

3   Trans. "Romeo i Dzhul'etta," "Gamlet," "Otello," "Korol' Lir," "Makbet," and "Antonii i Kleopatra" (Shakespeare's tragedies). In *Tragedii. Sonety*, by William Shakespeare. Moscow: GIKhL, pp. 25–690.

1969

1   [Letters to S. Spassky]. *VL* 13, no. 9: 165–81.

2   "Pervye opyty Borisa Pasternaka" [Boris Pasternak's first attempts]. *TZS*, no. 236, pp. 239–81.

3   "Slepaia krasavitsa" [The blind beauty]. Introduction by L. Ozerov. *Prostor*, no. 10, pp. 45–75.

4   *Slepaia krasavitsa* [The blind beauty]. London: Collins and Harvill Press, 78 pp.

5   *Slepaia krasavitsa* [The blind beauty]. London: Flegon Press, 80 pp.

6   Trans. *Dramy. Novelly* (Translations of Heinreich von Kleist). Moscow: GIKhL, 621 pp.

7   Trans. *Faust* [Goethe's *Faust*]. 5th ed. Moscow: GIKhL, 507 pp.
Fourth edition: 1960.4.

1970

1   [Drafts of Pasternak's cycle "Nachal'naia pora" [A primary time]]. *RZIa* 4: 128–41.

2 [Letters to M.M. Morozov and A.O. Naumov]. *Masterstvo perevoda 1969*, pp. 341–47; 356–58; 360–63.

3 *Okhrannaia gramota* [A safe conduct]. Rome: Edizioni Aquario, 93 pp.

1971

1 "Babochka-bur'ia" [Butterfly-storm], "Otplytie" [Sailing away], "Nastuplenie zimy" [The coming of winter], "Sed'moi etazh" [Seventh floor], "Petukhi" [Cocks], "Osen'" [Autumn], "Bodrost'" [Buoyancy], and "Perelet" [Flight]. *ZOR* 32: 214–19.

2 [Letter to Medvedev.] *UZTGU*, no. 284, pp. 528–31.

3 [A Letter to Rainer Maria Rilke.] In *Nesobrannye proizvedeniia*, by Marina Tsvetaeva. Munich: Wilhelm Fink Verlag, pp. 681–83.

1972

1 [A letter to Zinaida Nikolaevna Pasternak, Pasternak's second wife.] *VRSKhD*, no. 106, pp. 222–23.

2 [Letters to the Mandelstams.] *VRSKhD*, nos. 104–5, pp. 229–48.

3 [Letters to Stich, Gordeyev, Bobrov, Loks, Mandelstam, Froman, Akhmatova, Kuliev, Durylin, Baranovich, and Ruoff.] *VL* 16, no. 9: 142–71.

4 *Temy i variatsii. Chetvertaia kniga stikhov* [Themes and variations. The fourth poetry collection]. Ann Arbor, MI: Ardis, 125 pp.
    Reprint of 1923.7.

5 "Tri glavy iz povesti" [Three chapters from the tale]. *TeC* 1, no. 1: 84–96.

6 [An unfinished Blok article, and a letter to Vyacheslav Ivanov.] In *Blokovskii sbornik. Trudy vtoroi nauchnoi konferentsii, posviashchennoi izucheniiu zhizni i tvorchestva A.A. Bloka.* Vol. 2. Tartu: Tartutskii gosudarstvennyi universitet, pp. 447, 450–53.

1973

1 *Fragmenty romana* [Fragments of a novel]. London: Collins and Harvill Press, 34 pp.

2   [Letters to Nina Skorbina.] *NRS* (18 February): 2, 8.

3   Trans. "Oda k svobode," "Grob Agamemnona," "Puteshestvie na vostok," "Voskhod solntsa na Salamine," "Zakat na more," "Pesnia na Nile," "Razgovor s piramidami," "V Shveitsarii," "Tuchi," and "Moe zaveshchanie," by Juliusz Słovacki. *NM*, no. 49, pp. 164–85.

4   Trans. *Romeo i Dzhul'etta* [Shakespeare's *Romeo and Juliet*]. 5th ed. Moscow: Detskaia literatura, 189 pp.
        Fourth edition: 1951.5; Reprinted: 1980.7.

1974

1   "Istoriia odnoi kontroktavy" [A history of a contraoctave]. In *IAN*, no. 2, pp. 150–61.

2   [Letters to Anna Akhmatova.] *RLT*, no. 9, pp. 523–29.

3   [Letters to Zaitsev, his daughter (Natalie Sologub), and Michel Aucouturier] (Russian and French texts). *CMRS* 15, nos. 1–2: 220–33.

4   "Novyi sbornik Anny Akhmatovoi." *RLT*, no. 9, p. 530.

5   "Retsenziya na knigu izbrannykh stikhov Anny Akhmatovoi" [Review of Anna Akhmatova's collection of selected poetry]. *RLT*, no. 9, pp. 531–32.

1975

1   [Letter to F.I. Vitiazev.] *RLT*, no. 13, pp. 543–44.

2   [Letter to V. Mayakovsky.] *RLT*, no. 13, p. 508.
        Reprinted: 1990.20.

3   [Letters to Bely.] *RLT*, no. 13, pp. 545–51.

4   [Letters to D.E. Maksimov.] In *Tezisy Vsesoiuznoi (III) konferentsii "Tvorchestvo A.A. Bloka i russkaia kul'tura XX veka,"* edited by Z.G. Mints. Tartu, pp. 11–16.

5   [Letters to G. Kozintsev.] *VL*, no. 1, pp. 212–23.

6   Trans. *Stikhi. Mariia Stiuart* [Juliusz Słowacki's *Maria Stuart*]. Moscow: GIKhL, 176 pp.

1976

1 [Fragments (ten) of Pasternak's early prose (1911–1913) dealing with winter city images.] In *Boris Pasternak. Essays*, edited by Nils Åke Nilsson. Stockholm Studies in Russian Literature, no. 7. Stockholm: Almqvist & Wiksell International, pp. 35–51.

2 [Letters to V.E. Meierkhol'd.] In *Perepiska 1896–1939*, by V.E. Meierkhol'd, compiled by V.P. Korshunova and M.M. Sitkovetskaia. Moscow: Iskusstvo, pp. 277–79.

3 *My Sister, Life and other Poems* (Russian and English texts). Edited and with texts by Olga Andreyev Carlisle. 3d ed. New York and London: Harcourt Brace Jovanovich, 119 pp.
    Second edition: 1923.5.

4 *Sestra moia zhizn'. Leto 1917 g. Stikhi* [My sister, life. Summer, 1917. Poems]. Ann Arbor: Ardis, 115 pp.
    Reprint of 1923.5.

5 *Sister My Life. Summer, 1917* (Russian and English texts). Translated by Phillip C. Flayderman. New York: Washington Square Press, 170 pp.
    Reprint of 1967.4.

6 *Stikhotvoreniia i poemy* [Poems and tales in verse]. Edited and with comments by L.A. Ozerov. Leningrad: Sovetskii pisatel', 604 pp.

7 [Three sketches.] In *Pamiatniki kul'tury. Novye otkrytiia. Pis'mennost'*. Moscow: Nauka, pp. 110–18.

8 *Vozdushnye puti* [Aerial ways]. Ann Arbor, MI: Ardis, 139 pp.
    Reprint of 1924.3.

1977

1 "Dialog." In *Stat'i o Pasternake*, by L. Fleishman. Bremen: K. Presse, pp. 130–37.

2 "Interlude." *SH* 1: 33–35.

3 "Istoriia odnoi kontroktavy" [A history of a contraoctave]. *SH* 1: 257–92.

4 [A letter to A.L. Shtikh.] *SH* 1: 194.

5   [A letter to Yu. Yurkin.] *Glagol* 1: 189–93.
    Reprinted in 1981.7.

6   [Letters to V. Bryusov.] *Russia. Rossiia*, no. 3, pp. 239–65.

7   "Nikolai Aseev. Oksana. Stikhi 1912–1916 godov" [Nikolai Aseyev. Oksana. Poetry from the years 1912–1916]. *SH* 1: 301–5.

8   *Poemy* [Tales in verse]. Moscow: Sovremennik, 91 pp.

9   "Sem' fragmentov iz 'Detstva Liuvers'" [Seven fragments from the Childhood of Luvers]. In *Stat'i o Pasternake*, by L. Fleishman. Bremen: K. Presse, pp. 118–29.

10 "Tezisy doklada 'Simvolizm i bessmertie'" [Abstract of the lecture "Symbolism and immortality"]. In *Stat'i o Pasternake*, by L. Fleishman. Bremen: K. Presse, pp. 116–17.

11 "Tri nabroska" [Three drafts]. In *Pamiatniki kul'tury. Novye otkrytiia. Pis'mennost'. Iskusstvo. Arkhielogiia. Ezhegodnik 1976.* Moscow: Nauka, pp. 110–18.

12 Trans. *Gamlet, prints datskii* and *Korol' Lir* (Shakespeare's *Hamlet* and *King Lear*). Leningrad: Khudozhestvenaia literatura, 351 pp.

13 Trans. "Semeistvo Shroffenshtein" [Kleist's *Die Familie Shroffenstein*]. In *Izbrannoe. Dramy. Novelly. Stat'i*, by Heinrich von Kleist. Moscow: GIKhL, pp. 25–176.
    Reprinted from 1923.9.

1978

1   [Letters to R. Rilke and M. Tsvetaeva (1926).] *VL* 4: 233–81.
    Reprinted: 1987.2.

1979

1   [Fragments from Pasternak's early prose (1911–1913).] *SH* 4: 286–93.

2   *Il tratto di Apelle.* Letchworth-Herts-England: Prideaux Press (Russian Titles for the Specialist, no. 170), 25 pp.

3   [Letter to K.M.L. Lozinsky.] In *Boris Pasternak 1890–1960: Colloque de Cerisy-la-Salle, (11–14 septembre 1975)*. Biliotheque russe de l'Institut d'études slaves, no. 47. Paris: Institut d'études slaves, pp. 107–9.

4 [Letter to V. Sayanov.] In *Ezhegodnik rukopisnogo otdela pushkinskogo doma, 1977*. Leningrad: AN SSSR, pp. 193–202.

5 "O predmete i metode psikhologii" [About the subject and method of psychology]. *SH* 4: 274–84.

6 *Pis'ma iz Tuly* [Letters from Tula]. Letchworth-Herts-England: Prideaux Press, (Russian Titles for the Specialist, no. 171), 12 pp.

7 [Two letters to Jozsef Hóra.] *VL*, no. 7, pp. 182–85.
      Reprinted in part from 1965.2.

8 *Vozdushnye puti* [Aerial ways]. Letchworth-Herts-England: Prideaux Press, (Russian Titles for the Specialist, no. 169), 16 pp.

9 "Vystuplenie na plenume Soiuza Sovetskikh Pisatelei" [A lecture at the convention of the Union of Soviet Writers]. *SH* 4: 297–303.

1980

1 [Letters to N.A. Tabidze (2 May 1951–5 February 1960).] *LiG*, no. 2, pp. 22–40.

2 [Letters to Olga Freidenberg.] In *Perepiska s Ol'goi Freidenberg*. New York: Harcourt Brace Jovanovich, 377 pp.

3 "Magdalina" [Mary Magdalene], "Rozhdestveskaia zvezda" [Star of the nativity], "Gefsimanskii sad" [The garden of Gethsemane], and "Gamlet" [Hamlet]. *DP*, pp. 179–81.

4 "Nikolai Baratshvili (Publikatsiia 28 marta 1946)." *DN*, no. 2, pp. 267–68.

5 "Spektorskii" (A passage from *Spektorskii*). *VoR*, nos. 9–10, p. 206.

6 "Uezd v tylu" [A district in the rear], "Pered razlukoi" [Before parting], "Nadmennyi nishchii" [A haughty pauper], "Tetia Olia" [Aunt Olya], "Noch' v dekabre" [A night in December], and "Dom s galereiami" [The house with galleries]. *NM*, no. 6, 176–205.

7 Trans. *Romeo i Dzhul'etta* [Shakespeare's *Romeo and Juliet*]. Minsk: Narodnaia asveta, 141 pp.
      Reprint of 1973.4.

1981

1   [Excerpts from correspondence and original works, published and unpublished.] In *Boris Pasternak v dvadtsatye gody*, by L. Fleishman. Munich: Wilhelm Fink Verlag, *passim*.

2   [A fragment of an article on English poetry.] *AB* 2: 106–7.

3   "Gamlet" [Hamlet]. *WSJ* 27: 113.

4   [Letters.] *SH* 5–6: 535–42.

5   [Letters to Fedor Stepun.] *RuA*, pp. 475–77.

6   [Letters to his parents, brother, sisters, Olga Freidenberg, E.V. Pasternak (Pasternak's first wife), Stikh, Loks, Bobrov, Tsvetaeva, Rilke, Petrovsky, Chikovani, and Nina Tabidze.] *RES* 53, no. 2: 267–91.

7   [Letters to Yu. Yurkin.] *VL*, no. 7, pp. 225–32.
    Reprint in part of 1977.5.

8   [Letters to M.A. Voloshin, O.D. Forsh, and G.E. Sorokin.] In *Ezhegodnik rukopisnogo otdela Pushkinskogo doma 1979*. Leningrad: AN SSSR, pp. 191–227.

9   [Letters to P.I. Chagin.] *AB* 2: 100–106.

10 [Letters to Sergei Bobrov.] *SH* 5–6: 523–33.

11 "Piazza S. Marco," "Bestsvetnyi dozhd'" (Colorless rain), "Betkhoven mostovykh" (A Beethoven of Roads), "Zhizn'" (Life), and "Na strastnoi" (Holy week). *DP*, pp. 161–65.

12 *Slepaia krasavitsa* [The blind beauty]. Paris: Izdatel'stvo Algata, 80 pp.

13 Trans. *Stikhotvoreniia, poema*, by N. Baratshvili. Tbilisi: Merani, 109 pp.

1982

1   [Letters to Ariadna Efron.] In *Pis'ma iz ssylki (1948–1957)*, by Ariadna Efron. Paris: YMCA Press, pp. 15, 19–20, 41–42, 44–45, 48–49, 52–53, 63–64, 75–76, 81–82, 93–94.
    Reprinted: 1985.2.

2 [Letters to Elena Orlovskaya and Kaisyn Kuliev.] *PoR* 1: 33–47.

3 [Letters to K. Bogatyrev]. In *Poet-perevodchik Konstantin Bogatyrev: drug nemetskoi literatury*, edited by Wolfgang Kasack. Munich: O' Sagnori, p. 188.

4 [Letters to S.P. Bobrov.] *VsP* 4: 139–60.

5 ["Remeslo" and four letters to his family.] *ChR*, nos. 2–3, pp. 23–36.

6 *Stikhotvoreniia* [Poems]. Moscow: Detskaia literatura, 174 pp.

7 *Vozdushnye puti. Proza raznykh let.* [Aerial ways. Prose of various years], edited by E.B. Pasternak and E.V. Pasternak. Introduction by D.S. Likhachev. Moscow: Sovetskii pisatel', 493 pp.
    Reprinted: 1983.4.

8 Trans. *Gamlet, prints datskii. Sonety. Romeo i Dzhul'etta* (Translations of two of Shakespeare's tragedies and his sonnets). Moscow: Molodaia gvardia, 326 pp.

9 Trans. *Tragedii* (Translations of Shakespeare's tragedies). Leningrad: Khudozhestvenaia literatura, 380 pp.

1983

1 [Letters to Akhmatova, Tikhonov, Polonsky, Medvedev, Obradovich, Pozner, George Reavey, and Ozarovskaya; Includes the poem "Mne kazhetsia" (It seems to me).] *LiN* 93: 654–737.

2 [Letters to N. Muravina.] *RES* 55: 639–40.

3 *Stikhotvoreniia* [Poems]. San Francisco: Nostal'giia, 358 pp.

4 *Vozdushnye puti. Proza raznykh let* [Aerial ways. Prose of various years]. Moscow: Sovetskii pisatel', 494 pp.
    Reprint of 1982.7.

5 Trans. *Romeo i Dzhul'etta. Gamlet. Otello. Korol Lir. Makbet* (Shakespeare's tragedies). Moscow: Pravda, 670 pp.

6 Trans. *Sud'ba Gruzii* (Russian and Georgian texts. N. Baratasvili's *Bedi Kartlisa*). Moscow: Kniga, 318 pp.

1984

1   [Excerpts from correspondence and original works, published and unpublished.] In *Boris Pasternak v tridtsatye gody*, by L. Fleishman. Jerusalem: Magness Press, Hebrew University, *passim*.

2   [A letter to Kaverin.] *Oktiabr'*, no. 9, p. 148.

3   [Letters to John Harris.] *SSR*, no. 3, pp. 82–94.

4   [Poems ("Tochil'shchik," "Pristup," "Pamiati Mariny Tsvetaevoi," "Pamiati Tsvetaevoi," "Na strastnoi," "Gamlet," "Ob"iasnenie," "Snimi ladon' s moei grudi," "Improvizatsiia," "Poet, ne prinimai na veru," "Odessa," "Vtoroe iiulia. Tri chasa utra," "Dusha—dushna, i dal' tabachnogo," "Nakrapyvalo. No ne gnulis'," "Dom kazalsia chuzhim," "Speloi grusheiu v buriu sletet'," "Griaznyi, gremuchii, v postel'," "Vse utro golub' vorkoval," "I posviatiat emu," "On mozhet roshchi obla ... ," "Gde sinii svet, svoi zimnii vosk," "Kak byli bely eti zuby," "Ia ponial: vse zhivo," "Mne po dushe stroptivyi norov," "Poet, ne prinimai na veru," "Pokhorony tovarishcha," "V nastuplen'e," "Ustami druga," "On vstaet. Veka, Gelaty," "Zima v Tiflise," "Skromnyi dom, no riumka romu," "Vse naklonen'ia i zalogi," "Kak-to v sumerki Tiflisa," "Veterok zabubennyi," "O vesna, vsia—tomlen'e," "Osleplen'e sprosonok," "Iunoi zhizni oplot,") and letters to Vashnetsev, Yartsev, and Tarasenkov.] *NZh*, no. 156, pp. 5–52.

5   "Six fragments of Juvenilia." In *"Juvenilia" B. Pasternaka. Shest' fragmentov o Relikvimini*, compiled by A. Ljunggren. Stockholm: Alinquist & Wiksell International, pp. 3–62.

6   [Two inscriptions.] *JRS*, no. 47, pp. 29–33.

7   [Two notes on Hans Sachs and Ben Jonson.] In *Aspects of Russia 1850–1970. Poetry, Prose, and Public Opinion. Essays Presented in Memory of Dr. N.E. Andreyev*, edited by William Harrison and Avril Pyman. Letchworth, Herts, England: Avebury Publishing Co., pp. 201–13.

8   Trans. [Swinburne's sonnet]. *IAN* 43, no. 6: 544–50.

1985

1   *Izbrannoe v dvukh tomakh* [Selected works in two volumes], edited by E.V. Pasternak and E.B. Pasternak. Vol. 1, 624 pp. *Stikhotvoreniia i poemy*. Introduction by D.S. Likhachev. Vol. 2, 560 pp. *Proza. Stikhotvoreniia*. Moscow: Khudozhestvennaia literatura.

2   [Letters to Ariadna Efron.] In *Pis'ma iz ssylki (1948–1957)*, by Ariadna Efron. Paris: YMCA Press, pp. 15, 19–20, 41–42, 44–45, 48–49, 52–53, 63–64, 75–76, 81–82, 93–94.
     Reprint of 1982.1.

3   [Letters to D.N. Zhuravlev and his wife]. In *Zhizn'. Iskusstvo. Vstrechi*, by D.N. Zhuravlev. Moscow: Vserossiiskoe teatral'noe obshchestvo, pp. 337, 340–43.

4   Trans. "Gamlet, prints datskii" [Shakespeare's *Hamlet*]. In *Gamlet. Izbrannye perevody*, by William Shakespeare. Moscow: Raduga, pp. 447–560.

1986

1   [Drafts for "Zarevo" (Glow)]. *DP* (1985): 146–48.

2   [Letters to Gorky.] *IAN* 45, no. 3: 261–83.

3   [Letters to P. Suvchinsky.] *RES* 58, no. 4: 637–48.

4   *Sestra moia, zhizn'. Stikhotvoreniia i poemy* [My sister, life. Poems and tales in verse]. Alma-Ata: Zhalyn, 399 pp.

1987

1   [Letters to Olga Freidenberg.] *Ogonek*, no. 16 (April): 26–28.

2   [Letters to R. Rilke and M. Tsvetaevoi (1926)]. *DN*, nos. 6–8, pp. 219–68. Reprint of 1978.1. Reprinted in 1990.11

3   *Sestra moia—zhizn'* [My sister, life] (Includes Russian and German texts). In *"Sestra moja—žizn" von Boris Pasternak. Analyse und Interpretation*, by Angelika Meyer. Slavistische Beiträge, no. 207. Munich: Verlag Otto Sagner, pp. 164–245.

4   *Stikhotvoreniia i poemy* [Poems and tales in verse]. Ashkhabad: Turkmenistan, 400 pp.

1988

1   *Doktor Zhivago*. [Annotations by E.B. Pasternak and V.M. Borisov]. *NM*, nos. 1–4, pp. 5–112, 96–157, 90–174, and 48–128.

2 [Letters and notes to various individuals.] *NM*, no. 6, pp. 205–48.

3 [Letters to Ariadna Efron.] *Znamia*, nos. 7–8, pp. 134–54; 127–61.

4 [Letters to Bely and K.N. Bugaeva]. In *Andrei Belyi. Problemy tvorchestva*, compiled by St. Lesnevskii and A.L. Mikhailov. Moscow: Sovetskii pisatel', pp. 686–706.

5 [Letters to Bobrov.] *LiR*, no. 49, p. 18.

6 [Letters to Leonid Pasternak and Olga Freidenberg, and a fragment from an early essay.] *RLJ* 42, nos. 141–43, pp. 147–50, 154–57, 158–60.

7 [Letters to Olga Freidenberg.] *DN*, nos. 7–10, pp. 201–4, 237–61, 235–56, and 232–42.

8 [Letters to Shalamov.] *Iunost'*, no. 10, pp. 54–67.

9 [Letters to Shalamov.] *VsP*, no. 6, pp. 291–305.

10 [Letters to V.D. Avdeyev.] *LU*, no. 6, pp. 108–16.

11 "O predmete i metode psikhologii" [About the subject and method of psychology]. *VF*, no. 8, pp. 97–105.

12 *Stikhotvoreniia* [Poems], compiled by L.S. Fleishman. Paris: YMCA Press, 192 pp.

13 *Stikhotvoreniia i poemy* [Poems and tales in verse], compiled by E.V. Pasternak. Moscow: Khudozhestvennaia literatura, 511 pp.

1989

1 *Doktor Zhivago. Roman* [Doctor Zhivago. A novel]. Introduction by E.B. Pasternak. Afterword by V.M. Borisov. Moscow: Knizhnaia palata, 431 pp.

2 *Doktor Zhivago. Roman.* [Doctor Zhivago. A novel]. Moscow: Sovetskaia Rosiia, 639 pp.

3 *Doktor Zhivago. Roman, povesti, fragmenty prozy* [Doctor Zhivago. A novel, tales, fragments of prose]. Moscow: Sovetskii pisatel', 733 pp.

4 [Excerpts from correspondence and original works, published and unpublished.] In *Boris Pasternak. Materialy dlia biografii*, compiled by E. Pasternak. Moscow: Sovetskii pisatel', *passim*.

5   "Gamlet" [Hamlet], "Chirkali ptitsy i byli iskrenni" [The birds twittered and were sincere], "Bozhe, ty sozdal bystroi kasatku" [Oh, Lord you've created a swallow to be swift]. In *Boris Pasternak and His Times. Selected Papers from the Second International Symposium on Pasternak*, edited by Lazar Fleishman. Modern Russian Literature and Culture. Studies and Texts, no. 25. Berkeley, CA: Berkeley Slavic Specialities, pp. 190–93.

6   [Letter to G.F. Ustinov.] *SSR* 12–13: 37–46.

7   [Letters to Aseyev (1943 and 1953).] *LG*, no. 28, pp. 6–7.

8   "Maiakovskii v moei zhizni." *LG*, no. 40, p. 5.

9   *Okhrannaia grammota. Shopen* [A safe conduct. Chopin]. Moscow: Sovremennik, 94 pp.

10 [A response to *Evening Moscow's* questionnaire "My First Thing."] In *Boris Pasternak and His Times. Selected Papers from the Second International Symposium on Pasternak*, edited by Lazar Fleishman. Modern Russian Literature and Culture. Studies and Texts, no. 25. Berkeley, CA: Berkeley Slavic Specialties, pp. 416–17.

11 "Russkaia revoliutsiia" [The Russian revolution]. *NM*, no. 4, pp. 131–34.

12 "Severianin iavliaetsia v Odessu" [Severyanin appears in Odessa]. In *Intertextualität und Interpretierbarkeit des Texts. Zur frühen Prosa Boris Pasternaks*, by Erika Greber. Munich: Wilhelm Fink Verlag, pp. 272–73.

13 *Sobranie sochinenii v piati tomakh*. Vol. 1, 750 pp. *Stikhotvoreniia i poemy, 1912–1931*. Vol. 2, *Stikhotvoreniia, 1931–1959; Perevody*. Vol. 3, 733 pp. *Doktor Zhivago*. Moscow: Khudozhestvenaia literatura.

14 *Stikhotvoreniia* [Poems], compiled by E.A. Evtushenko. Petrozavodsk: Kareliia, 301 pp.

16 *The Year Nineteen-five. Deviat'sot piatyi god* (Includes Russian and English texts). Translated into English verse by Richard Chappell. London: Spenser, 96 pp.
     Russian text reprint of 1932.1.

1990

1   *Boris Pasternak. Ob iskusstve. "Okhrannaia gramata" i zametki o khudozhestvennom tvorchestve*. [Boris Pasternak on art. A safe conduct and notes on artistic creativity]. Moscow: Iskusstvo, 396 pp.

2   "Iz pisem raznykh let" [Letters from various years]. *Ogonek*, no. 6, pp. 2–47.

3   [Letter to D.I. Chizhevskii (26 May 1959).] *DN*, no. 3, pp. 242–43.

4   [Letter to Mandelstam (spring 1937) and letter to Nadezhda Mandelstam (10 April 1943).] *LO*, no. 3, pp. 97 and 99.

5   [Letter to P.P. Suvchinsky (31 October 1927).] *LO*, no. 12, p. 101.

6   [Letter to P.S. Kogan]. *VL*, no. 2, pp. 44–46.

7   [Letters to D.V. Petrovsky, N.K. Chukovsky, K.G. Paustovsky, and N.A. Pavlovich]. *LO*, no. 2, pp. 6–16.

8   [Letters to E.D. Orlovskaia and K.S. Kuliev (1947–1954).] *DN*, no. 2, pp. 259–70.

9   [Letters to his family.] *Znamia* (February): 194–204.

10   [Letters to M. Iudina (1941–1959).] *NM*, no. 2 (February): 166–91.

11   [Letters to Marina Tsvetaeva and Rainer Maria Rilke.] In *Pis'ma 1926 goda*. Moscow: Kniga, 255 pp.
       Includes reprint of 1987.2.

12   [List of popular sayings Pasternak composed during his stay in Chestopol]. *RuR*, no. 1, pp. 25–28.

13   "Neizdannye pis'ma" [Unpublished letters]. *NRS* (23 March): 3–4.
       Reprint of 1990.14.

14   "Neizdannye pis'ma" [Unpublished letters]. *Ogonek* (January): 23–25.
       Reprinted: 1990.13.

15   [Nine letters to Nina Muravina (19 February 1948; 20 August 1948; 28 November 1948; 12 February 1949; 16 May 1949; 3 March 1950; 8 February 1951; 18 November 1951; 19 January 1953)]. In *Vstrechi s Pasternakom*, by Nina Muravina. Tenafly, NJ: Hermitage, pp. 73, 80, 100, 115, 124, 132–33, 157, and 178.

16   ["Nobelevskaia premiia." (The Nobel prize) and letters to Freidenberg, the Tabidzes, and Shalamov.] In *"Doktor Zhivago" Borisa Pasternaka*, compiled by L.V. Bakhnov and L.B. Voronin. S raznykh tochek zreniia. Moscow: Sovetskii pisatel', pp. 118; 127–31; 133–38; 145–52; and 161–63.

17 "O Lili Kharazovoi' [About Lili Kharazova]. *LO*, no. 2, pp. 17–18.

18 "Pis'ma B.L. Pasternaka v sviazi s 'Doktorom Zhivago'" [B.L. Pasternak's letters in connection with Doctor Zhivago]. *RR*, no. 1 (January–February): 3–16.

19 "Pis'mo chitateliu" [Letter to the reader]. Introduction by A. Semenova. *LO*, no. 2, pp. 16–17.

20 "Pis'mo Vladimiru Maiakovskomu" [Letter to Vladimir Mayakovsky]. *LO*, no. 2, pp. 42–44.
       Reprint of 1975.2.

21 *Poems*, compiled by E. Pasternak. Moscow: Raduga, 316 pp.

22 [Six letters to Josephine Pasternak and two to his parents (1924–1937)]. *Znamia*, no. 2, pp. 194–204.

23 [Speeches on formalism and impressionism (13 March 1936 and 16 March 1936.] *LO*, no. 3, pp. 87–91.

24 *Stikhotvoreniia* [Poems], compiled and with an introduction by N. Bannikov. Moscow: Molodaia gvardiia, 224 pp.

25 *Stikhotvorenniia i poemy v dvukh tomakh* [Poems and tales in verse]. 2 vols, compiled by V.S. Baevskii and E.B. Pasternak. Introduction by V.N. Al'fonsov. Leningrad: Sovetskii pisatel', 504 pp. and 368 pp.

26 [Twelve letters to Pasternak's second wife, Zinaida Nikolaevna (1931–1954)]. *Ogonek*, no. 1, pp. 23–25.

27 [Two letters to Konstantin Loks (1913)]. *VL*, no. 2, pp. 30–31.

28 [Two letters to M.M. Morozov (30 September 1947 and 15 July 15 1942]. *Teatr*, no. 3, pp. 144–46.

29 "2-aia kartina. Peterburg" [The second scene. Petersburg] (A fragment of an unfinished tale). *NM*, no. 5, 166–77.

Criticism of Boris Pasternak
1914–1990

1914

1 SHERSHENEVICH, VADIM. Review of Pasternak's *A Twin in the Clouds* (in Russian). *SZh*, no. 11 (November): 134–35.

Finds fault with Pasternak's word choices in the collection ("an unbearable mixture of neologisms and antiquated words") and Pasternak's poetics, i.e., his "creativity methods," which are dubbed "chaotic." Argues that "the young poet is capable of using an ultra-modern turn of speech with turns which even to Pushkin would appear old-fashioned." Reprimands Pasternak for using mythological names along with "new themes on a contemporary city." Concludes all this is "a result of insipidness and inner muddle."

1922

1 ASEEV, NIK. "Pis'ma o poezii ('Sestra moia zhizn' Pasternaka)" [Letters on poetry (Pasternak's *My Sister, Life*)]. *KN*, no. 3, pp. 248–53.

Briefly discusses *My Sister, Life*; deems every line characteristic of Pasternak. Notes that the collection is "organically compact." Pasternak demonstrates "miraculous technical possibilities" based on freedom of improvisation. Insists this is not impressionism because the "choice of methods is strict and narrow" but the "achievements are many and various."

2 BRIUSOV, VALERII. "Vchera, segodnia i zavtra russkoi poezii" [Yesterday, today, and tomorrow of Russian poetry]. *PR*, no. 7, pp. 38–68.

An elaborate commentary on Pasternak's early poetry (mainly on *My Sister, Life*), with frequent comparisons of Pasternak to Mayakovsky. Sees Pasternak's influence on the younger generation as almost equal to that of Mayakovsky's; claims Pasternak contributed to the creation of the new rhyme more than Mayakovsky, and that Pasternak's poetry is more imitated than Mayakovsky's. Strongly argues that Pasternak's poetry has been honored more than anyone else's since the time of Pushkin and points out that Pasternak's poetry has been distributed in handwritten copies. Stresses Pasternak's individuality ("ability to see everything in meters"), and the boldness of "new syntatic constructions." Concludes that Pasternak "has no individual poems about the Revolution," though Pasternak's "poetry is permeated with the spirit of modernity."

3　CHERNIAK, IAKOV. Review of Pasternak's *My Sister, Life* (in Russian). *PR*, no. 6 (July–August): 303–4.

Praises Pasternak's collection, which reminds him of Pushkin in its "lucidity and simplicity." Also comments on Pasternak's other works.

4　ERENBURG, I. "Boris Leonidovich Pasternak" (in Russian). *NRK*, no. 6, pp. 10–12.

Describes his meeting with Pasternak in Moscow in 1922. Recalls Pasternak's appearance ("I was struck by his shy and challenging manner") and reading of "a poem about the scourged wings of the Demon." Notes the romanticism in Pasternak's poetry, though "not one of his poems could have been written before him." Comments on Pasternak's "complex associations and frank comparisons" and concludes that Pasternak's "magic" lies in his syntax. Points to Pasternak's musicality, which reminds him of Igor Severyanin, and to Pasternak's "violent and wild" rhythm. Believes that the title of one of Pasternak's poems, "The Urals for the First Time," could apply to Pasternak's other works that are labeled as "The World for the First Time." Compares Pasternak's lyric poetry to Akhmatova's and concludes that "in Pasternak there are no autumns, sunsets or other sweet inconsolable things. He has shown that the lyrical exists and can go on existing, outside the questions of social environment." Predicts that lyrical poetry (such as Pasternak's) might be abolished, but that future generations will appreciate it. Translated: 1969.7. Reprinted: 1972.8.

5　KUZMIN, M. "Govoriashchie (B. Pasternak)" [Those talking (B. Pasternak)]. In *ZI*, no. 31, pp. 8–15.

Notes that *The Childhood of Luvers* is an "event in art," and that the work's interest is not in child psychology, but in the "virtuous sincerity of the author's perception." Also notes that the plot development is barely noticeable, because it is embedded in various trivial scenes "interrupted by Pasternak's philosophical reflections." Concludes that Pasternak is a significant artist with great inner resources. Reprinted: 1923.4.

6　PRAVDUKHIN, V. "V bor'be za novoe iskusstvo" [In the struggle for the new art]. *SiO*, no. 5.

Insists that Pasternak is "an amazingly subtle master" who ascribes importance not so much to the whole of nature as to the "world of trifles and individual parts." Argues that Pasternak cannot become a creator equal to life, but rather remains a "homeless dweller in a new place," although one must welcome his attempt to "face the vistas opened by the Revolution." Reprinted: 1924.3.

7   TSVETAEVA, MARINA. "'Svetovoi liven'. Poeziia vechnoi muzhestvennosti" [Luminous downpour. Poetry of eternal courage]. *Epopeia*, no. 3, pp. 10–33.

A reaction to *My Sister, Life,* her first encounter with Pasternak's poetry, though she had met him three or four times before. Recalls Pasternak's poetry reading at the Polytechnic Museum in Moscow when he read in a "muffled" and "muttering" manner, "as if a bear awaking." Describes Pasternak's appearance, his face with "something of an Arab and his horse: an alertness, an attentiveness, the most complete readiness to run away at any moment. A large, also horselike, wild and shy slant of the eyes." Notes that Pasternak's poetic talent cannot be imitated, and emphasizes that Pasternak is "greater than all others: the majority of significant poets *were*, there were a few who *are*, only Pasternak *will be*." Sees Pasternak as belonging to the first day of creation—"he was created before Adam." Concludes that Pasternak "has no questions, only answers," and that the collection is an affirmation of everyone and everything. Believes that everyone should want to get to know it; it has miraculous power: "nobody would want to kill themselves or take it to their head to kill another." Reprinted: 1953.1. Translated: 1969.18.

1923

1   ASEEV, N. Review of Pasternak's *Themes and Variations* (in Russian). *PR* 6: 71–8.

Recounts his first encounter with Pasternak. Observes that "Pasternak's magic" is in his syntax and his rhythm ("furious and wild in its swiftness"), and that his poetry lacks sentimentality because of its irony and intelligence. Praises the "tautness of his syntactical devices," and calls Pasternak a "remarkable organizer of speech." Underlines the importance of similes in Pasternak's poetry, which are "always perfectly apt," and calls Pasternak a "master of comparison." Cites heavily from *Themes and Variations.* Reprinted: 1929.1. Translated: 1969.1.

2   GRUZDEV, IL'IA. "Utilitarnost' i samotsel'" [Utilitarianism and the end in itself]. In *Petrograd. Literaturnyi al'manakh.* Petrograd-Moscow: Petrograd, pp. 172–90.

Only a portion of the fifth part deals with Pasternak; it focuses on his language and "incomprehensibility." Affirms that Pasternak introduced a "household" language into poetry, "our everyday speech . . . substantiating it with lyrical themes." Insists that Pasternak's "incomprehensibility" is "only apparent. Pasternak is logical and utterly sober." Sees *Themes and Variations* as Pasternak's quest for "new courses."

3 GUSMAN, BORIS. "Boris Pasternak" (in Russian). In *Sto poetov. Literaturnye portrety*. Tver: Oktiabr', pp. 206–9.

Cites poetry from *My Sister, Life* and analyzes the use of particular sounds in two of the poems—"About These Verses" and "The Crying Garden." Characterizes the latter poem as the "melody of a garden." Elaborates on Pasternak's concept of art as a sponge, "not as [a] fountain." Comments on Pasternak the poet: "Boris Pasternak, cold, indifferent, and perplexed, wandering the groves of life." Lauds Pasternak's ability to hearken changes even in soft sounds and rustles.

4 KUZMIN, M. "Govoriashchie (B. Pasternak)" [Those talking]. In *Uslovnosti*. Petrograd: Poliarnaia zvezda, pp. 158–61.

Reprint of 1922.5.

5 MANDELSHTAM, O. "Vulgata. Zametki o poezii" [Notes on poetry] and "Boris Pasternak" (A two-part article). *RI*, no. 2, pp. 68–70; *Rossiia*, no. 6, p. 29.

Contends that Pasternak and Khlebnikov are the first poets since Iazykov to utilize secular, everyday Russian poetic speech. Compares Fet's "burning salt of undying words" with Pasternak's "high tide of images and feelings [that] sprang into being again with unprecedented force." Concludes that to read Pasternak's poetry is "to get one's throat clear, to fortify one's breathing, to renovate one's lungs; such poems must be a cure for tuberculosis. At present we have no poetry that is healther than this." Reprinted: 1928.1. Translated: 1969.15.

1924

1 PARNOK, SOFIA. "B. Pasternak i drugie" [B. Pasternak and others]. *RS*, no. 1, pp. 307–11.

An attempt to interpret Pasternak as a contemporary poet ("I think that of all of my coevals Pasternak is truly contemporary with our time"). Discusses Pasternak's rhymes, rhythm, and melodiousness; the musicality of his verse; and his language ("unlike any existing poetic language"). Praises *Themes and Variations* as Pasternak's best collection and compares Pasternak to other poets.

2 PERTSOV, V. "Vymyshlennaia figura" [An imaginary figure]. *NP*, no. 1, pp. 209–24.

Reviews Pasternak's early poetry: "Disintegration," "Earth's Diseases," "Our Thunderstorm," and "Definition of Soul." Dubs Pasternak a "living misunderstanding which occurred among futurists."

Blames him for not wanting to change his views of art and his continued "work for an individual consumer." Insists that Pasternak harms the "development of a new, proletarian literature," and clamors, "We don't need Pasternak."

3 PRAVDUKHIN, V. "B. Pasternak" (in Russian). In *Literaturnaia sovremennost'*. Moscow: Gosizdat, pp. 130–37.
  Reprint of 1922.6.

4 TYNIANOV, IURII. "Promezhutok" [Interval]. *RS*, no. 4, pp. 209–21.
  Argues that Pasternak's poetry is born among "sickness, childhood, generally those *accidental* things, those of one's vision's intimate corners coated with lacquer and usually forgotten." Discerns Pasternak's favorite image as "downpour," and observes that Pasternak's "difficult language is the most precise language, an intimate conversation, a conversation in a nursery," and that a "chance turns out to be a more powerful bond than a most intimate logical bond." Mentions common bonds with Lermontov, Fet, and Apukhtin, among others. Concludes that Pasternak "wanders" and "his wandering has affected others." Reprinted: 1929.3. Translated: 1969.19.

1925

1 MIRSKY, D.S. Review of Pasternak's *Rasskazy* (in Russian). *SZ* 25: 544–45.
  Mentions Pasternak's popularity as a poet ("occupies one of the highest places"). Notes that this prose collection (*The Line of Apelles*, *Letters from Tula*, *The Childhood of Luvers*, and *Aerial Ways*) is distinguished by new methods of perceiving the world's reality. *The Line of Apelles* reminds the author of Pasternak's association with "Centrifuge." *The Childhood of Luvers* is seen as a "psychological history of a girl," though it addresses ideas instead of feelings and thoughts. Singles out *Aerial Ways* for not having the "dry" prose of *The Childhood of Luvers* and labels it as a somewhat "stumbling and incoherent story." Comparisons or contrasts are made to Proust, Bely, and Mandelstam.

1926

1 LEZHNEV, A. "Boris Pasternak" (in Russian). *KN*, no. 8, pp. 205–19.
  Questions the controversy surrounding Pasternak: some see him as the greatest of contemporary masters, while others find him affected and incomprehensible. Argues that Pasternak's verse is built upon the principle of linear linkage of associations and that the omission of associative links is Pasternak's deliberate device. Insists Pasternak wishes to write unintelligibly. Through this dissolution of the emotional-objective world

into simple components of sensations, Pasternak appears as an impressionist, and in the mixing of these elements, as a futurist. Concludes that Pasternak discovers sensation as a new element of poetry. Believes that freshness and tension are fascinating ingredients in Pasternak's verse. Reprinted: 1927.2. Translated: 1969.13.

2 ———. Review of Pasternak's *Selected Verses* (in Russian). *KN*, no. 8, pp. 230–32.
   Reviews Pasternak's poetry in passing as a part of the collection *Uzel*, which includes poetry and prose of seven other contemporaries of Pasternak. Places Pasternak in "the first place" among the collection's contributors, and compares Pasternak to one of them, Antokolsky, deemed a Pasternak imitator. Ascribes certain qualities of "profundity and sincerity" to Pasternak and labels him "timid, intimate, and tongue-tied."

3 SELIVANOVSKII, A. "B. Pasternak" (in Russian). In *Poeziia i poety. Kriticheskie stat'i.* Moscow: Sovetskaia literatura, pp. 155–78. Reprint. 1933.
   Maintains that the sources of the worldview evident in Pasternak's poetry lay in bourgeois culture, that he never reconciled himself to the existence of social orders but did not struggle against them, and that his poetry is an attempt to exit from the battle. Concludes that Pasternak is not a bourgeois poet, yet it is difficult to be a revolutionary one (Pasternak is located "at the boundary of two cultures—the bourgeois and the socialist"). Reprinted: 1936.3.

1927

1 KRASIL'NIKOV, VIKTOR. "Boris Pasternak" (in Russian). *PR*, no. 5, pp. 78–91.
   A composite survey of Pasternak's works up to 1927. Registers journals that published Pasternak's works, surveys criticism and takes issue with some (Lezhnev [1926.1] and Pertsov [1927.4]), and analyzes Pasternak's poetry. Labels Pasternak a "city-poet" and a "poet-citizen," and explains Pasternak's "incomprehensibility" by his "intonational orientation." Credits Pasternak for his "poetic exactness" (he gave a "multitude of aphorisms" to the Russian language), lexical innovations (terms from contemporary science, Latin expressions, mythological characters, neologisms, and localisms), his "profound erudition," verse novelties, and his "self-perfection" (his poetry "goes its own way and will occupy a unique place in the history of Russian verse").

2 LEZHNEV, A. "Boris Pasternak" (in Russian). In *Sovremenniki. Literaturno-kriticheskie ocherki.* Moscow: Krug, pp. 32–54.
   Reprint of 1926.1.

3 ———. Review of Pasternak's *Two Books* and *The Year 1905* (in Russian). *Pravda*, no. 297 (28 December): 5.

Notes Pasternak's "enormous" influence on the contemporary literary scene and bemoans his unpopularity with the general reader. Bases his criticism of Pasternak's poetry on two previous collections, *My Sister, Life* and *Above the Barriers*, which comprise *Two Books*. Finds the philosophical aspect of Pasternak's poetry echoing Tyutchev, and lauds Pasternak's poetry for its novelty of poetic expressions. Singles out a number of poems from *My Sister, Life* as the most prominent examples of Russian lyrics. Thinks of *The Year 1905* as a significant turning point in Pasternak's career, a move from a closed to a more open "social space." Also lauds Pasternak's individuality, his "great talent," and his temperament.

4 PERTSOV, V. "Novyi Pasternak" [A new Pasternak]. *NLP*, no. 2, pp. 33–39.

Reviews Pasternak's poetry from the early collections to tales in verse, noting three forms of Pasternak's "technique": self-observation, observation, and "poetic influence." Finds "revolutionary" themes in Pasternak's poetry, notably in *Spektorsky* and *The Year 1905*, and concludes that Pasternak was then a "living force, no longer a cultural heritage, coming closer to the construction of the Revolution."

1928

1 MANDELSHTAM, OSIP. "Boris Pasternak" (in Russian). In *O poezii*. Moscow: n.p.
Reprint of 1923.5.

2 MIRSKY, D.S. Review (in Russian) of Pasternak's *The Year 1905*. *Versty*, no. 3, pp. 150–54.

Hails the appearance of *The Year 1905* as a "great literary event." Mentions that the collection consists of two pieces, *The Year 1905* and *Lieutenant Schmidt*, the latter of which is related to *Aerial Ways*. Finds the court scenes in *Lieutenant Schmidt* "striking" and "saturated with pining lyricism." Traces the tradition Pasternak retains, a tradition of Tyutchev, Fet, and Annensky. Concludes that all the bonds of the pre-revolutionary tradition have now converged in Pasternak, who is a "point of departure for all future Russian traditions."

3 OTSUP, NIKOLAI. "Boris Pasternak" (in Russian). *Zveno*, no. 5, pp. 260–66.

Offers sporadic remarks on Pasternak's verse and labels the poetry of *The Year 1905* and *Lieutenant Schmidt* as "tiresome and prosaic" and lacking in "quality." Sees this "failure" in Pasternak's endeavor "to explain himself and nothing came out of it." Feels that Pasternak acheives "an understandable and clear language" in these two pieces, though insists they turned out to be "much too weaker than the confusing poetry of *My Sister, Life.*"

4 POSTUPAL'SKII, I. "Boris Pasternak" (in Russian). *NM*, no. 2, pp. 229–37.

Notes that Pasternak spoke of the influence of Pushkin's aesthetics, but understood even Pushkin in an impressionistic way. Calls Pasternak a unique reformer of impressionism, rethinking and recreating it as a literary device. Considers Pasternak's first characteristic of an impressionistic worldview to be an anlaytical approach (transferring human sensations to the surrounding environment). Phonetic associations comprise the second characteristic, while a third is the changing of varied words from his literary palette. A fourth characteristic is the deliberate obfuscation of poetic syntax.

5 WEIDLE, WLADIMIR. "Stikhi i proza Pasternaka" [Pasternak's poetry and prose]. *SZ* 36: 459–70.

Criticizes Pasternak's "deficiency of taste" in his prose and poetry, arguing that Pasternak possesses an "insufficient realization of how words should be used." For Pasternak "poetry means above all confusion in tongues," and that "the kernel of genuine poetry hidden in all his verbiage is limited and meagre." Praises Pasternak's unusual skill of combining sounds with senses, underlining that in his poetry "the word itself has meaning, but the words taken together have no spiritual life." Discusses in detail Pasternak's usages of "near-meaningless un-Russian turns of speech, dubious stresses, incorrect cases, and wrongly abbreviated endings." Calls *The Line of Apelles* and *Letters from Tula* "unsuccessful, chaotic experiments" but admires *Aerial Ways*, in which Pasternak creates "a wholly original linguistic tissue, unlike any that has ever existed before in Russian prose." Makes a general conclusion that Pasternak's work "deserves our attention." Translated: 1969.20.

1929

1 ASEEV, N. "Melodika ili intonatsiia" [Melody or intonation]. In *Dnevnik pisatelia.* Leningrad.

Reprint of 1923.1.

2 ROZANOV, IVAN. "Boris Pasternak" (in Russian). In *Russkie liriki. Ocherki.* Moscow: Nikitinskie subbotniki, pp. 103–31.

Makes general remarks about Pasternak's early poetry collections; notes that Pasternak belonged to the right wing of the futurists. Contrasts Mayakovsky to Pasternak, the former seen as a poet of the street and the latter as a chamber poet. Notes that Pasternak's two poetry collections provoked negative criticism even though they contained "such remarkable poems as 'Marburg,' 'On a Boat,' and 'The Storm.'" Also notes that in *A Twin in the Clouds* a motif of solitude is clearly heard, and that *Themes and Variations* was unsuccessful. Claims that each collection of Pasternak's poetry exibits increasing simplification of style and greater comprehensibility.

3 TYNIANOV, IURII. "Promezhutok" [Interval]. In *Arkhaisty i novatory.* Leningrad: Priboi, pp. 563–68; 579–80.
    Reprint of 1924.4.

1930

1 EL'SBURG, Zh. "Mirovospriiatie B. Pasternaka" [B. Pasternak's world perception]. *NLP*, no. 7, pp. 42–50.
    Calls Pasternak an "artistic ideologue of a very thin layer of the petty-bourgeois intlelligentsia" that formed before the Revolution. Argues that Pasternak did not accept evolutionary change ("the ideological essence of Pasternak's work did not accept decisive changes"). Believes that Pasternak must recognize "his inner contradictions and the unsoundness of his dualism."

2 REAVEY, GEORGE. "First Essay Towards Pasternak." *Experiment* (October): 14–17.
    Compares Pasternak to Mayakovsky and Esenin; argues that Pasternak "does not dramatize himself"; labels his early poetry as "incomprehensible," noting that this complexity "purifies the poem until it is brought near to the creative act itself." Also argues that "tonality and harmony of words is the very spring of Pasternak," that Pasternak had created a revolution "in the eternal structure of the poem," and that Pasternak's "poetry may be *trobar clus*, but it is a parthenon of impersonality after the agonies and perorations of Esenin and Mayakovsky." Reprinted: 1959.58.

1931

1 LANZ, HENRY. *The Physical Bases of Rime. An Essay on the Aesthetics of Sound.* Stanford, CA: Stanford University Press, p. 92.
    Comments on rhymes in *Spektorsky*. Argues that Pasternak "hardly employs any other combinations but rhyphmoids," that "he succeeds in bringing into melodic unity ideas and words which otherwise would probably never occur to the poet's mind," and that Pasternak's rhymes "often result in daring intellectual adventures."

2 TARASENKOV, A. "Boris Pasternak" (in Russian). *Zvezda*, no. 5, pp. 228–35.

An overview of Pasternak's attitude toward the Revolution and a general commentary on Pasternak's poetry. Discusses Pasternak's syntax and imagery—dubs the latter "one of the forms of impressionistic subjectivism." Sees Pasternak's "societal neutrality" as a result of his "artistic method" formed at the time of destruction of the old world and the birth of the new. Cites Pasternak's three tales in verse to illustrate that Pasternak endeavored to adapt himself to new themes and "new processes"—but with "old methods." Urges Pasternak to "strengthen" his "phase of turning to us" and to "genuinely" master "the dialectics of the proletarian revolution."

1932

1 MILLER-BUDNITSKAIA, R. "O 'filosofii iskusstva' B. Pasternaka i R.M.Ril'ke" [On B. Pasternak's and R.M. Rilke's philosophy of art]. *Zvezda*, no. 5, pp. 160–68.

Draws similarities between Pasternak's and Rilke's views of the being and between their use of a child's psyche as "creative resources." Blames Pasternak for "fetishism" in act. Demands that Pasternak change his artistic views, including his rejection of Rilke's "philosophy of symbolism." Bases comments on Pasternak's *A Safe Conduct*, "The Death of a Poet," "New Verses," and "The Waves."

2 PROZOROV, A. Review of Pasternak's *Spektorsky* (in Russian). *NLP*, no. 7, pp. 26–35.

Contends that Pasternak incorrectly labeled his work a "novel in verse" because his creative method kept him from depicting "objective social reality." Pasternak locks himself "within the boundaries of subjective conciousness," and as a "consistently subjective idealist," Pasternak was unable to create an objective, rounded protagonist. Calls Pasternak a "writer-fellow traveler." Allows that within the limits of his faulty artistic method, *Spektorsky* stands at a "considerable height."

1933

1 BEM, A. Review of Pasternak's *Second Birth* (in Russian). *SZ*, no. 51, pp. 454–56.

Detects a thematical intertwinement of personal experiences with nature in the collection's cycle "The Waves." Notes the collection's Caucasus theme ("resurrection of Russian Romanticism"), and emphasizes Pasternak's simplification of syntax and lexica and diminishment of sound effects. Concludes that Pasternak's poetic gift lies in his ability of rejuvinating an "object".

2   SLONIM, MARK. "Boris Pasternak" (in Russian). In *Portrety sovetskikh pisatelei*. Paris: Parabola, pp. 38–47.
     Considers Pasternak the only innovator among the poets of the 1920s and the 1930s. Analyzes some aspects of Pasternak's poetics—his "unusual" metaphors and elliptical devices, including the omission of a vehicle or a tenor in similes and comparisons. Labels Pasternak's poetry as that of "individual consciousness," and claims that in *The Year 1905*, *Lieutenant Schmidt*, and *Spektorsky*, Pasternak glorifies "first of all the movements of a human soul." Compares Pasternak to Mayakovsky and Esenin, and concludes that Pasternak's poetry clashes with Mayakovsky's. While Pasternak's and Esenin's poetry have more in common, Pasternak's is "more profound."

3   TSVETAEVA, M. "Epos i lirika sovremennoi Rossii. Vladimir Maiakovskii i Boris Pasternak" [Epic and lyric of contemporary Russia. Vladimir Mayakovsky and Boris Pasternak]. *NG*, no. 6, pp. 28–41.
     Juxtaposes Mayakovsky and Pasternak. Finds Pasternak as the opposite of Mayakovsky, who is implicitly "a poet without a theme," and that Pasternak's *The Childhood of Luvers* is the "work of a genius." Reprinted: 1979.47. Translated: 1975.15.

4   ———. Review of Pasternak's *Stikhotvoreniia v odnom tome* (in Russian). *RA* 26–27: 104–42.
     An evaluation of Pasternak's early poetry and a perception of Pasternak as the poet and lyricist. Sees Pasternak, Akhmatova, and Mandelstam as poets-lyricists whose poetry had never "dried up." Emphasizes Pasternak's predilection for descriptions of nature ("Pasternak's entire book is nature") and, particularly, for describing rain. Discusses Pasternak's "revolutionary" themes, arguing that Pasternak reacted to all historical events of his time. Perceives *Lieutenant Schmidt* and *The Year 1905* as Pasternak's childhood recollections—written not by "chance" but by "conscience." Sees the plight and fate of women as the only contemporary issue that "captivated" Pasternak. Emphasizes that Pasternak did not change his political views after the Revolution. ("Pasternak sleeps . . . with the sleep of a lyricist"). Reprinted: 1981.22.

5   ZELINSKII, K. Review of Pasternak's *Second Birth* (in Russian). *GSh*, no. 1, pp. 394–407.
     A discussion of the collection's language, themes, structure, sound texture, and the influence of symbolism and romanticism. Classifies the works as love lyrics (deemed the best in Pasternak's poetry), nature poetry, the Caucasus (a new interpretation of the traditional theme), and poetry with social motifs. Sees "social egoism" and "infantilism" as char-

acteristic of Pasternak. Concludes that Pasternak's poetry exerted a great influence on many poets, even on those considered "proleterian," for Pasternak "possesses a remarkable gift of a poetic language and poetic expressiveness." Reprinted: 1934.3.

1934

1   SELIVANOVSKII, A. "Pasternak, Boris Leonidovich" (in Russian). *Literaturnaia entsiklopediia* 8: 465–71.

A composite commentary on Pasternak—his attitude toward the "proletarian Revolution," his work, and his poetics. Argues that Pasternak's poetry "avoids active interference in social practice," that the "acceptance of socialism is for him a sacrifice," and that Pasternak "sympathizes with socialism but still does not understand its real essence." Elaborates on Pasternak's musical compositional structure, rhythm, and metaphors. Concludes that a "variety of meters, an efficient combination of various themes and variations in a single small work, and a rich verse instrumentation—all this makes Pasternak's poetic technology musical and expressive." Cites examples of similes dubbed "domesticated metaphors."

2   TARASENKOV, AN. "Polden' liriki" [Midday of lyrics]. *LG* (20 May): 2.

Argues that a "great human love for woman" is one of the "leading motifs" in *Second Birth* and that this "love" is Pasternak's "individual, concrete catch on the revolutionary contemporaneity."

3   ZELINSKII, K. Review of Pasternak's *Second Birth* (in Russian). In *Kriticheskie pis'ma*. Vol. 2. Moscow: Sovetskaia literatura, pp. 240–57.

Reprint of 1933.5.

1935

1   JAKOBSON, ROMAN. "Kontury Glejtu" [The contours of *A Safe Conduct*]. In *Boris Pasternak. Gleijt*, translated by S. Pírková. Prague: Knihy Mánesa, pp. 149–62.

Discusses the general difference between verse and prose, the nature of poetry (its thematic structure, lyric and epic poetry, and the lyric hero, among others), and some features of modern literary movements and their representatives. Compares Pasternak to Bryusov, Bely, Khlebnikov, and Mayakovsky ("both are lyric poets of the same generation, and Mayakovsky, more than any other poet, deeply affected Pasternak in his youth"). Argues that Pasternak is a lyric poet, that he bases his poetics on a personal experience of reality, that his poetry continues the romantic tradtion of symbolism, and that Pasternak's "lyrical theme" is ruled not by metaphorical but by metonymical relations ("Nikoliv metaforické, n'ybrž *metonymické* vztahy vedou lyricke tema Pasternakovo"). Discusses Pasternak's early prose (sees the hero of *A Safe Conduct* as a "chronic bungler," and *Aerial Ways* as Pasternak's most dramatic story). Strongly repudiates Pasternak's association with literary movements, though "Pasternak's poetry provides clear evidence of his affinity with his generation." Recognizes that Pasternak's "debt to his age comes very strongly in his poetry." Links Pasternak to cubist painters in their decomposition and interpretation of objects. Reprinted: 1971.7. Translated: 1976.16.

2 ————. "Randbemerkungen zur Proza des Dichters Pasternak." *SlR* 7: 357–74.
    Modified version of 1935.1. Translated: 1969.12; 1987.9.

3 TARASENKOV, A. "Pasternak v krivom zerkale" [Pasternak in a distorting mirror]. *Znamia*, no. 10, pp. 228–35.
    Challenges the critic from *Literaturnaia gazeta*, Iaropolk Semenov, over his evaluation of Pasternak's work. Semenov accuses Pasternak of "subjective idealism," while Tarasenkov maintains that one must not "crudely or vulgarly identify philosophy with the creative methods of the artist." Both agree that much in Pasternak's poetry must be "critically overcome."

4 ————. Review of "Gruzinskie liriki" (in Russian). *Znamia*, no. 9, pp. 201–9.
    Remarks that Pasternak, with no knowledge of the Georgian language and using interlinear texts, made it possible for the reader to catch the feel of Georgian poetry. Contends that this is the first first-class work of poetic translation "in all the existence of Soviet poetry."

1936

1 BRÜGEL, FRITZ. "Rozmluva s Borisom Pasternakem" [Conversation with Boris Pasternak]. *LUK* 4, no. 1: 10–12.
    Records Pasternak's views of Jozsef Hóra's translations ("Boris Pasternak." In *Liryka*. Prague: Melantrich, 1935), his comments on Czech and other Slavic languages, views of Rilke and the meaning of Rilke to him, recollections of Larisa Reisner, views of Georgian poetry Pasternak was translating at that time, and his perception of lyricists ("lyric poets are a special bunch, almost a sect, they seize each others' meaning at once"). Translation included in 1979.29.

2 GUTNER, M. "Proza poeta (B. Pasternak)" [The prose of a poet (B. Pasternak)]. *LS*, no. 1, pp. 118–31.
    Claims that Pasternak is "always utterly serious," that Pasternak the prose writer stems from Pasternak the poet, and that plot is not cru-

cial to Pasternak. Discusses *The Childhood of Luvers, The Tale, Aerial Ways, Letters from Tula,* and *A Safe Conduct,* and concludes that Sergei (from *The Tale*) is "Heine's double" (from *The Line of Apelles*), that Zhenya Luvers's instinct is her "only teacher," and that a metaphor in *A Safe Conduct* "shortens the distance between the nature phenomena fixed by his metaphor and the reader's perception." Compares Pasternak's early prose to that of young Tolstoy, Proust (their similarity is deemed "outward"), Tyutchev, and Rilke—*Aus den Aufzeichnungen des Malte Laurids Brigge.*

3 SELIVANOVSKII, A. "B. Pasternak" (in Russian). In *Ocherki po istorii sovetskoi poezii.* Moscow: GIKhL, pp. 185–99.
    Reprint of 1926.3, with an addition that the *Second Birth* collection may be "a final, culminating link with the past, a summation of previous development."

1937

1 ALEKSANDROV, V. "Chastnaia zhizn'" [Private life]. *LK,* no. 3, pp. 55–81.
    Takes issue with Shklovsky concerning his terms "distortion, encumbrance, tongue-tie," and repudiates the charges of "encumbrance" in Pasternak. Compares Pasternak's poetry (sound instrumentation, in particular) to Balmont's. Discusses *The Childhood of Luvers* and *A Safe Conduct,* and mentions the meaning of detail to Pasternak and his indifference to politics. Analyzes "The Kremlin During the Snowstorm of the End of 1918," *Lieutenant Schmidt, The Year 1905,* and the collections *High Malady* and *Second Birth.* Concludes that Pasternak's "departure from social themes has predetermined the origin of specific features in Pasternak's poetics." Argues that Pasternak's use of Gogol's epigraph "Suddenly It Became Visible Far into All Ends of the World" (which Pasternak uses in his poem "Collapse" in *My Sister, Life*) is meant "to be applied" to the Revolution. Reprinted: 1956.1.

1940

1 ALEKSEEV, M. "'Gamlet' Borisa Pasternaka" [Boris Pasternak's *Hamlet*]. *IZh,* no. 8, pp. 14–16.
    A textual analysis of the second version of Pasternak's translation of *Hamlet* that mentions Pasternak's endeavors to produce a stage translation as opposed to a "serious academic rendition." Credits Pasternak for many accurate renditions of difficult passages (translated "with great mastery, ingenuity, and technical dexterity"), but blames him for "distortions, unnecessary and unjustified modernization, heavy, utterly incom-

prehensible lexical constructions," and "marked vulgarization." Cites numerous examples to support his views, and insists that the translation should not be used on the stage.

2   REZTSOV, L. "Prints Datskii v novom osveshchenii" [The prince of Denmark in a new light]. *LO*, no. 20, pp. 52–55.

Discusses the "defects in translation" of Pasternak's *Hamlet*, and concludes that the translation's style contradicts the original. Argues that it is less a matter of poverty of language on the part of the translator than an "excess of possibilities due to an insufficiently disciplined selection of words," evidenced by the translator's lapses and errors.

3   VIL'IAM-VIL'MONT, N.N. "'Gamlet' v perevode Borisa Pasternaka" [*Hamlet* in Boris Pasternak's translation]. *IL*, nos. 7–8, pp. 288–91.

An analysis of Pasternak's *Hamlet* translation that accompanies comments on other *Hamlet* renditions by Sumarokov, Kroneberg, Popovich, and Lozinsky. Lauds Pasternak for his unique conveyance of Shakespeare's tragedy, particularly for his language ("popular and everyday . . . a healthy, lusty language touched by a sudden frost of the historic tragedy"). Cites passages to illustrate his views, notably the scenes from the third act, in which Pasternak is deemed to have successfully recreated "the rhymed scene." Adds that in rendering Shakespeare's metaphors, Pasternak was guided by his poetics, "in which visual images lose the self-sufficing, sensual thingness owing to the mobility and inner metaphorical quality of his poetic language."

1941

1   MOROZOV, M. Review of Pasternak's translation of *Hamlet* (in Russian). *Teatr*, no. 2, pp. 144–47.

Sees Pasternak's translation as free from mechanical copying and literalisms. Comparison with the translations of Lozinsky and Radlova leads to the conclusion that Pasternak correctly pointed out the nature of his work: "I turned from the translation of words and metaphor to the translation of thoughts and scenes." Concludes that the result was not a literal translation but an artistic one. Notes the translation's shortcomings: "a collection of fuzzy spots" and affectations.

1943

1   ANTOKOL'SKII, P. "Boris Pasternak" (in Russian). *Znamia*, nos. 9–10, pp. 312–16.

Examines closely Pasternak's *On Early Trains* and makes observations on Pasternak's views of art in general. Calls Pasternak a "striking" and "serious" poet, an artist of remarkable resources, yet a poet who has been prone to immediately abandon "what he has just started to do." Reprinted: 1945.1.

2   KAUN, ALEXANDER. "Pasternak." In *Soviet Poets and Poetry*. Berkeley: University of California Press, pp. 60–63. Reprint. Freeport, NY: Books for Libraries, 1968.

Characterizes Pasternak as a lyricist who combines the involved syntax and estrangement of the futurists with his own directness, confidence, and unique view of life.

3   SIMONOV, K. "Pravil'nyi put'" [The correct way]. *Ogonek*, nos. 34–35, pp. 12–13.

Discusses Pasternak's *On Early Trains*. Praises Pasternak's "simplified" style as a sign of his internal growth and not artistic decline. Also discusses Pasternak's views of art and stresses his integrity and freedom of choice. Reprinted: 1971.16.

1944

1   COHEN, J.M. "The Poetry of Boris Pasternak." *Horizon* 10, no. 55 (July): 23–36.

Mentions major events in Pasternak's life, examines his early poetry, and draws parallels to other poets. An early Pasternak poem (1912), "The Sleepy Garden Scatters Beetles," reveals "already several characteristics of his mature style." Views *My Sister, Life* as containing "lyrics of appalling saccharinity, though of perfect craftsmanship," and "several poems of real beauty." Detects new themes in *Themes and Variations*, and deems it "smoother in texture." Insists that Pasternak's "affinities are with the brood of Laforgue," T.S. Eliot, and Auden, but concludes that "Pasternak's strength lies in his absolute independence."

2   MOROZOV, M. "Shekspir v perevode Borisa Pasternaka" [Shakespeare in Boris Pasternak's translations]. *Teatr. Sbornik statei i materialov*. Moscow: VTO, pp. 51–61.

Notes Pasternak's "enormous merit in his translations of Shakespeare's three plays—*Hamlet, Romeo and Juliet*, and *Anthony and Cleopatra*." Sees that merit in the fact that Pasternak has translated these tragedies primarily for the theater, and has finally eliminated literalism—striving instead toward inner and outward similarity. Notes Pasternak's tendency to simplify Shakespeare's language and claims that Pasternak has profoundly and truthfully resolved the problem of translating Shakespeare. Emphasizes Pasternak's skill of economizing language, a mastery perhaps most appreciated in theater. Singles out

Pasternak's translation of *Anthony and Cleopatra* as his most mature and perfect Shakespeare translation. Claims that in his translation of *Romeo and Juliet*, Pasternak conveyed a "natural and direct freshness of feelings." Concludes that Pasternak's three Shakespeare translations now belong to well-respected Russian literature. Reprinted: 1967.10.

1945

1 ANTOKOL'SKII, P. "Boris Pasternak" (in Russian). In *Ispytanie vremenem. Stat'i*. Moscow: Sovetskii pisatel', pp. 99–107.
    Reprint of 1943.1.

2 GROMOV, PAVEL. Review of Pasternak's *Earth's Expanse* (in Russian). *Zvezda*, nos. 5–6, pp.
    Compares this collection to Pasternak's early poetry: "In the past, a single poem by Pasternak was a flow of associations and of an extended, whimsical metaphor". Sees *Earth's Expanse* as "wiser and simpler."

3 SCHIMANSKII, STEFAN. Introduction to Pasternak's *Collected Prose Works*, edited by Stefan Schimanskii. London: Lindsay Drummond, pp. 11–44.
    Outlines Pasternak's biography, poetry, prose, and translations, centering on Pasternak's early prose (until 1945). Makes general observations on Pasternak as a writer and on his views of art. Believes that Pasternak's greatness lies in "the revolutionary correlation that governs his interpretation of time, space, and form." Summarizes Pasternak's views of art as "his ability to recreate emotional states by means of utterly trivial correlatives and the unusual choice of images." Discusses Pasternak's affinity to Mayakovsky, Bely, and Esenin, among others, and labels him a "direct decendant of Pushkin." Notes Pasternak's protest against the misuse of art. Focuses on *Letters from Tula, The Childhood of Luvers, The Line of Apelles*, and *Aerial Ways*, noting that "in every one of the four stories, therefore, something is lost: a notebook in the story from Italy; a life's purpose in the old actor's existence in the *Letters*; a child in *Aerial Ways*; and the innocence of childhood in the last story."

4 TARASENKOV, AN. Review of Pasternak's *Earth's Expanse* (in Russian). *Znamia*, no. 4, pp. 136–39.
    Compares the landscape descriptions to Levitan's and Serov's canvases. Draws parallels between this collection and Pasternak's "dry" and "chaotic" World War II poems. Praises the collection for its poetry of nature, art, and love.

1947

1 SURKOV, A.A. "O poezii B. Pasternaka" [On B. Pasternak's poetry]. *KZh*, no. 8 (21 March): 2.

Vehemently attacks Pasternak's poetry and his "scanty spiritual resources" deemed incapable of "giving birth to a great poetry." Cites examples of Pasternak's poetry (from *My Sister, Life* in particular), attempting to display Pasternak's isolation from "social human emotions."

1948

1 MASLIN, N. "Maiakovskii i nasha sovremennost'" [Mayakovsky and our modern times]. *Oktiabr'* 25, no. 4: 148–60.

Criticizes Pasternak's poetry for his supposed subjugation of content to form, and argues that Pasternak has turned the art into a catalogue of "subjective feelings." Also argues that Pasternak inflicted "severe damage on Soviet poetry."

1949

1 BOWRA, SIR MAURICE. "Boris Pasternak." In *The Creative Experiment.* London: Macmillan, pp. 128–58.

Discusses Pasternak's use of poetic elements from the symbolist, futurist, and acmeist movements while correcting their excesses, therefore creating a modern poetic vision and serving a twofold truth of fact and experience. Pasternak puts imagism at the service of a complex and unified vision, using paradoxical or unexpected images that convey an essential truth. The individuality and exactness of his technique is discussed as it applies to three basic themes: nature, love, and political events. Asserts that a sense of communion with unseen powers, of which nature, war, and history are various interpenetrating and interacting manifestations, gives Pasternak's verse its primeval directions and overall unity. Discusses and quotes at length "Spring," "Sparrow Hills," "In the Forest," "Spasskoye," "Do Not Touch," "Summer," "January 1918," "May it Be," and "Definition of Poetry."

1950

1 BERLIN, ISAIAH. Review of Pasternak's *Selected Writings*. *PaR*, no. 7 (September–October): 748–51.

Examines Pasternak's poetic approach. Emphasizes his sense of energy and the persuasiveness of cosmic categories that integrate the orders of creation. Likens Pasternak's prose to Bely's, and often sees it as obscure and artificial, which makes it resistant to translation. Discusses the quality of translations in this collection. Reprinted: 1978.4.

1951

1   ANSTEI, OL'GA. "Mysli o Pasternake" [Thoughts on Pasternak]. *LiS*, no. 2, pp. 89–96.
    Analyzes Pasternak's love poetry, and emphasizes musicality and innovations in his lyrics. Marvels at Pasternak's prosaisms (seen to "expand the arsenal of images which crowd his poetry") and his original similes of nature—all of which are signs of a great poet with a heritage of a "fatal stamp of Providence." Corroborates her views with passages from Pasternak's poetry.

2   STRUVE, GLEB. "Pasternak." In *Soviet Russian Literature 1917–1950*. Norman: University of Oklahoma Press, pp. 173–77.
    A general overview of Pasternak's career. Notes that as a romantic and an individualist, "Pasternak was never quite at home in Soviet literature," as he was "constitutionally incapable of prostituting his muse." Observes the "strangeness" in Pasternak's poetry, the clear influence of music on his work, and the strong connection with the romantic tradition in Russian poetry. Briefly examines *Spektorsky* ("as an attempt to outgrow lyricism and create a modern epic, the poem is a failure"), *The Year 1905*, *Lieutenant Schmidt*, and *Second Birth*. Characterizes Pasternak's prose as having the "same freshness of vision and felicity of expression" as his poetry. Comments on *Aerial Ways*, *A Tale* ("Rilke's influence is very strongly felt"), *The Childhood of Luvers*, and *A Safe Conduct* ("in which Pasternak's individualism is given free play"). Revised and reprinted: 1971.18.

3   WRENN, C.L. "Boris Pasternak." *OSP* 2: 82–97.
    Discusses Pasternak's early poetry, his translations, *Second Birth*, *Spektorsky*, and *A Safe Conduct*. Examines the originality and intensity of both his prose and poetry, and mentions Pasternak's inability to adapt to Soviet literary demands.

1952

1   GRONICKA, ANDRÉ von. "Rilke and the Pasternaks. A Biographical Note." *GR* 27, no. 4: 260–71.
    Traces Pasternak's links to Rilke, as revealed in Pasternak's father's (Leonid Pasternak) memoirs and correspondence with Rilke, Rilke's correspondence, and Pasternak's *A Safe Conduct*. Centers on

Pasternak's description (from *A Safe Conduct*) of his and his father's meeting with Rilke and contrasts that description against Rilke's letter to Sofia Schill and Leonid Pasternak's memoirs. Records "baffling" discrepancies between Pasternak's description ("Boris Pasternak's account opens with an outright contradiction of his father's version") and Rilke's ("Rilke's record must be considered if not definitive, then certainly far more reliable than Pasternak's"). Concludes that "Rilke's work came to have the greatest influence on Pasternak, broadened the young Russian's spiritual horizons," and "'opened doors for him.'" Points out that "as late as 1944 Pasternak still refers to Rilke with the greatest of admiration."

1953

1 TSVETAEVA, MARINA. "Svetovoi liven'" [Luminous downpour]. In *Proza*. New York: Izdatel'stvo imeni Chekhova, pp. 353–71.
Reprint of 1922.7.

1956

1 ALEKSANDROV, V. "Chastnaia zhizn' (O poezii B. Pasternaka)" [Private life (On Boris Pasternak's poetry)]. In *Liudi i knigi. Sbornik statei*. Moscow: Sovetskii pisatel', pp. 171–207.
Reprint of 1937.1.

1957

1 AUCOUTURIER, MICHEL. "Boris Pasternak" (in French). *Esprit* 25 (March): 465–77.
A general commentary on Pasternak the poet. Discusses Pasternak's style, language, and the role of his metaphors in particular. Draws parallels between Pasternak and Proust. Admires Pasternak's ability to preserve his individuality in spite of the Communist system he lived through. Supplies his own renditions of Pasternak's poems.

2 BRÜCK, MAX von. "Schnee, Blut und Tränen. Pasternaks Dr. Zivago." *Gegenwart* 12, no. 25: 791–92.
Gives a detailed content of the novel; compares *Doctor Zhivago* to *War and Peace*, Zhivago to Pierre, and Lara to Natasha. Believes that *Doctor Zhivago* describes "the passion of the twentieth century which came out of Russia." Sees the novel as the voice of a new, "timeless" Russia. Points out many conversations in the novel that make it a form of a "Bildungsroman."

3 CHIAROMONTE, NICOLA. "La parola di Pasternak." *TP* 2, no. 12: 905–9.

Sees the appearance of *Doctor Zhivago* as a "historical event," a resurgence and reaffirmation of the Russian "sense of truth, love of life, feeling of hope, and . . . faith in literary communication" suppressed by the turmoil, force, and violence of the postrevolutionary period. Argues that with *Doctor Zhivago*, Pasternak moves out of the "fragmentary" and "personal" realm, and into the sphere of history, not by chronicling events but by mediating in a spiritual solitude from which events and characters unfold like "muffled, tranquil memories." Discusses Zhivago's evaluation of the Revolution, his "mysticism of nature" and "mysticism of artistic creation," and his interpretation of Christ's message of "absolute faith in man's innerness and freedom." Also argues that the philosophical "solutions" Pasternak proposes are less important than the fact that he raises anew the "accursed questions" of Russian literature and philosophy "when it seemed that history itself had suppressed them forever." Translated: 1958.9.

4 MUCHNIC, HELEN. "Toward an Analysis of Boris Pasternak." *SEEJ* 15 (Summer): 101–5.

Defines Pasternak's poetry with philosophical statements from *A Safe Conduct* and calls it the "allegorical speech of direct feeling." Sees three parts as representative of the poet's developing relationship with poetry, culminating in the portrait of a poet, represented in *A Safe Conduct* by Mayakovsky. Also sees this theme of concentrating upon others in an autobiographical work as a symbolic interpretation.

5 SHIRIAEV, B.N. "Boris Pasternak: Il dottor Zivago." *VII* 7, no. 4: 118–23.

Recounts the history of the novel's appearance, noting that before its publication "practically no one had known Pasternak the prose writer." Mentions that the novel's composition is complex, with several main plots that "now converge, now diverge, yet at the end are connected through a common end." Also notes that there is nothing superfluous in the novel—"everything flows into a common harmony expressing the author's views," and that the novel has "pathetic tones," a fact regarded as an "enormous force which stimulates our dramatic perception of the novel." Concludes that *Doctor Zhivago* is an "epoch-making novel."

1958

1 ABEL, LIONEL. "On Doctor Zhivago: An Open Letter to Nicola Chiaromonte." *Dissent* 5: 334–41.

A rebuttal of another critic, Nicola Chiaromonte (1957.3). Expresses enthusiasm about *Doctor Zhivago*, but explains a number of misgivings that keep him from "admiring" it in the spirit of the other criticism. These misgivings include a falsely objective and "pure" style, the unconvincing depiction of Strelnikov and Lara, and the "monstrous" behavior of Zhivago in firing at the tree stump and abandoning his wife for Lara. Concludes that Pasternak's novel implies a great theme, but fails to realize it.

2 ADAMOVICH, GEORGII. "Nevozmozhnost' poezii" [Poetry's impossibility]. *Opyty*, no. 9, pp. 35–51.
    Notes that Pasternak, together with Khlebnikov, is a poet of the "innovative" type, whose use of words departs from the rational—he does whatever he wishes with them. Believes that all of his verses are well—and strongly—constructed, though one may read them and wonder to what purpose they were written. Argues that Pasternak is more of a poet than Tsvetaeva, though he lacks Tsvetaeva's "charm."

3 ANATOL'EVA, N. "Pasternak i mirovaia obshchestvennost'" [Pasternak and the world public]. *Grani* 13, no. 40: 54–77.
    A detailed survey of the reception of Pasternak in Western countries as recorded in American, African, Asian, and European newspapers. Recounts Pasternak's family background and highlights Pasternak's literary career. Discusses foreign correspondents' interviews and encounters with Pasternak in Peredelkino (a writers' colony near Moscow where Pasternak had a country house) and narrates their impressions. Traces and discusses writers' and newspapers' reactions to the Nobel Prize awarded to Pasternak and his subsequent victimization by the Soviet authorities. Occasionally comments on criticism.

4 ——. [Popliuiko-Anatol'eva]. "Tsel' tvorchestva—samootdacha. Etiud o Pasternake, poete i cheloveke" [The goal of creativity is self-giving. An étude on Pasternak the poet and the man]. *Grani*, no. 37, pp. 128–59.
    Believes three of Pasternak's works are crucial to an understanding of his creative path: *A Safe Conduct*, the poem "To Be Famous" and *Doctor Zhivago*. Notes that in *A Safe Conduct* Pasternak writes of how he came to poetry from music, which he loved "more than anything in the world." For him, the hush of nature is filled with sounds "audible only to him," and it is through music that he senses feelings of love and seeks out the way to truth. Asserts that Mayakovsky holds a special place in Pasternak's life. Claims that in Pasternak's account of Mayakovsky's last years of life and of their last meeting there is much in common with the death of Yury Zhivago.

5 BARSOV, VASILII. "O Pasternake. Moskovskie vpechatleniia" [About Pasternak. The Moscow impressions]. *Grani* 13, no. 40: 102–16.
    Recounts Pasternak's poetry reading, a public debate, and Pasternak's physical appearance. Recalls Pasternak's recital at the

Polytechnic Museum in Moscow and captures the audience's reaction to his reading manner ("he read languidly, slowly, with a toneless, faint voice"). Relates Pasternak's appearance as remembered from his portrait sittings with him at Pasternak's Moscow apartment at Volkhonka in the late 1920s. Describes Pasternak's face as "valiant, resolute, and carved," his face color as "slightly southern," and his eyes like those of a Vrubelian portrait. Attempts to convey Bryusov's defense of Pasternak's poetry deemed to have taken place at one of the public poetry disputes.

6   BEER, KARL WILLY. "Der *Doktor Schiwago* unter uns. Warum Boris Pasternaks Buch revolutionär und doch—naiv ist." *PM* 3, no. 31: 91–93.
     Insists that *Doctor Zhivago* gives a response to contradictory questions in recent Russian history and politics, even though Pasternak is "unpolitical." Singles out the "power of the language" in *Doctor Zhivago* as one of the strongest features of the novel, although the novel's language does not reflect the "new literary means of style." Sees the novel's narrative form as belonging to traditional Russian classical literature.

7   BERLOGIN, MIKHAIL. "Son o zhizni (Boris Pasternak)" [Dream of life (Boris Pasternak)]. *Grani* 13, no. 40: 98–101.
     Argues that *Doctor Zhivago* is "not so much a depiction of life itself as a dream about it, which makes the book more like a collection of verse." Insists that Pasternak did not work out the novel's plan, but only entrusted himself to life, allowing his soul to flow out into his work, and that *Doctor Zhivago* is one "of the most religious works of our era."

8   CHAMBERLAIN, JOHN. "A Judgement on Revolution." *NR* 6 (7 September): 215–16.
     Characterizes *Doctor Zhivago* as primarily a political testament, "500 pages of inspired criticism" of the fanaticism and cruelty that the Revolution brought to Russia. Calls *Doctor Zhivago* the second major work, following Igor Gouzenko's novel *The Fall of a Titan*, to come out of Russia in "decades."

9   CHIAROMONTE, NICOLA. "Pasternak's Message." *PaR* 25: 127–34.
     Translation of 1957.3. Reprinted: 1969.3

10   ———. "La replica di Chiaromonte." *TP* 3, no. 12: 972–80.
     Responds to Lionel Abel (1958.1), and expresses his misgivings with Abel's views of *Doctor Zhivago*. Argues that *Doctor Zhivago* is "one of the most beautiful novels written since Proust's," and that the characters (Zhivago, Lara, and Antipov) are true characters and "exist." Faults Abel's criticisms for their misunderstanding of Pasternak's intentions and too strict an adherence to "artistic purism," which values conventional representation of events. Translated: 1959.8.

11 DELGADO, F. "Boris Pasternak, premio nobel." *RF* 158 (December): 477–82.

A general discussion of *Doctor Zhivago* that centers on the Nobel Prize and the controversy following the publication of the novel. Strongly opposes the criticism that interprets the novel as anticommunist. Briefly discusses Pasternak's literary career, mentioning literary groups to which Pasternak is deemed to have belonged.

12 "'Delo' Pasternaka" [The Pasternak affair]. *Grani* 13, no. 40: 3–120.

Includes three segments: an introduction, a decree of the U.S.S.R. Union of Writers about the publication of *Doctor Zhivago*, and "Free Discussion." The introduction surveys the main events surrounding the publication of the novel, lauds Pasternak for "displaying a great fortitude," and blames the authorities for their adverse treatment of Pasternak. The second segment recaptures the Soviet writers' "unanimous conviction" of Pasternak, a reprint of *Literaturnaia gazeta's* report of 28 October 1958. The third section provides random samplings of Soviet citizens' reactions to Pasternak and the publication of *Doctor Zhivago*.

13 *"Delo Pasternaka"* [The Pasternak affair]. Munich: TsOPE, 112 pp.

Divided into five main segments: an outline of Pasternak's literary career, a chronicle of events surrounding the Nobel Prize awarded to Pasternak (detailed day to day from 23 October through 5 November 1958), a list of authors' and institutions' comments on the events as reflected in the press (including France, U.S.A., Sweden, Chile, Canada, Great Britain, Brazil, Italy, Japan, Norway, India, Pakistan, and Morocco), reactions of Russian émigré writers (including Zaitsev, Slonim, and Andreyev), and the *Doctor Zhivago* poems. Also includes Pasternak's two letters to Khrushchev (31 October 1958) and *Pravda* (published 6 November 1958).

14 DEUTSCH, BABETTE. "'Talent for Life' in a New Russian Novel." *HM* 217, no. 1300: 72–76.

Praises the broad scope and rich complexity of *Doctor Zhivago* in the course of an outline of Pasternak's career and the story of his novel. Predicts that the novel "will eventually be recognized everywhere as a classic" and discusses aspects of Pasternak's realism and symbolism, stating that the novel is "barbed with ideas" and full of latent meanings. Examines the themes of moral and physical death, "the impossibility of improving life by purely mechanical means," and Pasternak's use of coincidence, which is termed a daring enhancement of the novel's verisimilitude. Claims the "novel offers a broad and serene vision that lifts 'the particular to the level of the universal and familiar.'"

15 ERLICH, VICTOR. "A Testimony and a Challenge: Pasternak's *Doctor Zhivago.*" *PC* 7, no. 6: 46–49.

Outlines the "Pasternak Affair," compares *Doctor Zhivago* to *War and Peace*, and gives an account of Zhivago's evolving attitude toward the Revolution and a summary of his view of history, which is characterized as a mixture of poetic awe and Christian personalism. Credits the novel with "moral depth" and "enduring beauty," a tragic yet "life-affirming" testament to the author's "creative integrity." Reprinted slightly abridged: 1978.13.

16 FERNANDEZ, DOMINIQUE. "Sur Boris Pasternak." *NRF* 12: 487–93.

Argues that *Doctor Zhivago* is not an anti-Communist, anti-Soviet novel, but a meditation on life and death, and that it reflects a philosophy of life that cannot be reconciled with Marxist philosophy ("the active relationship between man and history"). Also discusses the novel's style, the main hero, and the function of history and nature in the novel.

17 FRANK, VICTOR S. "The Meddlesome Poet. Boris Pasternak's Rise to Greatness." *DR* 232 (Spring): 49–58.

Recalls the "discovery" of Pasternak in 1922 with the publication of *My Sister, Life*, and notes the originality and "magic" quality of Pasternak's verse. Provides a sketch of Pasternak's background that concentrates on his Russian-Jewish heritage and its possible influence on the freshness of his art. Follows Pasternak from his position as "master of poetry in Russia" through a personal religious crisis, which precipitates a change in his art from the personal to the epic preceding the composition of *Doctor Zhivago*.

18 ———. "A Russian Hamlet. Boris Pasternak's Novel." *DR* 232: 212–20.

Notes the "old-fashioned" quality of *Doctor Zhivago* and Pasternak's indifference to the strictures of socialist realism as well as his isolation from twentieth-century Western literary trends. A summary of the plot concludes by noting the "serene confidence" with which the novel ends, the explanation for which lies in the "humble submission and sacrifice" of the concluding poems. Translated: 1974.6.

19 ———. "Stikhi Borisa Pasternaka iz romana *Doktor Zhivago*" [Verses from Pasternak's novel *Doctor Zhivago*]. *Opyty*, no. 9, pp. 17–22.

Maintains that three to four poems in the novel have direct connections to the plot, while the rest reflect "the spiritual life of the protagonist." Argues that "The Dawn" is directed to Christ, and that Pasternak drastically changed his poetic views while making "genuine spiritual discoveries." The "road to happiness" lies in self-sacrifice, as manifested in "The Dawn," "Wedding," and "Hamlet." Argues that Pasternak understood that "a deed always presupposes and entails sufferings," and that parallel with the enrichment of Pasternak's "spiritual content" is the process of structure simplification—"an act of conscious self-sacrifice."

20   GAEV, A. "B.L. Pasternak i ego roman *Doktor Zhivago*" [B.L. Pasternak and his novel, *Doctor Zhivago*]. *VII* 3, no. 28: 100–121.
      Outlines Pasternak's biography and his literary career. Claims that the essence of *Doctor Zhivago* lies in a love conveyed in three forms: (1) love in an ordinary sense; (2) love for creativity; and (3) "love as worldview, as sense of life, as a basis of man's inner content." Notes that Pasternak's device of counterpoint, an interlacement of parallel themes in *Doctor Zhivago*, was borrowed from music. Also discusses Pasternak's use of landscape, the importance of secondary characters (deemed to play the role of symbols), the history of the novel's publication, the author's destiny, and criticism of the novel. Translated: 1959.22. Reprinted: 1962.11.

21   GIUDICI, GIOVANNI. "Zivago in Italia." *NoS* 2: 83–108.
      A detailed survey of Italian criticism of *Doctor Zhivago*. Registers various and contradicting views of the novel, claiming that this diversity stems from critics' political affiliations (Communists vs. Catholics, for example). Sees the diversity of interpretations as proof that *Doctor Zhivago* is "indeed a new literary genre" and "a masterpiece."

22   GUL', ROMAN. "Pobeda Pasternaka" [Pasternak's victory]. *NZh*, no. 55, pp. 111–29.
      Gives general observations of *Doctor Zhivago*. Underlines the novel's "Russianness," the abundance of details, the absence of lyrical plot development and plot motivations, the concocted collisions and coincidences, the absence of promulgations of philosophical systems and concepts, and the absence of "messages," among others. Believes that Lara is modeled on Tsvetaeva, whose thoughts and intonations are seen to be echoed in Lara's conversations with Zhivago—who, "like Pasternak, vehemently disclaimed the daily round and the so-called life's reality." Observes Pasternak's antithesis to Dostoevsky and Tolstoy, and concludes that *Doctor Zhivago* is an "amazing novel-confession, a novel-parable." Reprinted: 1973.6.

23   HAMPSHIRE, STUART. "*Doctor Zhivago*. As from a Lost Culture." *Encounter* 11, no. 5: 3–5.
      Asserts *Doctor Zhivago*'s dissimilarity to the fragmented, uncertain art of the twentieth century and its roots in the literary ambitions and philosophical culture of the nineteenth century. Discusses deep Russian patriotism, its affinity with Shakespeare as opposed to Tolstoy, and *Doctor Zhivago*'s concern with philosophical and religious rather than political issues. Concludes that the novel contains "one of the most profound descriptions of love in the whole range of modern literature." Reprinted: 1969.8; 1978.17.

24 HARARI, MANYA. "Pasternak." *TC* 164, no. 982: 524–28.

A response to the persecution of Pasternak following the publication of *Doctor Zhivago*. Lara is seen as Russia, Antipov as the
Revolution, and Komarovsky as "the ugly side of the old Regime" and as
"the old cynic." Antipov's desertion of Lara for politics is seen as the reason for his destruction and for Lara being "handed over" to Komarovsky.

25 HAYWARD, MAX. "*Doctor Zhivago* and the Soviet Intelligentsia." *SS*,
no. 24, pp. 65–69.

Classifies the frustrated Soviet intellectual as more an "outcast,"
bereft of his/her status as purveyor of ideas, than the "superfluous man"
or dispossessed gentry of the previous century. Views Zhivago's status as
social outcast as the determining factor in his spiritual and intellectual
makeup. Zhivago's objections to the pretensions of "science," appeals to
class conflict, and pragmatic ethos of Marxism are juxtaposed with his
own brand of individualism in the framework of Christianity. Sees isolation from friends and society as the mounting price exacted by the Soviet
regime, through NEP (New Economic Policy) and after, exemplified by
Zhivago's break with Gordon and Dudorov.

26 ———. "Pasternak's *Dr. Zhivago*." *Encounter* 10, no. 5: 38–48.

Gives a brief history of the suppression of *Doctor Zhivago* in the
Soviet Union, including an account of Pasternak's rivalry with Alexei
Surkov, secretary of the Union of Writers. Finds that the source of the
novel's troublesomeness for the Soviet authorities lies not in any "outright subversiveness," but in the novel's "rehabilitation of the 'obyvatel'
[philistine] attitude," which is traced from Pushkin through Gogol's
"Overcoat" to the figure of Yuri Zhivago. Contrasts the "aloofness from
all things political and social" with the "activist" attitude of
Antipov/Strelnikov, a contrast central to the novel. Cites Pasternak's earlier poetical work as illustrating the poet's highly personal, subjective
vision to which government interference would be politically inimical.
Doctor Zhivago's addressees are seen as "fellow obyvatels," "small" people in whom the novel would "instill a sense of dignity and superiority
over the 'activists.'" Reprinted: 1959.25.

27 HERLING-GRUDZINSKI, GUSTAV. "Zwycięstwo Borysa
Pasternaka" [Boris Pasternak's victory]. *Kultura*, nos. 1/2, pp. 35–48.

Acknowledges difficulty in labeling Pasternak's poetry either as
that of acmeists or symbolists. Notes that winter landscape description is
Pasternak's second favorite theme. Attempts to repudiate A.M.
Ripellino's assertion that in *The Year 1905* and *Lieutenant Schmidt*
Pasternak resorted to a "technique of film montage" similar to that of
Eisenstein's, and argues that in both pieces Pasternak strives to create
"natural" poetry deemed identical to "natural history" or a revolution as
an "inevitable element." Applies this interpretation to *Doctor Zhivago*, in

which the Revolution "most clearly" plays the role of an "inevitable element." Discusses the novel's content, themes, characters, worldviews, and parallels to *War and Peace*, among others, and cites lengthy passages from Pasternak's poetry and prose.

28 HYART, CHARLES. "Doudintsev et Pasternak, deux insoumis parmi les écrivains soviétiques." *RGB* 94, no. 3: 58–74.

Draws parallels between Dudintsev's *Not By Bread Alone* and *Doctor Zhivago*, centering on the political impact both works created. Examines "Socialist realism" against the background of the realistic trend in literature, the literary counterreaction following Stalin's death, and the official Soviet reaction to the two novels. Predicts that *Doctor Zhivago* "will never see the light in the Soviet Union unless the official position becomes favorable to it."

29 ISWOLSKY, HELEN. "The Voice of Boris Pasternak." *Commonweal* 69 (14 November): 168–70.

Views *Doctor Zhivago* as a novel with a strong religious undercurrent, an attempt to work out a "philosophy of events and historic destinies." Describes Pasternak's formative influences and temperament as a youth and the stages of his reaction to the 1917 Revolution. Notes that the novel belongs to the "terrible years" forseen by Tolstoy, Dostoevsky, and Turgenev, close in spirit to the worldview of Blok. Claims Pasternak's message is one of regaining inner freedom through Christ.

30 IVASK, IURII. "Stikhi Zhivago (Pasternaka)" [(Pasternak's) Zhivago poems]. *Opyty* 9: 29–31.

Points out that the theme of several of *Doctor Zhivago*'s poems is religious, but "the treatment of religion in the poetry of Zhivago-Pasternak arouses doubts." Concludes that in *Doctor Zhivago* there is much pretension and lack of logic.

31 KERMODE, FRANK. "Pasternak." In *Puzzles and Epiphanies: Essays and Reviews 1958–1961*. London: Routledge & K. Paul, pp. 108–20. Reprint. New York: Chilmark Press, 1962.

Consists of essay reviews of *Doctor Zhivago* and two autobiographies. Discusses the novel's structure and design and sees it as a historical novel but differing from Tolstoy in its detail. Notes the use of "Un-Tolstoyan" coincidence devices to "forward the plot." Lara is seen as being life and Russia. Singles out Pasternak's statement of his "symbolist aesthetic" from *A Safe Conduct* and cites a passage dealing with the death of Mayakovsky. Compares two autobiographies. Sees the first autobiography, *A Safe Conduct*, as an "imaginative production of isolated events" and as a "conscious work of art." Views the second autobiography, *An Essay in Autobiography*, as indispensable and as an "account of events and causes."

32   KORIAKOV, MIKH. "Termometr Rossii" [The thermometer of Russia]. *NZh*, no. 55, pp. 130–41.

The first part, "At Pasternak's Place," describes Pasternak's life in Peredelkino: the poet's appearance at age sixty-eight and his daily life and surroundings. Points out that Pasternak himself regarded *Doctor Zhivago* as an artist's testimony of the present era, and that he can thus be regarded as "a thermometer of Russia." The second part, "Stalin and Pasternak," tries to answer the question of Pasternak's survival during the Stalinist repression. Recounts situations in which Pasternak boldly stated his views, and when he was called an "enemy" from the platform of the board of directors of the Union of Writers, yet remained free. Thinks Stalin protected Pasternak in return for the sincere sympathy Pasternak expressed upon the death of Stalin's wife, Nadezhda Alliluyeva, in 1932.

33   KOVALENKOV, ALEKSANDR. "Poeziia v kachestve 'pristiazhnoi' (B. Pasternak)" [Poetry in the role of outrunner (B. Pasternak)]. *MG*, no. 12, pp. 211–15.

Insists that the Nobel Prize was awarded to Pasternak for the "anti-Soviet" quality of his novel *Doctor Zhivago* and that his poetry has played the role of a "shaft-horse runner" ("He has ridden on that 'crooked nag' for a long time"). Cites passages from Pasternak's poetry labeling him with various "isms"—"pessimism," "subjective idealism," "formalism," and "literary symbolism," for example.

34   KULLMANN, MICHAEL. Review of *Doctor Zhivago*. *ULR*, no. 5, pp. 80–82.

Praises *Doctor Zhivago* as "more than a novel, a piece of revela-tion" and its author as a "prophet." Several aspects of the novel's mes-sage are discussed: man's "anarchic relation to God," the salience of truth and beauty in the complexity of values, and the debilitating effects of "symmetric duplicity." Expresses the relevance of *Doctor Zhivago*'s message to the immediate present, and argues it is like a biblical "revela-tion brought to date."

35   KURLOV, G. "O Pasternake. Iz gimnazicheskikh vospominanii" [On Pasternak. From gymnasium memoirs]. *RM*, no. 1288 (18 November).

Recalls Pasternak's high school and university years, observing that Pasternak was punctual and that he hardly ever participated in his peers' pranks—though he voluntarily shared the punishment his friends received. Also offers a detailed description of Pasternak's appearance and bearing.

36   LINDSAY, JACK. "*Dr. Zhivago*." *ASJ* 19, no. 4 (Winter): 20–23.

A sharply critical review of the novel that stresses the inconsistency of characterization, disorder, and misuse of coincidence, all due to Pasternak's "clumsiness as a novelist." Cites passages that highlight the inconsistencey of the characters of Pasha Antipov and Zhivago. Argues that Pasternak attaches many of his own grievances to Antipov even though Antipov in no way embodies them, and that Zhivago is incomprehensibly transformed from a strongly positive character to a "worthless human being," a character that "cannot incarnate or express any protest at all except a neurotic one." Adds that the "endless intrusion of coincidence" upsets the balance of the narrative. Concludes that in spite of its many faults, *Doctor Zhivago* has redeeming qualities that reflect Pasternak's talent as a poet.

37   LOOSE, GERHARD. "Pasternak's *Doctor Zhivago*." *CQ* 7: 259–70.
     Discusses "the Pasternak Affair" and outlines Pasternak's career and the plot of *Doctor Zhivago*. Sees Zhivago as representative not only of the modern artist sensing "the shrinking of the atmosphere of free expression," but also as a figure of "metaphysical inquiry." *Doctor Zhivago*'s "epic quality" is seen to arise from Pasternak's skillful use of locale, a diverse cast of characters, and a complex portrayal of ideological struggle. Characterizes Pasternak's style as "brief, lucid, mosaic."

38   MAGARSHACK, DAVID. Review of *Doctor Zhivago*. *Nation* 187 (13 September): 134–35.
     Views the novel as "social commentary" with an undercurrent of genuine feeling and poetic gift, a "fearless work of observation." Traces Zhivago's critique of the Revolution, using his statements from the novel.

39   MANNING, CLARENCE A. "Pasternak and Khvylovy." *UQ* 14: 348–56.
     Likens the life and work of Pasternak to Ukrainian nationalist and writer Mykola Khvylovy, who committed suicide in 1933 under Stalinist persecution. The message of *Doctor Zhivago* is seen to have been foreshadowed by Khvylovy's story *I* and unfinished novel *The Woodcock*, both of which feature heroes disillusioned with the Revolution who advocate individual freedom as well as independence for the Ukraine. Asserts that Khvylovy's work shares with *Doctor Zhivago* a concern for humane, ethical values in the face of impersonal despotism, as well as a desire to warn the world of the increasing Soviet threat.

40   MCLEARY, WILLIAM. "Pasternak's Best Selling 'Doctor Zhivago' Portrays Russian People in Lyrical Style." *ST* (9 November): F4.
     A chronicle of Pasternak's career as a lyric poet. Biographical and historical data are combined with critical evaluations of each stage in the poet's development. Pays attention to Pasternak's creative relationship with the Revolution. Contrasts the title heroes of *Lieutenant Schmidt* and *Spektorsky* and compares them with their creator. After an account of the circumstances surrounding the creation of *Second Birth* and its reinterpretation of the image of the poet, Pasternak's later career is out-

lined, concluding with a discussion of *Doctor Zhivago*. Mentions points of contrast between Pasternak's career and Mayakovsky's.

41 MIŁOSZ, CZESŁAW. "Komentarz do komentarzy o nagrodzie Nobla" [A commentary on Nobel Prize commentaries]. *Kultura*, no. 12, pp. 8–16.

Comments on Pasternak's popularity in Poland (where he is considered "the first Russian poet" among the Polish writers), the Pasternak myths in the West, and on the American and Russian "mass culture." Also comments on Pasternak's translations (found to be of "very doubtful quality") and *Doctor Zhivago*: "for Pasternak history does not depend on human will, it is determined." Adds that Pasternak should have been awarded the Nobel Prize earlier—notably for his poetry and translations.

42 MONAS, SIDNEY. Review of *Doctor Zhivago*. *HR* 11: 612–19.

Concentrates on Zhivago's function as "mediator between nature and history" and his "gentle but vigorous rebuke" to the Bolsheviks and their supporters among the intelligentsia. Treats Zhivago's non-Orthodox religiosity, the importance of the three women whose paths cross and recross his own (especially the "life-light" represented by Lara), and his evolving attitude toward the Revolution as aspects of Zhivago's worldview.

43 MORAVIA, ALBERTO. "Visite à Pasternak. Un adolescent aux cheveux gris." *Preuves*, no. 88, pp. 3–7.

Briefly discusses the treatment of history in *Doctor Zhivago*, cursorily examines Pasternak's poetry, and provides a summary of Pasternak's significance in Russian literature. Recalls his visit to Pasternak's home in 1956 and reveals conversation topics touched upon during that visit—including the suicides of Fadeyev, Esenin, and Mayakovsky. Recalls Pasternak saying that Esenin's suicide was the result of his sense of isolation within modern Soviet society. Also recalls Pasternak's remarks that he had not read Proust and Kafka. Mentions that history is an underlying observer in *Doctor Zhivago*, and as such, history is pitiless and guileless, thus allowing Pasternak to portray various aspects of events in the U.S.S.R. faithfully and accurately. Compares the role of history in *Doctor Zhivago* to that in *War and Peace*.

44 MORELLI, A. *Dr. Zhivago:* A Pasternak Milestone." *SSU*, no. 2, pp. 77–86.

Translation of 1958.45.

45 ———. "Pasternak, *Doktor Zhivago* i postroenie sotsializma" [Pasternak, *Doctor Zhivago*, and the building of socialism]. *Vozrozhdenie*, no. 77, pp. 113–24.

Contains biographical information followed by a detailed retelling of *Doctor Zhivago*. Observes that the novel's chief heroine is Russia, finding rebirth and renewal in suffering: "The heaping of torment and suffering through the novel's seven hundred pages is resolved by a major chord sounding out the world's future grandeur." Translated: 1958.44.

46 NADEAU, MAURICE. "En marge. *Le Docteur Jivago.*" *LN*, no. 64 (October): 471–80.
  Comments on *Doctor Zhivago*, including its main hero (seen as a petty bourgeois, one of the last members of a social class annihilated by the Revolution) and the novel's structure (which centers on a love story, like a love story of "Tristan and Isolde"). Also mentions that Zhivago's isolation reflects Pasternak's own double solitude—that of the physician and of the artist, both of whose individuality tends to be killed by society.

47 NEGRI, ANTIMO. "Il messaggio di Pasternak." *TP* 3, no. 12: 980–85.
  An interpretation of *Doctor Zhivago*'s basic themes. Sees the novel as focusing on a common man (not on a "hero" of the Revolution), affirming artistic feedom, and displaying a strong religious message. Defends the use of symbolism and claims that the novel advances the image of a man the Revolution could not destroy.

48 NILSSON, NILS ÅKE. "Boris Pasternak och *Doktor Zjivago*" [Boris Pasternak and *Doctor Zhivago*]. *BLM* 27, no. 2: 139–44.
  A summary of Pasternak's biography, centering on Pasternak's study of music and philosophy. Explains how Pasternak avoided the Stalinist purges in the 1930s. Discusses Pasternak's early poetry, and mentions the influence of Proust, Conrad, and Joyce. Summarizes the plot of *Doctor Zhivago*, claiming that the novel's greatness lies in its style and language.

49 ———. "Hos Boris Pasternak" [At Boris Pasternak's]. *BLM* 27, no. 8: 618–22.
  Recounts his visit to Pasternak in Peredelkino in September 1958. Relates information about Pasternak's way of life and views: his living on income derived from translations, the background for writing *Doctor Zhivago*, the explanations that *Doctor Zhivago* was not published because it was thought a bad novel and would damage his literary reputation, his indifference to the possibility of being excluded from the Union of Writers and thus losing home and income, and his expectations of arrest. Also records Pasternak's views of Strindberg, Hamsun, Jacobsen, and Ibsen (whose *Peer Gynt* Pasternak endeavored to translate). Translated: 1959.46.

50 ———. "Pasternak: We are the Guests of Existence." *Reporter* 19 (27 November): 34–35.
  In a brief conversation with the author, Pasternak discusses the genesis of *Doctor Zhivago* and his reasons for considering the novel his

most important work. Pasternak outlines the philosophical justification for *Doctor Zhivago*'s "optimistic" conclusion, which he describes as humankind's development from materialistic to possessing more human and spiritual values. Abridged and reprinted: 1959.48.

51   OTSUP, NIKOLAI. "Podvig odinochki" [A deed of an individual]. *Grani*, no. 40, pp. 51–53.

Divides *Doctor Zhivago* by acts, with the first two as the appearance and self-assertion of the hero, the third as the writing and publishing of the novel, the fourth as the crowning and humbling of the hero, the fifth as the *dénouement*, and the epilogue as "the judgement of posterity." Argues that the link between Pasternak's spiritual autobiography and his versified prose is "one of the most vivid examples of *personalism* in contemporary literature." Concludes that the novel's huge success shows that *personalism* is a "central factor" in our time, "a reaction to atheism and the herd instinct," and a "defense of personal dignity in the name of each one's contemporaries." Affirms this is why Pasternak is so greatly loved.

52   PANICHAS, GEORGE A. "Boris Pasternak's Protest and Affirmation." *GOTR* 4, no. 2: 161–72.

Deplores the current state in which the "dogmatics of politics" have been excessively and indiscriminately applied to works of art, a fate that applies particularly to *Doctor Zhivago*. Seeks to go beyond political issues, as well as criticisms of the novel's "stylistic weaknesses" to discuss the moral and spiritual dimensions—the ingredients that make *Doctor Zhivago* an "everlasting monument to the divinity of all men." Includes a brief biography of Pasternak, in essence a discussion of the factors that led to his decision to become a poet, and of the life of "retirement and detachment" that enabled him to create such a unique literary work. Discusses such aspects of the novel as its debunking of the heroic epic of the Revolution, the "motif of loss," the depiction of moral breakdown and the "horror of the Mass-man." Sees Zhivago as embodying "the perennial struggle between freedom and despotism." Considers all other considerations secondary to the novel's main theme, "Christian love and faith, Christian truth and immortality." Reprinted: 1974.12.

53   "The Passion of Yurii Zhivago." *Time* 72, no. 24: 80–88.

An overview of the significance of *Doctor Zhivago* as a political and literary phenomenon, and a sketch of the personality, background, and early career of Pasternak. Believes that the novel's importance is more due to its "extraordinary moral passion" than to its literary value. The discussion of Zhivago centers on his "paralysis of the will" and unmistakable sympathies for the educated middle class, which are seen to reflect Pasternak's own views. Pasternak's career, traced from the emphasis on imagery that marked his early poetry through his later periods of silence, is seen to embody the philosophy of disengagement from ephemeral political causes and attachment to lasting aesthetic and moral values, combined with confidence in the future of humanity.

54   PAYNE, ROBERT. "Boris Pasternak." *LR* 2: 315–33.
     A thematic study of Pasternak's prose up to *Doctor Zhivago*. Pasternak's affinity with the Danish poet Jens-Paul Jacobsen is sketched out, along with several other early influences, both positive and negative. Passages from *Il Tratto di Apelle, The Childhood of Luvers, Letters from Tula*, and *Aerial Ways* illustrate Pasternak's prose style in its development toward "full orchestration" marked by a vivid command of imagery, elaborate intensity, and evocative set pieces. Sees thematic preoccupation with trains, journeys, and frontiers as significant.

55   PHILLIPS, WILLIAM. "Men and History. The Tragic Visions of Pasternak and Silone." *Commentary* 26, no. 6 (December): 529–33.
     Likens *Doctor Zhivago* to Ignazio Silone's *The Secret of Luca*, both of which assert that moral and intellectual autonomy is the true face of the "gendarmerie of power" represented by modern Communist movements. *Doctor Zhivago*'s "confrontation of history," set against the panoramic backdrop of historical events, is contrasted with Silone's work, a more oblique and personal moral statement.

56   PLETNEV, R., and W. GREBENSCHIKOW. "Le maître." *ESE* 3: 179–82.
     An evaluation of Pasternak's craft. Notes "the bewildering sincerity of Pasternak's verses, their new simplicity, [and] the limpid sonority of their form." Finds the dominant traits to be the gravity and purity of his ideas and forms, and stresses the autobiographical nature of *A Safe Conduct* and *Doctor Zhivago*. Observes that Pasternak admires all of life's aspects and particularly enjoys describing nature in action (rain, wind, and storms). Adds that the New Testament themes of Christ (as a child and crucified), the Resurrection, and the Last Judgement recur in *Doctor Zhivago*, and notes the absence of hate in Pasternak's works.

57   POGGIOLI, RENATO. "Boris Pasternak." *PaR* 25, no. 4: 541–54.
     Recounts Pasternak's struggle with Soviet authority, and examines various facets of Pasternak's dualism, a "modern baroque" sensibility founded on tension and paradox. Contrasts Pasternak's "dramatic and pathetic" imagery with the "hyperbolic and iconoclastic" imagery of Mayakovsky. Believes *Doctor Zhivago* and *War and Peace* both represent a prelude to the story of a different generation. Sees Pasternak's reconciliation with politics as ultimately impossible. Concludes that *Doctor Zhivago* is a "moral act and a psychological document of great value, though not the culmination of his work." Feels that Pasternak's poetry and prose are honest assertions of the spirit's "private rights."

58 ———. "Pasternak." *Opyty*, no. 9, pp. 23–28.

Discusses Pasternak's loyalty to the Soviet system and his endeavors to find a "poetic expression of the Revolution" in his works, such as *Spektorsky*, *The Year 1905*, and *Lieutenant Schmidt*. Singles out the early prose: *The Childhood of Luvers*, the "tone and style" of which remind him of Rilke's *Aus den Aufzeichunungen des Malte Laurids Brigge*; and *A Safe Conduct*, in which the figure of Mayakovsky eclipses everything else. Outlines Pasternak's career as a translator, and notes that he is bound to futurism (sees his word handling as reminiscent of Khlebnikov's experiments and tradition); observes that Pasternak's language of translation is a "mosaic" in which formless particles unite into a single poem with the aid of syntax and rhythm. Emphasizes that "complex toying with emotions and concepts" is characteristic of Pasternak's poetry, and that his poetics, like that of Blok, is closer to the poetics of romanticism than that of his immediate predecessors.

59 PROSS-WEERTH, HEDDY. "Boris Leonidowitsch Pasternak." *NDH* 5, no. 2: 921–29.

Claims that Pasternak has completely detached himself from futurism and symbolism, and that he has followed "a realism of his own coinage." Also claims that the Soviet Union completely "accepted" Pasternak, but at the same time the Soviet Union was "deeply strange" to him. Lists parallels between *Doctor Zhivago* and *War and Peace*; insists that *Doctor Zhivago* does not at all follow the prescripts of a traditional realistic novel, neither of the nineteenth century nor of the early twentieth century.

60 REDLIKH, R. "Filosofskie vypiski iz *Doktora Zhivago*" [Philosophical extracts from *Doctor Zhivago*]. *Grani* 13, no. 40: 78–97.

Notes that even though this is a historical novel, the only historic figure in *Doctor Zhivago* is Nikolas II, and that only one character, Vedenyapin, is "creatively equal to Zhivago." Asserts that *Doctor Zhivago* is a philisophical novel continuing "the path of Gogol, Dostoevsky, and Tolstoy," and argues that it is not a social novel, but a metaphysical one. Compares the charm of Natasha Rostova with that of Lara, a character he sees to be more complex, even though "the author's intent stems from the same root." Questions what Pasternak wanted to reveal in his epilogue and suggests that Yevgraf Zhivago "is the embodiment of will for struggle, for solutions, for a life structure." Concludes that the center of the novel is "a fate of a doctor and a poet," and that there is another fate, the "fate of a ruler, the fate of a judge."

61 RODE, HEINZ. "Ein tragischer Idealist namens Shiwago. Randbemerkungen zu Boris Pasternaks Roman." *WW* 13: 355–56.

Insists that by no means should *Doctor Zhivago* be regarded as "an epic work of literature of the highest quality." Also insists that political criticism of the novel is unfounded and inept, and that the novel does not portray a Stalinist Soviet Union. Pasternak is seen as "a Russian patriot."

62 RUGE, GERD. "A Visit to Pasternak." *Encounter* 10: 22–25.
Describes his visit to Pasternak's home at Peredelkino, including a description of Pasternak's domestic setting and of a dinner with several guests. Records a conversation that touched upon many topics: Pasternak's difficulties in publishing *Doctor Zhivago*, his dissatisfaction with the politicization of the novel, his political and religious views, and his brief remarks on Proust, Mann, Joyce, and Rilke, for example. Admires Pasternak's independence and calmness in the "eye of the hurricane" that surrounds him. Argues that Pasternak represents "another Russia," unknown in extent and essentially inaccessible to the West. Reprinted: 1959.65.

63 SALISBURY, HARRISON. "Gratitude for the Tender Moments." *SR* 41 (6 September): 20–21.
Credits *Doctor Zhivago* with rich and poetic execution, devastating power, a passionate Christian faith unmatched since Tolstoy, and an honest and noble purpose. Pays attention to the novel's imagery that survives "pedestrian prose translation and wooden rendering of his poetry."

64 SIMMONS, ERNEST J. "The Independence of Pasternak." *Nation* 186 (15 March): 235–37.
Outlines Pasternak's literary career, tracing the stages of how *Doctor Zhivago* developed within Pasternak's other works—his poetry, prose, and translations. Discusses his imagery and language, his early prose, and *Doctor Zhivago*. Gives an account of a 1958 interview between Pasternak and Gerd Ruge (1958.62).

65 ———. "Russia from Within. Boris Pasternak's First Novel." *AM* 202 (September): 67–72.
Praises Pasternak as "one of the great men of letters of our time" and *Doctor Zhivago* as "the most sincere, honest, and revelatory fictional treatment of the Soviet epoch to come out of Russia." Outlines the course of events in the novel, with special attention given to Zhivago, who "epitomizes man's quenchless thirst for sanity and survival in a time of madness and death." Discusses Zhivago's antipathy to Marxism and "the political mysticism of the Soviet intelligentsia," as well as the "extraordinarily frank" epilogue in which the "colossal lie" of life under Soviet rule is openly treated "for the first time in any Soviet novel."

66 SLONIM, MARK. "Roman Pasternaka" [Pasternak's novel]. *NZh*, no. 52, pp. 94–108.
Takes issue with interpretations of *Doctor Zhivago* as a political novel, underlining that it contains hardly "any attacks against the com-

munist system." Provides an informative analysis of the novel's literary values—its structure (i.e., "the flow of days"), narrative, language, imagery (particularly similes), and characters (Zhivago, Lara, and Vedenyapin)—and of the major issues treated in the novel (*"Doctor Zhivago* is, first of all, a novel about intelligentsia"). Discusses the novel's contents in detail, concluding that *Doctor Zhivago* is a "remarkable creation of genuine art."

67 SMIRNOV, S.S. "Filosofiia predatel'stva" [The philosophy of treason]. *Agitator*, no. 23, pp. 61–63.

Expresses his outrage regarding the publication of *Doctor Zhivago*—as a Soviet, a Russian, a member of the intelligentsia, a soldier during the "Fatherland War," and as a human being—particularly due to its thinly veiled antihumanism. Denies the possibility of apoliticism in art, calling the novel an "apology for treason." Demands that Pasternak leave the U.S.S.R. and "personally sample the joys of the capitalist paradise."

68 SOUKUP, MOJMIR. "Pasternak and the Cold War." *NeR* 139 (8 December): 17–19.

Traces the political events surrounding the publication of *Doctor Zhivago* and the misunderstandings on the part of both the East and West regarding Pasternak's intentions and the novel's literary merits. Maintains that the novel is neither as revelatory nor as universal as critics have claimed. Sees *Doctor Zhivago* as a "classical Christian tragedy" offering no judgement, but merely "bearing witness to the events surrounding the Revolution." Claims that both the East and West have mistakenly interpreted *Doctor Zhivago* as an "act of defiance," and blames this "joint East-West stupidity" for Pasternak's expulsion from the Union of Writers. Insists that the Nobel Prize for literature awarded to Pasternak triggered a chain of events leading to a condition in which "Pasternak, the great human being and *Doctor Zhivago*, his great human document, are being whittled down to paper pellets for propagandists."

69 STOJNIĆ, MILA. "Pasternakov *Doktor Živago*" [Pasternak's *Doctor Zhivago*]. *Savremenik* 4, no. 8: 250–61.

Recounts Zhivago's life against the backdrop of major events brought about by two revolutions, gives sporadic comments on Zhivago and the two main female characters, and offers conclusive views of the novel's originality and poetics. Interprets Zhivago not as a "man from a street," but rather as a "quintessence of a man of great moral and intellectual values." Sees the novel's originality in the "constant presence of a poet and an educated man," and in its lyricism, subtle symbolism, simultaneous landscape descriptions, and unwavering author's interventions—all of which make "the novel *Doctor Zhivago* a cerebral construction of an exceptional force and artistic suggestiveness." Cites passages from the

Italian translation of *Doctor Zhivago* and the Italian criticism of Pasternak—Alberto Moravia (1958.43), G.P. Angioletti, and Guido Piovene.

70 VERBIN, V. "Boris Pasternak und sein *Doktor Zivago.*" *Sowjetstudien*, no. 6, pp. 96–112.

Outlines Pasternak's literary career and briefly discusses his works, including major translations. Centers on *Doctor Zhivago*, its philosophic views and poetics in particular. Singles out similes ("multilayered" and "manysided") as the most prominent facet of Pasternak's imagery and discusses Pasternak's syntax, comparing it to Mayakovsky's. Makes general observations about the novel, claiming that human relationships are more important to Pasternak than his views on philosophy, that for Pasternak love in general is an integral part of Christian love, and that important personal events and catastrophies described in the novel are closely connected to descriptions of natural events, such as snowstorms, hurricanes, and thunderstorms. Details the novel's publication history, and elaborates on the "Pasternak Affair." Cites appreciative criticism of the novel.

71 VISHNIAK, M. "*Doctor Zhivago* i ego tolkovateli" [*Doctor Zhivago* and its critics]. *SV*, no. 12, pp. 246–47.

Asserts the need to evaluate *Doctor Zhivago* by using artistic terms rather than political, religious, or ideolgical yardsticks. Agrees with Zhivago's own conclusion that the presence of art in a literary work outweighs all other considerations. Concludes that despite its formal flaws and unfortunate adaptability to both Communist and anti-Communist propaganda, *Doctor Zhivago* is a unique and significant literary phenomenon.

72 WALL, BERNARD. "A Great New Russian Novel." *Listener* 60 (11 September): 387–88.

Hails *Doctor Zhivago* as "one of the great books of our time, the only masterpiece we have had from Russia since the Revolution." Uses excerpts to illustrate the various symbols, from the simple to the complex, that are seen to pervade the novel, creating tension that is "sometimes difficult to bear." Sees Zhivago portrayed through religious and liturgical symbols, which are opposed to "mere History, the machinery of society."

73 WEIDLE, WLADIMIR. "Boris Pasternak" (in German). *Hochland* 50, no. 4: 394–96.

Enumerates general qualities of *Doctor Zhivago*, which he sees as Pasternak's best and most significant work. Accentuates that the novel is not a book on politics, but rather a book in which the people, in their relationships to each other as well as regarding their inner freedom, are important. Notes also that the end of the novel gives us a foreshadowing of "freedom."

74 WILSON, EDMUND. "Doctor Life and His Guardian Angel." *NY* 34 (15 November): 213–38.
Criticizes Hayward and Harari's translation of *Doctor Zhivago*, citing many omissions, distortions, and "further evidences of haste," and labeling the translation an "abridgement" unworthy of the novel's solidity, subtlety, and intensity. A discussion of the philisophical content of the novel, seen as universal and not specific to Russia, follows. Deems Pasternak's "peculiar" religious position and disdain for Marxism a struggle between "positive values" and "barbarities," with immortality as an overarching concern. Characterizes the novel as a legend, and discusses the role of Yevgraf Zhivago at some length. Zhivago's poems are found to represent the "full, triumphant statement" of the novel, the main theme of which is death and resurrection. Concludes that *Doctor Zhivago* "will come to stand as one of the great events in man's literary and moral history." Reprinted: 1965.7.

75 WINSTEAD, WILFRED. "Russian Novelist and Poet Writes of Individualist." *NVP* (7 September): F4.
Hails *Doctor Zhivago* as "one of the literary masterpieces of this century." Praises its artistic qualities—a "tender love story," landscape descriptions (deemed as "some of literature's most significant"), the rapid narrative, and imagery bespeaking "a master story-teller"—and the novel's "indictment of man's inhumanity." Finds fault with one aspect: the author "rings more of the historian than the novelist."

76 WOLFE, BERTRAM D. "A Russian Poet's Great Novel in the Great Tradition." *NYHTBR* (7 September): 1, 8.
Hails *Doctor Zhivago* as a great novel in the tradition of Tolstoy with its vast sweep, deep humanity, and religious feeling. Gives an overview of the novel's plot and main characters, interpreting the novel as a "paradigm of the author's own life."

77 YOUNG, MURRAY. Review of *Doctor Zhivago*. *NWR* 26 (November): 74–76.
Surveys and comments on the *Doctor Zhivago* criticism that appeared after the publication of the novel. Relates the novel's "main story" by focusing on Zhivago and his attitude toward the Revolution. Finds fault with the novel's structure ("awkward in construction, obscure in continuity, wildly improbable in its use of coincidence") and its character descriptions ("does not make his characters really come alive for us, he is not able to employ those psychological insights"). Concludes that Pasternak "has not written either a great artistic, social or humanistic novel."

1959

1   AMMON, KURT. "Auf den Spuren Larissas." *Monat* 11, no. 126: 76–77.

Elaborates on Lara's prototype, supposedly the Russian female writer Larissa Reissner-Raskolnikova, to whom Pasternak devoted a poem, which is cited fully. Makes suggestive parallels between the name Rasstrelnikov and Raskolnikov (a hero of Dostoevsky's *Crime and Punishment*) in order to support his thesis.

2   ARNDT, WALTER. "*Doctor Zhivago*—Freedom and Unconcern." *SAB* 25, no. 1: 1–6.

Recognizes in *Doctor Zhivago* less of a daring challenge or gesture of defiance than a reflection of Pasternak's inner freedom and unconcern. Attributes much of the novel's ensuing controversy to circumstance and the unpredictability of the ever-shifting political climate. Points out Tolstoy's influence on Pasternak and identifies parallels between *Doctor Zhivago* and *War and Peace*, with the former seen as an affirmation of the values of the latter. Sees "the suffusion of a willfully private testimony of freedom with this gratuitous essence of unconcern that underlies much of the impact of Pasternak's remarkable novel."

3   AUDRY, COLETTE. "Poésie et révolution: L´aventure de Boris Pasternak." *TM* 14, no. 155: 1046–59.

Finds Pasternak's troubles with the Soviet system rooted in language usage, specifically in aesthetic and linguistic deviations from the Soviet norm. Points out that hymns, prayers, and other religious texts in *Doctor Zhivago*, despite their relevance within the context of the novel, incurred official disfavor. Adds that Zhivago's confusion about grandiose revolutionary pronouncements earned Pasternak official denunciation. Compares *Doctor Zhivago* to Yugoslav poets Popa, Lalić, and Ćosić, locating similarities between their poetic language and Pasternak's.

4   BAIRD, SISTER MARY JULIAN. "Pasternak's Vision of the Fair Rowan Tree." *CW* 189: 427–31.

Sees the chapter "The Rowan Tree" in *Doctor Zhivago* as the fulfillment of Zhivago's search for the ideal, incomparable woman, who is embodied by the rowan tree, Lara, and the Virgin Mary. Having lost or abandoned three other mother figures (his mother, the "mother" of Russia and the Revolution, and Tonia), Zhivago is seen to idealize Lara and to value their experiences together, the significance of which even Lara is unaware.

5   BARTON, PAUL. "L´épopée de Boris Pasternak." *PF* (May): 19–25.

An analysis of *Doctor Zhivago*'s language. Observes that the language has an aesthetic value of its own (independent of the plot), and that there is both an equilibrium and tension between the language and the plot, generating a meditative element. Names three peculiarities of metaphors: the "instinctive gesture," the "straightforward process," and the "deliberate step." Adds that long periods in the novel and historical tableaus are treated "in passing," allowing the introduction of descriptive motifs in the manner of classical epics. Draws parallels between *Doctor Zhivago* and *War and Peace*—intrigue, chronicling, and a philosophy of history, among others. Asserts that Pasternak has "renewed the genre of the epic."

6   BIENEK, HORST. "Das also ist es." *FH* 14, no. 1: 69–73.
    Insists that "a political aspect" of *Doctor Zhivago* cannot be separated from the novel's artistic value. Accentuates Pasternak's courage in creating *Doctor Zhivago*. Points out that Zhivago dies at the moment when he finds himself fitting "in a new form of society," after he had "relinquished himself as an individual, as a single man."

7   BOWMAN, HERBERT E. *"Doctor Zhivago." NoR* 2: 59–67.
    Outlines Pasternak's background and discusses several aspects of *Doctor Zhivago*: its continuity with the poet's earlier work, its "clear and coherent philosophy of life" based on the principle of the free individual, and the antithetical nature such "heresy" represented to the Soviet regime. Deems the reflections of the novel's hero more important than the external events. Characterizes the novel as a "defense of life" against the impersonal forces of the Revolution and regimentation.

8   CHIAROMONTE, NICOLA. *"Doctor Zhivago* and Modern Sensibility." *Dissent* 6: 35–44.
    Translation of 1958.10.

9   CLOUGH, WILLIAM O. "Dr. Zhivago's 'Hamlet.'" *WHR* 13: 425–28.
    Discusses "Hamlet" as the most personal of Zhivago's poems, depicting a "drama of duty and self-denial" illustrative not only of Zhivago, but of Pasternak as well. Traces events in Zhivago's life and excerpts from his writings with respect to the character's growth and increasing sense of hidden destiny, which is to drink the "bitter cup of his own isolation" as his "Mother Russia" binds herself to an alien, threatening destiny. Zhivago's comments on the importance of writing about the city are also seen to throw the poem into a new light, in which the "other drama" it refers to becomes the personal life of the poet against the backdrop of the roar of the city.

10 COHEN, J.M. Introduction to *Boris Pasternak: Prose and Poems*. Edited by Stefan Schimanski. London: Ernst Benn, pp. 1–7.
    Argues that Pasternak's early works justify "his claim to be among the best of modern writers." Mentions or discusses some of Pasternak's

early works—*Collected Poems* (1933 edition), *On Early Trains*, and translations. Notes the presence of Pasternak's earlier writings in *Doctor Zhivago*, and remarks that the novel is an attempt to achieve an understanding of the Revolution. Compares Pasternak with Rilke, pointing out their concern with transformation of objects and events into symbols. Discusses Pasternak's belief in the unity of man and nature ("To Pasternak there is no essential difference between convulsions of nature and those in the affairs of men") and observes that the chief motif of his stories is "of loss, and that of *Zhivago's* resurrection."

11   CRANKSHAW, EDWARD. *"Dr. Zhivago* and the *Novy Mir* Letter." In *Khrushchev's Russia.* Harmondsworth: Penguin, pp. 148–71.
      Reprints the rejection letter addressed to Pasternak by the editorial board of *Novy mir* (as it appeared in *Literaturnaia gazeta*, October 1958), outlining the journal's specific criticisms of the novel. The letter objects to Pasternak's failure to differentiate between the February and October revolutions; his heroizing of a man like Zhivago; his neglect of the reasons for the inevitability of the revolution; and his sympathetic portrayal of characters whose only goal is to preserve their individual lives and lifestyles ("It is hard to name outright another work in which heroes with pretenses to higher spiritual values have in the years of the greatest events, shown such concern for and talked so much about food, potatoes, firewood, and other comforts and discomforts of life . . ."). Concludes that "this letter testifies to the existence of a gulf between the human and the Soviet way of looking at the things that will be far more difficult to bridge than the political differences, which obsess us all today." Translated: 1960.6.

12   CUADRA, PABLO ANTONIO. "El mensaje de Boris Pasternak." *Abside* 23: 96–101.
      Discusses the controversy surrounding the publication of *Doctor Zhivago* and glosses over the novel. Emphasizes that the novel does not contain outright "propaganda," but rather something more profound: a humane message, a humanistic and Christian hope, seen as the provision of "freedom, true freedom."

13   DAVIS, MELTON S. "The Book That Shook the Kremlin: *Dr. Zhivago.*" *Coronet* 46 (May): 58–65.
      Recounts the events leading up to and following *Doctor Zhivago's* publication. Includes a brief biography of Giangiacomo Feltrinelli and his involvement with the Italian Communist Party, which led to his subsequent difficulties with party chief Palmino Togliatti after publishing *Doctor Zhivago*. The mediation of Sergio D'Angelo, including his smuggling of the manuscript from the U.S.S.R., and Feltrinelli's resistance to the pressure by Soviet and Italian Communist parties to return the man-

uscript are detailed, as are the considerations surrounding the decision to ignore Pasternak's telegram asking for the return of his manuscript. Soviet attempts to discredit Feltrinelli and the problem of "rights" to the novel are also mentioned.

14 "Delo Pasternaka" [The Pasternak affair]. *ND*, no. 1, pp. 12–20.

Outlines Pasternak's life and discusses his major works. Observes that the tragedy that befell Pasternak is the tragedy of the entire world confronted with the choice of whether to preserve man as a free individual or to condemn him to endless "humiliation and profanation." Chronicles events surrounding Pasternak's Nobel Prize "Affair." Defends Pasternak and illustrates his support with citations of various public figures, philosophers, critics, writers, poets, and teachers throughout the world. Cites and discusses poetry from *Doctor Zhivago*.

15 DERZHAVYN, VOLODYMYR. "The Case of Pasternak or the Self-exposure of Bolshevist Literature." *UR* 6, no. 1: 37–44.

Analyzes the controversy surrounding Pasternak in the West and the Soviet Union and the response generated by the Nobel Prize. Speculates that the Soviet authorities were unconcerned and indifferent about the novel's foreign publication until the prize was awarded, fearing then that a Russian text of the book would seep into the Soviet Union and radically destroy the "legend of the Russian cultural heritage." Asserts that "those who attack the Bolshevist claim to national Russian culture are attacking the Bolshevist claim to national Russian loyalty."

16 DEUTSCH, BABETTE. Introduction to *Boris Pasternak: A Safe Conduct; An Autobiography and Other Writings*. New York: Signet Books.

Acknowledges the influences of specific people, art, and events in Pasternak's personal history and on his work and views. Pays tribute to Pasternak's "gift, essential to durable writing, of particularizing even seemingly trivial events in such a way as to enhance them, so that they take on universality, while drenched with the here and now." Finds that "his poetry and his prose belong to that incredible organism which grows out of our lives and on which they depend for survival, the organism to which he gives the name art."

17 DEUTSCHER, ISAAC. "Pasternak and the Calendar of Revolution." *PaR* 26: 248–65.

Charges Pasternak with misreading history, "the calendar of the Revolution," by creating a novel that is anachronistic in content and form. Pasternak's critique of the Revolution in *Doctor Zhivago* is seen as archaic, attributing to the Bolsheviks promises they never made. The characters and incidents portrayed in *Doctor Zhivago* are regarded as irrelevant or peripheral, unequal to the momentous issues and events of the period described in the novel, and in contrast to the direct involvement of characters in *War and Peace*. Argues that Zhivago is more like Oblomov than Pierre Bezukhov, and that Pasternak overidealizes Zhivago without presenting any convincing characters to contrast or oppose him. Believes that stylistically, the novel is marked by a "perplexing contrast between masterful lyrical passages and an inept, confusing storyline." Reprinted: 1969.6.

18 DRAWDZIK, WITOLD. *"Doktor Żywago"* (in Polish). *Horyzonty*, no. 36, pp. 45–51.
A general commentary on *Doctor Zhivago*. Sees *Doctor Zhivago* as "gloomy as the world described" in it and its characters' introductions as "chaotic." Recognizes the presence of various language strata in the novel. Attempts to explain "the phenomenon of self-accusation," of which Strelnikov's suicide is an example. Cites his own translation of the poem "A Miracle."

19 ERLICH, VICTOR. "The Concept of the Poet in Pasternak." *SEER* 37, no. 89: 325–35.
Attempts to redefine the problem of Pasternak's paradoxical poetic craft by examing some of his "explicit and implicit notions" regarding the self and poetry. These include a view of the self as an "objectified" part of nature rather than the subject of artistic dramatization, a unique conception of passion and feeling as a cosmic and experimental rather than affective and romantic force in art, organizing and integrating experience and art into a whole of life, and a poetics that emphasizes language over personality. Sums up Pasternak's poetry as "the world becomes language," unique because of its attention to detail and craftsmanship over the "romantic temptations of prophesy." Pasternak's growing conflict with historical developments that became increasingly incompatible with "life by verses" is seen to culminate in *Doctor Zhivago*, the "crowning paradox" of his career due to the singularly personal and epic qualities it simultaneously possesses. Revised: 1964.4.

20 FOSTY, VERA. "Le vrai Boris Pasternak." *RGB* 95, no. 1: 40–55.
Surveys or discusses Pasternak's time and works: artistic influences exerted on Pasternak from different arts and literary trends and movements; major themes in Pasternak's poetry and his poetics; the government's attitude toward Pasternak (notably Stalin's tolerance of him); Pasternak's feelings toward Russia, political events he witnessed, and the reflection of these events in his works; and religious themes in Pasternak's works. Draws parallels between Pasternak and Zhivago, warning against blunders of total identification of the two as the same.

21 FRANK, VICTOR. "Realizm chetyrekh izmerenii" [Realism of four dimensions]. *Mosty*, no. 2, pp. 189–209.

Explains the so-called chronological confusion in *Doctor Zhivago* as Pasternak's intention to distinguish his work from the novel-chronicle. Argues that *Doctor Zhivago* is not a history but an autobiographical novel, partially in the external but mostly in the internal sense. Believes that the characters must not be viewed as copies of real life and that the laws of nature and probability lose their absolute quality in the novel. Deems that the novel's autobiographical nature should not be crudely literalized, that Zhivago is Pasternak and Hamlet is Saint George and Christ, and that Zhivago is the bearer of the power that, originating in Christ, is endowed to those who are ready to submit to it. Concludes that Zhivago's greatness lies in his humble readiness to enlighten the world around him with the aid of this spiritual reality. Reprinted: 1974.5.

22 GAEV, ARKADY. *Boris Pasternak and Dr. Zhivago*. Institute for the Study of the U.S.S.R. Soviet Affairs Analysis Service. Series 1, no. 46. Munich: Institut zur Erforschung der U.S.S.R., 20 pp.

Translation of 1958.20 (last two pages modified).

23 GIFFORD, HENRY. "*Dr. Zhivago*: The Last Russian Classic." *EC* 9: 159–70.

Doctor Zhivago is praised as a recovery of the Russian national voice representative of embattled, high European values such as humanity, intelligence, confidence in freedom, and modesty. Its structure, in contrast to that of a conventional novel, is seen to center on four "sustained moments at which 'the candle burns,'" which are, in turn, correlated to the poetry at the end of the novel, as well as on evocations of nature that both embody and symbolize the novel's "piety." Discusses *Doctor Zhivago*'s love story as a "plea for continuity" in the Soviet Union and abroad.

24 GRIGORIEFF, DIMITRY FELIX. "Pasternak and Dostoevskij." *SEEJ* 17, no. 4: 335–42.

A study of Dostoevsky's influence on *Doctor Zhivago*: the novel's plot structure centering on an "image of pure beauty," ideologies, characters, religious perceptions, and themes of life and death ("death is a gate to immortality"). Sees Pasternak and Dostoevsky as believing that with the coming of Christ all former ideas and orders will cease to exist and that man's individuality and a new world will be firmly established. Cites Sima Tuntseva's Bible interpretations, and discusses Pasternak's assertion that among the kingdom of plants, death, and life an inseparable bond exists. Concludes that both Pasternak and Dostoevsky treat a contemporary civilization and society with skepticism. Translated: 1960.11–12.

25 HAYWARD, MAX. "'Obyvatel' or the Superfluous Man." In *Boris Pasternak*, edited by K.K. Sinha. Calcutta: Congress For Cultural Freedom, pp. 16–42.
  Reprint of 1958.26.

26 ———. "'Zhivago's' Suppression—a New Theory." *LJ* 84, no. 10: 1562–63.
  Recounts *Doctor Zhivago*'s suppression, contending that the matter is less an ideological conflict than a result of professional and personal jealousy toward Pasternak on the part of Alexei Surkov, secretary of the U.S.S.R. Union of Writers.

27 HOWE, IRVING. "Freedom and the Ashcan of History." *PaR* 26: 266–75.
  Defends Pasternak and *Doctor Zhivago* against Isaac Deutscher's essay (1959.17), reckoning the essay an "unfortunate venture into literary criticism" that "ignores serious literary issues" and constitutes "neither more nor less than a political act." Seeks to refute Deutscher's charges that *Zhivago* deals inadequately with historical events, that Pasternak ascribed false hopes to the Revolution, and that *Zhivago* falls short of Tolstoyan breadth and social awareness, claiming instead that the novel is faithful to the "essential history of our time." Most vehemently disputes Deutscher's argument that Pasternak and his novel suffer from "archaism," citing several passages from the novel to show Pasternak's treatment of current political concerns, and adding that the novel portrays recurring, timeless truths such as freedom, conformism, and suffering. Reprinted: 1969.10.

28 HUGHES, RILEY. Review of *Doctor Zhivago*. *CW*, no. 188 (January): 335.
  Sees *Doctor Zhivago* as "one of the great religious novels of our time." Stresses the novel's human values ("values that ultimately are religious ones"). Links the novel's beginning with its end to establish "what has happened in Russia in the past forty years." Concludes that the novel's "end is, perhaps ironically, a serene one."

29 JOVANOVIĆ, MILIVOJE. "Na marginama *Doktora Živaga*" [On the margins *of Doctor Zhivago*]. *Izraz* 3, no. 1: 26–38.
  Discusses Pasternak's worldview (a notion of life regeneration, art, and the Revolution, among others) as reflected in *Doctor Zhivago*, while underpinning his comments with ideas expressed in Pasternak scholarship (including Aleksandrov and Mirsky) and Pasternak's works. Finds similarities between *Doctor Zhivago* and the poem "Waves" (from the *Second Birth* collection), seen in the poem's life self-regeneration "plan" as presaging Zhivago's "new spiritual orientation," and between Pasternak's *Tale* and Dostoevsky's *Crime and Punishment*. The hero of

Tale, Seryozha, is compared to Raskolnikov in his "demand for humility" and his "sacrificial readiness." This idea of sacrifice is also tied to *Doctor Zhivago*, which is seen as affirming an "identical motif"—Zhivago's intent to sacrifice Lara to Komarovsky.

30   KAROL, K.S. "Le cas de Boris Pasternak." *TM* 14, no. 155: 1030–81.
      Discovers and discusses paradoxes surrounding Pasternak: he was among the few Soviet writers still published in the 1930s, he continued to enjoy privileges, and he was untouched during the purges—even though he had already "fallen in disgrace." Cites excerpts from the speeches of Bukharin, Surkov, and Pasternak delivered at the First Soviet Writers' Congress in 1934. Comments on the speeches, particularly on Pasternak's definition of poetry and his urging to writers not to sacrifice their individuality.

31   KERNIG, C.D. "Menschenbild und Revolution. Zur Interpretation des Romans *Doktor Schiwago*." *MW* 1: 267–83.
      Attempts to draw similarities between *Doctor Zhivago* and Thomas Mann's *Doctor Faustus*. Centers on *Doctor Zhivago*'s philosophical (echoes of Hegel's and Schelling's alienation concepts and Goethe's nature philosophy) and ideological (the Revolution and the theory of Marxism) views. Also makes general remarks about the novel ("the seamless integration of individual fate and social events is perfect") and concludes that for Pasternak, "man's history is . . . comprised and sustained by the story of the salvation of man by God" and that "Zhivago's poems are Pasternak's 'Credo in unum Deum' soaring above the forward marching basses that give history dimension and consistency." Translated: 1961.15.

32   KONSTANTINOV, D.V. "*Doktor Zhivago* i bogoiskatel'stvo v SSSR" [*Doctor Zhivago* and the God-seekers in the U.S.S.R.]. *VII*, no. 2, pp. 75–86.
      Notes the abundance of religious/philosophical ideas in *Doctor Zhivago*, ideas seen to be similar to those of Fedorov's, which "perceive a sense of history in mankind in a collective struggle for annihilation of death." Insists that the novel negates a materialistic theory of social existence and consciousness patterned on the "recipes of communist theoreticians." Also observes other ideas of the novel, including "sacrificial love for fellow men" and "striving for higher ideals."

33   KORIAKOV, MIKH. "Afinogenov i Pasternak" [Afinogenov and Pasternak]. *NZh*, no. 56, pp. 159–86.
      Surveys Pasternak's friendship with Afinogenov. Finds common features in their works and their views—similar thematic treatments and composition interpretations of Doestoevsky's novels, among others. Draws parallels between Afinogenov's diary and *Doctor Zhivago*. Sees the commonality of their characters in their "gift for tears." Cites passages from Pasternak's Afinogenov essay and comments on it.

123

34 ———. "Zametki na poliax romana *Doktor Zhivago*" [Marginal notes on *Doctor Zhivago*]. *Mosty*, no. 2, pp. 210–23.

Singles out the Kamergersky Lane as the central point of the novel's composition ("its foothold, that focus in which all rays converge"), and elaborates on why the Kamergersky Lane is the central point, assuming that Dmitry Samarin had lived there and suggesting that Samarin is partly a prototype of the protagonist. Observes that Pasternak's remark that Zhivago "had an eye best of all" is linked with Pasternak's interpretation of the word *vzgliad* (glance) as "an uninterrupted dialogue between man's outside and inner world."

35 LEVITSKII, SERGEI. "Svoboda i bessmertie. O romane Pasternaka *Doktor Zhivago*" [Freedom and immortality. On Pasternak's novel *Doctor Zhivago*]. *Mosty*, no. 2, pp. 224–36.

Argues that *Doctor Zhivago* is not so much a novel as an artistic confession and sermon, containing much impressionism bordering on symbolism. Notes that the protagonist remains faithful to principles of the immortality of spiritual values, and that at the end of the novel he loses his family, Lara, and his livelihood as a doctor, while continuing to be free in spirit within. Adds that Pasternak shows the preeminence of the interior world over everything exterior. Concludes that Pasternak's novel displays a genre that combines realism, impressionism, and symbolism, and that the "Poems of Yury Zhivago" represent the summit and summation of Pasternak's creative path.

36 LÉVY, YVES. "Les trois femmes du docteur Jivago." *CS* 3, no. 3: 171–74.

Argues that *Doctor Zhivago* is structured around three women—Tonya, Lara, and Marina—who symbolize three different worlds: the old, the Revolution, and the new. Pays special attention to the scene describing Zhivago's death and draws comparisons with Hemingway's use of similar symbols ("On ne peut ici s'emprêcher de songer à la parabole de Hemingway symbolisant les États-Unis par un vieux colonel—cardiaque lui aussi").

37 LYONS, EUGENE. "The Book the Kremlin Is Afraid to Let the Russians Read." *RD* 74 (February): 58–64.

Discusses the publication of *Doctor Zhivago*, a novel seen as "an explosion that is rocking the Kremlin to its very foundations." The author's Nobel Prize is seen as a "crisis in the Kremlin." Recounts Pasternak's literary career, culminating in his novel whose "grim realism . . . strips the revolution of romantics." Several philosophical passages from the novel are quoted to support the contention that, although Pasternak's "quarrel is not political, the result adds up to a devastating indictment of Communism." Traces reactions to the novel from various sources, including Albert Camus, John Steinbeck, Chet Huntley, James Billington, and Marc Slonim.

38   MACDIARMID, HUGH. Foreword to Pasternak's *Poems*. Translated by L. Slater. London: Poets' and Printers' Press, pp. 5–7.

Considers Pasternak "a very good poet," even greater than Yeats, Valery, Rilke, and Blok. Argues that few poets share Pasternak's view of nature, and that Pasternak perceives nature as "alive and powerful, but doesn't make a god of it or expect it to reveal oracular messages." Contrasts Pasternak to symbolist poets, noting that Pasternak does not "project merely confused . . . impressions and decadent transpositions of one sense into another."

39   MARKOV, VLADIMIR. "Notes on Pasternak's *Doctor Zhivago*." *RR* 18: 14–22.

Characterizes *Doctor Zhivago* as a work of art and an ideological novel, and discusses various aspects of its content and style: the symbolic implications of its characters, its life-affirming philosophical content, its depiction of the Revolution as an "evil force," and its "conservative" link to the Russian classical tradition, especially to Pushkin and Tolstoy. Also discusses the novel's European influence and its connections with Pasternak's earlier prose. Criticizes B.G. Guerney's translations of the poems as "pale, monotonous, and bland" renderings of Zhivago's "exegi monumentum." Sums up the novel as a "moral victory for post-Revolutionary literature."

40   MATLAW, RALPH E. "A Visit with Pasternak." *Nation* 189 (12 September): 134–35.

Records Pasternak's views of the simplistic causality of the nineteenth-century novel and its debunking by Flaubert, Pasternak's disagreement with Edmund Wilson's symbolic interpretation of *Doctor Zhivago* (1959.78) and the degree to which various descriptions in the novel may be consciously or unconsciously symbolic, arguments about whether Zhivago's poems can be said to belong to Pasternak, and the process of the composition of the first three chapters of the novel.

41   MAURINA, ZENTA. "Licht und Finsternis in der russischen Literatur." In *Auf der Schwelle zweier Welten. Essays*. Memmingen/Allgau: Maximilian Dietrich Verlag, pp. 132–54. Reprint. 1961.

Outlines Russian classic and contemporary literature; singles out the writers who were either murdered or committed suicide. Sees Lara's love for Zhivago as an element of rebelliousness; considers Lara a "bearer of an idea . . . of the patient, all-caring, indestructible Russian earth."

42   MAZUROVA, ALEKSANDRA. "O teme *Doktora Zhivago*" [On *Doctor Zhivago*'s theme]. *Mosty*, no. 3, pp. 141–49.

Insists that the novel's theme is man against the "backdrop of history and this theme arose from life itself, and political threats gave it urgency." Argues that the hero represents the image of a "living" man, embodying both the struggle on one's own behalf and betrayal of self, and the incompatibility of one's aspirations and feelings. Attempts to prove that Zhivago hailed the February Revolution (1917) as the "flood of life." Also contends that Zhivago's "personal revolution" was meeting Lara, the embodiment of love; that the driving forces of life are not only love, but also faith; and that the image of Christ ceases to be merely a symbol, becoming "the living reality of the transformed human being."

43 MCDONNELL, THOMAS P. "From Ben Hecht to Pasternak." *CW* 189 (April): 39–43.

Contends that *Doctor Zhivago* conclusively refutes Ben Hecht's recent assertion that Christianity is "petering out" and that concepts of mysticism regarding the soul and immortality are sharply waning in the modern era. Compares Matthew Arnold's belief in the permanent need for "humane letters" to Pasternak's own preservation of "humanity" and "the continuity and tradition of literature." Sees the furor caused by awarding the Nobel Prize to Pasternak (while three Soviet physicists who also received the Nobel Prize the same year went virtually unnoticed) as evidence of the basic human concern for individual creativity and imagination over the depersonalized forces of science and technology.

44 MERTON, THOMAS. "The Pasternak Affair in Perspective." *Thought* 34: 485–517.

Recounts the "Pasternak Affair" (the controversies surrounding the publication of *Doctor Zhivago* and the awarding of the Nobel Prize to Pasternak), emphasizing the novel's "essentially spiritual character," its status as a deeply meaningful portent, a "miracle." Traces Pasternak's literary career from his early poetry (seen to express passive resistance to the evil repression of the Soviet regime), to his silent period (as equally instructive and inspirational in his refusal to take part in the totalitarian machine), to the *Doctor Zhivago* period (in which Pasternak's apolitical religious message reaches the world in its clearest and most emphatic form). Argues that *Doctor Zhivago* should not be compared to *War and Peace* and to Tolstoy because "Pasternak was a poet and a musician which Tolstoy was not." Also argues that Pasternak fought for "man's true freedom, his true creativity, against the false and empty humanism of the Marxists." Sees Pasternak's ideas as potentially subversive to the East and West alike. Translated: 1960.24. Reprinted: 1960.25.

45 NIEL, MATHILDE. "Boris Pasternak à la recherche d'un humanisme ouvert." *AN* 12, no. 106: 65–73.

Applies concepts of existentialist humanism ("open versus closed humanism") to *Doctor Zhivago*, citing examples from the novel seen to correspond to these concepts. Defines these concepts as man's indispensable dependence on his environment, and refers to Erich Fromm as the basis for a new type of humanism as well as to Julian Huxley's "evolutionary humanism."

46 NILSSON, NILS ÅKE. "Besuch bei Boris Pasternak: September 1958." In *Boris Pasternak: Bescheidenheit und Kühnheit*, edited by R.L. Meister. Zurich: Arche, pp. 102–13.
    Translation of 1958.49.

47 ———. "Life as Ecstasy and Sacrifice. Two Poems by Boris Pasternak." *ScS* 5: 180–98.
    A thorough textual and structural analysis of "With Oars at Rest" (from *My Sister, Life*) and "Hamlet" (from *The Poems of Yury Zhivago*). Sees in "Oars at Rest" several characteristic features of Pasternak's early poetry—dislocation, metonymy, "its emotionality, its intensive personal diction full of exclamations and repetitions," and its orchestration. Stresses Pasternak's intent to link living and dead objects, and discusses several effects of *kliuchitsy* (collarbones) and *vkliuchiny* (rowlocks)—effects created by their semantic similarity. Argues that in "Hamlet" Pasternak reveals a "firmer allegiance" to Pushkin, Lermontov, Tyutchev, and Blok, and that he shows a "striving toward simplicity, content, and essentials." Discusses elaborately the poet's task "Hamlet" is seen to offer and observes that "the connection between the poet and his work followed Pasternak through the years." Reprinted: 1978.31.

48 ———. "'Most Difficult of All.'" In *Boris Pasternak*, edited by K.K. Sinha. Calcutta: Congress For Cultural Freedom, pp. 64–68.
    Abridged reprint of 1958.50.

49 NORMANDIN, RODRIGUE. "Le Docteur Jivago." *RUO* 29, no. 2: 215–27.
    Surveys critical reception of *Doctor Zhivago* and discusses reasons why the novel was banned in the Soviet Union but was received so well in the West. Discusses the novel's style, the use of poetic language in prose, and glosses over the novel's story line. Believes that Zhivago does not oppose the Revolution, is not affected by it, rises above the Revolution, and isolates himself. Views *Doctor Zhivago* as a documentary novel, a psychological novel, and as a novel of "Christian humanism."

50 NOSTITZ, OSWALT von. "Was bezeugt *Doktor Schiwago?* Die Pasternak—Sensation und die stillere Wahrheit." *WoW* 14: 205–8.
    A negative criticism of *Doctor Zhivago*. Singles out "haziness and lack of execution of some details" and "interspersion of too novelistic elements" as the novel's weaknesses. Argues that Pasternak has rejected "Stalinism and the communist doctrine in general" due to his Christian beliefs. Reprinted: 1967.11.

51 OLDHAM, JANET. *"Dr. Zhivago* and *Babbitt." EJ* 48: 242–46.

Compares Pasternak's novel with Sinclair Lewis's *Babbitt*. Both writers are said to denounce conformity as "the cause of their societies" and explore the psychological and moral effects of standardization on individuals. Both novels are viewed as having emphasized ideas over specific characterization, and their characters are contrasted with respect to their attitudes toward nature and human companionship. Treats the dominant stylistic considerations in each novel—symbolism in *Doctor Zhivago*, satire in *Babbitt*—and hostile reactions to both authors in their native countries.

52 PAGE, ALEX. *"Doctor Zhivago* in the Classroom." *CEA* 21, no. 3: 1, 10–11.

Presents a synopsis of *Doctor Zhivago*, treating such subjects as the Revolution, Strelnikov, Evgraf, Zhivago, and Lara, and the novel's technique. Labels the novel a "chronicle," and claims that the problems that arise from this sort of novel are "what to exclude and how to maintain a drama." Also claims that "a chronicle by its very nature will remain inconclusive" and "the formlessness of the novel is the price paid for its achieved grandeur." Makes comparisons to Dostoevsky and Tolstoy, and concludes that *Doctor Zhivago* is a " 'novel of ideas.' "

53 PELTIER, HÉLÈNE, M. ANDRONIKOF, and JACQUES MADAULE. "Boris Pasternak et *Le Docteur Jivago*. Débat du 23 Avril 1959." *ReD*, no. 29, pp. 151–85.

A three-part critique of Pasternak and *Doctor Zhivago*, with Peltier conveying the discussion on *Doctor Zhivago* she had with Pasternak in 1956. Peltier argues that the novel is not a love story but a "judgement on this epoch by a man who experienced the tumult of the Revolution" and that it is a "hymn to life," an escape into Christian philosophy, offering an "ideal of life." Andronikof remarks on the novel's structure, seen as based on a religious perception of art, with inseparable form and content.

54 POREMSKII, A. "Politicheskie motivy v romane *Doktor Zhivago*" [Political motifs in the novel *Doctor Zhivago*]. *ND*, no. 1, pp. 33–45.

An interpretation of political views in *Doctor Zhivago*. Insists that the novel is "definitely apolitical, and in this lies its political effect." Also argues that Pasternak's approach to the Revolution is not "political at all." Names the novel's "political themes": attitude toward the prerevolutionary past, the Revolution and the Soviet system, issues of freedom and justice, and the relation between an individual and society. Surveys the "political views" of Zhivago, Antipov-Strelnikov, Gints, and Vedenyapin. Concludes that *Doctor Zhivago* is not a "freedom declaration" but a "freedom realization." Reprinted: 1961.23.

55 POWERS, RICHARD HOWARD. "Ideology and *Doctor Zhivago.*" *AR* 19: 224–36.

Criticizes reviewers of *Doctor Zhivago* who praise the novel and characterize it as an apolitical work. Condemns the novel's protagonist, who possesses a "limited vision" and seeks exemption from politics while indulging in "special pleading" for parochial, bourgeois values—an attitude summed up as "the rebelliousness of the spoiled and pampered." Sees the role of politics not only as a major factor, but a determinant of the critical reaction the novel has received.

56 PRAUSNITZ, WALTHER G. "*Doctor Zhivago.*" *Discourse* 2: 171–88.

Summarizes the novel's plot lines and discusses its great popularity as a preface to a study of the organizing and unifying techniques. Sees rhythmic devices as the novel's main chronological, organizing force. Mentions repeated images such as funerals and the "Moreau & Vetchinkin" signs as examples of such "signposts" marking the narrative. Symbolic, fortuitous appearances and reappearances of charcters such as Mademoiselle Fleury are seen to invest the narrative with a sense of purpose and meaning. Shows ways in which Pasternak mixes the omniscient point of view with direct dramatization through the characters' own speech, unifying time and action. Maintains that the use of images that "destroy the action of the moment" to suggest greater, more eternal associations is crucial to Pasternak's poetics. An overview of Zhivago's political views follows along with a brief assessment of his legacy as embodied in his poems.

57 RANNIT, ALEKSIS. "The Rhythm of Pasternak. His Early Poetry, 1912–1924." *BNYPL*, no. 11 (November): 555–69.

Examines rhythmic structures and metaphors in early collections: *A Twin in the Clouds*, *Above the Barriers*, *My Sister, Life*, and *Themes and Variations*. Surveys Pasternak's indebtedness to his predecessors and contemporaries. Sees Blok as having been present "through the whole of his [Pasternak's] production"; records other poets' influences (Balmont's, Severyanin's, and Rilke's); and stresses Pasternak's adaptation of the "loose framework of futurist poetics" to his affinity for classic verse. Underlines Pasternak's use of the caesura that is seen to come "at a different position in each line and is frequently employed for an exceptional emphasis." Singles out Pasternak's innovation in new rhymes ("In the invention of new rhymes Pasternak has probably no rivals in modern Russian poetry"). Pasternak's metaphors are seen to be achieved "through successive juxtaposition and superimposition and fragmentation of images"; finds that in Pasternak's metaphors "slang occurs next to the most sophisticated reinterpretations of Plato or the most subtle suggestions of tenderness." Concludes that in Pasternak's poetry, "what most strikes the student is its rhythmically creative zest and power." Continued: 1960.29.

58 REAVEY, GEORGE. "First Essay Towards Pasternak." *Chelsea*, no. 4, pp. 3–6.
    Reprint of 1930.2.

59 ———. Introduction to *The Last Summer*. Translated by George Reavey. London: Peter Owen, pp. 5–30.
    A condensed version of his introduction to *The Poetry of Boris Pasternak: 1914–1960* (1959.60), with added comments on *The Last Summer*. Points out the strong autobiographical and social commentary "on the objective and deteriorating situation of man" in the work, taking note of its similarity in this respect to *A Safe Conduct*. Praises Pasternak's prose as "extremely mobile" in conveying elusive impressions of nature when seen through the mercurial complexity of human emotion. Concludes that the richness of Pasternak's prosaic images can be traced to his early poetry and the influence of symbolist and imagist poets.

60 ———. Introduction to *The Poetry of Boris Pasternak: 1914–1960*. Selected, edited, and translated by George Reavey. New York: G.P. Putnam's Sons, pp. 13–100. Reprint. 1960.
    A three-part study that focuses briefly on Pasternak's life (family background, school and university education, music and literature experiences, and his life in the Soviet period); the author's correspondence and meetings with Pasternak; and on Pasternak's poetry. The third part divides Pasternak's poetry into three periods: the early (1914–1923), which reflects the influence of the philosophy of the symbolist movement; the middle (1923–1936), in which his main activity was writing prose; and the later (1940–1960), which is seen as the period of Pasternak's full maturity. Sees Pasternak as a universal poet, "a free citizen of spirit," and labels his poetic development as a "slow and even laborious progression from a rich complexity to a richer simplicity." Makes numerous observations on the poetics of Pasternak's early poetry—including sound instrumentation, meter ("the four-beat iambic quatrain"), imagery, and rhymes (apocopated and near rhymes). Affirms a link of continuity between Pasternak's early and later poetry.

61 REYNOLDS, J.F. "Reflections on *Dr. Zhivago*." *Studies* 48: 59–66.
    Stresses that non-Russian-speaking readers cannot judge the true nature of *Doctor Zhivago* or any Russian literary work, as it is weakened by translation. Argues that the conflict between Pasternak and the Soviet government is simply a repetition of the age-old conflict in Russia between writer and government. Supports Max Hayward's view that *Doctor Zhivago* is "the latest in a stream of writings in defence of the small man," such as the hero of Gogol's *Overcoat*. Laments the inability of Western literature to appreciate the depth and consciousness of Zhivago's love for his wife and for Lara, noting that in the West such

scenes are treated comically or with excessive concern for propriety. Concludes that "the miracle has happened" in that a "wayward human being has shown them that the human spirit cannot be confined, that man does not live by bread alone."

62 RINGBOM, LARS-PETER. *"Doktor Zjivago* kommenterar sitt verk. Några reflexioner" [*Doctor Zhivago* comments on its work. Some reflections]. *FT*, no. 1. pp. 17–22.

A commentary on *Doctor Zhivago*'s poetics—art in which comments about art become a part of the art itself. Contrasts this approach of Pasternak against that of Thomas Mann. Sees Pasternak's ideas reflected in quotes from the young Yuri on his literary goals and compares them to passages in *An Essay in Autobiography*. Notes that Zhivago does not fear death or anything else; the answer to death is to create beauty. Mentions influences on Pasternak, including Proust, and Pasternak's preference for Pushkin and Chekhov over Tolstoy and Dostoevsky. Discusses Pasternak's affinity with Blok.

63 ROUGEMONT, DENIS DE. "Nouvelles métamorphoses de Tristan." *Preuves*, no. 96, pp. 14–27.

Labels *Doctor Zhivago* an "amour passion" novel in which a Tristan prototype is a "dominating figure." Also sees all features of the Tristan legend adopted in the Zhivago-Lara love story. Points out similarities between Pasternak and Zhivago—Pasternak's decision not to emigrate and Zhivago's staying in Moscow after his family has gone abroad, for example. Insists that *Doctor Zhivago* is one of the last "love-as-passion" novels based on the Tristan archetype. Attributes the social and political conditions under which *Doctor Zhivago* was written to this inherent passion. Creates a "resume" that Pasternak might offer, including his "passionate" love for Russia, and his desire to "keep silent" in order to remain with Russia during the threat of exile. Translated: 1959.64; 1963.16.

64 ———. "Tristans neue Gestalt. Dr. Schiwago, Lolita und der Mann ohne Eigenschaften." *Monat* 11, no. 127: 9–21.
Translation of 1959.63.

65 RUGE, GERD. "The Other Russia." In *Boris Pasternak*, edited by K.K. Sinha. Calcutta: Congress For Cultural Freedom, pp. 53–63.
Reprint of 1958.62.

66 SIMMONS, ERNEST J. "Pasternak in the First Person." *VQR* 35 (Summer): 493–97.
Describes Pasternak's second autobiography (translates as *I Remember*) as "only partially successful" in achieving its stated goal of showing how Pasternak's life was "transmitted into art." Its contents are

outlined, with particular attention devoted to Pasternak's "obsession" with Mayakovsky and his "frank and courageous criticisms of the purge years." Compares *I Remember* unfavorably to *A Safe Conduct,* which is seen as richer, less fragmentary, and more evocative.

67   SINHA, K.K., ed. *Boris Pasternak.* Calcutta: Congress For Cultural Freedom, 148 pp.

A collection of previously published notes, articles, essays, and letters. In addition to 1959.25, 1959.48, and 1958.65, it includes notes by Buddhadeva Bose ("Zhivago's Poems: A Note on Boris Pasternak"), Francois Bondy ("Dr. Zhivago and the Literary Commisar"), Alberto Moravia ("Thoughts on Boris Pasternak"), Sibnarayan Ray ("The Creative Artist in a Totalitarian State"), Adib ("The Horror of It"), Ignazio Silone ("Will Survive All Polemics"), Victor Zorza ("Tortured History of the Revolution"), Leopold Labedz ("An Old Argument"), Jacques Croise ("Pasternak's Literary Works"), and A.M. Williams ("The Faust of Modern Society"). It also presents extracts from editorials (*New Statesman, Novy mir,* the *Manchester Guardian*), and discussions and statements by Indian and other writers (Sholokhov, among others).

68   SLONIM, MARC. *"Doctor Zhivago* and *Lolita." ILA* 2: 213–25.

Notes the controversy surrounding *Doctor Zhivago* and *Lolita,* and attributes much of *Doctor Zhivago*'s popularity to that controversy. Strongly argues that comparisons with *War and Peace* are misleading because *Doctor Zhivago* is supposed to be vastly different from the "river-like" quality of *War and Peace.* Comments on Pasternak's use of Christianity. Sees Zhivago's poems as "stanzas of love, nature, and passion."

69   STEPUN, FEDOR. "B.L. Pasternak" (in Russian). *NZh,* no. 56, pp. 187–206.

Questions Pasternak's belonging to literary movements, arguing that one can speak of Pasternak's inner ties to symbolism and of his closeness to futurism, and that readers unversed in symbolism cannot accept the form of *Doctor Zhivago* because they find its characters vague. Also argues that it is impermissible to identify Zhivago with Pasternak, and that *Doctor Zhivago* differs from the classical Russian novel in its characters' lack of plasticity and interconnectedness. Believes mutual contact among characters outside of the psychological plane and the portrayal of the novel's hero within the world-changing events are the most characteristic features of *Doctor Zhivago.* Cites a passage to illustrate this point. Reprinted: 1962.25; 1990.69. Translated: 1959.70; 1978.38.

70   ———. "Boris Leonidowitsch Pasternak. Der 'Fall' Pasternak." *NeuR* 70, no. 1: 145–61.

Translation of 1959.69.

71 STERN, RICHARD D. *"Doctor Zhivago* as a Novel." *KR* 21: 154–60.
      Criticizes *Doctor Zhivago* as a diffuse, confusing accretion of char-
acters and incidents, a failed attempt to follow Tolstoy and Stendhal.
Among the several "narrative sins" listed with examples from the text are
unsignalled transitions, coincidences, lack of proper sequence, and an
"intolerable profusion of simile and metaphor." Sums up the novel as a
"melancholy event" that fails to live up to its subject matter and the
expectations of many who awaited its appearance.

72 STEUSSY, R.E. "The Myth Behind *Dr. Zhivago.*" *RR* 18: 184–98.
      Unveils a complex of allegorical associations borne by each major
character in the novel, centering on the "myth of the inevitability of the
Revolution" on which the novel is supposedly built. Argues that the key
to the allegory is the character of Yevgraf, whose fragmentary, mysterious, and materially insubstantial role makes him a symbol of "cultural
Eurasia," the triumphant unknown quantity of Russia's destiny.
Komarovsky is seen as the embodiment of the degradation and evil of
the old Russian Empire; Lara is said to represent an idealized form of
the Revolution, with Antipov as the embodiment of its failure in practice; and Zhivago is seen as a representative of "Pasternak's own
Europeanized culture."

73 TARASOVA, N. "Ideinoe i religioznoe soderzhanie *Doktora Zhivago*"
[The ideological and religious content of *Doctor Zhivago*]. *ND*, no. 1, pp.
21–32.
      A general commentary on *Doctor Zhivago.* Compares the novel to
Chekhov and Tolstoy (for its "stylistic simplicity"), Pushkin (its "bright
purity"), and Dostoevsky (its "religious feeling"). Classifies the novel's
characters (Zhivago, Sima Tuntseva, and Vedenyapin, for example), and
discusses Zhivago's views of art, his place in the world, his attitude
toward Lara and Tonya, his belief in Christ, and his fortitude ("Not a single disease of our century was capable to overpower . . . Zhivago").

74 TSCHIŽEWSKIJ, DMITRIJ. "Nobelpreis für Literatur." *RC* 11, no. 25:
12–19.
      Records in detail misconceptions surrounding the "Pasternak
Affair" (carried out in the press in Germany, Israel, and Spain). Points out
errors concerning Pasternak himself, such as identification of Zhivago
with Pasternak, and parallels of Pasternak to many writers with whom
Pasternak had no close affinity. Underlines that Pasternak had received
the Nobel Prize for his poetry, even though his prose had been mentioned
as meritorious. Outlines Pasternak's literary career, centering on the early
period. Notes Pasternak's association with futurism, mentioning that
Pasternak inherited his novelty of rhymes from futurism, and that he had
been closely associated with Mayakovsky. Also mentions that Pasternak,
in his innovation of metaphor, stood out among futurists, and elaborates

in detail on Pasternak's poetics of metaphor. Concludes that Pasternak is first of all a thinker, and that his system of thinking is very "entangled." This concept is seen as a reason why a "living individual" stands in the center in Pasternak's works—not "people" or a "class." Of Pasternak's translations, *Faust* is singled out as his most remarkable achievement.

75 VICKERY, WALTER. "Symbolism Aside: *Doktor Zhivago*." *SEEJ* 17, no. 4: 343–48.
     Sees *Doctor Zhivago* as first and foremost a "human story," the principle impact and claim to greatness of which derives from the "doings, personalities, loves and fates of the main characters" rather than from the "abstruse and esoteric" realm of symbols. Discusses the parallels between Christ and Zhivago (an "important organizing function" in the novel) and Pasternak's use of coincidence (presented as useful in conveying his notion of the interrelatedness of all things).

76 WAGNER, GEOFFREY. "Notes on *Doctor Zhivago*." *CJF* 17: 157–61.
     Examines *Doctor Zhivago*'s stylistic inconsistencies. Pasternak is seen as mixing "careful realism" in the novel's first half with a philosophical-poetic treatment in the second, resorting to "old-fashioned tricks" such as premonition and coincidence. Maintains that far from "creating its own form," *Doctor Zhivago* is deliberately inconsistent. Believes that its coincidences, disparities, and detail create a sense of mystery and cosmic destiny.

77 WASIOLEK, EDWARD. "Review of *Doctor Zhivago*." *CR* 13, no. 1: 77–83.
     Calls *Doctor Zhivago* "a great book" only in terms of its author's "literary courage," while as a novel it is judged "almost mediocre." Argues that the novel is charged with looseness, clumsiness, incoherence, and failure to "dramatize what are essentially poetic utterances." Regards the Revolution as "the novel's central event."

78 WILSON, EDMUND. "Legend and Symbol in *Doctor Zhivago*." *Encounter* 12, no. 69: 5–16.
     Reprint of 1959.79. Revised and reprinted: 1965.8.

79 ———. "Legend and Symbol in *Doctor Zhivago*." *Nation* 188, no. 17 (25 April): 363–73.
     Notes parallels and symbols in *Doctor Zhivago* ("they lie at the center of the meaning of the book"), discussing also the meaning of the hero's name ("the Russian name Yury is a form of George, and a reference to the legend of St. George"). Argues that Zhivago is a "composite of all the characters who had influenced his childhood and youth," and that Zhivago represents the thinking and idealistic part of Russian society before and after the Revolution. Elaborates on the role of Yevgraf

("Evgraf in the Russian calendar means *writer*") and on the heroine's name ("Larisa means sea gull, sea bird"), which he links to wind ("because it is life's storm that casts Lara and Zhivago together"). Surveys Stalin's treatment of Pasternak, suggesting that Pasternak enjoyed "unique immunity." Cites numerous references to illustrate his arguments and constantly resorts to other Pasternak criticism. Explains the symbolism of the billboard signs ("Moreau and Vetchinkin. *Seeders. Threshers*") as being "very much in the manner of Joyce" and concludes that symbols and parallels are very important ("the whole story is organized around them"). Reprinted: 1959.78.

80 WINTER, HANNS. "Boris Pasternak: *Dr. Schiwago.*" *WZ* 5, no. 1: 9–15.
    Explains the novel as a "story of the living." Concludes that the novel describes "a man living for himself"; an apolitical man who is, however, conscious of history; a man who is patient, religious, and who "participates in his community." Also concludes that Zhivago's counterpart is representative of the Russian intelligentsia, which was then, as well as during the tsarist time, sensitive to the ideas of Russia. Defines Lara as an embodiment of "the Russian martyr."

81 ZANDER, L.A. "Filosofskie temy v romane Pasternaka *Doktor Zhivago*" [Philosophical themes in Pasternak's novel *Doctor Zhivago*]. *VRSKhD*, no. 52, pp. 36–44; and no. 53, pp. 37–48.
    Regards criticism of *Doctor Zhivago* as a social novel as one-sided because the main theme of the novel exists on a philosophical plane. Singles out destiny as a primary theme ("a part of that atmosphere in which biography and history are developed"), while the beauty and femininity theme occupies a secondary position. Discusses the latter theme in the context of Dostoevsky's and Solovyev's concepts of beauty.

1960

1 ALEKSANDROVA, VERA. "Po literaturnym adresam poeta" [Following the poet's literary addresses]. *VP*, no. 1, pp. 118–34.
    Mentions poets and writers seen as having influenced Pasternak: Shakespeare, Rilke, Kleist, Verlaine, Byron, Edgar Allan Poe, and Gogol. Discusses Pasternak's affinity with Rilke. Also mentions poets who have enriched Pasternak's works (Pushkin, Fet, Goethe, and Tyutchev). Concludes that the "roots of Pasternak's talent have deeply and widely made way into the soil of the world and Russian literature."

2 ANATOL'EVA, N. Introduction to *Poeziia. Izbrannoe* (in Russian). Frankfurt am Main: Posev, pp. 7–51.
    Describes and reflects upon the lifelong "dreams" of Pasternak's personal and artistic development, drawing upon the two autobiogra-

phies, critical prose and verse, *Doctor Zhivago,* and the writings of Pasternak's contemporaries such as Ehrenburg, Tsvetaeva, and Bryusov. Traces Pasternak's early encounters with music and philosophy to his early verse, seen as suffused with the theme of loss and searching. Emphasizes the inseparability of Pasternak's life and his poetry, as well as the fundamental unity of Pasternak's body of work throughout all periods of his career. Finds the motifs of chance encounters with personally familiar places or people to permeate all of the poet's work. Analyzes the wellsprings of Pasternak's freshness of vision and renewal of poetic language. Discusses the symbolism of such recurring Pasternakian images as the city, changes of the seasons, and snow. Finds Pasternak's love poetry to be unsurpassed, owing to his deep feelings of wonderment and tenderness toward women. Treats the significance of the Caucasus and the Urals in his work. Follows the evolution of Pasternak's relationship with Mayakovsky. Defends Pasternak against the charge that he wrote too little during the war years 1941–1945, tracing the theme of the *podvig* (deed) from his work of that period. Follows the *podvig* theme as it evolves from wartime grieving and martyrdom into the purposeful, optimistic expectancy of Pasternak's later work. Concludes that Pasternak's entire life and body of work are a victory of spirit over material chaos.

3   ANSTEI, O. "Novyi Pasternak" [A new Pasternak]. *Grani,* no. 45, pp. 101–9.

Mentions Pasternak's maxim, "The Almighty God of Details," and concludes that Pasternak realized that he has "to place the entire world on one page." Believes that the word "entire" is a novelty to Pasternak, because he went through a tedious emotional experience "to arrive at the very essence of the matter." Notes that nature has always been alive in Pasternak's poetry, but Pasternak "has found a new God in it." Concludes that the poem "You Meant All My Fate" is directed to Christ and that any changes that occured in Pasternak should be looked upon as a result of his new interpretation of the Christ figure.

4   CARLISLE, OLGA. "Three Visits with Boris Pasternak." *PaR* 6, no. 24: 45–69.

A recollection of her three visits to Pasternak in Peredelkino. Mentions Pasternak's views on literature and writers: Mayakovsky, Esenin, Tsvetaeva, Akhmatova, Bely, Hemingway, Nietzsche, Berdyaev. Recounts a fragment of *Blind Beauty*—an unfinished play of Pasternak's. Reprinted: 1963.4–5. Translated: 1961.5; 1988.20.

5   CHAKRAVARTY, AMIYA. "Pasternak: Poet of Humanity." *CC* 77 (6 July): 803–4.

A recollection of the interview with Pasternak on 28 December 1959. Claims that Pasternak "was anguished at thoughts of how his novel, *Doctor Zhivago,* had been made a tool in the cold war," that there were many reasons for his refusal of the Nobel Prize, and that "outside dictation" was not the reason. Relates that Pasternak acknowledged his work has similarities to Rimbaud, Rilke, and the symbolists, that Pasternak insisted "he had no philosophy of art except that gained from stark experience," and that Doctor Zhivago "was written 'with his heart's blood.'" Claims that Pasternak said he could not have endured the "agony of his age" without "'my discovery of Jesus, the Christ.' And he added: 'He came to me.'" Reprinted: 1962.7.

6 CRANKSHAW, EDWARD. *"Doktor Schiwago* und der Brief der *Nowy Mir."* In *Russland und Chruschschow.* Berlin: Colloquim Verlag, pp. 175–207.
   Translation of 1959.11.

7 DINFREVILLE, JACQUES. "La guerre de partisans dans le *Docteur Jivago." RDN,* n.s. 16, no. 1 (January): 40–50.
   An appreciation of the portrayal of partisans and guerrilla warfare in *Doctor Zhivago.* Praises Pasternak's treatment of the partisans: their prosecution of the war matches general Russian geostrategy; the characterization of the partisan leaders is true-to-life; the partisan army is heterogenous in makeup; the partisan bands receive little material support from a central authority; the partisans retain a cohesive framework throughout the war; and the partisans conduct their operations in locations favorable to guerrillas. Adds that just as partisans and their leaders are portrayed to live by a natural order, so is Zhivago bound by things he cannot change, and thus loses Lara to Komarovsky.

8 FITCH, ROBERT E. "The Sickness of an Affluent Society." *RIL* 29: 608–14.
   Sees the theology of *Doctor Zhivago* as bounded on pathos and self-pity, evidenced in the identification of Christ with Hamlet (and of Zhivago with both), and in the "truncated humanism" and lack of personality of the novel's characters. The novel is likened to Archibald MacLeish's *J.B.* insofar as they are the products of affluent societies. The use of the concept of theology based in pity is seen as indicative of a general trend away from the courageous, active theology of the prophets to a Job-like "naivete" concerning suffering and pain in life.

9 FORD, R.A.D. Review of *The Poetry of Boris Pasternak, 1917–1959.* Translated by George Reavey. *QQ* 67: 673–77.
   Discusses Pasternak's contemporaries in the "submerged literary treasure" of twentieth-century Russian poetry; the poetic, rather than prosaic, nature of his art; and the imagery and religious quality of the Zhivago poems.

10 GIBIAN, GEORGE. "The Climax with *Doctor Zhivago*." In *Interval of Freedom*. Minneapolis: University of Minnesota Press, pp. 145–58.

Outlines the unusual circumstances behind the appearance of *Doctor Zhivago* and *I Remember*, focusing on political considerations. The "far-reaching individualism" of *Doctor Zhivago* is seen as anathema to the Soviet regime and revelatory of the extent of its moral classes. Discusses Pasternak's judgements of his fellow writers and his own role as a poet as set forth in *I Remember*. Concludes with an outline of Pasternak's troubles with the Soviet regime, concentrating on the "central" role of *Doctor Zhivago* in the controversy and the novel's importance to world literature.

11 GRIGOR'EV, DMITRII. "Pasternak i Dostoevskii" [Pasternak and Dostoevsky]. *VM*, no. 2, pp. 79–87.

Translation of 1959.24. Reprint of 1960.12.

12 ———. "Pasternak i Dostoevskii" [Pasternak and Dostoevsky]. *VRSKhD*, no. 57, pp. 44–51.

Translation of 1959.24. Reprinted: 1960.11.

13 GUPTA, NOLINI KANTA. "Boris Pasternak. An Indian Viewpoint." *RR* 19: 248–53.

Acknowledges several aspects of Pasternak's personal philosophy as reflected in *Doctor Zhivago*. Describes Pasternak's three "articles of faith" as a "unanimist" perception that the world is one, a belief in dynamism and progress, and dedication to freedom of the individual. Relates sensitivity and suffering in terms of an "inner divinity" and "outer calvary." Believes that Pasternak's depiction of "the flow of existence" is exemplified by his descriptions of nature.

14 HAHN, KARL JOSEF. "Boris Pasternak. Die neue Freiheit und das Pfeifen der Traurigkeit." *Hochland* 52: 325–38.

Sees *Doctor Zhivago* as Pasternak's "life work," in which Pasternak treats diametrically opposed themes: the role of the individual, Christianity, and the Revolution, for example. States that Pasternak's condemnation of the Revolution stems from his affiliation with the "literary-aesthetic world of the turn of the century."

15 HECHT, ANTHONY. Review of Pasternak's *Poems*. Translated by E.M. Kayden. *HR* 13: 131–38.

While noting those qualities of Pasternak's poetry that show through Kayden's translation—its concreteness and density, its thematic interweaving of life, history, and art—criticizes Kayden's overly solemn tone, confusing syntax, and cumbersome inversions and additions. Three stanzas of "So Be It," in both Kayden's and C.M.

Bowra's translations, are printed side-by-side and compared with each other.

16   JACKSON, ROBERT L. *"Doktor Živago* and the Living Tradition." *SEEJ* 4, no. 2: 103–18.

Addresses areas of continuity and contrast between *Doctor Zhivago* and its predecessors in the "tapestry of Russian literature and thought," mainly Tolstoy's *War and Peace* but also works of Dostoevsky, Blok, and Pushkin. The "centripetal" nature of the upheaval of 1812 is contrasted with the "centrifugal" period of 1917; the two novels produced by those periods (*War and Peace* and *Doctor Zhivago*, respectively) are seen to share the concerns of societal cleavage, family, tradition, and the destiny of Russia, with the difference that the world of *War and Peace* is the "lost center" of *Doctor Zhivago,* due to the "crisis of Russian culture" brought on by the Revolution. Contrasts Zhivago's period of captivity with Pierre's wartime experiences, demonstrating that Zhivago's captivity exemplifies the retreat into self that came to replace communal identification among the Russian intelligentsia. Lara and Natasha Rostova are seen to represent the same process of dislocation, though only in the sphere of family life. Asserts that the line of "degeneration and ultimate resurrection" associated with the Revolution in *Doctor Zhivago* echoes the theme of Blok's *Retribution.* Reprinted: 1978.23.

17   KAUCHTSCHISCHWILI, NINA M. "L'arte di Boris Pasternak." *Aevum* 34: 234–52.

A commentary on Pasternak's poetics and his views on art. Discusses Pasternak's infatuation with music, and attributes that infatuation to Verlaine's influence ("Tutta la poesia di Pasternàk sembra essere dominata dal verso di Verlaine: 'De la musique avant toute chose'"). Cites *The Year 1905*, in which "acoustical and optical impressions overlap." Notes the use of color and cites "The Golden Autumn," in which "everything is painted with different hues of gold," making the poem resemble one of van Gogh's paintings. Discusses Pasternak's translations, those of Georgian poets in particular, and concludes that Pasternak's later poetry was influenced by his experience as a translator. Compares Pasternak's influence of poetry on prose to that of Baudelaire's (his *Petits poèmes en prose*). Concludes that Pasternak's art is life, and that Pasternak "takes everything that is common and transforms it into art."

18   KAZIN, ALFRED. "Pasternak's Wake." *Reporter* 22 (23 June): 37–40.

Contrasts the official Soviet attitude of condemnation, disapproval, or silence toward Pasternak at the time of his death with the sympathetic treatment he recieved from Konstantin Paustovsky at the Soviet Writers' Congress. Quotes Paustovsky's remarks to exemplify his dissatisfaction with the state of Soviet literature and regards them as a "generous homage" to Pasternak.

19   LAMONT, ROSETTE C. "'As a Gift . . .': Zhivago, the Poet." *PMLA* 75: 621–33.

    Offers, from the standpoint that Zhivago's poems hold the key to both Zhivago's and Pasternak's vision of life, a detailed commentary on each of Zhivago's poems, emphasizing the evolving tonal architecture of the cycle, its "harmonic" rather than chronological organization. Maintains that parallel to this development of rhythmic patterns is a seasonal succession of moods and ideas, culminating in the "stately resignation" and "transfiguration" of the lost poems. Traces both of these organizing principles as each poem is described and related to corresponding periods in Zhivago's life. Pays special tribute to religious and philisophical issues, and to varying facets of Pasternak's autobiography expressed in the poems.

20   LEHRMAN, EDGAR H. "A Minority Opinion on *Doctor Zhivago.*" *EUQ* 16: 77–84.

    Summarizes *Doctor Zhivago*. Notes the political reaction to the novel and the publicity it received in the West. Argues that evaluation of the novel rests primarily on an evaluation of its protagonist as a "morally deficient" individual who is compared to Dostoevsky's Raskolnikov. While credited with stimulating political discussion and moving descriptive passages, the novel is seen as marred by obscure language coincidence and lack of organization.

21   MALDONADO DENIS, MANUEL. "Boris Leonid Pasternak (1890–1960)" (in Spanish). *CA* 113, no. 6 (November/December): 210–16.

    Outlines Pasternak's life and his literary career, drawing heavily on his two autobiographies and Pasternak criticism. Singles out two basic themes of *Doctor Zhivago*: death and resurrection. Sees the novel as a multidimensional work, a claim substantiated through character examination.

22   MARCHAND, RENE. "Boris Pasternak" (in Spanish). In *Cuatro maestros de la literatura Rusa*. Cuadernos de la Facultad de Filosofia y Letras, 3. Veracruz: Universidad Veracruzana, pp. 118–55.

    An evaluation of Pasternak's works and an outline of his life. Traces the development of his literary career and mentions influences that contributed to his develpment as a writer. Discusses his prose and poetry and cites profusely from his works, particularly from *The Childhood of Luvers*. Compares Pasternak to Proust—but excludes Proust's "direct influence" on Pasternak. Provides the titles of *Doctor Zhivago*'s poems, and cites "The Miracle" and "The Garden of

Gethsemane" in his own renditions. Discusses the "Pasternak tragedy" (dubbed the "tragedy of Russian history") against the background of the Soviet system.

23 MARKOV, V. "Sovetskii Gamlet" [A Soviet Hamlet]. *Grani,* no. 45, pp. 119–24.

Contends that in Pasternak's translation of the monologue "To Be or Not to Be" one is bewildered by the discrepancy between the translation and the original. Concludes that Pasternak's translation "was a sort of inner immigration" and the most significant of his translations is *Faust.* Argues that Pasternak gave particular meanings to many words in his translation of *Hamlet,* and that these meanings are achieved through "the accent arrangements" Pasternak conveys to his translations. Also argues that in Pasternak's translations one reads the "description of his own fate, his polemics with the authorities, and his interaction with the contemporary life."

24 MERTON, THOMAS. "L'affare Pasternak in prospettiva." *Humanitas* 15, no. 1: 97–118; and no. 3: 184–97.

Translation of 1959.44.

25 ———. "The Pasternak Affair." In *Disputed Questions.* New York: Farrar, Straus & Cudahy, pp. 3–67. Reprint. London: Hollis & Carter, 1961. Reprint. New York: New American Library, 1965.

Reprint of 1959.44.

26 ———. "Postscript to 'The Pasternak Affair.'" In *Disputed Questions.* New York: Farrar, Straus & Cudahy, pp. 291–94. Reprint. London: Hollis & Carter, 1961. Reprint. New York: New American Library, 1965.

Relates events surrounding his correspondence with Pasternak after the "Pasternak Affair." Mentions Pasternak's illness and his struggle with it: "as early as November 1959, Pasternak himself was aware that he was gravely ill and was expecting to die." Comments that Pasternak's letter to him dated 7 February 1960 reflected "the titanic inner struggle which the poet was waging to keep his head above water." Includes this letter (written in English).

27 MONDRONE, DOMENICO. "La mortificata irriducibile umanità di Boris Pasternak." *CiC* 3, no. 1: 358–70.

An overview of Pasternak's poetic, political, and religious views. Emphasizes that Pasternak never "completely embraced" the ideals of the Revolution, which he looked upon as something "inevitable, but not necessarily positive." Also examines Pasternak's views of artistic freedom as displayed in his poetry and in his abandonment of LEF. Surveys Pasternak's poetry with religious themes, concluding that they do not fully attest to Pasternak's personal religious feelings.

28 POGGIOLI, RENATO. "Boris Pasternak: The Case of *Doctor Zhivago.*" In *The Poets of Russia 1890–1930.* Cambridge, MA: Harvard University Press, pp. 329–39.

Discusses various aspects of *Doctor Zhivago*'s significance as a "moral act and psychological document of great value." The novel's antihistorical message, contrasted with *War and Peace*, is seen to emphasize "I" over "we," the individual over the family or national unit. Sees the novel as a culminating point in a process of increasing engagement in moral obligations, both an apology and a defense of the "stubborn retreat of the spirit" found in Pasternak's work and practiced by Zhivago.

29 RANNIT, ALEKSIS. "The Rhythm of Pasternak. Part II. Poet in Search of his Place 1924–1936." *BNYPL* 64, no. 8 (August): 437–49.

A continuation of 1959.57. Offers fragmented observations of *High Malady, The Year 1905, Lieutenant Schmidt, Spektorsky, Second Birth*, Pasternak's place in Soviet poetry, and his relationship to his father. Sees *High Malady* as an attempt to construct "an ideological alliance between himself and contemporary Russia" and points out its "freshness of texture, the alliteration, the changes from poignant to rounder, cooler rhymes and assonances." All three tales in verse are deemed to express Pasternak's "northern mysticism" and to be void of "overriding supremacy of metaphor seen in his earlier works," though *Spektorsky* is also seen as "Pasternak's last demonstration of the full richness of his rhapsodic, ornamental, spectrally interwoven manneristic diction." Views *Second Birth* "as an example of his own kind of classical romanticism," a collection in which "Pasternak touches on socialist themes." Strongly argues against the view that Pasternak is "the greatest Russian poet since Blok," believing him to be "only *one* of the *three* great Soviet Russian poets" —together with Akhmatova and Mandelstam. Concludes that Pasternak was "the direct opposite of his father" and "opposed to any kind of egocentric philosophy." Includes the speech ("hitherto unpublished in English") Pasternak delivered at the First Soviet Writers' Congress in 1934.

30 REEVE, F.D. "*Doctor Zhivago*: From Prose to Verse." *KR* 22, no. 1: 123–36.

Observes that the Zhivago poems are an "integral part of the novel." Each poem is seen as Zhivago's "effort to transfix the beauty and the meaning of life's fluctuations" and the "idea of life in two aspects: life incarnate in an archetype personality and life as sacrifice." Notes that the "poems become the symbol—hopefully, the harbinger—of the world to come." Sees the novel as a completion of both Zhivago's poems and Pasternak's own poetry. Argues that the poems are "carefully organized" and "musically efficient," with an extension of imagery from

Pasternak's earlier poems. Also notes that the poems embody a consciousness of form that "holds the world together," turning depersonalization into the revelation of the Divine. Illustrates the poems' emotional context and expression of universal values with many quotes. Reprinted: 1966.17; 1967.13.

31 REXINE, JOHN E. "In Memoriam. The Spiritual Challenge of Boris Pasternak." *SVSQ* 4, no. 4: 20–25.
    A memorial to Pasternak after his death; strongly emphasizes Pasternak's Christian beliefs ("Pasternak was a Christian artist . . . an Orthodox convert of Jewish descent") and cites examples from *Doctor Zhivago* to illustrate Pasternak as a "faithful Orthodox believer." Argues that too much critical attention has been paid to the political controversy of *Doctor Zhivago* and not enough to its true focus, "Christian love and faith, truth and immortality." Concludes that Pasternak's "whole life and philosophy were a meditation on death and resurrection" and that he "never visualized death in the everyday sense of the word. He saw only immortality of life."

32 ROWLAND, MARY and PAUL. "Larisa Fedorovna: From Another World." *KR* 22: 493–501.
    Centers on the allegorical-historical treatment of the character of Lara, i.e., on Lara as namesake of the household god Lar in Roman mythology and the various forms of the name. Pasternak's association of Lara with the countryside, the sea, and the crossroads, in addition to textual clues and hints, establishes and reinforces this identification. Cites Lara's "multiple roles" as heroine, the Eastern Orthodox St. Lara, and Mary Magdelene. These associations and their historical and religious dimensions are seen to converge into an "eidolon of Russia"—Lara as the embodiment of her country's spirit on various levels. Reprinted in 1967.14.

33 RZHEVSKII, L. "O 'tainopisi v romane *Doktor Zhivago*" [On cryptography in *Doctor Zhivago*]. *Grani*, no. 48, pp. 150–64.
    Believes language analysis reveals that the novel's "dualism of style" is identical to the "dualism" of Pasternak's poetics, which combines traditionally realistic elements with a system "of figurative expressions and the non-realistic 'out.'" Expounds that "out" styles are symbolic in their nature (like the symbol of a burning candle) and that they bristle with "Blok associations" and "shadows." Argues that the image of the author is already reflected in this "dualism of styles." Sees the novel's poetry as a "deepening of the author's monologue in which authorial and Zhivagoian elements inseparably are flown together." Concludes that in the poetry section the image-symbol becomes "the image-cipher," and in this way "the form of the creative self-revelation creates a form of coding." Reprinted as chapter 6 in: 1962.23.

34 ŠAJKOVIĆ, MIRIAM TAYLOR. "Notes on Boris Pasternak's *Doctor Živago.*" *SEEJ* 4, no. 4: 319–30.

Regards Zhivago's chapter-by-chapter development as a passage from his youthful, idealistic formulation of immortality as memory in others to a higher sense of spiritual communication founded upon love. These two stages are seen to reflect Zhivago's evolving attitude toward the Revolution as well as an evolution in literary affinities from the restlessness of Gogol, Tolstoy, and Dostoevsky to the "childlike quality" of Pushkin and Chekhov. Discusses the growing importance of nature and religion in this transformation. Sees Pasternak's artistic method as three-fold, combining Tolstoy's epic structure, the symbolist poetics of metaphor and simile, and the polyphonic method of Dostoevsky.

35 SIMMONS, ERNEST J. "Boris Pasternak." *Nation* 190 (11 June): 503.

Eulogizes Pasternak, noting that the Soviet press was "almost silent on the occasion of his death." Notes that "political considerations appear to have been the primary criteria for artistic judgement of his novel" in the West and argues that "despite artistic lapses, *Doctor Zhivago* did revive the noble tradition of the Russian past that literature is the conscience of the nation." Foresees that the name Boris Pasternak will proudly be listed "as perhaps the greatest poet of the first incredible forty years of the existence of their country."

36 STRACHEY, JOHN. "The Strangled Cry." *Encounter* 15: 3–18, 23–37.

Analyzes the novel as a "simple but subversive" story of love between both Zhivago and Lara and Zhivago and his art. Discusses Pasternak's views on aesthetics and inspiration as well as his "humanist" interpretation of the Gospels, which is "richer than other such contemporary attempts" at making a religious statement. Pasternak's attitude toward the Revolution is "comprehension, but not acceptance," a "measured rejection." This attitude, along with the novel's basic apathy toward politics, is valued as the cause for Soviet alarm over the novel's publication, a reaction that is "pitiable." Discusses the possibilities for Pasternak's message to find a receptive audience and catalyze meaningful change in the prevailing materialist, totalitarian Soviet order. Reprinted: 1962.26.

37 STRUVE, GLEB. "Iz zametok o masterstve Borisa Pasternaka. Koechto ob ego rifmakh." [Notes on Boris Pasternak's craft. Something on his rhymes]. *VP*, no. 1, pp. 88–117.

Briefly surveys criticism of Pasternak's poetics and centers on the innovations of rhymes. Singles out past-tense verbal adverb rhymes as "a characteristic feature of Pasternakian rhymes" and provides examples from Pasternak's poetry. Traces other forms of rhymes—"grammatical

... verbal, and adjectival"—that are seen as preferred rhymes after Pasternak turned toward "formal simplicity" in 1940. Provides statistical data of various rhymes Pasternak used. Discusses "chain rhymes" and concludes that one finds "unusual richness and diversity" of rhymes in Pasternak's poetry.

38 SUNDGREN, NILS P. "Samtal med Pasternak" [Conversation with Pasternak]. *BLM* 29, no. 3: 210–15.

Recounts his visit to Pasternak in Peredelkino in January of 1960. Records Pasternak discussing aesthetic and philosophic topics in *Doctor Zhivago*, and gives reasons why Pasternak preferred writing broad epic and dramatic works. Relates Pasternak's reaction to Western criticism of *Doctor Zhivago* (views of Edmund Wilson's two Pasternak critiques). Cites Pasternak's perceptions of many writers, including Flaubert, Goncourt, Jacobsen (particularly his *Niels Lyhne*), Bang, Thomas Mann, and Rilke. Also mentions Pasternak's views of Chekhov, Turgenev, Balzac, Dostoevsky, and Stendahl (particularly his *Red and Black*, which is discussed in detail).

39 ULMER, JOSEF. "Boris Pasternaks Roman *Doktor Schiwago* ist auch ein religiöses Buch. Eine Besprechung." *Sammlung* 15: 1–11.

Suggests that one should not use a "Western" yardstick when assessing *Doctor Zhivago* and its religious and politcal aspects, but rather should evaluate the novel in relation to Greek Orthodox Christianity, with its "essential" virtue of "patient suffering" and the acceptance of evil without resisting it. Points out how "Christianity through the entire novel experiences undiminished respect." Notes that the revolutionary upheaval had been portrayed in the novel in a "Christian and eschatological" manner.

40 URBANSKI, EDMUND STEPHEN. "Novelas revolucionarias de Gironella y Pasternak." *USC* 51 (May–August): 99–105.

Juxtaposes *Doctor Zhivago* to José María Gironella's *Los Cipreses Creen en Dios* and finds features common to both works: a hatred of wars and revolutions, the character portrayal ("only loosely connected by the central figures"), and their treatment of religion. Offers additional observations on *Doctor Zhivago*'s style ("the frequent usage of metaphors and symbolism reveals Pasternak as a seasoned writer"), language ("uses the rich Russian colloquialism"), and structure ("has many loosely connected chapters and some unconvincingly presented personages which do not make the narrative congruous"). Translated: 1960.41.

41 ———. "Revolutionary Novels of Gironella and Pasternak." *Hispania* 43: 191–97.

Translation of 1960.40.

42 VISHNIAK, MARK. "Chelovek v istorii" [Man in history]. *VP,* no. 1, pp. 180–99.

  Argues that Pasternak's relationship with history is inwardly connected with an orthodox religious perception of the world, and that Pasternak follows Vladimir Solovyev. Observes that Pasternak remains alien to a tragic worldview and that he sings a hymn to life. States that Pasternak's attitude toward nature and man is akin to that of Tolstoy and characterizes both of them as possessing a combination of "pedantry" with a "free artistic creativity."

43 WINTER, HANNS. "Boris Pasternak." *WZ,* no. 7, pp. 46–47.

  Eulogizes Pasternak and provides a brief background sketch of his life. Mentions Pasternak's untranslatable poetry and some of his major collections. Also mentions Pasternak's relationship to Blok, Mayakovsky, and Gorky. Asserts that Pasternak had been able to create only within a "Russian world," concluding that within this "Russian world," Pasternak had written "in a Western spirit." Also concludes that Pasternak had fought for freedom of all people, the inviolability of the person, and belief in God.

44 ZAVALISHIN, V. "Boris Pasternak i russkaia literatura" [Boris Pasternak and Russian literature]. *Grani,* no. 45, pp. 110–18.

  Maintains that the influence of Russian literature on Pasternak is more significant in his later period. Draws parallels of influence with Chekhov and Blok. Points out similarities between the death of Zhivago and the death of Kovrin in Chekhov's *Black Monk* and between the image of Lara and that of Zarechnaya in Chekhov's *The Seagull.* Outlines the main points of similarity between Pasternak's and Blok's poetry, and the reflection of Blok's musicality and rhythm in Pasternak. Draws attention to the influence of Blok's prose on *Doctor Zhivago,* particularly Blok's tale *Neither Dreams Nor Reality.* Concludes that similarity between prosaic experiments of Blok and Pasternak's novel reminds one of the similarity between "a sketch and big canvas painted on the basis of these sketches."

1961

1 AUCOUTURIER, MICHEL. "L'image dans poésie de Pasternak." *RES* 38: 45–49.

  Examines Pasternak's similes and metaphors, claiming that their purpose is to clarify internal resonances rather than to describe isolated details, or to express concomitant circumstances rather than similarities. Observes that in many cases these similes are not accessories or ornaments for the poet but the very subject of a given poem, and that sensations take precedence over verbal understanding for the reader. Cites examples from *Above the Barriers*, *Themes and Variations*, and *My Sister, Life.*

2   BAIRD, SISTER MARY JULIAN. "The Lonely Greatness of Boris Pasternak." *Today* 16 (June): 34–35.

Focuses on some of Pasternak's Christian-like features—love of life, love of God, love of man, and joy of life, among others—as reflected in Pasternak and his writings. Mentions Pasternak's esteem for Tolstoy, from whom he learned "that God is love—and where love is, there is God." Offers comments on Pasternak's tale *The Last Summer*, some of his poetry, and on *Doctor Zhivago*, the poetry of which is "integral to the novel, not merely supplementary." Outlines the major events in Pasternak's life, culminating with a brief description of his funeral: "they came to his funeral from far and near, the rich and the poor—carrying to his coffin the wild flowers he loved."

3   ———. "Pasternak's Zhivago-Hamlet-Christ." *Renascence* 14: 179–84.

Traces the Christocentric symbolism of the poems of Yury Zhivago, from Hamlet's frustration and its links to the temptation of Gethsemane to the promise of hope and resurrection that is seen as the inspirational core of both the poems and the novel.

4   BOWMAN, HERBERT E. "Postscript on Pasternak." *Survey*, no. 36, pp. 106–10.

Exhorts readers to "look again at the central meaning" of *Doctor Zhivago*, which has been obscured by political considerations, overly sophisticated literary criticism, and "esoteric symbol-chopping." Sees a love of life and attachment to simple, ordinary human existence, especially in the face of extraordinary upheaval and violence, as the novel's message—its "gift." All other aspects of the novel—its religious, aesthetic, and ethical dimensions, as well as its descriptive passages—are reflections of Pasternak's "refusal to forsake the common earth." Charges that overly sophisticated interpretations of the novel have done the great disservice of "creating an attitude that is unreceptive to the lyrical simplicity of the book's major theme." Reprinted: 1973.1.

5   CARLISLE, OLGA. "Trois visites à Boris Pasternak." *Preuves* 11, no. 121 (March): 3–16.

Translation of 1960.4.

6   CHIBISOVA, L. "Vstrechi s Pasternakom" [Meetings with Pasternak]. *ND*, no. 8, pp. 91–101.

Summarizes Olga Carlisle's "Trois visites à Boris Pasternak" (1961.5), including descriptions of Peredelkino and its atmosphere and excerpts of Pasternak's remarks on various topics, including Leonid

Andreev, Nietzsche, Pasternak's attitude toward his early work, and a detailed outline of Pasternak's planned series of plays set in the period of emancipation.

7   CONQUEST, ROBERT. *Courage and Genius: The Pasternak Affair; A Documentary Report on Its Literary and Political Significance*. London: Collins & Harvill, 191 pp. Reprint. Philadelphia: Lippincott, 1962. Reprint. New York: Octagon Books, 1979.
       A detailed account of the "Pasternak Affair" and its documentary evidence. The first section focuses on many aspects surrounding the controversy regarding the novel, such as Pasternak's intention to publish the novel, general views of the novel, its publication problems, the Nobel Prize awarded to Pasternak, his death, and the role of Ivinskaya. It includes ten chapters, an introduction, and a conclusion. The second section publishes translations of material on the controversy: articles from *Literaturnaia gazeta* and *Pravda*, the resolution of the Union of Soviet Writers to expel Pasternak, Pasternak's letter to Krushchev and to *Pravda*, and radio Moscow's attack on Ivinskaya (21 and 27 January 1961). Contains a bibliography.

8   ———. "The Fate of Olga Ivinskaya." *Encounter* 17, no. 96: 86–92.
       Recounts the various means Soviet authorities used to persecute Olga Ivinskaya both before and after Pasternak's death. Pasternak's forebodings regarding Ivinskaya are seen as justified in the light of events subsequent to his death. Gives an account of radio Moscow's attempt to portray Ivinskaya as a false friend of Pasternak's, bent on misappropriating his royalties, charging her with involvement in illegal currency transfers to the West. Asserts that the authorities were more motivated by the desire to single Ivinskaya out for persecution rather than to impartially enforce the law due to the lack of evidence against her. Claims that the next stage in Ivinskaya's persecution is the authorities' portrayal of her as a bad influence on Pasternak in his later years.

9   DYMSHITS, AL. "Memuary i istoriia" [Memoirs and history]. *Oktiabr'*, no. 6, pp. 194–98.
       Charges Ilya Ehrenburg with selective memory and exaggeration in his depiction of various literary figures, especially Boris Pasternak. Faults Ehrenburg for neglecting Pasternak's wartime works and debt to Mayakovsky. Warns against oversimplifying Pasternak as an aesthete living outside the demands of political and social life.

10   ERENBURG, I. ["B. Pasternak"] (in Russian). *NM*, no. 2, pp. 87–92.
       Recollects his meetings with Pasternak during a period of twenty-four years. Notes that Pasternak named his poetry collection *My Sister, Life* because he lived in harmony with life and that the realism of

Pasternak's poetry is dictated by the poet's nature. Emphasizes that the manuscript of *Doctor Zhivago* was distressing and that it struck one with its lack of artistic truthfulness. Stresses that the "wonderful verse appended to the book throws the spirtiual inexactitude of the prose into relief" and that Pasternak's poetry will never be erased from the earth because it is alive. Reprinted: 1961.11.

11 ———. "Boris Pasternak" (in Russian). In *Liudi, gody, zhizn'*. Moscow: Sovetskii pisatel', pp. 407–20.
     Reprint of 1961.10.

12 GERSCHENKRON, ALEXANDER. "Notes on *Doctor Zhivago*." *MP* 58, no. 3: 194–200.
     Places *Doctor Zhivago* in the "main strain" of nineteenth-century Russian literature by virtue of its "language, central figure, and main theme." Sees the "miracle" of Pasternak's language as a reawakening of the old Russian language. Views the novel's philosophical concern with Russia's historical path and the role of intelligentsia as continuing the Russian literary tradition. Places Zhivago in the line of "superfluous men," though in Pasternak the characterization is said to be a positive one. Concludes with a discussion of philosophical differences with Tolstoy regarding the question of free will. Argues that the novel is a retelling in prose of Blok's poem "Russia, the Poverty-Ridden Russia." Reprinted: 1962.12.

13 GORIÉLY, BENJAMIN. "Pasternak cet inconnu." *Esprit*, no. 708, pp. 40–49.
     A summary of views on Pasternak's poetics of lexica, his affinity with Yazykov, Khlebnikov, Konevskoy, and Aseyev, and on the question of Pasternak's belonging to the school of futurism. Notes Pasternak's propensity for maintaining the "balance" between semantics and rhythm ("the image is created above all by rhythm"), his substitution of "idea with word," and his musicality of lexica. Sees echoes of Yazykov in Pasternak's use of archaisms and archaic accents; cites passages from Yazykov's "Spring Night" and Pasternak's "Marburg" to illustrate similarity in their use of "moon" imagery. Finds an affinity with Khlebnikov in Pasternak's evocation of images through phonetics and in his frequent use of alliteration. Insists that Konevskoy's "influence is more direct," Pasternak "consciously applies" Konevskoy's aesthetics, and that Pasternak and Aseyev have also influenced each other. Rejects the notion of Pasternak belonging to futurism—yet underlines the facts of his association with "Lirika" and "Centrifuge," and his signing of futurists' posters and placards. Briefly discusses *The Childhood of Luvers*, accentuating Pasternak's display of transformation "from the magic world of childhood to the moral world of adults." Translated: 1967.5.

14   JOBET, JULIO CÉSAR. "Pasternak y la realidad literaria soviética." *Combate* 3, no. 18 (September/October): 42–52.

An essay divided into four parts. The first three sections describe the Soviet milieu in which Pasternak lived and worked, and the last part outlines Pasternak's life, including his literary career. Details the Soviet government's policy toward Pasternak during and after the "Pasternak Affair." Discusses *Doctor Zhivago*'s content and the controversy that surrounded the novel.

15   KERNIG, C.D. "*Doctor Zhivago*—An Essay in Interpretation." *MoW* 1: 54–68.

Translation of 1959.31.

16   KHALAFOV, K. "O muzyke stikhov Pasternaka" [On the music of Pasternak's poetry]. *Mosty*, no. 8, pp. 120–29.

Maintains that Pasternak's poetry "stands between poetry and music," and that its musicality is subconscious in nature. Argues that its secret is not in its verse form, but in the very structure of its speech, "in the consonances of its word and rhythm combinations." Offers classification of the melodic devices used by Pasternak, such as repetitions of syllables and/or various sounds, "inversion of the interval," theme developments based on sound repetitions, various forms of rhymes (masculine, assonances, and inward rhymes), and fragmentations of lines. Concludes that the musicality of Pasternak's poetry makes it virtually untranslatable.

17   LOHENBILL, F. "*Dr. Zhivago* and the Russian Revolution." *CI* 11, no. 41: 1–10.

Traces the ideological development of Zhivago step-by-step to "thereby subject Pasternak's attitude to the Revolution to critical evaluation." Finds it "astonishing that Pasternak should show so little political understanding of the circumstances he is capable of describing with so much feeling." Takes Pasternak to task for his criticisms and contradictions toward the Russian revolutionaries: "The Stalin period is, according to him, an unavoidable episode in the unbroken continuity of the progressing revolution." Speculates whether *Doctor Zhivago* will ultimately find a place in Khrushchev's epoch of "enlightened barbarism."

18   MARKOV, VLADIMIR. "An Unnoticed Aspect of Pasternak's Translations." *SlaR* 20: 503–8.

Compares two excerpts from Pasternak's translations (*Hamlet* and *Faust*) with the originals and finds them to contain elaborations and alterations more illustrative of Pasternak's own personality and artistic concerns than the literal sense of the original. Thinks the passages are "lyrical confessions disguised as translations," a variation of "Aesopian language."

19 MUCHNIC, HELEN. "Boris Pasternak and the Poems of Yuri Zhivago." In *From Gorky to Pasternak. Six Writers in Soviet Russia.* New York: Random House, pp. 341–404. Reprint. London: Methuen, 1963.

Defines *Doctor Zhivago* and its poems as a "dramatization of the function of art"; illustrates this definition with several scenes from the novel. Sees the novel as a tissue of interlocking fates and coincidences, a mixture of pagan fate and Christian principle. Argues that continuity in the novel is elliptical, its philosophical approach goes beyond the rational, and that it is an inclusive symbol of life itself. Traces the gradual evolution of Pasternak's concept of life, from his early infatuation with Scriabin, through his experience with unrequited love, to his studies with Cohen. Sums up Pasternak's poetic technique as language composed of interchangeable images expressing the power of feeling. Explores Pasternak's consciousness of relations and connections among phenomena, his sense of the "community of all creation," and emphasizes the continuity of Pasternak's search for symbols of historical power in the epic poems of the 1920s. Contrasts Pasternak's metaphysical approach and its quiet, individual epiphanies with the rational approach of Tolstoy. Believes Pasternak's Kantian, transcendental sense of wonder distinguishes him from his literary predecessors, while his crucial approach to human behavior furthers the main tradition of Russian literature.

20 OBOLENSKY, DIMITRI. "The Poems of Doctor Zhivago." *SEER* 40: 123–35.

Traces the connections between the poems of Zhivago and the rest of the novel in three major thematic areas: nature, love, and the meaning of life. Sees the poems' nature imagery as urban and dynamic, with special emphasis on spring. Views Pasternak's treatment of love as "moving and profound," exploring aspects such as latent passion, union and separation, reverence for the loved one, and destruction potential. The allegory of the poem "Fairy Tale" is considered to link Zhivago's love story with his philosophy of life as sacrifice. Asserts that Zhivago's concern with death and resurrection is exemplified by (though not directly identified with) the passion of Christ. Translated: 1962.21. Reprinted: 1978.32.

21 OTSUP, NIKOLAI. "Venets Pasternaka" [Pasternak's crown]. In *Literaturnye ocherki*. Paris: Imprimerie coopérative étoile, pp. 233–43.

Comments on Pasternak's reaction to the events surrounding the publication of *Doctor Zhivago*. Justifies Pasternak's "repentance," triggered by the publication of *Doctor Zhivago* and expressed in his letter to *Pravda*, in which Pasternak asserted that the novel was "utterly 'in tune' with the building of the U.S.S.R." Also comments on Pasternak's love for Russia ("he is so amalgamated with Russia that he is unable to repudiate it despite its Bolshevik deformities"). Advocates these views with impressions made on him during meetings with Pasternak in Berlin in 1923—"I have decided to break off, he has [pledged] loyalty . . . Even his loyalty was well founded and serious, without a shadow of bitterness and servility." Compares the tragedy of Pasternak with that of Pushkin and cites Lermontov's lines, "Having taken of the former wreath, they have put on him a halo of thorns, wrapped in laurels," as applicable to Pasternak.

22 PAYNE, ROBERT. *The Three Worlds of Boris Pasternak.* New York: Coward-McCann, 228 pp. Reprint. London: R. Hale; Bloomington: Indiana University Press, 1962.

A detailed biography of Pasternak based on three dimensions: Pasternak as poet, prose writer, and political figure. Discusses or analyzes some of Pasternak's major works (*The Line of Apelles*, *Letters from Tula*, *The Childhood of Luvers*, *Aerial Ways*, "The High Malady," some poetry from *Theme and Variations*, *Doctor Zhivago*, and a few poems of the later years), using translations of poetry to support his arguments. Zhivago is considered "clearly a reflection of Pasternak himself." Retells the novel's content and offers a thorough account of its political controversy. Includes ten chapters and an introduction.

23 POREMSKII, ALEKSEI VLADIMIROVICH. "Politicheskie motivy v romane *Doktor Zhivago*" [Political motifs in *Doctor Zhivago*]. In *Siloi idei*. Frankfurt am Main: Posev, pp. 87–101.

Reprint of 1959.54.

24 PRUAIAR, ZHAKLINA DE [Proyart, Jacqueline de]. Foreword (in vol. 1) to Pasternak's *Sochineniia*, edited by G.P. Struve and B.A. Filippov. 4 vols. Ann Arbor: University of Michigan Press.

Draws her views of Pasternak from their correspondence. Cites Pasternak's letter to her of 2 May 1959, in which he expounds on his baptism. Notes that Pasternak's love of God was first of all a love of life, his "élan vital," and that Pasternak's attitude toward life, nature, and man was commanded to him "by love." Discusses many features of Pasternak's character: his humane attitude toward others, his "heart of an infant," his "childlike straightforwardness and ardor," his "lack of vindictiveness," and his "receptivity" to the world around him. Elaborates on Pasternak's views of reality ("realism is a response to the reality"), his love of man ("for Pasternak love of God is manifested in his love of man"), his moral views ("Pasternak placed a sign of equality between aesthetics and ethics"), and his formula for accepting truth ("each man should arrive at it by his own way"). Records Pasternak's comments on his works.

25 ROWLAND, MARY and PAUL. "*Doctor Zhivago*: A Russian Apocalypse." *RIL* 30: 118–30.

Argues that Pasternak's intention to continue the revelation of St. John in *Doctor Zhivago*, hinted at by Zhivago's statement to that effect, is supported by similarities between the two works. These include their status as works emerging from totalitarian societies; their use of unchaste women to symbolize a nation's idolatry and apostasy; the appearance in *Doctor Zhivago* of the four horsemen of the Apocalypse, and counterparts to the cherubim, seraphim, and angel of the revelation; and three instances in *Doctor Zhivago* where a parable is used. Sees the call to suffering and martyrdom that marks both works not as a message of despair, but a proclamation of eschatological hope. Points out that the major difference between the two works is the transformation of the supernatural events and beings portrayed in revelation into allegories in *Doctor Zhivago*, using real human characters whose carefully chosen names hint at their allegorical significance. Reprinted in 1967.14.

26 ———. "Pasternak's Use of Folklore, Myth, and Epic Song in *Doctor Zhivago*." *SFQ* 15: 207–22.

Characterizes *Doctor Zhivago* as a quasi-realistic allegory, and Pasternak's approach as mytho-historic; submits prototypes based on folklore, myth, and history for several characters in the novel. Divides these "charactonyms" into categories based on destructive and healing capabilities. On the destructive side are Komarovsky (regarded to be related to an Ostyak Samoyed myth about mosquitoes) and the Mikulitsyn family: Averky Stepanovich, whose prototype is the Russian "Paul Bunyan," Mikula Selyaninovich; Elena Proklovna, who is associated with Helen of Troy and the Neoplatonic philosopher Proclus; and Liberius, whose prototypes are Solovey-Razboĭnik and Volkh Vseslavevich, the Prince-Werewolf. Opposed to these are the positive figures of Kubarikha, whose other name, Medvedikha, is associated with Slavic myths about bears; and Zhivago himself, whose namesake, St. George, is related to the wolves that appear in the narrative. Discusses various legends about the Tree of Life, with respect to Pasternak's use of the rowan berry tree. Reprinted in 1967.14.

27 RZHEVSKII, L. "O nekotorykh osobennostiakh iazyka i stilia romana *Doktor Zhivago* B. Pasternaka" [On some language and style peculiarities in B. Pasternak's novel *Doctor Zhivago*]. *ScS* 7: 92–113.

Attempts to define "basic features" of *Doctor Zhivago*'s language and style, while examining modes of characterization and characters' speech patterns. Discusses similarities in sentence structure between *Doctor Zhivago* and *War and Peace*. Finds that some characters' turns of speech are individualized, Zhivago's Old Church Slavonic current is "extended in Sima Tuntseva's" speech, and that *Doctor Zhivago* is a "unique form of a novel—a parable." Cites numerous examples to prove his point. Some observations reprinted in 1962.23.

28 VEIDLE [Weidlé], W. Introduction (vol. 1) to Pasternak's *Sochineniia* (in Russian), edited by G.P. Struve and B.A. Filippov. 4 vols. Ann Arbor: University of Michigan Press.

Part 2 reprinted in 1961.29—except for the last paragraph, claiming that in volume 1 one will not find a great deal of faultless poetry and that one should not seek a perfection in it, yet one will find "to one's heart's content" evidence of high poetic gifts.

29 ———. Introduction (vol. 3) to Pasternak's *Sochineniia* (in Russian), edited by G.P. Struve and B.A. Filippov. 4 vols. Ann Arbor: University of Michigan Press.

Reprint of Part 2 of 1961.28.

30 ———. "O rannei proze Pasternaka" [On Pasternak's early prose]. *NZh*, no. 64, pp. 144–50.

Notes that in the 1920s when Pasternak's poetry was highly praised, no one talked about his prose, even though he had published *The Childhood of Luvers* in the same year as *My Sister, Life*. Argues that Pasternak's early prose (*The Line of Appeles* and *Letters from Tula*) displays the author's talent as well as his "youthful romantic muddle." Regards *The Childhood of Luvers* and *Aerial Ways* as exemplary in their mastery. Argues that in his early prose, Pasternak remained a poet. Concludes that Pasternak's prose of the 1920s is more easily linked to *Doctor Zhivago* than his poetry of that period. Translated: 1978.40.

31 ———. "Pasternak i modernizm" [Pasternak and modernism]. *Mosty*, no. 6, 119–32.

Consists of two parts. The first part surveys the history of Pasternak's reception in the 1920s and 1930s while offering views of his poetry and innovations, which are looked upon as "somewhat one-sided and affected." Elaborates on Pasternak's renouncement of his early "style," suggesting that Pasternak's reference to "trinkets" in his poetry should be interpreted as "words doomed by the concern for a word." Strongly believes that even in his early poetry Pasternak was not a modernist, and that he only became associated with modernism while growing in its environment. Cites Pasternak's poetry to illustrate changes in his poetics (including sense and sound relations, rhymes, meter, and sound instrumentation). The second part examines the transformation in Pasternak's poetry with *Second Birth* and *Spektorsky*. Notes that the "incoherence" that Tsvetaeva noted in his earlier poetry was much less apparent in these works, and that Pasternak had "shifted from a conspicuous to an inconspicuous style." Adds that the "dazzle of verbal texture" that inhibited Pasternak's early work was missing, and that it was transformed into an innate simplicity. Concludes that Pasternak's gift for creating striking images was not lost, but was simply "brought under control." Reprinted: 1973.15.

32 ZAMOYSKA, HÉLÈNE. "L'art et la vie chez Boris Pasternak." *RES* 38: 231–39.

Evaluates the role of art for Pasternak. Observes that art, the artist's fate, and the subjects of artistic reflection and inspiration preoccupied Pasternak in the later years of his life. Draws partly on her correspondence with Pasternak. Claims that art and life are inseparable for Pasternak, life is dynamic and constantly changing, and the artist's task is to view the world with originality and make its essence intelligible.

1962

1   ALEKSANDROVA, V.A. "Ranniaia proza Pasternaka" [Pasternak's early prose]. In *Sbornik statei, posviashchennykh tvorchestvu B.L. Pasternaka*. Munich: Institut po izucheniiu SSSR, pp. 190–203.

Argues that Pasternak is not fond of labeling art with names of various schools and movements (symbolism, acmeism, and futurism) because for him only poetry and prose are inseparable. Believes that Pasternak's early prose (*The Childhood of Luvers, Aerial Ways, The Tale,* and *A Safe Conduct*) is saturated with images and that the reader is stricken by a serene rhythm of narrative compounded with vivid everyday speech patterns. Links characters found in Pasternak's early prose with those in *Doctor Zhivago.*

2   BOWRA, C.M. Foreword to Pasternak's *In the Interlude. Poems, 1945–1960.* Translated into English verse by Henry Kamen. London: Oxford University Press.

Mentions that "in the last thirty years of his life Boris Pasternak published almost no original poetry." Discusses the transformation of Pasternak's style from his early poetry to that in *Doctor Zhivago.* Concludes that "the old shocks and surprises and paradoxes have been eliminated; the movement of the verse is much more regular; the experiences presented with such sincerity and self-knowledge are closer to those of other men"; and that the language "has been brought closer to modern speech."

3   BURFORD, WILLIAM S. "The Talent for Life. *Doctor Zhivago* in Perspective." In *Six Contemporary Novels. Six Introductory Essays in Modern Fiction*, edited by William Sutherland. Austin: University of Texas Press, pp. 22–45.

Discusses *The Childhood of Luvers, Aerial Ways, The Tale, The Last Summer, Letters from Tula,* and *Doctor Zhivago.* Believes that Pasternak himself is the central character in his works. Sees Pasternak's prose as poetic in nature—a result of his background in music. Argues that Pasternak considers the "talent for life" displayed in Zhenya Luvers and Lara as "the highest talent." Concludes that *Doctor Zhivago* is Pasternak's "final testament."

4   BUSHMAN, I.N. "O rannei lirike Pasternaka" [On Pasternak's early poetry]. In *Sbornik statei, posviashchennykh tvorchestvu B.L. Pasternaka*. Munich: Institut po izucheniiu SSSR, pp. 204–24.

Establishes that Pasternak has always been a lyrical poet, and that he entered Russian poetry through his love of music and painting. Believes

155

that Pasternak's early poetry is complex and not immediately understood by the reader; there is no shallow play on words and his sound instrumentation contains meaning. Also notes that meter is unique in Pasternak's early poetry and that he has used all classical meters. Sees Pasternak's rhymes as based on a frequent coincidence of vowel and consonant sounds and notes that alliteration plays a significant role. Argues that hyperbole is an important aspect of his poetry as well, and points out that many inanimate objects in his works (such as rain, trees, gardens, and photography) talk to each other, think, feel, and act.

5 ———. "Pasternak i Ril'ke (Iz raboty na temu 'Nemetskaia poeziia i tvorchestvo Pasternaka')" [Pasternak and Rilke (From the work on the theme 'German poetry and Pasternak's works')]. In *Sbornik statei, posviashchennykh tvorchestvu B.L. Pasternaka.* Munich: Institut po izucheniiu SSSR, pp. 233–39.

Sees Rilke's influence in Pasternak's interest in philosophy and theology. Notes differences between Rilke and Pasternak—Pasternak rarely uses blank verse and Pasternak's rhyme is one of his basic verse embellishments. Underlines that Pasternak has "much more heart," while Rilke has much more "intellect."

6 CARLISLE [ANDREYEV], OLGA. "Boris Pasternak. Portrait of a Poet." In *Voices in the Snow. Encounters with Russian Writers.* New York: Random House, pp. 183–224.

The first part, "A Walk in Peredelkino," describes in detail the domestic surroundings of Pasternak's country home. Also notes Pasternak's humility and the poetic quality of his speech. Points out that Pasternak compares his use of religious symbolism in *Doctor Zhivago* to putting stories into a house, and chides critics for getting too "wrapped up" in such symbols and theological interpretations. The second part, "A Conversation," is distinguished chiefly by Pasternak's own lengthy, detailed synopsis of a trilogy of plays set in the nineteenth century on which he was working. The conversation also touches on the merits of Hemingway and Faulkner, the excessive influence of Nietzsche on twentieth-century Russian authors, and Pasternak's brief evaluation of several Russian poets. The third part, "Pasternak Remembered," quotes an eyewitness account of Pasternak's funeral and records other Soviet writers' views of Pasternak (Evtushenko's, for example), who are said to have told Mrs. Carlisle (Andreyev's granddaughter) that *Doctor Zhivago* "is not a good novel. It is dull." Reprinted in part: 1963.4–5; 1976.10. Translated (first part): 1988.20.

7 CHAKRAVARTI, AMIYA. "Pasternak: Poet of Humanity." In *The Christian Century Reader*, edited by Harold E. Fey and Margaret Frakes. New York: Association Press, pp. 384–87.

Reprint of 1960.5.

8   DYCK, J.W. "*Doktor Živago*: A Quest for Self-Realization." *SEEJ* 6, no. 2: 117–24.

Argues that *Doctor Zhivago* carries on the romantic quest for some "unknown other" while shifting the emphasis to the seeker from that which is sought; that the novel's philosophical and metaphysical content lies in the process of self-realization undergone by Zhivago; that this process is achieved by an "almost violent individualness" in which the individual takes over the stage of history; and that in such a scheme, religion imposed from without is rejected in favor of religious autonomy, which enables a free space from which the universe's beauty can be experienced and its tasks fulfilled. Concludes that the question of self-realization is emphasized throughout as an ongoing dialogue with previous thinkers such as Goethe, Schelling, Shakespeare, Dostoevsky, and Socrates, taking the commands "know thyself" and "be thyself" into a new period of concentration on the individual.

9   FRANK, V.S. "Vodianoi znak (Poeticheskoe mirovozrenie Pasternaka)" [Water sign (Pasternak's poetic worldviews)]. In *Sbornik statei, posviashchennykh tvorchestvu B.L. Pasternaka*. Munich: Institut po izucheniiu SSSR, pp. 240–52.

Contends that Pasternak's favorite poetic symbol is running water—rain for Pasternak is tantamount to life. Also contends that water constantly accompanies Pasternak's heroes as a symbol of their inner experiences and changes in life, and adds that snow symbolizes death for Pasternak. Concludes that Pasternak has always been aware of the presence of a "water sign" in himself, that he has been aware of those "downpours which came to him in the form of poetic inspiration." Reprinted: 1974.7; 1990.22.

10   FROESE, LEONHARD. "Dr. Shiwago alias Boris Pasternak: 'Der Mensch wird geboren, um zu leben. . . .'" In *Der Mensch in der neueren russischen Literatur*. Ratingen: A. Henn, pp. 38–55.

Records some biographical data: the origin of Pasternak's parents and his early familiarization with Western cultures, concluding that Pasternak's life stems "from the art" and goes "into the art." Lists Pasternak's major works and discusses *Doctor Zhivago* in detail—centering on the novel's major message (seen as "allegoric"), its structure and themes (mainly religious and revolutionary), its characters (Lara is seen as embodiment of "the love of Mother Russia"), and on the impact the novel made with the "Pasternak Affair." Concludes that with *Doctor Zhivago* Pasternak had written not only his own history but the history of the "Russian people of today" as well.

11   GAEV, ARK[ADII]. "B.L. Pasternak i ego roman *Doktor Zhivago*" [B.L. Pasternak and his novel *Doctor Zhivago*]. In *Sbornik statei, posviashchen-*

nykh tvorchestvu B.L. Pasternaka. Munich: Institut po izucheniiu SSSR, pp. 20–44.
 Reprint of 1958.20 (last two pages modified).

12 GERSCHENKRON, ALEXANDER. "Notes on *Doctor Zhivago.*" In *Economic Backwardness in Historical Perspective.* Cambridge, MA: Harvard University Press, pp. 341–52.
 Reprint of 1961.12.

13 IVASK, GEORGE. Review of Pasternak's *Sochineniia*, edited by G.P. Struve and B.A. Filippov. *RR* 21: 293–95.
 A summary of Pasternak's career and significance as a poet accompanies an appreciative review welcoming Pasternak's collection. Describes Pasternak's style briefly, seeing no essential differences in Pasternak's later writings ("there have been no essential changes in Pasternak's way of expression since 1917").

14 KATKOV, GEORGE. Notes on Pasternak's *In the Interlude. Poems, 1945–1960.* Translated into English verse by Henry Kamen. London: Oxford University Press, pp. 224–47.
 Discusses "The Poems of Yuri Zhivago," the collection *When the Skies Clear*, and Pasternak's later poetry. In the first section explains the connection between individual poems; comments on the background of each poem and on their relation to other works (Pasternak's and others); and links them, where possible, to the prose section of the novel. Sees in "Hamlet" "the unexpected identification of Hamlet with Christ"; also sees "The Wedding Party" as "one of the gayest and most colourful poems of the series," and "A Fairy Tale" as "one of the central poems linking the contents of the lyrical part of the novel with the prose narrative." Interprets "My Soul" (from section 2) as "the most tragic poem of the series" and "Winter Festivities" (section 3) as continuing "a profound sense of disappointment with the circumstances of his private life."

15 MARKOV, VLADIMIR. Review of Pasternak's *Sochineniia*, edited by G.P. Struve and B.A. Filippov. *SlaR* 21: 772–75.
 Notes that many of the little-known works, unpublished items, and variant readings are enumerated and discussed, as well as general questions raised by the collection about Pasternak's life and work in general. Praises inclusion of a bibliography of Pasternak's works and the publication of his early poetry (in which "Rilke's influence is more clearly seen than elsewhere"). Argues that Weidlé "is clearly exaggerating when he says that 'no major poet was a modernist by nature,'" that the editors should not have placed *Autobiographical Sketch* "at the very beginning of the volume," and that Pasternak's translations should have been included because "without them the study of his poetry can only be one-sided."

16 MARTI, PAUL. "Tolstojs *Krieg und Frieden* und Pasternaks *Doktor Schiwago.*" *SM* 42: 79–90.

Singles out common features inherent to both *Doctor Zhivago* and *War and Peace:* (1) history is used as a background in both novels; (2) both novels portray characters who are thrown into the turmoil of events; (3) both authors represent their time; and (4) both authors believe that "evil means" cannot be justified by any "good goals."

17 MATLAW, RALPH E. "Mechanical Structure and Inner Form: A Note on *War and Peace* and *Dr. Zhivago.*" *Symposium* 16, no. 4: 288–95.

Points out several compositional features common to *Doctor Zhivago* and *War and Peace:* Both works are divided into fifteen parts and two epilogues; both consist of three broad sections or "eras"; and both portray in their early chapters the end of one generation and the rise of the next. Discusses similarities in the handling of characters and describes the opening chapters as "fragmentary." Tolstoy's second epilogue and the poems of *Doctor Zhivago* are likened in that they both represent attempts to transcend or modify the novel as a form, placing both works in the line of "idiosyncratic masterpieces" that transcend genre and "crown Russian literature."

18 MAYER, HANS. "*Doktor Schiwago.*" In *Ansichten zur Literatur der Zeit.* Reinbek bei Hamburg: Rowohlt Verlag, pp. 205–25.

Surveys the history of *Doctor Zhivago*'s publication while narrating the novel's content. Centers his discussion on Zhivago—a "non-hero of his time," whose essence is interpreted as a "conflict between an objective and subjective side of the case," and whose "non-engagement" is said to be his "most essential feature." Rejects identification of Zhivago with Pasternak and claims that Pasternak has knowingly acted against socialist realism by having chosen an intellectual for his hero and by having him "slowly withered away." Compares the novel's poems to Hermann Hesse's *Glasperlenspiel.* Also cites Pasternak's poetry. Translated: 1971.10.

19 MEZHAKOV-KORIAKIN, I. "K probleme lichnosti v romane *Doktor Zhivago*" [Toward a definition of personality in the novel *Doctor Zhivago*]. In *Sbornik statei, posviashchennykh tvorchestvu B.L. Pasternaka.* Munich: Institut po izucheniiu SSSR, pp. 84–102.

Centers on two aspects of the novel—personality and family, and personality and Zhivago's poetry. With regard to the former, traces the fate of two female characters—Lara and Tonya. Sees the love of Tonya as an embodiment of motherhood and the love of family. Views the love of Lara as a struggle against the atrocities of life, a struggle for existence worthy of man, and a struggle for confirmation of personality in one's labor. The aspect of personality in Zhivago's poetry is seen as a compliment to Zhivago's character, a description of his personality, and as a means for Pasternak to express his thoughts. Notes that the themes of Zhivago's poetry include lyrical, religious, and philosophical aspects and that lyrical poems reflect the personal experience of the hero.

20 MOTTLEY, ROBERT C. "Boris Pasternak: The Late Phase." *Shenandoah* 13, no. 1: 42–47.

Welcomes Conquest's account of "the Pasternak Affair" [1961.7], adding his own evaluation of the Soviet case against Pasternak. Uses the philosophical and descriptive passages from *Doctor Zhivago* to disprove the Soviet thesis that Pasternak changed his political views before he had written the novel. Elaborates on Pasternak's emphasis on resurrection, redemption, and affirmation of life as a "lesson to pessimists." Pasternak's "trinity" of religion (God, Russia, and a "shrewd sense of history") is credited for endowing him with "extraordinary powers of observation and understanding."

21 OBOLENSKII, D.D. "Stikhi doktora Zhivago" [The poems of Doctor Zhivago]. In *Sbornik statei, posviashchennykh tvorchestvu B.L. Pasternaka.* Munich: Institut po izucheniiu SSSR, pp. 103–14.

Translation of 1961.20.

22 POPLIUIKO-ANATOL'EVA, N.A. "Bezvinnoe stradanie (Filosofskie elementy v tvorchestve Borisa Pasternaka)" [Guiltless suffering (Philosophical elements in Boris Pasternak's works)]. In *Sbornik statei, posviashchennykh tvorchestvu B.L. Pasternaka.* Munich: Institut po izucheniiu SSSR, pp. 60–83.

Underlines that Pasternak does not regard philosophy as his calling; that Pasternak has tried, since his youth, to understand the real sense of poetry, soul, and creativity; and that he has endeavored to resolve the question of man's place in the world. As a result, love and suffering have become two predominant themes in his work. Concludes that Pasternak's worldview is a Christian-like view because it includes the general Christian commandments, such as love for one's neighbor and sympathy for the insulted. Also concludes that Pasternak has always believed that after death people are not destroyed completely—they continue to live in the memory of others and in the products of their creativity.

23 RZHEVSKII, L. "Iazyk i stil' romana B.L. Pasternaka 'Doktor Zhivago'" [Language and style of B.L. Pasternak's novel *Doctor Zhivago*]. In *Sbornik statei, posviashchennykh tvorchestvu B.L. Pasternaka.* Munich: Institut po izucheniiu SSSR, pp. 115–89.

A detailed analysis of the novel's language and style. Elaborates on the following aspects: (1) the language of the novel within the entire speech system of Pasternak's prose; (2) the author's language; (3) the language of the characters; (4) forms of stylistic dualism in the novel; (5)

the use of cryptography as a form of creative self-exposure; (6) *Doctor Zhivago* as a parable; and (7) Pasternak and Rilke, and Pasternak and Blok. Makes profound observations on the language and style, concluding that the author's language is many-layered, that the characters' language is clearly individualized ("each has his own speech manner"), that portrayal of characters is traditional, that the cryptographical device of self-exposure is best seen in the "interrelation between 'author's image' with the novel's hero," and that in the novel Russian nature has been portrayed "splendidly." Chapter 6 reprint of 1960.33. Reprint of some observations in 1961.27. Reprinted (portions of chapter 3 and 4 with modifications): 1970.15.

24 SINIAVSKII, A. Review (in Russian) of *Stikhotvoreniia i poèmy*, edited by N. Kriuchkova. *NM*, no. 3, pp. 261–62.
    Remarks that Pasternak's poetry's fundamental creative leitmotiv is "amazement at the miracle of existence." Sees as unfortunate that the collection is marked with significant changes and corrections, many works characteristic of Pasternak's were not included, and an introductory article is lacking.

25 STEPUN, FEDOR. "B.L. Pasternak" (in Russian). In *Sbornik statei, posviashchennykh tvorchestvu B.L. Pasternaka.* Munich: Institut po izucheniiu SSSR, pp. 45–59.
    Reprint of 1959.69. Translated: 1978.38.

26 STRACHEY, JOHN. "The Strangled Cry." In *The Strangled Cry and Other Unparliamentary Papers.* New York: William Sloane, pp. 11–77.
    Reprint of 1960.36.

27 STRUVE, GLEB. "Sense and Nonsense about *Doctor Zhivago*." In *Studies in Russian and Polish Literature. In Honor of Wacław Lednicki*, edited by Zbigniew Folejewski. Slavistic Printings and Reprintings, 27. The Hague: Mouton, pp. 229–50.
    Disputes or elaborates on some Pasternak criticism—the *Novy mir* editors' letter to Pasternak as well as views of Richard Stern (1959.71), Isaac Deutscher (1959.17), and Edmund Wilson (1958.74; 1959.78) on *Doctor Zhivago*. Concurs with the *Novy mir* editors' opinion that *Doctor Zhivago* is "antirevolutionary in the Soviet sense of the word." Takes issue vehemently with Stern, emphasizing that *Doctor Zhivago* "is a poet's novel, a novel of symbolic realism," that Pasternak uses "very ingeniously the device of 'inner monologue,'" and that coincidences in *Doctor Zhivago* "are deliberate, consciously willed, and skillfully contrived." Lectures Deutscher on the use of "inside émigré" and calls Deutscher's interpretation of *Doctor Zhivago* "unadulterated nonsense." Refers to some arguments in Wilson's articles as "meaningless and pointless" or "just plain gibberish" and repudiates Wilson's interpretations of some "significant

symbols." Concludes that *Doctor Zhivago* should be looked upon as "a rich, complex, multiplanar, modern poetic novel."

1963

1 ALEXANDROVA, VERA. "Boris Pasternak. (1890–1960)." In *A History of Soviet Literature*. Translated by Mirra Ginsburg. Garden City, NJ: Doubleday & Co., pp. 150–61. Reprint. Wesport, CT: Greenwood, 1971.

Recounts major events in Pasternak's life (as reflected in *A Safe Conduct*) and gives general views of his poetry, prose, and translations. Of Pasternak's early prose, *Letters from Tula* is considered his "most characteristic" piece. Compares *The Childhood of Luvers* to Pushkin's *The Captain's Daughter* (for its "rapidly sketched picture of a snowstorm which is almost as vividly powerful as the description of the blizzard in Pushkin's *The Captain's Daughter*"). Observes that Pasternak's talent "is remarkable for its sense of detail" and that his prose "bears the imprint of poetry." Mentions Pasternak's translations (from German and English—Kleist's *The Broken Jug* and *Prince of Hamburg* and nine of Shakespeare's tragedies) and Pasternak's three comments on his own translations. Finds that the core of *Doctor Zhivago* "is the history of the generation whose adolescence witnessed the revolution of 1905, and whose youth coincided with the First World War and the revolution of 1917."

2 AUCOUTURIER, MICHEL. *Pasternak par lui-même.* Paris: "Ecrivains de Toujours" aux éditions du seul, 190 pp.

Basically a biography of Pasternak. Describes his family background, his travels, and maturing events, with emphasis on the effect of the Revolution on his work and thought. Discusses Pasternak's relationship with Rilke, who is credited with inspiring Pasternak to write, and the place of Pasternak's work in world literature.

3 BROWN, EDWARD J. "The Way of Pasternak." In *Russian Literature Since the Revolution*. New York: Collier Books, pp. 268–76. Rev. ed. London: Collier-Macmillan, 1969. Rev. and enl. ed. Cambridge, MA: Harvard University Press, 1982 and 1985.

Mentions Pasternak's "subjectivity" and "non-involvement" that made him unique as a writer and allowed him to survive the purges. Characterizes Pasternak's artistic method as intuitive and associative, striving to name that which had not yet been named. Sees *Doctor Zhivago* as depicting a world where miracles and magic are possible (exemplified by Samdevyatov and Yevgraf), and concludes that the ultimate achievement of Zhivago is one of "apprehension of love and beauty, and joyful optimism at the prospect of living."

4 CARLISLE, OLGA. "Boris Pastenak." In *Writers at Work. The 'Paris Review' Interviews*. 2d ser. Edited by Malcolm Cowley. New York: Viking Press, pp. 113–36. Reprint. Middlesex, England: Penguin Books, 1972.
   Reprint of 1960.4. Reprint in part of 1962.6.

5 ———. "Boris Pasternak." In *Writers at Work. The 'Paris Review' Interviews*. 2d ser. Edited and with an introduction by Van Wyck Brooks. New York: Viking Books, pp. 97–117.
   Reprint of 1960.4. Reprint in part of 1962.6.

6 DISOPRA, NIKOLA. "Pasternakov *Doktor Živago*" [Pasternak's *Doctor Zhivago*]. *Mogućnosti* 10, no. 6: 653–64.
   Finds fault with *Doctor Zhivago* in its portrayal of the Revolution, its "old-fashion genre" (dubbed "literary method"), and the portrayal of the main hero and his relationship with Lara, among others. Sees the novel's "basic flaw" as its indetermination of the "problem of the Revolution and an individual," a problem deemed to be resolved in Sholokhov's *Quiet Flows the Don*. Sees another of the novel's defects in the portrayal of Zhivago, who lacks an active participation in the description of events, and in the conveyance of the love story, seen as absent of "any profound sense, any exceptional content . . . even any point [applicable] to the entire novel."

7 GORKII, MAKSIM. "Predislovie k povesti Pasternaka 'Detstvo Liuvers'" [Introduction to Pasternak's tale *The Childhood of Luvers*]. *LiN*, no. 70, pp. 308–10.
   A brief appreciation of Pasternak's poetry and prose and an evaluation of *The Childhood of Luvers*, praised for its "rich, capricious, perky, and turbulent language of a youth-romantic." Argues that in *The Childhood of Luvers*, Pasternak had tried to "narrate about himself" and that he did so "brilliantly" and "utterly originally."

8 JACKSON, ROBERT L. "The Symbol of the Wild Duck in *Dr. Zhivago*." *CL* 15: 39–45.
   The appearance of a wild duck is attributed a symbolic significance that "embraces the entire work," foreshadowing a crisis of Russian culture and the personal eclipse of Zhivago. The dead duck (accepted by Zhivago as a present from a chance acquaintance) is seen to echo the "whole range of hopes, dreams and illusions" represented by similar birds in Ibsen's *The Wild Duck* and Chekhov's *The Seagull*, and to represent the demise of these illusions in the face of imminent historical and personal catastrophe.

9 LEVITSKY, SERGE. "Rose Koffman-Pasternak: la mère du poète." *SEES*, no. 8, pp. 73–80.
   Points out the influence of Pasternak's parents on their son, particularly his mother's musical upbringing of and her influence on Pasternak.

Also discusses Pasternak's mother's career as a pianist and her devotion to the Pasternak family.

10 LIVINGSTONE, ANGELA. "The *Childhood of Luvers.* An Early Story of Pasternak's." *SoR*, no. 1, pp. 74–84.

Notes that through his heroine of the story Pasternak depicts the process of maturation, the encounter of the individual with the images and rhythms of life. Believes that this development is accomplished at first by employing the "motif of names," the patterning of real yet alien and vague perceptions, and as the story progresses, by extending the heroine's awareness to other people, leading to an understanding of what it means to be a woman and a human being. This is traced from the heroine's passive experience with guilt and shame about menstruation through the moral awakening of pity for the lame Tsvetkov. Pasternak's use of precise sensory detail, his sympathetic treatment of women, and the naturalness with which he invests the story with Christian morality are seen to make it a forerunner of *Doctor Zhivago.*

11 ——. "Pasternak's Last Poetry." *MQ* 22: 388–96.

A study of *When the Skies Clear.* Divides the collection into two groups: poems of confession and "poems that describe some urban scene." Compares these themes to Pasternak's early poetry and concludes that the "Pasternak of thirty years later has a different relation to reality." Deems that Pasternak no longer seeks to change the world, instead he waits for the world to act upon him and reveal its splendor, "promise," and "its own transformation." Discusses the imagery, insisting that some of Pasternak's later poetry is "unsatisfying." Praises Pasternak's early poetry for its portrayal of new life (with "jagged elements and intense perceptions, with always the risk of incomprehensibility"), and argues that now he "is chiefly concerned to avoid extravagance," and lays out "his verses like a planned garden. . . . All is to be modest and regular." Concludes with a discussion of how Pasternak's worldviews have changed since his youth. Reprinted: 1978.27.

12 MONAS, SIDNEY. Review of *From Gorky to Pasternak,* by H[elen] Muchnic. *MR* 5: 578–83.

Contrasts Pasternak's "private muse" with the chaos and violence of Blok and Mayakovsky, concluding that Pasternak's devotion to the "true substance of art" makes him a more lasting influence on the current generation of poets and readers than his more publicly celebrated contemporaries.

13 MÜLLER, LUDOLF. "Die Gedichte des Doktor Schiwago." *NS* 3: 1–16.

Sees the function of the poetry section in *Doctor Zhivago* as a harmonious reportrayal of Zhivago's life in a new, transfigured, and poetic form. Divides the poetry section into three cycles, with the poem "Hamlet" being a prologue to the first cycle, which extends from the second poem to the eleventh. The second cycle—the twelfth through the seventeenth poems—is seen to reflect Zhivago's meetings with Lara; and the third cycle, from the thirteenth poem to the last, correlates Zhivago's fate with Christ and gives Zhivago his "last meaning." Analyzes thoroughly "The Garden of Gethsemane"—Pasternak's "understanding of the resurrection"; concludes that the last judgement in the poem is "consummated in history" and that Zhivago has "somehow taken part in the fate of Christ."

14 PELTIER-ZAMOYSKA, HÉLÈNE. "Pasternak, homme du passé?" *Esprit* 31, no. 1 (January): 16–29.

A rebuttal against the Soviet authorities for their condemnation of Pasternak for idealizing prerevolutionary values. Sees in Pasternak a dual past—prerevolutionary and Soviet. Notes that Zhivago is both witness and judge to his time, but he judges by eternal standards and has the courage to maintain his convictions despite his experiences. Likens Zhivago's resistance to the imposition of a "sterile, predetermined order" to Pasternak's view that life is an eternal transformation. Finds Zhivago to be less developed than Pasternak in his faith in the future, drawing heavily on conversations with the writer—Pasternak contemplated not a system but an artistic vision. States that Zhivago's horror at destruction should not be regarded as an "anti-Soviet" tendency, but as a trait in a man who refuses to compromise his principles.

15 RÖHLING, HORST. "Gethsemane bei Rilke und Pasternak." *WS* 8: 388–402.

A comparison of Rilke's "Ölbaumgarten" to Pasternak's "The Garden of Gethsemane." Narrates the content of Pasternak's poem emphasizing the role of quotations, and draws parallels between the biblical text and the poem—particularly in stanzas 3 through 14. Observes that Pasternak's poem is not a response to Rilke's and that one of the concluding lines in Pasternak's poem ("The course of centuries is like a parable") reminds the reader of an excerpt from the second part of *Faust* ("Alles Vergängliche ist nur ein Gleichnis; Das Unzulängliche, Hier wirds Ereignis"). Enumerates differences and similarities between the two poems: (1) Pasternak's poem has more "dramatic highpoints"; (2) the name of Christ is not used in either poem; (3) the narrative differs in both poems and their dependence on biblical text is different; and (4) in Rilke's poem "a dramatic occurrence is resolved lyrically and is not epically ruled as with Pasternak."

16 ROUGEMENT, DENIS DE. "New Metamorphoses of Tristan." In *Love Declared: Essays on the Myths of Love.* New York: Pantheon Books, pp. 39–76.

Translation of 1959.63.

17 ROWLAND, MARY F. and PAUL. "The Mission of Yury and Evgraf Zhivago." *TSLL* 5: 199–218.

Seeks symbolic meanings in interpretations of *Doctor Zhivago*. Sees Zhivago the physician as caring for "his stricken patient," Russia; compares Zhivago to Jesus, noting that Zhivago's delirious dream was "the eternal struggle of life against Hate and Brutality and Death"; sees the Orthodox saints George and Eugraphos in Zhivago and Yevgraf. Concludes that Zhivago ends his life in kenotic fashion, paralleling the humble life and death of Christ. Reprinted in 1967.14.

18 RÜHLE, JÜRGEN. "Die Stimme Russlands: Boris Pasternaks *Doktor Schiwago.*" In *Literatur und Revolution. Die Schriftsteller und der Kommunismus*. Cologne and Berlin: Kiepenheuer and Witsch, pp. 148–65.

Asserts that the major characters in *Doctor Zhivago* "incorporate the best that Russian literature and the Russian people have given to humanity," and that the novel "is not determined by this or that political tendency, but by a universal spiritual attitude that suffuses its every page." Links Antipov to nihilists like Turgenev's Bazarov and Chernyshevsky's Rakhmetov; Lara to the saint-and-sinner prototypes of Tolstoy's Anna Karenina and Dostoevsky's Sonya; and Zhivago to a long line of "superfluous men" like Lermontov's Pechorin and Pushkin's Onegin. Suggests that the novel revolves around three underlying themes: the reverence for life, the mystery of the individual, and the idea of resurrection. Responds to criticism of Pasternak's political views as reflected in the novel, maintaining that "the novel is unmistakably a post-Revolutionary work . . . addressing the Russia of the future." Translated: 1969.16.

19 SELIVANOVSKII, A. "Boris Pasternak" (in Russian). In *V literaturnykh boiakh (Izbrannye stat'i i issledovaniia)*. 2d ed. Moscow: Sovetskii pisatel', pp. 452–66.

A summary of general views of Pasternak's poetic perceptions, some of which have been expounded in *A Safe Conduct*. Notes that Pasternak is a master of "concrete" detail, similes, and metaphors ("his poetry was born in a room interior, he saw life from afar, behind a window sash"). Concludes that Pasternak is a real poet, "from top to toe, one of a few poets for whom the entire world could become an object of poetic expression."

20 WILLIAMS, RAYMOND. "Tragic Resignation and Sacrifice." *CrQ* 5: 5–19.

Describes modern conceptions of martyrdom and sacrifice as ambiguous, defensive, and guilt-driven and compares the "rhythm of sacrifice" as it appears in T.S. Eliot's *The Cocktail Party* and *Murder in the Cathedral* with the same element in *Doctor Zhivago*. Contrasts Eliot's dogmatic, marginal treatment of sacrifice with Pasternak's hero, who is seen to represent life experience rather than "literary attitudes." Sees sacrifice in *Doctor Zhivago* as a Christ-like individual martyrdom, but as a dialectical process of which Zhivago and Lara are both victims and witnesses. Rejects overly simplistic, ethical views labeling Zhivago as hero or failure in order to penetrate to the novel's "paradoxical design," which has no hero and no victim, and is instead a vision of sacrifice interpreted as linking Christian redemption with the Marxist idea of history. Reprinted: 1966.20.

1964

1 BRÄUER, HERBERT. "Pasternaks Bedeutung als Dichter." *AMP* (Sommersemester), pp. 13–18.
   Accentuates the unique significance that lies in Pasternak's lyrics; Pasternak is seen as a lyricist even in his prose. Notes that Pasternak's earlier poetry belongs to futurism, that Pasternak had been fortunate to combine symbolism and futurism and to convey them in his unique manner, and that in Pasternak's poetry and prose an outer action is often placed completely in the background.

2 BURG, DAVID. "Um Pasternaks Platz in der Sowjetliteratur." *Osteuropa* 14: 640–45.
   Outlines Pasternak's years as a writer. Presents Paustovsky's article on Pasternak in which Paustovsky cites a Pasternak poem, thus acquainting Russian readers with both Pasternak's poetry and prose. Concludes that official Soviet literary criticism has not sufficiently acquainted Russian readers with Pasternak. Elaborates in detail on Pasternak's correspondence with Gorky, who is said to have greatly valued Pasternak as a prose writer, and to have even encouraged him to write prose work. Addresses Pasternak's treatment in the Soviet Union in two ways: (1) he was quoted without being named as author, and (2) that a liberal movement in favor of Pasternak's rehabilitation had emerged. Translated: 1964.3.

3 ———. "V bor'be za Pasternaka" [In the struggle for Pasternak]. *Grani*, no. 56, pp. 205–12.
   Translation of 1964.2.

4 ERLICH, VICTOR. "'Life by Verses': Boris Pasternak." In *The Double Image: Concepts of the Poet in Slavic Literatures*. Baltimore: John Hopkins Press, pp. 133–54.
   Redefines the paradoxical "problem" of Pasternak's poetics by tracing explicit and implicit notions regarding poetry, the self, and the world. Sees the reduction of self and humanization of nature as key elements of a process-oriented poetics that recreates the "primordial joy of existence," and that emphasizes the "internal laws and exigencies of poetic language" while downplaying the romantic self-dramatization of Mayakovsky or

Blok. Analyzes Pasternak's way of meeting the challenge posed by the 1917 Revolution to his "life by verses," with emphasis on the essential continuity of his poetic vision from his earliest lyrics to *Doctor Zhivago*, which is seen as a paradoxical insistence for privacy that turned him into a heroic figure. Contrasts Pasternak's role as "witness" with Blok's role as "seer" and with the utopianism of the symbolists and futurists. Pasternak's poetics is summed up as "Romanticism with a difference"; he is seen as a poet who cocreates and reshuffles existence with the force of language rather than personality. Revision of 1959.19. Revised: 1978.11.

5   FEIFER, GEORGE. "Art for Marx' Sake." *NYTM* (20 December): 12–13, 20–28.

Cites Alexander Chakovsky's [then the editor of *Literaturnaia gazeta*] views of *Doctor Zhivago*. Cites Chakovsky as having said that *Doctor Zhivago* is "a boring book, a bad novel," that Pasternak is "a poor novelist," that "Pasternak subjects to doubt what is most fundamental and most important for the entire Soviet people, the value of the October Socialist Revolution," and that "to reject the October Revolution in any literary creation is to deprive it of its moral substance as a work of art."

6   GHOSH, GOURIPRASAD. *"Doctor Zhivago*: A Literary Study." *Visva-Bharati* 30, nos. 1/2: 62–88.

Offers both general and analytical views of *Doctor Zhivago* as a work of art. Observes that the novel was written by a poet ("and to this its great merits and its curious failings are very much due"); it is autobiographical: "its portrayal of life is at times intense and moving"; it is "a bad historical novel"; its narrative "lacks vividness" and the dialogue "has at times a tiresome stiffness"; some coincidences are "bordering on the absurd"; and its central idea "is the freedom of the human spirit from the tyranny of systems." Strongly opposes the *Novy mir* editors' accusation of *Doctor Zhivago* and its author ("a malicious piece of writing"; "the life story of a malicious philistine"; and "a petty, worthless, wretched little job," for example). Focuses on the three major characters—Zhivago, Lara, and Antipov/Strelnikov—who are seen as "sharply contrasted . . . [with] one magnetic feminine entity that drives and animates and is the life and death of both [the others]." Takes issue with Edmund Wilson's article (1959.78), calling some of his interpretations (the "Moreau and Vetchinkin" sign, for example) a "sort of fantastic symbolism" and "extraordinarily farfetched and somewhat purposeless."

7   GIFFORD, HENRY. *"Doctor Zhivago*: A Novel in Prose and Verse." In *The Novel in Russia. From Pushkin to Pasternak.* London: Hutchinson University Library, pp. 185–94. Reprint. New York: Harper & Row, 1965.

Calls *Doctor Zhivago* a "poet's novel," "the last Russian classic," made of "hundreds of separate lyric notations." Notes the novel's "economy of design that helps to concentrate meaning." Pasternak's use of coincidence, transitions, and the poetry chapter allow his lyrical impulse to branch into "something like epic fullness." Contrasts the privacy of nature in Pasternak's vision with his "immediate witness" of political and social events. Defines history and nature in relation to each other, as exemplified by Zhivago's death in the street. Argues that Pasternak's concern for "vanishing tradition" is indicative of the novel's status as a "valedictory work, a singing of 'eternal memory'" to attitudes and themes of the past.

8   LIVINGSTONE, ANGELA. "Pasternak's Early Prose." *AUMLA*, no. 22, pp. 249–67.
    An analysis of content and modes of expression in six prose works. Traces their common tendency toward a uniquely Pasternakian concept of simplicity by which disparate physical details or particulars of existence form transcendant artistic wholes. Argues that the evolution of this creative simplicity is preceded by a shift in emphasis from the "outrageous self-confidence" of the poet in *The Line of Apelles* to its loss in *Letters from Tula*, a movement from intense self-dramatization to a fundamental stillness from which creativity can begin to exert its unifying force. Sees *A Safe Conduct* as a synthesis of the themes and techniques of the preceding stories, in which intense, focused description combines with metaphorical reflection to demonstrate a simple, organic unity of art and life.

9   LORA, GUILLERMO. "El caso Pasternak (bolchevismo y arte)." In *La frustración del novelista Jaime Mendoza (Crítica irreverente). Y otros ensayos.* La Paz: Ediciones Masas, pp. 103–19.
    Surveys Pasternak's literary career, offering insight into his style as a futurist. Discusses Pasternak's political "conduct" and the Kremlin's "relatively high tolerance for him and his work."

10 MALLAC, GUY DE. "Zur Aesthetik Pasternaks." *Sowjetstudien*, no. 16, pp. 78–101.
    An attempt to define Pasternak's aesthetic views, with an introduction that discusses Pasternak's notoriety ("Zauber um den Namen Pasternak") and literary circles in which Pasternak lived and worked. Elaborates on Pasternak's adages that art ought to "grasp reality" ("natural, human reality"); a work of art should contain a "rich and profound content"; art should reflect life with its "constant zest"; art should give the "whole show to the world"; and that creation of an "enlarged image of man," which art is supposed to achieve, is "possible only in the motion." Traces the evolutionary process Pasternak underwent from futurist poet-theoretician to a poet preaching superiority of "content over form." Discusses Pasternak's conception of dynamism and realism, and his views of form versus content and determinism versus arbitrary

chance, among others. Also discusses Pasternak's views of art in light of Kant's *Kritik der reinen Vernunft* and *Kritik der Urteilskraft*, contrasting Pasternak's notion of cognition (*poznanie*) against Kant's *Gemüt* (heart; soul) conception. Mentions Pasternak's reaction to Vyacheslav Ivanov's views of religious myths. Draws on *A Safe Conduct*, Pasternak's essays on Verlaine and Chopin, "Some Propositons," "Black Goblet," and on relevant criticism (including Ripellino, Mesterton, and Stepun). Translated (with modifications): 1979.30; 1981.14.

11 O'HARA, FRANK. "About Zhivago and his Poems." In *On Contemporary Literature: An Anthology of Critical Essays on the Major Movements and Writers of Contemporary Literature*, edited by Richard Kostelanetz. New York: Avon Books, pp. 486–97.

　　Explores various facets of Pasternak's presentation of Zhivago, "one of the most original heroes in Western Literature." Views Pasternak's own renunciation of the "Romantic prose" as a "recognition" that "the poet and life walk hand in hand," foreshadowing Zhivago's own role as an "instrument" of the "perceptions of life." Sees the novel's poems as Zhivago's unique creations, voicing a complex, dynamic interpretation of Christianity as social change rather than orthodoxy. Perceives Zhivago's unrelenting honesty in "clarification of feelings and thoughts" as the embodiment of love to which Pasternak dedicated himself. Reprinted: 1977.17.

12 PASTERNAK, JOSEPHINE. "Patior." *LM* 4, no. 6 (September): 42–57.

　　Recollections of Pasternak (her brother) and a summary of views of his works. Reveals Pasternak's views of Proust ("the best writer of the beginning of the century"), and recalls her meeting with Pasternak in Berlin in 1935. Claims that at that time the image of Lara as a partial reflection of Zinaida Nikolaevna (Pasternak's second wife) had been contemplated. Observes that names are repeated throughout Pasternak's works, "crossing" from one work to another. Strongly believes that *The Childhood of Luvers* should not be regarded as the beginning of *Doctor Zhivago* (their heroines are different, with various psychological characterizations). Elaborates on Lara's affinity with Zhivago—both are devoid of materialistic interests, they are inwardly free and open to unification with world and nature. Discerns *Doctor Zhivago*'s endeavors to comprehend life as the central theme to the novel. Reprinted: 1974.13. Translated: 1990.54.

13 PASTERNAK SLATER, LYDIA. Introduction to *Fifty Poems*. Translated by Lydia Pasternak Slater. New York: Barnes & Noble, pp. 9–23. Reprint. London: Unwin Paperbacks, 1984.

　　Details her early life with Pasternak (her brother) while offering insights into the relationship between him and his sisters. Mentions the musicality of Pasternak's poetry, the success of *My Sister, Life*, and some of Pasternak's other early poetry. Corrects innumerable errors she encountered in publications about Pasternak. Cites from Pasternak's letters to his parents to substantiate these corrections. Examines the last three years of Pasternak's life, noting her wonderment about the huge crowd that attended the funeral of Pasternak.

14 PROYART, JACQUELINE DE. *Pasternak* (in French). Paris: Gallimard, 317 pp.

A combination of Pasternak biography (an outline) with a discussion of his literary career (notably in two chapters—"A la recherche d'une signature" and "Seconde naissance") and a concise content narration of all of his poetry collections, major prose works, and articles. Cites Pasternak's correspondence, entries from Afinogenov's memoirs, and Evtushenko's comments on Pasternak; includes her own and others' renditions of Pasternak's poetry and prose.

15 SLONIM, MARC. "Boris Pasternak. The Voice of the Other Russia." In *Soviet Russian Literature. Writers and Problems*. New York: Oxford University Press, pp. 218–30. Reprint. London: Oxford University Press, 1967, 1969, 1977.

Defines Pasternak's place as a writer within Soviet literature, gives a brief biographical sketch, and mentions his major works, including his translations. Divides his literary career into three major periods: from his "debut to 1932," from 1932 to 1945, and from 1945 to his death. Finds that his poetry is a combination of "the classical tradition, a symbolist musicality and the colloquial bent of the futurist," that Pasternak "gets an approximation of concepts deriving from phonetic kinship of words and sounds," and that he "omits the links between the components of a metaphor." Narrates in detail the content of *Doctor Zhivago*, emphasizing its "two styles—the lyrical-poetic and the epic-descriptive," its autobiographical nature, its uniqueness ("it does not resemble other novels and remains a novel *sui generis*"), its "incredible originality," and its "beautiful descriptions of landscapes and seasons" that "put nature at the focal center of *Doctor Zhivago* in the same way as time and space are the main protagonists of Tolstoy's *War and Peace.*

1965

1 DAVIE, DONALD. Commentary on *The Poems of Dr. Zhivago*. Translated by Donald Davie. New York: Barnes & Noble, pp. 51–164. Reprint. Westport, CT: Greenwood Press, 1977.

A detailed commentary on the twenty-five Zhivago poems. Draws heavily on earlier criticism (Nilsson, Reeve, Gifford, Hayward, Katkov, and Obolensky, among others). Draws parallels between the poems and prose of *Doctor Zhivago*. Discusses sources and literary allusions (including Blok, Pushkin's *Eugene Onegin*, Eliot, and Yeats). Offers a particularly detailed analysis of "White Night," "The Wedding," and "The Garden of Gethsemane." Concludes from "Hamlet" that Pasternak believed "life is not a field of experience to be crossed, but the path of a destiny to be found and followed." Labels Pasternak's views of Christianity as "apocalyptic marxism" and argues that Pasternak's Jesus is a broad image: "Jesus can be very fully and seriously Jesus, yet also Zhivago, and also other men besides Zhivago."

2   PROYART, JACQELINE DE. "Boris Pasternak. 1890–1960" (in French). In *Les écrivains contemporains*, edited by G.E. Clancier. Paris: Éditions d'art, pp. 396–99.

A composite account of Pasternak's biographical and literary data. Mentions Pasternak's early works, his first contacts with intellectual life in Moscow, the influence of historical events on his life and works, and his translations. Also summarizes *Doctor Zhivago*.

3   SILBAJORIS, RIMVYDAS. "The Poetic Texture of *Doktor Živago*." *SEEJ* 9, no. 1: 19–28.

Argues that Pasternak transcends conventional considerations of genre in *Doctor Zhivago* by imbuing the prose with poetic texture, "a new artistic technique to express a new conception of reality." Believes that this enhancement can be felt in such things as: "miracle-metaphors" relating to mysterious natural forces; echoes of Zhivago's poetry in the text of the novel; symbolic images such as the shadows and trains; specific "symbol-hieroglyphics" such as the rowan tree; character-symbols such as Kubarikha and Samdevyatov; and juxtaposition of conventional and figurative causality. Concludes that the "poetic logic" leads to its "fulfillment" in the poems of Zhivago, which work with the text to transfer the novel to the "sphere of myth."

4   SINIAVSKII, A.D. Introduction to *Stikhotvoreniia i poemy* (in Russian), edited by A.A. Ozerov. Moscow: Sovetskii pisatel', pp. 9–62.

Analyzes Pasternak's poetry thematically (not chronologically). Consists of an introduction followed by six sections: (1) a history of Pasternak's publications; (2) a survey of recurrent nature motifs in his works; (3) an analysis of themes of life in Pasternak's poetry and the use of language; (4) a discussion of Pasternak's "imprint on contemporary literature"; (5) a survey of themes in Pasternak's poetry and their interrelationship; and (6) a conclusion aspiring to place Pasternak into a specific school with modernist poetry. Concludes that Pasternak's poetry retained a vital unity between 1917 and 1960; that nature plays a central role in his poetry, with Pasternak playing the role of an observer ("just as nature does"); that poetry for Pasternak is a direct consequence of life; that in his use of everyday language Pasternak bears a slight resemblance to other Russian poets (Bely, Blok, and Annensky); that Pasternak often intertwines images by choosing words that contain similar phonetic characteristics; and that the meaning of one's existence, one's destiny, and the essence of nature are the three most common themes in Pasternak's poetry. Translated: 1969.17; 1978.37. Selectively translated: 1966.18–19; 1967.16; 1975.14.

5 SSACHNO, HELEN VON. "Boris Pasternak" (in German). In *Der Aufstand der Person*. Berlin: Argon Verlag, pp. 183–208.
    Gives a brief background of the publication of *Doctor Zhivago* and examines Pasternak's poetry, citing from her own translations. Notes that although Pasternak had turned away from symbolists and had become a futurist, he stood closer to symbolists due to his origin. Sees *Doctor Zhivago* as a "heart confession"; a novel with two levels, "realistic and symbolic"; and as the pinnacle of Pasternak's literary career. Denies that Pasternak has the ability to create epic works ("Pasternak ist kein Epiker").

6 WAIN, JOHN. Review of *The Poems of "Doctor Zhivago."* Translated by Donald Davie. *NeR* 153 (27 November): 17–19.
    Finds Davie's commentaries on the poems of *Doctor Zhivago* too literal and narrow in their efforts to "tidy up" after inconsistencies and gaps in the relationship between the body of the novel and the poems. Sees, rather, the poems as an illumination of the novel's central themes of death and resurrection. Pasternak's intention in setting the poems apart rather than interspersing them throughout the text is interpreted as discouraging such searches for specific correspondences. Concludes that the correspondence between Zhivago and his creator signifies more than a conventional "autobiographical novel."

7 WILSON, EDMUND. "Doctor Life and his Guardian Angel." In *The Bit Between My Teeth. A Literary Chronicle of 1950–1965*. New York: Farrar, Straus, pp. 420–46.
    Reprint of 1958.74.

8 ———. "Legend and Symbol in *Doctor Zhivago*." In *The Bit Between My Teeth. A Literary Chronicle of 1950–1965*. New York: Farrar, Straus, pp. 447–72.
    Reexamines *Doctor Zhivago*'s "symbols and significant puns" (1959.78) and the novel's organizing principle. Includes a discussion of parallels with Pasternak's career and relations with Stalin in particular. The protagonist's surname is linked to a passage from the Gospels, as is Zhivago's first name to St. George. The names of Yevgraf and Lara are interpreted as symbols of creative genius and elemental freedom, respectively. Develops Lara's association with sea and wind in some detail. Analyzes the content of an "obsessive billboard" and claims the first

word is a compound of *mort* and *eau* (death and water). Revised reprint of 1959.78.

9   ZAITSEV, BORIS. "Pasternak v revoliutsii" [Pasternak in the Revolution] and "Eshche o Pasternake" [More about Pasternak]. In *Dalekoe*. Washington, DC: Inter-Language Literary Associates, pp. 107–118; 119–27.

Provides information on Pasternak's family and discusses futurists' influences on early Pasternak, and insists that Pasternak did not participate in their activities. Recalls his first meeting with Pasternak and discusses *The Childhood of Luvers*, stressing its novelty and originality. Remarks that Pasternak embraced the October Revolution, but distanced himself from it afterward. Discusses his correspondence with Pasternak and cites from it, noting, among other things, that "Pasternak's fate is the most astonishing one in our literature—embodying a tragic and heroic shade."

1966

1   ACHAR, K.R.H. "Boris Pasternak." *JKU* 10: 61–69.

Outlines a short biography of Pasternak and discusses his relation to other literary movements (symbolism, futurism, acmeism, and imaginism); profusely cites Pasternak's poetry and offers commentary on it (seen as "a series of accidentally preserved samples of that poetical vision which went on uninterruptedly as long as he breathed"). Surveys Pasternak criticism including Gerd Ruge's (1958.62), Edmund Wilson's (1958.74; 1959.78), John Strachey's (1960.36), C.M. Bowra's (1962.2), Stuart Hampshire's (1958.23), and Max Hayward's (1958.25), and argues that *Doctor Zhivago* is "a simple love story" whose central theme is the contrast between Zhivago and Antipov. Concludes that "only a man like Pasternak could know the pulse of the people in whose midst he lived and suffered."

2   ANNENKOV, IURII. "Boris Pasternak" (in Russian). In *Dnevnik moikh vstrech. Tsikl tragedii.* Vol. 2. New York: Mezhdunarodnoe literaturnoe sodruzhestvo, pp. 152–99.

Asserts that Pasternak was oblivious to "social problems" of his time and that "Universe" and "Eternity" were Pasternak's "fatherland." Underlines Pasternak's love for music (Pasternak's cult) and finds that this love is a reason for "phonetic texture" in Pasternak's poetry. Singles out the uniqueness of Pasternak's lexicon, a "collision of poetic abstractness and ordinary street talk, an interlacement of syntactic originality and everyday twitter." Records some events surrounding "the Pasternak Affair," notably the awarding of the Nobel Prize to Pasternak. Excerpt reprinted: 1990.4.

3   ARBELAEZ, FERNANDO. "Boris Pasternak" (in Spanish). *BCB* 9, no. 9: 1733–42.

Discusses Pasternak's Nobel Prize and the controversy ensuing from it—specifically during the period when *Doctor Zhivago* was translated into seventeen languages, yet banned in the Soviet Union. Also discusses the difficulty encountered when translating the novel's poetry into Spanish. Mentions the hermetic nature of the novel's poetry, suggesting that the Soviet society/culture might have contributed to it.

4   AUCOUTURIER, MICHEL. "The Legend of the Poet and the Image of the Actor in the Short Stories of Pasternak." *SSF* 3: 225–35.

Traces the theme of the poet-legend in *The Line of Apelles, Letters from Tula*, and *The Tale*. Narrates these stories in detail and argues that Pasternak's short stories "appear as isolated incursions of a poet into the domain of prose." Also argues that the legend of the poet is the "initial ferment of all the prose work of Pasternak," noting that for Pasternak a poet is an actor, such as Heine in *The Line of Apelles*, the old actor in *Letters from Tula*, and Y[3] in *The Tale*. Finds similarities between *The Childhood of Luvers, Aerial Ways*, and *Doctor Zhivago*. Sees the originality of *The Tale* in the insertion of "the legend of the poet into a realistic context that traces it back to its birth and illuminates its essence." Concludes that Pasternak's poet-legend theme reached its maturity in *The Tale*: "the poet is not the author of his legend, but the servant of the destiny it traces for him." Reprinted: 1969.2.

5   BUSCH, WOLFGANG. "Pasternak und Horaz. Zu zwei unbeachteten Übersetzungen." In *Orbis Scriptus. Dmitrij Tschižewskij zum 70. Geburtstag*, edited by Dietrich Gerhardt, Wiktor Weintraub, and Hans-Jürgen zum Winkel. Munich: Wilhelm Fink Verlag, pp. 151–54.

Analyzes Pasternak's translations of Horace's poem on Pompeius Varsus's homecoming ("Na vozvrashchenie Pompeia Vara") and his ode to Melpomene ("K Mel'pomene"). Lauds Pasternak for retaining the original meter (although he finds fault with Pasternak's caesura) and for his sound instrumentation that emulates "rustling of trees, burbling of streams, and sea waves." Also praises Pasternak's loyalty to the content and "artistic form" of the original and for "freshness and naturalness of the language." Mentions other Russian translations of the two poems (including Pushkin's) and contrasts them to Pasternak's.

6   BUSCHMANN, IRENE. "Boris Pasternak und die deutsche Dichtung. Zweiter Beitrag: Pasternak und Nietzsche." *Sowjetstudien*, no. 20, pp. 74–87.

Elaborates on Scriabin's influence on Pasternak's infatuation with music and insists that Scriabin introduced Pasternak to Nietzsche's work. Draws parallels between Pasternak and Nietzsche: Pasternak's essay "Some Propostions" and Nietzsche's *Thus Spake Zarathustra*, Pasternak's

"Bad Dream" and Nietzscheian pessimism, and *My Sister, Life* and Nietzsche's notion of "Übermensch." Suggests other similarities, including Pasternak's propensity for alliteration, inner rhymes, and hyperbole; corroborates his arguments with detailed examples. Mentions some of Pasternak's "direct" borrowings from Nietzsche, "toying" with titles of his poems, for example.

7   CHUKHOVSKII, KORNEI. Introduction (in Russian) to *Stikhi*, edited by V.M. Inber, V.O. Pertsov, A.A. Prokof'ev, and A.T. Tvardovskii. Moscow: Khudozhestvennaia literatura, pp. 5–26.
       Recalls his frequent meetings with Pasternak in the Peredelkino area. Compares some features of Pasternak's character to his poetry— "extreme sensitivity, impetuosity," and "ardency of emotions." Underlines Pasternak's closeness to nature, his ability to recreate "the reality which flashed before his eyes at that instance," thus giving the nature discriptions of his poetry "specificity, definitiveness, and accuracy." Cites from "Pinetrees," *My Sister, Life*, "Today in the Downpour," and *The Year 1905* while commenting on them; *The Year 1905* is praised for its stanzas "invented by Pasternak." Outlines the evolution that had occurred in Pasternak's poetry, ending with the last period when his verse "became laconic and harmonious, retaining all its initial Pasternakian power and clarity."

8   HARVIE, J.A. Review of *Stikhotvoreniia i poemy*, edited by L.A. Ozerov. *Meanjin* 25: 326–31.
       Discusses the omissions from this edition, and remarks that "the new material is unlikely substantially to affect the writer's reputation." Discusses many aspects of Pasternak's poetry, including: "rhythm and harmony as the basic metaphysical force"; relations between human and nonhuman, organic and inorganic, and nature and society; love poetry; reactions to the Revolution as they appear in Pasternak's works; and the vision of Christianity.

9   HERERRA, ONÉSIMO. "Boris Pasternak" (in Spanish). *Istmo* 42 (January/February): 83–87.
       An elaborate study of *Doctor Zhivago* that is broken down into five parts. The first focuses on Zhivago's character, the truth that speaks in him, his simplicity, his direct contact with life, and his abundance of love. The second part discusses the novel's Christian elements and attempts to explain what Christianity meant to Pasternak. The third treats Pasternak's attitude toward the Revolution, noting Pasternak's refusal to "divorce the pen of his conscious in order to prostitute it with politics." The fourth part underlines the novel's lack of political undertones—seeing the protagonist's protest on a spiritual level, and not on a political, sociological, or pragmatic one. A brief biography that traces Pasternak's life from his childhood to the end constitutes the last section.

10 HOWE, IRVING. "Boris Pasternak: Of Freedom and Contemplation."
    In *Steady Work. Essays in the Politics of Democratic Radicalism,
    1953–1966.* New York: Harcourt, Brace & World, pp. 159–69.
        Analyzes *Doctor Zhivago* within its major ideas and its similarity to
    War and Peace. Singles out remarkable passages—a scene that describes
    the Zhivagos as they help to clear the railroad trucks on their journey to
    Varykino, and the descriptions of Zhivago's and Lara's stay in Varykino.
    Marvels at "a series of clipped vignettes" describing prerevolutionary
    Russia, "apparently meant to suggest a Tolstoyan breadth and luxurious-
    ness of treatment." Views *Doctor Zhivago* as "a major work of fiction,"
    "an historic utterance," and as "a work of art toward which one's final
    response is nothing less than a feeling of reverence."

11 "Judgement on Pasternak. The All-Moscow Meeting of Writers 31
    October 1958. Stenographic Report." *Survey,* no. 60, pp. 134–63.
        Proceedings from the general meeting of Moscow writers that
    reveals comments (sincere or affected) by some Soviet writers on
    Pasternak and *Doctor Zhivago.* Includes fourteen speeches—all con-
    demning Pasternak for *Doctor Zhivago,* some demanding for him to
    leave the country, and one (Polevoy) labeling Pasternak "a literary
    Vlasov, a man who ... deserted to the enemy camp, and is now fighting
    on their side."

12 KOVALEVA, RAISA. "Togda" [Then]. *TRSF,* no. 9, pp. 270–87.
    (*UZTGU,* no. 184).
        Recalls her meetings with Pasternak in 1921 and 1922 when she
    frequently met him and and attended his poetry readings. Offers com-
    ments on some of Pasternak's early works and includes Mayakovsky's
    views of Pasternak's early poetry: "Lucky Pasternak. Look what a fine
    poetry he writes." Insists that Pasternak's views of Mayakovsky and the
    futurists in *Doctor Zhivago* were "incorrect." Translated: 1967.18.

13 KROTKOV, IURII. "Pasternaki" [The Pasternaks]. *Grani,* no. 60, pp.
    36–74; no. 63, pp. 58–96.
        Recollections of encounters with Pasternak and his family;
    chronicles major events in Pasternak's life from 1936 until his death.
    Divided into four sections: Pasternak's stay in Georgia in March 1959;
    a portrayal of Zinaida Nikolaevna, Pasternak's second wife; Pasternak
    the man; and a description of Pasternak's family. Records countless
    details about Pasternak's love for Georgian poets and Georgia; his
    thoughts about *Doctor Zhivago* and his work on it (begun in 1938);
    ordinary people's love for and admiration of Pasternak; Pasternak's
    unpretentiousness and simplicity in everyday life; his last days; and
    Russian writers' attitude toward him during the Pasternak Affair, his
    funeral, and other events. Many observations are revealed for the
    first time.

14 NAG, MARTIN. "Ibsen und Pasternak." *ScS* 12: 38–48.
    Records Ibsen's motifs in Pasternak. Believes Pasternak, like Ibsen, discovered the purpose of a poet in his internal struggle. Points out that the "gulfstream" metaphor in Pasternak also echoes Ibsen. Concludes that Pasternak accepted the Revolution as a necessity and that Ibsen's life and works were considered existential by Pasternak. This affinity with Ibsen notwithstanding, sees Pasternak as closer to Chekhov's "solution" in *The Seagull* than to Ibsen's interpretations of symbols in *Wild Duck.*

15 PLANK, DALE L. *Pasternak's Lyric. A Study of Sound and Imagery.* The Hague: Mouton and Co., 124 pp.
    Includes nine chapters, an introduction, and a selected bibliography. Centers on sound instrumentation, imagery, dictation from nature, sound as theme, sound as image, the voice of the image, the grammatical metaphor, and melody and metaphor. Confines analysis to a group of poems written between 1916 and 1932. Cites profusely from Pasternak critcism, such as Tsvetaeva, Weidlé, and Adamovich. Concludes that sound devices are an integral part of the figurative order and that the use of sounds in Pasternak's poetry can be limited to the "descriptive, denotative purposes of language."

16 PORMAN, R. "B.L. Pasternak v Chistopole" [B.L. Pasternak in Chistopol]. *RL*, no. 3, pp. 193–95.
    Recalls Pasternak's stay (winters 1941–42 and 1942–43) in Chistopol, his participation in poetry and prose readings, and his friendship with the Chistopol family of the Avdeevs. Also mentions that Aseyev recommended Pasternak to the Chistopol family of the Vavilovs, from whom Pasternak rented a room, and that Aseyev very frequently visited with Pasternak ("Aseyev usually brought along his poetry for discussion with B. Pasternak"). Includes two of Pasternak's poems, "When in My Recollections" and "The Future Will Change the View of Everything," and Pasternak's letter (dated 26 February 1951) to the Chistopol high–school students.

17 REEVE, F.D. "*Doctor Zhivago* (Pasternak)." In *The Russian Novel.* New York: McGraw-Hill, pp. 360–78.
    Reprint of 1960.30. Reprinted: 1967.13.

18 SINYAVSKY, ANDREI. "On Boris Pasternak." *Encounter* 26 (April): 45–50.
    Selective translation of 1965.4. Reprinted: 1975.14.

19 ———. "La poesia di Pasternak." *NA*, no. 497, pp. 310–29, 483–502; no. 498, pp. 40–57.
    Selective translation of 1965.4.

20 WILLIAMS, RAYMOND. "Tragic Resignation and Sacrifice. Eliot and Pasternak." In *Modern Tragedy*. Stanford, CA: Stanford University Press, pp. 156–73.
Reprint of 1963.20.

21 WILLIAMS-FOXCROFT, ELIZABETH. "Boris Pasternak and *Dr. Zhivago*." *Lantern* 16, no. 2 (December): 6–13.
Provides a biographical sketch of Pasternak, including an assessment of his early and later works, and the circumstances surrounding the publication of *Doctor Zhivago*. Summarizes the plot of the novel, with insights into the motivations of the primary characters. Argues that the living for Pasternak are those who awake from collective sleep and become individual seekers of truth like his main character. Views the descriptions of nature and natural phenomena as an attempt to establish a bond between man and the world: "Pasternak was not concerned with politics. What he wished to achieve was a true picture not of the upheavals that shook Russia, but of their effects on the lives of people . . . to show invisible forces at work in human destinies. This makes *Doctor Zhivago* unique in contemporary Soviet literature."

1967

1 ALLILUYEVA, SVETLANA. "To Boris Leonidovich Pasternak." *Atlantic* 219, no. 6: 133–40.
Compares the fate of Zhivago and Lara to her own tragic life, that of her children, and that of all of Russia. Evokes Pasternak's recurrent images of rebirth, such as spring and the rowan tree, among others. Reflects on what *Doctor Zhivago* has meant to her.

2 CAMPO, CRISTINA. "En profundo silencio, notas sobre el estilo de Pasternak." *ZF* 3, no. 46 (June): 22–27.
Focuses on the poetics of *An Essay in Autobiography*—"a great river of horror and eloquence." Partly attributes this style to Pasternak's childhood experience with music, notably the piano, and elaborates on how this experience transcended to bring about *An Essay in Autobiography*. Also discusses the general content of the autobiography.

3 CANG, JOEL. "Pasternak, Prophet of Jewish Assimilation. Is Russia Rehabilitating the Famed Author?" *JD* 12 (September): 9–12.
Mentions revival of interest in Pasternak in the late 1960s, most notably among the young Jewish writers in the Soviet Union. Claims that Pasternak's father, Leonid Pasternak, had been a "friend of Chaim Weizman and Nahum Sokolov, whose pictures he painted, and was himself in great sympathy with the Zionist movement." Acknowledges

Pasternak's estrangement from Judaism and his assimilation with Christianity and a "Russian Orthodox mysticism." Insists that Pasternak's philosophy of accepting Christianity has found "more and more followers among young Russian Jews." Also mentions that the poems in *Doctor Zhivago* are looked upon as "the Pasternak Bible of Jewish assimilation."

4   GIFFORD, HENRY. "Pasternak and the 'Realism' of Blok." *OSP* 13: 96–106.

Explores the "essential bond" between Blok and Pasternak by applying Pasternak's comments on realism (appearing in "Paul Marie Verlaine," "Chopin" and *An Essay in Autobiography*) to the major works of Blok. Compares Blok's and Pasternak's concepts of realism as "a cross" and "self-sacrifice," respectively. Calls Pasternak "the true successor" to Blok in Russian poetry, and compares Blok's destiny to Zhivago's.

5   GORIÉLY, BENJAMIN. "Pasternàk e il futurismo. Dalla magia della parola al senso morale dell'arte." In *Le avanguardie letterarie in Europa*. Milan: Feltrinelli, pp. 98–108.

Translation of 1961.13.

6   LIVINGSTONE, ANGELA. "Allegory and Christianity in *Doctor Zhivago*." *MSS* 1: 24–33.

Sees a metaphysical meaning as the generative, primary element of *Doctor Zhivago*, dictating the structure of plot and character. Notes that the key to the novel's metaphysics is the notion of immortality as articulated by Vedenyapin. Emphasizes Pasternak's unified, complete identification of the supernatural with the material dimension, giving his metaphysical assertions a literal rather than symbolic truth. Considers the overarching allegorical scheme enacted on the plane of narrative and character as another reason for the novel's awkwardness and lack of surface order.

7   MAGIDOFF, ROBERT. "The Life, Times and Art of Boris Pasternak." *Thought* 42, no. 166 (Fall): 328–57.

Studies the development of Pasternak and his art. Traces the evolution of his attitudes and writings, particularly his acceptance or rejection of aspects of the symbolist, acmeist, futurist, and imagist movements ("Since Pasternak was in some way heir to both the Symbolist revolution and the Acmeist revolution, it was inevitable that he became, however tenuously, a 'fellow traveller' of the Futurists"). Examines the impact of later events on Pasternak's work, suggesting that "the shattering moral and intellectual crisis he brought about by the purge seems to have resulted in the emergence of Christianity as a major theme in Pasternak's prose and poetry," and points out that religious themes cropped up in

Pasternak's writings only after that period: "In a sense, all of his prose that preceded the novel was a proving ground and a preparation for the writing of *Doctor Zhivago*. The book was . . . his credo, a summation of his views . . . a lifetime's heroic deed—testing his mastery as a writer, his depth and integrity as a thinker, his courage as a man."

8   MESHAKOV-KORJAKIN, IGOR. "K probleme lichnosti v romane *Doktor Zhivago* (Lichnost' i Khristianstvo)" [Toward a definition of personality in *Doctor Zhivago* (Personality and Christianity)]. *MSS* 1: 34–48.

Contends that Pasternak's ideological views are revealed not only by Zhivago, but by Vedenyapin, Sima Tuntseva, and Gordon through their religious and philosophical views. Argues that Pasternak's interpretation of immortality "bears no trace of Christianity," which professes "universal individual resurrection from the dead." Discusses the Apocalypse and "immortality as eternity." Regards Zhivago's religious feelings as detached from Christian piety and argues that Zhivago's resurrection is a transformation into a Christ figure. Concludes that the idealistic worldviews of Pasternak "are essentially different from the historical Christianity."

9   MONAS, SIDNEY. "The Revelation of St. Boris: Russian Literature and Individual Autonomy." In *Soviet and Chinese Communism. Similarities and Differences*, edited by Donald W. Treadgold. Seattle: University of Washington Press, pp. 255–87.

Examines *Doctor Zhivago* in the light of the relationship between art and society. Points out the views of Nietzsche, Jung, Marx, Engels, and Freud on this subject. Labels Pasternak "St. Boris" as a reflection of Pasternak's belief that "all art resembles and continues the Revelation of St. John." Describes *Doctor Zhivago* in terms of Christian motifs. Notes that "as a doctor Zhivago resembles Chekhov in his modest urge to be useful," and compares Zhivago with the characters of Strelnikov and Komarovsky. Concludes that neither Pasternak nor Zhivago completely rejected Marxism, but both felt that Marxism: (1) "claims too much for itself" in that it is not a science; (2) destroys man's "connection with the source of his own energies" by "exalting human consciousness and will above all else"; and (3) is "life-denying in its enormous emphasis on the future."

10   MOROZOV, M. "Shekspir v perevode Borisa Pasternaka" [Shakespeare in Boris Pasternak's translations]. In *Shekspir, Berns, Shou . . .* Moscow: Iskusstvo, pp. 218–38.
Reprint of 1944.2.

11   NOSTITZ, OSWALT VON. "Wofür zeugt 'Doktor Schiwago'? (1959)." In *Präsenzen/Kritische Beiträge zur europäischen Geistesgeschichte*. Nuremberg: Glock & Lutz, pp. 202–10.
Reprint of 1959.50.

12 PAYNE, ROBERT. Introduction to *Sister My Life. Summer, 1917.* Translated by Phillip C. Flayderman. New York: Washington Square Press.

Describes Pasternak's conception of art as expounded in *My Sister, Life*, *Doctor Zhivago*, and *The Childhood of Luvers*; his differing orientations toward the February and October revolutions; his nature imagery; and his views of human and natural influences. Sees Pasternak in his earlier art as "divorced entirely from the world of events, entering deeper and deeper into himself, losing himself in a world of sensations." Attributes Lermontov as the only influence upon Pasternak while he was writing *My Sister, Life*. Describes the influence the symbolists and futurists (including Mayakovsky) had upon Pasternak as "nil." Sees *My Sister, Life* as the stepping-stone of Pasternak's development as a poet. Concludes that "if, as he believed, *Doctor Zhivago* was the summit of his achievement, *My Sister, Life* first proclaimed his power over words and the delicacy of his enduring love affair with nature and with living things."

13 REEVE, F.D. *"Doctor Zhivago."* In *The Russian Novel.* London: Frederick Muller, pp. 360–78.

Reprint of 1960.30; 1966.17

14 ROWLAND, MARY F. and PAUL. *Pasternak's Doctor Zhivago.* With a preface by Harry T. Moore. Carbondale and Edwardsville: Southern Illinois University Press, 216 pp.

An attempt to explicate deeper levels of meaning in *Doctor Zhivago*, centering on the novel's artistic qualities—its mythological, allegorical, folkloristic, symbolic, and apocalyptic components. Sees character names as charactonyms and translates "meaningful" place and street names ("Flower Town" and "Gentleman-in-waiting Street," for example). Seeks to relate poems to the novel's prose. Explain Zhivago's "actions from the last days in Varykino to the last days in Moscow" as a "well-established kenotic ideal." Concludes that *Doctor Zhivago* is "an apocalyptic poem in the form of a novel" and that it shows "the power of great art to overcome death." Includes sixteen chapters, notes, and an exhaustive subject index. Reprint of 1960.32; 1961.25–26; 1963.17.

15 SILBAJORIS, RIMVYDAS. "Pasternak and Tolstoj: Some Comparisons." *SEEJ* 11, no. 1: 23–34.

Asserts that although direct comparisons reveal little in common between *Doctor Zhivago* and *War and Peace*, there is nevertheless a kinship, a spiritual bond between the two writers that requires further definition. Pasternak's "lyrical truth," founded on correspondence with "fact transformed by feeling," is contrasted with Tolstoy's literal truth, based on correspondence with fact alone. Their divergent views on art, especially Shakespeare's, are seen as a result of these different views of truth. They are shown to agree in their fundamental views of art as a means of illuminating reality and not as an empty manipulation of aesthetic forms. Argues that both writers strove for their own versions of simplicity and directness, and both saw meaning and purpose in existence. Concludes that both opposed the positive presence of nature to soulless cold mechanism, and both were deeply concerned with the overcoming of death, affirmation of life, and liberation from the bonds of self-consciousness.

16 SINIAVSKI, ANDRÉ. "La poésie de Pasternak." *Esprit*, no. 357, pp. 286–309.
    Selective translation of 1965.4.

17 TERRAS, VICTOR. "Boris Pasternak and Romantic Aesthetics." *PLL* 3: 42–56.
    Defines Pasternak's aesthetics in the Romantic tradition ("a view of poetry as a knowledge of the deepest reality of nature as a living whole, and of poetry as primarily myth and symbolism"). Considers two representative poems, "English Lessons" and "Definition of Poetry," to exemplify the philosophical and aesthetic underpinnings of all of Pasternak's work—animalistic metaphors, a notion of poetic "power," the "almighty god of details," a cosmic vision, a gift for "making it strange," childlike immediacy, and musicality. Links Pasternak's notions of "power" and conception of symbolism with Schellingian Romanticism, with Fet as a poetic imtermediary. Argues that central to Pasternak's romantic aesthetics is a concrete, direct identification.

18 WRIGHT-KOVALEVA, RITA. "Mayakovsky and Pasternak: Fragments of Reminiscence." *OSP*, no. 13, pp. 107–32.
    Part 4, entitled "Togda" [Then], is a translation of 1966.12; pp. 122–32 refer to Pasternak.

19 ZASLOVE, JERALD. "*Dr. Zhivago* and the Obliterated Man: The Novel and Literary Criticism." *JAAC* 26: 65–80.
    Charges Pasternak with replacing real concern for suffering with "cultural reverie" and failing to address the animal aspects of humankind as did Tolstoy and D.H. Lawrence. Believes the novel is permeated with stock scenes, moralistic pronouncements masquerading as insight, and an obliteration of facts and persons into literary symbols, adding up to a poetic and spiritualized abstraction of life. Contrasts the static, detached, and symbolic qualities of Pasternak's abstraction with the dynamics of Tolstoy's Bezukhov. Concludes that Pasternak fails to challenge perceptions because commitment to symbol and "addiction to poesy" push the living human community into the background.

1968

1 ANGELOFF, ALEXANDER. "Water Imagery in the Novel *Doctor Zhivago.*" *RLJ* 22, nos. 81/82: 6–13.

Singles out several aspects of "communion among men" and "man's communion with life's manifestations and with historical events" expressed by water imagery in *Doctor Zhivago*: the essence of death; fear, anxiety, and evil; the awakening of sexual emotions and the vitalization of human attachments; the vitality of man's relationships to nature and to man; and social chaos, war, and revolution. Cites two or three incidents from the novel to support each point. Concludes that Pasternak's water imagery "stops time" to unite the expressive power of language with the meaning of existence.

2 AUCOUTURIER, MICHEL. "*Il Tratto di Apelle*. Manifeste Littéraire du modernisme Russe." *RES* 47: 157–61.

An appraisal of *The Line of Apelles*. Observes that the title points to a symbolic illustration of a certain notion of art in the work, and relates this to tendencies during the 1910s, in part to Kuzmin. Finds that Pasternak already in 1915 surmounted the contradictory views on art propounded by symbolists, acmeists, and futurists in the character of Heine. Insists that it is futile to distinguish craft from talent or technique from creative gifts, which only results in a "hypocritical paradox."

3 CHIAROMONTE, NICOLA. "Pasternak fra la natura e la storia." *TP*, no. 13, pp. 10–21.

Traces Pasternak's concept of history in *Doctor Zhivago*. Believes that the novel is the result of Pasternak's desire to "rescue a crucial epoch in the story of the Russian people from the falsehoods of official history." In this respect Pasternak's view of history is compared to Tolstoy's. Argues that Pasternak focused on the conflict between nature and history. Points out the ambiguity of *Doctor Zhivago*, particularly in the Pasternak-Zhivago character's wavering attitude toward the Revolution. Insists that "*Doctor Zhivago* remains the most passionate and most serious effort by a contemporary writer to represent with love and judge with equity the men and events into whose midst history has thrown him." Translated: 1970.3; 1973.8.

4 COSTELLO, D.P. "*Zhivago* Reconsidered." *FMLS* 4: 70–80.

Ascribes the "incomprehensible vogue" of *Doctor Zhivago* to the overeager readiness of Western readers and critics to hear something profound and significant from Pasternak. Acknowledges Pasternak's gift for descriptive passages. Lack of characterization, defective storytelling, and the "megalomania" of the protagonist are points of contention. Particular exception is taken to vague and misleading use of the word "life" in meaningless metaphysical "gush."

5   DE MICHELIS, CESARE G. "Il tentativo epico di Boris L. Pasternak."
    AnN 11: 57–81.
       A discussion of Pasternak's attitude toward the Revolution. Argues
    that Pasternak preferred the 1905 Revolution to that of 1917, and claims
    that both revolutions played a significant role in Pasternak's works, par-
    ticularly in his prose. Insists that Pasternak does not see a "new salva-
    tion" in any of the two revolutions ("Pasternak non si e mai detto corifeo
    della Rivoluzione, non ha mai annunciato, come Esenin nel poematto
    Inonija 'una nuova salvazione'").

6   GAVRUK, IU. "Nuzhen li novyi perevod 'Gamleta' na russkii iazyk?"
    [Do we need a new Russian *Hamlet* translation?] In *Masterstvo perevoda.
    1966*. Moscow: Sovetskii pisatel', pp. 119–33.
       Registers shortcomings in Pasternak's *Hamlet* translations—lan-
    guage modernization, imagery misinterpretations, lack of expressiveness
    in prose sections, and inadequacy of the "To Be or Not to Be" mono-
    logue, among others. Cites examples to support his contentions.

7   IGNATIEFF, LEONID. "A Philosopher Who Lived His Philosophy:
    Yuri Zhivago." *QQ* 75: 703–17.
       Sees the "main interest" of *Doctor Zhivago* in the life thoughts of
    its hero, which refute the tenets of Marxism and the demands of the rev-
    olutionary regime. Episodes from Zhivago's life and excerpts from his
    philosophical pronouncements are seen to center on the themes of life,
    religion, and love. Offers comparisons between Zhivago and
    Dostoevsky's Prince Myshkin, deemed similar in their Christ-like posi-
    tive attributes yet differing in their strength of character and attitudes
    toward sexual love, suffering, and individualism.

8   LEVIK, V. "Nuzhny li novye perevody Shekspira?" [Do we need new
    Shakespeare translations?] In *Masterstvo perevoda. 1966*. Moscow:
    Sovetskii pisatel', pp. 93–104.
       Comments on Pasternak's Shakespeare translations. Praises
    Pasternak for his simplification of Shakespeare's language (he removed
    "conventionality, harangue"), and argues that Pasternak's use of spoken
    language has "narrowed" Shakespeare's lexica and diminished
    Shakespeare's "contrasts of style."

9   MAGIDOFF, ROBERT. "The Recurrent Image in *Doktor Živago*." In
    Studies in Slavic Linguistics and Poetics in Honor of Boris O. Unbegaun,
    edited by Robert Madigoff. New York: New York University Press, pp.
    79–88.
       Outlines the background of Pasternak's preoccupation with figura-
    tive language and singles out its domains—inanimate nature, details of
    daily life, and Lara ("the very epitome of radiance, purity, and beauty").
    Proves that recurrent imagery "is reserved exclusively for Lara," in

Lara's association with water imagery, the rowan tree, light, air, Russia, and the "miracle of life itself," for example. Discerns similarities of light, sea, rain, and "'water's sighs and tears'" imagery found in *Doctor Zhivago* and *Romeo and Juliet* and *Anthony and Cleopatra*. Argues that the major difference in Shakespeare and Pasternak is Shakespeare's use of all things in his works (good or evil), whereas Pasternak limits his use of recurrent imagery to the good. Underlines that Shakespeare's recurrent imagery "seems to have prompted" Pasternak, yet one cannot "speak of imitation or borrowing on Pasternak's part." Cites examples from *Doctor Zhivago* (in his own translations) and *Romeo and Juliet*.

10   MIHAILOV, MIHAILO. "Pasternak's *Doctor Zhivago*." In *Russian Themes*. New York: Farrar, Straus & Giroux; London: MacDonald, pp. 250–63.

Delineates several areas of fault in *Doctor Zhivago*: a "naive, sprawling, disjointed structure, a lack of drama"; "pale and invisible" characters who all speak with the same voice; "sermonizing and proselytizing"; and untenable ideas on Christianity and the Revolution. Pasternak's passages on love and nature are seen as "transfixingly poetic," and the poetry of Zhivago is regarded as "excellent" and "a flight back to childhood." Argues that *Doctor Zhivago* is only "unequaled" by comparsion with the norm of socialist realism, and is undeserving of its critical acclaim in the West.

11   MOSSMAN, ELLIOTT DUNBAR. "The Prose of the Poet Pasternak." Ph.D. diss., Princeton University, 213 pp.

Examines a correlation between poetry and prose in *My Sister, Life*, *Spektorsky*, *A Tale*, *A Safe Conduct*, and *Doctor Zhivago*. Concludes that: *My Sister, Life*, in addition to being a collection of lyrics, also "depicts the objective history of the summer of 1917 through the objective experience of the poet"; *Spektorsky* and *A Tale* have "the same main character and narrative plot"; *A Safe Conduct* "portrays changes in his [Pasternak's] own life as changes in the lives of his contemporaries"; and the prose in *Doctor Zhivago* is "based upon the workings of the temporal, spatial and casual in the tradition of 19th-century Russian novel." Sees the unifying factor between prose and poetry in the "theme of autobiography—the need to present a life complete within a given segment of time."

12   OZEROV, L. "Zametki Pasternaka o Shekspire" [Pasternak's notes on Shakespeare]. In *Masterstvo perevoda. 1966.* Moscow: Sovetskii pisatel', pp. 111–18.

A general commentary on Pasternak's Shakespeare translations. Emphasizes that Pasternak's Shakespeare goes beyond his Shakespeare renditions and includes his poetics and his works—his poems, prose, and a play all possess Shakespearean reverberations. Sees the gist of Pasternak's poetics in Shakespeare translations in Pasternak's maxim, "like an original, a translation should produce an impression of life, not of literature." Praises Pasternak for his "enormous and multivalent" Shakespearean language.

13 POMORSKA, KRYSTYNA. "Pasternak and Futurism." *RiS* 16: 228–46.
    Highlights Pasternak's association and common features with the futurists, despite the general belief in Pasternak scholarship that he defies classification. Outlines his association with "Centrifuge" and the neofuturist group LEF, with comments on some of the works he authored during those periods (*The Wassermann Test, The Black Goblet*). Provides detailed contextual examinations of the poems "Poetry" (from *Themes and Variations*), "Certain Poetry," and *My Sister, Life*. Observes many characteristics in these works that Pasternak shares with the futurists: strong paronomastic structure (which creates rich sound images), parenthetical constructions, a tendency toward anacolutha and ellipses (resulting in the futurists' colloquialism of the "rough surface" of poetry), the idea of "poetry growing out of everything, even out of trivialites," strong consonantal orientation ("characteristic for Futuristic sound repertory"), and the varied use of the instrumental. Concludes with a comparison of the thematic and psychological features of Pasternak's poetry and prose with those of the futurists.

14 STORA, JUDITH. "Pasternak et le judaïsme." *CMRS* 9: 353–64.
    Insists that Pasternak's vision was enriched by his origins and that until *Doctor Zhivago*, the image of Christ appeared almost exclusively in poems singing glory to God. Analyzes the attitudes Pasternak expressed in *Doctor Zhivago* toward Judaism and Christianity and finds four themes reminiscent of Judaic teaching: (1) throughout the novel the joy of living is affirmed (a fundamental concept in Judaism); (2) certain characters (Sima Tuntseva, for example) regard the soul and the body to be inseparable rather than distinct entities; (3) Pasternak often emphasizes the importance of small details in daily life that grant human existence its substance; and (4) in passages pertaining to immortality, human creative action is regarded as the driving force behind perpetuation of the universe.

15 STRUVE, GLEB. "Some Observations on Pasternak's Ternary Meters." In *Studies in Slavic Linguistics in Honor of Boris O. Unbegaun*, edited by Robert Magidoff. New York: New York University Press, pp. 227–44.
    Counts stress omissions in Pasternak's poetry's ternary meters: (1) three-foot dactyls ("the omission is in the first or second foot"); (2) four-foot dactyls ("the omission of the initial stress is quite usual"); (3) three-foot anapests (predominantly in the second foot); (4) four-foot amphibrachs (either in the first, second, or third foot); and (5) three-foot amphibrachs ("particularly rich in metrical deviations"). Concludes that "there seems to be no doubt that Pasternak should be regarded as an outstanding renovator of Russian ternary verse."

16 TERRAS, VICTOR. "Boris Pasternak and Time." *CSS* 2, no. 2: 264–70.
Contrasts Pasternak's "panchronistic, ahistorical" view of time with the "historical" Mandelstam and "ahistorical" Mayakovsky in terms of philosophy and language. Links Pasternak's optimistic, constantly renewing embrace of the wave of time rushing to the future, to Schelling, Bergson, and *élan vital.* The identification of natural time with human time is said to transcend metaphor to achieve a unique "panpsychistic," "pantheistic," and "panchronistic" vision. Sees Pasternak's "ahistorical, classless, unstylized" language as reflecting this philosophy in contrast to Mayakovsky's "conscious handling of language."

17 TOMAŠEVSKIJ, NIKOLAJ. "Boris Pasternak (Ritratto letterario)." *Annali* 11: 33–51.
An outline of Pasternak's literary career—with a contrastive analysis of two versions of "Venice." Emphasizes the importance of music and philosophy in Pasternak's poetry. Uses the second version of "Venice" to explicate Pasternak's detachment from symbolism. Discusses Pasternak's association with LEF and advances reasons why Pasternak abandoned it (he could not accept the idea of subjugating his art "to the rules of a group"). Elaborates on the poetics of Pasternak's translations, claiming that Pasternak founded a new school of literary translation based more on the recreation of the spirit of the original than a lexical truthfulness to the original. Cites both versions of "Venice"—1913 and 1928.

18 VOZNESENSKII, ANDREI. Review (in Russian) of *Zvezdnoe nebo. Stikhi zarubezhnykh poetov v perevode B. Pasternaka. InL,* no. 1, pp. 199–203.
Conveys his impressions of Pasternak the poet and translator, prompted by Pasternak's last collection of translations, which are summed up as a "dactyloscopic imprint of the master's fate." Detects Pasternak's poetics in translations—"faces and places" of what Pasternak has experienced and seen (Venice and Marburg, among others). Relates his attraction to Pasternak, his reading of *A Safe Conduct* as "the Bible of [my] childhood," a visit to Marburg to reexperience Pasternak, and an attendance (with Pasternak) of the premiere of *Romeo and Juliet* in Pasternak's translation. Concludes that Pasternak "over-turned" poets he translated, including Goethe's *Faust,* the heroine of which is of "minor importance" in the original but in Pasternak's translation "acquires a matter, breathes the life, the pain into it."

19 WAIN, JOHN. "The Meaning of *Dr. Zhivago." CrQ* 10: 113–37.
Views Pasternak as "a major, and perhaps the last, writer of the Symbolist novel . . . arguably the greatest writer of the twentieth century." Points out Pasternak's adherence to symbolist practices and masterful use of imagery; his abandonment of art "experiments" in favor of art

as "an elemental force, a condition of life as urgent as sex or hunger"; his method of expressing by literary methodology a "reverence for the wholeness of life"; his "general contempt" for the conventional rules of the novel, including his tendency to "introduce walloping coincidences"; and his utilization of "linking devices that bind the huge, episodic narrative into a unity" assisted by "unobtrusive threads stitched into a larger design which tend to pull it towards a centre." Emphasizes the use of the New Testament as "back-projection." Suggests that if Shakespeare had lived in the twentieth century and written a novel, "this is the kind of novel it would have been." Defends the novel's coincidences as "primarily a way of reminding us of the extent to which our lives are woven with other people's. The conventional novel avoids coincidences because it feels a need to demonstrate that character is destiny . . . to allow chance into the story is to spoil the neatly ruled pattern. Pasternak delights in spoiling the pattern, or rather in opening it up to show the deeper pattern underneath." Reprinted: 1968.20.

20 ———. "The Meaning of Dr. Zhivago." In *A House for the Truth. Critical Essays.* New York: Viking Press, pp. 128–60. Reprint. 1972. Reprint. London: Macmillan, 1973.
Reprint of 1968.19.

1969

1 ASEEV, NIKOLAI. "Melody or Intonation." In *Pasternak. Modern Judgements*, edited by Donald Davie and Angela Livingstone. London: Macmillan, pp. 73–84.
Translation of 1923.1.

2 AUCOUTURIER, MICHEL. "The Legend of the Poet and the Image of the Actor in the Short Stories of Pasternak." In *Pasternak. Modern Judgements*, edited by Donald Davie and Angela Livingstone. London: Macmillan, pp. 220–30.
Reprint of 1966.4.

3 CHIAROMONTE, NICOLA. "Pasternak's Message." In *Pasternak. Modern Judgements*, edited by Donald Davie and Angela Livingstone. London: Macmillan, pp. 231–39.
Reprint of 1958.9.

4 DAVIE, DONALD. Introduction to *Pasternak. Modern Judgements*, edited by Donald Davie and Angela Livingstone. London: Macmillan, pp. 11–34.
Breaks the introduction into four parts: "Pasternak: the Early Collections," "Pasternak and the Formalists," "Pasternak: the Middle

Period," and "From 1934 to the End." Examines three means by which non-Russian-speaking readers can understand the essence of Pasternak: sound, symbolism, and syntax. Notes the difficulty of translating Pasternak's syntax from highly inflected Russian into English. Compares Pasternak to Hart, Crane, Dryden, Mallarme, Verlaine, and Valéry, among others. Points out Pasternak's "revolution in poetic method," and cites from Mandelstam, Bryusov, and Tynyanov. Discusses *A Safe Conduct* and mentions Pasternak's avoidance of biography as spectacle.

5   DAVIE, DONALD, and ANGELA LIVINGSTONE, eds. *Pasternak. Modern Judgements*. Verse translations by Donald Davie. London: Macmillan, 278 pp.
    In addition to 1922.4; 1922.7; 1923.1; 1923.5; 1924.4; 1926.1; 1928.5; 1935.2; 1958.9; 1959.17; 1959.27; 1965.4; and 1966.4, includes Akhmatova's poem "Boris Pasternak" in its original form and in the English translation.

6   DEUTSCHER, ISAAC. "Pasternak and the Calendar of the Revolution." In *Pasternak. Modern Judgements*, edited by Donald Davie and Angela Livingstone. London: Macmillan, pp. 240–58.
    Reprint of 1959.17.

7   EHRENBURG, ILYA. "Boris Leonidovich Pasternak." In *Pasternak. Modern Judgements*, edited by Donald Davie and Angela Livingstone. London: Macmillan, pp. 39–41.
    Translation of 1922.4.

8   HAMPSHIRE, S.N. *"Doctor Zhivago."* In *Modern Writers and Other Essays*. London: Chatto & Windus, pp. 136–42. Reprint. New York: Knopf, 1970.
    Reprint of 1958.23. Reprinted: 1978.17.

9   HAYWARD, MAX. Foreword to *The Blind Beauty. A Play by Boris Pasternak*. Translated by Max Hayward and Manya Harari. London: Collins and Harvill Press, pp. 5–12.
    Relates Pasternak's views of *The Blind Beauty* and the way he was working on it—as reported in Pasternak's correspondence and an interview Pasternak gave to Olga Carlisle. Narrates in detail the play's content—both the written part (the prologue and the first act), and the then-unwritten remainder, later published by Olga Carlisle following her interview with Pasternak (1962.6). Compares the play to Gogol's *Dead Souls* and to *Doctor Zhivago*, the latter in terms of Pasternak's philosophy of history, noting that "he was concerned to show in this play, as well as in his novel, that the history in which we are trapped is only a mirage, always about to dissolve into another one."

10   HOWE, IRVING. "Freedom and the Ashcan of History." In *Pasternak.*
Modern Judgements, edited by Donald Davie and Angela Livingstone.
London: Macmillan, pp. 259–68.
       Reprint of 1959.27.

11   IVASK, IURII. "Tsvetaeva—Maiakovskii—Pasternak" (in Russian).
NZh, no. 95, pp. 161–85.
       Argues that the hero of *Doctor Zhivago* is the last superfluous man
in Russian literature. Sees Zhivago and Lara not as holy people, but as
wandering pilgrims. Believes that all themes have greater resonance in
Pasternak's poetry than in his prose. Views the novel as striking in its
spiritual power, but cannot call it a success at the artistic level, due particularly to its unconvincing plot. Finds errors in Zhivago's poetry. Sees
the poem "In the Hospital" as Pasternak's last farewell to life, a "personal, private talk with God."

12   JAKOBSON, ROMAN. "Marginal Notes on the Prose of the Poet
Pasternak." In *Pasternak. Modern Judgements*, edited by Donald Davie
and Angela Livingstone. London: Macmillan, pp. 135–51.
       Translation of 1935.2.

13   LEZHNEV, A. "The Poetry of Boris Pasternak." In *Pasternak. Modern
Judgements*, edited by Donald Davie and Angela Livingstone. London:
Macmillan, pp. 85–107.
       Translation of 1926.1.

14   LOTMAN, IURII M. "Stikhotvoreniia rannego Pasternaka i nekotorye
voprosy strukturnogo izucheniia teksta" [Pasternak's early poetry and
some questions of structural text analysis]. *TZS* 4: 206–38.
       Conducts a profound semantic analysis of sketches and rough
drafts of Pasternak's early poetry, elaborating on the range of "referents" and vocabulary variants that Pasternak used to correlate motifs
and to synthesize images needed "to describe an actual situation produced jointly by the nature of these referents, their actions, and interre-
lationships." Notes Pasternak's shifting of semantic relations to draw
nearer to the "reality" of his themes. Discusses Pasternak's concept of
seeing the world ("it is a world actually *seen and experienced*") as noted
by Tsvetaeva ("In his verse Pasternak *sees* and I *hear*"); his "humanization of the world"; and his attempts at philosophical self-determination.
Argues strongly against identification of Pasternak's early poetry as symbolist or acmeist. Reprinted: 1971.9. Translated and abridged: 1978.28.

15   MANDEL'SHTAM, OSIP. "Notes on Poetry." In *Pasternak. Modern
Judgements*, edited by Donald Davie and Angela Livingstone. London:
Macmillan, pp. 67–72.
       Translation of 1923.5.

16 RÜHLE, JÜRGEN. "The Voice of Russia." In *Literature and Revolution. A Critical Study of the Writer and Communism in the Twentieth Century.* London: Pall Mall Press, pp. 117–29.
   Translation of 1963.18.

17 SINYAVSKY, ANDREI. "Boris Pasternak." In *Pasternak. Modern Judgements*, edited by Donald Davie and Angela Livingstone. London: Macmillan, pp. 154–219.
   Translation of 1965.4. Reprinted: 1978.37.

18 TSVETAYEVA, MARINA. "A Downpour of Light: Poetry of Eternal Courage." In *Pasternak. Modern Judgements*, edited by Donald Davie and Angela Livingstone. London: Macmillan, pp. 42–66.
   Translation of 1922.7.

19 TYNYANOV, YURI. "Pasternak's 'Mission.'" In *Pasternak. Modern Judgements*, edited by Donald Davie and Angela Livingstone. London: Macmillan, pp. 126–34.
   Translation of 1924.4. Reprinted: 1978.39.

20 WEIDLE, WLADIMIR. "The Poetry and Prose of Boris Pasternak." In *Pasternak. Modern Judgements*, edited by Donald Davie and Angela Livingstone. London: Macmillan, pp. 108–25.
   Translation of 1928.5.

1970

1 AUCOUTURIER, MICHEL. "The Metonymous Hero or the Beginnings of Pasternak the Novelist." In "Symposium in Memory of Boris Pasternak (1890–1960)." *BA* 44: 222–27.
   Traces the Pasternakian hero in *The Tale* and *Spektorsky*, in which, for the first time, a childlike spontaneity and a feminine receptivity appear as traits of an "individual character" in Sergey Spektorsky. Sees this "metonymous hero" as the touchstone of Pasternak's poetics with its effacement of the subject and its allusive narrative method that results in a lack of intrigue, drama, or psychological analysis. The development of Pasternak's hero is discussed from Spektorsky's "organ of . . . reception, . . . incapable of acting" to the symbolic, ineffective reaction of the hero of *The Tale*; this hero forshadows the Zhivago-Hamlet-Christ images, the "social and moral justification" of which is presented in *Doctor Zhivago*. Reprinted: 1978.1.

2 BARNES, CHRISTOPHER. Introduction to Pasternak's *Dramatic Fragments.*" *Encounter* 35, no. 1: 15–16.
   Explicates Pasternak's *Dramatic Fragments* and compares it to *Doctor Zhivago*, *The Year 1905*, *Lieutenant Schmidt*, and *A High*

Malady. Claims that the difference between early and later Pasternak is that the "'Dramatic Fragments' contain little of that fatalism and pessimism which marked Pasternak's later attitudes to the Revolution." Notes that the setting for the first two *Fragments* is during the French Revolution—"a simple translocation of the Russian revolutionary scene." Sees the main character in the third *Fragment* acting "as the vehicle for some recognizably Pasternakian thoughts as he replies to a French Police interrogation." Concludes that the "'Dramatic Fragments' are perhaps the first clear forecast in Pasternak's work of the characters and fates of his later heroes" and that this is "his first work on an overtly historical theme."

3 CHIAROMONTE, NICOLA. "Pasternak, Nature and History." In *The Paradox of History: Stendhal, Tolstoy, Pasternak and Others*. London: Weidenfeld Nicolson, pp. 117–32. Reprint. Philadelphia: University of Pennsylvania Press, 1985.
      Translation of 1968.3.

4 FARYNO, JERZY. "Wybrane zagadnienia poetyki Borysa Pasternaka" [Chosen themes of Boris Pasternak's poetics]. *SO* 19, no. 3: 271–89.
      An examination of Pasternak's poetics and "poetic world" as reflected in early poetry, primarily in "The Crying Garden," "A Girl," "With Oars at Rest," "Early Frosts," "Improvization," and "Do Not Touch." Conducts a thorough textual, contextual, and intertextual analysis of these poems. Compares Pasternak's poetics to that of Tsvetaeva, Akhmatova, and Khlebnikov. Observes that Pasternak tries to create an image of the world without using physical elements; rather, he uses elements that are unnoticeable by traditional standards. Stresses Pasternak's use of the subject created through continuum; insists that a correct interpretation of Pasternak's artistic message requires a profound analysis of his numerous texts. Concludes that Pasternak's poetic world is very complex and unique and has deep roots in the philosophy of that time as well as in physics (Einstein), psychology, and linguistics (in the works of Ferdinand de Saussure). Claims that Pasternak's poetics reflects other Russian writers (Tyutchev, Fet, and Dostoevsky—his "philosophical system," in particular).

5 HUGHES, OLGA RAEVSKY. "Pasternak and Cvetaeva: History of a Friendship." In "Symposium in Memory of Boris Pasternak (1890–1960)." *BA* 44: 218–21.
      Draws upon Tsvetaeva's letters to Pasternak, Pasternak's *An Essay in Autobiography*, and the poems that Tsvetaeva and Pasternak addressed to each other to produce a chronology and analysis of their relationship. Themes that emerge from the materials include the depth of their literary and poetic friendship versus the disappointment of their real-life

meetings, the contrast between the exuberance of Tsvetaeva's poetic tributes and Pasternak's reticence, and the position of both poets in a small minority of poets of their generation.

6   KASACK, WOLFGANG. "Die Funktion der Erzählschlüsse in Pasternaks *Doctor Živago.*" *ZSP* 25: 170–86.

Gives a brief history of the novel's reception. Compares the novel's epilogue to Turgenev's, Dostoevsky's, and Tolstoy's novels and to Eberhard Lämmert's theory of "Bauformen des Erzählens." Argues that sentences ending sections and chapters either emphasize the plot already narrated, hint at the narrative to unfold, or are used as a surprise or tension device. Discusses the relationship between the two concluding chapters and the "Poems by Yury Zhivago" chapter.

7   KASHIN, ALEJANDRO. "La peligrosidad de Pasternak." *Arco* 11, no. 112 (February): 144–46.

Outlines Pasternak's literary career, focusing on his early poetry, notably *My Sister, Life* and his poetry of the early 1930s. Claims that the central points of Pasternak's writing are the word and man, never political ideas, and that Pasternak "looked at the world through the eyes of a child."

8   MALLAC, GUY DE. "Zhivago Versus Prometheus." In "Symposium in Memory of Boris Pasternak (1890–1960)." *BA* 44: 227–31.

Discusses Pasternak's "philosophy of natural authenticity," the clash between nature and Promethean man, in which Pasternak is seen as mounting a protest against the excesses of "technological" society in favor of a more contemplative, autonomous existence. Draws parallels to the eighteenth-century vitalists, who similarly revolted against the scientifically based mechanization of nature. Cites Bergson and Hamsun as sources of influence. Reconciles Pasternak's interest in urban aesthetics and praise of labor with the primacy of nature by the overarching concept of organic nature accessible through mediation of human labor. Revised: 1981.14.

9   MIŁOSZ, CZESŁAW. "On Pasternak Soberly." In "Symposium in Memory of Boris Pasternak (1890–1960)." *BA* 44: 200–209.

Discusses several aspects of Pasternak's writings, concentrating on the poet's role and image. Sees Pasternak's achievement as a poet as his emerging out of the dialectical cross-pressure of various contradicting aspects of his art such as narcisstic self-renunciation, strength through weakness, and "atheological" Christianity. Mentions Pasternak's "Sovietness"; the anti-intellectual and linguistically founded perceptions of his poetry; and his integral, organic conception of symbolism. Reprinted: 1977.16.

10 MOREAU, JEAN-LUC. "The Passion According to Zhivago." In "Symposium in Memory of Boris Pasternak (1890–1960)." *BA* 44: 237–43.

Explores religious and philosophical echoes of Christ's Passion in *Doctor Zhivago*, beginning with the premise that the novel picks up where Blok left off in *The Twelve*, completing a modern Passion cycle. Traces "Star of the Nativity," "Hamlet," and "Garden of Gethsemane" with respect to the cycle of seasons and spiritual progress they depict. Examines thematic resonances with Rilke and Dostoevsky. The symbolic importance of women and the earth are fitted into the scheme. Emphasizes the centrality of the Gospel to Pasternak's thought.

11 ODABASHIAN, PETROS. "An Onomastic Study of *Doktor Živago*, a Novel by B. Pasternak." Ph.D. diss., University of Pennsylvania, 241 pp.

A thorough study of personal names and nicknames in *Doctor Zhivago*, with emphasis on the formation of names, their derivative, diminutive, and patronymic forms. Claims to have verified all names against dictionaries of names, with surnames checked against "the Moscow Telephone Directory, the Petrograd Address Directory (1916), the Leningrad Address Directory (1935), the Moscow Address Directory (1930), the Biographical Dictionary and the Large Soviet Encyclopedia." Finds that only less than one-third of surnames in *Doctor Zhivago* are in dictionaries, that Pasternak "makes excessive use of diminutive forms," and that some "surnames are given a stylistic function."

12 PASTERNAK, E.V. "Rabota Borisa Pasternaka nad tsiklom 'Nachal'naia pora'" [Boris Pasternak's work on the cycle "A Primary Time"]. *RZIa* 4: 124–28.

A commentary on Pasternak's reworking of the *A Twin in the Clouds* collection into the "A Primary Time" cycle published in the 1929 edition of *Above the Barriers*. Cites and discusses some textual/lexical modifications that display "textological movement from the conception to completion." Suggests that these criteria were observed in the revision process: (1) "rhythmical and intonational inertia of the verse"; (2) "norms of unaffected language"; (3) "absolute substance and pithiness" of the text; and (4) "the utmost exactness and power of expressiveness." Includes all corrected poems originally contained in the *A Twin in the Clouds* copy Pasternak presented to A.L. Shtikh.

13 PAUL, SHERMAN. "An Art of Life: Pasternak's Autobiographies." *Salmagundi* 16: 17–33.

Summarizes Pasternak's two autobiographies and places them in the context of his art and life—the historical, personal and artistic factors that affected his "choice" to look back at two different points in his life in two different ways. Sees *A Safe Conduct* as a "recreation of self," an autobiographical assessment prompted by the "vicarious death" of Mayakovsky and a creative impasse caused by events in his personal life. Perceives *An Essay in Autobiography* as a complement to *A Safe Conduct* (as well as a code to *Doctor Zhivago*), rather than a renunciation of it. Sees Pasternak's relationship with Mayakovsky, deemed central to both works, as "renounced" in *An Essay in Autobiography* as part of a "simple and direct" affirmation of life in the face of the extraordinary adverse pressures to which Mayakovsky succumbed.

14 POSELL, ELSA Z. "Boris Leonidovich Pasternak. February 10, 1890–May 30, 1960." In *Russian Authors.* Boston: Houghton Mifflin Co., pp. 184–203.

A concise biography of Pasternak and a brief discussion of his major works. Details the political and ideological sources of Pasternak's persecution by some Soviet critics, the Soviet government, and neighbors. Accompanies this description with mixed Soviet and foreign reception of some of his works. Describes the Nobel Prize controversy and Pasternak's expulsion from the Writers' Union. Briefly touches on Pasternak's later years, heart condition, painful cancer, and funeral.

15 RZHEVSKII, L. "Roman 'Doktor Zhivago' B. Pasternaka: Stil' i zamysel" [B. Pasternak's novel *Doctor Zhivago*: The style and design.] In *Prochten'e tvorcheskogo slova. Literaturovedcheskie problemy i analizy.* New York: New York University Press, pp. 83–192.

Reprint (with modifications of chapters 3 and 4) of 1962.23.

16 SILBAJORIS, RIMVYDAS. "The Conception of Life in the Art of Boris Pasternak." In "Symposium in Memory of Boris Pasternak (1890–1960)." *BA* 44: 209–14.

Explains Pasternak's conception of individual consciousness and its integration by means of art into a larger and more significant whole. Sees this process as illustrative of Pasternak's fundamentally optimistic worldview, differing from the posture taken by many modern artists. Argues that Pasternak conveys the unity and dynamism of life through such devices as fusion of disparate elements, distortion of physical phenomena, and dissolution of the personal "I." Concludes that such a dissolution, achieved by an artistic self-awareness that continues and perfects life rather than opposing it, is a biological camouflage and part of Pasternak's conception of immortality.

17 STERPELLONE, ALPHONSO. "A dieci anni dalla morte. Ricordo di Pasternak." *NA* 509, no. 2033: 46–65.

Evaluates Pasternak's popularity ten years after his death. Details Pasternak's life in the 1950s, centering on the difficulties Pasternak experienced after the Nobel Prize controversy. Supplements his arguments with information obtained from the correspondence with Zinaida

Nikolaevna, Pasternak's second wife. Claims that Pasternak's fame was growing within the new generation of writers and critics, both in the Soviet Union and abroad.

18 STRUVE, GLEB. "The Hippodrome of Life: The Problem of Coincidences in *Doctor Zhivago.*" In "Symposium in Memory of Boris Pasternak (1890–1960)." *BA* 44: 231–36.

Recounts in detail several coincidences in the plot of *Doctor Zhivago*, labeling them "a deliberate structural pattern" that provides compositional underpinnings of foreshadowing and relationships between diverse characters—as well as expressing a deeper theme of predestination and intertwined destinies. In addition to coincidences of the plot, Pasternak is said to use "symbolic coincidences" such as those between the rowan berry tree and the berrylike drops of blood in the snow after Strelnikov's suicide.

19 "Symposium in Memory of Boris Pasternak (1890–1960)." *BA* 44: 195–243.

A collection that consists of a brief introduction by Ivar Ivask, four previously unpublished letters by Pasternak, eight articles: 1970.1; 1970.5; 1970.8; 1970.9; 1970.10; 1970.16; 1970.18; and 1970.20; and a bibliography of articles dealing with Pasternak that appeared in *Books Abroad* from 1935 to 1970.

20 WEIDLÉ, WLADIMIR. "A Contemporary's Judgement." In "Symposium in Memory of Boris Pasternak (1890–1960)." *BA* 44: 215–17.

Reviews his previous critique of Pasternak's early poetry (1928.5) and confirms his earlier judgments. Still argues that Pasternak's chief shortcoming is the "unintelligibility of means," that Pasternak's feeling for the word does not go deep enough, and that Pasternak's word choice is not always apt or accurate. Commends Pasternak for his renunciation of his earlier style of "approximation of meaning," which sacrifices accuracy to style. Translated: 1970.21.

21 ———. "Pogljadev nazad, o Pasternake" [On Pasternak, with hind sight]. *NZh*, no. 98, pp. 105–11.

Translation of 1970.20.

22 ZELINSKY, K. "Pasternak." In *Soviet Literature. Problems and People.* Moscow: Progress Publishers, pp. 110–17. Reprint. 1973.

General views of Pasternak's poetry and his attitude toward the Soviet system. Observes that: (1) "Pasternak's subjectivity, capriciousness, and paradoxicality were indeed unprecedented in poetry"; (2) "Pasternak became so completely carried away by the play of sounds or the fascination of his unorthodox comparisons that he had no thought for their meaning"; (3) "Pasternak shocks you twice: first, with the sound and structure of his poetry, its monophonism and the startling unpredictability of the metaphors and comparisons . . . and then comes the second shock: the narrowness of his social horizon"; and (4) Pasternak "is unequalled in his genius for creating a monophonic surge of sounds and words." Argues that "Pasternak thought socialism the most important thing of the age, and the Russian Revolution its foremost event," and that he wrote *Doctor Zhivago* from a position "ideologically unprepared to understand the principle aims of the Revolution." Cites excerpts from Pasternak's letter (6 November 1958) to the editors of *Pravda*, concluding that "Pasternak himself deplored the consequences resulting from the publication of his novel." Includes some remarks based on personal encounters with Pasternak ("I knew this remarkable man and poet too well to think so ill of him").

1971

1   ARNOLD, JOHN. "Hamlet in Gethsemane. A Study of Boris Pasternak." *Theology* 74, no. 609 (March): 111–18.
    Compares the ficticious lives of Zhivago and Hamlet with the real-life dramas of Pasternak and Jesus. Points out parallels in the goals, development, and "transfiguration" of all four as manifested in the poems "Hamlet" and "The Garden of Gethsemane." Interprets the reference to drowning in Pharisaism, for example, as "the universal pharisaism in Jerusalem at that fateful Passover, in the court at Elsinore and the rotten state of Denmark, in Zhivago's experience of the Civil War, of Pasternak's experience, of our experience, and of others' experience of us. It is a universal flood . . ."

2   BURKIN, IVAN. "Metonymy in the Poetry of Pasternak." In *Zbirnyk na poshanu profesora doktora Iuriia Shevelova. Symbolae in honorem Georgii Y. Shevelov*, edited by William E. Harkins, Olexa Horbatsch, and Jacob Hursky. Ukrains'kyi vil'nyi universytet. Naukovyi zbirnik, no. 7. Munich: Logos, pp. 91–103.
    Analyzes the metonymy in *The Year 1905* on lexical and syntactical levels. Lists lexical metonymic substitutions involving nouns (ten types), adjectives, numerals, verbs, and adverbs as well as syntactic subsitutions ("Here, metonymy embraces a larger context and even extends to the discourse level"). Adds that "metonymy may even affect the structure of the sentence"—in elliptical constructions, nominal sentences, and the use of passive instead of active." Concludes that metonymy on the syntactical level is a manifestation of futurism while on the lexical level it is a reflection of "Pasternak's excessive use of colloquialisms and a prosaic style in general."

3 CHUDAKOVA, M.O. "Novye avtografy B.L. Pasternaka" [B.L. Pasternak's new manuscripts]. In *Zapiski otdela rukopisei*. Vol. 32. Moscow: Gosudarstvennaia biblioteka imeni Lenina, pp. 208–19.

Discusses eight of Pasternak's poems—two published for the first time—found in the A.M. Efros archive. Elaborates on the poems' publication history, explains lexical changes in the text, establishes the correct variants, and mentions the poems' contextual bonds to other poets (Pushkin and Fet, for example). Includes "Butterfly-Storm," "Sailing Away," "The Coming of Winter," "The Seventh Floor," "Roosters," "Autumn," "Buoyancy," and "Flight."

4 DEBENEDETTI, GIACOMO. "Pasternak e Moravia." In *Il romanzo del Novecento*. Milan: Garzanti, pp. 114–25.

Records differences and similarities between Pasternak and Moravia. Argues that Pasternak uses the probability of a subject he writes about to make an episode occur. Thinks that the "modern romance" in Pasternak hinges on "probability"—and not on certainty. Adds that Pasternak uses this probability to show the dramatic effects of the realization of a situation.

5 DYCK, J.W. "Ambiguity and Paradox in *Doctor Zhivago*: Coincidence or Design? Dualism, Duplicity, and Paradox in Pasternak's *Dr. Zhivago*." In *The Language Learner: Reaching His Heart and Mind. Proceedings of the Second International Conference*. Toronto: Ontario Modern Language Teacher's Association, pp. 232–38.

Sees notions of duplicity, duality, contrapositions, plurality, and paradox as the most prominent features of *Doctor Zhivago*. Applies these notions to Zhivago (his wishes and desires, his two dreams, and "circumstances and events" surrounding him), Lara, Yevgraf, Antipov, Komarovsky, and "the entangled relationship between the major characters." Details the Zhivago-Lara relationship: the Lara-Yury-Tonya triangle is one "of the most opportune love stories in modern literature," it "is not as intricate as it is providential," and "Yury's relationships to Tonya and to Lara have their beginning in sources which are diametrically opposed to each other." Concludes that the novel's characters "are endowed with a plurality which does not lend itself to a traditional classification of characters, such as good and bad, positive and superfluous, or simply protagonists and antagonists," and " it is within the interplay of his characters that Pasternak designs man's anxieties and concerns." Reprinted in 1972.7.

6 FILIPPOV, BORIS. "O proze Pasternaka" [On Pasternak's prose]. *Vozrozhdenie*, no. 228, pp. 69–83.

A general commentary on Pasternak's prose, which is labeled a "new prose"—"breaking a system of images, character modes, plot development devices ... and changing a syntax." Also notes that

Pasternak's prose is an "intersection" between Gogol's and Dostoevsky's, that it is "impetuous," with details surfacing instantaneously, and that it strives to perceive the world spontaneously and in its original appearance. Concludes that Pasternak's *oeuvre* "has been a preparation for his life's work"—*Doctor Zhivago*. Reprinted: 1981.5.

7 JAKOBSON, ROMAN. "Kontury Glejtu" [The Contours *of A Safe Conduct*]. In *Studies in Verbal Art. Texts in Czech and Slovak*. Ann Arbor, MI: Czechoslovak Society of Arts and Sciences in America and the Department of Slavic Languages and Literatures, University of Michigan, pp. 386–94.
   Reprint of 1935.1.

8 LOTMAN, IU. M. "Analiz dvukh stikhotvorenii" [An Analysis of two poems]. In *Teksty sovetskogo literaturovedcheskogo strukturalizma. Texte des sowjetischen literaturwissenschaftlichen Strukturalismus*. Centrifuga: Russian Reprintings and Printings, no. 5. Munich: Wilhelm Fink Verlag, pp. 191–224.
   Analyzes "A Woman Substitute"—structure, literary associations (Lermontov), semantics, rhythms, and its dependence on the poetics of Russian Romanticism. Shows that the poem's title reflects "the double tradition" of Lermontov and Heine ("Ich stand in dunkeln Träumen"). Detects the avant-garde's conception of sameness between words and objects (i.e., the poem's depiction of a photo as if it were a sweetheart). Also detects the abrupt meter shift, which makes the last five stanzas almost a separate poem. Demonstrates how a "text configuration makes up a semantic structure of a movement identical to life."

9 ———. "Stikhotvoreniia rannego Pasternaka i nekotorye voprosy strukturnogo izucheniia teksta" [Pasternak's early poems and some questions of structural text studies]. In *Teksty sovetskogo literaturovedcheskogo strukturalizma. Texte des sowjetischen literaturwissenschaftlichen Strukturalismus*. Centrifuga: Russian Reprintings and Printings, no. 5. Munich: Wilhelm Fink Verlag, pp. 206–38.
   Reprint of 1969.14.

10 MAYER, HANS. *"Doctor Zhivago."* In *Steppenwolf and Everyman*. New York: Cromwell, pp. 256–80.
   Translation of 1962.18.

11 MORGAN, JAMES. Introduction to *The Poems of Doctor Zhivago*. Translated by Eugene M. Kayden. Kansas City: Hallmark Cards, pp. 4–10.
   Offers a short synopsis of events in *Doctor Zhivago* that lead up to the writing of the Zhivago poems. Notes that through all of Zhivago's

poems "runs the assertion of the value of life, of beauty, of nature," and concludes that "Zhivago is a man caught between two realities—the reality of history, of the everyday world and the reality of his own poetic vision."

12 MOSSMAN, ELLIOTT. "Pasternak's Prose Style: Some Observations." *RLT*, no. 1, pp. 386–98.

Investigates several stylistic traits of Pasternak's shorter prose works, accompainied by specific examples. Sees these as an accordance of neologisms and phonetic progressions instead of "substantial and verifiable" bridges of association based on etymology and regionalisms. Sees traces of "ornamentalism" in the "comprendia of associations" and various types of rhythmization, including alliteration, anaphora, and mimetic prose containing secondary associations. Argues that relativity of time and space distinguishes Pasternak's short prose. Views such stylistic traits as "eccentricities" that, though not necessarily peculiar to Pasternak alone, do not represent a systematized effort to forge a consciously experimental normative style.

13 NOVIKOVA, M. "Kits—Marshak—Pasternak (Zametki ob individual'nom perevodcheskom stile)" [Keats—Marshak—Pasternak (Notes on a specific translation style)]. In *Masterstvo perevoda. Sbornik vos'moi.* Moscow: Sovetskii pisatel', pp. 28–54.

Compares Pasternak's and Marshak's translation styles as reflected in their renditions of Keats's sonnet "Grasshopper" and a lyric poem "To Autumn." Finds that in the sonnet rendition, Pasternak "gravitates" toward a spoken language, does not often "preserve" details of the original, and truthfully renders "philosophical" nature descriptions. Claims that in Pasternak's rendition of "To Autumn," the style of Keats becomes more agitated and "viscous" due to the abundance of adverbial participles, participles, and "exclusive" expressions.

14 PENICHE VALLADO, LEOPOLDO. "*El Dr. Jivago*, una gran novela contrarrevolucionaria." *CA* 175: 217–29.

Focuses on the political aspect of *Doctor Zhivago*. Discusses the role it played in the political environment of the time, and mentions the novel's historical content, its ideological substance, and Pasternak's stance toward the Revolution. Cites lengthy passages from the novel to illustrate his points.

15 REAVEY, GEORGE. "Translation as Experience." In *The World of Translation. Papers Delivered at the Conference on Literary Translation Held in New York City in May 1970*. New York: P.E.N. American Center, pp. 223–30. Reprint. 1987.

A commentary on Pasternak's poetry, prose, and development as a poet. Contrasts two of Pasternak's poems, "Lines on Pushkin's 'The

Prophet'" (1918) and "The Thrushes" (1941), to demonstrate changes in Pasternak's style. Investigates similar stylistic shifts in Pasternak's prose ("its simplification and, as it were, its movement towards a broader, more conscious reality than in the earlier prose"), while discussing *The Childhood of Luvers*, *The Tale*, and *Doctor Zhivago*. Comments on Pasternak's responses to his queries posed to Pasternak during their meeting "shortly before his [Pasternak's] death."

16 SIMONOV, K. "Pravil'nyi put'" [The correct way]. In *DP*, pp. 170–71.
      Reprint of 1943.3.

17 STONE, HAROLD. "The Enigma of Yurii Zhivago." *PP* 2: 52–63.
      Analyzes Zhivago's personality and offers sporadic comments on other major characters—Lara, Tonya, Yevgraf, Antipov, and Komarovsky. Finds Zhivago's character enigmatic due to some of his contradictory qualities—noticing evil in the Revolution and power in Antipov but not "in himself," and being unable to "bridge the gap between the scientific and literary disciplines" ("He was a physician ... also a poet and artist. These two worlds were not reconciled in him"). Attempts to decode symbolism in the novel's four dreams as they regard Zhivago's personality, such as a symbol of Sashenka as "the potential for [Zhivago's] masculine development" and the image of Lara, "this powerful image of the anima."

18 STRUVE, GLEB. "Pasternak (1890–1960)." In *Russian Literature under Lenin and Stalin 1917–1953*. Norman: University of Oklahoma Press, pp. 180–85.
      Revised reprint of 1951.2.

19 TERRAS, VICTOR. "'Im Walde'—Goethe und Boris Pasternak." *WS* 16, no. 3: 283–88.
      Cites Pasternak's poem "In the Forest," which is considered equal to Griboedov's *Woe From Being Smart*, Goethe's *Sorrows of a Young Werther*, and one of Solomon Gessner's idylls. Bases his parallels on the motif of "cosmic hour" reflected in the penultimate line from "In the Forest": "The happy ones do not observe the hours"—and notes Pasternak borrowed the line from *Woe From Being Smart*.

1972

1 ANNING, N.J. "Introduction: 'One and the Same Life.'" *TeC*, no. 1: 71–96.
      An analysis of links (lexical, structural, and thematic) and allusions between *Three Chapters from a Tale* and *The Tale*, *Spektorsky*, two autobiographies, and *Doctor Zhivago*. Argues that *Three Chapters* "is an

important stage in the evolution of Pasternak's plans in writing both *Spektorskii* and *The Story*" and that it "establishes an indisputable continuity between his writing in the 1920s and ... *Doctor Zhivago.*" Sees the title of part 2, "The Maid of Woe," as taken from *The Lay of the Host of Igor'*. Includes the Russian text of *Three Chapters from a Tale*.

2   BARNES, CHRISTOPHER J. "Boris Pasternak and Rainer Maria Rilke: Some Missing Links." *FMLS* 8, no. 1: 61–78.
    Surveys thoroughly the criticism of the Pasternak-Rilke relationship; examines Rilke's influence on *A Twin in the Clouds* (which shares the "introspective mood and subdued imagery" of Rilke's *Das Stunden Buch*) and on Pasternak's rough draft translations of Rilke's poetry (from his *Das Buch der Bilder*). Publishes the original text (hitherto unpublished) of Pasternak's letter to Rilke (12 April 1926) and elaborately comments on the text of the letter, comparing, among other things, Pasternak's views of history expressed in it to similar views in *Doctor Zhivago*. Discusses Pasternak's translations of Rilke's requiems (the poems "Für eine Freundin" and "Für Wolf Graf von Kalckreuth") and finds echoes of Rilke in Pasternak's poem "To the Meyerholds" and in the poetry of the *Second Birth* collection. Also sees similarities between *Aus den Aufzeichnungen des Malte Laurids Brigge* and *A Safe Conduct* (in their artistic personalities and their aesthetic theories) but concludes that in spite of their "textual echoes," "the impact of Rilke on Pasternak was ultimately a spur to individual and original activity."

3   BEN-ASHER, NAOMI. "Jewish Identity and Christological Symbolism in the Work of Three Writers." *JF* 39 (November): 9–15.
    Discusses three Jewish-born authors, Pasternak, Andre Schwarz-Bart, and Bernard Malamud, with respect to their Jewish backgrounds, on the principle that "the irrelevance of man's Jewishness to his work rarely applies to the Jew who is also a writer." Traces Pasternak's formative influences with respect to his assimilation into non-Jewish culture, including Tolstoy, mysticism, and his first marriage. Discusses general themes of *Doctor Zhivago*, focusing on its "Christological tone" and the paradox between his Christian principles and his willingness to consign the Jews to "spiritual suicide."

4   BOYD, ALEXANDER F. "After the Storm. Boris Pasternak and *Doctor Zhivago.*" In *Aspects of the Russian Novel*. London: Chatto & Windus, pp. 109–30.
    Discusses the significance of *Doctor Zhivago* from the point of view of Pasternak's position as a poet-novelist. Retells the controversy over the novel's publication, and places the work within the nineteenth-century Russian literary tradition because of its concern for spiritual and philosophical matters. Contrasts the poetic bent of its descriptive passages with Pilnyak, and claims that its use of history as framework rather

than subject distinguishes it from the work of other Soviet authors. Traces its theme ("the spirit of Zhivago/Pasternak") to Pasternak's earlier poetry, and likens the poet's goal of penetrating rather than abandoning reality to the work of Pushkin and Blok. Links Pasternak with Lermontov. Believes that facets of *Doctor Zhivago*'s "expression of life," its vitality and "exhilaration in the elements," make the work a fundamentally religious expression of faith.

5 DAL', ELENA. "Evoliutsiia instrumentovki ot varianta k variantu v pervykh opytakh Borisa Pasternaka" [Sound instrumentation evolution from variant to variant in Boris Pasternak's first attempts]. *ScS*, no. 18, pp. 79–90.
    Examines sound texture of the 1911–13 poems, focusing on word and stanza changes to determine the extent of sound instrumentation. Concludes that Pasternak intentionally employed sound effects (notably a repetition) that frequently were causes for text changes. Elaborates on other causes for text changes.

6 DREISTADT, ROY. "A Unifying Psychological Analysis of the Principal Characters in the Novel *Dr. Zhivago* by Boris Pasternak." *Psychology* 9, no. 3: 22–35.
    Subjects the characters of Zhivago, Tonya, Lara, and Antipov to psychological analysis, based on their interpersonal interactions, with recourse to Freudian, Adlerian, Jungian, and Maslowian psychological theories. Discusses anxiety-driven tendencies toward excessive identification and role playing as manifest in Pasha Antipov's transformation into Strelnikov. Classifies Zhivago as an "oral dependent Freudian character type" with an aggressive "will to power." Explains two of his dreams as wish fulfillment directed toward Lara and rehearsal for a future time when he will lose her. Sees Komarovsky's status as fulfillment of both Zhivago's and Lara's oedipal wishes as impacting on their interrelationship throughout the novel. Labels Zhivago's later decline in health as psychosomatic in origin.

7 DYCK, J.W. *Boris Pasternak.* Twayne's World Authors Series, no. 225. New York: Twayne Publishers, 208 pp.
    A detailed study of Pasternak's prose and poetry. Outlines Pasternak's life and discusses his parents' background, his formative years, and the importance of Scriabin, Rilke, and Marburg in his life. Analyzes biographical writings focusing on Pasternak's concept of art, which is seen to be "traced to two major sources—the author himself and the world in which he lives." The poetry is analyzed in chronological order, with each collection, the epic poems, and the *Doctor Zhivago* poetry treated individually and profoundly. The *Doctor Zhivago* chapter discusses the novel's genesis, personae, plot, concept of art, dualism, duplicity, paradox, concept of man, concept of man in history, illusions,

disillusions, perception of the meaning of life, and idea of death and immortality, among other things. Also discusses Pasternak's short stories and translations, which are "colored with his own emotions." Incorporates Pasternak criticism into his evaluations. Section 4 of chapter 5 is a reprint of 1971.5.

8   ERENBURG, I.G. "Boris Leonidovich Pasternak" (in Russian). In *Portrety russkikh poetov. Porträts russischer Dichter*. Nachdruck der Ausgabe Berlin 1922 mit einer Einleitung von Friedrich Scholtz. Centrifuga. Russian Reprintings and Printings, no. 20. Munich: Willhelm Fink Verlag, pp. 127–30.
      Reprint of 1922.4.

9   IVINSKAIA, O. *V plenu vremeni. Gody s Borisom Pasternakom* [A captive of time. Years with Boris Pasternak]. Munich: n.p., 437 pp. Reprint. Paris: Fayard, 1978.
      Recounts in detail her years with Pasternak—from 1946 to 1949 and from 1953 until his death in 1960. Provides a detailed account of Pasternak's decision to write and publish *Doctor Zhivago*, his day-to-day reaction to the pressure exerted on him by the Soviet authorities after the publication of the novel, the campaign of persecution against Pasternak after he was given the Nobel Prize in 1958, and the events occurring during the last year of Pasternak's life. Records Pasternak's views of Stalin and Khrushchev, his literary peers (notably Mayakovsky, Mandelstam, Akhmatova, and Tsvetaeva), and gives a background of Pasternak's working habits and views of many of his books—finished and unfinished—including his unfinished play, *The Blind Beauty*. Offers hitherto unrecorded information valuable for a better understanding of Pasternak as a human being. Includes four chapters, three appendices, notes, comments, and an index. Translated: 1978.21.

10 KODJAK, ANDREJ. *"Dr. Zhivago* in the Classroom." *TLL* 12, no. 1: 23–31.
      Recommends utilizing *Doctor Zhivago* for advanced language instruction due to Pasternak's preoccupation with "detailed descriptions of nature and human life" and his obsession with "the barely perceptible structure of objects and events." Suggests that the novel makes the trivia of life more meaningful to students struggling with tedious vocabulary lists, provides endless opportunities for analysis, stimulates intellectual involvement with the text, and offers a diversity of themes and linguistic textures that affords the teacher "an excellent opportunity to adjust his course to the capabilities of his students."

11 MIHAILOVICH, VASA D. "Pasternak, Boris (1890–1960)." In *Modern Slavic Literatures*, edited by Vasa D. Mihailovich, vol. 1. New York: Frederick Ungar Publishers, pp. 231–43.

A collection of twenty-two excerpts, each one to three paragraphs in length, from writings on Pasternak by poets, scholars, and critics such as Tsvetaeva, Mandelstam, Renato Poggioli, Nicola Chiaromonte, Isaac Deutscher, C.M. Bowra, and Robert Conquest, among others. Relates various points of view on Pasternak's work, especially on *Doctor Zhivago*.

12   MØLLER, PETER ULF. "Delineation of Character in Pasternak's Novel *Doktor Zivago*." *ScS* 18: 69–78.

Seeks to show how the "spirit" or "tendency" of *Doctor Zhivago* finds expression through characterization, which is seen as evaluative in nature. Develops five catagories of personal qualities (A, B, C, D, E) with respect to their presence in Zhivago, Vedenyapin, and other positive characters, namely "genius," "receptive," "living," "articulate," and "unpretentious," each with several specific subheadings. This is followed by a corresponding list of the opposite qualities (-A, -B, -C, etc.) and the extent to which they occur in such characters as Antipov (Strelnikov). The characters are viewed to exemplify and proclaim fixed sets of values, resulting in the novel's consistency of "spirit" and the static nature of its characters.

13   MOODY, C. "Boris Pasternak's *Doctor Zhivago*." *UES* 10, no. 1: 37–48.

Argues that assumptions about Pasternak's intention to imitate classical realists in *Doctor Zhivago* are precluded by his personal and literary history. Views the novel as a quasi-realistic, late by-product of symbolism that represents a mytho-poetical and mytho-historical approach mirroring Pasternak's philosophy of life and humanity. Points out a deliberate, intricate web of allegory, metaphor, and other imagery that symbolizes (among other things) Zhivago's attempt to preserve Russia, the conflict between paganism and Christianity, and man's immortality. Surveys and discusses *Doctor Zhivago* criticism, such as that by Wilson, Kermode, Hayward, Stern, Deutscher, Costello, Gifford, Struve, Wain, Rowlands, and Davie.

14   MOSSMAN, ELLIOTT. "Pasternak's Short Fiction." *RLT*, no. 2, pp. 279–302.

Traces Pasternak's short fiction, valued as a unique record of the poet's "coming of age," from one of his earliest works, *Story of a Contraoctave*. Sums up the tale's rich imagery, extended metonymy, and unique fabric of detail as "tonal realism," a concept seen to be extended later to the realism of *Doctor Zhivago*. Traces the theme of art and life through *The Line of Apelles* to *The Childhood of Luvers*, and its moral, "biographical" realism, seen as inspired by Lermontov and representative of the coming age of romanticism. Sees the place of the individual in history as a developing concern in *Aerial Ways* and *The Tale*, which presages the coincidence and noncausational view put forth in *Doctor Zhivago*.

15 PALMER, CHRISTOPHER. "A Note on Skryabin and Pasternak." *MT* 113 (January): 28–30.

Describes Pasternak's relationship with Scriabin, Scriabin's friendship with Leonid Pasternak (Pasternak's father), Pasternak's six years of musical studies under Scriabin, and his subsequent disillusionment with his idol. Scriabin's influence is found in the use of synaesthesia and interplay of light and color in Pasternak's poems, as well as in descriptive passages of *Doctor Zhivago*. Raises the possibility that the figure of Vedenyapin may possess certain traits akin to those of Scriabin.

16 PASTERNAK, E.V. "Pasternak o Bloke" [Pasternak on Blok]. In *Blokovskii sbornik*. Vol. 2. Tartu: Tartutskii gosudarstvennyi universitet, pp. 447–53.

Cites in detail Pasternak's views of Blok and his poetry as recorded in Pasternak's two autobiographies, Pasternak's notes written for an unfinished Blok article, his letter to Vyacheslav Ivanov, his unpublished essay on Akhmatova, and his essay on Verlaine. Mentions specific features of Blok's poetry Pasternak is said to have singled out—"Blok's impetuosity, velocity of his observations," among others. Presents Pasternak's unfinished Blok article, "Toward a Characterization of Blok."

17 PEVEAR, RICHARD. "Sinyavsky in Two Worlds." *HR* 25: 375–402.

Credits Pasternak with a decisive influence on Sinyavsky and proposes a fundamental similarity of poetic vision between the two—"inclusive, associative, simultaneous" and opposed to the rigid reasoning of totalitarian secularization. Cites Sinyavsky's own observations on Pasternak's poetic outlook.

18 PLANK, D.L. "Readings of *My Sister, Life*." *RLT*, no. 2, pp. 323–37.

Offers a host of interpretations of *My Sister, Life* and of one of its poems in detail. Suggests lexical affinity between the collection and *Doctor Zhivago* ("Was Doctor Life the author of *My Sister, Life*?"). Equates the collection's title with Alexander Dobrolyubov's *From the Unseen Book* (its line "So whispered to me a girl, my sister—Life") and Dobrolyubov's image of "sister" ("she is an accomplice in the conspiracy of childhood, a promptress and a temptress"). Analyzes the collection's poem "Sultry Night" on four levels—descriptive, thematic, symbolic, and in its literary context (Balmont's "Rain" and Annensky's "October Myth"). Suggests that the collection's sister might be interpreted as "a symbol and not as an allegory," serving "a profound psychic purpose, uniting subject and object, inner and outer, self and other." Cites his own rendition of "Sultry Night."

19 POMORSKA, KRYSTYNA. "*Ochrannaja gramota*" [*A Safe Conduct*]. *RuL*, no. 3, pp. 40–46.

An analysis of *A Safe Conduct*, with emphasis on its relation to Pasternak's fiction. Sees this relationship in the static main hero present in all of Pasternak's works. Looks at the relationship between Pasternak and the people he mentions in *A Safe Conduct*: Mayakovsky, Scriabin, Pushkin, and others. Analyzes these relationships to show the effect each had on Pasternak's poetry. Discusses how Pasternak meets and parts from them due to his inability to exist with each individual on an equal level. Asserts that "the alteration of meeting and parting is thus a compositional principle of the book," and an essential indication of the presence of a poet in Pasternak.

20 ROGERS, THOMAS F. "Pasternak, *Doctor Živago*—Jurij Andreevič Živago." In *Superfluous Men and the Post-Stalin 'Thaw.' The Alienated Hero in Soviet Prose During the Decade 1953–1963*. The Hague: Mouton, pp. 160–86.

Provides characterizatons of Zhivago and Antipov. Surveys poetic and ideological issues raised in the novel: (1) Zhivago's rebelliousness and irresponsibility; (2) the contrast between Zhivago, Komarovsky, and Antipov/Strelnikov; (3) the nature of Zhivago's death and legacy; (4) the autobiographical nature of Zhivago in relation to Pasternak; and (5) the complexity of symbolic names, images, and events that surround Zhivago. Gives particular attention to death-and-rebirth symbolism.

21 RÖHLING, HORST. "Boris Leonidovič Pasternak und die russische Rilke-Rezeption." *WS* 17, no. 1: 118–54.

A general commentary on Pasternak's bonds to Rilke and an analysis of Pasternak's two Rilke renditions. Elaborates on Rilke's impact on Pasternak as described in Pasternak's two autobiographies. Surveys and discusses Pasternak's Rilke translations and mentions Pasternak-Rilke ties in their religious poetry, notably in Rilke's "Der Ölbaumgarten" and Pasternak's "The Garden of Gethsemane." Examines in detail Pasternak's renditions of Rilke's "Der Lesende" and "Der Schauende" ("their translations are for the most part admirably successful"). Praises Pasternak for conveying the "tone" of the original ("Das Wesentliche bei Rilke liegt im Ton") and for his contribution to Rilke's reception in Russia.

22 STATKOV, DIMITER. "Pasternaks *Faust*-Übersetzung und der Gegensatz von Poesie und Prosa im Original." *Arcadia* 7: 43–47.

Examines Pasternak's translation of *Faust*, centering on his tendency to use poetry instead of the prose of the original. Finds that Pasternak's shifts are not arbitrary, that the translation as a whole is consciously executed, and that the beginning and the end are dominated by forms closer to prose, while poetry dominates the middle ("Hier ist ein Kompositionsplan verwirklicht, der . . . das Lied zum tragenden Element macht"). Concludes that the translation is a simplification of the original.

23 TAUBMAN, JANE ANDELMAN. "Marina Tsvetaeva and Boris Pasternak: Toward the History of a Friendship." *RLT*, no. 2, pp. 304–21.

Analyzes the relationship between Pasternak and Tsvetaeva as reflected in some correspondence and poetry. Points out similarities, and discusses their attitudes towards art, literary groups, and reality or life in general. Identifies poems dedicated to each other, and develops a central theme. Traces the nature of their relationship, which is seen to evolve from literary to emotional. Claims that Tsvetaeva developed her own personal myth about Pasternak that was intensified due to the epistolary nature of their friendship.

24 THOMSON, BORIS. "Boris Pasternak." In *The Premature Revolution*. London: Weidenfeld and Nicolson, pp. 260–76.

Chronicles Pasternak's career as a lyric poet and combines biographical and historical data with critical evaluations of each stage in Pasternak's development. Contrasts the heroes of *Lieutenant Schmidt* and *Spektorsky* and compares them with Pasternak. Recounts the circumstances surrounding the creation of *Second Birth* and its reinterpretation of the image of the poet. Outlines Pasternak's later career, concluding with a discussion of *Doctor Zhivago*. Mentions points of contrast between Pasternak's career and Mayakovsky's.

1973

1 BOWMAN, HERBERT E. "Postscript on Pasternak." In *Major Soviet Writers: Essays in Criticism*, edited by Edward J. Brown. London: Oxford University Press, pp. 138–45.

Reprint of 1961.4.

2 DÖRING, JOHANNA RENATE. *Die Lyrik Pasternaks in den Jahren 1928–1934*. Slavistische Beiträge, vol. 64. Munich: Verlag Otto Sagner, 416 pp.

An elaborate examination of the *Second Birth* collection. Emphasizes the poetics (new genres, the art-and-life relationship, the meaning of *sila* [power], the double meanings of time and space, the "aesthetics of creation," the structure of stanzas, imagery [function and anaphoras], rhythm, rhymes, and lexica) and the significance of the period on Pasternak's artistic development. Discusses Pasternak and Mayakovsky and the break between them; Pasternak and Gorky (their correspondence, Gorky's "correction" of Pasternak's translations, his influence on Pasternak's prose, and his criticism of Pasternak's poetry); and Pasternak's translations from the Georgian. The appendix lists the most frequent nouns, adjectives, and verbs in *Second Birth*, and contains a word-for-word German rendition of the poems in the collection.

3   FEINBERG, LAWRENCE E. "The Grammatical Structure of Boris Pasternak's *Gamlet.*" In *Slavic Poetics. Essays in Honor of Kiril Taranovsky*, edited by Roman Jakobson, C.H. Van Schooneveld, and Dean S. Worth. The Hague: Mouton, pp. 99–124.

Elaborately analyzes the grammatical structure of each word of the poem "Hamlet." Recognizes a heretofore unnoticed "masterly verbal design" characterized by "an intricate system of imagery and a sophisticated utilization of poetic grammar" that is strikingly demonstrated by its tendency toward "polar equality or antisymmetry" and antiparity. Perceives this design as "an elaborate network of inverse, antisymmetrical relations which inform every level of organization."

4   FRANCE, ANNA KAY. "Boris Pasternak's Interpretation of *Hamlet.*" *RLT*, no. 7, pp. 201–26.

Finds omissions and shifts of emphasis in *Hamlet* to reveal Pasternak's understanding of the play and "the nature of tragedy itself." Sees Pasternak's texts as downplaying the strong images of decay, corruption, and disease used by Shakespeare, de-emphasizing the capability of evil to overcome the virtuous; brings forth the Christlike image presented by Pasternak in his "Garden of Gethsemane." Sees the play's reference to sexual corruption as represented by Ophelia as "bowdlerized" by Pasternak, whose emphasis is seen to shift to images that suggest Ophelia's beauty and fragility. Argues that Pasternak lessens some of the tragic implications of the play as a whole, and thus tips the balance from Hamlet's despair and destructive impulses to the redemptive promise of his sacrifice, all of which likens Hamlet to Pasternak's earlier hero, Lieutenant Schmidt. Reprinted (with modifications) in 1978.15.

5   GLADKOV, ALEKSANDR. *Vstrechi s Pasternakom* [Meetings with Pasternak]. Paris: YMCA Press, 159 pp.

Recalls his meetings with Pasternak from 1936 to 1948 and from 1954 to Pasternak's death. Gives a detailed account of their meetings at Chistopol in the winter of 1941–42, focusing on Pasternak's spartanlike style ("simplicity and modesty were, it seemed, his need"), his "eccentricities" and contrasts with his literary peers (he was the "black sheep"), his work habits and views of his translations (which Pasternak is said to have regarded as a "substitute for a genuine activity"), his views of his own works, and, above all, his views of literary figures, poetry, and art in general. The latter views are recorded in diary entries, presenting Pasternak as preferring Bedny to other Soviet poets, Pushkin to Lermontov, Chekhov to Dostoevsky and Tolstoy, and his *Hamlet* translation to his other Shakespeare translations, as well as indicating his views of Mayakovsky and his supposed envy of the authors of *Cement* and *Rout.* Cites Pasternak's poem recorded in an album of a Chistopol doctor. Chapter 4 recalls several chance encounters, including one on 18

August 1957 when Gladkov met Pasternak in Peredelkino and recorded Pasternak's views of the *Zhivago* affair. Comments on Pasternak's escape from the purges of the Stalin years, on *Doctor Zhivago* ("the novel disappointed me," "everything in the book that smacks of a novel is weak," "it does not add up to a great novel"), and on the campaign against Pasternak. Chapter 5 recounts in detail Pasternak's funeral—the crowd ("two to three thousand, or four"), the procession, and the burial ceremony, among other occurences. Reprinted in part: 1978.16; 1980.6; 1990.28. Translated: 1977.10.

6   GUL', ROMAN. "Pobeda Pasternaka" [Pasternak's victory]. In *Odvukon'. Sovetskaia i emigrantskaia literatura.* New York: Mosty, pp. 44–62.
     Reprint of 1958.22.

7   KESTNER, JOSEPH A. "The Spatiality of Pasternak's 'Aerial Ways.'" *SSF*, no. 10, pp. 243–51.
     A contextual analysis of *Aerial Ways* as it relates to spatial and temporal elements. Contains three sections, with each examining a specific spatial art (painting, sculpture, or architecture). Claims that in Pasternak's art the aesthetic is linked to the ethic. Uses symbolism, juxtaposition, anthropomorphism, metonymy, synecdoche, and synaesthesis as devices of analysis.

8   K'IAROMONTE, NIKOLA. "Priroda i istoriia u Pasternaka" [Pasternak's views of nature and history]. In *Paradoks istorii. Stendal', Tolstoi, Pasternak, i drugie.* Florence: Edizione Aurora, pp. 163–86.
     Translation of 1968.3.

9   MALLAC, GUY DE. "Pasternak and Religion." *RR* 32, no. 4: 360–75.
     Attempts to pin down Pasternak's "unorthodox orthodoxy," his synthesis of religious values and doctrine, drawing mainly upon *Doctor Zhivago* and elements of Pasternak's upbringing. Addresses various theologians' reservations about the theological tenability of Pasternak's faith with respect to issues such as immortality, individual freedom, historical progress, and the nature of Christ. Finds Pasternak's religion to contain pre-Christian and generalized mystical elements, seen as an eclectic nondenominationalism stemming from his mixed Judeo-Christian upbringing. Sums up Pasternak's faith as intensely moral, optimistic, and founded on a personal rather than a generalized concept of God. Revised: 1981.14.

10 ———. "Pasternak's Critical-Esthetic Views." *RLT*, no. 6, pp. 503–32.
     Traces the development of Pasternak's aesthetic views from his youthful emphasis on form to his mature assertion of the primacy of "experience-content." Surveys Pasternak's involvement with

"Centrifuge" and other futurist groups, his use of the term "realist" with respect to Verlaine and Chopin, his negative identification of romanticism with the fantastic, and various other aspects of his nineteenth-century aesthetics. Discusses the significance of Pasternak's move from poetry to prose as well as the philosophy of Kant (his *Critique of Judgement*), which is linked to Pasternak's lyricism-history dichotomy. Perceives the synthesis of romantic conception—ideals, transcendant values, inspiration—together with Pasternak's contrasting advocacy of realism and content rooted in everyday experiences as a synthesis of life and art, regarded to go beyond the limitations laid out by Kant. Revised as "The Poet as Critic: Views on Art and Literature" in 1981.14.

11 MOSSMAN, ELLIOT. "Pasternak's *Blind Beauty.*" *RLT*, no. 7, pp. 227–42.

Provides a textual history of Pasternak's unfinished historical drama *The Blind Beauty*, with a synopsis of Act I, scenes 1–4 (the scenes Pasternak completed), and outlines of the unfinished portions of the work. Centers analysis on historical and thematic-theatrical parallels between twentieth-century drama and that of the nineteenth-century (the play focuses on a nineteenth-century serf actors' troupe). Pasternak's fascination with *Hamlet* is seen as central to the theatrical parallel, a line of analysis that is traced from Pasternak's 1941 play *In the Other World.*

12 NAUMOV, E. "O vremeni i o sebe. Maiakovskii i Pasternak" [About time and oneself. Mayakovsky and Pasternak]. In *O spornom i besspornom. Stat'i.* Leningrad: Sovetskii pisatel', pp. 133–213. Reprint. 1979.

Interprets the Mayakovsky-Pasternak relationship as a social and literary phenomenon due to their different "tendencies manifested in Soviet poetry." Mentions that both had entered literature in 1912, that in their early poetry some similarities could be found, and that their personal contacts at that time were close. Argues that after the Revolution, Pasternak had endeavored to "stand behind the barriers of life itself" (whereas Mayakovsky had lived within the Soviet social life). Concludes that "time has proven that Pasternak's poetry is linked to the past but not to the current day of history." Also concludes that the "anti-socialistic essence of *Doctor Zhivago* finds its root in Pasternak's views of the 1920's and 1930's." Strongly argues that Pasternak cannot be counted a member of Soviet poetry.

13 SKORBINA, NINA. "Boris Pasternak. Vstrechi i pis'ma" [Boris Pasternak. Encounters and correspondence]. *NRS* (18 February): 2, 8.

Recalls her encounters with Pasternak in the late 1940s, and cites from his correspondence to her. Describes Pasternak the man, notably his fears of arrest. Reveals Pasternak's views of Fedin, Alexey Tolstoy, Stalin, and other subjects.

14 THOMPSON, EWA M. "The Archetype of the Fool in Russian Literature." *CSP* 15, no. 3: 245–73.

Finds that the title character in *Doctor Zhivago* "may well be the most prominent twentieth-century link in the chain of variations on the fool archetype" in Russian literature. Thinks Zhivago's unsettled, materially undemanding existence and the intensity of his participation in life place him after Prince Myshkin, Alesha Karamazov, and Pierre Bezukhov in a succession of literary incarnations in historical and fictional books. Sees the development of a transrational spirituality unattainable to the common person, yet elevating humankind by example as Zhivago's important "holy fool" characteristic.

15 VEIDLE [Weidle], V. "Pasternak i modernizm" [Pasternak and modernism]. In *O poetakh i poezii*. Paris: YMCA Press, pp. 84–101.

Reprint of 1961.31.

16 VOROBIOV, ALEX. "The Significance of Style in Pasternak." In *Proceedings: Pacific Northwest Conference on Foreign Language*, edited by Walter C. Kraft. Corvalis: Oregon State University Press, pp. 326–39.

Argues that sentences with words of the same root are characteristic of *Doctor Zhivago*'s poems and considers it a significant stylistic device. Points out that Pasternak uses words with the same root in common expressions, in active formations, and sometimes as autonomous constructions, for example. Argues that words with an identical root "not only emphasize content, but, due to their mutual roots and semantics, facilitate the creation of associations."

1974

1 BEAUNE, DANIÈLE. "Les influences religieuses dans la formation intellectuelle de Pasternak." *CLOS*, nos. 3–4, (August–December): 1–29.

A summary of religious influences on Pasternak—centering on religious diversity. Discusses Pasternak's Jewish background, his family's well-established place among the Russian intelligentsia, Pasternak's high-school years (including a list of subjects he studied and their influence on him), his father's art and Scriabin's music, philosophical interests, attraction to symbolism and futurism, his aesthetic views of religion as opposed to Tolstoy's ethical (moral) views, Fedorov's theory as an attempt to reconcile religion and natural sciences, and Cohen's rationalized views of religion, among other influences.

2   BIRKMANN, KARL. "Pasternak oder dann kommt ein Orkan übers Land . . ." In *Ich schlage langsam ein Kreuz . . . Russland zwischen Bunin und Solschenizyn.* Munich: Markus-Verlag, pp. 93–176.

Outlines Pasternak's biographical data, recording his major works. Sees the *Themes and Variations* collection as his "high point." Argues that Pasternak was influenced by Blok and Akhmatova. Discusses a number of historic events—the revolution of 1905, the revolutions of 1917, the Civil War—in connection with their treatment in *Doctor Zhivago.* Observes that *Doctor Zhivago* is not an autobiographical novel, though the author's features have been "distributed" to the novel's characters; that Pasternak juxtaposes "his idea of radical individualism" against "the ideas of collective human happiness"; and that in the novel an artist appears as a "chosen one, thrown into the world" at a moment at which "an individual, a soul" is crucified. Also discusses the novel's poetry—the comparison of Zhivago to Christ and Lara to Mary Magdalene. Concludes that the novel ends with a "Whitsun miracle, promise, hope, and reconciliation."

3   DYCK, J.W. "Boris Pasternak: The Caprice of Beauty." *CSP* 16, no. 4: 612–26.

Explores "the face of beauty" in Pasternak's work, concentrating on its two primary manifestations—the word and the woman. Sees the relationship of beauty's power with art and life itself as the enigma to which Pasternak devoted his creative energy, resolving the tension between physical and moral beauty, creative free will, and moral duty. Uses excerpts from Pasternak's early prose and the long poem "Waves" to illustrate the evolution of beauty with respect to both Pasternak's art and his own personal life. Regards Lara as a "total, absolute" embodiment of beauty, a force that transfigures life to become one with destiny.

4   FORTIN, RENÉ E. "Home and the Uses of Creative Nostalgia in *Doctor Zhivago.*" *MFS* 20 (Summer): 203–9.

Concurs with criticism acknowledging the symbolic quality of *Doctor Zhivago* and focuses on the novel's "home" imagery in its "historical, religious, and aesthetic dimensions." Thus, the home imagery is "an expression of Zhivago's resentment of the Bolshevik Revolution," for it endangers "the very values associated with home." Argues that home imagery in *Doctor Zhivago* is likewise "the primary symbol of man's nature and of his destiny" and that it includes "the problems of death and immortality," for "man is at home in the universe in death as in life, death being a return to the All—the final homecoming." Also argues that home imagery encompasses the novel's conception of art ("art is a homecoming in that it involves a return to the intuition of childhood"), seen to be reflected in the creation of poetry ("to name, suggests Zhivago, is to give a home to that which is named"). Compares the home imagery to Heidegger's aesthetic theory that places "strong emphasis on the central poetic acts of naming and returning to the source," and concludes that *"Doctor Zhivago* is on one level a parable lamenting a lost Russia, a lost home place."

5 FRANK, VICTOR. "Realizm chetyrekh izmerenii" [Realism of four dimensions]. In *Izbrannye stat'i*, edited by L. Shapiro. London: Overseas Publications Interchange, pp. 62–85.
    Reprint of 1959.21.

6 ———. "Russkii Gamlet: Roman Borisa Pasternaka" [A Russian Hamlet: Boris Pasternak's novel]. In *Izbrannye stat'i*, edited by L. Shapiro. London: Overseas Publications Interchange, pp. 37–42.
    Translation of 1958.18.

7 ———. "Vodianoi znak" [The water sign]. In *Izbrannye stat'i*, edited by L. Shapiro. London: Overseas Publications Interchange, pp. 103–19.
    Reprint of 1962.9.

8 HARRIS, JANE GARY. "Pasternak's Vision of Life: The History of a Feminine Image." *RLT*, no. 9, pp. 389–421.
    Discusses the development of Pasternak's views of life, love, and art through his feminine images—underlining that "to comprehend Pasternak's feminine image is to come to an understanding of his overall aesthetic vision." Examines such imagery in *My Sister, Life, The Childhood of Luvers*, and *Spektorsky* (compared to Pushkin's *The Fountain of Bakhchisarai* for their presentations of a "dual vision of woman") in which the feminine image is seen to be "empowered to inspire the poet." Sees Lara as a "representative of life" and "as Pasternak's ultimate feminine image."

9 HUGHES, OLGA R. *The Poetic World of Boris Pasternak.* Princeton Essays in European and Comparative Literature. Princeton, NJ: Princeton University Press, 192 pp.
    A thorough analysis of Pasternak's poetry and Pasternak the poet. Traces Pasternak's development as a poet, emphasizing continuity and unity of his work. Contends that Pasternak abhorred any adherence to schools and movements—argues, though, that Pasternak's poetry is that of "aesthetic realism," which fits "as the imaginative realism of post-symbolist poetry," and that Pasternak's realism "does not share some elements with traditional realism." Singles out Blok and Scriabin as Pasternak's most striking influences during his formative years. Examines themes and poetics. Concludes that "art is one of the permanent themes in Pasternak's works" and that "the originality of Pasternak's language is the inevitable result of and the function of the poet's new vision of the world." Includes four chapters: "The Origin and Nature of Poetry," "Art and Reality," "Time and Eternity," and "The

Responsibility of a Poet," as well as an introduction, conclusion, bibliography, and index.

10   MOORE, HARRY T., and ALBERT PARRY. "The Battle Against Pasternak." In *Twentieth-Century Russian Literature.* With a preface by Harry T. Moore. Carbondale: Southern Illinois University Press, pp. 124–29.

Outlines Pasternak's career, stressing his faithfulness to his art in the face of Stalinist repression. Quotes Pasternak's "Prophet" as an example of his refusal to "write poetry to order" despite the threats of party idealogues. Cites passages from *The Year 1905, A Safe Conduct, On Early Trains,* and *The Wide Earth* as further examples of this. Observes that Pasternak was "fairly lucky" in the prewar years, his only penalty the suppression of his second volume of *A Safe Conduct.* Discusses Pasternak's repeated defiance of the Congress of Soviet Writers and the resulting denouncement by inferior colleagues. Concludes that despite the harassment Pasternak suffered from Soviet officials, he was enormously popular among the Russians, as he was a "poet of magnitude."

11   NIVAT, GEORGES. "Six lettres inédites de Boris Pasternak." *CMRS* 15, nos. 1–2: 220–33.

A commentary on Pasternak's letters to Zaitsev, his daughter (Nathalie Sollogub), and to Michel Aucouturier. Discusses the letters' content—the Zaitsev letters exhibit "certain formulas dear to Pasternak" and echo his second autobiography. Reveals Pasternak lamenting in the letter to Zaitsev's daughter that his contact with "respectable" people and frank conversations with them began too late in his life. Includes Pasternak's remarks in a letter to Aucouturier on the influence of Rilke on his work. Concludes with reporting portions of a December 1959 conversation in which Pasternak discussed *Blind Beauty.*

12   PANICHAS, GEORGE A. "Boris Pasternak's Protest and Affirmation." In *The Reverent Discipline. Essays in Literary Criticism and Culture.* Knoxville: University of Tennessee Press, pp. 283–91.
      Reprint of 1958.52.

13   PASTERNAK, JOSEPHINE. "Patior." *RLT,* no. 9, pp. 371–88.
      Reprint of 1964.12.

14   ROGERS, THOMAS F. "The Implication of Christ's Passion in *Doktor Živago.*" *SEEJ* 18: 384–91.

Interprets the mythopoetic imagery of *Doctor Zhivago* as endorsing the Revolution by associating it with Christ's passion and death. Mentions a general kinship between the elemental apocalypse of the

Revolution and the supernatural, kenotic nature of Christ's death and transfiguration. Singles out the chapter "The Forest Soldiery" as abundant in specific associations that are not systematic or rational, but seek to exert a cumulative effect on the reader.

15 SCHERR, BARRY P. "The Structure of *Doctor Zhivago.*" In *Proceedings of the Northwest Conference on Foreign Languages*, edited by Walter Kraft. Vol. 25, part 1. Corvalis: Oregon State University Press, pp. 274–79.

A detailed analysis of the novel's structure. Thoroughly groups sections and chapters. Identifies "interlocking devices."

16 ZELINSKY, BODO. "Definitionen der Poesie bei Pasternak." *ZSP* 37: 275–90.

Seeks to define Pasternak's "definition" of poetry and claims that Pasternak never presented a coherent theory as the basis for his writings. Notes that after Pasternak's futuristic period, the term *poezia* (poesy) instead of *lirika* (lyric poetry) began to dominate Pasternak's theoretic views in his essays. Believes that this shift is a result of Tyutchev's, Rilke's, and Blok's influences. Also believes that Pasternak's claim "prose is poetry" indicated that prose is supposed to include poetic categories, such as rhythm and rhymes. Strongly argues that Pasternak's definition of poetry is "Bilderrede," by which an image serves as a "means of essential expression—and never of a beautiful speech." Accepts Pasternak as a "realistic writer," and his "realism" as possessing the highest possible degree of preciseness in mimetic depiction of nature: "Poesie ist metaphorischer Detailrealismus."

1975

1 BARNES, CHRISTOPHER J. "Boris Pasternak's Revolutionary Year." *FMLS* 11: 334–48.

Traces and characterizes Pasternak's attitude toward the Revolution through various published and unpublished writings of the period. Contrasts Pasternak's views with Zhivago's views. Discusses two different "psychologies of revolution"—initial enthusiasm and subsequent disillusionment—as they appear in both Pasternak and Zhivago. Sees the presence of revolutionary enthusiasm in *My Sister, Life* as more of a psychological revolutionary character akin to that of the "Scythian" group of poets than as a concrete political endorsement. Pasternak's *Dramatic Fragments* of 1917 receives particular attention by virtue of its revolutionary hero, Saint-Just, who exemplifies this Scythian brand of "mystical patriotism." Reprinted: 1976.4. Translated (with modifications): 1979.4.

2   FLEISHMAN, L. "B. Pasternak i A. Belyi" [B. Pasternak and A. Bely]. *RLT*, no. 13, pp. 545–52.

Argues that Pasternak's ties to Bely were twofold—biographical and literary. Gives a chronology of Pasternak's encounters with Bely, such as Pasternak's attendance of Bely's readings and the MUSAGET "Rhythmic Circle," and their meetings during the first postrevolutionary years. Comments on Pasternak's, Bely's, and Pilnyak's intent to found the journal *Three Borises*, a project viewed as revealing Pasternak's literary interests of the 1910s—a shift to prose and a "large verse epic." Sees this shift as prompting Pasternak to do "his experiment" on "'antiautobiographical' autobiography—*A Safe Conduct.*" Concludes that for Pasternak, Bely was first of all a prose writer and that Pasternak's interpretation of the origin of the "first Soviet prose" (in Pasternak's essay "Some Propositions") refers to Bely's *Symphonies* and *Petersburg.* Pasternak's three unpublished letters to Bely follow the introduction.

3   ——. "Iz perepiski B. Pasternaka" [From B. Pasternak's correspondence]. *RLT*, no. 13, pp. 543–44.

Gives additional information on Pasternak's essay "Some Propositions," on which he has previously published his comments. Explains that Pasternak's own views of "Some Propositions" are to be found in his letter (published here for the first time) to F.I. Sedenko (pseudonym for F.I. Vityazev), who in 1928–29 intended to publish a collection of essays, *Book Garland*, to which Pasternak had submitted his essay "Some Propositions."

4   ——. "K kharakteristike rannego Pasternaka" [Toward a characterization of the early Pasternak]. *RuL* 12: 79–126.

A detailed analysis of Pasternak's early works (1913–1918). Argues that Pasternak's conception of art formed during this period is applicable to all his work, because Pasternak's "poetical biography" is cyclical, not evolutionary. Claims that the resource of Pasternak's worldviews should not be sought in the neo-Kantian Marburg school but in the philosophy of E. Husserl, whose philosophical system is seen to have influenced Pasternak's *My Sister, Life*; his unpublished cycle of "Articles of Man"; and a draft, "Tale in Verse about Fellow Man." Bases his analysis on Pasternak's essay "Symbolism and Immortality." Also claims that Husserl's philosophy determined the reduction of the author's "I" in Pasternak's poetry. Analyzes poetic devices in Pasternak's early prose. Reprinted: 1977.8.

5   FOMENKO, I.V. "Muzykal'naia kompozitsiia kak cherta romanticheskogo stilia (na primere tvorchestva Pasternaka 20-kh godov)" [Musical composition as a feature of romantic style (on the example of Pasternak's works of the 20s]. *VR* 2: 75–90.

A study of the influence of music on Pasternak's poetry and the significance of musical compositions as a means of embodiment of romantic worldviews. Underlines Pasternak's infatuation with music and discusses his musical upbringing. Analyzes compositional variations of "Petersburg," in which Pasternak uses "musical forms" as a decisive principle of the poem's composition. Summarizes compositional structures of *My Sister, Life* and notes similarities between the collection's compositional features and the composition of Scriabin's "Third Symphony." Concludes that Chopin is for Pasternak an embodiment "of life's truth in small forms" while "Scriabin is a summit of symphony."

6 FRANCE, ANNA KAY. "Prosody and Verse Structure in Pasternak's Translations of Shakespeare's Plays." *CASS* 9, no. 3: 336–51.

Argues that Pasternak's Shakespeare translations show remarkable sensitivity to the sound structure and meaning of the original verse, displaying great ingenuity in recreating its verbal effects. Demonstrates how rhyme and sound patternings, maintenance of enjambements, and line length preserve the verbal effects of the original without slavish imitations of formal aspects. Draws parallels between Pasternak's renditions and those of other translators, whose more literal faithfulness to the original achieves cumbersome results that fall short of Pasternak's more imaginative and original recreations.

7 GOLDMAN, HOWARD ALLEN. "Shakespeare's *Hamlet* in the Work of Boris Pasternak and Other Modern Russian Poets (Aleksandr Blok, Anna Axmatova, and Marina Cvetaeva)." Ph.D. diss., Indiana University, 292 pp.

The section on Pasternak discusses Pasternak's interpretations of Hamlet and Ophelia—seen to be linked to "Shakespeare's Desdemona" and to "various characters" in *Doctor Zhivago*. Argues that Pasternak emphasizes Hamlet's "philosophy of life," repudiates "the traditional interpretation of Hamlet as indecisive," and uses Hamlet "to rebuke the practitioners of Socialist Realism for oversimplifying literature and such activist figures as Strel'nikov and his comrades in *Doktor Zhivago*."

8 GURCHINOV, MILAN. "Antinomiia 'romantizm-realizm' v poetike B.L. Pasternaka" [The antinomy "romanticism-realism" in B.L. Pasternak's poetics]. *SlS*, no. 1, pp. 49–57.

An examination of Pasternak's views of romanticism ("Romantic manner") and realism. Discusses these views as they appear in Pasternak's correspondence, his three critiques, and two autobiographies. Notes that in *The Wassermann Test*, Pasternak "paves principles for the new metonymical perception of the poetic image"; in "Black Goblet," he "fundamentally breaks off with Impressionism and Symbolism"; and in "Some Propositions," he finally "ends with Futurists' aesthetics." Concludes that a "genuine" debate over romanticism and realism occurs in his two autobiographies, that Pasternak looked upon romanticism as a "variety" art and a "false pathos," and that Pasternak "clearly" accepts realism in his essays of the 1940s. Reprinted: 1979.10.

9   KATANIAN, V.A. "O Maiakovskom i Pasternake" [On Mayakovsky and Pasternak]. *RLT*, no. 13, pp. 499–518.

A chronological account of meetings between Pasternak and Mayakovsky compounded with the author's comments on their relationship. Draws information from Pasternak's two autobiographies, his meetings with Pasternak and Mayakovsky, archive material, questionnaires, book inscriptions, Pasternak's two letters to Mayakovsky, and literary works. Elaborates on Pasternak's break with LEF, Pasternak's and Mayakosky's meeting in April of 1928, their last meeting on 30 December 1930, and on Polonsky's views of Mayakovsky, which are said to have continued to change after Mayakovsky's death. Concludes that Mayakovsky's death prompted Pasternak's *A Safe Conduct*. Also concludes that Pasternak had tried to play down the extent of his friendship with Mayakovsky while flatly denying that an inscription ("To Boris from Vol with friendship, tenderness, love, respect, comradery, habit, sympathy, admiration, etc., etc., etc.") Mayakovsky wrote on one of his poems was addressed to him.

10   KAYDEN, EUGENE M. "On Re-reading the Poems of *Doctor Zhivago*." *CQ*, no. 23, pp. 396–401.

Notes the universality of the poems' message of Christian love, freedom, and self-renewing exultation in life. Argues that differences between political systems, among individuals, and even between past and future are transcended by organic, eternal intimations of the poet, whose perceptions and insights refute the modern "compulsive need of autonomy."

11   LUKIĆ, SVETA. Introduction (in Serbo-Croatian) to Pasternak's *Doktor Živago*. Translated by Olga Vlatković. Savremeni strani pisci, no. 10. Belgrade: Prosveta, pp. 7–30.

Divided into three parts: a concise, informative Pasternak biography followed by two sections, "Love and Freedom—A Kernel of *Doctor Zhivago*" and "Lights and Shadows of Pasternak's Novel," respectively. Makes observations on the novel's notion of freedom (seen in heroes' enjoyment of simple, mundane things and in their ability to achieve freedom through love), its alienation concept (asserted to originate from Rousseau and Hegel), and on the novel's poetics, its structure and similes in particular. Regards that similes have become richer and "more rational" ("at the expense of excessive manneristic decorativeness") and that the novel's structure is "compact" and "closed," "as if modeled on a geometric system"—even though the novel is seen to display numerous digressions and asides, such as descriptions of nature and soil tilling.

Summarizes the novel as an "anthology of Pasternak's fine pieces: poems in prose, pure prose fragments, and poetry."

12 MATHEWSON, RUFUS W. "Pasternak: 'An Inward Music.'" In *The Positive Hero in Russian Literature*. 2d ed. Stanford, CA: Stanford University Press, pp. 259–78.

Retells stages of Zhivago's "personal mission" (a series of choices that gives him the sense of a cummulative fatality). Discusses these stages in terms of the progressively greater disharmony between "ethos of production" and "continuum of life," which are seen as the two opposing forces in *Doctor Zhivago*. Traces the evolution of Zhivago's attitude toward the Revolution from initial acceptance and welcome to ultimate rejection of Soviet power as antithetical to Zhivago's Christian-mythological worldview. Such actions as Zhivago's decision to leave Moscow with his family, his desertion of the partisans, and tricking Lara into leaving with Komarovsky are characterized as reflecting various stages in this evolution.

13 POMORSKA, KRYSTYNA. *Themes and Variations in Pasternak's Poetics*. Lisse: Peter de Ridder Press, 92 pp.

A study of Pasternak's poetics, broken down into five chapters: "Pasternak and Futurism," "Music as Theme and Structure," "The Fate of the Artist," "*A Safe Conduct*," and "*Doctor Zhivago*." Details various aspects of Pasternak's poetics—structure and composition, sound texture (sound repetition devices, "sound repertory," paronomasia), "symbolic content," metonymic structure, imagery, tonality, rhythmical and intonational principles, metric structure, and thematic development. Finds features akin to those of futurism in Pasternak's early poetry, such as "sound-images," "words at freedom" poetics, "inter-syntactical connectness," and "consonantal orientation," among others. Explores the notion of art and the fate of an artist in "musical" poems of *Second Birth*. Identifies "the five main complexes of the protagonist's experiences" in *A Safe Conduct*. Sees *Doctor Zhivago*'s main plot line as structured around "the form of coincidences," and elaborates on the novel's principle of characterization, "puzzling chords of experiences" (a psychological approach), the concept of human fate, and the role of the epilogue. Cites entire poems and passages to support her thesis. Chapter 4 reprinted (in slightly adopted form): 1990.59.

14 SINYAVSKY, ANDREI. "On Boris Pasternak." In *Twentieth-Century Russian Literary Criticism*, edited by Victor Erlich. New Haven, CT: Yale University Press, pp. 235–46.

Reprint of 1966.18. Selective translation of 1965.4.

15 TSVETAEVA, MARINA. "Epic and Lyric in Contemporary Russia: Mayakovsky and Pasternak." *RLT*, no. 13, pp. 519–42.

Translation of 1933.3.

16 ZELINSKY, BODO. "Selbstdefinitionen der Poesie bei Pasternak. Prof. Dr. Dmitrij Tschiževskij zum 80. Geburtstag." *ZSP* 38: 268–78.

A sequel to his earlier essay (1974.16); reiterates his argument that Pasternak did not make statements reflecting his own writings. Notes that "poesy" is often thematically reflected in his poems, most significantly in his "Definition of Poetry," in which "poesy" is defined as nature ("Poesie ist Natur"). Argues that the poem's title should be translated in the plural—"definitions of poetry." Insists that defining "poesy" through poetry writing or through theoretical essays is impossible: "Die Selbstdefinitionen der Poesie zeigen bei Pasternak letztlich, was bereits die Definitionen gezeigt haben: die Unmöglichkeit, Poesie, zumindest vorliegende Art von Poesie, zu definieren."

1976

1 ABUASHVILI, A. "Dva tsveta" [Two colors]. *VL*, no. 3, pp. 111–27.

Comments on Pasternak's translations of Baratashvili, with emphasis on his translation "The Sky-blue Color." Concludes that an enormous discrepancy between the original and Pasternak's version exists, notably in the worldview of the authors and the poems' heroes. Finds that the translation's hero is an "inhabitant of the earth," while the original poem's hero is an "eternal seeker." Concludes that the original and its translation are "two different poems"—connected only by an identical theme.

2 ANNING, N.J. "Pasternak." In *Literary Attitudes from Pushkin to Solzhenitsyn*, edited by Richard Freeborn. New York: Macmillan, pp. 99–119.

Outlines major events in Pasternak's life while giving a detailed chronology of his works. Comments on the evolution of Pasternak's views of art, observing that *A Safe Conduct* "sums up Pasternak's position with an irony made more telling by the fact that" Mayakovsky was "as much a victim of RAPP's hostility as of his own fatally divisive drives." Labels Pasternak a "post-Symbolist by inclination and philosophy" and defines *A Twin in the Clouds* as a "blend of total, musical effects with glimpses into the world of nature inspired by love and passion." Traces influences on Pasternak's prose (Rilke, Proust, Hoffmann, and Bely). Sees *My Sister, Life* constructed "as a 'novel' with 'chapters,' and 'Spektorsky' is a long 'novel in verse' that finally spilled over into a prose format in *The Story*." Mentions Pasternak's views of the intimacy between prose and poetry (reflected in his essay of 1922 and in *A Safe Conduct*) and concludes that *Second Birth* was a more "dramatic watershed in his poetic evolution." Offers insights into Pasternak's development as a writer and comments on Pasternak's attitude toward women. Views *Doctor Zhivago* as Pasternak's "crowning work," "the product of a lifetime," a work that "should be read as a poetic rhapsody." Sees the essence of the novel in its form, with Pasternak highlighting character and philosophical content while avoiding "conventional elements of the novel."

3 BARKSDALE, E.C., and DANIEL POPP. "Hamsun and Pasternak: The Development of Dionysian Tragedy." *Edda* 76, no. 6: 343–51.

Applies the Apollonian/Dionysian dichotomy principles to *Doctor Zhivago* and links *Doctor Zhivago* to Hamsun and his *Pan*. Sees Zhivago pinioned between the Apollonian (Tonya) and the Dionysian (Lara)—"and therefore Zhivago is a Dionysian hero whose life is wracked with paradox." Explains the paradoxes in Zhivago with Pasternak's adherence to Hamsun and draws parallels between *Doctor Zhivago* and *Pan*: "unmetered poetry," "man's mystic union with Nature," "references to the force" as "the controlling factor behind both historical and personal events," and "many religious references and motifs." Interprets Lara as "Nietzschean in seeing the wonders of life through its horrors." Concludes that Zhivago, "bereft of his Dionysian source of strength, . . . becomes a drone, a nothing," and that "Hamsun and Pasternak both when they paralleled one another and when they diverged added a new page to the distinguished lineage of the [Dionysian] tragedy."

4 BARNES, CHRISTOPHER J. "Boris Pasternak's Revolutionary Year." In *Studies in Twentieth Century Russian Literature. Five Essays*, edited by Christopher J. Barnes. New York: Barnes & Noble, pp. 46–60.

Reprint of 1975.1.

5 BIRNBAUM, HENRIK. *Doktor Faustus und Doktor Schiwago. Versuch über zwei Zeitromane aus Exilsicht.* Lisse: Ridder, 66 pp.

Contains six chapters: (1) general characterizations; (2) common and parallel features; (3) main and side characters; (4) religion and history; (5) patriotism, politics, and the national question; and (6) life's syntheses. Concludes that both Mann's and Pasternak's novels come from the same source, and sees two themes as prevalent in both novels—religion and history. Analyzes and cites the poetry from *Doctor Zhivago*. Insists that for Pasternak art and religion are single powers, which symbolically can make the tragedy of life and death conquerable and more bearable. Argues that Pasternak's conspicuous religious worldviews are a main reason for his nonacceptance of the Revolution. Discusses thoroughly the Pasternak criticism in English and German.

6 BJÖRLING, FIONA. "Aspects of Poetic Syntax. Analysis of the Poem 'Sestra moja—žizn' i segodnja v razlive' by Boris Pasternak." In *Boris Pasternak. Essays*, edited by Nils Åke Nilsson. Stockholm Studies in Russian Literature, no. 7. Stockholm: Almqvist & Wiksell International, pp. 162–79.

A syntactic analysis of Pasternak's poem "My Sister, Life and Today in the Downpour"—with emphasis on the word association within a sentence and the relationship between sentences and the entire poem. Examines the function of conjunctions, semantic meanings of almost each word, linking devices of and connections between stanzas, general syntactic organizations, and the function of similes (discussed in the notes). Concludes that: (1) "grammatical irregularities rarely occur"; (2) "the logic of Pasternak's poetry is reminiscent of the logic of impassioned speech"; and (3) "the syntax of individual sentences is difficult in that it frequently points to two movements within the limits of one sentence."

7   BODIN, PER ARNE. *Nine Poems from 'Doctor Živago': A Study of Christian Motifs in Boris Pasternak's Poetry.* Stockholm Studies in Russian Literature, no. 6. Stockholm: Almqvist & Wiksell International, 176 pp.

Analyzes nine poems from the collection "The Poems of Yury Zhivago" ("Hamlet," "Holy Week," "Fairy Story," "Christmas Star," "The Miracle," "The Bad Days," "Magdalene I," "Magdalene II," and "The Garden of Gethsemane"). Centers on the use of Christian motifs and argues that Pasternak employed them to emphasize "the importance of Christianity in European civilization" and "to express the idea of a common Christian culture." Compares Pasternak's notes found in his personal Bible to the poems, and records the highlighted biblical passages that had influenced Pasternak's poetry. Summarizes the common features in the nine poems as: (1) "a struggle between an active and a passive principal of living"; (2) "miracles and miracle making"; and (3) the Resurrection. Labels the most important features as "the abandonment of a passive way of life, a belief in the future and . . . an apology of Christianity not on the first hand as a mystical, but as a moral system of thought." Concludes that "Hamlet" is an introductory poem to the eight remaining poems, all of which "are either variants or developments of the motifs introduced or alluded to there." Includes a bibliography and an appendix (the original text of the nine poems).

8   ———. "Pasternak and Christian Art." In *Boris Pasternak. Essays*, edited by Nils Åke Nilsson. Stockholm Studies in Russian Literature, no. 7. Stockholm: Almqvist & Wiksell International, pp. 203–14.

Suggests that Pasternak utilized Christian art as a source for the poems in *Doctor Zhivago* and that he was influenced by works of Russian, Byzantine, Dutch, Flemish, and Italian artists. Hypothesizes a link between the poems and among Christian paintings and Orthodox iconography, finding evidence of both elements and influences in the topographical concreteness of the poems. Points out examples (i.e., the raising of Lazarus, the Resurrection) in which Pasternak diverges from New Testament interpretations of biblical events in favor of motifs depicted in Western art or icons. Identifies an "overlapping of

Byzantine and Western elements in Pasternak's interpretation of Christian motifs" that "underscores an important idea in his authorship—the unity of Christian culture." Maintains that "Pasternak sees the dividing line to run not between Orthodoxy and Catholicism, but between Christianity and materialistic ideologies. *Doctor Zhivago* can be regarded as a defense and an apology for such a universally Christian world-view."

9 BOROWSKY, KAY. *Kunst und Leben. Die Ästhetik Boris Pasternaks.* Germanistische Texte und Studien, vol. 2. Hildesheim and New York: Georg Olms Verlag, 136 pp.

Discusses briefly Pasternak's aesthetic, ethical, religious, and philosophical views on his poetry. Examines perfunctorily the poetics (language, style, form, and content). Makes distinctions between Pasternak's usages of "life," "art," "beauty," and "truth of art and reality." Surveys the meaning of art, antiquity, society, and creativity in Pasternak's works. Discusses the themes of "self-sacrifice," "self-denial," "death" and "immortality" (chiefly drawn from *Doctor Zhivago*).

10 CARLISLE, [ANDREYEV] OLGA. "Conversations with Pasternak." In Pasternak's *My Sister, Life and Other Poems*, edited with texts by Olga Andreyev Carlisle. Color photographs by Inge Morath. New York and London: Harcourt Brace Jovanovich, pp. 105–18.

Reprint of the first part of 1962.6.

11 ———. "Prologue." In Pasternak's *My Sister, Life and Other Poems*, edited with texts by Olga Andreyev Carlisle. Color photographs by Inge Morath. New York and London: Harcourt Brace Jovanovich, pp. 7–15.

Recalls several highlights in Pasternak's life, drawing on his two autobiographies. Dwells on the importance of the summer of 1917 in Pasternak's life "because it inspired him to write a cycle of poems, *My Sister, Life.*" Views *My Sister, Life* as a collection with exceptionally "harmonious artistic personality," and as a collection with "no literary clichés." Ranks Pasternak "with the greatest, Alexander Blok and Osip Mandelshtam." Gives the background of the publication of *Doctor Zhivago* and labels its lyrics "original and immensely fluid." Recalls Pasternak's own views of *Doctor Zhivago* as expressed to her during her 1960 interview with Pasternak.

12 FARINO, EZHI. "Dva poeticheskikh portreta" [Two poetic portraits]. In *Boris Pasternak. Essays*, edited by Nils Åke Nilsson. Stockholm Studies in Russian Literature, no. 7. Stockholm: Almqvist & Wiksell International, pp. 52–66.

Analyzes Pasternak's poem to Akhmatova and Akhmatova's poem to Pasternak. Pasternak's "To Anna Akhmatova" is discussed in terms of the epistolary genre in Russian poetry (Zhukovsky's and Pushkin's).

Concludes that Pasternak's Akhmatova portrait is structured on a "certain Akhmatova-like archi-text" that embraces "three aspects: a realia 'world-text'; a comprehensive spatial structure of that text's world; Akhmatova's poetic path." Cites Pasternak's poem in its entirety.

13 FRANCE, ANNA KAY. "Iago and Othello in Boris Pasternak's Translation." *SQ* 28: 73–84.

Discusses Pasternak's conception of Iago and Othello by analyzing his *Othello* translation and quoting from Pasternak's "Notes on Translations." Labels Pasternak's Iago as less "cunning" and "persuasive," "lacking in subtlety," and displaying "absence of good" ("The very assertion of the power of the individual to mold his life according to his desires loses force in Pasternak's translation"; "Pasternak chooses not to use his own powerful poetic and imaginative gifts to suggest their perversion to evil uses by another"). Also points out differences between Pasternak's and Shakespeare's images of Othello and Desdemona. Reprinted (with modifications) in 1978.15.

14 GIFFORD, HENRY. "Mandelstam and Pasternak: The Antipodes." In *Russian and Slavic Literature*, edited by Richard Freeborn, R.R. Milner-Gulland, and Charles A. Ward. Columbus, OH: Slavica Publishers, pp. 376–86.

Reformulates the standard criticism of Pasternak through a comparison to Mandelstam based on the memoirs of Nadezhda Mandelstam. Defines Pasternak's literary position in Western society as embodying "the best hope for Russian poetry" and its renaissance. Points out differences between Pasternak and Mandelstam: Pasternak's more lenient treatment by the Soviet authorities and feelings of self-importance due to his belief in the "elite" position of an artist, conceptions of art and the artist, preferences in European literature, religious beliefs, and others. Concludes that "the notes of Pasterank and of Mandelstam are distinct, but they belong to the same species."

15 JACKSON, LAURA [RIDING]. "About *Story*." *Chelsea* 35: 82–86.

Applies her theories on the function and origins of *Story* and its place in human consciousness to *Doctor Zhivago* in a brief note discussing the Russian approach to the novel, which entails a sense of the enclosure of human beings in terms of their strengths and weaknesses, and the supplementing of the "story-scene" with commentary on "wisdom" (seen as "beauty" in *Doctor Zhivago*).

16 JAKOBSON, ROMAN. "The Contours of *A Safe Conduct*." In *Semiotics of Art. Prague School Contributions*, edited by Ladislav Matejka and Irwin R. Titunik. Cambridge: MIT Press, pp. 188–96.

Translation of 1935.1.

17   JENNINGS, ELIZABETH. "Boris Pasternak. A Vision from Behind Barriers." In *Seven Men of Vision. An Appreciation*. London: Vision, pp. 224–46.

Examines several aspects of Pasternak's status as forerunner of the "modern visionary"—defined as the artist who creates a world from within the confines of political repression. Uses poems from *Themes and Variations*, *When the Skies Clear*, and *Doctor Zhivago* to illustrate the religious, affirmative, and unified vision of Pasternak. Sees an all-embracing love, moral courage, and aesthetic receptivity as the salient character traits underpinning Pasternak's vision. The poems "Christmas Star," "The Miracle," "Holy Week," "Mary Magdelene II," and "The Garden of Gethsemane" form a unit of analysis where the reader is seen to find the essence of Pasternak's personal religious vision, which illuminates Pasternak's love poems and all of his other works as well.

18   LEVIN, Iu. I. "Zametki o 'Leitenante Shmidte' B.L. Pasternaka" [Notes on B.L. Pasternak's *Lieutenant Schmidt*]. In *Boris Pasternak. Essays*, edited by Nils Åke Nilsson. Stockholm Studies in Russian Literature, no. 7. Stockholm: Almqvist & Wiksell International, pp. 85–161.

A thorough analysis of *Lieutenant Schmidt's* poetics—its metric structure (including meter, rhymes, and stanzas), the dependence on historic sources and documents published on Schmidt (criticism, memoirs, and correspondence), the thematic composition, and its language ("speech spheres"). Establishes that twenty-three chapters (out of twenty-eight) are structured monometrically (with sixteen various meters); that chain, ring, and pair rhymes abound; that three basic "thematic spheres" (history, nature, and personal life) could be singled out; that Schmidt's letters to Rizeberg and various memoirs (those of Rizeberg and Schmidt's sister in particular) are used profusely; and that the authorial language stratum, with a polyphonic absorption of other strata, dominates over dialogical and other speeches.

19   LUR'E, A.N. "Istoricheskaia osnova v poeme B. Pasternaka 'Leitenant Shmidt'" [A historic basis in B. Pasternak's tale in verse *Lieutenant Schmidt*]. *NDVSh*, no. 4, pp. 14–22.

An analysis of *Lieutenant Schmidt*—historical background, composition, and style. Compares Schmidt's biographical facts (including trial and correspondence) with Pasternak's Schmidt portrayal, and concludes that the plot is historically documented. Argues that the protagonist incorporates features of a revolutionary of the 1870s (is a nobleman and navy officer, and suffers estrangement from his circle). Finds that Pasternak characterizes Schmidt through his speech, reflections, and actions, and that he also renders his thoughts and feelings.

20   MAL'TSEV, IU. *"Doktor Zhivago"* [*Doctor Zhivago*]. In *Vol'naia russka-ia literatura, 1955–1975*. Frankfurt am Main: Possev-Verlag; New York: Atheneum, pp. 16–36.

Calls the appearance of *Doctor Zhivago* "a historical event" and believes that one can understand the essence of the novel only in the context of Soviet literature and Soviet life. Sees the novel's central point in it's "personalism," which determines the novel's "sketchiness of characters," "compositional friability," abundance of metaphors and similes, multitude of styles, and coincidences, among other aspects. Elaborates on the difference between a "traditional" novel and *Doctor Zhivago*, in which "both characters and their world are portrayed by a lyrical monologue even though that monologue is portrayed in a third person." Underlines the novel's high poetic quality and concludes that "brilliant verses full of lyricism and sadness, purity, inspired trepidation and music crown this astounding book."

21   NILSSON, NILS ÅKE. "'With Oars at Rest' and the Poetic Tradition." In *Boris Pasternak. Essays*, edited by Nils Åke Nilsson. Stockholm Studies in Russian Literature, no. 7. Stockholm: Almqvist & Wiksell International, pp. 180–202.

Examines the link between "With Oars at Rest" and literary tradition, regarding the poem as a variation on the "in the boat" [*na lodke*] theme seen as popular among the Russian poets—including Derzhavin, Fet, Balmont, Bryusov, Bely, and Sologub. Thoroughly analyzes the poem's poetics—its structure, semantics, and sound instrumentation, among other things. Concludes that Pasternak's poem "breaks down a commonplace situation ... and a poetic statement ... into pieces and segments"; that it "is an illustrative example of Pasternak's way of handling a question very topical"; that "it is romantic in a quite different sense than the traditional genre of the theme 'na lodke'"; and that "it abolishes the common Romantic opposition of 'I'-'you', 'I'-'world' and replaces them with a new kind of relationship between the poet and man, between man and the world." Translated: 1979.34.

22   ———, ed. *Boris Pasternak. Essays*. Stockholm Studies in Russian Literature, no. 7. Stockholm: Almqvist & Wiksell International, 215 pp.

Includes: 1976.6; 1976.8; 1976.12; 1976.18; 1976.21; 1976.23; 1976.25; 1926.27.

23   PASTERNAK, ELENA. "Iz pervykh prozaicheskikh opytov Borisa Pasternaka. Publikatsiia II" [On Boris Pasternak's first prose experiments. Second publication]. In *Boris Pasternak. Essays*, edited by Nils Åke Nilsson. Stockholm Studies in Russian Literature, no. 7. Stockholm: Almqvist & Wiksell International, pp. 26–51.

A continuation of her first publication on Pasternak's unpublished early prose fragments concerning the "genesis of literary inspiration."

Includes fragments that develop further the previous theme in their descriptions of "winter city" images. Cites examples of these images in Pasternak's poetry and records the evolution of "city impressions." Concludes that "winter city" images are a recurrent theme in Pasternak's poetry—beginning with *A Twin in the Clouds* of 1913 and ending with his "Winter Holidays" poetry of 1959. Comments in detail on the previously unpublished fragments.

24 ROWE, ELEANOR. "Pasternak and *Hamlet*." In *Hamlet. A Window on Russia*. New York: New York University Press, pp. 147–66.

Links Pasternak's "departures" from and "distortions" of Shakespeare's original to facets of the translator's own life and the Russian literary tradition in general. These include Hamlet's greater objectivity and dispassionateness, an increased emphasis on Ophelia's sexual innocence, and a muting of the theme of contamination. Grigory Kozintsev's 1954 stage and 1964 film adaptations of *Hamlet* are subjected to analysis, illuminated by excerpts from Kozintsev's correspondence with Pasternak. An analysis of Zhivago's poem "Hamlet," and comments on *Hamlet* from Pasternak's plays *The Blind Beauty* and *The Here and Now* show that Pasternak saw Hamlet as a resigned, reluctant sacrifice rather than the hero many Soviet critics have seen him to be.

25 TRENIN, V.V., and N.I. KHARDZHIEV. "O Borise Pasternake" [On Boris Pasternak]. In *Boris Pasternak. Essays*, edited by Nils Åke Nilsson. Stockholm Studies in Russian Literature, no. 7. Stockholm: Almqvist & Wiksell International, pp. 9–25.

Makes random observations on Pasternak's poetry (the first four collections, *A High Malady*, the three tales in verse, and the *Second Birth* collection) and records shifts in Pasternak's poetics—from the lyric intonational spaciousness and word repetitiousness of *A Twin in the Clouds*, the lyric word play of *Themes and Variations*, sound metaphors and attentiveness to details of things and objects in *My Sister, Life*, and contemporary epic forms in *A High Malady* and the three tales in verse to a romance tradition of Fet and Polonsky and the poetry with "music" themes in *Second Birth*. Also draws parallels between Pasternak's and Fet's "poetic culture"—between their "methods of associative leaps."

26 ZELINSKY, BODO. "Der Poesiebegriff Pasternaks." In *Proceedings of the VIIth International Congress of Aesthetics*. Bucharest, 28 Août–2 Septembre 1972. Bucharest: Editura Academiei Republicii socialiste Romania, pp. 509–13.

Incorporates major notions and views expounded in his two previous essays (1974.16; 1975.16). Adds that Pasternak's statement "poetry is prose" does not fit into traditional concepts of prose. Argues that Pasternak's notions of prose imply depiction of reality, truthfulness, clarity, sobriety, and naturalness. Concludes that Pasternak's creative act of writing is the transformation of poetry from a stationary condition into the poetry of a living word.

27 ZHOLKOVSKII, A.K. "Zametki o tekste, podtekste, i tsitatsii u Pasternaka (k razlicheniiu strukturnykh i geneticheskikh sviazei)" [Notes on Pasternak's text, subtext and quotations (toward a differentiation of structural and genetic bonds)]. In *Boris Pasternak. Essays*, edited by Nils Åke Nilsson. Stockholm Studies in Russian Literature, no. 7. Stockholm: Almqvist & Wiksell International, pp. 67–84.

Provides various readings of a Pasternak text and subtext and discusses types of quotations as applied to Pasternak. Cites a line and offers nine readings—including a "metaphoric equation of objects" and "lexical and phonetic object approximation." Elaborates on Pasternak's device of "metaphoric transference into a subtext" and gives examples of such a "technique." Subdivides *tsitatsii* (quotations) into five quotation types—a quotation used "consciously"; a quotation "simply 'rooted' in a literary tradition"; a quotation "obviously" influenced by a literary work (Pasternak's poetry about other poets, and epigraphs or paraphrases from the Bible and poetry); a quotation based on "correlative description" of text; and a quotation involving a repetition of Pasternak's own text (an epigraph from his own poetry or a repeated use of rhymes).

1977

1 BARNES, CHRISTOPHER J. "Boris Pasternak, the Musician-Poet and Composer." *SH* 1: 317–35.

Discusses Pasternak's "youthful period of musical studies" while mentioning his mother's musical influence on him. Centers on Scriabin's influence on Pasternak's musical compositions, and on Pasternak the musician turned poet and prose writer. Details Pasternak's penchant for music as reflected in titles of some of his lyric poems, in his association with friends who were musicians and composers, and in the musicality of Pasternak's "verse and prose." Identifies and elaborately discusses numerous features of Scriabin's "musical impact" in Pasternak's own musical pieces, pointing out an affinity with Scriabin by analyzing the rhythmic patterns, schemes, melodic motifs, and more, and citing in full the notes of Pasternak's "Prelude" (8 December 1906). Translated: 1983.3. Reprinted: 1977.4.

2 ———. "Boris Pasternak: A Review of Nikolaj Aseev's *Oksana* (1916)." *SH* 1: 293–305.

Details Pasternak and Aseyev's literary affinity during 1913–1915: their involvement "in the 'Lirika' publishing enterprise," their reciprocal poetry dedications to each other, their tributes to Mayakovsky and Mayakovskian elements in their poetry, and Aseyev's "strong influence on

Pasternak's own evocations of medieval Moscow in the consciously avant-garde poems." Surveys their friendship during subsequent years concluding that after 1936 "there is no evidence of any close artistic relationship, mutual influence or collaboration." Comments in detail on Pasternak's review of Aseyev's *Oksana*, a review published for the first time.

3   ———. Introduction to Pasternak's *Collected Short Prose*, edited by Christopher Barnes. New York: Praeger Publishers, pp. 3–18.

Discusses briefly the presence of Pasternak the poet and prose writer in all of his works. Evaluates Pasternak's early prose: (1) *The Story of a Contraoctave* ("a plain restatement of neoromantic themes"); (2) *The Line of Apelles* ("an expression of the author's own dilemma and conflict with romanticism"); (3) *Letters from Tula*; (4) *A Safe Conduct* ("a series of fascination and original discourses on art, culture, history, psychology, and many other topics"); (5) *Aerial Ways* ("a form of Aesopian comment on the fate of modern Russia"); (6) *The Story* ("records its haunting memories of the prewar period"); (7) *The Childhood of Luvers*; (8) *The Haughty Beggar* (translated as "A Beggar Who Is Proud"); and others. Also comments on *Second Birth* and other poetry. Draws parallels between the early prose and *Doctor Zhivago*, referred to as Pasternak's "crowning achievement," in which Pasternak developed "Christian motifs, aesthetic, ethical, and historical views, and strands of literary and personal experience, combining them in a bold new poetic revelation of man's place in the modern world."

4   ———. "Pasternak as Composer and Scriabin-Disciple." *Tempo*, no. 121 (June): 13–19.
     Reprint of 1977.1.

5   FLEISHMAN, L. "Avtobiograficheskoe i 'Avgust' Pasternaka" [The autobiographical elements and Pasternak's "August"]. In *Stat'i o Pasternake*, by L. Fleishman. Studien und Text, 11–12. Bremen: K-Presse, pp. 102–12.
     Reprint of 1977.6.

6   ———. "Avtobiograficheskoe i 'Avgust' Pasternaka" [The autobiographical elements and Pasternak's "August"]. *SH* 1: 194–98.

Juxtaposes Pasternak's descriptions of a biographical fact—his "fall from a horse"—recorded in two autobiographies, and links these to his poem "August." Argues that only two motifs in the texts of both autobiographies are unchanged: the story of his broken leg and his first musical impressions. Cites and discusses Pasternak's letter to A.L. Shtikh, seen as a direct connection between the facts "of Pasternak's fall from a horse" and the tenth "musical anniversary"—6 August 1913. Argues that the letter's content helps the reader better understand the hidden intent of the poem "August." Traces symbolic meanings of the "fall from a horse" in Pasternak's works. Reprinted: 1977.5.

7 ———. "Istoriia 'Tsentrifugi'" [The history of "Centrifuge"]. In *Stat'i o Pasternake*, by L. Fleishman. Studien und Text, 11–12. Bremen: K-Presse, pp. 62–101.

Regards Pasternak's role in the literary group "Centrifuge" and the history of "Centrifuge" as important to the formation of Pasternak's literary views. Traces interrelations among various literary groups of the 1920s, notably between "Centrifuge" and "Lirika," and "Centrifuge" and "The First Journal of Futurists." Discusses Pasternak's association with his contemporaries, Mayakovsky in particular. Records the contents of the first two "Centrifuge" issues and discusses the material for the third unpublished issue. Traces how Pasternak's independent views and his final break from futurism were formed parallel to "Centrifuge"'s shift to the futurists' platform. Reprinted: 1979.16.

8 ———. "K kharakteristike rannego Pasternaka" [Toward a definition of early Pasternak]. In *Stat'i o Pasternake*, by L. Fleishman. Studien und Text, 11–12. Bremen: K-Presse, pp. 4–61.

Reprint of 1975.4.

9 GIFFORD, HENRY. *Pasternak: A Critical Study*. Cambridge: Cambridge University Press, 294 pp.

Examines chronologically and thoroughly Pasternak's poetry (*My Sister, Life*; *Themes and Variations*; *Second Birth*; *On Early Trains*; *The Poems of Yury Zhivago*; and *When the Weather Clears*), prose (*Letters from Tula*; *The Childhood of Luvers*; *The Line of Apelles*; *Safe Conduct*; *Doctor Zhivago*; and *An Essay in Autobiography*), and his unfinshed play, *The Blind Beauty*. Discusses Pasternak's translations (from Shakespeare, Goethe, and Schiller) and surveys other renditions (from Jonson, Byron, Shelley, Kleist, Rilke, Petöfi, Słowacki, Shevchenko, Tsereteli, and Pshavela). Recounts in detail the main events in Pasternak's life. Concludes that *My Sister, Life* and *Themes and Variations* are Pasternak's lasting accomplishments; believes they proved Pasternak is "an original poet" and an "innovator," and they "give a matchless impression of a unique period in Russian history." *Doctor Zhivago* is seen as "an extension" to *A Safe Conduct*; asserts that "particular episodes of the novel (the spring in Melyuzeevo, the long journey to the Urals, the return to Varykino) have evolved from the most successful experiments in his earlier fiction." Makes conclusive parallels with Mayakovsky, Mandelstam, Solzhenitsyn, Tsvetaeva, Blok, and Akhmatova (mentions her poem "The Four of Us," the title of which refers to Akhmatova, Mandelstam, Pasternak, and Tsvetaeva).

10 GLADKOV, ALEXANDER. *Meetings with Pasternak*. Translated from the Russian and edited with notes and introduction by Max Hayward. London: Collins & Harvill Press; New York: Harcourt Brace Jovanovich; New York: Helen & Kurt Wolff, 224 pp.

Translation of 1973.5.

11 HAYWARD, MAX. Introduction to *Meetings with Pasternak*, by Alexander Gladkov. Translated from the Russian and edited with notes and introduction by Max Hayward. London: Collins & Harvill; New York: Harcourt Brace Jovanovich; New York: Helen & Kurt Wolff, pp. 7–30.

Briefly recounts the history of meetings between Pasternak and Gladkov (1977.10). Records the most important statements in Gladkov's memoirs for the first time. Offers his own observations and comments on Pasternak's early poetry, his "self-centeredness," his rightness, and his survival of Stalin's purges, concluding that Stalin's personal protection might have saved Pasternak. Also notes that Pasternak's translation activities were for Pasternak a refuge from the restriction of the period, an avenue through which Pasternak could say things that he "could no longer express in his own name." Believes that *Doctor Zhivago* was a new experiment in genre, a "successful embodiment of what Pasternak set out to do," and that through the novel's coincidences "Pasternak was only emphasizing the reality of his approach." Calls *Doctor Zhivago* a "lyrical kaleidoscope." Reprinted 1983.10.

12 LAMONT, ROSETTE C. "Yury Zhivago's 'Fairy Tale': A Dream Poem." *WLT* 51: 517–21.

Analyzes the context of Zhivago's poem "Fairy Tale" regarding its creation in the body of *Doctor Zhivago*, its personal significance for Zhivago, and its cultural and historical symbolism. Sees the close identification between the poet and his mythical hero as reflecting Zhivago's status as poet and doctor ("twice healer") catalyzed by a special mental and spiritual state at the moment of creation—a "shamanic trance" or "Apollonian ecstasy."

13 LIVINGSTONE, ANGELA. "The Poet and the Revolution. Zhivago and Strelnikov: Pasternak and Mayakovsky." *PNR* 5, no. 2: 21–23.

Objects to simplistic interpretations of Antipov by noting evidence of "paradoxical admiration" and fascination on Pasternak's part toward the character. Traces this mysterious attraction back to precursors of Antipov in Pasternak's previous works, as well as to Pasternak's ambiguous relationship with Mayakovsky. Sees the two meetings between Antipov and Zhivago, as well as the "incompleteness and awkwardness" of Antipov's transformation into Strelnikov, to support the idea that Pasternak felt himself posing and role-playing much like the sincere revolutionary zealots Antipov and Mayakovsky.

14 ———. "Wherefore Poets in Destitute Times. A Commentary on Two Early Prose Fragments by Pasternak." *PNR* 5, no. 4: 14–18.

Analyzes the content of Pasternak's two fragments (one untitled, the other "Ordering a Drama") both separately and in relation to *A Safe Conduct*, *The Black Goblet*, and *Doctor Zhivago*. Asserts that both texts are "rich in motifs characteristic of Pasternak's entire life's work" and that they embody "the idea that the world needs to be rescued—or let loose—or completed—by art." Includes fragments in her own translations.

15 MASING-DELIĆ, IRENE. "Some Alternating Opposites in the Zhivago Poems." *RR* 36: 438–62.
    Contends that the poems of Zhivago contain a unified system of thought organized philosophically and structurally under the principle of "alternation of opposites." Contrasting concepts and images characteristic of the poems include darkness and light, oblivion and remembrance, sickness and health, seasonal contrasts, sleep and vigil, and the central opposition: death and life. These clusters of positive and negative elements make up interchangeable "metaphoric synonyms," giving the cycle an organic unity. Discerns the pattern of alternating opposites in the sequence of the poems. The two elements of this pattern are "recurrences" (positive) and "intervals" (negative), both of which lead to "disfunctions" when carried to excess, but are essential to the maintenance of a fresh, creative perception of reality.

16 MIŁOSZ, CZESŁAW. "On Pasternak Soberly." In *Emperor of the Earth: Modes of Eccentric Vision.* Berkeley, Los Angeles, London: University of California Press, pp. 62–78.
    Reprint of 1970.9.

17 O'HARA, FRANK. "About Zhivago and His Poems." In *Standing Still and Walking in New York.* Bolinas, CA: Grey Fox Press, pp. 99–109.
    Reprint of 1964.11.

18 PASTERNAK, E.V. "Iz rannikh prozaicheskikh opytov B. Pasternaka" [From B. Pasternak's early prose attempts]. In *Pamiatniki kul'tury. Novye otkrytiia. Pis'mennost'. Iskusstvo. Arkhielogiia. Ezhegodnik. 1976.* Moscow: Nauka, pp. 106–18.
    A textual analysis of Pasternak's three rough prose drafts dated 1911–1913 that reveals a "symbolic meaning" of Relinquimini, Pasternak's pen name for his earliest and lost works, and a hero of the three drafts and *The Line of Apelles.* Links the drafts thematically with *My Sister, Life* ("for the first time, we can here see a personified life image entering a trusting relationship with the poet") and other works (*Spektorsky, A Safe Conduct,* and *Black Goblet,* for example). Expounds on the drafts' leitmotifs and "recurrent images" that reach out to later works. Includes three rough drafts published for the first time.

19 SEGAL, D. "Pro Domo Sua: The Case of Boris Pasternak." *SH* 1: 199–250.
    A study of the problem of Pasternak's conception of Judaism as expounded in his "treatment of being Jewish" in *Doctor Zhivago.*

Presents a number of themes (totality, nonobligatoriness, holistic art with collective significance, everyday experience as a subject, vividness, and Christianity, for example) as central to understanding Pasternak and extensively explicates them. Asserts that in *Doctor Zhivago* there is a "system of aesthetic and ethic oppositions between the Jews and 'the rest.'" Uses Vedenyapin, Zhivago, and Lara to illustrate the treatment of Jews. Strongly believes that Pasternak presents Christianity as "good" and Judaism as "bad." Claims "Pasternak draws clear parallels between the fate of Jurij Živago and the fate of Jesus." Outlines the Russian cultural tradition, and places Pasternak within that scheme. Relates Pasternak's "Judaism conception" to his ethic and aesthetic views.

20 TOOMRE, JOYCE STETSON. "The Narrative Structure of Pasternak's *Doctor Zhivago.*" Ph.D. diss., Brown University, 271 pp.
      Seeks to correct an "imbalance" in Pasternak criticism by understanding the book and its themes "within terms of the fabric of its language." Surveys criticism, reexamining the assumption that *Doctor Zhivago* is a "realistic" novel (chapter 1). Pasternak's conception of the ideal poet and his idiosyncratic theory of realism are found to be complementary notions that hierarchically govern the book's structure and provide a rationale for "the two distinct types of narrative prose which occur in the novel" (chapter 2). Links thematic material with distinctive syntactic patterns in a discussion of modality and ornate prose (chapters 3–4). Pasternak's emphasis on language is linked thematically to the death of the Russian language and its resurrection "through the creation of a verbal work of art" (chapter 5). Provides a bibliography.

21 WILSON, EDMUND. "Boris Pasternak." In *Letters on Literature and Politics 1912–1972*, edited by Elena Wilson. New York: Farrar, Straus & Giroux, pp. 582–89.
      Presents seventeen letters (1958–60) and discusses various Zhivago-related topics related to the novel's first appearance, including the quality of the translations, publishing history, remarks on the names of Zhivago and Lara, and a reaction to Pasternak's death. Correspondents are William Shawn, Helen Muchnic, Avrahm Yarmolinsky, Janet Flanner, Gleb Struve, George L. Kline, and Eugene Lehovich.

1978

1 AUCOUTURIER, MICHEL. "The Metonymous Hero or the Beginnings of Pasternak the Novelist." In *Pasternak. A Collection of Critical Essays*, edited by Victor Erlich. Englewood Cliffs, NJ: Prentice-Hall, pp. 43–50.
      Reprint of 1970.1.

2   BARNES, CHRISTOPHER. "Boris Pasternak and the 'Bogeyman of Russian Literature.'" *RuL* 6, no. 1: 47–68.

Characterizes Pasternak's critical evaluations of Kruchenykh as a mixture of the new thematic possibilities radical futurism brought to Russian literature tempered with antipathy for the lack of unity and "malarial" shifts from formal to semantic and objective concerns. Details several of Kruchenykh's publishing ventures that involved Pasternak, especially the 1934 edition of *Poet's Tournament*, from which Pasternak's entry is reproduced in full and seen to exemplify Pasternak's rhyming prowess and stylistic originality even in light verse. Concludes with the texts of two poems Pasternak dedicated to Kruchenykh to typify the appreciative yet antipathetic feelings Pasternak held toward the futurist poet.

3   BARTLING, NATALIE. "Les poèmes religieux du docteur Živago." In *Slavistische Studien zum VIII. Internationalen Slavistenkongress in Zagreb 1978.* Cologne and Vienna: Böhlau-Verlag, pp. 15–26.

A study of the relationship of *Doctor Zhivago*'s poems to an annual, seasonal, and religious cycle, with a detailed discussion of the poems "Hamlet" and "The Garden of Gethsemane." Bases her interpretations on Russian Orthodox rituals and biblical stories. Draws parallels between Blok's *The Twelve* and "Star of the Nativity."

4   BERLIN, ISAIAH. "The Energy of Pasternak." In *Pasternak. A Collection of Critical Essays*, edited by Victor Erlich. Englewood Cliffs, NJ: Prentice-Hall, pp. 39–42.

Reprint of 1950.1.

5   BJÖRLING, FIONA. "Textual Coherency in Pasternak's Early Poetry." *SlaL* 6: 117–30.

Analyzes two of Pasternak's poems ("Ennui" and "Balashov") to demonstrate textual coherency despite the existence of "simultaneously two mutually interferential possibilities of language." Exhibits how the semantics in "Ennui" "are revealed as being coherent and well organized." Proves that "Balashov" "is organized around the use of the repeated connective phrases." Concludes that Pasternak "does not create images ... but predicates one image upon another"; "saturates his imagery with ... metaphorical substitutions"; and "assumes the familiarity of that which he has made strange." Provides a diagram to illustrate the composition of "Balashov."

6   BONAMOUR, JEAN. ["Pasternak et *Jivago.*"] In *Le roman russe.* Paris: Presses Universitaires de France, pp. 187–89.

Interprets *Doctor Zhivago* as a symbol of a "Renaissance" in Russian literature while discussing the novel's style, characters, the role of coincidences (as a symbol of fate, providence), and the novel's symbolism.

7 CHUDAKOVA, M.O. "Neizvestnyi korrekturnyi ekzempliar sbornika perevodov B.L. Pasternaka" [An unknown galley-proof copy of B.L. Pasternak's translation collection]. In *Zapiski otdela rukopisei.* Vol. 39. Moscow: Gosudarstvennaia biblioteka im. Lenina, pp. 106–18.

Describes the proofs of Pasternak's translation collection—*Selected Translations*—dated 14 December 1948. Itemizes the collection and elaborates on the publication data of major translations (*Hamlet* and *Faust*, for example). Comments on Pasternak's corrections and the collection's textological significance. Notes that the collection excludes some of Pasternak's most accomplished renditions (from Rilke, Tabidze, and Iashvili, for example), and attributes this omission to "time requirements." Concludes that the proofs shed light on Pasternak's work habits reflected in this, the penultimate collection of Pasternak's life.

8 CLAYTON, J. DOUGLAS. "The Hamlets of Turgenev and Pasternak: On the Role of Poetic Myth in Literature." *GS* 2, no. 6: 455–61.

Cites contrasting attitudes toward Hamlet that evolved between the writings of Turgenev and Pasternak, and sees Pasternak as having reinterpreted Hamlet as a self-sacrificing innocent who truly loves Ophelia but is victimized by evil and political circumstances. Suggests that Pasternak may have viewed Hamlet as an allegory of events in Russia during Pasternak's lifetime.

9 DAL', ELENA. *Nekotorye osobennosti zvukovyx povtorov Borisa Pasternaka* [Several peculiarities of Boris Pasternak's sound repetitions]. Commentationes Slavicae Gothaburgenses, no. 2. Göteborg: Institutum Slavicum Universitatis Gothaburgensis, 169 pp.

Analyzes sound repetitions in Pasternak's four poetry collections—*A Twin in the Clouds*; *My Sister, Life*; *Second Birth*; and *The Poems of Yury Zhivago*. Supplies phonetic transcriptions and counts of sound repetitions in them. Establishes four repetition types: Type A, containing a stressed vowel; Type B, a stressed vowel with a consonantal echo; Type C, a pure consonantal repetition; and Type D, a repetition with an unstressed vowel alone or followed by a consonantal echo. Concludes that Type-A repetitions are "significantly longer than Type C and D," a fact that is seen to prove that stressed vowels have overwhelmingly been used for sound repetition devices in Pasternak's poetry.

10 DYCK, SARA. "In Search of a Poet: Buckler and Pasternak." *GS* 2, no. 5: 325–36.

Likens *Doctor Zhivago* to Ernest Buckler's *The Mountain and the Valley*, arguing that the two works provide a "fourfold portrait" (through both their authors and their heroes) of the artistic process. Discusses personal attributes necessary to an artist as they apply to the two novels' heroes. Examines the heroes' similarities: their struggle with death, their apparent lack of will, their receptivity to life's colors and rhythms, and the chaos and suffering they experience due to historical conditions.

11   ERLICH, VICTOR. "Categories of Passion." In *Pasternak. A Collection of Critical Essays*, edited by Victor Erlich. Englewood Cliffs, NJ: Prentice-Hall, pp. 1–20.
　　　Revision of 1964.4.

12   ———. Reviews of *A Captive of Time*, by O. Ivinskaya, and *Meetings with Pasternak*, by A. Gladkov. *YR* 68, no. 1: 133–40
　　　Traces the conditions surrounding the creation of the two memoirs and each author's relationship with Pasternak. Ivinskaya's memoirs (though "generally uninspired") are seen as informative and occasionally moving, especially with respect to their account of Pasternak's struggle with Soviet authorities before and after the publication of *Doctor Zhivago*. Praises Gladkov's biography as "vivid and affectionate." Believes that Gladkov has shown an unguarded, relaxed Pasternak, graceful under wartime hardships and idiosyncratic and astute in his literary judgements. Differs with Gladkov in his negative appraisal of *Doctor Zhivago*. Singles out Gladkov's depiction of Pasternak's funeral as particularly vivid and moving.

13   ———. "A Testimony and a Challenge—Pasternak's *Doctor Zhivago*." In *Pasternak. A Collection of Critical Essays*, edited by Victor Erlich. Englewood Cliffs, NJ: Prentice-Hall, pp. 131–36.
　　　Reprint of slightly abridged text of 1958.15.

14   FARINO, EZHI [JERZY]. "K probleme koda liriki Pasternaka" [Toward a coding problem of Pasternak's poetry]. *RuL* 6, no. 1: 69–101.
　　　Exemplifies a coding system by textually and contextually analyzing Pasternak's poem "About these Verses," while centering on the poem's "spatial characteristics" and not its "title problem." Associates the poem's winter images ("its agents like frost, hoarfrost, and snow") with similar winter images (even "blizzard" and "snowstorm") in Pasternak's other poems and points out Pasternakian codes—a candle as a symbol of "human life"; a Christmas tree as "eternity and a myth of childhood"; and a window as an "entrance through which the demonic winter world strives to penetrate," among others. Concludes that Pasternak's poetry "is strictly systemized," that "Pasternak's code obviously breaks down to separate sub-codes," and that each of Pasternak's worlds ("summer," "winter," and "reality") is coded in its own way.

15   FRANCE, ANNA KAY. *Boris Pasternak's Translations of Shakespeare*. Berkeley: University of California Press, 288 pp.
　　　Analyzes in detail Pasternak's translations of Shakespeare's four tragedies (*Hamlet, Othello, King Lear*, and *Macbeth*) and elaborately

comments on Pasternak's translation style, often comparing it to the style used in Pasternak's original works. Concludes that Pasternak has reacted against the "implication of certain images, turns of phrase, and textual details." Thus, Pasternak avoids or changes sexual allusions in his *Hamlet* ("That's a fair thought to lie between maids' legs" becomes "But what a wonderful thought that is—to lie at a young girl's feet!"), *Othello*, and *King Lear*. He softens Iago's "malignant genius," accentuates "what is most positive and affirmative in the works," and strengthens Christian elements while freely using biblical terminology. Looks upon Pasternak's translations as an integral part of the rest of his creative work, and believes that his style of translation does not suggest the "displacement of reality by feeling, but an effort to define reality sharply." Contains reprints (with modifications) of 1973.4; 1976.13.

16 GLADKOV, ALEKSANDR. "Zima v Chistopole. Vospominaniia o B.L. Pasternake" [A winter in Chistopol. Recollections about B.L. Pasternak]. *LO*, no. 4, pp. 103–11.
    Partial reprint of 1973.5.

17 HAMPSHIRE, STUART. "*Doctor Zhivago*. As From a Lost Culture." In *Pasternak. A Collection of Critical Essays*, edited by Victor Erlich. Englewood Cliffs, NJ: Prentice-Hall, pp. 126–30.
    Reprint of 1958.23; 1969.8.

18 HARDWICK, ELIZABETH. Review of *A Captive of Time*, by Olga Ivinskaya. *NYRB* 25, no. 8: 6–14.
    Meditates on the fate of great writers at the hands of "wives and mistresses" who write of their lives together. Notes that Ivinskaya idealized her treatment of Pasternak and compares Ivinskaya's version of their relationship with the "tragic exhaustion" of the Countess Tolstoy's diaries and the "unaccountable deceit" of Lady Byron. Recounts Pasternak's relationship with Ivinskaya, emphasizing its effects on the personal lives of the two of them and Pasternak's second wife. Concludes Ivinskaya's account is distorted by excessive self-absorption, exaggeration of the importance of their relationship in Pasternak's life and work, and jealousy of Pasternak's wife.

19 HAYWARD, MAX. Introduction to *A Captive of Time*, by Olga Ivinskaya. Translated by Max Hayward. Garden City, NY: Doubleday & Co.
    Describes Pasternak's family background and records numerous events and aspects of Pasternak's life and work, such as his education and upbringing, love for music and philosophy, four poetry collections (*A Twin in the Clouds*, *My Sister, Life*, *Themes and Variations*, and *Second Birth*), the "Centrifuge" association, the rupture with LEF and Mayakovsky, his two marriages, the horrors of the 1930s, the periods during and after World War II, and the *Doctor Zhivago* affair, among

others. Outlines Ivinskaya's biography, followed by an explanation of the structure of her book. Reprinted: 1983.9.

20   IAKOBSON, A. "'Vakkhanaliia' v kontekste pozdnego Pasternaka" ["Bacchanalia" in the context of later Pasternak]. *SH* 3: 302–79.

Asserts that a more definitive interpretation of the poem "Bacchanalia" is possible only within the context of Pasternak's later works (written after 1945)—such as *Doctor Zhivago* and the collection *When the Skies Clear*. Believes the theme of immortality emerged from the theme of death—which is seen to have become a "triune entity: life-death-resurrection"—a plot theme in Pasternak's later works. Also sees a "transformation of life" into death—and the reverse—as a basis for all metamorphoses in Pasternak's later works. Compares "Bacchanalia" to the poem "Winter Night" in terms of the former's duality of space; the outward space is seen as "dark" and the inner as "light."

21   IVINSKAYA, OLGA. *A Captive of Time.* Translated by Max Hayward. Garden City, NY: Doubleday & Co., 498 pp.

Translation of 1972.9.

22   JACKSON, CAROL ANN. "Teleological Coincidence and Eternity in Pasternak's Prose." Ph.D. diss., New York University, 347 pp.

Sees the teleological nature of coincidences in Pasternak's prose, their status as evidence of guiding power or purpose in the universe, to rise from Pasternak's own personal experience, becoming manifest in his prose works as they connect the eternal and historical dimensions of existence. Identifies three types of coincidences: happenstance (physical), synchronicity (psychic or spiritual), and prophetic (destiny-related). These occur on three levels: obvious, subtle, and transcendent. Perceives Pasternak's early prose—*The Childhood of Luvers, Letters from Tula, The Line of Apelles*, and *Aerial Ways*—to operate more on the level of obvious and transcendent levels of coincidence. Argues that coincidence is the structural element that integrates Pasternak's teleological concept of eternity into all of his prose works. Relates Pasternak's beliefs to this structural device in each work.

23   JACKSON, ROBERT L. "*Doctor Zhivago*: *Liebestod* of the Russian Intelligentsia." In *Pasternak. A Collection of Critical Essays*, edited by Victor Erlich. Englewood Cliffs, NJ: Prentice-Hall, pp. 137–50.

Reprint of 1960.16.

24   LAYTON, SUSAN. "Poetic Vision in Pasternak's *The Childhood of Luvers.*" *SEEJ* 22, no. 2: 163–74.

Asserts the centrality of *The Childhood of Luvers* to Pasternak's work as a whole, and its importance as a forerunner of *Doctor Zhivago* in particular. Sees the story as built upon Pasternak's analogy between artistic vision and the spontaneous perception of a child, an approach shared by other postsymbolist Russian writers. Considers the work's central poetic principle of metonymy to link the perceptual and philosophical planes as the complex changing emotional states of immediate perception. Considers these absolute categories as central to all of Pasternak's work. Sees two of these philosophical concerns—Zhenya's realization of the interconnectedness of humankind and her embodiment of a feminine essence to which Pasternak felt a special kinship—as finding their later fuller realization in the character of Lara.

25   LEVIN, Iu. "Razbor odnogo malopopuliarnogo stikhotvoreniia B. Pasternaka" [An analysis of B. Pasternak's not very popular poem]. *RuL* 6: 39–45.
    A contextual analysis of "When [I hear] the Mortal Crackling of a Creaking Pine Tree"—originally published in 1928 and excluded from further publications during Pasternak's life. Sees the poem as structured on the "ambivalence of reality and illusion." Discerns the poem's "underlying death motif," stressing the poem's message as a "warning" of political events—a rout of New Political Economy and the emergence of the Trotsky opposition.

26   LINDSTROM, THAIS S. "Boris Pasternak: *Dr. Zhivago.*" In *A Concise History of Russian Literature.* Vol. 2, *From 1900 to the Present.* New York: New York University Press, pp. 207–17.
    Discusses the history of *Doctor Zhivago*'s creation and publication, and analyzes its artistic and philosophical content. Draws brief parallels between *Doctor Zhivago* and Mann's *Magic Mountain*, Eliot's *The Waste Land*, Joyce's *Ulysses*, and Dostoevsky's *Notes from Underground* and *The Idiot*. Identifies the significant themes in *Doctor Zhivago* as "uprooted man looking for certainties," "the spatially limited world," "the celebration of personal fulfillment," "the intimate involvement of the natural order in human affairs," the poet's role and creativity in relation to art and life, and others.

27   LIVINGSTONE, ANGELA. "Pasternak's Last Poetry." In *Pasternak. A Collection of Critical Essays*, edited by Victor Erlich. Englewood Cliffs, NJ: Prentice-Hall, pp. 166–75.
    Reprint of 1963.11.

28   LOTMAN, YURY. "Language and Reality in the Early Pasternak." In *Pasternak. A Collection of Critical Essays*, edited by Victor Erlich. Englewood Cliffs, NJ: Prentice-Hall, pp. 21–31.
    Translated and abridged text of 1969.14.

29   MASING-DELIĆ, IRENE. "Some Allusions to *Besy* in *Doktor Živago.*" *BIDS* 8: 31–41.
    Cites Dostoevsky's *Besy* as one of many subtexts used to expand and deepen the ideological structure, mood, and message of *Doctor*

Zhivago. Argues that both novels portray fanatical and materialist revolutionaries as leading Russia into disintegration and chaos. Centers on the parallel father-son relationship between Stepan Trofimovich Verkhovensky and Petr Stepanovich Verkhovensky (in *Besy*) and Averky Stepanovich Mikulitsyn and Livery Averkievich Mikulitsyn (in *Doctor Zhivago*), and finds patterns of revolutionary destructiveness. Concludes that "the basic structure of the world models in *B* and *DZ* is similar, as both works postulate values above Man. The allusions to *B* in *DZ* therefore find a functional place, increasing the connotative richness of Pasternak's novel."

30   MASLENIKOVA, ZOIA. "Portret poeta" [A poet's portrait]. *LiG*, nos. 10–11, pp. 267–94.
     Recollections of her meetings with Pasternak recounted in diary entries—from 22 June 1958 through 17 October 1958. Records Pasternak's reminiscences of his childhood; infatuation with music; and views of Bely, Gorky, Tolstoy, Nekrasov, Paustovsky, Grin, Rodin, and French impressionists. Also records Pasternak mentioning his family background, parents, brother, and two sisters. Pays special attention to Pasternak's views of Tsvetaeva, his works (*A Safe Conduct*, in particular), and his translations (Goethe's *Faust*, among others). Continued: 1979.32. Reprinted: 1988.31, with slight modifications; and 1990.43, with text modified and added.

31   NILSSON, NILS ÅKE. "Life as Ecstasy and Sacrifice: Two Poems by Boris Pasternak." In *Pasternak. A Collection of Critical Essays*, edited by Victor Erlich. Englewood Cliffs, NJ: Prentice-Hall, pp. 51–67.
     Reprint of 1959.47.

32   OBOLENSKY, DIMITRI. "The Poems of *Doctor Zhivago.*" In *Pasternak. A Collection of Critical Essays*, edited by Victor Erlich. Englewood Cliffs, NJ: Prentice-Hall, pp. 151–65.
     Reprint of 1961.20.

33   O'CONNOR, KATHERINE TIERNAN. "Boris Pasternak's *My Sister—Life*: The Book Behind the Verse." *SlaR* 37: 399–411.
     Examines the "underlying narrative and thematic structure of *My Sister—Life.*" Divides the collection into two halves. Provides schemas of both halves and the double conclusion of *My Sister, Life*, and analyzes each section independently, showing how they interrelate. Claims the collection's narrative form is similar to that of a novel. Looks at garden and mirror imagery, analyzes the interrelations between the first and second halves, and extensively explicates what is seen as a love theme that runs through the collection. Believes that Pasternak's "definition" poems of poetry, soul, and creation are slightly ironic.

Examines the motifs of separation, trains, seasons, and nature imagery, and concludes that Pasternak's art follows and frames life. Comments on the "thematic, spatial, and temporal" levels of the collection. Reprinted (with modifications) in 1988.36.

34 PERELMUTER, JOANNA. "Reflection of Urban Speech in the Language of *Doctor Živago.*" *RLJ* 32, no. 113: 13–20.

Argues that Pasternak's nonnarrative language is exemplified in the speech of both upper- and lower-class Moscow inhabitants. Sees foreign loanwords, substandard use, colloquialisms, folkloric expressions, abusive expressions, archaic vocables, and folk etymologies as characteristic of the varying degree and quality of these two urban classes. Finds substandard lexical phenomena marking the direct speech of the intelligentsia in third-person narrative and represented in discourse as well (giving the narrator's language such distortions as changing Zhivago's name to Zhilvok); these are examined as typical of the special role played by the vernacular in Pasternak's prose.

35 SEGAL, D. "Zametki o siuzhetnosti v liricheskoi poezii Pasternaka" [Remarks on plot in Pasternak's lyrics]. *SH* 3: 282–301.

Investigates the presence and evolution of plot in Pasternak's poetry—with emphasis on the poetry from *Themes and Variations.* Demonstrates the existence of plot in Pasternak's lyrics—a "semantic coherence of the poetic text." Detects this coherence on four levels: logical, topical, referential, and semantic. Concludes that a "theme of an integrated impetuous movement" is one of Pasternak's rudimentary structural pivots. Discusses "micro-plots" (often generated from "tropes and figures") and Pasternak's predilection for "impetuous eventfulness," which he contrasts against a "traditional form of plot narration in *Doctor Zhivago.*" Cites numerous examples to demonstrate his thesis. Reprinted: 1979.41.

36 SENDICH, MUNIR. Review of "Max Hayward and Manya Harari, translators. *Boris Pasternak. Doctor Zhivago.*" *RLJ* 32, no. 113: 241–49.

Translators Max Hayward and Manya Harari are taken to task for a "plethora of distortions and mistranslations" of *Doctor Zhivago.* Many such errors are enumerated, with textual comparisons. Desires to add to the demand for a new, more accurate rendition. Singles out omissions, additions, concoctions, and onomastic errors as the most egregious of the translators' distortions.

37 SINYAVSKY, ANDREY. "Pasternak's Poetry." In *Pasternak. A Collection of Critical Essays*, edited by Victor Erlich. Englewood Cliffs, NJ: Prentice-Hall, pp. 68–109.

Reprint of 1969.17.

38 STEPUN, FYODOR. "Boris Pasternak." In *Pasternak. A Collection of Critical Essays*, edited by Victor Erlich. Englewood Cliffs, NJ: Prentice-Hall, pp. 110–25.
     Translation of 1959.69.

39 TYNYANOV, YURY. "Words and Things in Pasternak." In *Pasternak. A Collection of Critical Essays*, edited by Victor Erlich. Englewood Cliffs, NJ: Prentice-Hall, pp. 32–38.
     Reprint of 1969.19.

40 WEIDLÉ, VLADIMIR. "The End of the Journey." In *Pasternak. A Collection of Critical Essays*, edited by Victor Erlich. Englewood Cliffs, NJ: Prentice-Hall, pp. 176–83.
     Translation of 1961.30.

41 ZHOLKOVSKY, A.K. "Mesto okna v poeticheskom mire Pasternaka" [The role of the window in Pasternak's poetic world]. *RuL* 6, no. 1: 1–38.
     Views the basis of Pasternak's imagery through two themes, that of heightened awareness and that of "plastics contact" or linkage between levels of being, of which some fifteen varieties are identified and exemplified. Argues that Pasternak has frequently used the image of a window in many of its derivative forms and in many plot constructions employed as central themes in Pasternak's poetics. The window is also seen as a recurrent image in Pasternak's entire poetry, as recurrent as art, spring, garden, night, or candle images. Cites examples of a peculiar role a window has played in Pasternak's poetic designs: (1) a window is an "opening" through which air and fragrances penetrate; (2) a window is a gleam through which visual impressions penetrate; and (3) a window is "part of one's living quarters open to the outside world." Concludes that a window is a "sort of recurrent character" in Pasternak's works. Translated: 1978.42.

42 ———. "The Window in the Poetic World of Boris Pasternak." *NLH* 9, no. 2: 1–38.
     Translation of 1978.41. Reprinted: 1984.24.

1979

1 AROUTUNOVA, BAYARA. "Zemlia i nebo. Nabliudeniia nad kategoriiami prostranstva i vremeni v rannei lirike Pasternaka" [Earth and sky. Observations of space and time categories in Pasternak's early poetry]. In *Boris Pasternak 1890–1960: Colloque de Cerisy-la-Salle (11–14 septembre 1975)*. Bibliothèque russe de l'Institut d'études slaves, no. 47. Paris: Institut d'études slaves, pp. 195–224.
     Studies the function of spatial and temporal categories in Pasternak's early poetry. Applies Pasternak's statement "I'm amazed

how important the clarity of time and space is to me" to her study, and connects the statement to Pasternak's philosophic worldviews. Analyzes the early collections, notably *Above the Barriers* and *My Sister, Life*, to demonstrate the structure and artistic function of temporal and spatial categories. Concludes that Pasternak perceives life as an eternal movement.

2   AUCOUTURIER, ALFREDA. "Semantika ritma v sbornike *Sestra moia zhizn*'" [Semantics of rhythm in *My Sister, Life*]. In *Boris Pasternak 1890–1960: Colloque de Cerisy-la-Salle (11–14 septembre 1975)*. Bibliothèque russe de l'Institut d'études slaves, no. 47. Paris: Institut d'études slaves, pp. 225–62.

   A detailed study of *My Sister, Life's* rhythmic patterns—meters, composition, closures, acaldectics, repetition devices, anaphora, stanzaic instrumentation, and rhymes. Divides the collection into three parts, with a multitude of meters prevailing in the first, an absence of that multitude in the second, and variations of the first part's structural schemes in the third. Finds that compositional rhythm singles out two basic structural principles—circular structure and dynamic movement, both deemed to occur on various levels. Concludes that compositional rhythmics conditions the completeness and linear design of narration, thus "strengthening the position of poetic units." Elaborates on poems' individual meters and rhythmic patterns.

3   AUCOUTURIER, MICHEL. "Ob odnom kliuche k *Okhrannoi gramote*" [On one key to *A Safe Conduct*]. In *Boris Pasternak 1890–1960: Colloque de Cerisy-la-Salle (11–14 septembre 1975)*. Bibliothèque russe de l'Institut d'études slaves, no. 47. Paris: Institut d'études slaves, pp. 337–49.

   Singles out three features distinguishing *A Safe Conduct* from *An Essay in Autobiography*—*A Safe Conduct*'s poetic (artistic) aspect, the displacement of a traditional autobiographical plot, and its philosophical quality. Claims that *A Safe Conduct* is closely interwoven with Pasternak's poetry and that it fulfills a poetic function. Sees the third part of *A Safe Conduct* as an example of the plot displacement, because a Mayakovsky story became the part's "thematic kernel" and not the summer of 1917 when *My Sister, Life*, deemed a beginning of the mature Pasternak, was created. Finds the source of *A Safe Conduct*'s title in Pasternak's "To a Friend," the theme of which—a conflict between poetry and the Revolution—is seen as the most important of Pasternak's themes in the 1920s. Concludes that *A Safe Conduct* is an "attempt to protect art from the encroachment of time-enslaver and to secure to art a road into eternity."

4   BARNES, CHRISTOPHER. "Boris Pasternak i revoliutsiia 1917 goda" [Boris Pasternak and the revolution of 1917]. In *Boris Pasternak*

1890–1960: Colloque de Cerisy-la-Salle (11–14 septembre 1975). Bibliothèque russe de l'Institut d'études slaves, no. 47. Paris: Institut d'études slaves, pp. 315–27.

A rehashed version of his previous essay, some parts of which have been translated. Concludes that from the 1920s on, Pasternak began to "belittle the air of history" more freely than he had before, and that from *My Sister, Life* and *Dramatic Fragments* to *Doctor Zhivago* lies a single line of development; sees all three works to speak directly or indirectly of the Revolution. Translation (with modifications) of 1975.1.

5 ———. "The Original Text of 'O skromnosti i smelosti.'" *SH* 4: 294–303.

Compares a stenographic transcript of Pasternak's speech ("On Modesty and Courage") at the Third Plenary Session of the Board of the Union of Writers (February 1936) with the official version published in *Literaturnaya Gazeta*. Discusses issues in Pasternak's address such as the undesirability of "ranking" poets, ordinariness versus mediocrity, and Pasternak's hesitation to give recitations of his poetry. Is fully annotated, with a list of Pasternak's public speeches and lectures.

6 BODIN, PER-ARNE. "Three Soviet Poets Round the Epitaphios." *ScS*, no. 25, pp. 5–17.

An analysis of the genre of the Easter poem in the works of Pasternak, Akhmatova, and Surkov as it relates to "Orthodox Russia's preoccupation with the *epitaphios* motif." Analyzes from Pasternak "excerpts, which the poet took from the service books of the Orthodox Church in the late forties," and some poems. Claims that these "excerpts" have been used in *Doctor Zhivago*, that Pasternak's writings have typical features of the Easter-poem genre (such as the coming of spring and the celebration of Easter), and that the "sacral element" in Pasternak's poetry is an "open symbol with a multitude of potential interpretations."

7 CHERTKOV, LEONID. "K voprosu o literaturnoi genealogii Pasternaka" [Concerning Pasternak's literary genealogy]. In *Boris Pasternak 1890–1960: Colloque de Cerisy-la-Salle (11–14 septembre 1975).* Bibliothèque russe de l'Institut d'études slaves, no. 47. Paris: Institut d'études slaves, pp. 55–62.

Examines Pasternak's literary genealogy—similarities with Khlebnikov, Esenin, Tyutchev, Sluchevsky, Shtikh, Severyanin, and Annensky (intonation, imagery, and lexica, for example). Notes Pasternak's "hidden competition" with Bely and affinity with Bryusov, Tsvetaeva, Nabokov, Tikhonov, and Selvinsky.

8 CRONE, ANNA LISA, and PATRICIA SUHRCKE. "Pasternak's 'Pushkin Variations.'" *WS* 24: 316–36.

Examines Pasternak's interpretations of Pushkin's poetics as presented in "Theme with Variations." Centers an analysis of the poem on nature imagery, references to Greek and Egyptian mythology, European folklore, Judeo-Christian tradition, and Beethoven. Views Pasternak as trying to answer the riddle "'What is Pushkin? What is poetry?'" Concludes that "the riddle itself is used as a metaphor for Pushkin, and for great poetry."

9   DÖRING, JOHANNA RENATE. "Semantizatsiia zvukovykh struktur v poeme Pasternaka 'Vysokaia bolezn'" [Semantization of sound structures in Pasternak's tale in verse *A High Malady*]. In *Boris Pasternak 1890–1960: Colloque de Cerisy-la-Salle (11–14 septembre 1975)*. Bibliothèque russe de l'Institut d'études slaves, no. 47. Paris: Institut d'études slaves, pp. 143–54.

An analysis of sound repetitions in *A High Malady* that attempts to prove that Pasternak consciously employs sound repetitions, and argues that these sounds are manifested as motifs combined into larger thematic units. Contends that sound repetitions are "carriers of lyric action"; they are not metaphor conduits but have an associative role. Concludes that "semantization of sound repetitions is an important evolutionary step in the development of Pasternak's poetic language because it contributes to the collision of poetic and referential language."

10 DRJUČINOV, MILAN. "Antinomiia 'romantizm-realizm' v poetike Pasternaka" [Antinomy "romanticism-realism" in Pasternak's poetics]. In *Boris Pasternak 1890–1960: Colloque de Cerisy-la-Salle (11–14 septembre 1975)*. Bibliothèque russe de l'Institut d'études slaves, no. 47. Paris: Institut d'études slaves, pp. 95–103.
Reprint of 1975.8.

11 ERLICH, VICTOR. "'STRASTI RAZRIADY.' Zametki o "'Marburge'" ["PASSION DISCHARGES." Notes on "Marburg"]. In *Boris Pasternak 1890–1960: Colloque de Cerisy-la-Salle (11–14 septembre 1975)*. Bibliothèque russe de l'Institut d'études slaves, no. 47. Paris: Institut d'études slaves, pp. 282–88.

Analyzes "Marburg" from various angles—imagery, its relation to corresponding passages in *A Safe Conduct*, and its "centrality" within Pasternak's poetic world. Mentions five versions of the poem ("obviously this poem meant a great deal to Pasternak") and discusses the poem's plot simplicity. Elaborates on the meaning of the "image of passion" used in *A Safe Conduct* as "love" and "feeling." Concludes that the image of "passion," a metonymy for a "gradual withering away," changes its role of a "main motivator of the lyric action to the role of its passive and powerless witness."

12 ETKIND, EFIM. "O 'Gamlete' v perevodakh B. Pasternaka i M. Lozinskogo" [On B. Pasternak's and M. Lozinsky's translations of *Hamlet*]. In *Boris Pasternak 1890–1960: Colloque de Cerisy-la-Salle (11–14*

septembre 1975). Bibliothèque russe de l'Institut d'études slaves, no. 47. Paris: Institut d'études slaves, pp. 471–74.

Comments on Pasternak's views of his Shakespeare translations in general and *Hamlet* in particular. Sees Pasternak's *Hamlet* as aimed at a stage production (to "reach the audience immediately"), a translation "saturated with spoken idiomatic turns," bordering "at times on vulgarity." Cites passages from Pasternak's and Lozinsky's *Hamlet* translations to support his arguments.

13 ———. "Pasternak, novator poeticheskoi rechi" [Pasternak, an innovator of poetic speech]. In *Boris Pasternak 1890–1960: Colloque de Cerisy-la-Salle (11–14 septembre 1975).* Bibliothèque russe de l'Institut d'études slaves, no. 47. Paris: Institut d'études slaves, pp. 117–42.

A general commentary on innovations in Pasternak's poetics—metrical system, rhymes, and poetic language—that establishes Pasternak did not violate the Russian classical metrical system and made his innovations within the five basic traditional meters. Also argues that Pasternak remained loyal to "exact" classical rhymes. Sees Pasternak's major innovations in his ability to absorb various lexical strata into his poetic language.

14 FLEISCHMANN, IVO. "Les Écrivains tchèques devant Pasternak." In *Boris Pasternak 1890–1960: Colloque de Cerisy-la-Salle (11–14 septembre 1975).* Bibliothèque russe de l'Institut d'études slaves, no. 47. Paris: Institut d'études slaves, pp. 451–60.

An account of and commentary on a discussion between Pasternak and four Czech writers in Moscow in 1956. Presents the poetics of Pasternak as reflected in the Czech cultural life of 1935 (the publication of the Czech edition of *A Safe Conduct*); the role of Jozsef Hóra, a Pasternak translator and correspondent; Pasternak's influence on Czech poets; the Marburg philosophy; and the Rilke tradition, among other topics.

15 FLEISHMAN, L. "Fragmenty 'futuristicheskoi biografii' Pasternaka" [Fragments of Pasternak's "futuristic biography"]. *SH*, no. 4, pp. 79–113.

An attempt to resolve the question of Pasternak's belonging to the futurist movement. Resorts to Pasternak's two autobiographies, Pasternak's essay *The Wassermann Test*, and his own analysis of Pasternak's "Lyrical Space" to establish Pasternak's views of the movement. Mentions Pasternak's closeness to Mayakovsky and Bolshakov, who is seen as a mediator between Pasternak and Mayakovsky. Draws parallels between Pasternak and Bolshakov, drawing heavily on results of textual analysis of a number of Pasternak's and Bolshakov's poems. Also contrasts the text of *The Wassermann Test* against Bolshakov's article on the topic. Finds a number of similarities between their two works. Concludes that "aesthetic declarations of *A Safe Conduct* fully correspond to artistic principles in a futurist painting—a dynamic portrayal of displacement, a registration of several dynamic aspects, with an 'image' of man portrayed in the fixation of 'transition.'"

16 ———. "Istoriia Tsentrifugi" [The history of "Centrifuge"]. In *Boris Pasternak 1890–1960: Colloque de Cerisy-la-Salle (11–14 septembre 1975)*. Bibliothèque russe de l'Institut d'études slaves, no. 47. Paris: Institut d'études slaves, pp. 19–43.
      Reprint of 1977.7.

17 ———. "Problems in the Poetics of Pasternak." *PTL* 4: 43–61.
      Examines Pasternak's poetics "in a wide theoretical perspective" and thoroughly surveys criticism on the subject. Presents a composite view of Pasternak's poetics. Decodes the plot of Pasternak's prose and verse with "non-coincidence of codes." Describes the structure of Pasternak's thematics. Asserts that at *Doctor Zhivago*'s basis are the compositional devices of geographical texts.

18 FRANCE, PETER. "Pasternak et le romantisme." In *Boris Pasternak 1890–1960: Colloque de Cerisy-la-Salle (11–14 septembre 1975)*. Bibliothèque russe de l'Institut d'études slaves, no. 47. Paris: Institut d'études slaves, pp. 83–92.
      Demonstrates a similarity between the views of European romanticists and Pasternak's tendency to depict reality from a fresh, individual perspective. Discusses Pasternak's definition of romanticism (a declaration of individuality and personal integrity, and a protest against immodest literary "pharisees"). Provides a detailed appraisal of romantic elements in Pasternak's texts. Asserts that Pasternak's art can be considered an extension of trends initiated by European romanticists.

19 GELLERSHTEIN, S.G. Commentary on Pasternak's "O predmete i metode psikhologii" [On the subject and methods of psychology]. *SH* 4: 284–85.
      A generalized commentary on Pasternak's essay on P. Natorp's conceptions of psychology, an essay written in 1913 and published for the first time in this issue (pp. 274–84). Places the essay within Pasternak's other articles, treating the relationship between art and conscious, particularly within Pasternak's essay "Symbolism and Immortality." Sees the essay as an "exceptionally important document throwing additional light on the early roads of the formation of Pasternak's spiritual make-up."

20 HAMILTON, TATIANA NICOLAEVNA. "Osnovnaia tematika proizvedenii Borisa Pasternaka" [The basic themes in Boris Pasternak's works]. Ph.D. diss., Georgetown University, 130 pp.
      Defines five themes—God, woman, nature, avocation, and death—as Pasternak's "distinctive landmarks," and discusses them in detail. Examines these themes in their relationship to literary forms, schools,

and movements—symbolism, futurism, acmeism, and impressionism. Chapter 6 tries to elaborate on Pasternak's views of and his endeavors to preserve "freedom of thought under a totalitarian regime."

21   HUGHES, OLGA. "Stikhotvorennie 'Marburg' i tema 'vtorogo rozh-deniia.' Nabliudeniia nad raznymi redaktsiiami stikhotvoreniia 'Marburg'" [The poem "Marburg" and the theme of "second birth." Observations on various versions of the poem "Marburg"]. In *Boris Pasternak 1890–1960: Colloque de Cerisy-la-Salle (11–14 septembre 1975)*. Bibliothèque russe de l'Institut d'études slaves, no. 47. Paris: Institut d'études slaves, pp. 281–302.
      Juxtaposes various versions of the poem "Marburg" and discusses the theme of "second birth" ("birth of a poet" and "rebirth") in the poem and Pasternak's works. Provides a textual history of all the poem's versions, supporting her views with references to *A Safe Conduct*. Concludes that the development of the poem's main theme (birth of a poet) was completed in the second version and that all subsequent changes were primarily limited to text abridgments.

22   JONES, DAVID L. "History and Chronology in Pasternak's *Doctor Živago*." *SEEJ* 23: 160–63.
      Offers a detailed chronology of the events of the novel, noting "glaring inconsistencies" in references to Kolchak and the formation of the Far Eastern Republic, which are seen as contradictory to historical data. Discusses and resolves inconsistencies raised by other critics. Offers possible solutions to discrepancies; concludes that historical spirit is more important to *Doctor Zhivago* than historical accuracy.

23   KATKOV, GEORGE. "'Bezliub'e'—rannii nabrosok *Doktora Zhivago*" [*Without Love*. An early draft of *Doctor Zhivago*]. In *Boris Pasternak 1890–1960: Colloque de Cerisy-la-Salle (11–14 septembre 1975)*. Bibliothèque russe de l'Institut d'études slaves, no. 47. Paris: Institut d'études slaves, pp. 329–35.
      Regards *Without Love* "almost as the embryo of *Doctor Zhivago*, containing not only hints of specific episodes which later evolved into the novel, but its fundamental philosophical structure as well," and interprets it as a sketch descending into the journey of two friends who, upon learning of the February Revolution, hurry back to Petrograd from the Urals. Points out that in the character of Goltsev one finds the image of Zhivago, and in Kovalevsky the image of Antipov-Strelnikov, to whom dreams of revolution were dearer than all else. Believes that "Kovalevsky thought that Goltsev slept when it was he, and not Goltsev, who was sleeping" and that this carries a symbolic significance. Concludes that the revolutionary dreams of Kovalevsky-Antipov-Strelnikov are a state of sleep in which one loses everything and that *Without Love* confirms that even at the beginning of his career, Pasternak knew what he "had to say to mankind."

24 KAZARKIN, A.P. "Tema poeta v tvorchestve Borisa Pasternaka" [The theme of a poet in Boris Pasternak's works]. In *Khudozhestvennoe tvorchestvo i literaturnyi protsess*. No. 2. Tomsk: Izdatel'stvo tomskogo universiteta, pp. 61–74.

An attempt to define Pasternak's adherence to literary movements (futurism and symbolism, in particular) and literary norms. Claims that Pasternak's "interest in the world of nature," "breadth of cultural reminiscences in his poetry, and a particular cosmism" stem from symbolism. Concludes that Pasternak's early and later poetry belong to one and the same "system"—but that the later poetry is still "complex, multilinear, for in it the lines of a branched gradition leading toward Romanticism are alive."

25 KOPELEV, LEV. "Faustovskii mir Borisa Pasternaka" [Boris Pasternak's Faustian world]. In *Boris Pasternak 1890–1960: Colloque de Cerisy-la-Salle (11–14 septembre 1975)*. Bibliothèque russe de l'Institut d'études slaves, no. 47. Paris: Institut d'études slaves, pp. 491–515.

Evaluates Pasternak's translation of Goethe's *Faust* as "inspired, emotional, sometimes arbitrary." Observes that the characters of *Faust* and its mood and thinking can be seen in the poems "Margarita," "Mephistopheles" and "Love of Faust," which appeared in the 1930s before the translation. Points out that it is hard to find traits of Faust's "sweetheart" in Margarita and that most important for Pasternak was the unity of woman with nature. Argues that in the poem "Mephistopheles" there appear several external traits resembling those of *Faust*. Concludes that in translating *Faust*, Pasternak created a "newly poetic, musically—which means spiritually—and emotionally different atmosphere" and that Pasternak's Faustian world "is closely linked with the world of Goethe's *Faust*, but it is a particular creative link, and therefore goes both ways."

26 LIVINGSTONE, ANGELA. "At Home in History: Pasternak and Popper." *SH* 4: 131–45.

Compares and contrasts the "metaphysical" philosophies of Pasternak and Popper. Details Popper's concept of a third or objective world ("world 3") that exists in parallel with the other two worlds, the physical and subjective, and that acts as a source of human knowledge. Believes Pasternak's early work *Theses* (1922), as well as *A Safe Conduct* and *Doctor Zhivago* evidence a similar concept of an objective world, but as a source for art. Popper's theory that knowledge, or science, is expanded through one's attempt to prove or disprove current knowledge is compared to Pasternak's view of art as an endeavor to solve the enigmas put forth in the art of one's predecessors. Draws comparisons with the pessimistic philosophies of Rilke and Blok, pointing out that Pasternak and Popper were optimistic in their concept that the "world 3" is created by humans, who are "at home" in the sense that the objective world provides a link between the physical and subjective worlds. Argues that because of Pasternak's views on this subject, one should not overly stress the importance of religious symbolism in *Doctor Zhivago*, as Pasternak "does not need 'religion'"—he only shows respect for it in the novel.

27 ———. "Pasternak i Ril'ke" [Pasternak and Rilke]. In *Boris Pasternak 1890–1960: Colloque de Cerisy-la-Salle (11–14 septembre 1975)*. Bibliothèque russe de l'Institut d'études slaves, no. 47. Paris: Institut d'études slaves, pp. 431–40.

Establishes similarities and dissimilarities between Pasternak's *A Safe Conduct* and Rilke's *Aus den Aufzeichnungen des Malte Laurids Brigge* while focusing on the works' themes and notions, the language, and the poets' temperament and *Weltanschauung* (the "sense of duty," the concept of "la condition humaine," for example). Concludes that Pasternak's perception of life "begins with a feeling that man is at home in the universe, which, though mysterious and not created by us, becomes ours more and more all the time." Labels Pasternak's worldview an "ontology of joy," contrasted to "Rilke's existentialism." Further develops these ideas in her next essay (1983.18).

28 LUKIĆ, SVETA. *Dileme i sinteze Borisa Pasternaka* [Boris Pasternak's dilemmas and syntheses]. Belgrade: "Slovo Ljubve"—"Prosveta," 116 pp.

Mentions major biographical events in Pasternak's life, borrowing information from *A Safe Conduct*. Examines the evolution of Pasternak's poetics by comparing two of his biographies and concludes that Pasternak simultaneously "handles" two of his tools—metaphor and commentary, which "cannot be alone for themselves, there is no gap between them, they grow into each other." Finds Pasternak's prose a reflection of European "intellectual, philosophical, and essay prose" and compares his prose to Proust's (*A Safe Conduct* and *A la recherche du temps perdu*) and Rilke's (*The Childhood of Luvers* and *Das Buch der Bilder*). Centers prose discussions on two biographies (in *A Safe Conduct* Pasternak is deemed to convey himself through Scriabin, Cohen, and Mayakovsky); *The Childhood of Luvers*; *Letters from Tula*; *Doctor Zhivago*; and *A Story of a Contraoctave*. Draws parellels between prose and poetry. Emphasizes in *Doctor Zhivago*'s objectivity the meaning of one's freedom, the meaning of love, and the function of nature. Finds shortcomings of the novel—lack of structural coherence (particularly the ending), style, open confrontations between the heroes, and an abundance of participles that are profusely used as adjectives.

29 MALEVICH, O., and E.V. PASTERNAK. "Iozef Gora i Boris Pasternak (K istorii odnogo perevoda)" [Jozsef Hóra and Boris Pasternak (Toward the history of a translation)]. *VL*, no. 7, pp. 177–87.

Breaks the analysis into three segments—comments on Jozsef Hóra's translations of Pasternak's lyrics (*Liryka*. Prague: Melantrich, 1935) and Pasternak's reaction to the translation; an interview with Pasternak by Fritz Brügel (1936.1); and two of Pasternak's letters to Hóra.

30 MALLAC, GUY DE. "Esteticheskie vozzreniia Pasternaka" [Pasternak's aesthetic views]. In *Boris Pasternak 1890–1960: Colloque de Cerisy-la-Salle (11–14 septembre 1975)*. Bibliothèque russe de l'Institut d'études slaves, no. 47. Paris: Institut d'études slaves, pp. 63–81.

Translation (with modifications) of 1964.10. Translated (with modifications): 1981.14.

31 ———. "Pasternak and Marburg." *RR* 38: 421–33.

Recounts major events and impressions from Pasternak's stay in Marburg, quoting from *A Safe Conduct*, "Marburg," and *Doctor Zhivago*. Discusses the influence of Cohen, the significance of Pasternak's unrequited love for Ida Vysotsky, and Pasternak's subsequent plunge into poetry. Summarizes Pasternak's time in Marburg as a "crossroad experience" of existential opposites (the Middle Ages versus the contemporary world, and reason versus love) that provided the basis for Pasternak's literary development. Revised: 1981.14.

32 MASLENIKOVA, ZOIA. "Portret poeta" [A poet's portrait]. *LiG*, no. 2, pp. 132–54.

Continuation of 1978.30; includes diary entries from 11 February 1959 through 30 July 1959. Adds to information about Pasternak the man. Records Pasternak's views of Voznesensky ("he is on a right path, will achieve a great deal, and already has"), his play *Blind Beauty* (on which Pasternak was working), and on Pasternak's reaction to foreign criticism of his works (a German translation of his poetry and two English critiques), among others. Reprinted: 1988.31, with slight modifications; and 1990.43, with text modified and added.

33 MÜLLER, LUDOLF. "Pasternak. *Doktor Schiwago*." In *Der russische Roman*, edited by Bodo Zelinsky. Düsseldorf: Bagel, pp. 354–80.

Singles out art as the main theme of *Doctor Zhivago*; mentions other themes: Russia, Russian history, World War I, "a sense of history," "the image of Christ," and "a captivating earnestness of a human life." Sees art as a vehicle for the "unriddling and overcoming of death." Considers the poems integral to the novel's goal.

34 NILSSON, NILS ÅKE. "Stikhotvorenie Pasternaka 'Slozha vesla' i literaturnaia traditsiia" [Pasternak's poem "With Oars at Rest" and literary traditions]. In *Boris Pasternak 1890–1960: Colloque de Cerisy-la-Salle (11–14 septembre 1975)*. Bibliothèque russe de l'Institut d'études slaves, no. 47. Paris: Institut d'études slaves, pp. 273–80.

Translation of 1976.21.

35 NIVAT, GEORGES. "Les matins de Pasternak." In *Boris Pasternak 1890–1960: Colloque de Cerisy-la-Salle (11–14 septembre 1975)*.

Bibliothèque russe de l'Institut d'études slaves, no. 47. Paris: Institut d'études slaves, pp. 361–72.

Expresses views on Pasternak's poetic world, namely mornings, which are seen as "favored moments" but not as a time when objects are "revealed" or "contrasted." Finds the present as Pasternak's only tense—fraught with "menace" and never "already completed." Sees Venice as the only "positive hero" of *A Safe Conduct*, a city that "exists, and, at the same time, does not." Concludes that Pasternak preferred Christmas, a "holiday of beauty," to Easter, a "tragic moment in Christianity." Reprinted: 1982.13.

36 POLLAK, SEWERYN. "Pol'skie stikhi v perevodakh Borisa Pasternaka" [Polish verses in Boris Pasternak's translations]. In *Boris Pasternak 1890–1960: Colloque de Cerisy-la-Salle (11–14 septembre 1975)*. Bibliothèque russe de l'Institut d'études slaves, no. 47. Paris: Institut d'études slaves, pp. 475–90.

Discusses Pasternak's translations of Słowacki, Broniewski, and Lesmian. Mentions the background surrounding the translations—their original locations (and how they were found) and Pasternak's poetics of an artistic translation as examined in his "Notes of a Translator." Believes that Pasternak was drawn to Słowacki through his translations of Kleist and Schiller (his *Maria Stuart*). Observes that in his Słowacki translations, Pasternak departed from the original, changed "realia," and shortened or added "entire pieces"; concludes that Pasternak did not treat anyone else "so high-handedly" as Słowacki.

37 PONOMAREFF, CONSTANTIN. "Boris Pasternak (1890–1960): Art of Self-Concealment." In *The Silenced Vision. An Essay in Modern European Fiction*. Frankfurt am Main: Peter Lang, pp. 63–78.

Asserts Pasternak's tendency to conceal himself in his prose through "masked speech" that hides essentials and maintains a distance between authorial content and the text's symbolic action (particularly in *Doctor Zhivago*). Cites examples of such self-concealments from *The Childhood of Luvers, Letters from Tula, Aerial Ways, A Tale, A Safe Conduct*, and others of Pasternak's works that express his views of poetic creation and the nature of art. Argues that Pasternak's own nature and intent combined with a historically imposed ordeal encouraged these tendencies toward self-concealment. Theorizes that to understand *Doctor Zhivago* one has to study its twenty-five poems, deemed to be a comprehensive sequence of the meaning of human life that transcends the thematic content.

38 PRITCHETT, V.S. "Pasternak. Unsafe Conduct." In *The Myth Makers. Essays of European, Russian, and South American Novelists*. London: Chatto & Windus, pp. 9–20.

An overview of Pasternak's early life as set forth in his *An Essay in Autobiography*, followed by a discussion of *A Safe Conduct*, seen to represent the early, "affected Pasternak" and considered difficult and dense to reader and translator alike. Discusses various features of *Doctor Zhivago*, among them its apolitical nature as a human "confession of anguish." Excerpts some of the philosophical observations of Zhivago; sees his status as "saint" and "complete Soviet non-hero" as contributing to the novel's return to the "compassion of the great Russian tradition." Places Pasternak's observant eye for details and "gratuitous actions" in the context of his individualism; labels *A Safe Conduct* an "autobiography turned novel," a "romance" on the "texture of fate."

39 PROYART, JACQUELINE DE. "Une amitié d´enfance. Souvenirs recueillis." In *Boris Pasternak 1890–1960: Colloque de Cerisy-la-Salle (11–14 septembre 1975)*. Bibliothèque russe de l'Institut d'études slaves, no. 47. Paris: Institut d'études slaves, pp. 517–19.

Describes Pasternak's friendship with Ida Vysotskaya. Provides an account of Vysotskaya's own memoirs attesting to the role she considers to have played in Pasternak's life and works, most notably in *Doctor Zhivago*, in which Vysotskaya said Pasternak had aptly conveyed "the mood of their generation."

40 ———. "La nature et l'actualité de l'oeuvre de Pasternak. Réflexions sur la structure du cycle *Kogda razguljaetsja*." In *Boris Pasternak 1890–1960: Colloque de Cerisy-la-Salle (11–14 septembre 1975)*. Bibliothèque russe de l'Institut d'études slaves, no. 47. Paris: Institut d'études slaves, pp. 373–410.

A thematic and structural analysis of *When the Skies Clear*. Elaborates on the publication history of each poem in the collection and attempts to decode the poems' basic themes, the nature and the significance of the season changes in particular. Finds autobiographical elements adapted to the poems' themes. Discerns the polyphonic features (up to four voices) of the language. Examines a continuation of Pasternak's "conversation with his 'regular companions'—God, woman, nature, and death." Contains six charts that underpin her analysis.

41 SEGAL, DMITRI. "Zametki o siuzhetnosti v liricheskoi poezii Pasternaka" [Remarks on plot in Pasternak's lyrics]. In *Boris Pasternak 1890–1960: Colloque de Cerisy-la-Salle (11–14 septembre 1975)*. Bibliothèque russe de l'Institut d'études slaves, no. 47. Paris: Institut d'études slaves, pp. 156–77.

Reprint of 1978.35.

42 SHORE, RIMA. "A Note on the Literary Genesis of *Doctor Zhivago*." *UlR* 2, no. 1: 186–93.

Elaborates on Zhivago's remark that the art, rather than the crime, of Dostoevsky's *Crime and Punishment* is what moves the reader. By virtue of various similarities between *Doctor Zhivago* and *Crime and Punishment*, *Doctor Zhivago* is analyzed as its "continuation, a transportation of *Crime and Punishment* into the realm of the ordinary."

Among these similarities are the life stories of Dunya and Lara, the personalities of Svidrigaylov and Komarovsky, and the occurrence of axe murders in both novels. Cites Raskolnikov and Antipov-Strelnikov as representative of revolutionary ideals to which both authors are opposed. Compares Zhivago's guilt and irresolution over whether to confess his adultery to Raskolnikov's feelings about his own crime.

43 SIEGEL, PAUL. "Boris Pasternak's *Doctor Zhivago*: The Russian Revolution and the 'Hereditary' Intelligentsia." In *Revolution and the Twentieth Century Novel.* New York: Monad Press, pp. 173–94.

Outlines the novel's plot, with a summary of Zhivago's philosophical views, followed by a critique of the novel's artistic shortcomings and ideological inconsistencies. Disputes Pasternak's defense of the novel's coincidences on the grounds that they make the novel more, rather than less, predictable. Charges Pasternak with fuzzy characterization, exemplified by Dudorov and Antipov. Sees Lara and Zhivago as inconsistent to some degree. Views Pasternak's attitude toward the Revolution as equivocating and contradictory as reflected in Zhivago's words and deeds.

44 SIMPLICCIO, D. DI. "Iz rannikh prozaicheskikh opytov B. Pasternaka" [B. Pasternak's early prose attempts]. *SH* 4: 286–93.

A sequel to Elena Pasternak's previous publication on Pasternak's unpublished prose fragments dated 1911–1913 (1976.23). Includes fragments with a "'European,' romanticized background" and with "figures from medieval history." Elaborates on the fragments' history, describes them in detail, and annotates and comments on them.

45 SINIAVSKI, ANDRÉ. "Odin den' s Pasternakom" [A day with Pasternak]. In *Boris Pasternak 1890–1960: Colloque de Cerisy-la-Salle (11–14 septembre 1975).* Bibliothèque russe de l'Institut d'études slaves, no. 47. Paris: Institut d'études slaves, pp. 11–17.

Records Pasternak's views: (1) that he considered the period of *My Sister, Life* to be "unique in its intensity"; (2) that during that period he did not consider the field of poetry to be very promising; (3) that transition from poetry to prose was for him an "escape from stereotyped ways of thinking"; and (4) that Pasternak chose such a form for *Doctor Zhivago* because incoherence of form offered an opportunity to bring out ideas, and that Christ was the "most natural and closest reality." Reprinted: 1990.65. Translated: 1981.18.

46 STRUVE, GLEB. "Koe-chto o Pasternake i Ril'ke" [Something about Pasternak and Rilke]. In *Boris Pasternak 1890–1960: Colloque de Cerisy-la-Salle (11–14 septembre 1975).* Bibliothèque russe de l'Institut d'études slaves, no. 47. Paris: Institut d'études slaves, pp. 441–49.

Discusses E.V. Pasternak's "Pasternak's First Attempts" (1976.23), identifies eight lines as Pasternak's rendition from Rilke's *Das*

Stundenbuch ("Jetzt reifen schon die roten Berberitzen"), and cites Pasternak's eight lines as well as other Russian translations of Rilke's poem.

47 TSVETAEVA, MARINA. "Epos i lirika sovremennoi Rossii. Vladimir Maiakovskii i Boris Pasternak" [Epic and lyric poetry of contemporary Russia. Vladimir Mayakovsky and Boris Pasternak]. In *Izbrannaia proza v dvukh tomakh. 1917–1937*, edited by A. Sumerkin, vol. 2. New York: Russica Publishers, pp. 7–26.
    Reprint of 1933.3.

48 WILSON, ROBERT N. "Boris Pasternak. Ideology and Privacy." In *The Writer as Social Seer.* Chapel Hill: University of North Carolina Press, pp. 105–17.
    Sees the central theme of *Doctor Zhivago* in the conflict between the individual's responsiblity or duty to the public good and the private search for one's own destiny and happiness. Views the novel as standing "firmly in the classic tradition of the Russian novel" and as "a story of love in the chaotic welter of social revolution." Compares Pasternak to Camus, Ibsen, and Shaw. Draws parallels between Zhivago's fictional and Pasternak's real-life struggles for individuality in an atmosphere where the role of writer clashes with the interests of the state. Elaborates on Lara and the novel's underscoring love story as the epitome of that struggle, and calls Lara "a conspiratorial companion in full rebellion against political dogma and comfortable middle-class morality."

49 ZAMANSKII, L.A. "O zhanrovo-stilevom svoeobrazii tsikla 'Volny' B. Pasternaka" [The genre and style peculiarity of B. Pasternak's cycle "The Waves"]. *PSZhSL* 10: 56–66.
    An attempt to define the style and genre of "The Waves," while examining the cycle's imagery, motifs, lyrical plot, and hero, among other features. Sees the meaning of "The Waves" in the "trinity of time: was, is, will be." Observes that the cycle's musicality is "Pasternak's means of world perception," and that the plot of the cycle "'springs up' in the third poem." Discusses the motifs of the cycle—the birth of a new man," "contemporaneity," and "the flow, the movement." Concludes that the cycle is a "mixture and even contradiction of different genres."

50 ZAMOYSKA, HÉLÈNE. "L'actualité du *Docteur Jivago*." In *Boris Pasternak 1890–1960: Colloque de Cerisy-la-Salle (11–14 septembre 1975)*. Bibliothèque russe de l'Institut d'études slaves, no. 47. Paris: Institut d'études slaves, pp. 411–25.
    Outlines the novel's historical background ("Le *Docteur Jivago* est centré ... sur la révolution russe de 1917"). Elaborates on the novel's interpretation of life as a "mighty force" that brings together man and the universe, and man and God; such a bond is experienced on biological, his-

torical, and spiritual levels. Concludes that the question of humankind's very existence is for Pasternak an eternal question reminding us that life is an appeal to a free, spiritual transfiguration of the individual.

1980

1   AUCOUTURIER, MICHEL. "Pasternak témoin de l´actualité de Tolstoï." In *Tolstoï aujourd'hui. Colloque international Tolstoi tenu à Paris du 10 au 13 octobre 1978, à l´occasion du cent-cinquantième anniversaire de la naissance de Léon Tolstoï.* Bibliothèque russe de l'Institut d'études slaves, no. 57. Paris: Institut d'études slaves, pp. 277–84.

Surveys Pasternak's affinity with Tolstoy, noting that *Letters from Tula* are proof of Tolstoy's impact on Pasternak, that the concept of life's vitality was common to both of them, and that both of them displayed common traits in their views of the historical process. Also finds traits of dissimilarities, including their opposing attitude toward religion, with Tolstoy denying the supernatural (Christ's miracles) and Pasternak being inspired precisely by the supernatural.

2   BAEVSKII, V.S. "Mif v poeticheskom soznanii i lirike Pasternaka (Opyt prochteniia)" [Myth in Pasternak's poetic consciousness and lyrics (A reading experiment)]. *IAN* 39, no. 2: 116–27.

Seeks to define Pasternak's "mythological stratum." Divided into five sections: an analysis of "Rainy Weather," general views of Pasternak's myth, analyses of "Ploughing" and "The Only Days," a survey of "cosmogonic presentations," and an outline (entitled "Axis mundi") of Indo-European and non-Indo-European mythologies. Sees "Rainy Weather" as structured on folklore, myth, and rituals and as an echoing of Nekrasov's lyrics. Finds that Pasternak "orientates" his poetic system on classical antiquity. Mentions that Pasternak's infatuation with folklore is also evidenced by his notes on the Uralian folklore he wrote during his stay in the Urals. Also mentions Pasternak's interest in old Hittite legends and old Georgian poetry.

3   BERLIN, ISAIAH. "Conversations with Akhmatova and Pasternak." *NYRB* (20 November): 25–35.

Prefaces the interviews with a sketch of the Russian literary scene in the 1930s and 1940s. Gives accounts of two conversations with Pasternak, dating from 1945 and 1956, in which he records Pasternak's evaluations of other literary figures, his reflection on the literary and historical fate of Russia since the Revolution, and his concern over the perception that he was cooperating with the Soviet regime in his work. Recounts Pasternak's telephone conversation with Stalin about Mandelstam, discusses the unavailability of various leading Western and émigré authors in the Soviet Union, and mentions the importance to Pasternak of *Doctor Zhivago*'s publication in the West. Translated: 1981.2.

4 ———. "Meetings with Russian Writers in 1945 and 1956." In *Personal Impressions*, edited by Henry Hardy. Introduction by Noel Anman. London: Hogarth Press, pp. 156–210.

Recalls his meetings with Pasternak in 1945 (first at Peredelkino and then at Pasternak's appartment) and in 1956 at Peredelkino. Comments on Pasternak's appearance; his way of talking ("his use of words was the most imaginative I have ever known"); how Pasternak related his 1935 trip to London and his speech delivered at the World Writers' Congress in Paris; Pasternak's admiration of Mayakovsky, Bryusov, Rilke, Verhaeren, and Tsvetaeva, among others; his "negative" feelings toward his Jewish origins; and, recorded in detail, Pasternak's telephone conversation with Stalin about Mandelstam's arrest. Records, from the last Peredelkino visits (in 1956), Pasternak's views of *Doctor Zhivago* ("It's my last word"), Pasternak's staunchest defense of his decision to publish *Doctor Zhivago* abroad, and Berlin's own impressions of the novel ("I thought it a work of genius"). Reprinted: 1981.1.

5 BIRNBAUM, HENRIK. "On the Poetry of Prose: Land- and Cityscape 'Defamiliarized' in *Doctor Zhivago*." In *Fiction and Drama in Eastern and Southeastern Europe. Evolution and Experiment in the Postwar Period. Proceedings of the 1978 UCLA Conference*, edited by Henrik Birnbaum. UCLA Slavic Studies, vol. 1. Columbus, OH: Slavica Publishers, pp. 27–60.

Includes five major sections: (1) "Controversial Assessment and Place in Overall Oeuvre"; (2) "Semiotic (Structural-Poetic) Background"; (3) "Landscape 'Defamiliarized' in *Doctor Zhivago*"; (4) "Cityscape 'Defamiliarized' in *Doctor Zhivago*; and (5) "Man and His Ambience in *Doctor Zhivago*." Elaborately surveys criticism of *Doctor Zhivago*. Views the novel "against the broad background of the total poetic oeuvre of the writer himself," referring to Pasternak's artistic prose as a "literary phenomenon of the postwar period." Illustrates the employment of defamiliarized imagery, particularly in landscape and cityscape descriptions, seen as adding realism and sharpening reader perceptions with "displaced" graphic depictions of images from everyday life. Comments on Pasternak's use of language: "a language more saturated, within the confines of a few sentences, with rich imagery ... can hardly be conceived of." Concludes that the predicament of man—not only of the poet—on earth is the central theme.

6 GLADKOV, A.K. "Vstrechi s Pasternakom (Iz vospominanii)" [Meetings with Pasternak (From memoirs)]. In *Teatr. Vospominaniia i razmyshleniia*. Moscow: Iskusstvo, pp. 385–437.

Partial reprint of 1973.5.

7   GRIFFITHS, F.T., and S.J. RABINOWITZ. *"Doctor Zhivago* and the Tradition of National Epic." *CL* 32: 63–79.

Compares *Doctor Zhivago's* place in the "strong and unbroken" tradition of the epic form to that of other national epics, including Virgil's *Aeneid*, which shares with *Doctor Zhivago* the attribute of distilling the experience of a nation in "the myth of a single life," carrying on a dual national/religious epic tradition. Declares the importance of both biblical and pagan elements in Pasternak's frame of reference. Discusses the parallels between the careers of Virgil and Pasternak, historical affinities between Imperial Rome and Soviet Russia, the two authors' similar use of space, the adherence of Zhivago to the *Aeneid's* symbolic plane, and several ways in which the adventures of Zhivago and Aeneas follow parallel courses. Mentions similarities between Pasternak's and Virgil's relationships with their predecessors in the epic genre (Tolstoy and Homer, respectively). Concludes that Pasternak's conscious use of the epic tradition is intended to give universality to the novel's message regarding national destiny and the individual.

8   HINGLEY, RONALD. Review of *Boris Pasternak's Translations of Shakespeare*, by Anna Kay France. *Encounter* (October): 21–24.

Expresses regret over the flatness of the translations. Uses examples from the plays, especially *King Lear*, to advance the opinion that Pasternak cut and toned down Shakespeare's language more than necessary. Regrets that Pasternak did not do the translations at a less cautious, more youthful stage of his career, concluding that Pasternak's translations do not live up to his potential as a poet.

9   HOSKING, GEOFFREY. "Two Key Works: *Doctor Zhivago* and *One Day in the Life of Ivan Denisovich.*" In *Beyond Socialist Realism. Soviet Fiction Since 'Ivan Denisovich.'* London: Granada Publishing, pp. 29–49.

Credits Pasternak (and Solzhenitsyn) with the rediscovery of folk culture and the initiation of a process by which literature moved away from Marxist teleology to a more sober, honest, and immediate portrayal of life. Centers on Pasternak's conflict between personalist and Marxist concepts of history, as seen embodied in Zhivago and Antipov.

10 IAKOBSON, ANATOLII. "O stikhotvorenii Borisa Pasternaka 'Roslyi strelok, ostorozhnyi okhotnik'" [On Boris Pasternak's poem "A Burly Shooter, a Careful Hunter"]. *Kontinent*, no. 25, pp. 323–33.

Attempts to pinpoint the theme of "A Burly Shooter, a Careful Hunter." Argues that the poem centers on feeling—a "key to the poem's theme," and pursues this theme in Pasternak's other poems, notably in "Oh, Had I Known That So Happens." Concludes that the poem's theme of feeling is "ambivalent," with the last stanza indicating that a "victorious march of the *feeling* with Pasternak is inevitable in the future," and that this was "declared by the poem 'Oh, Had I Known That So Happens' three years later" (i.e., in 1931).

11   IL'IN, V.N. "Predchuvstvie vtorogo vozrozhdeniia. Pasternak" [Presentiment of second rebirth. Pasternak]. In *Arfa Davida*. San Francisco: Globus, pp. 403–15.

Maintains that *Doctor Zhivago* consists of several layers: the biography of the hero; his wanderings, which symbolize life; the Revolution; Zhivago's philosophy of life and religion; the professional life; and Zhivago's love and poetry. These layers are seen as interwoven without interfering with one another. The novel's first volume is seen as a prelude to the oncoming catastrophe and the second as "the tragedy of the human personality" ("crushed between the white and red millstones, yet nevertheless remaining alive and invulnerable"). Concludes that Pasternak understood that the novel was an "epic of the Russian rational soul."

12   KHAEV, E.S. "Problema kompozitsii liricheskogo tsikla (B. Pasternak. 'Tema s variatsiiami')" [Compositional problems in a lyrical cycle (B. Pasternak. "Theme with Variations")]. In *Priroda khudozhestvennogo tselogo i literaturnyi protsess. Mezhvuzovskii sbornik nauchnykh trudov*, edited by N.D. Tamarchenko. Kemerovo: Kemerovskii gosudarstvennyi universitet, pp. 56–68.

An attempt to define compositional and cyclic principles in "Theme with Variations." Discusses the poem's lexica, its affinity with Pushkin, "associative chains," "saturated" rhythm, rhyme uniformity, repetition sounds, predomination of stresses in a trochaic meter, syntax uniqueness, compositional "montage" ("thesis-antithesis-synthesis"), and types of variations—three "strong" and three "free."

13   KOVALEV, V.A. "Lirika Borisa Pasternaka" [Boris Pasternak's lyrics]. *RL*, no. 4, pp. 59–70.

A general commentary on Pasternak's poetry and his poetic perception that surveys Pasternak's literary career, mentioning his infatuation with Rilke, the Lermontov connection, Gorky's interpretation of "deep roots of Pasternak's artistic system," Pasternak's translations of the Georgian poets, and Pasternak's "social" attitude (in "*Second Birth* a realistic, new world perception takes shape"). Sees Pasternak as "prone to chamber themes" (like Tsvetaeva and Akhmatova), and notes that Pasternak "attributed a great significance to the sound texture."

14   MALLAC, GUY DE. "The Voice of the Street in Pasternak's *Doctor Zhivago*." In *Fiction and Drama in Eastern and Southeastern Europe. Evolution and Experiment in the Postwar Period. Proceedings of the 1978 UCLA Conference*, edited by Henrik Birnbaum. UCLA Slavic Studies, vol. 1. Columbus, OH: Slavica Publishers, pp. 103–19.

Analyzes Pasternak's concept of history in *Doctor Zhivago* as to its variance with Marxist thought and Soviet doctrine. Sees Pasternak's creation not as a chronicle, but an aesthetic complex of symbols and allusions refuting the old and new orders and pointing to a revival of freedom of the individual. Quotes the statements of Zhivago, Vedenyapin, and Sima Tuntseva to illustrate Pasternak's critique of the Soviet experiment and it's Roman-like dehumanization of society. Reprinted and revised in 1981.14.

15 MARIANI, DANISA. "L'Organizzazione dello spazio nell'opera di Pasternak." *RiS* 27–28: 299–323.

Analyzes Pasternak's conception of space and his attempt to describe the artistic and ideological world of the lyrical subject and Zhivago in *Doctor Zhivago*. Finds that the same forms of communication and contact between the external and internal world exist in both Pasternak's poetry and *Doctor Zhivago*. Also sees Pasternak as identifying himself and Zhivago with Christ and Hamlet.

16 SEYMOUR-SMITH, MARTIN. "Boris Pasternak." In *A Reader's Guide to Fifty European Novels*. London: Heinemann; Totowa, NJ: Barnes & Noble, pp. 487–97.

Retells *Doctor Zhivago*'s content, identifies its central motif as the "relationship between the personality of Zhivago ... and the twenty-five poems," and surveys the novel's criticism (including Gifford, Katkov, and Boyd). Passes judgement on Pasternak the poet (an "exceedingly erotic poet") and finds fault with the novel—"a failure to fuse fiction and poetry," with "highly obtrusive" metaphors. Sees Lara as "never alive except as a metaphor or symbol," Sima as "a puppet," and Komarovsky as a "ridiculous figure from Victorian melodrama."

17 TALL, EMILY. "Correspondence between Albert Camus and Pasternak." *CSP* 23: 274–78.

Details several external biographical links between Pasternak and Camus, as well as asserting an "inner bond" of devotion to individual integrity, spiritual freedom, and artistic independence. Includes the texts of two letters from Pasternak to Camus and one from Camus to Pasternak from the spring and summer of 1958, in which they discuss the views of several other authors.

18 TARANOVSKII, K.F. "'Zhizn' daiushchii kolos.' Zametka o Pasternake i Akhmatovoi" ["Ear-giving life." A note on Pasternak and Akhmatova]. In *Voz'mi na radost'. To Honour Jeanne van der Eng-Liedmeier*. Amsterdam: University Slavic Seminar, pp. 149–56.

A general commentary on Pasternak's poetics and a contrastive analysis of Pasternak's and Akhmatova's poems. Notes that Pasternak's grass images have "strongly impressed" Akhmatova (in "To the Memory of a Poet" she calls Pasternak "an interlocutor of forests"). Contrasts Pasternak's usage of rain (an "enormous topic") with that of

Akhmatova's and discusses other echoes of Pasternak in Akhmatova's verse (the theme of death, among others). Cites and discusses Pasternak's "My Sweetheart—of Sugary Rumor," and connects its rhymes with Lermontov's "Dream."

19 VANECHKOVA, GALINA. "'Fevral' Borisa Pasternaka i ego perevody na cheshskii iazyk" [Boris Pasternak's "February" and its Czech translations]. *ČeR* 25, no. 5: 204–9.

Relates the content of "February" (1912) and discusses its three Czech translations. Analyzes the poem's poetics and finds echoes of Bely, Blok, and Annensky in it. Argues that Annensky's "Black Spring" is reflected in "February's" image of "black spring" ["*vesnoiu chernoiu*"]. Discusses the poem's imagery.

20 VOZNESENSKII, ANDREI. "Mne chetyrnadtsat' let . . ." [I'm fourteen . . .]. *NM*, no. 9, pp. 155–74.

Recollections revealing numerous features of Pasternak the poet and the man. Records, among other details, that "until 1936 he himself lived . . . in a communal apartment, a separate family occupied the bathroom; at night going to the bathroom, one had to step over the sleeping people"; "he did not celebrate birthdays, regarded them as mourning days"; he "considered Tvardovsky a great poet"; he "never separated poetry from life"; "in his work there is generally a lot of Moscow with its streets, buildings, and roads"; "the later Pasternak worked hard on the purity of his style"; and "his teacher was Andrei Bely. . . . He especially valued [Bely's] collection *Ashes*." Describes his visits to the Pasternaks's, dinners he had there, guests attending these dinners, and Pasternak's last days and funeral.

21 ZHOLKOVSKII, A.K. "Invarianty i struktura poeticheskogo teksta: Pasternak" [Invariants and the structure of poetic text: Pasternak]. In *Poetika vyrazitel'nosti. Sbornik statei*, by A.K. Zholkovskii and Iu. K. Shcheglov. Wiener slawistischer Almanach. Sonderband, no. 2. Vienna: Wiener slawistischer Almanach, pp. 205–43.

Attempts to define poetic principles of Pasternak's verse organization. Discerns the following devices on which Pasternak's verse organization is founded: (1) development; (2) expansion; (3) repetition; (4) modification; (5) contrast; (6) matching/combination; and (7) presentation. Concludes that Pasternak uses a combination of these devices to modify themes and thus enhances the themes' expressiveness in the text. Profusely cites thirteen poems to support his thesis.

22 ———. "Tema i variatsii. Pasternak i Okudzhava: opyt sopostavitel'nogo opisaniia" [Theme and variations. Pasternak and Okudzhava: A contrastive description experiment]. In *Poetika vyrazitel'nosti. Sbornik statei*, by A.K. Zholkovskii and Iu. K. Shcheglov. Wiener slawistischer

Almanach. Sonderband, no. 2. Vienna: Wiener slavistischer Almanach, pp. 61–85.

A contrastive textual analysis of Pasternak's "Out of Superstition" and "No One Will Be at Home" and two of Okudzhava's poems—all seen as variations on the theme of Pushkin's "I Remember a Marvelous Moment." Identifies each author's typical features applied to the same theme and establishes similarities and dissimilarities between the authors' poetics. Suggests that the creation of a common method and corresponding metalanguage for each author is one of the most urgent theoretical tasks of contrastive poetics.

1981

1   BERLIN, ISAIAH. "Meetings with Russian Writers in 1945 and 1956 [Axmatova, Pasternak]." In *Selected Writings*. Vol. 4, *Personal Impressions*. New York: Viking Press, pp. 156–210.
Reprint of 1980.4.

2   ———. "Stalins Nachtasyl. Gespräche mit Boris Pasternak und Anna Achmatowa." *Trans-Atlantik*, no. 6, pp. 56–68.
Translation of 1980.3.

3   BJÖRLING, FIONA. "The Uses of the Present and Future Tenses in Pasternak's *Vozdušnye puti.*" In *The Slavic Verb. An Anthology Presented to Hans Christian Sørensen. 16th December 1981*, edited by Per Jacobsen et al. Copenhagen University, Institute of Slavonic Studies. Studier, no. 9. Copenhagen: Rosenkilde and Bagger, pp. 14–24.
Examines Pasternak's use of present and future tenses in *Aerial Ways* in light of the traditional conception of narration that emphasizes the use of the past tense. Sees the present tense as lifting "the narration from the timebound, historical dimension to the level of timelessness . . . this device gives direct expression to the fact that human beings are not in active control of their own destinies." Also examines the switch from present to future narration. Uses the principle of metonymy to explain Pasternak's digression from traditional narration, and comes "to the conclusion that the principle of metonymy contradicts the essence of narrative discourse."

4   DANOW, D.K. "Epiphany in *Doctor Zhivago.*" *MLR* 76: 889–903.
Argues that epiphanies occur in *Doctor Zhivago* through "transformations of images to achieve a transcendant effect." Sees the novel as a complex network of "clusters of related images" manipulated to instill in the reader the transrational insights afforded to Zhivago. Contends that Pasternak favors this method of "striking, brief revelations" in which "conventional logic has no place whatever" over conventional psycho-

logical analysis. Cites Zhivago's vision of Lara in the rowan tree, his horror at the sight of the wounded soldier who keeps adjusting his cap to the
detriment of his own wounds, and recurrent images of death and trains
as examples of such "striking" revelations. Comments that most elements in Pasternak's "mosaic of images" are bound up with Lara—the
focal point of Zhivago's epiphanies.

5   FILIPPOV, BORIS. "O proze Pasternaka" [On Pasternak's prose]. In
    Stat'i o literature. London: Overseas Publications Interchange, pp.
    154–68.
        Reprint of 1971.6.

6   FLEISHMAN, LAZAR. *Boris Pasternak v dvadtsatye gody* [Boris
    Pasternak in the 1920s]. Munich: Wilhelm Fink Verlag, 344 pp.
        Discusses events surrounding Pasternak's association with the
    futurists' group "Centrifuge," Pasternak's trip to Berlin, and Pasternak's
    revolt against Zamyatin's and Pilnyak's persecution during the 1928
    purge. Provides a textual analysis of *A Safe Conduct* (origin, the title, the
    genre, the Moscow chapters, the Marburg and Venice sections, and sec-
    tions dealing with Mayakovsky); *Spektorsky* (structure, themes, genre, the
    Pushkin "layer," semantics of names, and the "history" of the text);
    Beyond the Barriers (some of its poems); and Pasternak's poems to
    Tsvetaeva, Akhmatova, and Meyerhold. Draws parallels within
    Pasternak's works (*Doctor Zhivago, A Safe Conduct*, and *Spektorsky*).
    Elaborates on Pasternak's relationship with Kruchenykh, Bryusov (the
    Bryusov 50-year jubilee), and Mayakovsky (particularly with Pasternak's
    break with him); cites Pasternak's correspondence with Polonsky and
    mentions Pasternak's reaction to the Bakhtin school of literary criticism.
    Corrects data registered in the Pasternak scholarship. Bases research on
    published and unpublished material. Includes twelve chapters and an
    index.

7   GUTSCHE, GEORGE. "Sound and Significance in Pasternak's 'Leto.'"
    SEEJ 25, no. 3: 83–93.
        Attempts to determine if sound "patterns of ornamentation serve
    more than a melodic function in Pasternak's 'Summer.'" Uses criticism
    (Pomorska's and Plank's) as the starting point for the two-part study: a
    close reading of the poem and its relationship to Plato's *Symposium* and
    Pushkin's *Feast During the Plague*. Asserts that the notion of a "prototyp-
    ical feast" in light of a plague (literal or metaphorical) is central to all
    three works and that this explains the connection between sound and
    meaning in "Leto." Concludes that the sound and thematic relation
    between the words "Irpen'" and "pir" (feast) is the keystone to discover-
    ing the poem's poetic intent: "The poet has effectively incorporated the
    sounds of *Irpen'* into the phonetic and thematic structure of the poem so
    that both word and theme seem indissollubly united in sound and sense."

Claims that the ending *-en* is the poem's major recurring rhyme. Reprinted (with the beginning and end rewritten and the rest slightly modified): 1986.6.

8 JOVANOVIĆ, MILIVOJE. "Beleske o Pasternakovoj pesmi 'Noć'" [Notes on Pasternak's poem "The Night"]. *Književnost* 71, no. 3: 486–99.

Analyzes the poem "The Night," centering on its composition ("clearly divided into three segments"), semantic "spheres" (the function of the words "night" and "pilot" in the poem and in Pasternak's poetry, for example), themes, stanzaic structures, imagery, worldviews, and the "rhythmic-metric organization" (a three-foot iambic). Notes the object selection in the poem's second segment is accomplished from "above" ("reminding one of a traditional manner of 'world observation' from a 'flying carpet'"). Sees the poem's third segment as a "synthesis" in which "a few key pronouncements of Pasternak's philosophy of creativity are established." Footnotes an exhaustive listing of international criticism on the subject.

9 KOLONOSKY, WALTER. F. "Perception and Perspective: The Function of Windows in *Doctor Zhivago.*" *MFS* 27: 638–45.

Extends Zholkovsky's work on the imagery of windows (1978.41) with inclusion of optic/artistic effects of windows in *Doctor Zhivago*. Argues that windows can be translucent screens, apertures transmitting light from one dimension to another; natural thresholds at which images adjoin or change; devices for expressing parallels and correspondences that synchronize visual elements; points of access from enclosed spaces into nature; and symbolic junctures of plot and character. Singles out two specific windows—those of Misha Gordon's apartment and Pasha Antipov's room—as serving a number of such functions. Compares Pasternak to Zola and Flaubert—all seen to associate closed windows with fears and uncertainties.

10 KOVALEV, KONSTANTIN. "Za shekspirovskoi strokoi" [Behind a Shakespearean line]. *AB* 2: 100–107.

Throws light on Pasternak's life in Chistopol and his translations of Shakespeare's *Romeo and Juliet*, *Antony and Cleopatra*, and *Othello*. Bases his views on Pasternak's letters to P.I. Chagin. Includes Pasternak's six letters to Chagin and a fragment of Pasternak's article on English poetry.

11 LEVIN, IU. I. "Zametki k stikhotvoreniiu B. Pasternaka 'Vse naklonen'ia i zalogi'" [Notes on B. Pasternak's poem "All Moods and Voices"]. *RuL* 9: 163–74.

Explains concealed meanings of "All Moods and Voices," focusing on the poem's dialogic echoes with Tsvetaeva and Mandelstam. Cites the poem in full and footnotes relevant criticism.

12 LILLY, IAN K. "Moscow as City and Symbol in Pasternak's *Doctor Zhivago." SlaR* 40: 241–50.

Examines at various levels the primary importance of Moscow in Zhivago's life and the novel as a whole. Sees Moscow as exemplifying the contrast between the intellectual vital big city and the culturally and politically backward countryside shown in the novel. Contends that the historical and documentary aspects of the novel focus on Moscow as the axis around which the depicted events and periods revolve. Notes Pasternak's selection of actual names for locations associated with Moscow, as opposed to fictitious ones for other places. Gives examples of Pasternak's precise Moscow geography and explains its significance to the plot and characters (Zhivago's Moscow is a beloved "preeminent heroine" for which he leaves Tonya and Lara). Concludes that Moscow also achieves a symbolic status— an identification with Russia's destiny and historical continuity.

13 LOCHER, JAN PETER. "Ist Boris Pasternak ein Dichter der Avantgarde?" In *Colloquium Slavicum Basilense. Gedenkschrift für Hildegard Schroeder*, edited by Heinrich Riggenbach. Bern: Peter Lang, pp. 407–41.

Examines scholarship according to the definition of the avant-garde poetry movement as discussed in world literary criticism (in Alexander Flaker's *Symbolism or Modernism in Slavic Literatures,* for example), and applies the avant-garde concept to Pasternak's early poetry. Cites and thoroughly discusses Pasternak's lyrics of the early period exemplifying the characteristic features of the avant-garde movement. Strongly believes that "Boris Pasternak is, in decisive impulses of his poetics, a poet of the Avant-garde."

14 MALLAC, GUY DE. *Boris Pasternak. His Life and Art.* Norman: University of Oklahoma Press, 475 pp.

The first part, in twelve chapters, recounts a most comprehensive biography of Pasternak with events either hitherto recorded or discovered by the author in published or unpublished works by, about, or related to Pasternak. The second part, six chapters, analyzes Pasternak's views of the February and October revolutions, history, the role of the individual, Christianity, and critical-aesthetic views—as reflected in *Doctor Zhivago*, its criticism, and in the works of other authors. Contains numerous illustrations, a few newly published, two appendices, and a selective bibliography. Includes revisions of 1970.8; 1973.9–10; 1979.31; 1980.14. Includes translation (with modifications) of 1964.10; 1979.30.

15 MASING-DELIĆ, IRENE. "Zhivago as Fedorovian Soldier." *RR* 40: 300–316.

Explains Zhivago's behavior when he seizes a gun and shoots blindly at a tree on the battlefield, with recourse to Fedorov's philosophy of the "common cause." Describes Fedorov's utopian vision of men banding together to enlist in a mutual war against death itself. Sees the charred tree at which Zhivago fires as a "tree of death" laden with war-like associations. In firing at the tree, Zhivago is enlisting in Fedorov's army against the "heathen" gods of war who hypnotize men into believing in the inevitability of death and willingly enter into the "Golgotha" of war. Relates Zhivago's rescue of Seryozha, as well as the poem "Evil Days," to the great importance ascribed by Fedorov to the biblical resurrection of Lazarus.

16   MOSSMAN, ELLIOTT, and MICHEL AUCOUTURIER. "Perepiska Borisa Pasternaka" [Boris Pasternak's correspondence]. *RES* 53, no. 2: 267–91.

An attempt to classify Pasternak's correspondence and to correlate it with Pasternak's life, literary career, and works. Makes general remarks about Pasternak's penchant for the epistolary genre and suggests reasons for it. Singles out Pasternak's correspondence to: (1) his parents, brother, and sisters; (2) Olga Freidenberg: (3) E.V. Pasternak (Pasternak's first wife); (4) literary figures (including Shtikh, Loks, Bobrov, Tsvetaeva, Rilke, Petrovsky, Chikovani); and (5) Nina Tabidze. Cites excerpts from the correspondence and elaborately discusses them.

17   PILLING, JOHN. "Boris Pasternak: *Safe Conduct* (1931)." In *Autobiography and Imagination. Studies in Self-Scrutiny.* London: Routledge & Kegan Paul, pp. 50–62.

Defines *A Safe Conduct* as a "conventional self-portrait," as a "history of how Pasternak became a poet, and what the life of a poet actually means." Points out its complexity (its "oblique angle of vision"), which is a "perfect illustration" of the "estrangement" technique. Believes that Pasternak demonstrates that he "is not self-centered, but rather stands at the center of life." Examines Pasternak's views of art, the structure of *A Safe Conduct*, the use of coincidence, and Pasternak's "idiosyncratic theory of time." Concludes that in *A Safe Conduct* Pasternak had tried "to see how the lyric poet and historical circumstances are related" and that "'external integrity'" makes *A Safe Conduct* even more satisfying than a more confessional account would have been."

18   SINIAVSKI, ANDRÉ. "Une journée avec Pasternak. (Intervention au colloque de Cerisy)." In *Syntaxis: Réflection sur le sort de la Russie et de la culture russe*, edited by Maria and André Siniavski. Paris: Albin Michel, pp. 103–11.

Translation of 1979.45.

19   STABLEFORD, TOM. "Boris Leonidovich Pasternak (1890–1960)." In *The Literary Appreciation of Russian Writers.* New York: Cambridge University Press, pp. 121–26.

Primarily a structural, though also thematic, analysis of "Winter night'," with the text given in Russian. Analyzes overall structure, rhythmic structure, and metrical features stanza by stanza. Notes sparing abstract language amid concrete images. Concludes that thematically the poem is less a love poem than a meditation on the integrity of the human spirit, embodied by the recurring image of the candle.

20 SUHRCKE, PATRICIA. "The Place of 'Ja višu na pere u tvorca' in Pasternak's Work." *SEEJ* 25, no. 3: 71–82.
       Focuses on "I Hang on the Pen of the Creator" and relates it to Pasternak's views on "the relationship between poetry and the poet" and the writing process. Sees this poem as unique because in it "Pasternak speaks in the voice of the poet" about poetry. Discusses the "subordination and dependence" of the poet as an instrument of a higher power, Pasternak's reliance on reality, and the "'special vision'" of the poet who views the world in a new way, among other things. Believes that to understand Pasternak, a "'poet's poet' . . . an understanding of his view of poetry is essential."

21 TARANOVSKY, KIRIL. "On the Poetics of Boris Pasternak." *RuL* 10: 339–57.
       Confines his study of Pasternak's poetics to language, sound texture, metric structure, and Pasternak's "favorite poetic devices." Emphasizes Pasternak's preference for the language of "everyday things," his "esteem for the 'particles of reality,'" and his ability "to put together objects from completely different spheres of human life." Identifies sound texture with paronomasia—"based on repetition of consonantal clusters which tie together words giving cohesion and compactness to the text"—and underpins his views with quotations from various poems. Cites texts of "The Steppe" and "In the Hospital" for a more detailed analysis of Pasternak's poetics, focusing on lexical phenomena and metric structures. Footnotes some criticism relevant to the subject.

22 TSVETAEVA, MARINA. Review (in Russian) of Boris Pasternak's *Stikhotvoreniia v odnom tome*. *Glagol* 3: 197–240.
       Reprint of 1933.4.

1982

1 BAEVSKII, V.S. "Etnograficheskie temy v lirike Pasternaka" [Ethnographic themes in Pasternak's lyrics]. In *Tipologicheskii analiz literaturnogo proizvedeniia. Sbornik nauchnykh trudov*, edited by N.D. Tamarchenko. Kemerovo: Kemerovskii gosudarstvennyi universitet, pp. 148–54.
       A continuation of his previous essay on the role of mythology in Pasternak's lyrics (1980.2). Studies the poetics of "July" (from *When the Skies Clear*), centering on the poem's structural, mythological, and

ethnographic qualities. Sees prosopopoeia "running through the entire poem," with a number of associations personifying nature. Divides the poem into two parts—separated by the central quatrain in which the "question is formed." Underlines that the word "thunderstorm" (*groza*) was replaced by the word "hobgoblin" (*domovoi*)—a change indicating Pasternak's interest in folklore and ethnography ("the final version of 'July' has an ethnographic basis and is submitted to the image of HOB-GOBLIN"). Ties the poem to Bryusov's "Hobgoblin" and a Sologub poem cited in its entirety. Also mentions the Gnostic nature of "July."

2 BJÖRLING, FIONA. "Child Perspective: Tradition and Experiment. An analysis of 'Detstvo Ljuvers' by Boris Pasternak." In *Studies in Twentieth Century Russian Prose*, edited by Nils Åke Nilsson. Stockholm: Almqvist & Wiksell International, pp. 130–55.
    Places *The Childhood of Luvers* against presentations of the childhood theme in Russian literature. Observes that Pasternak "gives emphasis to the organic rather than to the social, ethical" and that *The Childhood of Luvers* differs from other childhood portraits "in the relationship between the narrator and the object of narration." Responds to her own query "to what principle of authenticity is the adult, surely masculine, narrator able to enter the mind of an adolescent girl?" Also discusses the story's composition ("fragmentary, erratic") and imagery (similes in particular). Elaborates on the heroine's "relationship towards the language" and her potential for creativity—with the latter linked to the equating of "the creativity of giving names" with "the creativity of giving birth."

3 FLAKER, ALEKSANDAR. "Railway Lyrics: The Slavic Forms." *CRCL* 9 (June): 172–87.
    Looks at the motifs of the railway and the train in many Slavic authors, one of whom is Pasternak. Claims that this type of poetry ("based on the motifs of rhythms of twentieth-century civilization") was extensively developed by Pasternak, who "also gave it some new qualities" (syntactic and semantic displacements). Identifies the topos of a train as a "demon-serpent" in Pasternak's "Railway Station," utilizing the window image in analyzing the poem. Discusses *My Sister, Life* as "a new unity of contradictory motifs . . . an aesthetic provocation and de-hierarchization of literary and cultural tradition."

4 FRANCE, PETER. "Boris Pasternak." In *Poets of Modern Russia*. London: Cambridge University Press, pp. 73–98.
    Textual analyses (accompainied by detailed narrations) of "Hamlet," "In Everything I Want to Reach," "A Definition of Creativity," "The Weeping Garden," "Storm, Instantaneous for Ever," "Death of a Poet," and "Pine Trees." Discusses Pasternak's three tales in verse; poetry from *Themes and Variations*, *Second Birth*, and *On Early Trains*; and the relationship between Mayakovsky and Pasternak. Traces

the "sacrificial note" and the role of a poet expressed in the poem "Hamlet" and Pasternak's other works. Concludes that "Pasternak's gift was above all to write of how the world feels to an individual—full of the life that poetry should live by." Calls *Doctor Zhivago* "a beautiful and moving book."

5 FREEBORN, RICHARD. *"Doctor Zhivago."* In *The Russian Revolutionary Novel. Turgenev to Pasternak.* Cambridge: Cambridge University Press, pp. 210–38.

Retraces the narrative of *Doctor Zhivago* with an eye toward Zhivago's spiritual development as he meets the challenge of the Revolution. Analyzes Zhivago as emerging from a "three-fold heritage" (new Christianity, practical life, and poetic vocation); going through experiences of war, revolutions, periods of creativity, and brushes with death and Providence; and arriving at a highly personal "choice" of "transferring ideals" of love and the "miracle of apotheosis."

6 GIFFORD, HENRY. "How Much Light There Is Already." *GrS* 1, no. 4: 113–24.

Reviews *The Correspondence of Boris Pasternak and Olga Freidenberg 1910–1954* (1982.11) and examines the relationships and lives of Pasternak and Freidenberg. Looks at their relationship as evidenced from their letters and their gradual change in sentiment. Claims Pasternak's "first letters are high-minded, freely flowing, with more than a hint of poetic inspiration in his side—already he views the world through intuition flowering into metaphor, already he has found his own imaginative territory on the border between the human city and nature beyond." Believes that the "true significance" of their friendship was Freidenberg's belief in "history as the realm of imperishable values" and the importance of family relationships as "the only real thing in life," both of which were "rooted in common memories of youth and loyalty to a family ideal."

7 HINGLEY, RONALD. "Two Voices Calling." In *Nightingale Fever. Russian Poets in Revolution.* London: Weidenfeld and Nicolson, pp. 236–47.

Discusses the relationship between Pasternak and Akhmatova and examines *Doctor Zhivago.* Looks at each poet's "long, complex evolution," particular instances of their interactions with the government, and shifts in literary styles. Recounts and explains the controversy surrounding both the Nobel Prize and the publication of *Doctor Zhivago,* and analyzes the work as a "philosophical, poetical, and atmospheric study that should, perhaps, never have been called a novel at all." Contrasts *Doctor Zhivago* to "run-of-the mill Socialist Realist novels." Asserts that the novel is actually a "non-novel about a non-hero" with "non-events" and "non-characters" that has "an exhilarating and life-enhancing impact."

8   IUNGGREN, ANNA. "Nekotorye sintaksicheskie osobennosti rannei poezii B. Pasternaka" [Some syntactical peculiarities of B. Pasternak's early poetry]. *ScS*, no. 28, pp. 223–34.

Examines syntactical constructions in Pasternak's three early collections—*Above the Barriers, My Sister, Life*, and *Themes and Variations*. Lists anomalies, such as ellipses, verb ellipses, disruption of anaphoric links within a text, changes in a word's syntactic role, contamination of syntactical constructions, and imbalance between main and subordinate clauses. Concludes that these digressions are syntactical and semantic—but not purely grammatical.

9   ———. "O poeticheskom genezise *Doktora Zhivago*" [On the poetic genesis of *Doctor Zhivago*]. In *Studies in Twentieth Century Russian Prose*, edited by Nils Åke Nilsson. Stockholm: Almqvist & Wiksell International, pp. 228–49.

A three-part study of *Doctor Zhivago*'s modes of character descriptions, polyphony, and coincidence devices. Applies Bakhtin's theory of the "ideal" novel to the composition of *Doctor Zhivago*, noting the novel's digression from Bakhtin. Also observes that the absence of complete portrait descriptions of the main heroes "likens them to poetry heroes," that the main heroes' speech patterns are "homogeneous, identical to the author's, they have no individual manner of speaking," and that chance encounters have a "character" of "spatial coincidences." Concludes that "prose anomalies can be explained by poetry norms," and that the reader has to opt which of the "two maxims" (prose or poetry) should be regarded as the prevailing one. If the option chosen is the poetry, then the novel should be read from the end, "as a gigantic poetic text aspiring to cope with the task of a historic novel whose connecting threads break off under the novel's weight."

10 MASING-DELIC, IRENE. "Bergsons 'Schöpferische Entwicklung' und Pasternaks *Doktor Shiwago*." In *Literatur-und Sprachentwicklung in Osteuropa im 20. Jahrhundert. Ausgewählte Beiträge zum Zweiten Weltkongress für Sowjet-und Osteuropastudien*, edited by Eberhard Reissner. Berlin: Arno Spitz, pp. 112–30.

Surveys criticism regarding Bergson's influence on *Doctor Zhivago*. Finds the influence in *Doctor Zhivago*'s structure, character descriptions, and, in particular, in Lara's relationship with Komarovsky, Antipov, and Zhivago—the latter seen as reflecting a Bergsonian concept of "élan," i.e., a development "from simple to complex forms of consciousness."

11 MOSSMAN, ELLIOTT. Introduction and explanatory prefaces to *The Correspondence of Boris Pastenrak and Olga Freidenberg, 1910–1954*. Translated by Elliott Mossman and Margaret Wettlin. New York and

London: Harcourt Brace Jovanovich, pp. 1–2, 33, 51–55, 91–94, 139–40, 173–74, 201–2, 241–43, 287–88.

Using the correspondence as a background, the introduction focuses on major events in Pasternak's and Freidenberg's lives, their literary and scholarly activity, and their relationship to each other. Explanatory prefaces heading each of nine chapters supplement the correspondence with detailed information.

12 NEKRASOVA, E.A., and M.A. BAKINA. "Sravneniia v kontekste tvorchestva B. Pasternaka" [Comparisons and similes in the context of B. Pasternak's works]. In *Iazykovye protsessy v sovremennoi russkoi poezii.* Moscow: Nauka, pp. 84–148.

A study of the role and function of Pasternak's comparisons and similes that analyzes lexical and semantic idiostyles, the cohesion of imagery and themes, semantic and contextual functions of similes and comparisons, and their structural and compositional role. Finds that two essential lines—"a principle of sensual vision and a compositional principle of purely verbal associations"—run through Pasternak's system of comparisons and similes. Numerous examples are cited to illustrate the authors' views.

13 NIVAT, GEORGES. "Le 'point du jour' pasternakien." In *Vers la fin du mythe russe. Essais sur la culture russe de Golgol à nos jours.* Lausanne: L'age d'homme, pp. 350–61.

Reprint of 1979.35.

14 PASTERNAK, EVGENII BORISOVICH. Foreword to *Boris Pasternak. Selected Poems.* Translated from the Russian by Jon Stallworthy and Peter France. New York: W.W. Norton & Co., pp. 11–14. Reprint. 1983.

Records Pasternak's views of artistic translation, his reactions to translations of his poetry, and his translation accomplishments (Goethe's *Faust*; Shakespeare's tragedies and historical plays; the lyric poetry of Byron, Shelly, Verlaine, Rilke; and others), concluding that the "volume of his translations is greater than that of his own collected works." Gives a brief account of the intellectual atmosphere ("the world of spiritual happenings") in which Pasternak grew up. Cites from unpublished materials preserved in the Pasternak family archives in Moscow.

15 PETERSON, RONALD E. "Andrej Belyj and Nikolaj Vedenjapin." *WSA* 9: 111–17.

Mentions criticism of prototypes for Vedenyapin—a character in *Doctor Zhivago*. Draws parallels between Bely and Vedenyapin, citing passages from *Doctor Zhivago* to exemplify connecting features between them. Surveys Bely's and Pasternak's encounters and Pasternak's comments on Bely and his works as recorded in Pasternak's correspondence, his two autobiographies, and Pasternak criticism. Concludes that

"Pasternak and Bely not only shared certain interests and participated in some of the same activities, they made concerted efforts to record their impressions of a stimulating and vibrant time," and that in *Doctor Zhivago* "Pasternak was able to use his recollections of Bely to help shape a character for the book that served as the capstone of his career."

16 PILLING, JOHN. "Boris Pasternak (1890–1960)." In *A Reader's Guide to Fifty Modern European Poets*. London: Heinemann; Totowa, NJ: Barnes & Noble, pp. 206–14.

Summarizes Pasternak's life and examines the *My Sister, Life* collection, in which Pasternak "blended the two traditions" (romanticism and symbolism). Discusses Pasternak's views of the poet (seen as "a universal figure of continuity") and of art and life (as reflected in *A Safe Conduct*). Comments on other poems by Pasternak—*Second Birth, On Early Trains, Earth's Expanse*, and others. Observes that Pasternak "must have known that in the furor aroused by the publication abroad of his novel . . . he would have to play a similarly sacrificial role and be publicly vilified."

17 RAYFIELD, DONALD. "Pasternak and the Georgians." *ISS*, no. 3, pp. 39–46.

A survey of Pasternak's affinity with Georgian poets (Paolo Iashvili, Titsian Tabidze, and Simon Chikovani) and a discussion of his translations from Tabidze and Vazha Pshavela. Reveals principles of "Pasternak's philosophy of translation," his penchant for discarding and reordering of original text, and the implementation of his own poetic creeds in the translations. Mentions that one of Pasternak's Tabidze translations, "Verses About the Mukrani Valley," was done by Olga Ivinskaya and that the accuracy of Pasternak's translation of Vazha Pshavela's *The Snake-Eater* was questionable ("Vazha's beeches and elms become puny planes and maples"). Cites translated texts in Russian, Georgian, and English.

18 STALLWORTHY, JON, and PETER FRANCE. Introduction to *Boris Pasternak. Selected Poems*. Translated by Jon Stallworthy and Peter France. New York: W.W. Norton & Co., pp. 15–42.

Offers an elaborate account of Pasternak's early life—his childhood, student years, parents, and associations with poetry groups, among other events—drawing heavily on Pasternak's two autobiographies. Discusses Pasternak's formation of ideas and views of art, his "feeling for history," culminating with a brief analysis of *Doctor Zhivago* and mention of *The Blind Beauty*. Elaborates on Pasternak's reworking of his poem "Marburg," singles out predominant themes in his works (the "sacrificial view of the artist's calling which is central to his latter writing," for example) and concludes that Pasternak has thought of his poems as "forming 'cycles' or 'books' and not isolated units." Draws parallels between the structure of poems in *My Sister, Life* and that of the Zhivago poems, noting that the poems of the former have chapter headings and the latter poems make up a "dynamic unity in which the movement of the seasons echoes the story of Christ." Mentions English criticism of Pasternak—Gifford's, Davie's, Livingstone's, Ehrlich's, and others.

19 TARANOVSKI, KIRIL. "Pasternakova pesma 'U bolnici'" [Pasternak's poem "In the Hospital"]. *ZS*, no. 23, pp. 15–20.

A detailed analysis of the poetics of "In the Hospital" that centers on the absence of ellipses and inversions and the presence of a more simplified imagery language. Claims the poem contains certain features of Pasternak's early poetry—the use of metonymy (both as a trope and a compositional device) and a conspicuous sound texture. Details the poem's structure (divided into three parts—an introduction, a plot development, and a conclusion), relates the content, and discusses its syntactical construction and the image of "window." Concludes that the poem conveys a real experience, Pasternak's stay at a hospital after his heart attack in 1952. Translated: 1984.19.

20 ZHOLKOVSKY, ALEXANDER. "Distributive Contact: A Syntactic Invariant in Pasternak." *WSA* 9: 119–49.

An attempt to define and analyze "distributive contacts" in Pasternak's "poetic diction." Essay breaks down into three major segments—introduction, cognate constructions, and distributive contacts. Divides the last segment into coordinative, comparative, and "quasi" distributive contacts: "'Ellipses' of the zero." Concludes: "In this paper I tried (i) to isolate and document an abstract component of the poet's diction . . . (ii) to examine it in light of the poet's other thematic and syntactic invariants," and "(iii) to envision it as a *sign*, the syntactic features that define the construction forming its *expression plane* and the effects it implements, . . . forming its *content plane*." Cites numerous examples to illustrate his thesis.

1983

1 ANTIPOV, S.N. "O nekotorykh osobennostiakh kharakterov v romane v stikhakh B. Pasternaka 'Spektorskii'" [On personae peculiarities in B. Pasternak's novel in verse *Spektorsky*]. In *Problema kharaktera v khudozhestvennoi literature. Sbornik nauchnykh trudov*, edited by A.G. Zhakov. Minsk: Minskii gosudarstvennyi pedinstitut, pp. 60–68.

A general commentary on forms of characterization in *Spektorsky*. Insists Pasternak does not focus so much on character portrayal as he does on the depiction of "atmosphere" and "historic panorama." Sees a double "aesthetic function" in Spektorsky's "ordinariness"—typological qualities of an individualized hero and a "generalized portrayal of a man's spiritual essence." Finds autobiographical features in Spektorsky ("Spektorsky is also a poet," for example). Adds that Pasternak also portrays the role of a woman in the Revolution and that *Spektorsky* displays Pasternak's attitude toward the Revolution—both his enthusiasm and bewilderment.

2 BARNES, CHRISTOPHER. "Biography, Autobiography and 'Sister Life': Some Problems in Chronicling Pasternak's Earlier Years." *ISS*, no. 4, pp. 48–58.
   Chronicles segments and aspects of Pasternak's life that lack information or accountability—the period of 1911 (when Pasternak "left his parents' home shortly after their move to an apartment on the Volkhonka"); Pasternak's "amatory interest" in Fani Zbarskaya (during his stay in the Urals with the Zbarsky family), Nadezhda Sinyakova, and Yelena Vilograd; and "evasiveness of Pasternak's autobiographical accounts" in both of his autobiographies. Elaborately records "slips of memory and factual errors" in the two autobiographies, concluding that "this cult of elusiveness goes to the foundation of Pasternak's artistic method."

3 ———. "Poeziia i muzyka. Vtoraia stikhiia Borisa Pasternaka" [Poetry and music. Boris Pasternak's second element]. *RM*, nos. 3455–56, pp. 11, 14.
   Translation of 1977.1.

4 BERLIN, MIRIAM H. "A Visit to Pasternak." *AS* 52, no. 3: 327–35.
   Describes her trip to the Soviet Union in 1957 to bring Pasternak the English translation of *Doctor Zhivago*. Quotes some of Pasternak's comments on *Doctor Zhivago*, including his letter of 13 October 1946, expressing his goals and reasons for writing the novel. Gives an account of events surrounding the English publication of *Doctor Zhivago*. Details the events of the day spent with Pasternak at his home in Peredelkino. Draws attention to the autobiographical nature and "last word" quality of *Doctor Zhivago*, and Pasternak's belief that "'it is the most important piece of work I have been able to do so far in the whole of my life.'"

5 DÖRING-SMIRNOV, JOHANNA RENATE. "'Uznat', čto budet ja, kogda. . . .' Vergleichende Anmerkungen zu den Autobiographien von B. Pasternak und I. Brodskij." *WS* 28, no. 2: 339–53.
   Draws parallels between Pasternak's *A Safe Conduct* and Brodsky's *Less than One* to explore the poetics of an "autobiography of a poet." Establishes three main features of an "autobiography of a poet": strong defiance of chronology, resistance to genuine epic thinking, and replacement of events with definitions. Surveys a genre of "artistic biographies."

6   FILONOV GOVE, ANTONINA. "The Poet's Self: Images of Soul in Four Poems of Pasternak." *SEEJ* 27, no. 2: 185–99.

Analyzes "Soul" (*Above the Barriers*), "Definition of Soul" (*My Sister, Life*), "The Voice of the Soul" (*Themes and Variations*), and "Soul" (*When the Skies Clear*) to discern each poem's "presentation of an image of the soul." Defines images of the soul emerging from each poem: "a soul-self that is imprisoned by its epoch"; a soul that is "an event or occurrance, one that is not bound to performance by a particular individual or time"; an "anti-lyrical soul"; and a soul that seeks in the face of surrounding death to preserve "what is witnessed through the poet's memory formed into verse."

7   GIBIAN, GEORGE. "*Doctor Zhivago*, Russia, and Leonid Pasternak's *Rembrandt*." In *The Russian Novel From Pushkin to Pasternak*, edited by John Garrard. New Haven and London: Yale University Press, pp. 203–24.

Asserts that *Doctor Zhivago*'s central themes, "embodying the ideas which animated Pasternak, represent a double journey backward in time—leading him to confrontations (with reversals and transmutations), first, with his father's views on the special character of Judaism (set down in a booklet on Rembrandt); and second, with traditional Russophile conceptions of the historic mission and special qualities of the Russian nation and Russian literature." Compares views expressed by Leonid Pasternak on Zionism with those seen as reflected or twisted in the novel: "Boris Pasternak overturns his father's opinions on the subject of identity [individual versus national]; second, he substitutes the New Testament for the Old Testament. In both cases, the new overcomes the old, the 'son' principle conquers the 'father' one." Examines Pasternak's conceptions of Russia and the Russian character and destiny as reflected in his attitudes toward the views of the characters in the novel. Translated: 1988.12.

8   GRINSHTEIN, A.L. "Chetyre perevoda stikhotvoreniia P. Verlena 'Effet de nuit'" [Four translations of P. Verlaine's poem "Effet de nuit"]. *FN*, no. 6, pp. 30–34.

A comparative study of four renditions (Bryusov's, Pasternak's, Levik's, and Geleskul's) of Verlaine's "Effet de nuit." Observes that Pasternak succeeded—"better than Bryusov"—in conveying the poem's concluding chain of tropes, and that Pasternak rendered the musicality "inherent in the original poem" by using alliteration, repetition of vowels, and inward rhymes. Reprimands Pasternak for using spoken language—absent in the original.

9   HAYWARD, MAX. "Life into Art: Pasternak and Ivinskaya." In *Writers in Russia: 1917–1978*, edited and with an introduction by Patricia Blake. Preface by Leonard Shapiro. London: Harvill Press, pp. 216–41.

Reprint of 1978.19.

10 ———. "Meetings with Pasternak." In *Writers in Russia: 1917–1978*, edited and with an introduction by Patricia Blake. Preface by Leonard Shapiro. London: Harvill Press, pp. 188–215.
Reprint of 1977.11.

11 HINGLEY, RONALD. *Pasternak. A Biography*. London: Weidenfeld and Nicolson, 304 pp. Reprint. 1985.
Divides Pasternak's life into three periods: part one (1890–1923), part two (1923–1946), and part three (1946–1960). Chronicles a detailed account of events and aspects: Pasternak's family background, formative years, attitude toward the Soviet system (and Stalin), stance toward his literary coevals (Mayakovsky, Tsvetayeva, Akhmatova, and Mandelstam), women in his life (the two marriages, love for Vysotskaya, affair with Ivinskaya), years of terror, the war years, the Zhdanovshchina period, the events surrounding the publication of *Doctor Zhivago*, and the Nobel Prize affair, among others. Draws heavily upon memoir literature (Gladkov's, Ivinskaya's, Chukovskaya's, Nadezhda Mandelstam's, Ehrenburg's), literary criticism, media, interviews (personal and others), and, above all, Pasternak's works, many of which (translations included) are discussed or thoroughly examined.

12 JENSEN, EJNER J. "*Hamlet* in Twentieth-Century Poetry." In *Reconciliations: Studies in Honor of Richard Harter Fogle*, edited by Mary Lynn Johnson and Seraphia D. Leyda. Salzburg Studies in English Literature. Salzburg: Institut für Anglistik und Amerikanistik, pp. 17–40.
A summary of observations on Pasternak's poem "Hamlet"—"power," "immediacy," "urgency," and "a brilliant, complex analogy." Incorporates Zhivago's notes from chapter 15 in *Doctor Zhivago* and Pasternak's own comments on the "To Be or Not to Be" soliloquy into the analysis. Makes other comparisons to T.S. Eliot's *Prufrock*. Sees Pasternak's "Hamlet" as the "quest for identity, for a means of asserting one's being, and its vehicles are the poet, Christ, Hamlet, the actor."

13 KAVERIN, V. Review of Pasternak's *Vozdushnye puti. Proza raznykh let. NM*, no. 6, pp. 260–64.
Interprets Pasternak's prose as "complex, difficult to read, packed with thoughts," and lacking plots ("it's impossible to render *A Safe Conduct, The Line of Apelles* in one's own words"). Sees Pasternak's heroes as "genuine, not fictionalized," and often "only named as if intentionally not delineated." Characterizes the portrait of Mayakovsky in the autobiographies as "unriddled." Praises Pasternak's correspondence—"a letter form is, perhaps, for him the most easy-going and active form." Recalls his walks and encounters with Pasternak in Peredelkino and at Vsevolod Ivanov's.

14 LEKIC, MARIA. "The Genesis of the Novel *Doctor Zhivago*: Four Modes of Literary Borrowing." Ph.D. diss., University of Pennsylvania, 218 pp.

Examines Pasternak's incorporation of four pieces into *Doctor Zhivago*: (1) a fragment from a 1936 prose piece (adapted in part 12 of the novel); (2) a passage from the play *Here and There* (adapted in the novel's epilogue); (3) Pasternak's unpublished notes on Dostoevsky's *Diary of a Writer*; and (4) Pasternak's notes on the folklore of the Urals—the latter two pieces thought to be "scattered throughout the novel." Elaborates on Pasternak's poetics of "adaptive assimilation," focusing on "stylistic development and language of the four sources."

15 LILLY, IAN. Review of *Boris Pasternak. Perepiska s Ol'goj Frejdenberg*, edited by Elliott Mossman. *WSA* 12: 387–97.

Gives chronological and circumstantial details of the Pasternak-Freidenberg relationship. Comments elaborately on their correspondence, classifying the material by period. Thoroughly reviews themes in Freidenberg's "Notes." Centers on several aspects of the relationship—the mutual encouragement Pasternak and Freidenberg offered each other in their careers, the development of *Doctor Zhivago* (especially the second volume), Pasternak's translating activities, and Freidenberg's own efforts to gain credibility as a significant scholar. Concludes that the collection is rich in content and is of long-term importance to the study of both writers.

16 LIUBIMOV, NIKOLAI. "Zemnoi prostor" [Earth's expanse]. In *Nesgoraemye slova*. Moscow: Khudozhestvennaia literatura, pp. 291–303.

A general commentary on Pasternak's translation poetics that underlines Pasternak's employment of all "creative means" in his translations (his language "is not less multi-layered than the language of his poetry"). Ranks Pasternak with the most prominent nineteenth-century Russian translators, noting Pasternak's "temperament of unique force" and his ability to masterfully convey the sound texture of the original.

17 LIVINGSTONE, ANGELA. "Donald Davie and Boris Pasternak." In *Donald Davie and the Responsibilities of Literature*, edited by George Dekker. Manchester, England: Carcanet New Press, pp. 8–30.

Compares many aspects of Donald Davie's poetry (including metaphysics, imagery, and word choice) to the poetry of Pasternak. Sees some similarities reflected in the purpose of the poetry, their poetic personae, use of nature and its imagery, outlooks on Russia and history, and presentations of reality and life, among other traits.

18 ———. "Some Affinities in the Prose of the Poets Rilke and Pasternak." *FMLS* 19: 274–84.

Enumerates differences and similarities between Pasternak's and Rilke's worldviews and literary styles as reflected in *A Safe Conduct* and

Pasternak's other early prose (1911–1913) and Rilke's *Aus den Aufzeichnungen des Malte Laurids Brigge*. Details Pasternak's penchant for evocation of "the most positive and affirmative in life," his happiness "with the human condition," and "Pasternak's conception of man in the world as 'movement.'" Identifies "elements of Rilke" (metaphors and themes in particular) in Pasternak's *A Safe Conduct* (its beginning and ending and the image of Venice) and in the prose of 1911–1913 ("it is here that a very Rilkean respect for *things*, that is material objects . . . is first found"). Cites criticism relevent to the topic. Developed the first three sections from her previous publication (1979.27).

19 MARCHENKO, ALLA. "'. . . Vse chishche, vospriimchivei, vernei.' Poeticheskoe zrenie Borisa Pasternaka" ["Clearer and clearer, more receptive, more accurate." Boris Pasternak's poetic vision]. *LU*, no. 1, pp. 148–57.
      Draws parallels between poems originally published in *A Twin in the Clouds* (1914) and *Above the Barriers* (1917) and their later revised versions. Defines a "general direction of new avenues" and analyzes Pasternak's unique labor on lexica in the modified texts. Concludes that the modifications led Pasternak to "structural simplifications" and that his early poetry displays more simplicity than his "mature" verses.

20 MLIKOTIN, ANTHONY M. "The Concepts of Inwardness in Kierkegaard and Pasternak. An Agonizing Dialogue on the Horizon of Our Age." In *As Literature Speaks. Voices of Intellect and Conscience in Modern Literature*. University of Southern California Series in Slavic Humanities. Los Angeles: University of Southern California Press, pp. 103–12.
      Outlines similarities in worldviews of "inwardness" of Pasternak and Kierkegaard and notes that they found refuge in turning inward "to create for themselves a more acceptable world." Dwells on three "stations" through which the two passed: (1) agonizing over the reality of life, lamenting the "lack of individuality among their contemporaries"; (2) excessiveness of inwardness (as in *Zhivago*) that led to "spiritual stultification or the negative phenomenon of self-centeredness, pure egoism"; and (3) the experience of the "salutary feeling of homecoming" or returning from inwardness to "unity with the whole." Also observes that both died "*persona non grata* to the authorities," that "it is doubtful whether . . . both Kierkegaard and Pasternak had ever left their 'inward' world," and that "they irrevocably asserted that man's return to normal existence is assured to him only through Christ."

21 ———. "Metaphysics and Poetry in *Doctor Zhivago*. A New Source of Inspiration and Interpretation." In *As Literature Speaks. Voice of Intellect and Conscience in Modern Literature*. University of Southern California

Series in Slavic Humanities. Los Angeles: University of Southern California Press, pp. 113–21.

Offers random criticism: (1) compares Pasternak (as a poet-thinker) to Nietzsche (his Zarathustra, who, like Zhivago, is seen as "unable to be happy among men"), Rilke, and Eliot and *Doctor Zhivago* to *Divine Comedy* (in both works "verse was essential to appreciation" of the philosophical meaning); (2) observes that in *Doctor Zhivago* Pasternak interweaved philosophy and poetry to the extent that "the disassociation of poetry from philosophy would destroy both the thought and art of Pasternak"; and (3) finds that "the very level of appreciation of *Doctor Zhivago* depends on our understanding and even on our final acceptance of Pasternak's thought." Concludes that *Doctor Zhivago* is "a result of a poetical as well as metaphysical inspiration." Reprinted: 1988.33.

22 NEKRASOVA, E.A. "Slovesno-assotsiativnye riady v stikhotvornom tekste. (K probleme slovesno-obraznoi sinonimii)" [Semantic and associative series in a poetic text. (A question of semantic and imagery synonymity)]. *IAN* 42, no. 5, pp. 451–63.

Analyzes the semantic structure (lexical and paradigmatic connectives) of "The Dawn Will Blaze a Candle" and "The Milky Way." Distinguishes four modes Pasternak used to organize semantic connectives in these poems: semantic units comprising synonyms of various degrees, lexical and semantic paradigms in imagery synonyms, lexical units combined by periphrastic means, and thematic connectives for broader lexical units.

23 OZEROV, LEV. "Ot metafory k epitetu" [From metaphor to epithet]. In *Neobkhodimost' prekrasnogo. Kniga statei*. Moscow: Sovetskii pisatel', pp. 267–82.

A general commentary on the evolution of Pasternak's poetics. Cites reasons for difficulties in comprehending Pasternak's early poetry: an unusually poetic lexicon, unusual syntax that disrupts accepted norms, complex and unusual associative series of images, and an indivisibility of associations. Strongly argues that toward the end of the 1920s, Pasternak completely detached himself from symbolism and began to strive for simplicity and naturalness in his poetry. Concludes that "it would be risky to ascertain that extended metaphor prevailed in the early Pasternak and that epithet prevails in the mature, later Pasternak." Cites examples to support his arguments.

24 PARAMONOV, BORIS. "Chastnaia zhizn' Borisa Pasternaka (Zametki o romane 'Doktor Zhivago')" [Boris Pasternak's personal life (Notes on *Doctor Zhivago*)]. *Kontinent* 35: 315–45.

Registers Pasternak's propensity for descriptions of everyday life scenes, a tendency seen as a "call for middle-class conventionality." Comments on some of Pasternak's views of the *byt* (way of life) descriptions recorded in Ivinskaya's and Gladkov's memoirs (1972.9 and

1973.5). Analyzes the *byt* fragments from Pasternak's early prose (*Aunt Olya*, in particular) in which an "image of the harmonious *byt* is created." Concludes that *A Haughty Beggar* and *A District in the Rear* "come right up to" *Doctor Zhivago*, and that fragments from the early works "are very powerful prose . . . more powerful than the basic text of *Doctor Zhivago*." Takes issue with *Doctor Zhivago* criticism published in the West that interpreted *Doctor Zhivago* as a Dostoevskian novel. Insists that the main heroes of the novel disrupt "abruptly" the novel's "stylistic entity." Also records Pasternak's views of the Revolution.

25 PASTERNAK, ALEKSANDR LEONIDOVICH. *Vospominaniia* [Memoirs]. Munich: Wilhelm Fink Verlag, 298 pp.
    Reminiscences of Pasternak's brother, Alexander. Sheds some light on Pasternak, especially on his family background, but not limited to material that is relevant to Pasternak. Translated: 1984.17.

26 PILLING, JOHN. "A Traveller Between Two Stations: Boris Pasternak." *PNR* 10, no. 34: 25–27.
    Traces Pasternak's dual creative approach through various stages of his career from the perspective of his assertion in "Symbolism and Immortality" that the artist conveys his experience of the "joy of living" in his work in such a way as to make his experience immortal. This concept of vitalism stems from the "objectively inspired and subjectively experienced" aesthetic of Pasternak's earlier poetry and correspondence through his self-motivated change of direction in the mid-1920s and the reduced "I" of *A Safe Conduct*. Discusses Pasternak's paradoxical development from a "modest boldness" to "bold modesty," which culminates in *Doctor Zhivago*.

27 SCHULTZ, JEAN MARIE. "Pasternak's 'Zerkalo'" [Pasternak's "Mirror"]. *RuL* 13, no. 1: 81–100.
    Analyzes the semantic meanings and imagery of each stanza of "Mirror" while taking into account two versions of the poem—the earlier published in 1920 (entitled "I Myself") and the second included in *My Sister, Life*. Points out that the existence of two texts makes one aware of "the doubled readings that Pasternak thereby incorporated." Argues that multitextuality of the poem is Pasternak's aim, that the poem offers a conflict between both illusion and reality, and between the lyrical self and exterior perception, and that the main metaphor of the poem is "the comparison of the self to a mirror, exemplified in the two titles of the text." Concludes that "there is essentially no end to the interpretive possibilities. There is no end to the definitions of the self."

28 SEEMANN, KLAUS DIETER. "Analyseprobleme der avangardistischen Dichtung. Boris Pasternaks 'Vse sneg da sneg. . . .'" *WS* 28: 141–54.
    An analysis of "All Is Snow" that emphasizes the question of a hermetic character in Russian avant-garde poetry. Concludes that "dark-

ness, hermetic features, and montage" are typical traits of Pasternak's poetry before the 1930s—deemed to characterize Pasternak as an avant-garde poet.

29 SMIRNOVA, I.P. "Dostoevskii i poeziia Pasternaka ('Marburg')" [Dostoevsky and Pasternak's poetry ("Marburg")]. In *Dostoevskij und die Literatur*, edited by Hans Rothe. Schriften des Komitees der Bundesrepublik Deutschland zur Förderung der Slawischen Studien, no. 7. Cologne and Vienna: Böhlau Verlag, pp. 275–96.

An intertextual analysis of Dostoevskian echoes in Pasternak's "Marburg." Discusses themes and motifs from *Crime and Punishment, The Idiot, The Brothers Karamazov,* and *The Devils* that are present in "Marburg." Concludes that Dostoevsky's theme of overcoming one's desire to break off a bond with life and finding the way toward one's rebirth lies in the "semantic basis" of "Marburg."

30 TOIT, PIETER DU. "Kierkegaard and Pasternak. A Literary-Philosophical Essay." *SAJP* 2, no. 4: 187–95.

Surmises that Rilke (directly or indirectly) introduced Pasternak to Kierkegaard and attempts to identify affinities between Pasternak and Kierkegaard. Focuses on their concepts of the poet, love, the individual, subjectivity, religion, and on their interest in Shakespeare. Argues that Pasternak "was always the *philosophical* poet, the thinker preoccupied with *existential* problems," and that the individual ("the self is always central") and human love ("one of the basic themes of Pasternak's work") occupy the central place in Pasternak's work. Corroborates his viewpoints by illustrating passages from Pasternak's works and references to Pasternak scholarship.

31 WARD, MARYANNE C. "Eliot and Pasternak: Restoring the Waste Land of Lost Culture and Tradition." *PCL* 9: 3–11.

Compares *Doctor Zhivago* to T.S. Eliot's *The Waste Land*. Claims that both works present a quest for the regeneration of the wasteland, and that "Pasternak intends us to believe that art, not decisive action, is the key to the regeneration." Applies Joseph Campbell's framework of myth to *Doctor Zhivago* to determine the "exact nature of Zhivago's quest." Concludes that *Doctor Zhivago* is "testimony" to Pasternak's faith "to make meaningful once again the traditions of the past by reinterpreting them from age to age thus insuring the regeneration of the waste land."

32 ZHOLKOVSKII, A.K. "Poeziia i grammatika pasternakovskogo 'Vetra'" [Poetry and grammar of Pasternak's "Wind"]. *RuL* 14: 241–86.

An analysis of the poem "Wind" (from *Doctor Zhivago*)—centering on its syntactic and compositional structure, its "poetry of grammar," rhythm, rhymes, "phonetic echoes" (dubbed "weaving of sounds"), affinity with the novel and its other poems, and its place within the poetics of the later Pasternak. Finds, among other observations, that the poem is structured as "a single elliptical period broken up by pauses," that its "syntactic and stanzaic structure is simultaneously complicated and simplified by the mention of the cradle-song," that "exposition is conducted in a languid, monotonous, and 'simple' tone," that "tropes are unimposing," and that "effects are muffled." Also discusses motifs of "wind" and "tree" in Pasternak's other works.

1984

1   BAEVSKII, V.S. "Stikhoslozhenie B. Pasternaka" [B. Pasternak's versification]. *PSL*, pp. 137–51.

Breaks down Pasternak's versification—its metric system, rhythmics, syntactic pauses, rhymes, stanzaic closures, and periodization. Concludes that "metrical variations" are moderate, with a four-foot iamb prevailing ("a sign of bondage with the Pushkin tradition"); that Pasternak omits stresses in ternary meters; that the "movement of verse syntax" corresponds to "the evolution of sound repetitions"; that approximate rhymes abound (33 percent), with inexact rhymes employed less frequently (12.5 percent); and that the average length of Pasternak's verse is 30.2 lines. Divides Pasternak's work into three major periods: (1) 1911–1913 (the first two collections, overcoming of symbolism, and first Rilke translations); (2) 1914–1930 (divided into two "phases": 1914–1922 and 1923–1930); and (3) 1931–1959 (also divided into two "phases": 1931–1945 and 1946–1959). Draws parallels between Pasternak's versification, general Russian versification, and that of some of Pasternak's contemporaries.

2   BARNES, CHRISTOPHER. "Some Background Notes on Pasternak's Early Translations, and Two Notes by Pasternak on Hans Sachs and Ben Jonson." In *Aspects of Russia 1850–1970. Poetry, Prose, and Public Opinion. Essays Presented in Memory of Dr. N.E. Andreyev*, edited by William Harrison and Avril Pyman. Letchworth, Herts, England: Avebury Publishing Co., pp. 201–13.

Offers a detailed history of Pasternak's early (until 1926) translating activity, including lost or unpublished manuscripts. Includes Russian texts of two unpublished introductory notes Pasternak wrote in 1926 to his translations of poems by Hans Sachs and Ben Jonson.

3   BIRNBAUM, HENRIK. "Gedichtroman und Romangedicht im russischen Postsymbolismus. Zu einigen tiefgründigen Übereinstimmungen und oberflächlichen Unterschieden zwischen *Doktor Schiwago* und dem *Poem ohne Helden*." In *Text. Symbol. Weltmodell. Johannes Holthusen zum 60. Geburtstag*, edited by Johanna Renate Döring-Smirnov, Peter

Rehder, and Wolf Schmid. Sagners slavistische Sammlung, no. 6. Munich: Verlag Otto Sagner, pp. 19–36.

An attempt to define the genre of *Doctor Zhivago*—with a comparison to Akhmatova's *A Poem Without a Hero*. Argues that *Doctor Zhivago* is a novel that is neither in the traditional nor modern, avant-garde genres. Opts for the label of "Romangedicht," as contrasted to Akhmatova's *A Poem Without a Hero*, deemed a "Gedichtroman." Admits that none of the suggested terms completely corresponds to the genre of *Doctor Zhivago*.

4 BRISTOL, EVELYN. "Pasternak: In Search of Literary Simplicity." In *Russian Literature and American Critics. In Honor of Deming B. Brown*, edited by Kenneth N. Brostrom. Papers in Slavic Philology, no. 4. Ann Arbor: University of Michigan Press, pp. 77–84.

Asserts that Pasternak's work from early to late shows a concern for simplicity. Chronologically examines the different "definitions" of simplicity and "power." Comments on Pasternak's relation to the futurists, "his recourse to imagery, and specifically to everyday details, his admiration of naturalness, as well as his understanding of images as symbols of feeling." Characterizes the early poems as having "passion and a sense of entering history," and the major theme of the later poems as "happiness and a gratitude for life."

5 DÖRING-SMIRNOV, JOHANNA RENATE. "Ein karnevaleskes Spiel mit fremden Texten. Zur Interpretation von B. Pasternaks Poem 'Vakchanalija.'" In *Text. Symbol. Weltmodell: Johannes Holthusen zum 60. Geburtstag*, edited by Johanna Renate Döring-Smirnov, Peter Rehder, and Wolf Schmid. Sagners slavistische Sammlung, no. 6. Munich: Verlag Otto Sagner, pp. 59–80.

A profound analysis of the "semantic structure" of Pasternak's poem "Bacchanalia," defined as "determined by a paradigmatic principle." Points out the poem's three segments and sees the first as reflecting a Moscow church service, the second as a description of a theater performance ("a premier of Schiller's *Maria Stuart* in Pasternak's rendition"), and the third segment as a narrative of a "private party." Also observes that the theme in the first two parts is portrayed as "solemn," switching to "trivial" in the third. Sees segment transitions signaled by "carnivalesque motifs," and concludes that Pasternak not only transforms a sense of his borrowed text or switches places of these texts, but that he also "substitutes a poet (Mayakovsky) with another poet (himself)." Cites examples of "echoes" from other literary works—Blok's, Bely's, Pushkin's, Grigoryev's, and Swinburne's.

6 EPP, GEORGE K. "Boris Pasternak." In *Rilke und Rußland*. Frankfurt am Main, Bern, New York: Peter Lang, pp. 85–94.

Recounts Pasternak's views of Rilke as recorded in *A Safe Conduct* and in Pasternak's correspondence. Suggests that Pasternak might have been drawn to Rilke because of Rilke's involvement with religious issues even though their views were opposite ("Rilke seeks God" while Pasternak's God is already there—"creates everything, including art and artist.") Compares Rilke's poem "Frühling" with Pasternak's "Mirror" (stressing their "Geistesverwandtschaft") and Rilke's *Aufzeichnungen des Malte Laurids Brigge* with *The Childhood of Luvers*, which he sees as an autobiographical tale that penetrates "like 'Malte' into the depths of a human soul." Contends that Rilke's influence on Pasternak was more in form than content and that Pasternak should not be regarded as an epigone of Rilke. Cites Pasternak's and Rilke's previously published correspondence.

7   FLAKER, ALEKSANDAR. "Pomaknuti svijet Pasternakov" [Pasternak's displaced world]. In *Ruska avangarda*. Zagreb: Sveučilišna naklada Liber/Globus, pp. 233–42.

A thematical and structural analysis of "Inspiration." Discusses the poem's publication history, its place within Pasternak's poetry, and the correlation between its content and title ("the feeling is named succinctly and clearly—as inspiration—and is singled out in the title"). Details the poem's images of the Revolution and discusses Pasternak's views of them. Elaborates on the role of a poet presented in the poem, a "lyrical subject" who "does not only interpret the events but creates" and "moves them." ("Because everything in this poem has been displaced, everything moves.") Also discusses "syntactic displacements" originating from "spoken speech." Compares Pasternak's "lyric subject to that of Mayakovsky's, and concludes that "Pasternak's poet [in the poem] does not portray the world from inside—his views are from inside."

8   FLEISHMAN, LAZAR. *Boris Pasternak v tridtsatye gody* [Boris Pasternak in the 1930s]. Jerusalem: Magnes Press, 450 pp.

A detailed study of the period 1930–1937. Argues that the 1930s should not be interpreted as a period of stagnation and "art of silence," as generally has been done by Pasternak criticism, but as a period of two opposite "twins": Pasternak's rapprochement with the Soviet system (1933–1935) and his abrupt rupture with it (1936–1937) when he became "one of the major objects of the struggle by various groups inside Soviet literature." Adds much information to primary details related to or surrounding Pasternak's life of the period, such as his participation in the two writers' congresses (Moscow and Paris), a letter to Stalin on the posthumous canonization of Mayakovsky, the telephone call from Stalin (arrest of Mandelstam), Pasternak's refusal to sign a joint letter from Soviet writers endorsing the death sentence of Tukhachevsky and others, Pasternak's "rebellion," and the movement to officially accept Pasternak as the foremost poet of the country. Discusses Pasternak's works, notably his *Second Birth* collection, his relationship to his literary peers (Russian and foreign), and his survival during the Yezhovshchina purges. Corrects errors discovered in Pasternak scholarship. Bases research on published (includ-

ing books, monographs, newspapers, and periodicals—Russian and foreign)
and unpublished (from private and public archives) material, numerous
interviews, and correspondence. Includes eleven chapters and an index.

9 ———. "Sredi filosofov (Iz kommentariev k *Okhrannoi gramote*
Pasternaka)" [Among philosophers (From commentaries on Pasternak's
A Safe Conduct)]. In *Semiosis. Semiotics and the History of Culture. In
Honorem Georgii Lotman.* Michigan Slavic Contributions, no. 10. Ann
Arbor: University of Michigan Press, pp. 70–76.

Explicates a passage in the "Marburg" section of *A Safe Conduct*
that describes the "visitors" of a café terrace Pasternak and other students of philosophy at the Marburg University frequented. Identifies one
of these "visitors," a "Spanish lawyer," as Fernando de los Rios, and supplements his hypothesis with a brief outline of Rios's life and a commentary on him.

10 FOMENKO, I.V. "Ob analize liricheskogo tsikla (na primere stikhov B.
Pasternaka 'Peterburg'")" [On an analysis of a lyric cycle (on the example
of B. Pasternak's poem "Petersburg")]. In *Printsipy analiza literaturnogo
proizvedeniia*, edited by P.A. Nikolaev and A. Ia. Esalnek. Moscow:
Moskovskii universitet, pp. 171–78.

Advances basic criteria for a poetic cycle—correlation between a
poem's title and content; themes; rhythmic, spatial, and temporal organization; and leitmotifs, among others—and applies these criteria to
Pasternak's poem "Petersburg." Interprets the poem's title as a symbol, a
variation on a traditional theme of Russian literature. Concludes that the
poem's rhythmic, spatial, and temporal organization attests to the
poem's completeness and cohesiveness, displaying a "sufficiently strong
system." Discusses the poem's content in detail.

11 IUNGGREN, ANNA. *"Juvenilia" B. Pasternaka: 6 fragmentov o
Relikvimini* [Pasternak's "Juvenilia": Six fragments about Relikvimini].
Stockholm: Almqvist & Wiksell International, 192 pp.

Based on Pasternak's earliest prose works, five of which are published
in this work for the first time. Describes the six fragments "not only in their
own right as relatively self-contained entities written in markedly individual
style, but also with respect to their potential as the embryo of the later works."
Divided into three major sections: chapter 1 establishes links with later works
(up to *Doctor Zhivago*); chapter 2 discusses structure and imagery of
Relinquimini; and chapter 3 relates the inner history of the texts.

12 KREPS, MIKHAIL. "'Doktor Zhivago.' Khristianstvo i revoliutsiia"
[*Doctor Zhivago*. Christianity and the Revolution]. In *Pasternak i
Bulgakov kak romanisty.* Ann Arbor, MI: Hermitage, pp. 4–65.

A textual interpretation of *Doctor Zhivago*. Sees the novel's originality in its structure, dictated by the hero's interaction with other characters,

with time conveyed not by historical events but by "profound feelings of the characters and events of local significance." Defines the philosophical aspect of the novel as a conflict between Christian morality and the Revolution and sees the disillusionment with the Revolution as a result of personality losses. Advances the idea of Zhivago's affinity with Christ while examining Zhivago's Christ-like actions and behavior seen to be demonstrated both in Zhivago's views and in his poetry. Analyzes the novel's poetry, faulting the poetry's criticism (the criticism's inability to correctly interpret the poems' symbolism), and sees the essence of the poems as "a road between the individual and the universal understandable to all and applicable to each." Provides a thorough analysis of "Fairy Tale," deemed to embody the novel's main theme in its most symbolic manner.

13 LIVINGSTONE, A.M. "Lou Andreas-Salomé and Boris Pasternak." *BRG*, nos. 11–12, pp. 91–99.

Explores the artistic and philosophical affinity between Pasternak and Andreas-Salomé. Makes comparisons between Rilke and Pasternak, and Rilke and Andreas-Salomé to show the similarities between Pasternak and Andreas-Salomé. Believes the significant affinity between them exists "in the unusually positive and resilient relation between self and world, in both of them; in their deep instinctual optimism." Asserts that another similarity between them is "the idea each of these writers held that there is no need to put oneself through rigorous and strenuous efforts to create art, to work, to construct the 'second universe.'" Concludes they "were both bound to Rilke with an intense love, yet both differed from him fundamentally, in ways that make them strangely akin to each other."

14 LOTMAN, IURII M. "Dorogoi drug!" [Dear friend!] *WSA* 14: 13–16.

A thematic, structural, and contextual analysis of "The Thrushes" that describes the poem's semantic structure as centered upon two "spatial models," the first created by a "collision of the initial stanza with the second and third," and the second introduced through the "image of a bird's 'colony.'" Identifies the colony as Peredelkino, "in which Pasternak had lived since 1936." Also sees the poem structured by a contrastive correlation of autobiographical details (a shift of visual impressions and the poet's thoughts during a real movement from the railroad station to Peredelkino) and Goethe's famous lines: "'Ich singe, wie der Vogel singt,/Der in den Zweigen wohnet:/Das Lied, das aus der Kehle dringt,/Ist Lohn, der reichlich lohnet.'" Concludes that the "abstract image of a Goetheian bird has been replaced by Pasternak's happy and free Thrush."

15 MASING-DELIC, IRENE. "Živago's 'Christmas Star' as Homage to Blok." In *Aleksandr Blok Centennial Conference*, edited by Walter N. Vickery. Columbus, OH: Slavica Publishers, pp. 207–23.

Explains Zhivago's emphatic yet "enigmatic" conception of Blok as a "Christmas poet" for whom "Christmas Star" was written as an artistic homage. Links Zhivago's conception of Christmas as an urban "culture holiday" with Blok's position as a prophet of "the city of God." Claims that thematic, allusive, and phonetic links between "Nativity Star" and *The Twelve* bespeak a shared commonality of goals—if not means. Argues that allusions to *The Twelve* in *Doctor Zhivago* show Pasternak to share Blok's innermost aspirations and fears while rejecting his insistence on "apocalyptic showdowns" and mass solutions. Summarizes Pasternak's view of Blok as that of an adult to an idealistic, impatient, beloved child representing a stage Pasternak/Zhivago passed through in their more spiritual growth.

16 PAPERNYI, Z.S. "Boris Pasternak i drugie: dom i mir" [Boris Pasternak and others: home and world]. *ZS*, no. 27, pp. 81–106.
    Examines the theme of home-world correlation in Pasternak (and in other poets), and strongly argues that Pasternak easily ties together "home and world, a way of life and existence." Maintains that Pasternak both rejected and embraced the Revolution, and endeavored to establish a rapprochement with people and his native country. Mentions nature, man, art, and love ("personifying" the bond between home and world) as Pasternak's prevalent themes. Cites Pasternak's poetry to demonstrate his arguments.

17 PASTERNAK, ALEKSANDR LEONIDOVICH. *A Vanished Present: The Memoirs of Aleksandr Pasternak*. Edited and translated by Ann Pasternak Slater. Oxford: Oxford University Press, 238 pp.
    Translation of 1983.25.

18 RASHKOVSKAIA, M.A., and E.B. RASHKOVSKII. "Sonet Suinberna v perevode Borisa Pasternaka" [Swinburne's sonnet in Boris Pasternak's translation]. *IAN* 43, no. 6: 544–50.
    Records the publication history of Pasternak's translation of Swinburne's sonnet "John Ford" and comments on it: "Pasternak changed a great deal in the sonnet's formal structure ... [and] deciphered the imagery structure of Swinburne's sonnet." Underpins the comments with unpublished correspondence and cites the English original along with Pasternak's translation.

19 TARANOVSKI, K.F. "Stikhotvorenie Pasternaka 'V bol'nitse'" [Pasternak's poem "In the Hospital"]. In *Semiosis. Semiotics and the History of Culture. In Honorem Georgii Lotman*. Michigan Slavic Contributions, no. 10. Ann Arbor: University of Michigan Press, pp. 221–27.
    Translation of 1982.19.

20 TOPORSKAIA, BARBARA. "Zhivago—svidetel' epokhi" [Zhivago—a witness to an epoch]. *Kontinent* 61: 363–80.
    Argues that *Doctor Zhivago* "often stumbles and often downright limps," that the novel's construction is "based on the principle of chance

coincidences," and that due to this construction the novel's actions appears somewhat artificial. Contends that the reference to Zhivago's mother as a woman possessing a "nobleman's feeling of equality among all that live" is characteristic of Pasternak the prosaist, deemed to be convinced of the uniqueness of each human personality. Concludes that Zhivago is the "antithesis of the positive hero of the socialist-realist novel" (because he leaves the hospital during a typhoid epidemic in order to save his loved ones, his work, and his personal happiness) and that the novel is a great literary work.

21 WESTSTEIJN, WILLEM G. "Author and Implied Author. Some Notes on the Author in the Text." In *Signs of Friendship. To Honour A.G.F. van Holk, Slavist, Linguist, Semiotician*, edited by J.J. van Baak. Amsterdam: Rodopi, pp. 553–68.

Uses *Doctor Zhivago* as a test case to distinguish between "implied author in the text" (a consistent, on-going phenomenon occurring throughout the text) and the more intermittent "author in the text." Analyzes Zhivago's language patterns to prove that they coincide with those of the author and thus discerns an "author in the text." Takes into account Pasternak's own status and his philosophical views expressed elsewhere in his works.

22 ZHOLKOVSKY, ALEXANDER. "Seven 'Winds': Translations of Pasternak's 'Veter.'" In *Language and Literary Theory. In Honor of Ladislav Matejka*, edited by Benjamin A. Stolz, I.R. Titunik, and Lubomir Doležel. Papers in Slavic Philology, no. 5. Ann Arbor: University of Michigan, Department of Slavic Languages and Literatures, pp. 623–43.

Breaks an examination of seven English texts of Pasternak's "Wind" into two segments—a summary of the poetics of the original, detailed earlier (1983.32) and a detailed analysis of the seven renditions. Examines (in both segments) design, rhymes, line structure, meter, phonetics, lexicon, syntax, and morphology. Ranks each rendition according to the poetics discussed in each segment. Concludes that "all seven versions clearly strive for accuracy . . . they match the cognitive meaning of the original line by line," and "judging by the seven renditions . . . adequate translation is not impossible—if not in details, at least in major outlines."

23 ———. "The 'Sinister' in the Poetic World of Pasternak." *IJSLP* 29: 109–31.

Examines the motif of the "sinister" in Pasternak's poetic world and compiles lists of the "sinister" submotifs. Divides these lists into six sections: "Literal Evil," "The Supernatural," "The Suspicious," "Evil Behavior," "Transgression," and "Law Enforcement." Desires to identify the place the "sinister" motif "occupies in the hierarchy" of

Pasternak's other motifs; proposes an explanation of the literary functions of the "sinister." Quotes extensively to support his arguments.

24 ———. "'Window' in the Poetic World of Boris Pasternak." In *Themes and Texts: Toward a Poetics of Expressiveness*, edited by Kathleen Parthé. Ithaca, NY; London: Cornell University Press, pp. 135–58.
Reprint of 1978.42.

1985

1 AL'TSHULLER, MARK, and ELENA DRYZHAKOVA. "Nobelevskaia golgofa Borisa Pasternaka" [Boris Pasternak's Nobel Prize Golgotha]. In *Put' otrecheniia. Russkaia literatura 1953–1968.* Tenafly, NJ: Ermitazh, pp. 45–58.
Surveys Pasternak's literary background, mentioning his participation in "Centrifuge," endeavors to adapt to demands of contemporary movements (the portrayal of Lenin, for example), his return to his own themes ("role of nature and art in man's life"), and the *Doctor Zhivago* period. Examines the poetry of *Doctor Zhivago*, particularly nature and love themes, and the role of Hamlet and his affinity with Christ, an embodiment of the "personal, individual outset of the world history."

2 GLAZOV, YURI. "Pasternak, Solzhenitsyn, and Sakharov." In *The Russian Mind Since Stalin's Death.* Dordrecht: D. Reidel Publishing Co., pp. 158–79.
Compares the lives and careers of three Russian Nobel Prize winners. Greatest attention is given to the similarities and differences between Pasternak and Solzhenitsyn, "two great Russians" who "belong to different eras and complement each other." Contrasts several aspects of the two authors' lives and work: Pasternak's privileged background and Sozhenitsyn's provincial roots, the subtlety of Pasternak's Hamlet-like characters and the decisive fearlessness of Solzhenitsyn's, Pasternak's idolatry of women and Solzhenitsyn's wariness of them, and Pasternak's distanced curiosity with Solzhenitsyn's identification with the common people. Describes the two as similar in their hermitlike, religious ways of life, with Solzhenitsyn's religion resembling that of the "Old Testament" more than Pasternak's.

3 LIKHACHEV, D.S. Introduction (in Russian) to *Izbrannoe v dvukh tomakh.* Vol. 1. Moscow: Khudozhestvennaia literatura, pp. 3–28.
Divided into two sections, a biographical account and an analysis of his works. The former mentions some basic details: Pasternak's family background, his love for music, participation in the association "Lirika," rapprochement with Mayakovsky (in whose poetry "he saw a high model and the justification for revolutionary novelty"), his several poetry collec-

tions (excluding the poetry of *Doctor Zhivago*), and major Shakespeare translations; conludes that the Pasternak style has been formed "under the influence of art, music, and traditions of Russian and world poetry." The latter section examines several aspects of Pasternak's poetics: his metaphors and similes (the vehicle of which is deemed to be seen by Pasternak as *the* reality), propensity for animation of inanimate objects ("a typical feature of Pasternak's creativity"), and his "expressionism" ("his poetic system was expressionistic"). Points out "echoes" of Shakespeare, Fet, Rilke, Tsvetaeva, Blok, Pushkin, Tyutchev, Tolstoy, Dostoevsky, and Picasso ("both felt to be condensers of the world energy"). Concludes that during all of his creative life Pasternak strove for simplicity but his poetry "combines in itself simplicity and incomprehensibility"—the latter being a result of "personal impressions [and] events from personal, every-day life unfamiliar to the reader." Draws numerous observations, pertaining to his life and works, on Pasternak's *A Safe Conduct.*

4   LIVINGSTONE, ANGELA. Introduction to and comments on *Pasternak on Art and Creativity.* Edited by Angela Livingstone. Cambridge: Cambridge University Press, pp. 1–17, 21–27, 49–64, 151–70, 201–13, and 252–62.

Consists of an introduction, four commentaries preceding four chapters, and a "Concluding Essay," all centering on Pasternak's conception of art. The introduction traces the motifs of art as a cry for help and of the "need" for "speed" in art ("speed is particularly characteristic of Pasternak's more youthful writings about art"). Concludes that Pasternak has no "complete theory of art" but "makes claims for certain abstract terms" (his "concept of a 'force' or 'power,'"). Relates Pasternak's conception of art to Tsvetaeva, Mandelstam, and Mayakovsky. Commentaries comprise detailed interpretations of Pasternak's statements and ideas about art and his views of nature and the origin of art as expressed in Pasternak's prose writings, notably his essays, stories, and tales, two autobiographies, speeches, and *Doctor Zhivago.* The "Concluding Essay" interprets and narrates some passages from *Doctor Zhivago* as related to Pasternak's conception of art and literature in particular.

5   NIVA, ZHORZH [NIVAT, GEORGES]. "'I ne bylo oshibkoiu rodit'sia'" [And it was no mistake to be born]. *Sintaksis* 14: 67–76.

Examines themes in "Blank Verses," focusing on Pasternak's interpretation of Balzac's last year, a theme deemed Pasternak's "realization dream of a universal artist" (Balzac in Paris, in Berdichev, or at the Paris Stock Exchange—"all these images are appended to each other"). Emphasizes Pasternak's ability to "witness" Balzac's last year and to harken to his "prophetic voice of life" that it was worthy to "suffer . . . and that it was no mistake to be born"; sees this theme repeated in *Doctor Zhivago*'s "August."

6   SMIRNOV, I.P. *Porozhdenie interteksta. Elementy intertekstual'nogo analiza s primerami iz tvorchestva B.L. Pasternaka* [The origin of intertextuality. Elements of intertextual analysis with examples from B.L. Pasternak's works]. Special Issue, no. 17. Vienna: Wiener slawistischer Almanach, 208 pp.

Defines the device of intertextuality within ideological, semantic, and communicative text interdependence; focuses on nonrepresentative and representative intertexts, converse sense, intertextual operations and signals, intertextuality and diachrony, and "memory of memory." Traces intertextuality in Pasternak's works and finds "echoes" in works by other authors—Lermontov, Bely, Rilke, Dostoevsky, Solovyov, Bryusov, Pushkin, Nietzsche, Narval, Minsky, Bunin, and Fet, among others. Pays particular attention to Pasternak's "Waves," "Dream," two poems on Venice, some poems from *My Sister, Life*, excerpts from *A Safe Conduct*, "The Wassermann Test," and others. Concludes that the result of intertext is linked to a writer's literary/semantic memory that retains information on semantically saturated texts/sources, and that a "writer retains information which an older writer has [already] retained."

7   STRADA, VITTORIO and CLARA. "Gamlet Borisa Pasternaka" [Boris Pasternak's Hamlet]. *Obozrenie*, no. 15 (July): 24–27.

Draws parallels between Pasternak's conception of Hamlet and Dostoevsky's Prince Myshkin, Goncharov's Oblomov, and Blok's and Mayakovsky's interpretations of Hamlet. Sees "elements of theater and Gospel universalism" in Pasternak's poem "Hamlet," in which Pasternak implements a "double mytho-structure" (endowment of "Christ featrues"). Cites passages from *A Safe Conduct* to illustrate Pasternak's comments on Hamlet and interprets *Doctor Zhivago* as "a sort of second *A Safe Conduct*." Points out similarities between *Doctor Zhivago* and Bulgakov's *Master and Margarita*.

8   WESTSTEIJN, WILLEM G. "Metaphor and Simile in *Doktor Živago*." *EP* 10, no. 2: 41–57.

Surveys criticism of *Doctor Zhivago*, particularly criticism that compares *Doctor Zhivago* with *War and Peace*; notes the difference between these two works. Discusses the terminology of metaphor and simile (both seen as "the figures of analogy"), and concludes that: (1) in *Doctor Zhivago* there exist "entire pages without any metaphor or simile" yet "some pages bristle with them"; (2) figures of analogy are "confined to . . . the narrator's discourse"; (3) metaphor and simile occur "in all kinds of forms" and are "rather complex"; (4) the large part of metaphors and similes "combine elements of nature with aspects of human life," a combination enhanced by "frequent use of personification"; and (5) figures of analogy are "essential techniques for the author to express his view of life."

9 ZHOLKOVSKII, A.K. "Mekhanizmy vtorogo rozhdeniia. O stikhotvorenii Pasternaka 'Mne khochetsia domoi, v ogromnost' ...'" [Mechanisms of second birth. On Pasternak's poem "I Want to Go Home, into Enormousness"]. *Sintaksis* 14: 77–97.

Provides notes on Pasternak's and Mandelstam's relationship, with a textual comparison of their two poems, an overview of Pasternak's views in *Second Birth*, and a semantic study of "I Want to Go Home, into Enormousness." Draws dissimilarities between Pasternak and Mandelstam as reflected in Nadezhda Mandelstam's memoirs. Sees *Second Birth* as a breakup in Pasternak's aesthetics, and cites four "moves" Pasternak demonstrated in the collection: (1) subjugation to force; (2) hope for positive changes and collectivism; (3) stand-by on tradition; and (4) a view of socialism as a landscape. Sees "I Want to Go Home, into Enormousness" as a realization of "Pasternak's program of acceptance of a socialistic virgin soil," and as "verses ... about a poet's calling and destiny." Reprinted: 1990.73.

10 ZHURAVLEV, D.N. "Boris Pasternak" (in Russian). In *Zhizn'. Iskusstvo. Vstrechi.* Moscow: Vserossiiskoe teatral'noe obshchestvo, pp. 332–46.

Recalls his meetings with Pasternak—beginning in 1939 and ending in 1960. Records many personal qualities of Pasternak: his childlike character, his kindness to and fondness of other people, and his knowledge of "stage life." Includes Pasternak's three unpublished letters to the author and his wife.

1986

1 AUCOUTURIER, MICHEL. "L'image de la révolution de 1905 dans l'oeuvre de Pasternak." In *1905. La première révolution russe*, edited by François-Xavier Coquin and Céline Gervais-Francelle. Collection historique de l'Institut d'études slaves, no. 32. Paris: Institut d'études slaves, pp. 405–11.

Attempts to characterize Pasternak's perception of the 1905 Revolution as reflected in *The Year 1905* and *Lieutenant Schmidt*. Claims Pasternak had three images of the Revolution: from the perspective of his childhood; through the eyes of the idealist, intellectual, and revolutionary Schmidt; and through Lara, who supposedly symbolizes the Revolution.

2 BAKINA, M.A., and E.A. NEKRASOVA. "Idiostil' B.L. Pasternaka" [B.L. Pasternak's idiostyle]. In *Evoliutsiia poeticheskoi rechi XIX–XXvv. Perifraza. Sravnenie*, edited by A.D. Grigor'eva. Moscow: Nauka, pp. 123–29.

Sees Pasternak's lexical and semantic units, including comparisons and similes, as diverse. Insists that the thematic bond between these units and the basic theme of a poem does not necessarily exist—a fact to be looked upon as a special artistic device; mentions that such a device is closer to Benediktov's idiostyle than to Vyazemsky's.

3   BARNES, CHRISTOPHER. Introduction to *The Voice of Prose*, edited by C. Barnes. Vol. 1, *Early Prose and Autobiography*. Edinburgh: Polygon Books, pp. 7–19.

Discusses Pasternak's early prose included in this volume and offers numerous comments on Pasternak's views of art, the Revolution, emergence in literature, adherence to literary trends ("if Pasternak is a romantic, he is so in the manner of Keats rather than of Byron"), "attitudes on public issues," and on oneness and similarities within Pasternak's prose. Links *The Line of Apelles* and *The Story of a Contraoctave* to Kleist and Hoffmann. Claims that "the idea of the artist as medium rather than agent ... shown once again in 'Letters from Tula'" is "of central importance for Pasternak's art." Continued: 1990.9.

4   BODIN, PER-ARNE. "God, Tsar and Man. Boris Pasternak's Poem *Artillerist*." *SSR* 6: 69–80.

A lexical analysis of "The Artilleryman"—including the publication background (both variants, 1914; 1917), imagery (political, metaphoric, and metonymic), themes, semantic references, and links between other authors' and Pasternak's poetry. Relates the content in detail, explains the word *Zao* (in Greek "I live"), and associates it with the New Testament. Sees the central meaning in the poem's "total lack of communication between the protagonist, God and the surrounding world." Identifies the protagonist as Nicholas II, suggesting details for an "encoded portrait of the Tsar." Concludes that the poem "unites a historical theme with a religious" one, is "intricately encoded not merely to enrich its content, but also to outwit the censor," and has "the embryo of the religious themes that were to be ... transformed in the Zhivago cycle."

5   CORNWELL, NEIL. *Pasternak's Novel: Perspectives on "Doctor Zhivago."* Essays in Poetics Publications, no. 2. Keele: Essays in Poetics, 166 pp.

Surveys the early criticism by themes, evaluation, protagonist, the novel's genre, suitability for publication in the Soviet Union, and the novel's shortcomings (including sermonizing, plot/narrative technique, transitions, style, speech patterns, dialogues, and characters). Groups criticism of the past decade, focusing on structure and form, correlation between prose and poetry sections, feminism, intertextuality (quotations, influences, allusions, parallels, borrowings, adaptations), and the "Joycean approach." Discusses criticism of authorial-narratorial discourses, temporal/spatial clusterings, allegory, symbolism/imagery (wind, lime tree, water), and coincidences; narrates the novels's first chapter. Contains a selective bibliography.

6   GUTSCHE, GEORGE J. "Pasternak's Lyric 'Summer.'" In *Moral Apostasy in Russian Literature*. Dekalb: Northern Illinois University Press, pp. 117–29.
      Reprint (with modifications) of 1981.7.

7   HASTY, OLGA PETERS. "Multiplicity of Perspective as Metaphor for Poetic Creation in Pasternak's 'Opredelenie poèzii' and 'Opredelenie tvorčestva.'" *IJSLP* 34, no. 34: 113–21.
      Analyzes the function of metonymies and the manner in which they interconnect in Pasternak's "Definition of Poetry." Finds that this poem "opens with seven statements," that "the second stanza continues that anaphoric pattern, meter, and rhyme scheme of stanza one," and that "the entire poem is constructed of ambiguous and shifting images, which taken together serve as a metaphor for poetry or its definition." Also analyzes "acoustic links and syntactic displacements" in "Definition of Creativity," seen as displaying "metonymic links as well as the distinctions among them."

8   KUN, ÁGNES. "Memories of Pasternak." *NHQ* 27, no. 104: 90–109.
      Discusses Pasternak's translations of Sándor Petöfi and Pasternak as a translator and a human being. Argues that Pasternak's poetry is not "based on associations of thoughts" but that "Pasternak marvelled at the world at every moment, like a child." Recalls Pasternak's way of talking ("Niagara of words"), his appearance ("With his buck-teeth I always saw Pasternak as an ugly, almost hideous man"), and his Petöfi translations "beyond doubt wonderful." Also recalls Pasternak's view of Petöfi's poetry, which Pasternak compared to his own. Includes Pasternak's three letters to the author.

9   LEECH-ANSPACH, GABRIELE. "Bemerkungen zum Verständnis von Zeit und Erinnerung in Romanen Boris Pasternaks, Andrej Bitovs und Jurij Trifonovs." *ZSP* 46: 218–29.
      Examines the importance of time and memory in *Doctor Zhivago* and Bitov's and Trifonov's novels. Establishes that many repeating character configurations in *Doctor Zhivago* symbolize fateful linkages between individuals of the identical historic period. Points out similarities between Pasternak's worldviews and Bergson's philosophy.

10 LIAPUNOV, VADIM, and SAVELII SENDEROVICH. "Ob odnoi poslovitse i trekh funktsiiakh plana vyrazheniia poslovits" [About one proverb and the three functions of proverbs plan expressions]. *RuL* 19: 393–404.
      An analysis of the functions (textual, contextual, and sound) of the last line (the proverb "To live one's life is not to cross a field") from the poem "Hamlet." Sees the proverb structured "by the same laws of a poetic word compression" as Pasternak's "complex poetry"—with the

only difference being that the poetry "amplifies expressive means which the proverb avoids." Interprets the proverb's first segment, "To live one's life," as defined by a "temporal measurement," and the second part, "to cross a field," as a "spatial measurement." Discerns and discusses the proverb's twelve variants, all seen as inferior to Pasternak's "formula of semantic complexity." Concludes that the proverb is a "complex microworld ... living in the inner interaction of its own parts," and "a sort of a minimal poetic text."

11 MOSSMAN, ELLIOTT. "Metaphors of History in 'War and Peace' and 'Doctor Zhivago.'" In *Literature and History. Theoretical Problems and Russian Case Studies*, edited by Gary Saul Morson. Stanford, CA: Stanford University Press, pp. 247–62.

Compares Tolstoy's "mechanical" metaphors of history in *War and Peace* to the "biological" metaphors of *Doctor Zhivago* in order to examine the "ways art renders history." Claims that Pasternak's novel "compels the reader to contrast its depiction of history with that in *War and Peace*." Asserts that there are three sources for Pasternak's biological metaphors of history: Darwinism, Dickens's celebration of natural rights in *A Tale of Two Cities*, and Einstein's special theory of relativity. ("The final scene of Zhivago's life is carefully modeled after Einstein's popular discussion of the relativity of simultaneous events, one of the facets of his Special Theory of Relativity.") Quotes extensively from *Doctor Zhivago* and uses specific examples such as Antipov/Strelnikov and Zhivago's funeral to illustrate different uses of the novel's mechanical and biological metaphors.

12 NÖLDEKE, ELISABETTA. *Boris Leonidovič Pasternak und seine Beziehungen zur deutschen Kultur*. Tübingen: n.p., 300 pp.

Surveys Pasternak's German connections (his study of German language, literature, philosophy, culture, his stay in Marburg, and his poem "Marburg") and his translations of German poets and writers. Pays special attention to Pasternak's renditions of Johannes Becher, Georg Herwegh, Georg Heym, Jakob van Hoddis, Hans Sachs, Franz Werfel, Paul Zech, and Schiller. Thoroughly evaluates the poetics of Pasternak's renditions of *Faust* and Rilke's poetry, noting that some translations of Rilke read like Pasternak's "own work," due to Pasternak's "simplification of syntax" and the use of everyday "expressions." Cites Russian originals to collaborate her findings. Formerly a "Philosophische Dissertation," defended at the University of Tübingen in 1985.

13 ORLOWA-KOPELEVA, RAISA, and LEW KOPELEV. *Boris Pasternak* (in German). Stuttgart: RADIUS-Verlag Gmbh, 62 pp.

Consists of three major sections: an outline of Pasternak's life with sporadic commentary on his works; Pasternak's letters to Rolf-Dietrich Keil; and a German translation of Pasternak's Chopin essay. Surveys

Pasternak's literary career, focusing on difficulties Pasternak experienced with the Soviet authorities (particularly during and after the "Pasternak Affair"), and on Pasternak's attitude toward the Revolution and the Soviet system (his belief in the Revolution was always accompanied by doubts and distance). Sees *Doctor Zhivago* as the climax of Pasternak's literary career.

14 SALYS, RIMA. "'Izmeritel'naja edinica russkoj žizni': Puškin in the Work of Boris Pasternak." *RuL* 19: 347–92.

Traces the influence of Pushkin in Pasternak's conception of art and the artist, highlighting several stages of Pasternak's literary career. Shows how various aspects of Pushkin interested Pasternak at different times, illuminating Pasternak's own path of literary development. Sees Pushkin as Pasternak's "antidote" to the romantic conception of the poet. Cites economy of expression and an effort to secularize the Russian literary language as Pushkin-influenced traits of Pasternak's style.

15 SMOLITSKII, V.G. "Iazyk ulitsy v poezii B. Pasternaka" [Street language in B. Pasternak's poetry]. *IaSPFL*, pp. 103–9.

Focuses on Pasternak's "imagery of spoken language," "expressions of colloquialisms," dialects, proverbs, sayings, and descriptions of "folk rituals" (Shrovetide and Christmas trees). Pays special attention to "street" language of the "big city" where "one can hear 'splinters' of the most various dialects." Contrasts variants of "Marburg" (1915 and 1928) and "Venice" (1913 and 1928) to demonstrate Pasternak's tendency for "lexical vulgarization" and pursues this tendency in Pasternak's later poetry. Cites numerous examples to illustrate his arguments.

16 VENTSLOVA, TOMAS. "B.L. Pasternak. 'Mchalis' zvezdy . . .'" [B.L. Pasternak. "The Stars Were Tearing Along"]. In *Neustoichivoe ravnovesie: vosem' russkikh poeticheskikh tekstov*. Yale Russian and East European Publications, no. 9. New Haven, CT: Yale Center for International and Area Studies, pp. 115–34.

Gives a brief background of Pasternak's poem "The Stars Were Tearing Along" (belonging to the cycle "The Theme With Variations" and the collection *Themes and Variations*) and surveys criticism of the poem—its musicality, "obscurity of the language," "semantic saturation," and its comparison to Beethoven's sonatas. Analyzes the poem's structure, language, meter, sound instrumentation, imagery (particularly synecdoche and hyperbole), and its phenomenology. Concludes that the poem has an abundance of nouns and only two adjectives (of a total of sixty-one words); that the motifs of sphinx and time play an important role; that links to Lermontov, Pushkin, and Fet exist; that the poem's rhymes are unique ("Pasternak avoids verbal rhymes"); that alliteration is employed from the first line; that Pasternak uses certain vocabularies more frequently than others; and that the poem "is one of the most perfect Pasternak works." Strongly argues that the poem is "about the birth of a 'Prophet' and simultaneously about its own birth" and "about singularity, inimitability of a poet—and about the unity of poetry."

17   VISHNIAK, VLADIMIR. "Pasternak's 'Roslyy strelok' and the Tradition of the Hunter and the Duck." *ISS*, no. 7, pp. 53–64.

Draws heavily on Pasternak criticism (Anatoly Yakobson, Robert Jackson, and Lazar Fleishman, among others), Pasternak's works (*A Safe Conduct* and *Doctor Zhivago*), and Pushkin's *Eugene Onegin*, while interpreting the symbolism of the poem "Sturdy Marksman" and the relationship between a poet, a hunter, and a wild duck. Sees the parallel between *Doctor Zhivago* and the poem in the image of the hunter as "a metaphor of the cruel age, a metaphor of the times." Sees Pasternak's identification in the poem of a poet with a wild duck as borrowed from Pushkin's *Eugene Onegin* (chapter 4, stanza 36), in Pasternak's line " 'Kill me with one shot, on the wing,' " and Pushkin's "One sees a duck and aims his gun/One raves in verse like me," for example. Also mentions Zabolotsky's poem "The Cranes" as in the "spirit of this tradition."

18   ZHOLKOVSKII, A.K., and IU. K. SHCHEGLOV. "Liubovnaia lodka, upriazh' dlia pegasa i pokhoronnaia kolybel'naia (Tri stikhotvoreniia i tri perioda Pasternaka)" [Love boat, harness for Pegasus, and the funeral lullaby (Three poems and Pasternak's three periods)]. In *Mir avtora i struktura teksta. Stat'i o russkoi literature*. Tenafly, NJ: Ermitazh, pp. 228–54.

Follows up Nils Åke Nilsson's (1959.46 and 1959.47) diachronic approach to Pasternak's poetry. Thoroughly analyzes Pasternak's three poems ("With Oars at Rest" [1918], "I Want to Go Home, into Enormousness" [1931], and "The Wind" [1958]) that represent the early, middle, and late periods. Focus on the poems' poetics—themes, structures, metrics, rhymes, syntaxes, and sound intrumentations, among others. Concludes that Pasternak's poetics during the forty years remained the same, and yet experienced an "obvious evolution": in syntax ("expanded steadily"), rhymes ("originality was achieved by a skilled altering of corrected forms"), composition ("structured on a clear, three-part pattern"), and sound instrumentation.

1987

1   ANDERSON, ROGER B. "The Railroad in *Doktor Živago*." *SEEJ* 31, no. 4: 503–19.

Enumerates and discusses train motifs in *Doctor Zhivago*, focusing on imagery and symbolism. Believes that "trains and related images of the railroad" significantly figure in the novel's treatment of history and revolutions, particularly in the character portrayal. Finds that the train imagery is associated with many characters, notably with Antipov-Strelnikov, Tonya, Kolya, Prolenko, Lara, and Zhivago. Thus, Zhivago's "integrative perception of the world" is seen "largely conveyed in Pasternak's imagery of the railroad" and his death refers "to Pasternak's imagery of the railroad as a system made up of many different intersecting private journeys." Argues that Zhivago's "religious beliefs, his views on history and art, and his own biography . . . are complementary statements that are served by the symbolism of the train-as-system."

2 ARKHANGEL'SKII, ALEKSANDR. Review (in Russian) of Pasternak's *Vozhdushnye puti. Proza raznykh let; Izbrannoe v dvukh tomakh; and Sestra moia—zhizn'. Stikhotvoreniia i poemy. DN*, no. 4, pp. 263–66.
Offers general views of Pasternak's prose and poetry, while taking issue with Pasternak criticism. Sees criticism as unjust and failing to record, for example, links between Pasternak's early poetry and his "farewell cycle 'When the Skies Clear.'" Discusses in detail Pasternak's poetic perceptions, interpreted as having the poet "in the center of the universe" ("only his [Pasternak's] metaphoric thinking is capable of interlocking together isolated world phenomena"). Pays special attention to *A Safe Conduct*, characterized as one of Pasternak's "high prose accomplishments."

3 BAEVSKII, V. "Temy i variatsii. Ob istoriko-kul'turnom kontekste poezii B. Pasternaka" [Themes and variations. On the historically-cultural context of B. Pasternak's poetry]. *VL*, no. 10, pp. 30–59.
Analyzes literary contexts of Pasternak's poetry in general and of his poems "Hoar-Frost," "Wind," "Spring in the Forest," and "Fairy Tale" in particular. Compares each of these poems in its historically cultural and historically literary context to the poetry of other poets, i.e., "Hoar-Frost" to Blok, Fet, and Heine; "Wind" to Blok; "Spring in the Forest" to Blok, Grigoryev, Zhukovsky, and Goethe; and "Fairy Tale" to Bely, Blok, Vrubel, Polonsky, Solovyev, Pushkin, Cervantes, and to the Russian icon paintings. Pays special attention to Pasternak's recurrent imagery, such as "mask" (*maska*), "cast" (*slepok*), "make-up" (*grim*), "bust" (*biust*), for example, all used repeatedly in Pasternak's works.

4 BARLAS, VLADIMIR. "O Pasternake" [On Pasternak]. *Neva*, no. 8, pp. 188–95.
Prompted by Gladkov's Pasternak memoirs (1973.5), relates his impressions of both Pasternak's poetry and poetry readings (five), which are described in detail—Pasternak's appearance and bearing, interaction with the audience, and the content of the readings. Elaborates on the fate of the publication of *Doctor Zhivago* and on Pasternak's funeral ("three individuals in civilian clothes were standing at the coffin and

photographed from two sides each one who came up to bid a farewell to the poet").

5   BODIN, PER-ARNE. "The Sleeping Demiurge: An Analysis of Boris Pasternak's Poem 'Durnoj son.'" In *Text and Context. Essays to Honor Nils Åke Nilsson*, edited by Peter Alberg Jensen et al. Stockholm Studies in Russian Literature, 23. Stockholm: Almqvist & Wiksell International, pp. 86–95.

   Cites Pasternak's poem "A Bad Dream" in its entirety and analyzes the poem's semantic meanings and imagery while mentioning its structure, rhymes, and meter. Discusses the poem's "key concept" ("the storm wind blowing through the landscape"); its bonds with Dostoevsky (Ivan Karamazov's "accusation against God" and the poem's line "How dared he, man, to play a heaven?") and Rilke (his "Geschichten vom lieben Gott" seen as "a sort of starting point or raw material for Pasternak's poem"); and its sounds, similes, and metaphors. Concludes that the answer to the "question of the relation between God and man is "a negative one—God is sleeping and perhaps even dying."

6   BUKHSHTAB, B. IA. "Lirika Pasternaka" [Pasternak's lyrics]. *LO*, no. 9, pp. 106–12.

   The first part of an unfinished study meant to be published in the late 1920s. Elaborates on the poetics of *My Sister, Life* and *Themes and Variations*, centering on the language, sound instrumentation, metric system, themes, and Pasternak's penchant for detail. Discusses the use of everyday lexica (for which Pasternak "found new sense angles"), defines sound texture as "sound approximation" and punning, notes the predominance of four-foot iambics ("his meters are classical"), and discovers and examines "lyrical movements" of Pasternak's verse and the "principle of object calling" ("For Pasternak, there are no, for example, 'flowers' or 'plants' in general; there are asters, dalles, phloxes, hyacinths, aleanders, anemones"). E.B. Pasternak prepared the introduction explaining the publication background of Bukhstab's study; G.G. Shapov contributed the notes to it.

7   FARYNO, JERZY. "Arkheopoetika 'Pisem iz Tuly' Pasternaka" [Archipoetics in Pasternak's *Letters from Tula*.] In *Mythos in der Slawischen Moderne*, edited by Wolf Schmid. Wiener slawistischer Almanach. Sonderband, no. 20. Vienna: Gesellschaft zur Förderung slawisticher Studien, pp. 237–75.

   Applies a *deshifrovka* (decoding) concept of the avant-garde approach to text analysis in *Letters From Tula*. Singles out ten key motifs, or lexical levels, in decoding the most concealed meanings of lexica in the story: (1) "In a Train They Transported the Sun"; (2) "The Railway Station and the Hotel"; (3) "A Stoker on the Tender"; (4) "The Sun in the Beer"; (5) "The Agronomist"; (6) "A Trial"; (7) "Buddy, You Got

Change For a Three"; (8) "Luggage Room Counter and Astapovo"; (9) "Well, That's Tula"; and (10) "Petr Bolotnikov and Savva Ignat'evich." Deciphering is executed within the story's lexical etymology and the poetics of Pasternak's other works.

8 ————. "Bul'var, sobaki, topolia i babochki (Razbor odnoi glavy 'Okhrannoi gramoty' Pasternaka)" [A boulevard, dogs, poplars and butterflies (A study of a chapter in Pasternak's *A Safe Conduct*)]. *SSASH* 33, nos. 1–4: 277–303.

A detailed textual analysis of part 3, chapter 4 of *A Safe Conduct*—with an attempt to decode allusions and quotations concealed within lexical strata of that section and the entire work. Makes the general conclusion that in *A Safe Conduct* a code is transmitted by communication, and not communication by code. Also makes numerous parallels to Pasternak's other works.

9 IAKOBSON, ROMAN. "Zametki o proze poeta Pasternaka" [Notes on the prose of the poet Pasternak]. In *Raboty po poetike*. Moscow: Progress, pp. 324–38.

Translation of 1935.2.

10 JENSEN, PETER ALBERG. "Boris Pasternak's 'Opredelenie poezii.'" In *Text and Context. Essays to Honor Nils Åke Nilsson*, edited by Peter Alberg Jensen et al. Stockholm Studies in Russian Literature, 23. Stockholm: Almqvist & Wiksell International, pp. 96–110.

Scrutinizes Pasternak's poem "Definition of Poetry" on three levels: phraseology, content ("syntax, meter, rhythm, and rhyme"), and its literary echoes. Finds that the poem displays "a peculiar chameleon-like quality," with its words "complex and difficult to disentangle," moved "away from their habitual lodgings," and "reaching out towards one another." Also finds "that in both form and content the poem establishes a metapoetical discussion for and against Futuristic poetics." Concludes that the poem "reaches back into Greek mythology and reminds us that the bad poet is doomed to perish in the waters of Lethe."

11 KAVERIN, V. "B.L. Pasternak" (in Russian). *Znamia*, no. 8, pp. 109–21.

A summary of his encounters with Pasternak, beginning in 1926 and ending with Pasternak's death. Conveys data about Pasternak the man, stressing Pasternak's courage and his efforts to remain a free man, and calls him an "enormous writer, a creator of a thousand pages of poetry, prose, and letters." Describes Pasternak's funeral, which reminds him of descriptions of Tolstoy's burial ("such a moving simplicity"), and summarizes his views of Pasternak: "he was a democrat in a real sense of the word," "he loved his homeland—its nature, its great spiritual culture, its great people," and "he did not force himself on the contemporaneity . . . and firmly knew that a time will arrive when the contemporaneity will once again appeal to him." Reprinted: 1988.21.

12 MARGVELASHVILI, GEORGII. "'Gruziia, revoliutsiia, Shekspir . . .'" [Georgia, Revolution, Shakespeare]. *LiG*, no. 11, pp. 141–73; no. 12, pp. 126–47.

Cites and discusses Pasternak's poetry that attests to his affinity with Soviet Georgia and its poets (particularly Tabidze). Discusses Pasternak's two stays in Georgia, his renditions of Georgian poets, participation in the First Congress of Soviet Writers, and his trip to Paris with Tabidze, among other topics. Elaborates on Pasternak's works of the 1930s, particularly *Second Birth*, *A Safe Conduct*, and "An Artist," and on Pasternak's correspondence, articles, lectures, and poetry recitals of the 1930s—all to define Pasternak's poetic views of the time. Attempts to manifest a poetic affinity between Pasternak and Pushkin, Mayakovsky, Shakespeare, and Vazha Pshavela.

13 MEYER, ANGELIKA. *Sestra moja—žizn' von Boris Pasternak. Analyse und Interpretation*. Slavistische Beiträge, no. 207. Munich: Verlag Otto Sagner, 253 pp.

Presents a multifarious analysis of *My Sister, Life*—its publication history (with a thorough discussion of all textual variants), its place within Pasternak's works, structure (including space and time criteria), meter, rhymes, sound instrumentation, themes (including nature, time, love, art, music, and music and poetry), motifs, and language. Sees *My Sister, Life* as a poetry collection in which "single elements achieve their complete meaning only in the context of the whole," a device Pasternak is believed to have borrowed from Blok. Also discusses the meaning of the subtitle *(Summer 1917)* and Pasternak's influence on other poets. Concludes that Pasternak has contributed a great deal to the development of a metrical system and sound instrumentation and that the content of his poetry did not fade in its importance despite all of Pasternak's "virtuosity." Includes the collection's Russian text accompanied by the author's German renditions.

14 MEZHAKOV-KORIAKIN, IGOR. "Dukhovnyi aspekt obraza Iuriia Zhivago" [The spiritual aspect of the character of Yury Zhivago]. *ASEES* 1, no. 2: 125–36.

Focuses on the personality of Zhivago and his worldviews, mentioning autobiographical features of Zhivago: egocentrism, originality, his "vivid mind," his "creative nature," sensitivity for the beauty of the world, and "joy of existence," among others. Also notes that Zhivago's "egocentrism" is lost in his love for Lara, and that for Pasternak a personal, family life was more precious than all revolutions and his "social" life. Reprinted (with slight changes): 1988.32.

15 PANIUSHEVA, M.S. "Slovo v poeticheskoi rechi" [The word in a poetic speech]. In *Znachenie i smysl slova. Khudozhestvennaia rech', publitsis-
   tika*, edited by D.E. Rozental'. Moscow: Izdatel'stvo Moskovskogo
   universiteta, pp. 23–40.
      Explores the function of a poetic phrase—the first snow—in
   Pasternak's "The First Snow," and notes that snow, blizzard, and winter
   storm occupy a "conspicuous place" in Pasternak's verse. Analyzes the
   poem's semantic structure on two semantic planes ("clearly breaks down
   into two parts") and details the meaning of snow in Pasternak's other
   poems and in works by other poets (Martynov, Vyazemsky, Esenin,
   Bryusov, and others).

16 PASTERNAK, EVGENII. "Priblizit' chas" [To bring the time nearer].
   VMK, no. 5, pp. 26–32.
      Recollections of Pasternak's life during the 1957–1959 period and
   a commentary on drafts and poems Pasternak created during that time.
   Discusses some of the drafts that "speak of a multistage serious work on
   the poems," a work that "did not follow a successive change of a line by
   another line or a quatrain by another quatrain but entire compositional
   structures." Cites variants to the poems "Soul," "Bacchanalia,"
   "Silence," "A Feeling of Life," "The Future," and "After the Storm,"
   among others. Mentions Pasternak's interpretation of Proust's conep-
   tion of time ("In Proust, the past is always a part of the present, it exists
   in it, in images and thoughts of man living at a given moment, as his recollections").

17 POLUKHINA, VALENTINA. "Diagnoses and Verdicts on Dr.
   Zhivago's Malady." *EP* 12, no. 1: 81–91.
      Reviews Neil Cornwell's survey of *Doctor Zhivago* criticism
   (1986.5). Sifts through the various strategies of approach to Pasternak's
   novel, focusing on the relationship between prose and poetry,
   Pasternak's use of metaphor, and accessibility of the novel.

18 PROFFER, CARL R. "A Footnote to the Zhivago Affair or Ann
   Arbor's Strange Connections with Russian Literature." In *The Widows
   of Russia and Other Writings*. Ann Arbor, MI: Ardis, pp. 132–41.
      Explores the events and persons surrounding the Italian and
   Russian publications of *Doctor Zhivago*. Focuses on the events from
   the standpoint of the editors who published the manuscript,
   Pasternak's friends, the CIA's involvement, and the University of
   Michigan Press's publication of the novel's Russian edition. Believes
   that "the Zhivago affair must be seen in the context of Soviet attitudes toward publication abroad." Details covert activities involving
   the CIA's attempt to publish *Doctor Zhivago*. Provides a short history
   of how the different editors obtained manuscripts and went about publishing *Doctor Zhivago*.

19 RISHINA, IRINA. "Nakanune stoletiia poeta. S zasedaniia komissii po literaturnomu naslediiu B.L. Pasternaka" [On the eve of the poet's centenary. From the meeting of the committee on B.L. Pasternak's literary legacy]. *LG*, no. 5127 (25 February): 6.

An interview with Voznesensky and Kaverin expressing their views of Pasternak. Voznesensky mentions Pasternak's "encyclopedical legacy"—"there exists hardly any spiritual sphere in which the great artist was not involved." Also mentions Pasternak's correspondence ("in his letters the poet appears on a level with leading Russian philosophers"). Kaverin recalls his encounters with Pasternak going back to 1926: "My meetings with him are a special page in my life . . . I often visit his grave. Flowers are always there. People place them. He is a people's writer. Even his funeral was the people's funeral."

20 SCHWARZBAND, S. "Pasternak's *Marburg*. On the Evolution of Poetic Structure." *SSR*, no. 8, pp. 57–74.

A semanitc and structural analysis of the two variants—1915 and 1928—of "Marburg." Details the first variant's structure, intonation, the "lyrical monologue," lexical repetitions, and other features. Contrasts the two variants and establishes that there are changes in semantic meanings, composition, metaphors, "in the organs of perception," the "development of poetic conflict," and "disintegration of the 'I' into 'trifles.'" Concludes that "in the first variant, everything is built upon oppositions and conflicts . . . whereas in the second the foundation is the transformation and re-creation of reality as a model of that reality." Strongly argues that one is "tempted to speak of two Pasternak poems bearing the identical title 'Marburg.'"

21 VIL'MONT, N. "Boris Pasternak. Vospominaniia i mysli" [Boris Pasternak. Recollections and thoughts]. *NM*, no. 6, pp. 165–221.

Recounts his impressions of his friendship with Pasternak, particularly during their frequent encounters during the 1920s. Reveals many sides of Pasternak the man and poet—his "poetic world and secret motives of his creativity," his poetry readings, and his infatuation with Pushkin and Chekhov. Suggests that Chekhov's *Student* and *Bishop* might have influenced *Doctor Zhivago*'s religious poetry, notably "Holy Week," "Miracle," and "The Garden of Gethsemane." Attests to Pasternak's religiousness apparent in the "Christocentrism" of his poetry. Cites Pasternak's poetry and records verbatim his thoughts and views. Reprinted with slight modifications: 1989.38.

22 VOROSHIL'SKII, VIKTOR [WOROZSYLSKI, W.]. "Epos i etos. (Sravnenie razlichnykh variantov kontsovki poemy Borisa Pasternaka 'Vysokaia bolezn')" [Epos and ethos. (A comparison of different ending variants of Boris Pasternak's tale in verse A *High Malady*]. *Sintaksis*, no. 20, pp. 72–89.

A textual analysis of *A High Malady*'s closures and an attempt to explicate changes in these variants. Centers on the first variant of

1924 (version 1), and the third and fourth variants of 1957 (versions 2A and 2B). Sees the first variant's closure as having "no finale," a text "broken off abruptly . . . a narrative . . . that has not and cannot have any more distinct, 'punch-like' denouement," and concludes that the "absence of finale" is not accidental. Elaborates on the closure changes in the second variant, notably the inclusion of "two heroes"— Lenin and history. Discusses in detail Pasternak's perception of Lenin and history (which "cooperates and supports" Lenin), and concludes that Pasternak extols Lenin's historic role more than Mayakovsky. Notes that two stanzas (describing the role of history) were expunged from the 1957 versions, and details the reasons for text changes. Sees *Doctor Zhivago* ("an epic in prose") intersecting with *A High Malady* ("an epic in verse") in their perceptions of history. Discusses criticism of *A High Malady*.

1988

1   *Acta Universitatis Szegediensis de Attila Jozseff Nominatae*. Sectio historiae litterarum Slavicae, no. 19. Szeged: Józseff Attila Tudományegyetem Összehasonlító Pító Irodalomtudományi Tanszéke, 350 pp.

A collection of twelve articles by Hungarian (Budapest and Szeged) and Polish contributors. Is divided into four sections: section 1 (Pasternak's prose), section 2 (Pasternak's philosophy and early aesthetics), section 3 (Pasternak's poetry), and section 4 (papers by students). The last section publishes articles on *The Line of Apelles* (the use of theater) and *Letters from Tula* (philosophy and artistic prose), and analyses of "The Weeping Garden" (the poetics and basic cosmological elements—earth, garden, darkness, and rain) and "Summer" (the poem's two language layers—existence and creativity). Other articles include 1988.6; 1988.7; 1988.19; 1988.22; 1988.25; 1988.43.

2   AL'FONSOV, V.N. "'Zapis' so mnogikh kontsov razom' (printsipy poeticheskogo povestvovaniia v 'Spektorskom' Borisa Pasternaka")" ["A simultaneous record coming from many sides" (principles of poetic narration in Boris Pasternak's *Spektorsky*)]. *RL*, no. 3, pp. 32–59.

A detailed analysis of Pasternak's *Spektorsky*—with emphasis on its poetics and the "fate of personality during a revolutionary epoch." Sees *Spektorsky* as the most complex and complete Pasternak work of the 1920s, a work structured without a "single plot line." Also analyzes *Spektorsky* in its literary context (Pushkin's *Bronze Horseman*, Goethe's *Faust*, Shakespeare's *Hamlet*, and Pasternak's *The Tale*, which is seen as completing *Spektorsky*'s central hero ["incomplete and cut short"]). Reprinted with slight modifications as chapter 2 of 1990.2

3   BAEVSKII, V.S. "Lirika Pasternaka v istoriko-kul'turnom kontekste" [Pasternak's poetry in a historically cultural context]. *IAN* 47: 130–41.

Examines Pasternak's poetry in its literary context—its genealogy from Russian romanticism and symbolism in particular. Draws parallels between Pasternak's "Wedding" and Zhukovsky's "Svetlana," Pasternak's "Night" and Tyutchev's poetry in general, as well as between Pasternak and romanticism and symbolism, Sluchevsky, and the Swiss poet K. F. Meyer. Pays special attention to echoes of Blok and Verlaine in Pasternak's "Winter" (Blok) and "Improvisation" (Verlaine). Also discusses reverberations of Bach, Beethoven, and Rembrandt in Pasternak's lyrics.

4   BORISOV, V.M., and E.V. PASTERNAK. "Materialy k tvorcheskoi istorii romana B. Pasternaka 'Doktor Zhivago'" [Materials on the creative history of Pasternak's *Doctor Zhivago*]. *NM*, no. 6, pp. 205–48.

Records events surrounding *Doctor Zhivago*'s affinity with Pasternak's early prose. Discovers echoes of *Doctor Zhivago* in the prose of the 1910s, the 1920s, and the 1930s, particularly in the story *Without Love*—in which "one of the basic antitheses of the future *Doctor Zhivago*, the loyalty to life and obsession with abstraction, is outlined." Closely links the titles of the two fragments of Pasternak's destroyed prose, "When Boys Grew Up" and "Zhivul't's Notes," and the variant for the hero of *The Line of Apelles*, i.e., Purvit [from the French *pour vie*] to *Doctor Zhivago*. Also chronicles dates of production of each of the novel's chapters, including poems, and elaborates on the novel's various Russian editions and on Pasternak's attempts to publish the novel. Includes a host of information beyond the genesis of *Doctor Zhivago*. Based on archival documents, published and unpublished diaries of Pasternak's contemporaries (including Chukovskaya's), Pasternak's notes and letters (published and unpublished), and Pasternak scholarship and criticism, among other sources. Abridged and translated: 1989.8. Selections from Chukovskaya's diaries reprinted: 1990.15.

5   BUTLER, HUBERT. "Zhivago's Creator." In *The Children of Drancy*. Mullingar, Ireland: Lilliput Press, pp. 157–63.

Makes observations on Pasternak's prose and on Pasternak as an artist. Views *An Essay in Autobiography* as being "stilted and slow, as though a grasshopper were trying to walk," while *The Childhood of Luvers* is seen as "an epitome of all the merits and defects of the early Pasternak." Points out Pasternak's "obsession with trains" ("there is hardly a story without its train"). Interprets *Doctor Zhivago* as having "all the marks of irrepressible genius but it also has grave blemishes."

6   FARINO, E. "Nekotorye voprosy poetiki Pasternaka ('Vecherelo. Povsiudu retivo ...'")" [Some questions of Pasternak's poetics. "Night

was coming on. Far and wide it was sprightly"]. In *Acta Universitatis Szegedienis de Attila Jozseff Nominatae*. Sectio historiae litterarum Slavicae, no. 19. Szeged: Józseff Attila Tudományegyetem Összehasonlító Pító Irodalomtudományi Tanszéke, pp. 135–80.

Notes that the poem's spatial and temporal structure attracts attention and that the poem is structurally divided into three parts: (1) stanzas 2, 3, and 4 give a panoramic view of the "accomplished ascent"; (2) stanzas 6, 7, and 8 are extensions of the panorama—"into the distance" and "high into the air"; and (3) stanzas 10, 11, and 12 are a view "down into" Tbilisi. Adds that temporal fragmentation of the poem is somewhat different: stanzas 2, 3, and 4 are the present time; stanza 5 is "memory of the past"; stanzas 6, 7, and 8 are "lyrical past"; and stanzas 10, 11, and 12 are "legendary history." Concludes that the Pasternakian "I" has a "poet's quality" and that a "poet" is created as a "result of autotransformation on the given world."

7 FEJÉR, A. "Chelovek, istina, universal'nost' (Analiz romana B. Pasternaka novel 'Doktor Zhivago'") [Man, truth, universality (Analysis of B. Pasternak's *Doctor Zhivago*)]. In *Acta Universitatis Szegedienis de Attila Jozseff Nominatae*. Sectio historiae litterarum Slavicae, no. 19. Szeged: Józseff Attila Tudományegyetem Összehasonlító Pító Irodalomtudományi Tanszéke, pp. 1–28.

Observes that: (1) the funeral scene opening *Doctor Zhivago* gives the tone to the entire work; (2) the novel's protagonist has been able to retain "idealistic values in the hostile world"; (3) Lara had no "illusions"; (4) the tragedy of Antipov proves that it is impossible for an individual to transform history; (5) Zhivago, compared to his friends, is more right though "human problems are not resolved exclusively on spiritual bases"; (6) the protagonist cannot see "the same problems" the reader is able to see; and (7) the protagonist "escapes the degradation of the personality."

8 FLEISHMAN, LAZAR. Introduction (in Russian) to Pasternak's *Stikhotvoreniia*. Paris: YMCA Press, pp. 7–22.

Chronicles the development of Pasternak's poetry. Analyzes the poetics of the early collections, notably *My Sister, Life*, which is seen as a "classic" of the twentieth century and the unique structure of which (each poem is individually complete and yet textually dependent on other poems) is seen as influenced by Heine, Baudelaire, Annensky, Ivanov, Blok, and Bely. Points out that the combination of "saturated lyricism" and "total disappearance of the authorial 'I'" is the collection's "most astonishing quality." Mentions Pasternak's ties to Khlebnikov, Mayakovsky, Bobrov, and Aseyev; Pasternak's break with LEF; the view of him as the "greatest Russian poet" in the 1930s; his disillusionment with the Soviet system in the late 1930s; and the poetry of "Yury Zhivago" and the collection *When the Skies Clear*—both of which are seen as "internally kindred" with Pasternak's early poetry collections.

9   FROLOVSKAIA, TAT'IANA. "Goriashchaia svecha, ili strasti po Iuriiu" [A burning candle, or the passion of Yury]. *Prostor*, no. 9, pp. 194–200.

A general commentary on Pasternak and a thematical study of *Doctor Zhivago*. Argues that Pasternak strove to depict two "faces of the world" and that Pasternak's penchant for "incompleteness and disjointedness" is a part of his "esthetic system." Sees a sacrificial theme as central to *Doctor Zhivago*. Claims that the novel is about the destruction of the conception of sacrificial art as the only possibility to salvage one's spiritual values. Draws sporadic parallels between *Doctor Zhivago* and works of other authors (Gorky's *The Life of Klim Samgin*, for example). Takes issue with Kaverin's argument that *Doctor Zhivago*'s main theme is a description of the "destruction of Russian intelligentsia." Concludes that *Doctor Zhivago* completes the theme of a "contemporary Christ."

10   GACHEV, G., et al. "'Doktor Zhivago' vchera i segodnia" [*Doctor Zhivago* yesterday and today]. *LG*, no. 24 (15 June): 3.

A "roundtable" conversation conducted among writers, philosophers, critics, and newspeople voicing their interpretations of *Doctor Zhivago* published in *Novy mir* (nos. 1–4, 1988). A. Gulyga remarks that one of the most rudimentary problems of the novel is "unprotectedness of the writer" while E. Starikova comments that nothing can be understood in the novel beyond Pasternak's poetics and the time within which it was created. G. Gachev notes: "Zhivago is life. History and Life—this is the problem, this is the subject of the novel. History in the twentieth century revealed itself as an enemy of Life, the Existence." Gachev believes that Pasternak's heroes are *personalities*, but they are also a "challenge to the creation of love and to the power of Spirit." R. Kireev contends that Pasternak's prose "is organically devoid of any fictionalizing." For A. Turkov, "Zhivago is not an individualist because he is a doctor, a healer, because he cures people and lives just for them. As a true Christian he is appealing to people, to all [of them]."

11   GASPAROV, M.L. "Semantika metra u rannego Pasternaka" [Early Pasternak's meter semantics]. *IAN* 47, no. 2: 142–47.

An elaborate discussion of the metrical imitations and echoes Pasternak displays in his early poetry: (1) the second poem in the *Themes and Variations* collection ("a brilliant rhythmically syntactic copy" of Pushkin's *Bronze Horseman*); (2) "Mein Liebchen, was willst du noch mehr?" and Fet's "Bad Weather-Autumn-You Smoke"; and (3) "The Dawn in the North" and Bely's "Ashes," among many others. Concludes that Pasternak "transplanted new contents with new intonation to old meters and the old meters became unrecognizable."

12 GIBIAN, DZHORDZH. "Leonid Pasternak i Boris Pasternak. Polemika ottsa i syna" [Leonid Pasternak and Boris Pasternak. The polemics of father and son]. *VL*, no. 9, pp. 104–29.
   Translation of 1983.7.

13 GIMPELEVICH-SHARTSMAN, ZINA. *Intelligent v romanakh Doktor Zhivago i Master i Margarita* [The intellectual in *Doctor Zhivago* and *Master and Margarita*]. Orange, CT: Antiquary, 194 pp.
   Investigates the term "intellectual" in *Doctor Zhivago* and *Master and Margarita*—with parallels drawn against the novels' motifs, plots, structures, contexts, and histories of publication, among other things. Defines the term "intellectual" as "an individual who has spiritually imbibed basic principles of a literary romantic hero." Classifies "intellectuals" using various criteria—such as their personality, talent, creativity, and their attitude toward religion and love. Sees such "creative individuality" in *Doctor Zhivago*'s Vedenyapin, Lara, Sima Tuntseva, Aleksandr Gromeko, Yevgraf, Strelnikov, Zhivago, and others.

14 GORELOV, PAVEL. "Razmyshleniia nad romanom" [Reflections on the novel]. *VL*, no. 9, pp. 54–81.
   Records his reflections on *Doctor Zhivago*. Takes issue with Soviet Pasternak scholarship (particularly with Likhachev's views of *Doctor Zhivago*) and cites passages taken at random—supposedly attesting to Pasternak's misinterpretation of the Soviet reality and to Pasternak's ineptitude as a writer ("Pasternak demonstrates very little and unskillfully. He, as a rule, narrates"). Praises Pasternak only for his integrity ("an honest novel, an honest, valiant author").

15 GREBER, ERIKA. "Pasternak's 'Detstvo Lyuvers' and Dostoevsky's 'Netochka Nezvanova': An Intertextual Approach." *ISS* 9: 62–79.
   An intertextual analysis of Pasternak's *The Childhood of Luvers* and Dostoevsky's *Netochka Nezvanova*. Centers on the heroines' family backgrounds (Netochka's "defective socialization" and Zhenya's family's "outward intactness"), plot similarities, roles of narrators, relationships between the parental couples, the motif of the fallen woman and children's secret readings, "homoerotic features," and the theme of feminine adolescence. Concludes that "Pasternak's recapitulation of NN is selective and deals only with partial elements of the text's structural levels" and that "Pasternak's reference to Dostoevsky is disguised and can be decoded only in roundabout ways." Reprinted: 1989.17.

16 IVANOV, VIACH. VS. "Pasternak i OPOIAZ (k postanovke voprosa)" [Pasternak and OPOIAZ (toward a formulation of the question]. In *Tynianovskii sbornik. Tret'i tynianovskie chteniia*. Riga: Zinatne, pp. 70–82.
   Mentions Pasternak's attitude toward OPOIAZ (a literary association) and discusses his affinity with some of the Russian avant-garde

poets. Elaborates on Pasternak's metrical experimentations, such as his acceptance of Bely's innovations with four-foot iambics. Also mentions the influence of Severyanin on the beginning of the first version of "Marburg." Concludes that Pasternak's participation in the experiments of futurists, avant-garde poets, and OPOIAZ was "only a part of the material on which Pasternak . . . hurried to build his aesthetics."

17 ———. "'Vechnoe detstvo' Pasternaka" [Pasternak's "eternal childhood"]. In *Literatura i iskusstvo v sisteme kul'tury*, edited by B.B. Piotrovskii. Moscow: Nauka, pp. 471–80.

Surveys Pasternak's childhood and the adolescent impressions ("imprints") perpetuated in Pasternak's works—in *A Safe Conduct*; in the poems "Butterfly-Storm," "The July Thunderstorm," and "Ballad"; and in *Spektorsky*. Decodes and discusses these impressions while commenting on their intertextuality within Pasternak's works. Elaborates on Pasternak's poetics in general.

18 IVANOVA, NATAL'IA. "Smert' i voskresenie Doktora Zhivago" [Death and resurrection of Doctor Zhivago]. *Iunost'*, no. 5, pp. 78–82.

A textual interpretation of *Doctor Zhivago*—publication background, philosophical views, literary tradition, and its symbolism. Concurs with a sentence, "The truth is rarely a companion of bitterness," from *Novy mir*'s letter of *Doctor Zhivago*'s publication rejection. Perceives the novel as structured around several motifs, some of them "crossing" each other: poetry and nature, heroine's sacrificial propensity, and characters' tragical destinies. Sees in the name of Zhivago and Lara's daughter, Tatyana, a reverberation of Pushkin's Tatyana Larina. Discusses railroad symbolism ("a metaimage of inexorable Time, ignoring man") and nature symbolism ("personifying Russia and the entire history of mankind"). Mentions similarities (the notion of "people's diversity") between *Doctor Zhivago* and Grossman's *Life and Fate*. Reprinted: 1990.29.

19 JAVOR, GY. "Traktovka stikhotvorenniia Borisa Pasternaka 'Raskovannyi golos' v svete ucheniia Platonovskogo Sokrata ob erose" [Interpretation of Boris Pasternak's poem "Uninhibited Voice" in the light of what Plato's Socrates teaches about Eros]. In *Acta Universitatis Szegediensis de Attila Jozseff Nominatae. Sectio historiae litterarum Slavicae*, no. 19. Szeged: Józseff Attila Tudományegyetem Összehasonlító Pító Irodalomtudományi Tanszéke, pp. 241–54.

Analyzes the semantics of "Uninhibited Voice" within the poetics of Pasternak's *Above the Barriers*, in which it appeared, and points to Blok's motifs found in the poem. Compares the poem to the dialogue "Feast" by Plato, whose Eros teachings form the poem's "semantic basis." Establishes that the poem defines the "poetization of man's personal life," that the poem's lyrical "I" "praises the desire and creativity born in desire [and], having freed itself from the author's 'I,' strives for immortality." Concludes that all this is "in accordance with Plato's teaching," because for Plato the love in immortality and "Feast" permeates "all spheres of existence."

20 KARLAIL [CARLISLE], OL'GA. "Tri vizita k Borisu Pasternaku" [Three visits to Boris Pasternak]. *VL*, no. 3, pp. 162–82.
    Translation of 1960.4. Translation of first part of 1962.6.

21 KAVERIN, V. "B.L. Pasternak" (in Russian). In *Literator. Dnevniki i pis'ma*. Moscow: Sovetskii pisatel', pp. 183–201.
    Reprint of 1987.11.

22 KHAN, A. "Osnovnye predposylki filosofii tvorchestva B. Pasternaka v svete ego rannego esteticheskogo samo-opredeleniia" [Main premises of B. Pasternak's philosophy of creativity in the light of his early aesthetic self-determination]. In *Acta Universitatis Szegediensis de Attila Jozseff Nominatae. Slavicae*. Sectio historiae litterarum Slavicae, no. 19. Szeged: Józseff Attila Tudományegyetem Összehasonlító Pító Irodalomtudományi Tanszéke, pp. 39–127.
    Discusses criticism of Pasternak's early aesthetic views (Fleishman's, Smirnov's, Ljunggren's, Oblomievsky's, and Aroutunova's). Remarks that Pasternak's philosophy of creativity ought to be analyzed within the Russian culture of the early twentieth century. Examines early Pasternak prose works (*Letters from Tula, The Line of Apelles, The Childhood of Luvers*, and *A Safe Conduct*), his early theoretical articles and lectures (*The Wassermann Test*, "The Black Goblet," "Some Propositions," and "Symbolism and Immortality"), and his early correspondence (the letter of 23 July 1910 to Olga Freidenberg)—as programmatic works expressing aspects of Pasternak's creativity philosophy: category of quality, category of conscious, category of originality, lyrical themes as "quantité imaginaire," art as an imbibing sponge, similarity and contiguity metaphors, "mirror reflection," and concept of time. Concludes that Pasternak does not believe in a "real, effective, transforming force of art capable of recreating the reality by laws of aesthetic creativity"; the process of recreation is, rather, "in the sphere of textual reality."

23 KOLONOSKY, WALTER. "Pasternak and Proust: Towards a Comparison." *RLT*, no. 22, pp. 183–93.
    Draws parallels—on thematic, structural, imagery, stylistic, and perceptual levels—between Pasternak and Proust. Sees their kinship in their metonymy (its preference over metaphor) and in certain similarities between *Doctor Zhivago, The Tale*, and *A Safe Conduct* and *A la recherche du temps perdu*. Compares Zhivago's and Marcel's "artistic vocation" and argues that "through Marcel and Yury's perception,

architectual, musical, meteorological, pastoral, and urban images may cross into any semantic field." Cites passages from *A Safe Conduct* deemed to echo "Proustian ingredients" and Proust's views of "memory and time." Concludes "that privileged moments add up to the most important kinship between these two authors."

24 LEKIĆ, MARIA. "Pasternak's *Doctor Živago*: The Novel and Its Title." *RLJ* 42, nos. 141–43: 177–91.

Centers on five draft titles of *Doctor Zhivago* and ties them to *Doctor Zhivago*, Pasternak's other works, and Pasternak criticism. Discusses one of the titles, "The Living, Dead, and Resurrecting," within the immortality theme that is "integral to the work that evolved into *Doctor Zhivago*." Another title, "Boys and Girls," is believed to be an "allusion" to Blok's poem "Little Willows" (seen as having served as the novel's epigraph) and a part of the novel's text, notably in its chapter "The Girl from Another Circle." Links the title "A Candle Was Burning" to *Doctor Zhivago*'s prose and its poem "Winter Night" and to Pasternak's early prose works (*An Order for a Play* and "A Willow of Life"). Also discusses two additional draft titles, "Rynva" (the name of a river) and "An Experiment of a Russian Faust." Bases study on Pasternak family archival materials preserved in Moscow. Cites one draft passage from *Doctor Zhivago*.

25 LEPAKHIN, V. "Ikonopis' i zhivopis', vechnost' i vremia v 'Rozhdestvenskoi zvezde' B. Pasternaka" [Iconography and painting, eternity, and time in B. Pasternak's "Star of Nativity"]. In *Acta Universitatis Szegediensis de Attila Jozseff Nominatae*. Sectio historiae litterarum Slavicae, no. 19. Szeged: Józseff Attila Tudományegyetem Összehasonlító Pító Irodalomtudományi Tanszéke, pp. 255–75.

Analyzes the poem within its three parts. The detailing and concreting of Christmas as a historic and human event is seen as characteristic of the first part, in which Pasternak portrays the Icon with his glance directed toward the movement of the sun. Sees the second part as a philosophically lyrical digression during which the theme of eternity arises. Claims the third part reiterates the compositional plane of the first part—the shepherds go to worship the Infant and the Mother of God. Concludes that in contrast to the Icon, the poem lacks two scenes—Joseph's conversation with the shepherd and the bathing of the Infant. This is not seen as an error because Pasternak did not intend "to write a poetical version of the Nativity Icon." The Icon is but one source of inspiration, as a pre-image of "the compositional organization of the temporal and spatial layers in the poem."

26 LIKHACHEV, D.S. "Razmyshleniia nad romanom B.L. Pasternaka *Doktor Zhivago*" [Thoughts about B.L. Pasternak's *Doctor Zhivago*]. In

Vzgliad. Kritika. Polemika. Publikatsii. Moscow: Sovetskii pisatel', pp. 363–75.

An examination of *Doctor Zhivago*'s genre (a "lyrical confession, a spiritual autobiography"), characters, and ties to Tolstoy. Equates Pasternak with Zhivago ("Zhivago's poetry is Pasternak's poetry"; "Zhivago is a mouthpiece of the innermost Pasternak"), Zhivago to Antipov-Strelnikov ("not only contrasted, but compared as well"). Sees an image of Russia and life in Lara, and elaborates on the influence of Tolstoy's historic views on Pasternak. Reprinted in 1990.72.

27   LIVINGSTONE, ANGELA. "'Integral Errors': Remarks on the Writing of *Doctor Zhivago.*" *EP* 13, no. 2 (September): 83–94.

Focuses on "integral errors" in *Doctor Zhivago*, and divides them into two groups—inadvertent and deliberate. Claims that the "'motif' of mistakes" is integral to the novel and a "reflection of, the indefinite, hazy, chance-guided, vacillation and creative personality of Yury Zhivago the poet." Also examines how Pasternak "foregrounds 'mistakes'" and links these to the notion of "'metonymy' that is often associated with this writer."

28   MACKINNON, JOHN EDWARD. "Boris Pasternak's Conception of Realism." *PL* 12, no. 2 (October): 211–31.

Appeals to Pasternak's theory of art (from *A Safe Conduct*) and Iris Murdoch's *The Sovereignity of Good* to present a portrait of Pasternak's "moral realism." Claims Pasternak associates realism with "richness of content," "impressionability, collaboration with real life, seriousness, conscientiousness, and moral responsibility." Further defines Pasternak's realism as one that "documents the involvement of the attentive self with its world . . . [and] constitutes a necessary response to the implicit command of revealed order."

29   ——. "From Cold Axles to Hot: Boris Pasternak's Theory of Art." *BJA* 28, no. 2: 145–61.

Advances a definition of Pasternak's theory of art. Insists "that Pasternak *has* a theory of art"—seen as such "throughout his writings, correspondence and recorded discussions." Perceives the essence of Pasternak's theory within three categories: "movement and interaction"; "transformation and reunion"; and "naming and the lyric truth." Substantiates each category with references to Pasternak's formulations of art, Pasternak scholarship on the subject, and perceptions of art recorded in general criticism. Details Pasternak's theory of art by observing his use of metonymy ("the instrumental role of movement in Pasternak's art"), his statement "that art must aim to depict *living* reality," his "reliance on contiguity," his principle of "likening between subjective and objective worlds," and his view of the importance of love ("love is an elemental force, the very paradigm of human feeling"). Concludes that Pasternak "is most preoccupied . . . with the relation between art and feeling, art and life, art and the individual, art and humanity." Adapted from the author's thesis, "All Things Human: Pasternak on Art and the Artist," University of Exeter, 1986.

30 MAL'TSEV, IURII. "Lichnost' Borisa Pasternaka" [Boris Pasternak's personality]. *Grani* 42, no. 147: 92–142.

Attempts to characterize Pasternak's personality as reflected in Pasternak criticism, his correspondence, and memoirs. Takes issue with critics who have distorted Pasternak's image by accusing him of egoism, duplicity, and indifference to politics. Also discusses Pasternak's views on Christianity, the October Revolution, and the Soviet system. Underpins his arguments with references to facts and documents.

31 MASLENIKOVA, ZOIA. "Portret Borisa Pasternaka" [The portrait of Boris Pasternak]. *Neva*, no. 9, pp. 135–57; no. 10, pp. 130–51.

The first part is a reprint of 1978.30, with slight modifications and the addition of four entries, inclusive of 2 January 1959. The second part is a reprint of 1979.32, with slight modifications and the addition of entries up to May 1961. Both parts reprinted: 1990.43, with final modifications. The added entries detail Pasternak's funeral; eulogies; and farewell speeches delivered by his wife and two sons, his closest friends (including Tagerov, Asmus, and Richter), and others.

32 MEZHAKOV-KORIAKIN, IGOR'. "Dvoistvennost' izobrazheniia i vospriiatiia obraza Iuriia Zhivago v romane Borisa Pasternaka *Doctor Zhivago*" [Duplicity in the portrayal and perception of Yury Zhivago's image in Pasternak's novel *Doctor Zhivago*]. *SO* 37, no. 3: 443–58.

Divided into two sections—"social" and "spiritual" aspects of Zhivago—with the first section characterizing Zhivago as an egoist, an antisocial individual, a bad family man, and a "trimmer," all of which is seen to bespeak of "Zhivago's heartlessness." Insists that Zhivago's family life is "duplicitous" like his social life, that Zhivago's "demoralization and degradation progresses" with his third marriage and his disinterest in his family after their emigration to Paris, and that the death of Zhivago "rescues Pasternak from the need to correctly question the psychologically ethical problem of human destinies." The second part is a reprint (with slight changes) of 1987.14.

33 MLIKOTIN, ANTHONY M. "*Doctor Zhivago* as a Philosophical and a Poetical Novel." *ASEES* 2, no. 1: 77–88.

Reprint of 1983.21.

34 NEIGAUZ, GALINA. "O Borise Pasternake" [On Boris Pasternak]. *LiG*, no. 2, pp. 194–212.

Memoirs of Pasternak recording events from 1929 until his death—describing Pasternak as a human being, his attitude toward people, his kindness, his trust toward others, his burning desire to help others, and his work habits. Also recalls circumstances of Pasternak's telephone converstation with Stalin, the impact of events surrounding the awarding of the Nobel Prize, Pasternak's last days, and his funeral—"The coffin was carried from home to the Peredelkino cemetery. The entire road was crowded with people. Candles burned on the grave the entire night, and people stayed until the dawn."

35 NOVIKOV, V.I. "'My vovlekaem prozu v poeziiu. . . .' L. Tolstoi i B. Pasternak" ["We are drawing the prose into poetry. . . ." L. Tolstoy and B. Pasternak]. *RuR*, no. 4, pp. 20–26.

Juxtaposes Pasternak's and Tolstoy's poetics while examining intercommunication between their prose and poetry. Defines Pasternak's poetic lexica and Tolstoy's prose as a "rapid torrent," a result of their unique syntax. Believes lexical "oddities" of both authors are artistically justified.

36 O'CONNOR, KATHERINE TIERNAN. *Boris Pasternak's My Sister— Life: The Illusion of Narrative.* Ann Arbor, MI: Ardis, 208 pp.

Basically a commentary on the narrative discussed in chronological order of the poems' original appearance. The collection's epigraph, Pasternak's "composite creation," is textually linked through Lenau (his image of an artist), Goethe (his *Faust*'s Helen of Troy), and Lermontov (his tragi-romantic hero of *The Demon*) to the rest of the collection. Themes, certain lexica, circular patterns and models, metaphors, ellipses, images, allusions, illusions, motifs, parallels (with Genesis, Gogol's *The Terrible Vengeance*, and *The Igor Tale*, for example), echoes (including Hamlet), diversions, the poet's "imitations" and his pursuits, and definitions (poetry, the soul, and creativity, among others) are all singled out, linked to, or dovetailed within the collection's chapters, their headings, and the poems. Includes ten chapters, a preface, an introduction, a conclusion, and notes. Reprint (with modifications) of 1978.33.

37 PASTERNAK, E.V., and E.B. PASTERNAK. "Iz perepiski Borisa Pasternaka s Andreem Belym" [From Boris Pasternak's and Andrei Bely's correspondence]. In *Andrei Belyi. Problemy tvorchestva*, compiled by St. Lesnevskii and A.L. Mikhailov. Moscow: Sovetskii pistael', pp. 686–706.

Surveys Pasternak's and Bely's friendship as reflected in their correspondence, encounters, and works—from 1904 ("I was poisoned with the latest literature, I was mad on Andrei Bely") until Bely's death in 1934, when Pasternak cosigned a Bely eulogy, declaring himself a Bely disciple. Contains five of Pasternak's letters to Bely, three to K.N. Bugaeva (Bely's widow), and two of Bely's letters to Pasternak.

38 PASTERNAK, E.V., and M.K. POLIVANOV. "Vtorzhenie voli v sud'bu. Pis'ma Borisa Pasternaka o sozdanii romana 'Doktor Zhivago'"

[The intrusion of will into fate. Boris Pasternak's letters about the creation of *Doctor Zhivago*]. *LO*, no. 5, pp. 97–107.

Discusses Pasternak's letters to N. Ia. Mandelstam, N.A. Tabidze, M.K. Baranovich, S.I. Chikovani, and L.A. Voskresenskaia. Annotates the letters and adds new information about the completion of *Doctor Zhivago* and about Pasternak's life after the publication of the novel: his expulsion from the Writers' Union, his persecution by the Soviet media, the forced refusal of the Nobel Prize, threats of citizenship revocation, and forcible expulsion from the country.

39   PISKUNOVA, S., and V. PISKUNOV. Review (in Russian) of *Doctor Zhivago*. *LO*, no. 8, pp. 48–54.

Makes general observations on the novel, the meaning of history seen as a "history-eternity," for example, and details the immortality theme, characterizing the major protagonists and discussing the novel's metamorphosis and the problem of space and time. Draws parallels to Trifonov's *Time and Place* and Zalygin's *After the Storm*. Concludes that *Doctor Zhivago* is a novel "ending an epoch and not announcing it."

40   RANCOUR-LAFERRIERE, DANIEL. "Linguistic and Folkloristic Notes on Pasternak's 'Khmel'.'" *CASS*, nos. 1–4, pp. 157–62.

A textual analysis (including language and metrical structure) of the poem "Hopbine." Details the poem's sexual undertones, resorts to the use of hopbine in Russian folk songs, and cites such a song. Quotes Ivinskaya's and Akhmatova's reactions to "Hopbine" to further allege the poem's "sexual message."

41   SALYS, RIMGAILA. "Boris Pasternak on Leonid Pasternak and the Critics: Two Early Texts." *RLJ* 42, nos. 141–43: 147–68.

Surveys in detail the relationship between Pasternak and his father, Leonid Pasternak, as recorded in their correspondence (some of which is published in this work for the first time) and in criticism. Finds that their relationship was "unusually close," that Pasternak viewed his father as a role model, that he saw in his father's works "an aesthetic which significantly paralleled his own emerging credo," that in their correspondence Pasternak often evaluated "himself" when discussing his father's works, that "like his father, Pasternak came to draw his inspiration from life itself," and that in their correspondence two leitmotifs emerge—"youthfulness vs. premature aging." Establishes the date of a Pasternak manuscript preserved in the Josephine Pasternak Archives (Oxford, Engand). Cites unpublished Pasternak correspondence and manuscripts.

42   SIMMONS, CYNTHIA. "An Autobiography for the Twentieth Century: Pasternak's *Oxrannaja gramota*." *RLJ* 42, nos. 141–43: 169–75.

Surveys criticism of Pasternak's *A Safe Conduct* (Pomorska, Aucouturier, and Fleishman). Discusses the autobiography genre as it applies to *A Safe Conduct.* Concludes that not only the style, the philosophical quality, and the displacement of the autobiographical subject determine the genre of *A Safe Conduct* but the "revelation itself" as well. The latter is seen in the articulation of "man's realization of self, of the 'Absolute,' and ultimately, of the community of man, by means of art." Elaborates on Pasternak's views of art as "the vehicle for fellowship between men and for communion with God." Concludes that *A Safe Conduct* is "an important representative autobiography of the twentieth century."

43 SZOKE, KATALIN. "'Nazyvanie' i 'naimenovanie' v 'Detstve Liuvers' B. Pasternaka" ["Naming" and "appellation" in B. Pasternak's *The Childhood of Luvers*]. In *Acta Universitatis Szegediensis de Attila Jozseff Nominatae.* Sectio historiae litterarum Slavicae, no. 19. Szeged: Józseff Attila Tudományegyetem Összehasonlító Pító Irodalomtudományi Tanszéke, pp. 29–38.

Argues that *The Childhood of Luvers* does not focus on the coming of age and upbringing but on the "artistic awakening" of the heroine, Zhenya, in an "impersonal world," and that naming and appelation, the major issues of the tale, are beyond the realm of the personality "question." Thus, by creating a ring-type composition of the tale, naming and appellation play a central role in the tale's first and last scenes. Sees this as a reason why everything meaningful to Zhenya has no name, and if it is named, it abandons "the kingdom of poetry." Explains that Zhenya frequently cries because she fears the impersonalness and is the "third person," not a doer, but an instrument of external and internal circumstances. Contends that naming of the tale's characters is in itself a "source of paradoxicality"; for example, Zhenya remembers the name of an English woman who "has not left the vestige" in Zhenya's life, but does not remember the name of the French woman who "was the source of her emotions." Sees the uniqueness of naming in its "strangeness," "alienness," and "foreignness," like Zhenya's last name or the name of her brother, all of which are seen to underline the fact of impersonalness. Concludes that Pasternak let the name speak in its full "strangeness" and that the problem of naming is tied to the appearance of "objective, twentieth-century lyric poetry reflecting perception in the world."

44 URNOV, DMITRII. "'Bezumnoe prevyshenie svoikh sil. O romane B. Pasternaka 'Doktor Zhivago'" [A senseless exceeding of one's powers. On B. Pasternak's *Doctor Zhivago*]. *Pravda*, no. 322 (27 April): 3.

Believes that Pasternak felt "historically obliged to express himself on a subject already drained"—on individualism for the intelligentsia. Finds contradictions in *Doctor Zhivago*: (1) for a certain group of people "Zhivago is a mind and talent incarnate," yet nothing from his life remains in one's memory; (2) with a description of the battle scene in the taiga during which Zhivago "unwillingly shoots and accidentally kills and believes that after this he should be pitied"; (3) in the fact that Zhivago despises revolutionaries for their cruelty and asks himself: "Why did I kill him?" never recalling that in the future; and (4) in his relationship with women Zhivago shows heartlessness behind his pretentious language, and Zhivago's poetry is "not better and not deeper than his views." Reprinted in 1990.72.

45 VOZDVIZHENSKII, VIACHESLAV. "Proza dukhovnogo opyta" [Prose of spiritual experience]. *VL*, no. 9, pp. 82–103.

Praises *Doctor Zhivago* for its rebirth of the "value of man's existence" and offers observations on the novel's structure (seen as determined by "a strong lyrical dominant") and its treatment of the Revolution, among others. Argues that Zhivago's attitude toward the Revolution is the novel's epicenter and that Pasternak's contradictory interpretations of the Revolution (i.e., that one's life cannot be changed "by outside efforts" and that the Revolution was "a miracle of history") should be understood as a virtue and not as a weakness.

46 VOZNESENSKY, ANDREI. "Svecha i metel'" [Candle and snowstorm]. *Pravda*, no. 158 (6 June): 4.

Sees *Doctor Zhivago* as poetical, "a novel about how one lives by verses and how the verses are born from life." Notes that the novel "cannot be read objectively today" because of the lies and invectives that have accompanied the novel for many years. Responds to Dmitry Urnov (1988.44), who saw Zhivago as "a second degree poet," by saying that Urnov cannot but know that "the novel is written as a metaphoric autobiography." Concludes that one can judge the novel from various angles, "but one has to enter the world of genius, like a temple, with trepidation." Reprinted in 1990.72.

1989

1 ARUTIUNOVA, BAIARA. "Zvuk kak tematicheskii motiv v poeticheskoi sisteme Pasternaka" [Sound as a thematic motif in Pasternak's poetic system]. In *Boris Pasternak and His Times. Selected Papers from the Second International Symposium on Pasternak*, edited by Lazar Fleishman. Modern Russian Literature and Culture. Studies and Texts, no. 25. Berkeley, CA: Berkeley Slavic Specialties, pp. 238–70.

Defines the role of sound as a thematic motif in Pasternak's poetic system and claims that four sound themes prevail in Pasternak's poetry: man/crowd, creativity/absence of creativity, harmony/absence of harmony, and love/absence of love. Also mentions other sound motifs and theories—a city with its streets, shapes, and railroad stations; houses with their windows, doors, and stairs; earth; and sky. Demonstrates the use of sounds as thematic motifs in a variety of poems: "February," "Inspiration," "Courtyard," "Balashov," "A Disease," "Winter," "Marburg," "Mirror," "About These Verses," "Spring Rain," "The End," "Stuffy Night," and "Happiness," for example. Underlines that Pasternak was a poet of nature and that nature was a "total world" of his work. Concludes that sound motifs are an integral part of his poetry, that Pasternak opts for particular sound themes by contiguity and similarity associations, and that his "concept of amalgamation of everything with everything justifies the most unexpected shifts and options of poetic tropes."

2   AUCOUTURIER, MICHEL. "Pasternak et la révolution française." *CMRS* 30, nos. 3–4: 181–91.
Discusses literary and historical sources for Pasternak's *Dramatic Fragments* (1917), focusing on two scenes that symbolize two aspects of the French Revolution. Sees portraits of Robespierre and Saint Just depicted as symbols in *Dramatic Fragments*. Draws parallels between *Dramatic Fragments* and Pushkin's *Little Tragedies*.

3   BAEVSKII, V.S. "Pushkin i Pasternak. K postanovke problemy" [Pushkin and Pasternak. Towards formulating the problem] *IAN* 48, no. 3: 231–43.
Centers on major links of Pasternak's affinity with Pushkin, such as 10 February—the anniversary of Pushkin's death and Pasternak's birthday. Surveys in detail Pasternak-Pushkin literary criticism (Bryusov, Parnok, Krasilnikov, Chumakov, Rozanov, Mirsky, Lezhnev, and Zelinsky, among others), and discusses similarities noted by critics between *Spektorsky* and *Eugene Onegin*. Also observes that Pasternak has frequently adopted Puskin's themes, motifs, and images, and that his *Themes and Variations* collection is the "most conspicuous example of it." Adds that Pasternak has produced two "large novels" plus *The Tale*, in which "poetry and prose are combined" (*Spektorsky* and *Doctor Zhivago*), and that "Pasternak became a bridge connecting Soviet poets with a Pushkin tradition."

4   BARNES, CHRISTOPHER. *Boris Pasternak. A Literary Biography*. Vol. 1, *1890–1928*. Cambridge: Cambridge University Press, 508 pp.
A detailed chronological account of Pasternak's life from his birth in 1890 through 1928 and an analysis of his works during that period—the first four poetry collections, all early prose, and three tales in verse. Adds valuable information on many details of Pasternak's life and works hitherto ignored by critics and scholars. Draws on other Pasternak biographies, archive material, correspondence (published and unpublished), Pasternak criticism (scrupulously examined), memoirs and diaries, Pasternak's works, and on encounters with individuals who met and knew Pasternak. Elaborates on Pasternak's affinity with his literary

peers—Tsvetaeva, Mayakovsky, Akhmatova, Aseyev, Blok, Kuzmin, Zamyatin, Bryusov, Bely, Lili Khorozova, Gorky, and Rilke, among others. Concludes that Pasternak's life and works had during that period changed from being "rooted in nature, family, art, and private experience" into "becoming increasingly and inescapably bound up with human affairs and history." Includes fourteen chapters, notes, a bibliography, an index, and a list of illustrations.

5 ———. "Notes on Pasternak." In *Boris Pasternak and His Times. Selected Papers from the Second International Symposium on Pasternak*, edited by Lazar Fleishman. Modern Russian Literature and Culture. Studies and Texts, no. 25. Berkeley, CA: Berkeley Slavic Specialties, pp. 398–413.

An explication of Pasternak's love for Elena Vinograd, and an account of Pasternak's lost prose works. Claims that in relation to Pasternak's other "amorous attachments," Vinograd, "in terms of the number of verses she inspired, ... emerges as the most important of four." Cites some of Pasternak's writings that reveal his feelings toward Vinograd (from *My Sister, Life* and *Doctor Zhivago*). Believes that the conclusion of the relationship was for Pasternak "as protracted and painful as it was artistically fruitful." Identifies prose works that were or are lost, excluded by Pasternak, or unpublished. Discusses a children's fairy tale, *The Tale of the Carp and Naphttalain*, and Pasternak's comments on *The Line of Apelles*, which reveal "how close the genres of verse and prose were for Pasternak."

6 BELENCHIKOV, V. "Lirika nemetskikh ekspressionistov v russkikh perervodakh (B. Pasternaka, Vl. Neishtadta, S. Tartakovera)" [Lyrics of German expressionists in Russian translations (of B. Pasternak, Vl. Neishtadt, and S. Tartakover)]. *ZeS* 34, no. 5: 692–708.

Examines translations of nine German expressionists (Rubiner, Lichtenstein, Leongard, Heym, Hoddis [Hans Davidsohn], Hasenclever, Wolfenstein, Werfel, and Becher) that Pasternak did during 1924–1925 and makes observations on Pasternak's "art of translation." Notes that Pasternak's renditions are "free"; that he did not retain the original's rhyme, lexica, tone, and even stanzas; and that he paid attention to rhymes that he used for sound instrumentation, melodiousness, and musicality. Adds that Blok influenced Pasternak as a translator.

7 BIRNBAUM, HENRIK. "Further Reflections on the Poetics of *Doktor Živago*: Structure, Technique, and Symbolism." In *Boris Pasternak and His Times. Selected Papers from the Second International Symposium on Pasternak*, edited by Lazar Fleishman. Modern Russian Literature and Culture. Studies and Texts, no. 25. Berkeley, CA: Berkeley Slavic Specialties, pp. 284–314.

A reexamination of the poetics of *Doctor Zhivago* (structure, genre, imagery, and style) and a comparison of the novel to Mann's

Doktor Faustus and Akhmatova's *A Poem Without a Hero*. Discusses in detail the relationship between the novel's prose and poems, and asserts that the poems are aesthetically the "most significant and successful section of the book as a whole rather than as merely 'preliminary steps toward the novel,' which is how the poet himself obviously viewed them." Puts forth the statement that "Pasternak's poetically embellished story is neither a novel nor a poem." Provides a history of the "metonymy/metaphor distinction" criticism about *Doctor Zhivago*. Repeats or reexamines some views previously expounded (1984.3).

8 BORISOV, VADIM, and EVGENI PASTERNAK. "The History of Boris Pasternak's Novel 'Doctor Zhivago.'" *SL* 2, no. 491: 137–50.
      Abridged translation of 1988.4.

9 CONQUEST, ROBERT. "Pasternak and *Doctor Zhivago*." In *Tyrants and Typewriters. Communiqués From the Struggle for Truth*. Lexington, MA: D.C. Heath and Co., pp. 49–56.
      Discusses Pasternak's pronouncements on art, notably as they apply to *Doctor Zhivago*—including the notion of suffering, attachment to Russia, and the rate-of-coincidences device. Takes issue with criticism of *Doctor Zhivago* (for example, with Philip Toynbee's interpretation of Lara). Insists that in Pasternak's "poetry, too, the formal, structual aspect receives the utmost stress," and that Pasternak "commonly observes his own dictum that rhyme is 'the entrance ticket' to poetry." Cites passages from Pasternak's correspondence written in English.

10 ENDRIUS, E. [ANDREWS, E.] "'Lingvistika i poetika' i interpretatsiia teksta: 'Zimniaia noch' Pasternaka" [*Linguistics and Poetics* and text interpretation: Pasternak's "Winter Night"]. In *VLGU* 4, no. 23: 89–97.
      Applies principles of textual interpretation from Roman Jakobson's *Linguistics and Poetics* to the analysis of the poetics of Pasternak's poem "Winter Night." Discusses the poem's lexical phenomena (the use of imperfective verbs only, for example), metric structure (four-foot and two-foot iambics), stanzaic structure, the concept of inside and outside world, and imagery (metaphor, metonyms, and synecdoches), among other aspects.

11 ERLICH, VICTOR. "Boris Pasternak and Russian Poetic Culture of His Time." In *Boris Pasternak and His Times. Selected Papers from the Second International Symposium on Pasternak*, edited by Lazar Fleishman. Modern Russian Literature and Culture. Studies and Texts, no. 25. Berkeley, CA: Berkeley Slavic Specialties, pp. 32–45.
      A chronological study of Pasternak's affiliations with and adherence to literary schools. Denies the validity of attributing "the Futurist label to any significant body of his verse" because Pasternak lacks "ideational extremism." Sees the "eternal" themes such as love and

nature as prevalent over the "temporal" ones of politics. Believes that Pasternak's position shows his "keen sense . . . of mounting pressures toward political regimentation of literature." Defines Pasternak's later literature as "striving for maximal directness of communication . . . to bear witness . . . to the world." Describes Pasternak as a romantic with the emphasis on "self-transcendence" and "language rather than on inspiration."

12 FARYNO, JERZY. *Poetika Pasternaka* ("Putevye zapiski"— "Okhrannaia gramota") [Pasternak's poetics ("Travel Notes"—*A Safe Conduct*)]. Wiener slawistischer Almanach. Sonderband, no. 22. Vienna: Gesellschaft zur Förderung slawistischer Studien, 322 pp.

A textual, contextual, and intertextual study of Pasternak's poetry cycle "Travel Notes." Thoroughly analyzes each of the thirteen poems to define major poetic principles of a given poem and of Pasternak's poetics in general. Singles out referential lexical units and motifs in the poems and relates them to identical referents in Pasternak's works. Elaborates on intertextuality of numerous motifs, tracing them through a poem, the cycle, and other works by Pasternak. Thus, compares *A Safe Conduct* or contrasts a candle motif in "Incessant Splash of Salts" against candle symbolism in *Doctor Zhivago* poems, notably in "Winter Night." Strongly argues that a definition of Pasternak's poetics hinges on the interconnectedness between the poetics of Pasternak's singular work and the poetics of the whole.

13 FLEISHMAN, LAZAR. "Pasternak and Bukharin in the 1930s." In *Boris Pasternak and His Times. Selected Papers from the Second International Symposium on Pasternak*, edited by Lazar Fleishman. Modern Russian Literature and Culture. Studies and Texts, no. 25. Berkeley, CA: Berkeley Slavic Specialties, pp. 171–88.

Focuses on Pasternak's relation with Bukharin and his "about-face in accepting Soviet reality." Claims two reasons account for the change: conditions and events in Germany, and the desire for "liberalization inside Soviet Russia." Attempts to recreate and interpret the political events of the period, and brings Mayakovsky, Mandelstam, and Stalin into the discussion. Strongly argues that Pasternak was a leading figure in the liberalization of Soviet literature between 1934 and 1936, and that his "passionate involvement" in the literary issues of the time "explain many of the actions and statements which today seem so enigmatic and so inconsistent with the later utterances of the author of *Doctor Zhivago*."

14 GASPAROV, BORIS. "Vremennoi kontrapunkt kak formoobrazuiushchii printsip romana Pasternaka 'Doktor Zhivago'" [Temporal counterpoint as a compositional principle in Pasternak's novel *Doctor Zhivago*]. In *Boris Pasternak and His Times. Selected Papers from the*

Second International Symposium on Pasternak, edited by Lazar Fleishman. Modern Russian Literature and Culture. Studies and Texts, no. 25. Berkeley, CA: Berkeley Slavic Specialties, pp. 315–58.

A detailed analysis of *Doctor Zhivago's* poetics that centers on temporal counterpoint as a compositional principle. Examines the novel's concerted/polyphonic compositional principle, and "timbre" compositions. Finds that temporal counterpoint has two basic forms: a simpler and a more developed one. In the former, an uneven, inconstant rhythm is attached to a series of events (similar to the novel's train movement); in the latter, a combination of series of events, moving with a different speed, a different rhythm, and in a different direction takes place (analogous to the polyphony of a railway junction). Also discusses the novel's composition as a whole—the multitude of language strata, time, and semantic rhythm—in both the prose and poetry sections. Concludes that *Doctor Zhivago* is a novel of "religious searches and pluralization of scientific and artistic thinking," and "of an era of violating unshakeable norms" and "social catastrophes."

15 GIFFORD, HENRY. "Pasternak and His Western Contemporaries." In *Boris Pasternak and His Times. Selected Papers from the Second International Symposium on Pasternak*, edited by Lazar Fleishman. Modern Russian Literature and Culture. Studies and Texts, no. 25. Berkeley, CA: Berkeley Slavic Specialties, pp. 13–31.

Seeks to determine Pasternak's position "in the broad stream of European or Western culture, . . . Pasternak's attitude to art, and the nature and origin of his singularity." Focuses on Pasternak's stay in Marburg and his association with Rilke to show Pasternak's relation to European culture. Uses Edmund Wilson's criticism and Faulkner's works to establish links between Pasternak and America. Also draws upon Tolstoy, Mandelstam, Mann, Eliot, Mayakovsky, Blok, Scriabin, Tsvetaeva, Nietzsche, and Proust to explicate Pasternak's work. Discusses Pasternak's relation with the Russian futurist and modernist schools. Lauds *Doctor Zhivago* for looking "to the future as none of these others do."

16 GIRZHEVA, G.N. "Stikhotvorenie B. Pasternaka 'Edinstvennye dni'" [B. Pasternak's poem "The Unique Days"]. *RIaSh*, no. 4, pp. 63–65.

A lexical and structural study of "The Unique Days." Sees the poem as divided into two segments, with the first two stanzas introducing the theme and the remaining three unfolding it. Explains contextual significance of the lexica, emphasizing the anaphoric links that bond "the poem's lines into a single semantic whole." Notes the absence of similes and the poem's lexical simplicity (no "words needed a linguistic interpretation"), and concludes that the "poem's expressiveness is not achieved by abundance of lexical means but by an unexpected unification of the most simple, familiar words."

17 GREBER, ERIKA. *Intertextualität und Interpretierbarkeit des Texts. Zur frühen Prosa Boris Pasternaks.* Theorie und Geschichte der Literatur und der schönen Künste. Reihe C., Ästhetik, Kunst und Literatur in der Geschichte der Neuzeit, no. 8. Munich: Wilhelm Fink Verlag, 314 pp.

An intertextual and contextual analysis of Pasternak's *The Childhood of Luvers, Three Chapters from the Tale,* and *The Tale.* Focuses on literary, historical, religious (including the Bible), musical, philosophical, psychological, anthropological, and lexical text interpretations. Contrasts *The Childhood of Luvers* with Dostoevsky's *Netochka Nezvanova* and decodes Dostoevsky's echoes in *The Childhood of Luvers* (see 1988.15). Traces the "prostitute motif" ("in the Russian line from Gogol to Kuprin") in *The Tale* and alludes to "Chekhov-Dostoevsky-Tolstoy" "intertextual" metaphors ("national symbols," for example). Discusses philosophical and musical implications in *Three Chapters from the Tale* and ties it to *The Lay of Igor's Campaign.* Concludes that Pasterank's dependency on *Netochka Nezvanova* is "selective," and that Pasternak's poetics of intertextuality could be defined as a "metonymic system." Provides an exhaustive bibliography on the subject and appends Pasternak's two-page text, "Severianin iavliaetsia v Odessu" [Severyanin appears in Odessa]. Chapter 1 is a reprint of 1988.15.

18 GROSSMAN, JOAN DELANEY. "Variations on the Theme of Puškin in Pasternak and Brjusov." In *Boris Pasternak and His Times. Selected Papers from the Second International Symposium on Pasternak,* edited by Lazar Fleishman. Modern Russian Literature and Culture. Studies and Texts, no. 25. Berkeley, CA: Berkeley Slavic Specialties, pp. 121–40.

Looks at "the relationship between Pasternak and Brjusov" and examines their two poems, Pasternak's "To Valery Yakovlevich Bryusov" and Bryusov's "Variations on the Theme of 'Bronze Horseman.'" Claims that these poems point to a previous dialogue between Pasternak and Bryusov, that Pasternak improved his vision of Pushkin "with images far beyond Brjusov's repertoire," and that "for both Puškin was a sign of what they valued most highly in art: individuality, dynamism, creative freedom." Concludes that Bryusov communicated to Pasternak the difficulties involved when long-held personal ideals came into conflict with internal and external forces of Pasternak's [or any other poet's] life.

19 HUGHES, ROBERT P. "Nabokov Reading Pasternak." In *Boris Pasternak and His Times. Selected Papers from the Second International Symposium on Pasternak,* edited by Lazar Fleishman. Modern Russian Literature and Culture. Studies and Texts, no. 25. Berkeley, CA: Berkeley Slavic Specialties, pp. 153–70.

An assessment of Nabokov's interpretation of *Doctor Zhivago*—based on sentences and marginal notes "sprinkled throughout" Nabokov's copy of an English translation of the novel. Divides Nabokov's comments into "the translation," "stylistic observations," "political ideology," "the Jewish question, and the novel's religiosity." Claims that disagreements Nabokov had with *Doctor Zhivago* "are profound" and "both aesthetic and ideological." Argues that in "some respect, however, Nabokov was a poor reader, and he confuses the author and his hero." Concludes that given Nabokov's personal and historical outlook "it is not surprising that Nabokov found *Doctor Zhivago* unacceptable as a work of art."

20   HUGHES-RAEVSKY, OLGA. "O samoubiistve Maiakovskogo v *Okhrannoi gramote* Pasternaka" [On Mayakovsky's suicide in Pasternak's *A Safe Conduct*]. In *Boris Pasternak and His Times. Selected Papers from the Second International Symposium on Pasternak*, edited by Lazar Fleishman. Modern Russian Literature and Culture. Studies and Texts, no. 25. Berkeley, CA: Berkeley Slavic Specialties, pp. 141–52.

Examines Pasternak's views of Mayakovsky and his suicide as described in *A Safe Conduct*. Remarks that Pasternak describes Mayakovsky "in motion" (a desire to capture the "dynamysm" of a Mayakovsky-futurist), and that Pasternak portrays Mayakovsky's death "directly," including detailed descriptions of weather, nature, and people—their impressions and experiences. Identifies "rupture-breaking-off" occurrences (Pasternak's rupture with "music and philosophy," for example) as a sort of "suicide," an experience leading to Pasternak's creative maturity ("emphasizing the youth of Mayakovsky in his death, Pasternak meant . . . an eternal youth of art. . . . Speaking about the poet's last year in *A Safe Conduct*, Pasternak asks . . . : 'Then this is not second birth? So this is death?'"). Adds that *A Safe Conduct* contains "still another biographical 'concurrence-non-concurrence' between the two poets—an opposite solution to the question of death and immortality."

21   IUNGGREN, ANNA. "'Sad' i 'Ia sam': Smysl i kompozitsiia stikhotvoreniia 'Zerkalo'" ["Garden" and "I Myself": Sense and composition of the poem "Mirror"]. In *Boris Pasternak and His Times. Selected Papers from the Second International Symposium on Pasternak*, edited by Lazar Fleishman. Modern Russian Literature and Culture. Studies and Texts, no. 25. Berkeley, CA: Berkeley Slavic Specialties, pp. 244–37.

Contrasts three versions (1920, 1922, and 1957) of "Mirror," centering on Pasternak's principles of perception and the poem's "semantic gist." Applies Pasternak's artistic views (from "Some Propositions" and *A Safe Conduct*) to her analysis. Sees the poem's structure as divided into three segments: "Garden," "Mirror," and "I Myself." Thinks that the first version's title "I Myself" bespeaks "elements of poetic self-portrait," and that the poem's second version (1922) is "the most extensive." Adds that the poem reflects Pasternak's common poetics of a combination of a most diverse story with a story "about himself." Concludes that the poem also reads as a "succession of mirror reflection extending into an illusory depth."

22 KARLINSKII, SEMEN [KARLINSKY, SIMON]. "Pasternak, Pushkin i okean v poeme Mariny Tsvetaevoi 'S moria'" [Pasternak, Pushkin and the ocean in Marina Tsvetaeva's poem "From the Sea"]. In *Boris Pasternak and His Times. Selected Papers from the Second International Symposium on Pasternak*, edited by Lazar Fleishman. Modern Russian Literature and Culture. Studies and Texts, no. 25. Berkeley, CA: Berkeley Slavic Specialties, pp. 46–57.

An attempt to reveal yet-undetected features of Pasternak's affinity with Tsvetaeva. Contrasts Pasternak's "Theme with Variations" and Tsvetaeva's "A Meeting with Pushkin," which is deemed grossly inferior to Pasternak's poem. Equates the image of "objects washed away by the sea" in Tsvetaeva's "From the Sea" with *Doctor Zhivago*'s passage describing additional features of Lara's image. Elaborates on Pasternakian images in "From the Sea."

23 LILLY, IAN K. "Binary vs. Ternary in the Early Lyrics of Pasternak." *In Boris Pasternak and His Times. Selected Papers from the Second International Symposium on Pasternak*, edited by Lazar Fleishman. Modern Russian Literature and Culture. Studies and Texts, no. 25. Berkeley, CA: Berkeley Slavic Specialties, pp. 271–83.

An examination of final-consonant truncation in "masculine, or one-syllable, rhymes" and "feminine, or two-syllable, rhymes." Shows that "this rhyme type is encountered more often in Pasternak's ternary measures than in his binary." Constructs three tables: the "Frequency of Final Consonant Truncation in Feminine Rhyme Pair Binary and Ternary Lyrics in Perfect AbAb Quatrains," the "Mean Syllable Count of Key Part of Speech Binary and Ternary Lyrics in Perfect AbAb Quatrains," and the "Verbs and Adjectives by Number of Syllables Early Binary and Ternary AbAb Lyrics." Claims that this analysis offers "objective criteria for discriminating between the early (1912–28) and later (1928–59) lyric canons."

24 LIVINGSTONE, ANGELA. *Boris Pasternak. Doctor Zhivago.* Cambridge: Cambridge University Press, 118 pp.

An overview study of *Doctor Zhivago*, including a thorough survey of its criticism, composition (presented chronologically, and with "time-distortion" devices, among others), themes and motifs, bonds with Pasternak's early prose (*The Line of Apelles*, *The Childhood of Luvers*, *Aerial Ways*, *The Tale*, and *A Safe Conduct*), characters, the poetry section, the Rilke connection, and the novel's style; groups characters (active versus passive, for example) and discusses their similarities and differences. Takes issue with the novel's English translators and registers their errors.

25 MALMSTAD, JOHN E. "Binary Oppositions: The Case of Xodasevič and Pasternak." In *Boris Pasternak and His Times. Selected Papers from*

the Second International Symposium on Pasternak, edited by Lazar Fleishman. Modern Russian Literature and Culture. Studies and Texts, no. 25. Berkeley, CA: Berkeley Slavic Specialties, pp. 91–120.

An examination of the relationship between Pasternak and Khodasevich and an evaluation of Khodasevich's criticism of Pasternak. Centers on Khodasevich's criticism of Pasternak's "overuse of metaphor, incomprehensibility, excessive complexity (for its own sake), and deliberate obscurity masking a fundamental emptiness." Asserts that Khodasevich did not consider Pasternak to be following the literary tradition of Pushkin, and that this is at the "roots of this crisis in a general decline of culture." Claims that Khodasevich also objected to Pasternak's close affiliation with futurism. Concludes that Pasternak's later work would have appealed to Khodasevich. Translated: 1990.41.

26 MASING-DELIC, I. "Capitalist Bread and Socialist Spectacle: The Janus Face of 'Rome' in Pasternak's *Doctor Zhivago*." In *Boris Pasternak and His Times. Selected Papers from the Second International Symposium on Pasternak*, edited by Lazar Fleishman. Modern Russian Literature and Culture. Studies and Texts, no. 25. Berkeley, CA: Berkeley Slavic Specialties, pp. 372–85.

Explores the meaning of "historical allegory" in *Doctor Zhivago*. Asserts that the novel represents capitalism and socialism through the "historical models which Roman history has to offer." Links Pasternak to Fedorov's *Philosophy of the Common Task*—seen to concentrate "on the Roman Janus-Face of history." Analyzes allegorically Komarovsky, Antipov, Zhivago, and Lara and makes comparisons to Blok's *The Twelve* and Dostoevsky's *Spanish Legend*. Concludes that "steeped in 'spectacle' as Socialist Rome is, it cannot deal with reality."

27 MOSSMAN, ELLIOTT. "Toward a Poetics of the Novel *Doctor Zhivago*: The Fourth Typhus." In *Boris Pasternak and His Times. Selected Papers from the Second International Symposium on Pasternak*, edited by Lazar Fleishman. Modern Russian Literature and Culture. Studies and Texts, no. 25. Berkeley, CA: Berkeley Slavic Specialties, pp. 386–97.

Attempts to define the meaning of the "fourth typhus" in *Doctor Zhivago* ("Zhivago's first bout with typhus is an instance of the disease raised to the level of metaphor, his second encounter is with the metaphorical disease itself, the fourth typhus") and its consequent connection to the fourth horseman of the Apocalypse and the Revelation. Believes that "the dislocation of both temporal and spatial unity in connection with typhus strengthens the association with the apocalyptic literary tradition." Claims the "Elizabethan concept of sleep and death contributes to the condition of the fourth typhus," and through this determines that "catachresis—sleep is the death of recurring life"—is central to the poetics of *Doctor Zhivago*. Incorporates the nightingale motif into the "typhus metaphor." Insists "that the metaphor *simple* is not the basis of Pasternak's poetics"; rather, it is catachresis.

28 PASTERNAK, E. *Boris Pasternak. Materialy dlia biografii* [Boris Pasternak. Texts for the biography]. Moscow: Sovetskii pisatel', 686 pp.

A comprehensive biography of Pasternak that chronicles events and includes a detailed commentary on the background of Pasternak's works—"how the life was materialized into an artistic transformation." Based on close readings of all Pasternak's works (in published and unpublished drafts), his correspondence (some of which is published in this work for the first time), memoirs and comments of his contemporaries, and on the author's personal observations and experiences. Throws much light on copious aspects of Pasternak's works and literary views, on Pasternak as the man, and on his relationship with his peers (notably Tsvetaeva, Mayakovsky, and Akhmatova). Offers criticism of Pasternak's works—including "the gist of *The Childhood of Luvers* is the formation of conscience", and "Tolstoyan nonacceptance of violence and cruelty . . . found its total incarnation in the novel." Sums up Pasternak's view of his life as a "one-man struggle against the prevailing and triumphant tackiness for man's free and active talent." Divided into nine chapters, five of which are named after Pasternak's works: *Above the Barriers*; *My Sister, Life*; *Second Birth*; *Doctor Zhivago*; and *When the Skies Clear*. Includes illustrations—some of which are published in this work for the first time.

29 ——. "'Russkaia revoliutsiia.' Neizvestnye stikhi Borisa Pasternaka" ["The Russian Revolution." Boris Pasternak's unpublished poem]. *NM*, no. 4, pp. 131–34.

Surveys revolutionary motifs deemed abundantly present in Pasternak's works—notably in "High Malady" and *Doctor Zhivago*. Cites Pasternak's "The Russian Revolution"—hitherto unpublished—and comments elaborately on the poem, placing it within Pasternak's works on the Revolution. Also cites a passage from Pasternak's letter (dated 1927) to the poet Obradovich: "I am used to seeing in the October Revolution a chemical peculiarity of our air, a chaos and element of our historic day," which is said to have been realized toward the end of *Doctor Zhivago* ("where changes of an artistic image in the creativity process of a live, rhythmic form are discussed").

30 ROLL, SERAFIMA. "Writing One's Self: Boris Pasternak's Autobiography *Ochrannaja Gramota*." *RuL* 26, no. 3: 407–16.

Examines the role of the narrator in *A Safe Conduct*, and sees that role as "displacement of reality"—by "feelings" and "consciousness perception." Discusses three descriptions of Marburg (in *A Safe Conduct*) in order to exemplify the process of creating the nonreferential meaning of proper names, a process identified as "the poetics of Modernism."

Concludes that "the process of writing in *Ochrannaja gramota* is intricately linked with the creation of non-referential meaning of proper names that constitute the fictional nature of the autobiography. Thus the creation of the fictional world of the work reflects the self-created image of the author."

31 SHANSKII, N.M. "Sredi poetisheskikh strok B.L. Pasternaka" [Amid B.L. Pasternak's poetic lines]. *RIaSh*, no. 6 (November/December): 60–64.

A study of Pasternak's language—syntax and lexica—that demonstrates that, contrary to some critics' views, it is not difficult and artificial; rather, it is easy to comprehend, except for imagery demanding an occasional "linguistic commentary." Notes that only a small number of archaisms and dialects are present.

32 SIMPLICHIO, DASHA DI. "B. Pasternak i zhivopis'" [B. Pasternak and painting]. In *Boris Pasternak and His Times. Selected Papers from the Second International Symposium on Pasternak*, edited by Lazar Fleishman. Modern Russian Literature and Culture. Studies and Texts, no. 25. Berkeley, CA: Berkeley Slavic Specialties, pp. 195–211.

Traces Pasternak's affinity for painting, and discusses his indebtedness to his parents, particularly to his father. Sees his father's influence in Pasternak's "chamber poetry" and "childhood themes," in Pasternak's interpretations of his father's concepts of impressionism and cubism, and in Pasternak's motif of light ("the most insistent motif" in Pasternak, and "one of the major tasks" of his father). Surveys criticism on the subject and argues with some of the critics (G. de Mallac, for example).

33 SINIAVSKII, A. "Nekotorye aspekty pozdnei prozy Pasternaka" [Some aspects of Pasternak's later prose]. In *Boris Pasternak and His Times. Selected Papers from the Second International Symposium on Pasternak*, edited by Lazar Fleishman. Modern Russian Literature and Culture. Studies and Texts, no. 25. Berkeley, CA: Berkeley Slavic Specialties, pp. 359–71.

A general commentary on Pasternak's later prose, *Doctor Zhivago* in particular. Labels *Doctor Zhivago* a "book of thoughts," similar to *A Safe Conduct*. Sees the novel's main characters as "dematerialized," i.e., intentionally incomplete, and "flowing" into each other (Zhivago into Lara and vice versa). Interprets the novel's structure as based on parables and as a "mythologization of everyday material." Insists that Pasternak's claim of his "inconspicuous style" is exaggerated.

34 STRUVE, N.A. "Zateriannaia zametka Borisa Pasternaka" [Boris Pasternak's lost note]. In *Boris Pasternak and His Times. Selected Papers*

from the Second International Symposium on Pasternak, edited by Lazar Fleishman. Modern Russian Literature and Culture. Studies and Texts, no. 25. Berkeley, CA: Berkeley Slavic Specialties, pp. 414–17.

Attempts to prove authorship of a note (dated October 1928) that Pasternak presumably wrote for the newspaper *Evening Moscow* as a reponse to the questionnaire "My First Thing." Annotates the note and provides arguments for Pasternak's authorship. Appends the note believed to be published in this work for the first time.

35 THOMPSON, R.D.B. "Cvetaeva and Pasternak 1922–1924." In *Boris Pasternak and His Times. Selected Papers from the Second International Symposium on Pasternak*, edited by Lazar Fleishman. Modern Russian Literature and Culture. Studies and Texts, no. 25. Berkeley, CA: Berkeley Slavic Specialties, pp. 58–90.

A continuation of Olga Hughes's essay on "the friendship between Tsvetaeva and Pasternak" (1970.5) centering on "its first years, 1922–24, from Tsvetaeva's point of view." Contends that Tsvetaeva's imitation of Pasternak's style indicates her "absorption" in him at that time. Concludes that "her love for Pasternak may have been displaced . . . but it returned to him deepened and enriched."

36 TIERNAN-O'CONNOR, KATHERINE. "Elena, Helen of Troy, and the Eternal Feminine: Epigraphs and Intertextuality in 'Sestra moya zhizn'." In *Boris Pasternak and His Times. Selected Papers from the Second International Symposium on Pasternak*, edited by Lazar Fleishman. Modern Russian Literature and Culture. Studies and Texts, no. 25. Berkeley, CA: Berkeley Slavic Specialties, pp. 212–23.

An examination of subtexts generated by the Lenau epigraph to *My Sister, Life*. Views the epigraph as "a poet's creation," and argues that the epigraph presents a "composite photo" of all the artists to whom Pasternak "served a primary apprenticeship." Examines inter-textual connections with Lenau ("Dein Bild"), Goethe (*Faust*), Poe, Shakespeare, and Byron, among others. Looks at the different mani-festations of Helen of Troy to complete the analysis. Claims the most significant intertextual connections run from Lenau to Goethe to Lermontov and back to *My Sister, Life*, and examines the subtexts of each. Some views expounded in her book (1988.36) are reiterated or reexamined.

37 TOLSTAIA, E. "Pasternak i Kuzmin (k interpretatsii rasskaza 'Vozdushnye puti')" [Pasternak and Kuzmin (toward an interpretation of the story *Aerial Ways*)]. In *In Honor of Professor I. Serman. Russian Literature and History*, edited by Wolf Moskovich et al. Jerusalem: Hebrew University of Jerusalem, pp. 90–96.

Traces echoes of Kuzmin in Pasternak's "Some Propositions," *Aerial Ways* (dedicated to Kuzmin), and *A High Malady*. Finds

Kuzminian "textual reminiscences" in "Some Propositions" and cites examples to support her thesis of Kuzmin echoes. Sees the image of an "enormous eye" (in *Aerial Ways*) as a reflection of Kuzmin (via Hoffmann): a "well-known and central episode in the aesthetics of Romanticism from Hoffmann's story *Ritter Gluck*, a mystical dissolution of a musician in music, culminating in his elevation and in his absorption by sun—an eye, a symbol of Holy Spirit. I perceive exaclty here a structural parallel supporting the story's [*Aerial Ways*'s] dedication to Kuzmin." Mentions Pasternak's meeting with Kuzmin during Pasternak's visit to Petrograd in 1922; discusses Pasternak's letter to Yurkin, Kuzmin's friend.

38 VIL'MONT, N. *O Borise Pasternake. Vospominaniia i mysli* [On Boris Pasternak. Memoirs and thoughts]. Moscow: Sovetskii pisatel', 224 pp.

Includes two additional chapters (6 and 7) of his "memoirs and thoughts" published earlier (1987.21). Provides a great amount of first-hand information, most of which is hitherto unrecorded, on Pasternak's life and works. Mentions Pasternak's views of Bely ("excessive penchant for experimentation"), acmeist poets ("none of them was a great poet"), futurists (Bobrov, among others), and of his poetry. Discusses Pasternak's attempts to "simplify" his poetics and relates conversations he had with Pasternak about *A High Malady*. Elaborates on the development of Pasternak's love for Zinaida Nikolaevna (his second wife) and labels it "the only great love" in his life. Cites verbatim Pasternak's phone conversation with Stalin he overheard while at the Pasternaks' home. Comments in detail on Pasternak's early prose ("I was enraptured and charmed with *The Childhood of Luvers*") and narrates the content of the continuation of *The Tale* Pasternak had conveyed to him before *The Tale* came out. Insists that in "We Are a Few. We Could Be Three," Pasternak identified the three as Bobrov, Aksenov, and himself. Includes reprint (with slight modifications) of 1987.21.

1990

1 AFINOGENOV, ALEKSANDR. "Iz dnevnika 1937 goda. Ianvar'–fevral' 1937 g." [From a diary for 1937. January–February 1937]. *VL*, no. 2, pp. 108–21.

Reveals information about Pasternak the writer and man, his habit of writing each day and his love for discussions about the meaning of art ("the most important thing to him is art"; "he is kind and humane"; "an exceptionally complete and interesting man"). Discusses *Doctor Zhivago* ("condensed sentences, unusual imagery, simplicity") and Pasternak's fondness of Chekhov ("Pasternak loves Chekhov and has been rereading him"). Also mentions Pasternak's Kleist translations.

2   AL'FONSOV, V. *Poeziia Borisa Pasternaka* [Boris Pasternak's poetry]. Leningrad: Sovetskii pisatel', 368 pp.

An attempt to analyze Pasternak's poetry in its evolution—its themes, motifs, and the poetics—while discerning the poetry's peculiarities, Pasternak's worldviews, and his creative methods. Observes that "vocational" motifs are inherent to both *A Twin in the Clouds* and to *Doctor Zhivago*'s poetry, that the *My Sister, Life* collection's main themes are "nature, love, and art," that *Themes and Variations* is Pasternak's "most expressive" book, and that *Second Birth* "echoes" of Pushkin. Also analyzes *Spektorsky*, the relationship of personality to history in particular, and its similarity to *The Tale*. Throws light on some aspects of Pasternak's art and the use of metaphor (compared to that of Blok, Mayakovsky, and Annensky), and on Pasternak's affinity with his peers (Blok, Mayakovsky, and, above all, Tsvetaeva). Concludes that Pasternak is "inimitable" and is an "extraordinary phenomenon." Chapter 2, with slight modifications, is a reprint of 1988.2.

3   AL'MI, I.L. "Ballady B.L. Pasternaka" [B.L. Pasternak's ballads]. *IAN* 49, no. 5: 420–31.

Aspires to define the poetics of three poems Pasternak designated as ballads. Analyzes "The Ballad" (both versions, 1916 and 1928) in detail, linking it to Chopin and the genre of a Zhukovsky ballad (for its "rhythm of a mad horse race"). Stresses the ballad's musicality ("its verses imitate sounds of a piano") pointing to a "chain of metaphors." Elaborates on the differences between the two versions. Discusses Pasternak's two other ballads, "The Ballad" and "The Second Ballad," written in 1930. Concludes that a ballad was not Pasternak's separate "artistic sphere" (as with Zhukovsky), "but, formed up in a single row, it gives a notion about important features" of Pasternak's "spiritual past."

4   ANNENKOV, IURII. "Boris Pasternak." Includes an introductory note (in Russian) by I.A. Vasilyev. *LO*, no. 3, pp. 101–4.
Excerpt of 1966.2.

5   ASMUS, V.F. Introduction (in Russian) to *Boris Pasternak ob iskusstve. "Okhrannaia gramota" i zametki o khudozhestvennom tvorchestve* [Boris Pasternak on art. *A Safe Conduct* and notes on artistic creativity]. Moscow: Iskusstvo, pp. 8–35.

Seeks to register Pasternak's views of art as reflected in his "specific works" (dubbed "aesthetic prose")—critical essays, reviews, and two autobiographies. Notes that Pasternak's "aesthetic prose" is a constituent of his poetry and prose ("*A Safe Conduct* is not only an autobiography but an artistic tale and an aesthetic confession as well. The article on Chopin is not only a musical and an aesthetic étude but also a poetic piece in its literary sense"). Sees Pasternak's perception of art as a "proclamation of whole truth about things endured and experienced."

Elaborates on Pasternak's views on the content-form relation, insisting that Pasternak "first of all" sought content in his poetry ("in art 'everything boils down to *content*'"). Explicates Pasternak's views on realism: "Pasternak approximates the quality of an artistic originality with art's realism," and "art is not simply a description of life but an expression of singularity of existence." Stresses Pasternak's definition of his calling as "craft" (*remeslo*). Comments in detail on a number of Pasternak's essays, particularly those on Chopin, Kleist, Blok, and Verlaine ("In his own—brilliant—rendition of Verlaine's manifesto Pasternak corrected a common error of the manifesto's intent").

6   AUCOUTURIER, MICHEL. "Boris Pasternak (1890–1960)" (in French). In *Histoire de la littérature russe. Le XXe siècle*** Gels et Dégels*, edited by Efim Etkind et al. Paris: Fayard, pp. 466–87.
      A detailed appraisal of Pasternak, divided into five major sections: (1) education and debuts; (2) views of *My Sister, Life*; (3) Pasternak's attitude toward the Revolution as reflected in his works of the 1920s; (4) views of *Second Birth* and a discussion of Pasternak's crisis in the 1930s; and (5) views of *Doctor Zhivago*. Notes Pasternak's rejection of Khlebnikov's and Kruchenykhs's doctrine of the "word as it is" in favor of Mayakovsky's dynamism in *My Sister, Life*. Discusses in detail Pasternak's poetry of the 1920s and the 1930s. Elaborates on historical and literary events surrounding Pasternak's official disgrace in 1936. Details principal characters of *Doctor Zhivago*, while discussing conflicts between them. Comments on Zhivago's simultaneous identification with Shakespeare's Hamlet (notably with his "To Be Or Not to Be" monologue) and Christ, noting Pasternak's rejection of the concept of a final death. Some views are expressed in his previously published works.

7   AZADOVSKII, K.M. Introduction (in Russian) to "Pozitsiia khudozhnika. Pis'ma Borisa Pasternaka" [An artist's view. Boris Pasternak's letters]. *LO*, no. 2, pp. 3–6.
      Elaborates on Pasternak's views of the Revolution, i.e., Pasternak's condemnation of the "base murder" of ministers Shingarev and Kokoshkin in a hospital ward—as reflected in Pasternak's poems "The Russian Revolution" and "My Brains Are Stirring Up. Imagine. In a Ward!," "whose publication in the fatherland's press could not have been imagined prior to 1989." Includes and comments on Pasternak's letters to Petrovsky, Chukovsky, Paustovsky, and Pavlovich.

8   BAEVSKII, V.S. "'Faust' Gete v perevode Pasternaka" [Goethe's *Faust* in Pasternak's translation]. *IAN* 49, no. 4: 341–51.
      An analysis of the metrics of Pasternak's translation of *Faust*. Contrasts excerpts from Goethe's original against Pasternak's rendition, observing that, as a rule, Pasternak retained the original's four-foot iambic while in other instances he digressed from the meters of the

original. Thus, Pasternak substituted five-foot dactyls for Goethe's "tonic verse with a tendency towards four stresses," or Pasternak preferred a two-foot amphibrach for a two-foot iambic, for example. Cites Pasternak's correspondence that sheds some light on views of his *Faust* translation and comments on other critics' views of Pasternak's translation (W. Pohl and E.G. Etkind). Concludes that Pasternak "saturated the text with spoken and colloquial lexicon . . . and various rhetoric figures of speech," and that his rendition is "artistically adequate to its original."

9   BARNES, CHRISTOPHER. Introduction to *The Voice of Prose*, edited by Christopher Barnes. Vol. 2, *People and Propositions*. Edinburgh: Polygon, pp. 12–25.
        A sporadic commentary on Pasternak's earlier prose, critical essays, literary career, *Second Birth* collection, *Doctor Zhivago*, and on echoes of early prose in *Doctor Zhivago*. Finds that *"Aerial Ways* falls into two main episodes, a 'situational rhyme' consisting of a narrative motif followed by its transformed echo," and that "lyricism and history have here converged." Draws parallels between *Seryozha's Story, Three Chapters from a Tale*, and *Spektorsky*. Concludes that *Doctor Zhivago* is Pasternak's "crowning achievement. It fed on, and grew naturally out of, his earlier writings, developing Christian motifs, aesthetic, ethical and historical views, and strands of literary and personal reminiscence, combining them in a bold new poetic revelation of the place of a creative personality in the modern world." Continuation of 1986.3.

10   ———. "Pasternak, Dickens and the Novel Tradition." *FMLS* 26, no. 4: 326–41.
        Establishes "the Dickensian element" in *Doctor Zhivago*, from the naming of *A Tale of Two Cities* in *Doctor Zhivago* to philosophical and textual parallels between the two works: (1) neither of them features "the magic personalities of their respective revolutions"; (2) both authors ascribe "the cause of the revolution to previous generations of social oppressions"; (3) "both works harmonize in their general religious and moral messages"; (4) they are similar in their character portrayal; and (5) they are alike in their use of recurrent imagery ("railways, names, and certain situational allusions"). Also mentions Tolstoyan and Dostoevskian echoes in *Doctor Zhivago*. Concludes his study does not suggest that "Pasternak's *Doctor Zhivago* is little more than an 'identikit' product, an imitation, or clone derived from certain nineteenth-century models."

11   ———. "A Poetic Dedication and a Response from the Commissariat." *SSR*, no. 14, pp. 191–98.
        A study of Pasternak's relations with Lunacharsky and Lunacharsky's views of Pasternak's poetry. Mentions favors Lunacharsky

did for Pasternak's family, providing data hitherto unrecorded. Concludes that their relations on a personal level were cordial, though Lunacharsky showed a "lack of sympathy with his poetry." Excerpts Lunacharsky's public comments on Pasternak the poet: "very talented, but extremely unintelligible and unsuited to our epoch" and "profoundly talented yet evidently muddled." Cites complete texts (previously unpublished) of the dedication Pasternak wrote to Lunacharsky in a copy of *My Sister, Life*, and Lunacharsky's letter to Pasternak. The letter strongly rejects Pasternak's poetry of *My Sister, Life*, though Pasternak is labeled "a genuine poet."

12 BODIN, PER-ARNE. "Boris Pasternak and the Christian Tradition." *FMLS* 26, no. 4: 382–401.

Claims that Christianity is present throughout Pasternak's works, not only within obvious themes of *Doctor Zhivago*, and "not so much thematically as in the structure of his works" (as in *A Safe Conduct*). Traces various facets of Christianity mirrored in Pasternak's oeuvre: (1) "Christiantiy as a unifying force"; (2) ideas of "*imitatio Christi*" ("Christ as judge," in "The Garden of Gethsemane"); (3) as the principle of linkages in history (affirmation of life and love); (4) as influenced by Chekhov's stories with Christian themes (*The Student, Holy Night*, and *The Archdeacon*); (5) as Goethe's ideas of "das Ewigweibliche" ("Pasternak's view of the connection between the Bible and everyday human life"); (6) as Sophian principle ("Sophia, or heavenly widsom")—which "finds expression in Pasternak's creative output from beginning to end"; (7) as "life as sacrifice and disunion"; and (8) as "motif of Resurrection." Sees Pasternak "as a modern Russian author who offers a deep interpretation of the Christian message."

13 BOGOMOLOV, N. "Vybor putei" [A choice of paths]. *LO*, no. 2, pp. 60–64.

Endeavors to pinpoint Pasternak's and Khodasevich's attitudes towards one another. Admits that any rapprochement between them seems impossible. Attempts to find similarities between them through their poetics, in Khodasevich's textual references to Russian literary works and Pasternak's textual intertextuality, for example.

14 CHERNIAK, IA. "Zapisi 20-kh godov" [Entries for the 1920s]. *VL*, no. 2, pp. 35–49.

Records Pasternak's collaboration with the journal *Press and the Revolution* (of which he had been a managing editor). Cites Pasternak's poetry dedicated to the Bryusov jubilee and offers views of Pasternak as entered in the author's diary entry for 16 April 1924: "Life has taught him to be keenly aware of his own right, I believe that he will grow up at this difficult stage of his life, as he has grown up during the past two years, hewing his poetic genius." Includes Pasternak's letter to P.S. Kogan; in the letter Pasternak interposed on behalf of N.N. Vilyam-Vilmont, arguing that he should not be expelled from Kogan's institute.

15 CHUKOVSKAIA, LIDIIA. "Iz dnevnikovykh zapisei" [From diary entries]. *LO*, no. 2, pp. 90–95.

    Recollections of Pasternak—with entries from 6 February 1947 through 6 June 1952. Records Pasternak's readings (at private gatherings) of excerpts from *Doctor Zhivago* and public readings of his translations. Also records Pasternak's views of Fedin, Ehrenburg, and Chekhov's *Uncle Vanya*. Adds to knowledge of Pasternak the man. Reprint (selections) of 1988.4.

16 CHUKOVSKII, KORNEI. "Iz dnevnika (O B.L. Pasternake)" [From a diary (About B.L. Pasternak)]. *VL*, no. 2, pp. 123–53.

    Records his impressions of Pasternak during their meetings from 1930 through 1960; entries from 1960 to 1965 add information about the cause of Pasternak's death and about the circumstances of his burial, notably the entry for 28 June 1962—as recorded from a conversation between the author and Pasternak's second wife, Zinaida Nikolaevna. Mentions Pasternak's infatuation with Pushkin and Chekhov, his immediate reaction to the news of the Nobel Prize award, his illness and hospitalization in February 1958, and Fedin's attitude toward Pasternak; above all, provides valuable information about Pasternak the man.

17 CLOWES, EDITH W. "Characterization in *Doktor Živago*: Lara and Tonja." *SEEJ* 34, no. 3: 322–31.

    Endeavors to define modes of characterization of Lara and Tonya in *Doctor Zhivago*. Views Tonya as "a relatively flat character precisely because of her role as conformist epic heroine" and Lara as "the type of the non-conformist heroine" ("Her non-conformist nature finds a certain legitimization through comparison to non-conformist archetypes of quite unepic cast"). Makes no conclusions.

18 DANIN, DANIIL. "Eto prebudet s nami. Iz 'Knigi bez zhanra'" [That will remain with us. From "The Book without a Genre"]. *RuR*, no. 1, pp. 29–48.

    Reminiscences of the author's encounters with Pasternak, Pasternak's poetry readings, and his impressions of Pasternak's poetry. Recalls in detail a poetry reading performed in 1932, during which Pasternak also responded to the audience's queries ("Can you logically decipher each of your lines?" "Oh, no! I cannot decipher each line individually!"). Includes Pasternak's letter to the author (dated 3 January 1944), responding to the author's comments on Pasternak's poetry and revealing Pasternak's thoughts on the poetry of *On Early Trains*.

19 DOZORETS, ZH. A. "B.L. Pasternak. Kogda razguliaetsia (Kniga stikhov kak tseloe)" [B.L. Pasternak's *When the Skies Clear* (Poetry collection as a whole)]. *RIaSh*, no. 1, pp. 60–66.

Analyzes the poetics of *When the Skies Clear*, its "compositional streamlining and the metric unity," claiming that Pasternak looked upon the collection as an "independent organism." Establishes the succession of the collection's poems, indicating their thematic and structural unities and cycles. Singles out two major "principles" governing the "collection's imagery, and lexical systems": "splitting up of phenomenon, image, and word" and a principle of "unification, approximation of various, distant, and dissimilar things." Cites numerous examples from the collection displaying these "principles."

20 FLEISHMAN, LAZAR. *Boris Pasternak. The Poet and His Politics.* Cambridge, MA: Harvard University Press, 360 pp.

A well-researched Pasternak biography—with an attempt to closely interrelate biographical data with Pasternak's works and his time. Elaborates on Pasternak's origin (with information on both parents), Pasternak's childhood and youth (including infatuation with music and university years), literary beginnings (a "literary debut" involving an examination of Pasternak's association with literary circles and movements), revolutionary years, and the Soviet period—with emphasis on literary factions in the 1920s, the period of "Thaw," the purges, the Great Terror of the 1930s, the years of World War II, and the postwar years, ending with the *Doctor Zhivago* period. Offers new information on numerous aspects of Pasternak's life and works—including his translations and shifts in his views of art. Attempts to correct some misconceptions regarding Pasternak scholarship, including Pasternak's assimilation into Christianity and his baptism—the latter deemed to be a myth ("though he loved to attend church services, the poet was never baptized"), among others. Also comments on the autobiographical nature of *Doctor Zhivago*. Includes thirteen chapters, an index, and illustrations.

21 FRANCE, PETER. "Pasternak and the English Romantics." *FMLS* 26, no. 4: 315–25.

Traces "direct contacts between Pasternak and the English romantics: Swinburne, Keats, Byron, and Shelley. Discusses in detail Pasternak's renditions of the four poets: Swinburne's sonnet to John Ford and *Chastelard*, Keats's *Endymion* and "To Autumn," Byron's "Stanza to Augusta," and Shelley's "Ode to the West Wind." Discusses Pasternak's affinity with these poets, particularly with Keats ("both stress receptivity as an essential poetic attribute"; "for both, the poetry of the past is a still living presence"). Concludes that the four poets "were none the less a significant point of reference for him, from the beginning to the end of his poetic career."

22 FRANK, V.S. "Vodianoi znak. Poeticheskoe mirovozrenie Pasternaka" [Water sign. Pasternak's poetic world views]. *LO*, no. 2, pp. 72–77.
    Reprint of 1962.9.

23 GASPAROV, M.L. "'Bliznets v tuchakh' i 'Nachal'naia pora' B. Pasternaka: ot kompozitsii sbornika k kompozitsii tsykla" [*A Twin in the Clouds* and *The Beginning Time* of B. Pasternak: From the collection's composition to the cycle's composition]. *IAN*, no. 49, pp. 218–22.
    A detailed study of compositional revisions of Pasternak's first collection, *A Twin in the Clouds* (1914), as they occurred in *The Beginning Time* (1929), the second variant of the first collection. Cites numerous examples of compositional changes as reflected in themes, emotions, and imagery. Concludes that the compostion of *A Twin in the Clouds* was based on three themes. Two of these, love and friendship, unified the collection's two untitled parts, and the third theme, creativity, bonded together the first two themes. The composition of the revised version centered only on two themes, love and creativity. Suggests that the absence of the friendship theme in the revised version is a result of "Pasternak's general re-evaluation of his own past and the present during the late 1920s."

24 ———. "Rifma i zhanr v stikhakh Borisa Pasternaka" [Rhyme and genre in Boris Pasternak's poetry]. *RuR*, no. 1, pp. 17–22.
    A study of the rhyme-simplification process in Pasternak's poetry. Provides percentages of inexact rhyme occurrences in masculine and feminine rhymes, concluding that a marked reduction of the use of inexact rhymes developed throughout Pasternak's poetry. Cites poetry from *A High Malady* to display Pasternak's choice of rhymes in an epic genre ("*A High Malady* is an epic about the birth of an epic"). Also concludes that the frequency of exact rhymes has increased in Pasternak's later poetry, reaching 100 percent in the poetry for 1958/1959.

25 GERSHTEIN, EMMA. "O Pasternake i ob Akhmatovoi" [About Pasternak and Akhmatova]. *LO*, no. 2, pp. 96–102.
    Sheds light on Pasternak's life in 1946 and 1947, his meetings with Akhmatova, public and private poetry and prose readings (of excerpts from *Doctor Zhivago*), and Pasternak's attempts to have *Doctor Zhivago* published in *Novyi mir*. Notes that the chapter of the novel describing Lara and Antipov meeting in an apartment on Kamergersky Lane originally had "a very spicy love scene." Records Akhmaktova's views of Pasternak, particularly of *Doctor Zhivago* ("which she did not accept at all").

26 GIFFORD, HENRY. "Pasternak and European Modernism." *FMLS* 26, no. 4: 301–14.
    An attempt to identify Pasternak's closeness to European modernism. Mentions Pasternak's association with Russian futurism, his

propensity for urbanism, and his affinities with European poets looked upon as modernists. These include Rilke, Baudelaire, Verlaine ("What Pasternak admired in Verlaine he had wanted to achieve himself"), Blake ("Pasternak has something of Blake's alert innocence"), Proust ("The notation of a child's awareness in both Proust and Pasternak is expressed with an elaboration and subtlety that are surprisingly close"), Joyce, and Eliot (his "attention to ambiguities," his "placing of the unusual words"— with Pasternak seen as proceeding "somewhat in this manner" in his *Themes and Variations*). Finds *Doctor Zhivago*'s concluding segment (in which Zhivago's friends gather to read his poetry after his death) as "the Modernist ambition [that] was perhaps never expressed more modestly, or with such quiet confidence." Concludes that Pasternak "became a Modernist in so far as he took the utmost freedom in expressing his bewilderment before the spectacle of life forever changing."

27 GIRZHEVA, G.N. "Nekotorye osobennosti pozdnei liriki Borisa Pasternaka" [Some peculiarities of Boris Pasternak's later lyrics]. *RIaSh*, no. 1, pp. 54–59.

Examines the poetics of the "later" Pasternak—*On Early Trains* and *When the Skies Clear*—focusing on his syntax, stanzaic structure, phraseologies, metaphors, and similes. Finds that: (1) the "use of a long chain of simple sentences is one characteristic of Pasternak's syntax"; (2) "anaphora is a leading stylistic figure of Pasternak's later poetry"; (3) stanzaic structure varies ("a stanza can consist of four . . . to ten lines"); (4) "phraseologisms could be divided into two groups: changed and unchanged"; and (5) "structural and semantic organization of metaphor is utterly diversified."

28 GLADKOV, ALEKSANDR. "Vstrechi s Pasternakom" [Meetings with Pasternak]. *Oktiabr'*, no. 3, pp. 171–200.

Partial reprint of the author's *Meetings with Pasternak* (1973.5)— random passages taken mainly from the opening and concluding chapters. Includes an introduction by L. Levitsky that conveys his impressions of Gladkov, Gladkov's memoirs in general, Gladkov's reaction to *Doctor Zhivago*, and the novel's reception in the past and recently—both by government officials, critics, and the general public.

29 IVANOVA, NATAL'IA. "Smert' i voskresenie Doktora Zhivago" [Death and resurrection of Doctor Zhivago]. In *Voskreshenie nuzhnykh veshchei*. Moscow: Moskovskii rabochii, pp. 83–105.

Reprint of 1988.18.

30 KATS, BORIS. "'. . . Muzykoi khlynuv s dugi bytiia'" ["'. . . Having Gushed with Music from the Gist of Existence"]. *LO*, no. 2, pp. 79–84.

A commentary on the role of music in Pasternak's life and works. Divides the article into three parts: "Awakening"; "The Rupture"; and

"Farewell." Strongly questions Pasternak's claims of his lack of a "perfect pitch" as a reason to abandon music as a vocation. Suggests that Pasternak waited for the "vacancy of a poet" and once that vacancy appeared, he chose poetry over music.

31 KAZAKOVA, SVETLANA IA. "Tvorcheskaia istoriia ob"edineniia 'Tsentrifuga' (Zametki o rannikh poeticheskikh vzaimosviaziakh B. Pasternaka, N. Aseeva i S. Bobrova)" [Creative history of the association "Centrifuge" (Notes on the early poetic interactions of B. Pasternak, N. Aseyev, and S. Bobrov)]. *RuL* 27, no. 4: 459–82.

A study of Pasternak's involvement with "Lirika" and "Centrifuge." Sheds light on Pasternak's activity in "Centrifuge"—while discussing in detail his contributions to it (his poetry and his participation in the writing of the manifestos), and his poetics and aesthetics of that period, 1912–1916. Analyzes Pasternak's poem "Feasts," stressing the motif of a "poetry-healer." Mentions Pasternak's interest in a "poet's personality." Claims that futurism's influence on Pasternak during that time could easily be discerned. Also claims that Pasternak's poems included in "Centrifuge"'s *Second Collection* ("Gypsies," "Cupronickle," and "About Ivan the Great") were influenced by Aseyev—seen in Pasternak's use of archaic lexica and neologisms. Concludes that in their "artistic experiences," Pasternak and Aseyev have "brilliantly developed" futurism's "'doctrine'"—by their "transformation of contemporary life into poetry" and by their "new work on word."

32 KHAZAN, V.I. "'Takim ia vizhu oblik vash i vzgliad . . .' (O tvorcheskom sodruzhestve A. Akhmatovoi i B. Pasternaka)" ["Such I see your face and your glance . . ." (On the literary cooperation of A. Akhmatova and B. Pasternak)]. *IAN* 49, no. 5: 432–43.

Surveys the "literary" relationship between Pasternak and Akhmatova. Finds Pasternakian echoes in Akhmatova's poetry and concludes that Akhmatova "most of all" valued Pasternak's credo of the "awareness of being a poet." Also comments that their relationship, a "complete trust to each other notwithstanding," was not "simple and smooth." Concludes that in addition to their "love and adoration," there were "unforgiven insults, stung pride, and unquenched vanity."

33 KONDAKOV, I.V. "Roman 'Doktor Zhivago' v svete traditsii russkoi kul'tury" [*Doctor Zhivago* in light of Russian cultural tradition]. *IAN* 49, no. 6: 527–40.

An attempt to place *Doctor Zhivago* ("novel and Russian culture") within Russian and European literature and culture. Picks out faults of Soviet critics' interpretations of *Doctor Zhivago*, criticism that generated "the tragic destiny of the novel." Repudiates the Soviet critics' intentions to "read" the novel "from the point of view of the time of its creation," and argues that *Doctor Zhivago* "stood in opposition" to the ideology, psychology, and politics of Soviet totalitarianism only as a "work of art"—unlike Zamyatin's, Pilnyak's, Platonov's, Zoshschenko's, and Solzhenitsyn's works. Analyzes *Doctor Zhivago*'s "multitude of cultural contexts," Russian and foreign, attending even to the characters' names reminiscent of those of Dostoevsky (Amaliya, Karlovna, Rodya, Komarovsky) and Ostrovsky (Nil Feoktistovich, Kupriyan Savelyevich, Lipochka, Felisata Semenovna)—in addition to links to Tolstoy, Pushkin, Chekhov, Turgenev, Bely, Gorky, Mann, Hesse, Dickens, Shakespeare, Goethe, and the Bible. Equates Zhivago with Christ ("Pasternak's hero, like the Gospel's Jesus, is a spiritual doctor, a Doctor of Spirit") and stresses Pasternak resorting to Old and New Testaments, and to Old Church Slavonic. Concludes that *Doctor Zhivago* is a "concentrated and 'rolled up' *unity*" of Pasternak's "entire preceding literary path."

34   KSHONDZER, MARIIA. "Gruziia v poezii Pasternaka" [Georgia in Pasternak's poetry]. *LiG*, no. 10, pp. 172–83.
        Finds "realia and atmosphere of Georgia" in Pasternak's cycle "Waves," while discussing in detail all twelve of the cycle's chapters and its major versions. Also finds that the "type" of Pasternak's "perception of Georgia" could be defined as "subjective, but this is a special Pasternakian subjectivism." Concludes that Pasternak saw "harmony and wholeness in Georgia."

35   LEVI, PETER. *Boris Pasternak. A Biography*. London: Hutchinson, 310 pp.
        Basically follows biographic contours established in other Pasternak biographies: family background and the early years ("Family and Boyhood to Sixteen"; "Youth and Folly—He Becomes a Young Poet"; "The Young Poet"), and major events of the 1930s and 1940s. Ends with a more detailed description of the 1950s (the chapters "*Dr. Zhivago*"; "The Nobel Prize"; and "The Hands of Time"). Offers judgements on Pasternak's works, particularly *Doctor Zhivago* (seen as still retaining "its freshness and its mystery"), and on his poetry cited profusely in the author's and others' renditions. Ventures explanations of some overlooked details of Pasternak's life, suggesting, for example, that part of the trouble surrounding Pasternak's divorce from his first wife was "her Judaism and her insistence on 'Jewish values.'" Draws heavily on other Pasternak biographies, memoirs, criticism, correspondence, some of Pasternak's works, and on information collected from encounters with people who knew Pasternak. Contains ten chapters, an appendix (with renditions of nine of Pasternak's poems), a bibliography, and an index.

36   LEVINA, T. "'Stradatel'noe bogatstvo'" ["Suffering richness"]. *LO*, no. 2, pp. 84–89.
        An attempt to juxtapose Pasternak's poetics and views of art against "unofficial art of the late 1920s through the early 1940s"—

painters like Drevin, Sokolov, Basmanov, Kozlov, and others. Sees, for example, a similarity between Pasternak's "interpenetration of inner and outer spaces, fractured in a prism" and the cubo-futurists' people images. Cites examples from Pasternak's *The Tale, The Childhood of Luvers*, and the poem "The Mirror" (and it's version "I Myself") to demonstrate links between Pasternak and the paintings of the late 1920s through the early 1940s.

37   LIUBIMOV, NIKOLAI. "Neslykhannaia prostota (fragmenty vospomi-nanii)" [The unheard-of simplicity (fragments from memoirs)]. *LiG*, no. 2, pp. 151–63.

Applies Pasternak's dictum of "unheard-of simplicity" to his rendi-tions of Georgian poets and regards the renditions "a turning point in his 'own' poetry." Regards Pasternak's translation of Shevchenko's "Mary" as evidence of a change in Pasternak's "stylistic system," a beginning of "Pasternak's longing for philosophical and biblical themes." Comments on Pasternak's translations in general—varied lexica, temperament of rare force, impressiveness, and the use of sound instrumention. Credits Pasternak for having proved to "the Russian reader" that Shakespeare is "a great poet" and "a great playwright."

38   LIVINGSTONE, ANGELA. "Pasternak and Faust." *FMLS* 26, no. 4: 353–69.

A study of *Faust* motifs and echoings in *Doctor Zhivago*, including a list of references to *Faust* in Pasternak's other works (the poems "Marburg," "To Helen," "Faust's Love," "Margarita," and *A Safe Conduct*), and a brief commentary on Pasternak's *Faust* translation. Takes issues with criticism linking Zhivago to Faust, denying any similar-ities between the two of them. Sees, rather, "Zhivago as Faust's antithe-sis." Supports her arguments with detailed instances of divergences distinguishing Zhivago from Faust: "Faust is essentially alone"—"Zhivago is never alone"; "Faust is split"—"Zhivago is intergrated"; and "Faust is primarily a desirer"—"Zhivago has no such desires." Discerns "Faustian traits" in the novel's "three other male characters"—Vedenyapin, Strelnikov ("a man of action"), and Komarovsky ("modeled on both Faust and Mephistopholes"). Draws other parallels between the two works, and elaborates on Pasternak's interpretations of *Faust* and the "Faustian world." Highly values Pasternak's *Faust* rendition, a "mag-nificent verse, in which the literal reductions and losses are overwhelmed by waves of expansive rhythms."

39   LOKS, K. "Povest' ob odmom desiatiletii (1907–1917 gg.)" [A story about a decade (1907–1917)]. *VL*, no. 2, pp. 5–34.

Recollections of the author's encounters with Pasternak during the early 1910s, with comments on Pasternak's poetry readings and the poet-ry of *A Twin in the Clouds* and *Above the Barriers*. Sheds light on

Pasternak's life during that period—his parents' apartment at Volkhonka in Moscow, Pasternak's relationship with Ida Vysotskaya (including the author's thoughts about her character), Pasternak's association with "Lirika" and "Centrifuge," and Pasternak's studies at the Moscow University. Contrasts Mayakovsky with Pasternak. Includes Pasternak's two letters (1913) to the author.

40 MAGOMEDOVA, D.M. "Sootnoshenie liricheskogo i povestvovatel'nogo siuzheta v tvorchestve Pasternaka" [The correlation of lyrical and narrative plots in Pasternak's works]. *IAN* 49, no. 5: 414–19.

Identifies similarities between prose and poetry sections of *Doctor Zhivago* and focuses on the links between the poem "Autumn" and the rest of the novel. Sees "Autumn" as a "point of intersection" between part 14 of the novel ("Again in Varykino") and chapters 1 and 2 of Pasternak's *The Beginning of the Prose of 1936*, stressing that despite these similarities, all three pieces have no "common plot." Also identifies similarities of "plot structures" between the poem "Winter Night" (both versions, 1913 and 1928) and *Three Chapters from The Tale* (1922), *The Tale* (1929), and *Spektorsky* (1925–1931). Concludes that the correlations between prose and lyrical plots in Pasternak's works "grow into one of the central problems of his poetics, a problem of genre and genesis transformation of singular plot invariants."

41 MALMSTAD, DZHON E. "Edinstvo protivopolozhnostei. Istoriia vzaimootnoshenii Khodasevicha i Pasternaka" [Unity of oppositions. A history of interactions between Khodasevich and Pasternak]. *LO*, no. 2, pp. 51–59.
    Translation of 1989.25.

42 MARKOVIĆ, VASILIJE. "Vijek Borisa Pasternaka. Jedan pogled na stvaralaštvo velikog pisca i prilike u kojima je stvarao" [Boris Pasternak's century. A glance at the great writer's creativity and circumstances in which he created]. *Stvaranje* 45, nos. 5–6: 576–602.

A summary of evaluative remarks on Pasternak's major works, way of writing, his worldviews, background, and his biography. Concludes that "both his family and the state, Communist ideologists and Freemasons, Russians and Jews, and legal wives and mistresses have fought for Pasternak."

43 MASLENIKOVA, ZOIA. *Portret Borisa Pasternaka* [The portrait of Boris Pasternak]. Moscow: Sovetskaia Rossiia, 288 pp.

Reprint (with text modified and added) of 1978.30 and 1979.32; reprint of 1988.31. Includes an introduction detailing reasons for the publication of her memoirs, summarizing her impressions of Pasternak as interlocutor, and mentioning that her diary entries have appeared in an abridged form.

44 MURAVINA, NINA. *Vstrechi s Pasternakom* [Meetings with Pasternak]. Tenafly, NJ: Hermitage, 224 pp.

Recollections of her meetings with Pasternak from 1946 through early 1950. Recalls Pasternak's public and private poetry readings ("he read his poetry easily and freely"; he read it "more confidently than the prose"), and excerpts of *Doctor Zhivago* ("the first volume was completed in 1948"). Comments on *Doctor Zhivago* (its "main heroes did not become the revolutionaries, but their victims, the anti-heroes"). Argues that she was a prototype for Zhivago's brother, Evgraf ("the brother's portrait was made from me"). Discusses Pasternak's relationships with Zinaida Nikolaevna, his second wife (he "was attached to her by [the force] of habit, his youngest son, and the adjusted home life") and Ivinskaya, citing Pasternak's poetry reflecting his views of Ivinskaya and commenting on this poetry. Also comments on Pasternak's poetry that reflects his views on women; divides this poetry into two groups: "the first, including abstract poetry about Eva, about woman's body ... and the second—intimate descriptions which he calls 'seconds of feeling.'" Describes her own feeling towards Pasternak ("I suddenly realized that this perhaps was exactly the love or that it could become it"). Includes nine letters (hitherto unpublished) Pasternak wrote to her between 19 February 1948 and 19 January 1953.

45 MUSATOV, V.V. "K probleme genezisa liriki Borisa Pasternaka" [Toward the question of genesis in Boris Pasternak's lyrics]. *IAN* 49, no. 5: 403–13.

An attempt to identify Pasternak's affinity with the poetics of Fet's poetry. Cites Mandelstam's and other poets' and critics' views of the Fet-Pasternak connection. Sees Fet-Pasternak similarities as an "affinity of starting aesthetic principles," with views of poetry as an "organic force of perception (sponge)." Underpins his views with numerous citations of Pasternak's and Fet's poetry, while discussing similarities between the two poets in detail.

46 NOVIKOV, VL. "Otzvuki i grimasy. Pasternak v parodiiakh i epigrammakh" [Echoes and grimaces. Pasternak in parodies and epigrams]. *LO*, no. 3, pp. 105–12.

A survey of parodies and epigrams written about Pasternak and his works from 1922 through 1990: *My Sister, Life*; individual poems; translations (*Faust*, in particular); Pasternak's identification with Pushkin, and *Doctor Zhivago* (Nabokov's views). Concludes that the "Pasternakian word has become not only a part of poetry but of the very life as well. And, therefore, the dialogue of literature with Pasternak will perpetually continue."

47 OZEROV, LEV. "Chudotvorstvo. K 100-letiiu so dnia rozhdeniia Borisa Pasternaka" [Miraculousness. Toward Boris Pasternak's centennial]. *Izvestiia*, no. 39 (8 November): 3.

Mentions Pasternak's training in music and philosophy, which is reflected in his works. Underlines Pasternak's inalienability from life professed in his collection *My Sister, Life*. Applies Karolina Pavlova's identification of poetry as a "holy craft" to Pasternak, noting that Pasternak had early on mastered that craft, which has naturally flowed into mastery and further into magic, defined by Pasternak as "miraculousness." Contrasts Pasternak's poetics (his concept and the use of the lexica of everyday life) with that of the symbolists. Mentions hostile Soviet criticism of Pasternak's poetry in *Doctor Zhivago*. Expands on many observations in his later publication (1990.48).

48 ———. "O Borise Pasternake" [About Boris Pasternak]. *Znanie*, no. 1, pp. 3–59.

Divided into five sections: (1) "Days and Works"; (2) "The Foundation and Destiny"; (3) "Let's Drop Words"; (4) "To Come to the Very Point"; and (5) "The Pasternak Lessons." Outlines Pasternak's life, often repeating data from *A Safe Conduct* and occasionally recording new information (such as the content of Pasternak's birth certificate and his association with the poet Anisimov's circle). Surveys Pasternak's attitude toward the Revolution and his detachment from the Soviet system (views of Lenin and tales in verse, notably *The Year 1905* and *Lieutenant Schmidt*). Singles out difficult aspects of Pasternak's poetry: his lexica (approximation of his prose language with the language of poetry); syntax (sentence structures and some poems' omission of subjects named in the titles); unusual associative links in imagery; and sound instrumentations (a trinomial simile, for example). Surveys Pasternak's path toward simplification, centering on his reexamination of his poetic "system" during the 1928–29 and 1956–57 periods. Records his meetings with Pasternak (beginning in 1935) and offers a myriad of impressions of him: as a poet, a translator (his "translations are exemplary"), and as a human being ("was childlike, trusting and candid"; loved "cordial, natural witticism"; and "always seemed to me a disinterested and fearless person, harsh on himself and kind toward his friends").

49 PAS, OCTAVIO. "O Pasternake" [About Pasternak]. *InL*, no. 1, pp. 193–96.

A translation of the author's essay published in Spanish in 1958. Sees *Doctor Zhivago* as "recollections of favorite shadows as well as a reunion with them." Emphasizes that Pasternak perceives the world "with the eye of a poet"; "he is from a tribe of lyric poets, not novelists." Interprets *Doctor Zhivago* as "a novel about love," "about undying love, steadfastness of life." Offers numerous other comments on the novel (denial of similarities to *War and Peace*, for example), Pasternak's poetry in general, and on *A Safe Conduct*.

50 PASTERNAK, E.B. "Namerennyi risk. Vystupleniia B.L. Pasternaka na diskussii o formalizme v 1936 godu" [A deliberate risk. Pasternak's speeches at the discussion on formalism in 1936]. *LO*, no. 3, pp. 86–91.

Consists of two parts: a commentary and the texts of two speeches (published in this work for the first time) on formalism and impressionism that Pasternak delivered on 13 and 16 March 1936. The commentary includes Pasternak's reaction to the discussion on formalism and impressionism, A.K. Tarasenkov's diary entries, and excerpts from ariticles published in *Pravda* and *Izvestiya*.

51 PASTERNAK, El. V. "Leto 1917 goda. 'Sestra-moia—zhizn' i 'Doktor Zhivago'" [The summer of 1917. *My Sister, Life* and *Doctor Zhivago*]. *Zvezda*, no. 2, pp. 158–65.

An analysis of contextual concurrences between *My Sister, Life* and *Doctor Zhivago*: use of the word 'life,' meaning of the summer of 1917 (in the novel's section "Melyuzeevo"), and, above all, the reflection of the image of the collection's heroine (deemed to be a prototype of Elena Vinograd) in Lara, among other similarities. Relates in detail Pasternak's encounters with Vinograd and quotes from their correspondence.

52 ———. "'Novaia faza khristianstva'" ["The new phase of Christianity"]. *LO*, no. 2, pp. 25–29.

An examination of Pasternak's acceptance of Tolstoy's preachings as demonstrated in Pasternak's works and correspondence, particularly in *The Story of a Contraoctave, The Childhood of Luvers*, "Blank Verses," *The Tale, Lieutenant Schmidt, Doctor Zhivago*, and "The Dialogue." Names and comments on Pasternak's adaptation to Tolstoy's preachings of nonviolence, the "image of outraged woman," refusal of parasitism, accomplishment of life's sustenance by one's own labor, soil tilling, plain living, and attainment of one's own perfection. Cites excerpts from Pasternak's works and correspondence to support her thesis.

53 PASTERNAK, E.V., and E.B. PASTERNAK. "Koordinaty liricheskogo prostranstva" [Coordinates of the lyric space]. *LO*, no. 3, pp. 91–100.

Details Pasternak's relationship with Mandelstam in the early 1930s and Pasternak's notorious telephone conversation with Stalin about Mandelstam. Restores the complete text of that conversation using Pasternak's own narrative as he had related it to Nadezhda Mandelstam, his wife Zinaida Nikolaevna, Ivinskaya, Vyacheslav Ivanov, and to the authors—his daughter-in-law and older son. Comments on Pasternak's views of Mandelstam's poetry collection *The Voronezh Notebooks*, and includes Pasternak's letter to Mandelstam reviewing the collection and Pasternak's letter to Nadezhda Mandelstam. Sheds light on Pasternak's life in the 1930s and early 1940s.

54   PASTERNAK, JOSEPHINE. "Patior." *Znamia*, no. 2 (February): 183–93.
      Translation of 1964.12.

55   PASTERNAK, Z. "Vospominaniia" [Memoirs]. *Neva*, no. 2, pp. 130–46; no. 4, pp. 124–38.
      First Segment includes recollections of her relationship with and marriage to Pasternak, beginning with their first encounter in Pasternak's apartment in Moscow (at Volkhonka) in 1929 and ending with her evacuation from Moscow in late June of 1941. Elaborates on Pasternak's flirting overtures that were begun in Irpen (summer 1930) and continued on a train from Kiev to Moscow, in Moscow, in Georgia, and again in Moscow, ending with her husband's consent for her to marry Pasternak (21 August 1933) after Pasternak attempted suicide by drinking a small bottle of iodine. Adds information about countless features of Pasternak the man, his caring for others in particular ("I was struck . . . by [the] profundity of his compassion for misfortunes of others"). Describes their trips to the Urals (1932) and to Leningrad (1934 and 1935), and mentions Pasternak's participation in the International Congress of Writers in Paris (21–25 June 1935) and in the Soviet Writers' Plenum in Minsk (winter 1935). Details Pasternak's views of and meetings with his literary peers—Akhmatova, Tikhonov, Andronikov, Pilnyak, and Mandelstam (Mandelstam "rode the high horse, jumped at Borya, criticized his poetry and constantly read his own [poetry] . . . talked with him [Pasternak] like a teacher with his pupil, was arrogant, and, at times, was blunt with him"). Records Pasternak's conversation with Stalin, insisting that "Borya suggested: 'Summon me to your place.'" Reports on the ongoing arrests of 1937 and Pasternak's refusal to add his signature to the list of other writers expressing their approval of death sentences for Tukhachevsky, Yakir, and Eydeman. Second Segment records Pasternak's life in Chistopol during the evacuation ("Borya liked very much to be in Chistopol") and in Moscow from June 1943 through his death and funeral (on 2 June 1960). Adds information about: (1) her relationship with Pasternak during that time ("I lived with him in a very close harmony"); (2) Ivinskaya; (3) Pasternak's love for reading the Bible ("learned psalms by heart and was in raptures over their super-moral content and poeticality"); (4) Fedin's attitude toward Pasternak; and (5) Pasternak's everyday work habits. Discusses events surrounding the publication of *Doctor Zhivago* and the "Pasternak Affair." Offers her views of the Lara character ("I was convinced that he took only appearance from that dame [Ivinskaya], but the fate and character were copied from me literally to the smallest details"). Details Pasternak's last two years, ending with

the description of his death, funeral, and her thoughts of Pasternak at the moment of the "last kiss" ("Farewell, the real great communist, throughout your life you sought to prove that you're worthy of such a title").

56   PODGAETSKAIA, I. IU. "Genezis poeticheskogo proizvedeniia (Boris Pasternak, Osip Mandel'shtam, Marina Tsvetaeva) [Genesis of a poetic work (Boris Pasternak, Osip Mandelstam, Marina Tsvetaeva]. *IAN* 49, no. 3: 203–22.

An investigation into the "means of writing" of Pasternak's drafts as displayed in manuscripts of *When the Skies Clear*. Observes that Pasternak drafted his poetry on the blank sides of his published poetry ("he confined a draft's scope to one page"). Elaborates on the genesis of the poem "A Linden Alley," noting that Pasternak's way of writing ("completion of the first stanza retained in the final draft") was "inherent to Horace's and Ronsar's verses and other poets of the 'rhetoric epic.'" Emphasizes that "Pasternak's work on the text is always a successive removal of a personal and concrete depiction" and that "Pasternak's drafts in their succession are a transition from 'absorption' of reality towards 'wringing' of that reality." Mentions that Pasternak originally wrote *Themes and Variations* on the back of the typewritten manuscripts of *My Sister, Life* ("It is not accidental that Pasternak published them together in 1927 and 1929, under the title of *Two Books*"). Compares Pasternak's manner of draft writing of his poetry to that of Mandelstam and Tsvetaeva.

57   POLIVANOV, M.K. "Tainaia svoboda" [Secret freedom]. *LO*, no. 2, pp. 103–9.

Recalls Pasternak's poetry readings (particularly "Earth's Expanse"), and describes Pasternak's "manner of reading." Records Pasternak's views of his early poetry and of art ("art is a dialogue, it presupposes itself from that very air which nurtures the life"). Comments on *Doctor Zhivago* in detail—its views of Christianity, the image of Lara ("a symbol of Russia"), and the epilogue, in which "the first Gulag story in Russian literature is outlined." Describes Pasternak's last days ("the last hours of the disease"), Pasternak's funeral, and his reading of Pasternak's poem "Hamlet" over his coffin before the interment.

58   POMERANTS, G. "Neslykhannaia prostota" [Unheard-of simplicity]. *LO*, no. 2, pp. 19–24.

Attempts to apply Pasternak's adage of "unheard-of simplicity" to Pasternak's poetry and worldviews—those poems in which supernatural naturalness encompasses "the plane of expression" and the "plane of content"; finds that "Pasternak's tendency towards simplicity embraces Pasternak's entire works." Bases much of the discussion on the poem "Rendezvous."

59   POMORSKA, KRYSTINA. "Boris Pasternak's *Safe Conduct*." In *Autobiographical Statements in Twentieth-Century Russian Literature*, edited by Jane Gary Harris. Princeton, NJ: Princeton University Press, pp. 114–22.

Reprint of chapter 4 (slightly adapted) of 1975.13.

60   RAINE, CRAIG. Introduction to *Poems 1955–1959*, translated by Michael Harari, and *An Essay in Autobiography*, translated by Manya Harari. London: Collins Harvill.

Records differences and similarities between *A Safe Conduct* and *An Essay in Autobiography*, focusing on the author's "I," Pasternak's "gifts and susceptibilities," and themes and topics treated in both autobiographies (the image of Venice, for example), among other aspects. In *A Safe Conduct*, Pasternak is seen as "convinced of the importance of being earnest," whereas in *An Essay in Autobiography* Pasternak "wryly observes himself as a young boy." Also observes that "moments of vivid brilliance" and economy of "writerly gifts" seen to be displayed in *An Essay in Autobiography* "can be matched by quotations from the rich and wayward pages of *Safe Conduct*." Provides a brief history of the publication of both autobiographies.

61   RAYFIELD, DONALD. "Unicorns and Gazelles: Pasternak, Rilke and the Georgian Poets." *FMLS* 26, no. 4: 370–81.

An examination of Pasternak's poetic bonds with Rilke, Paolo Iashvili, and Titsian Tabidze. Compares Rilke's "Das Einhorn" to Pasternak's "Margarita"—thematic structure ("both poets combine a primæval sexuality with reworked myth of inspiration") and imagery. Provides a list of lexical similarities between Rilke's "Der Ölbaumgarten" and Pasternak's "The Garden of Gethsemane," concluding that "the later Pasternak seems very much closer to the early Rilke, just as the later Rilke uncannily echoes the early Pasternak." Adds new interpretations of Iashvili and Tabidze as a continuation of his previous article on the Georgian poets (1982.17), noting Iashvili's "femininity" ("must have predisposed Pasternak to Iashvili"), the presence of Iashvili's themes in Pasternak's "Grass and Stones," and that "Pasternak rediscovered his own self" in Tabidze.

62   ROLL, SERAFIMA. "De-historicising the Self: Boris Pasternak's *Safe Conduct* and Osip Mandelshtam's *The Egyptian Stamp*." *FMLS* 26, no. 3: 240–49.

Deems both works to present "a literary form which will challenge the accepted pattern of thinking." Discusses Nietzsche's influence on both poets. Claims both works "differ from traditional autobiographies in their approach to the idea of self." Argues that Pasternak's "ability to imaginatively recast history and tradition is limited," and advances theories as to why Pasterank "has difficulty in distancing himself from the past and affirming himself in the present."

63 RUDOVA, LARISSA. "On Pasternak's 'Aerial Ways.'" *CASS* 24, no. 1: 33–46.

A detailed analysis of poetic devices in *Aerial Ways*—metaphoric, spatial, temporal, stylistic, aesthetic, and philosophic, among others. Finds that synesthesia is used to produce "the effect of simultaneity," and that Pasternak opposes "the free space of nature and man to the constructing space of the revolution." Discerns "the spatial form," Pasternak's "profoundly innovative stylistic idiom," as composed of "the features that distinguish 'Aerial Ways' as a piece of modern prose." Concludes that "the unexpected mixture of animate and inanimate, color and sound, as well as Pasternak's conception of transformation" attest to Pasternak's "affinity with Russian Symbolism."

64 SCHREINER, JANA. "Boris Pasternak als Musiker. Die Besonderheiten der Klang-, Laut- und Geräuschmetapher in seiner Dichtung." *WS* 35, no. 2: 276–304.

Surveys Pasternak's infatuation with music in his youth, centering on Scriabin's influence. Sees this influence reflected not only in Pasternak's propensity for music but in his involvement with philosophy and aesthetics. Mentions musical works (mainly operas), composers (Chopin, Tchaikovsky, Beethoven, Bach, and Brahms), and musical themes—all mirrored in Pasternak's works. Argues that "music plays an important if not prevalent role in Pasternak's poetry." Pays attention to Pasternak's use of sounds made by humans, nature, and animals. Cites statistics of "sound producers"—living creatures (notably birds, followed by humans and animals) and nature (trees with their leaves and twigs, succeeded by thunderings).

65 SINIAVSKII, ANDREI. "Odin den' s Pasternakom. K stoletiiu so dnia rozhdeniia Borisa Pasternaka" [A day with Pasternak. Toward Boris Pasternak's centennial]. *Iunost'*, no. 2, pp. 83–85.

Reprint of 1979.45.

66 SMITH, ALEXANDRA. "Tsvetaeva and Pasternak: Depicting People in Poetry." *EP* 15, no. 2: 94–101.

Discusses and contrasts Pasternak's and Tsvetaeva's portraiture techniques. Sees Pasternak as depicting individuals in an elliptical fashion and offering complex, multidimensional images. Cites Pasternak's portrait of Peter the Great in "Petersburg" to illustrate this principle.

67 SMOLITSKII, V.G. "B. Pasternak. Sobiratel' narodnykh rechenii" [B. Pasternak. The collector of popular sayings]. *RuR*, no. 1, pp. 23–28.

Insists that colloquial speech is Pasternak's "native tongue," and that in Pasternak "'coarse' words lose their coarseness," while they become a "necessary integral part of his poetics." Discusses Pasternak's use of dialects and gives examples. Includes a list of popular sayings

Pasternak composed during his stay in Chistopol. Concludes that the list (hitherto unpublished) attests to "how Pasternak attentively listened to the spoken speech, and how he was interested in everything new the life brought into the language."

68 ———. "V gimnazii" [At the gymnasium]. *LO*, no. 2, pp. 30–34.
Sheds light on Pasternak's school years at the Moscow Fifth Boys Gymnasium, the subjects Pasternak had studied, teachers who had taught him, and Pasternak's attitude towards his studies ("in reality Boris Pasternak took his studies very seriously"). Mentions that Pasternak graduated with honors and that his closest school buddies were Alexander Vladimirov and Leonty Rig.

69 STEPUN, FEDOR. "B.L. Pasternak." *LO*, no. 2, pp. 65–71.
Reprint of 1959.69.

70 TARASENKOV, AN. "Pasternak. Chernovye zapisi. 1934–1939" [Pasternak. Draft entries. 1934–1939]. *VL*, no. 2, pp. 73–107.
Records his meetings with Pasternak from 1930 through 1939, with comments on Pasternak's writings (including his translations), Pasternak's speeches, Pasternak as a human being, and Pasternak as a Soviet citizen. Excerpts Pasternak's Lermontov speech delivered at the Lermontov celebration on 26 October 1934 ("Pushkin and Lermontov to me are a couple. Pushkin had done everything for Lermontov"). Also records Pasternak's views of Tsvetaeva ("She is an excellent poet, but I did not know she is so crazy"), Tvardovsky ("is a real man"), and Ehrenburg ("I am not so fond of how Ehrenburg writes. All this is somehow spineless, all in him is frivolous. Even his style"). Details Pasternak's views of his *Hamlet* translation and of Shakespeare in general.

71 VILENKIN, V. "O Borise Leonidoviche Pasternake. Vospominaniia i dnevnik" [About Boris Leonidovich Pasternak. Memoir and diary]. *Teatr*, no. 3, pp. 129–42.
Recounts his meetings with Pasternak from 1939 to 1946, particularly during the winter of 1939–40, when Pasternak was completing his rendition of *Hamlet* to be staged at the Moscow Art Theatre. Recalls rehearsals of *Hamlet* at the Moscow Art Theatre and Nemirovich-Danchenko's reaction to Pasternak's *Hamlet* and poetry. Surveys Pasternak's public poetry readings, and provides an insight into "the manner" in which Pasternak read his poetry.

72 VORNIN, L.B., and L.V. BAKHNOV, comps. *Doktor Zhivago Borisa Pasternaka*. S raznykh tochek zreniia. Moscow: Sovetskii pisatel', 286 pp.
Divided into two parts, "Yesterday" and "Today," the former republishing the material reflecting the reaction to *Doctor Zhivago* in 1958 and the latter including articles published after the Soviet publica-

tion in 1988. The first part also includes the text of Pasternak's poem "The Nobel Prize" and the second includes some of Pasternak's correspondence (to Freidenburg, the Tabidzes, and Shalamov). The volume's introduction, "The Book of Destinies and the Destiny of the Book" (by Voznesensky), elaborates on the impact *Doctor Zhivago* has made abroad and in the Soviet Union. Three items of this volume (1988.26; 1988.44; 1988.46) have been annotated.

73   ZHOLKOVSKY, ALEXANDRE. "Mekhanizmy vtorogo rozhdeniia. O stikhotvorenii Pasternaka 'Mne khochetsia domoi v ogromnost' . . .'" [Mechanisms of Second Birth. On Pasternak's poem "I Want to Go Home, into Enormousness . . ."]. *LO*, no. 2, pp. 35–41.
      Reprint of 1985.9.

74——. "La poétique de Boris Pasternak." In *Histoire de la litterature russe. Le XXe siècle*** Gels et Dégels*, edited by Efim Etkind et al. Paris: Fayard, pp. 488–505.
      Claims that the central theme of Pasternak's poetry is a communion of the everyday with the eternal and finds evidence of this within Pasternak's language, imagery, and style. Discerns two recurring motifs—referential and stylistic—as prevalent in Pasternak's works. Insists the former includes "situation-themes," "object-themes," a combination of the two, and "event-themes." The latter is seen to include alliterative/phonetic blendings, "gravelly" accumulation of consonants, an abundance of plural forms, and a dense syntax, among other things. Discusses the intertextuality of Pasternak's poetics, tracing its evolution in detail. Notes a period of ambivalent adaptation to the new social order, a postwar shift toward simplicity and eternal (Christian) wisdom, and, ultimately, both an outward permanence and fluctuation of individual traits. Consists of a summarized account of notions expressed in earlier publications.

Author Index

Abel, Lionel, 1958.1
Abuashvili, A., 1976.1
Achar, K.R.H., 1966.1
Acta Universitatis Szegediensis De
    Attila Jozeff Nominatae, 1988.1
Adamovich, Georgii, 1958.2
Afinogenov, Aleksandr, 1990.1
Aleksandrov, V., 1937.1; 1956.1
Aleksandrova, Vera, 1960.1; V.A.,
    1962.1; 1963.1
Alekseev, M., 1940.1
Al'fonsov, V.N., 1988.2; V., 1990.2
Alliluyeva, Svetlana, 1967.1
Al'mi, Il., 1990.3
Al'tshuller, Mark, 1985.1
Ammon, Kurt, 1959.1
Anatol'eva, N., 1958.3–4; 1960.2. *See
    also* Popliuiko-Anatol'eva, N.A.
Anderson, Roger B., 1987.1
Andrews, E., 1989.9. *See also* Endrius, E.
Andronikof, M., 1959.53
Angeloff, Alexander, 1968.1
Annenkov, Iurii, 1966.2; 1990.4
Anning, N.J., 1972.1; 1976.2
Anstei, Ol'ga, 1951.1; O[lga Nikolaev-
    na], 1960.3
Antipov, S.N., 1983.1
Antokol'skii, P., 1943.1; 1945.1
Arbelaez, Fernando, 1966.3
Arkhangel'skii, Aleksandr, 1987.2
Arndt, Walter, 1959.2
Arnold, John, 1971.1
Aroutunova, Bayara, 1979.1;
    Arutiunova, Baiara, 1989.1
Aseev, Nik., 1922.1; N., 1923.1; 1929.1;
    Nikolai, 1969.1
Asmus, V.F., 1990.5
Aucouturier, Alfreda, 1979.2

Aucoururier, Michel, 1957.1; 1961.1;
    1963.2; 1966.4; 1968.2; 1969.2;
    1970.1; 1978.1; 1979.3; 1980.1;
    1981.16; 1986.1; 1989.2; 1990.6
Audry, Colette, 1959.3
Azadovskii, K.M., 1990.7

Baevskii, V.S., 1980.2; 1982.1; 1984.1;
    1988.3; 1989.3; V., 1987.3; 1990.8
Baird, Sister Mary Julian, 1959.4,
    1961.2–3
Bakhnov, L.V., 1990.72
Bakina, M.A., 1982.12; 1986.2
Barksdale, E.C., 1976.3
Barlas, Vladimir, 1987.4
Barnes, Christopher, 1970.2; 1978.2;
    1979.4–5; 1983.2–3; 1984.2;
    1986.3; 1989.4–5; 1990.9–11;
    Christopher J., 1972.2; 1975.1;
    1976.4; 1977.1–4
Barsov, Vasilii, 1958.5
Bartling, Natalie, 1978.3
Barton, Paul, 1959.5
Beaune, Daniéle, 1974.1
Beer, Karl Willy, 1958.6
Belenchikov, V., 1989.6
Bem, A., 1933.1
Ben-Asher, Naomi, 1972.3
Berlin, Isaiah, 1950.1; 1978.4; 1980.3–4;
    1981.1–2
Berlin, Miriam H., 1983.4
Berlogin, Mikhail, 1958.7
Bienek, Horst, 1959.6
Birkman, Karl, 1974.2
Birnbaum, Henrik, 1976.5; 1980.5;
    1984.3; 1989.7
Björling, Fiona, 1976.6; 1978.5; 1981.3;
    1982.2

Bodin, Per Arne, 1976.7–8; 1979.6; Per-
  Arne, 1986.4; 1987.5; 1990.12
Bogomolov, N., 1990.13
Bonamour, Jean, 1978.6
Borisov, V.M., 1988.4; Vadim, 1989.8
Borowsky, Kay, 1976.9
Bowman, Herbert E., 1959.7; 1961.4;
  1973.1
Bowra, Sir Maurice, 1949.1; C.M.,
  1962.2
Boyd, Alexander F., 1972.4
Bräuer, Herbert, 1964.1
Bristol, Evelyn, 1984.4
Briusov, Valerii, 1922.2
Brown, Edward J., 1963.3
Brück, Max, 1957.2
Brügel, Fritz, 1936.1
Bukhstab, B. Ia., 1987.6
Burford, William S., 1962.3
Burg, David, 1964.2–3
Burkin, Ivan, 1971.2
Busch, Wolfgang, 1966.5
Bushman, I.N., 1962.4–5; Buschmann,
  Irene, 1966.6
Butler, Hubert, 1988.5

Campo, Cristina, 1967.2
Cang, Joel, 1967.3
Carlisle, Olga, 1960.4; 1961.5; 1963.4–5;
  Carlisle [Andreyev], Olga, 1962.6;
  1976.10–11. *See also* Karlail,
  Ol'ga
Chakravarty, Amiya, 1960.5;
  Chakravarti, Amiya, 1962.7
Chamberlain, John, 1958.8
Cherniak, Iakov, 1922.3; Ia., 1990.14
Chertkov, Leonid, 1979.7
Chiaromonte, Nicola, 1957.3;
  1958.9–10, 1959.8; 1968.3; 1969.3;
  1970.3. See also K'iaromonte,
  Nikola
Chibisova, L., 1961.6
Chudakova, M.O., 1971.3; 1978.7
Chukovskaia, Lidiia, 1990.15
Chukhovskii, Kornei, 1966.7; 1990.16
Clayton, J. Douglas, 1978.8
Clough, William O., 1959.9
Clowes, Edith, W., 1990.17
Cohen, J.M., 1944.1; 1959.10
Conquest, Robert, 1961.7–8; 1989.9
Cornwell, Neil, 1986.5
Costello, D.P., 1968.4
Crankshaw, Edward, 1959.11; 1960.6
Crone, Anna Lisa, 1979.8
Cuadra, Pablo Antonio, 1959.12

Dal', Elena, 1972.5; 1978.9
Danin, Daniil, 1990.18
Danow, D.K., 1981.4
Davie, Donald, 1965.1; 1969.4–5
Davis, Melton S., 1959.13
Debenedetti, Giacomo, 1971.4
Delgado, F., 1958.11
De Michelis, Cesare G., 1968.5
Derzhavyn, Volodymyr, 1959.15
Deutsch, Babette, 1958.14; 1959.16
Deutscher, Isaac, 1959.17; 1969.6
Dinfreville, Jacques, 1960.7
Disopra, Nikola, 1963.6
Döring, Johanna Renate, 1973.2;
  1979.9; Döring-Smirnov, Johanna
  Renate, 1983.5; 1984.5
Dozorets, Zh. A., 1990.19
Drawdzik, Witold, 1959.18
Dreistadt, Roy, 1972.6
Drjučinov, Milan, 1979.10. See also
  Gurchinov, Milan
Dryzhakova, Elena, 1985.1
Dyck, J.W., 1962.8; 1971.5; 1972.7;
  1974.3
Dyck, Sara, 1978.10
Dymshits, Al, 1961.9

El'sburg, Zh., 1930.1
Endrius, E., 1989.10. *See also* Andrews,
  E.
Epp, George, K., 1984.6
Erenburg, I., 1922.4; 1961.10–11; I.G.,
  1972.8; Ehrenburg, Ilya,
  1969.7
Erlich, Victor, 1958.15; 1959.19; 1964.4;
  1978.11–13; 1979.11; 1989.11
Etkind, Efim, 1979.12–13

Faryno, Jerzy, 1970.4; 1987.7–8;
  1989.12; Farino, Ezhi, 1976.12;
  [Jerzy] 1978.14; 1987.7–8; Farino,
  E., 1988.6
Feifer, George, 1964.5
Feinberg, Lawrence E., 1973.3
Fejér, A., 1988.7
Fernandez, Dominique, 1958.16
Filippov, Boris, 1971.6; 1981.5
Filonov Gove, Antonina, 1983.6
Fitch, Robert E., 1960.8
Flaker, Aleksandar, 1982.3; 1984.7
Fleischmann, Ivo, 1979.14
Fleishman, L., 1975.2–4; 1977.5–8;
  1979.15–17; Lazar, 1981.6;
  1984.8–9; 1988.8; 1989.13;
  1990.20

Subject Index

"About Ivan the Great," 1990.31
"About These Verses," 1923.3; 1978.14;
　　1989.1
Above the Barriers, 1927.2; 1959.57;
　　1961.1; 1970.12; 1979.1; 1981.6;
　　1982.8; 1983.19; 1988.19; 1990.39
Acmeism, views of, 1949.1; 1958.27;
　　1962.1; 1966.1; 1967.7; 1968.2;
　　1969.14; 1979.20
Aerial Ways, 1925.1; 1928.2, 5; 1935.2;
　　1936.2; 1945.3; 1951.2; 1958.54;
　　1961.22; 1962.1, 3; 1966.4;
　　1972.14; 1973.7; 1978.22; 1979.37;
　　1981.3; 1989.24; 1990.9, 63
Aesthetic views, 1964.10; 1967.17;
　　1973.10; 1976.9; 1988.22; 1990.31,
　　44
Afinogenov, Aleksandr Nikolaevich,
　　1959.33
"After the Storm," 1987.16
Akhmatova, Anna. *See* Gorenko, Anna
　　Andreevna.
"All Is Snow," 1983.28
"All Moods and Voices," 1981.11
Andreas-Salomé, Lou, 1984.13
Andreev, Leonid Nikolaevich, 1961.6
Anisimov, Ivan Ivanovich, 1990.48
Annensky, Innokenti Fedorovich,
　　1928.2; 1965.4; 1972.18; 1979.7;
　　1980.19; 1988.8; 1990.2
Antokolsky, Pavel Grigoevich, 1926.2
Apukhtin, Aleksei Nikolaevich, 1924.4
Art, views of, 1922.4; 1923.3; 1943.3;
　　1945.3; 1960.4–5, 17, 27; 1962.1,
　　22, 32; 1963.3, 12; 1964.10;
　　1967.7, 12, 15; 1968.19; 1970.16;
　　1972.7, 23; 1973.5; 1974.3, 8, 16;
　　1975.4, 16; 1976.2, 9; 1979.19, 37,
　　45; 1981.6, 13–14, 20; 1982.16, 18;

1983.23, 26, 30; 1985.4; 1986.3;
　　1987.12, 21; 1988.22, 28–29, 42;
　　1989.4, 15, 28; 1990.1, 5, 20, 36,
　　42, 58
"The Artilleryman," 1986.4
"An Artist," 1987.12
"August," 1977.5; 1985.5
Aseyev, Nikolai Nikolaevich, 1961.13;
　　1966.16; 1977.2; 1988.8; 1989.4;
　　1990.31
Auden, Wystan Hugh, 1944.1
Aunt Olya, 1983.24
Autobiographies, 1960.2, 21; 1970.13;
　　1972.16, 21; 1975.2, 8–9; 1976.11;
　　1977.5; 1979.15; 1981.17; 1983.5;
　　1985.4; 1988.42; 1990.72
"Autumn," 1971.3; 1990.40

"Bacchanalia," 1978.20; 1984.5; 1987.16
Bach, Johann Sebastian, 1988.3;
　　1990.64
"The Bad Days," 1976.7
"Bad Dream," 1966.6; 1987.5
Bakhtin, Mikhail Mikhailovich, 1982.9
"Balashov," 1978.5; 1989.1
"Ballad," 1988.17
Balmont, Konstantin Dmitrievich,
　　1937.1; 1959.57; 1972.18; 1976.22
Balzac, Honoré de, 1960.38; 1985.5
Bang, Hermann Joachim, 1960.38
Baptism, 1961.24; 1990.20
Baudelaire, Charles Pierre, 1960.17;
　　1988.8; 1990.26
Beethoven, Lugwig van, 1986.16;
　　1988.3; 1990.64
The Beginning of the Prose of 1936,
　　1990.40
Bely, Andrei. *See* Bugaev, Boris
　　Nikolaevich

Correspondence/Epistolary (*continued*)
1972.2, 23; 1973.13; 1974.11;
1975.2, 8; 1977.5, 21; 1980.17;
1981.6, 10, 16; 1982.6, 11, 15;
1983.13, 15; 1984.18; 1986.13;
1987.19; 1988.22, 30, 37–38;
1989.4, 28–29; 1990.7, 35, 44, 53,
60, 72
Ćosić, Dobrica, 1959.3
"Courtyard," 1989.1
Crane, Stephen, 1969.4
Critiques, views of. *See* Essays, views of
"The Crying Garden," 1923.3; 1970.4
"Cupronickle," 1990.31

Davie, Donald, 1983.17
"The Dawn," 1958.19
"The Dawn in the North," 1988.11
"The Dawn Will Blaze a Candle,"
1983.22
"The Death of a Poet," 1932.1; 1982.4
"A Definition of Creativity," 1982.4;
1986.7
"Definition of Poetry," 1949.1; 1967.17;
1975.16; 1986.7; 1987.10
"Defintion of Soul," 1924.2; 1983.6
"Delo Pasternaka," 1958.12; "'Delo'
Pasternaka," 1958.13; 1959.14
"The Dialogue," 1990.56
Dickens, Charles, 1990.10, 33
"The Disease," 1989.1
"Disintegration," 1924.2
A District in the Rear, 1983.24
"Do Not Touch," 1949.1; 1970.4
Doctor Zhivago
allegory in, 1959.72; 1961.20, 25–26;
1967.6, 14; 1972.13; 1988.5;
1989.26
Antipov, 1958.1, 10, 24, 26, 36;
1959.18, 52, 54, 72; 1963.18;
1964.6; 1966.1; 1970.18; 1971.5,
17; 1972.6, 20; 1975.7; 1977.13;
1979.23, 42–43; 1980.9; 1982.10;
1986.11; 1987.1; 1988.7, 13, 26;
1989.26; 1990.25, 38
autobiographical features in, 1958.56,
76; 1959.21, 29, 34, 40, 47, 63;
1960.31; 1962.10; 1964.6, 15;
1965.6; 1974.2; 1983.4, 24;
1987.14; 1988.46; 1989.5; 1990.9,
20
characters, general, 1958.76–77;
1959.17, 21, 24, 51, 56, 69, 73;
1960.7; 1961.26; 1962.1; 1963.18;
1966.21; 1967.6, 8, 14; 1970.11;

1971.5, 17; 1972.12; 1978.10;
1979.43; 1982.9–10; 1984.12;
1986.9; 1987.1; 1989.24, 33;
1990.6, 33, 44
characters, minor, 1958.24, 67;
1959.29, 54, 72; 1961.26; 1963.3;
1967.8–9; 1968.14; 1971.5, 17;
1977.19; 1978.29; 1979.23, 42–43;
1980.15–16; 1981.15; 1982.10, 15;
1987.1; 1988.13; 1990.38
christianity theme in, 1958.25, 52, 63,
68; 1959.12, 21, 24, 42–43, 49, 53,
68, 73, 75; 1960.8, 14, 31, 39;
1961.2; 1963.17, 20; 1964.11;
1966.9; 1967.8–9; 1968.14;
1970.10; 1972.3; 1973.9; 1976.8;
1977.3, 19, 33, 50; 1979.6;
1981.15; 1984.12; 1985.1; 1988.9;
1990.6, 9, 12, 33, 57
coincidences in, 1958.14, 22, 36, 77;
1959.71, 76; 1960.2, 20; 1961.19;
1962.27; 1964.6–7; 1968.19;
1970.18; 1972.14; 1975.13;
1976.20; 1978.6; 1979.43; 1982.9;
1984.20; 1986.5; 1989.9
comparisons with/juxtapositions to,
1958.8, 28, 39, 55; 1959.24, 27, 29,
31, 33, 36, 39, 44–45, 51–52, 61,
68, 73; 1960.8, 16, 20, 40, 44;
1961.25; 1963.6, 8, 15, 18, 20;
1967.9; 1968.7, 9; 1969.9; 1970.2,
6, 10; 1973.14; 1975.7; 1976.5;
1978.10, 26, 29; 1979.42, 48;
1980.7, 9; 1982.7; 1983.14, 21, 31;
1984.15; 1985.7; 1986.9, 11;
1987.21; 1988.9, 13, 18, 23, 39;
1989.7, 22, 26; 1990.10, 33, 38.
See also War and Peace
contradicting views within, 1958.6, 36,
77; 1959.17, 21, 76; 1960.14, 20,
33, 40; 1965.6; 1979.28, 43;
1986.5; 1988.9–10, 27, 44
criticism of ideas in, 1958.20–21;
1968.4, 10; 1969.11; 1979.28;
1980.5, 15; 1986.5; 1987.17;
1988.4, 10, 14, 24; 1989.19, 26;
1990.33, 46, 60
death theme in, 1958.14, 74; 1959.6,
10, 24, 32, 36, 62; 1960.16, 21, 31;
1961.3, 20; 1962.20; 1963.18;
1965.6; 1967.8, 15; 1972.20;
1976.9; 1978.20; 1981.4; 1989.27;
1990.6, 12, 26
descriptions of nature in, 1958.16, 20,
69–70, 75; 1959.19, 68; 1961.20;

Subject Index

"*Fairy Tale*" *(continued)*
"Fairy Story," 1976.7
Faulkner, William, 1962.6
Faust, translation of, 1959.74; 1960.23;
    1961.18; 1968.18; 1972.22; 1978.7,
    30; 1979.25; 1982.14; 1986.12;
    1990.8, 38, 46. *See also* Shake-
    speare, William, translation of
"Faust's Love," 1990.38
"Feasts," 1990.31
"February," 1980.19; 1989.1
Fedin, Konstantin Aleksandrovich,
    1973.13; 1990.15–16, 55
Fedorov, N.F., 1959.32; 1989.26
"Feeling of Life," 1987.16
Fet, Afanasy Afanasievich, 1923.5;
    1924.4; 1928.2; 1960.1; 1967.17;
    1970.4; 1971.3; 1976.22, 25;
    1985.3, 6; 1986.16; 1987.3;
    1988.11; 1990.45
"The First Snow," 1987.15
Flaubert, Gustave, 1960.38
"Flight," 1971.3
Freidenberg, Olga Mikhailovna,
    1981.16; 1982.6, 11; 1983.15
"Future," 1987.16
Futurism, views of, 1924.2; 1926.1;
    1929.2; 1943.2; 1949.1;
    1958.58–59; 1959.57, 69, 74;
    1961.13; 1962.1; 1964.1, 4, 9–10,
    15; 1965.5, 9; 1966.1, 8, 12;
    1967.7, 12; 1968.2, 13; 1974.1;
    1975.8, 13; 1977.7; 1978.2;
    1979.15, 20, 24; 1981.6; 1984.4;
    1986.3; 1987.10; 1988.16; 1989.11,
    14, 24; 1990.26, 31. *See also*
    "Centrifuge" and "Lirika"

"The Garden of Gethsemane," 1960.22;
    1963.13, 15; 1965.1; 1970.10;
    1971.1; 1972.21; 1973.4; 1976.7,
    17; 1978.3; 1987.21; 1990.12, 61
Georgian poetry, translation of, 1935.4;
    1936.1; 1960.17; 1973.2; 1976.1;
    1980.13; 1982.17; 1986.8; 1987.12;
    1990.37. *See also* Translation
Gessner, Salomon, 1971.19
"A Girl," 1970.4
Gironella, Jose Maria, 1960.40
Goethe, Johann Wolfgang von, 1959.31;
    1960.1; 1971.19; 1987.3; 1988.2,
    36; 1989.36; 1990.12, 33
Gogol, Nikolai Vasilievich, 1937.1;
    1958.26, 60; 1959.61; 1960.1, 34;
    1969.9; 1971.6; 1988.36

"The Golden Autumn," 1960.17
Goncharov, Ivan Aleksandrovich,
    1985.7
Goncourt, Edmond Louis Antoine
    Huot de, 1960.38
Gorenko, Anna Andreevna [pseud.
    Akhmatova, Anna Andreevna],
    1922.4; 1933.4; 1960.4, 29; 1970.4;
    1972.9; 1974.2; 1976.12; 1977.9;
    1979.6; 1980.13, 18; 1981.6;
    1982.7; 1983.11; 1984.3; 1989.4, 7,
    28; 1990.25, 32, 55
Gorky, Maksim. *See* Peshkov, Aleksei
    Maksimovich
"Grass and Stones," 1990.61
Griboedov, Aleksandr Sergeevich,
    1971.19
Grigoryev, Apollon Aleksandrovich,
    1987.3
Grin, Aleksandr. *See* Grinevsky,
    Aleksandr Stepanovich
Grinevsky, Aleksandr Stepanovich
    [pseud. Grin, Aleksandr],
    1978.30
Grossman, Vasily Semyonovich,
    1988.18
"Gypsies," 1990.31

"Hamlet," 1958.19; 1959.9, 47; 1962.14;
    1963.13; 1965.1; 1970.10; 1971.1;
    1973.3; 1976.7, 24; 1978.3; 1982.4;
    1983.12; 1985.7; 1986.10
Hamlet, translation of, 1940.1–3;
    1941.1; 1944.2; 1960.23; 1961.18;
    1968.6; 1973.4–5; 1976.24;
    1978.7–8, 15; 1979.12;
    1990.70–71. *See also*
    Shakespeare, William, transla-
    tion of
Hamsun. *See* Pedersen, Knut
"Happiness," 1989.1
A Haughty Beggar, 1977.3; 1983.24
Heidegger, Martin, 1974.4
Heine, Heinrich, 1971.8; 1987.3;
    1988.8
Hemingway, Ernest (Miller), 1959.36;
    1960.4; 1962.6
Hesse, Hermann, 1962.18; 1990.33
"The High Malady," 1961.22; 1989.29
High Malady, 1937.1; 1960.29; 1970.2;
    1976.25; 1979.9; 1987.22; 1989.29;
    1990.24
"Hoar-Frost," 1987.3
Hoffmann, August Heinrich, 1976.2;
    1986.3